THEOLOGICAL DICTIONARY
OF THE
OLD TESTAMENT

THEOLOGICAL DICTIONARY

OF THE

OLD TESTAMENT

EDITED BY

G. JOHANNES BOTTERWECK

AND

HELMER RINGGREN

Translator

JOHN T. WILLIS

Abilene Christian College

Volume I

בָּדָד–אָב

'ābh – bādhādh

Revised Edition

WILLIAM B. EERDMANS PUBLISHING COMPANY

GRAND RAPIDS, MICHIGAN

Library of Congress Cataloging in Publication Data

Botterweck, G   Johannes.
    Theological dictionary of the Old Testament.

    Translation of Theologisches Wörterbuch zum
Alten Testament.
        1. Bible.   O. T.—Dictionaries—Hebrew.
    2. Hebrew language—Dictionaries—English.
    I. Ringgren, Helmer, 1917–   joint author.
    II. Title.

BS440.B5713   221.3   73-76170
ISBN 0–8028–2325–4

EDITORS' PREFACE

A Theological Dictionary of the Old Testament is a bold venture any time it is undertaken. At no time can the claim be made that scholarship has attained such a conclusive position in its research that the results will continue to be valid for all time. And yet, one may cherish the hope that the present is not a bad time to launch out on such a project. The form-critical and traditio-historical methods have been refined to such a point that one can expect rather certain results. Advances in related scholarly fields make it possible to use Akkadian and Egyptian material with greater certainty and Ugaritic material with a proper degree of caution. Finally, semantic research in general philology has given us insights into the problems involved to the extent that we can justifiably expect help from this area too, even though a general consensus probably has not yet been achieved.

This dictionary cannot intervene in the methodological discussion among the various schools of semantics, neither can it favor a particular theory of semantic fields. Its approach can be outlined as follows: Etymologies are carefully explored, word families defined, cases of borrowing and semantic transfer established. A semantic field is constructed and delineated by examination of the semantic relationships among synonyms and antonyms. Syntactic analysis exhibits lexemic distinctive features, contrastive pairs, etc. The use of fixed combinations of words in formulas and schemata is noted. Structural analysis reveals the use of signals, verbal metaphors, and tense metaphors. The situational context, finally, brings space and time closer to us with information about the historical setting. Thus a comprehensive analysis enables a single word to reveal a bit of history, culture, religion, society, and human self-understanding.

But in this context, what is meant by "theological"? Since the Old Testament certainly "speaks about God," the purpose of this dictionary is to analyze its religious statements with the aid of all accessible resources and to present them in their peculiarity, in order to shed as much light as possible on the connections of the content of Old Testament thought in a given text, tradition, or institution. Thus "theology" is understood primarily in a descriptive sense, just as one might speak of the theology of Augustine or the theology of Luther.

It is obvious that such an undertaking could not be accomplished by one, or even by a small group of scholars. To be sure, a small group might be able to produce a work that would be essentially more homogeneous, but this would be done at the cost of completeness and reliability. The only way to attain a well-rounded discussion of the problems of Old Testament theology is to draw upon the knowledge of a large number of scholars.

Viewed from its international perspective, contemporary Old Testament scholarship is not characterized by homogeneity. In light of this, the range of potential understanding would be severely narrowed if the contributors were limited to a single exegetical school. But if a Theological Dictionary is produced on a more international and interconfessional basis, a broader treatment of the issues can be expected. Fortunately, in our science there have already been cooperative efforts transcending national and confessional lines, making it possible to undertake the present project along similar lines. It is the hope of the editors that such an approach will encourage objectivity in this work and make possible a more comprehensive interpretation of the material involved. What is lost in homogeneity will, one hopes, be regained in the diversity of viewpoints.

Since this dictionary is restricted to Old Testament material throughout, the emphasis in each article is on the Hebrew terminology that is used. At the same time, the interconfessional structure of the work necessitates that attention be given to the Septuagint. The Qumran texts are taken into consideration briefly (as much as possible), but it is extremely difficult to arrange material in the Pseudepigraphic literature under Hebrew words. Also, little attention can be given to Rabbinic literature, since it is very hard to determine the post quem dates of materials in this corpus. Likewise the New Testament adoption and application of Old Testament ideas falls outside the scope of this work. The reader should consult the *Theological Dictionary of the New Testament,* edited by Kittel and Friedrich, for the use of pertinent synonyms to Old Testament terms in Rabbinic and New Testament literature.

It is impossible to understand the Old Testament fully without comparing it with extrabiblical literature of the ancient Near East. To be sure, such a comparison can be carried to an extreme, so as to make Old Testament faith appear to be only a particular form of ancient Near Eastern thought. But at the same time it can serve to emphasize more clearly the uniqueness of Old Testament faith as it is expressed in the credo, the cult, and the law, and thus to enhance greatly one's understanding of Old Testament thought. In this latter endeavor we have not intended to spare ourselves the trouble of elaborating on the extrabiblical material as fully as possible in the narrow scope of a dictionary. Therefore, we have not been content merely to examine words that are etymologically related to the Hebrew term being discussed, but have also given attention especially to similar thoughts and ideas even in cases where no word exists that corresponds etymologically with the Hebrew word.

There is great value in analyzing words semantically. However, the major goal of all the studies in this work is to present the fundamental concepts intended by the respective words and terms, the traditions in which they occur, and the different nuances of meaning they have in each tradition. It is in this area that lexical contributions can render a worthwhile service as individual building blocks in the process of reconstructing an Old Testament theology.

The conclusion of the first volume of the German edition is an appropriate occasion for us to thank all those who have contributed to the realization of this dictionary. Its initiators, Christel Matthias Schröder and Cardinal Augustine Bea (†), encouraged the publishers to undertake this project. Valuable consultants have been G. W. Anderson, Henri Cazelles, David N. Freedman, Shemarjahu Talmon, and Gerhard Wallis. J. Bergman, O. Loretz, and W. von Soden have served as technical advisers for egyptology, ugaritology, and the ancient Near East, respectively. We owe a special debt of gratitude to the authors of the articles for their cooperation in producing the *Theological Dictionary of the Old*

Testament. The publishers and editors hope it will prove to be a useful tool not only for exegetical research but also for pastoral work.

G. Johannes Botterweck / Helmer Ringgren

NOTE TO THE REVISED ENGLISH EDITION

The present edition incorporates a number of corrections and revisions suggested by the contributors, by reviewers, by Geoffrey W. Bromiley, and by David Green, to each of whom the publishers wish to express sincere gratitude.

Where the chapter or verse numbering is different in the Hebrew (or Septuagint) text and in the English versions, the Hebrew (or Greek) numbering has been noted first, and then the English in parentheses or brackets.

CONTRIBUTORS

Sverre Aalen, Oslo

G. W. Ahlström, Chicago

Arnulf Baumann, Hannover

Jan Bergman, Linköping

Karl Heinz Bernhardt, Berlin

G. Johannes Botterweck, Bonn (Editor)

N. P. Bratsiotis, Agia-Paraskevi-Attikis, Greece

Henri Cazelles, Paris

Ronald E. Clements, Cambridge, England

Frank M. Cross, Cambridge, Mass.

Otto Eissfeldt (†), Halle

Seth Erlandsson, Uppsala

A. O. Haldar, Uppsala

Vinzenz Hamp, Munich

Jean-Georges Heintz, Strasbourg

F. J. Helfmeyer, Bonn

Harry A. Hoffner, Waltham, Mass.

Alfred Jepsen, Greifswald

Bo Johnson, Lund

Elsie Johnson, Lund

Arvid S. Kapelrud, Oslo

Diether Kellermann, Tübingen

Klaus Koch, Hamburg

Joachim Krecher, Münster

Norbert Lohfink, Frankfurt/Main

Fritz Maass, Mainz

Günter Mayer, Münster

J. C. de Moor, Kampen

Magnus Ottosson, Uppsala

Benedikt Otzen, Aarhus, Denmark

Josef Plöger, Bonn

Horst Dietrich Preuss, Göttingen

Helmer Ringgren, Uppsala (Editor)

Josef Scharbert, Munich

Josef Schreiner, Würzburg

Horst Seebass, Münster

Siegfried Wagner, Leipzig

Gerhard Wallis, Halle

Hans-Jürgen Zobel, Halle

CONTENTS

ABBREVIATIONS

AANLR	*Atti dell'Accademia Nazionale dei Lincei, Rendiconti*
AASOR	*Annual of the American Schools of Oriental Research*
AB	*The Anchor Bible*
ABAW	*Abhandlungen der Akademie der Wissenschaften*, Berlin
ABL	R. F. Harper, *Assyrian and Babylonian Letters*, 1-14, Chicago, 1892-1914
ABR	*Australian Biblical Review*, Melbourne
ABRT	J. Craig, *Assyrian and Babylonian Religious Texts*, Leipzig, 1895-97
abs.	absolute
acc.	accusative
AcOr	*Acta Orientalia*
act	active
adj.	adjective
adv.	adverb
ÄF	*Ägyptologische Forschungen*, Glückstadt
AfK	*Archiv für Kulturgeschichte*
AFNW	*Arbeitsgemeinschaft für Forschung des Landes Nordrhein-Westfalen*
AfO	*Archiv für Orientforschung*
ÄgAbh	*Ägyptologische Abhandlungen*
AH	*Analecta Hymnica*, ed. G. Dreves and C. Blume, Leipzig, 1886-1922
AHAW	*Abhandlungen der Heidelberger Akademie der Wissenschaften*
AHDO	*Archives d'Histoire du Droit Oriental*
AHw	W. von Soden, *Akkadisches Handwörterbuch*
AION	*Annali dell'Istituto Universitario Orientale di Napoli*
AJA	*American Journal of Archaeology*
AJSL	*The American Journal of Semitic Languages and Literatures*
Akk.	Akkadian
AKM	*Abhandlungen zur Kunde des Morgenlandes* (Leipzig), Wiesbaden
AN	J. J. Stamm, *Die akkadische Namengebung. MVÄG*, 44 (1939)
AnAcScFen	*Annales Academiae Scientiarum Fennicae*
AnAeg	*Analecta Aegyptiaca*
AnBibl	*Analecta Biblica*, Rome
AncIsr	R. de Vaux, *Ancient Israel: Its Life and Institutions*, trans. 1961
ANEP	*The Ancient Near East in Pictures*, ed. J. B. Pritchard, Princeton, 1954, [2]1969
ANET	*Ancient Near Eastern Texts Relating to the Old Testament*, ed. J. B. Pritchard, [2]1955, [3]1969
AnOr	*Analecta Orientalia*
AnSt	*Anatolian Studies*, London
ANVAO	*Avhandlinger utgitt av det Norske Videnskaps-Akademi i Oslo*
AO	*Der Alte Orient*, Leipzig
AOAT	*Alter Orient und Altes Testament*, Neukirchen-Vluyn
AOB	*Altorientalische Bilder zum Alten Testament*, ed. H. Gressmann, [2]1927
AOT	*Altorientalische Texte zum Alten Testament*, ed. H. Gressmann, [2]1926
AP	A. E. Cowley, *Aramaic Papyri of the Fifth Century B.C.*, Oxford, 1923
APAW	*Abhandlungen der Preussische Akademie der Wissenschaften*, Berlin
APNM	H. B. Huffmon, *Amorite Personal Names in the Mari Texts*, Baltimore, 1965
Arab.	Arabic
Aram.	Aramaic
ArbT	*Arbeiten zur Theologie*, Stuttgart
ARM	*Archives Royales de Mari*, Paris
ArOr	*Archiv Orientâlní*, Prague
ARW	*Archiv für Religionswissenschaft*, Leipzig, Berlin
ASAW	*Abhandlungen der Sächsischen Akademie der Wissenschaften in Leipzig*
ASKT	P. Haupt, *Akkadische und Sumerische Keilschrifttexte*, Leipzig, 1882
Assyr.	Assyrian
ASTI	*Annual of the Swedish Theological Institute in Jerusalem*, Leiden
AT	*Alte Testament*

ATA	*Alttestamentliche Abhandlungen*, Münster
ATD	*Das Alte Testament Deutsch*
AThANT	*Abhandlungen zur Theologie des Alten und Neuen Testaments*, Zurich
ATR	*Anglican Theological Review*, Evanston
Aug	*Augustinianum*
AuS	G. Dalman, *Arbeit und Sitte in Palästina*, 1928-1942
BA	*The Biblical Archaeologist*, New Haven
Bab.	Babylonian
BAfO	*Beihefte zur Archiv für Orientforschung*
BAH	*Bibliothèque Archéologique et Historique*, Paris
BASOR	*Bulletin of the American Schools of Oriental Research*
BAss	*Beiträge zu Assyriologie*
BBB	*Bonner Biblische Beiträge*
BDB	Brown-Driver-Briggs, *A Hebrew and English Lexicon of the Old Testament*
BE	Babylonian Expedition of the University of Pennsylvania, Philadelphia
BeO	*Bibbia e Oriente*
BethM	*Beth Mikra*
BETL	*Bibliotheca Ephemeridum Theologicarum Lovaniensium*
BFChTh	*Beiträge zur Förderung Christlicher Theologie*, Gütersloh
BHHW	*Biblisch-Historisches Handwörterbuch*, ed. L. Rost and B. Reicke, 1962ff.
BHK	*Biblia Hebraica*, ed. R. Kittel
BHS	*Biblia Hebraica Stuttgartensia*, ed. K. Elliger and W. Rudolph, 1968ff.
BHTh	*Beiträge zur Historischen Theologie*, Tübingen
Bibl	*Biblica*, Rome
BiblRes	*Biblical Research*
BietOr	*Biblica et Orientalia*
BiLe	*Bibel und Leben*
BiLi	*Bibel und Liturgie*
BIN	*Babylonian Inscriptions in the Collection of James B. Nies*, New Haven
BiOr	*Bibliotheca Orientalis*, Leiden
BJRL	*Bulletin of the John Rylands Library*, Manchester
BK	*Biblischer Kommentar zum Alten Testament*, ed. M. Noth and H. W. Wolff
BL	*Bibel-Lexikon*, ed. H. Haag
BLA	H. Bauer-P. Leander, *Grammatik des Biblisch-Aramäischen*, 1927
Blachère-Chouémi	R. Blachère-M. Chouémi-C. Denizeau, *Dictionnaire Arabe-Français-Anglais*
BLe	H. Bauer-P. Leander, *Historische Grammatik der hebräischen Sprache*, 1922
BMAP	E. G. Kraeling, *The Brooklyn Museum Aramaic Papyri*, 1953
BMB	*Bulletin du Musée de Beyrouth*
Bo	Unpublished Boğazköy tablets (with catalog number)
BoSt	*Boghazköi Studien*
BOT	*De Boeken van het Oude Testament*, ed. Grossow, van der Ploeg, *et al.*
BRL	K. Galling, *Biblisches Reallexikon*, 1937
BS	*Bibliotheca Sacra*, Dallas
BSAW	*Berichte über die Verhandlungen der Sächsischen Akademie der Wissenschaften zu Leipzig*
BSGW	*Berichte der Sächsischen Gesellschaft der Wissenschaften*
BSt	*Biblische Studien*, Neukirchen
BT	*The Bible Translator*, London
BThH	*Biblisch-Theologisches Handwörterbuch zur Lutherbibel und zu neueren Übersetzungen*, ed. E. Osterloh and H. Engeland
BuA	B. Meissner, *Babylonien und Assyrien*, I 1920, II 1925
BuK	*Bibel und Kirche*
BVC	*Bible et Vie Chrétienne*
BWA(N)T	*Beiträge zur Wissenschaft vom Alten (und Neuen) Testament*, Stuttgart
BWL	W. G. Lambert, *Babylonian Wisdom Literature*, Oxford, 1960

BZ	*Biblische Zeitschrift,* Paderborn
BZAW	*Beihefte zur Zeitschrift für die Alttestamentliche Wissenschaft,* Berlin
BZfr	*Biblische Zeitfragen*
BZTS	*Bonner Zeitschrift für Theologie und Seelsorge*
CAD	*The Assyrian Dictionary of the Oriental Institute of the University of Chicago,* 1956ff.
CahRB	*Cahiers de la Revue Biblique*
CahTD	*Cahiers du Groupe F. Thureau-Dangin,* I, Paris, 1960
CANES	*Corpus of Ancient Near Eastern Seals in North American Collections,* I, Washington, 1948
CAT	*Commentaire de l'Ancien Testament*
CBQ	*Catholic Biblical Quarterly*
CBSC	*The Cambridge Bible for Schools and Colleges*
CChr	*Corpus Christianorum,* Turnhout
CD A, B	Damascus Document, Manuscript A, B
CH	Codex Hammurabi
ChrÉg	*Chronique d'Égypte*
CIH	*Corpus Inscriptionum Himjariticarum* (=*CIS,* IV)
CIS	*Corpus Inscriptionum Semiticarum,* 1881ff.
CML	G. R. Driver, *Canaanite Myths and Legends,* Edinburgh, 1956
CollBG	*Collationes Brugenses et Gandavenses,* Gent
comm.	commentary
ComViat	*Communio Viatorum,* Prague
conj.	conjecture
const.	construct
ContiRossini	K. Conti Rossini, *Chrestomathia Arabica meridionalis epigraphica,* 1931
Copt.	Coptic
COT	*Commentaar op het Oude Testament,* ed. G. C. Aalders, Kampen
CRAI	*Comptes-rendus de l'Académie des Inscriptions et Belles-Lettres,* Paris
CRRA	*Compte Rendu de . . . Recontre Assyriologique Internationale*
CT	Cuneiform Texts from Babylonian Tablets, etc. in the British Museum, London, 1896ff.
CT	*The Egyptian Coffin Texts,* ed. A. de Buck and A. H. Gardiner, 1935ff.
CTA	A. Herdner, *Corpus des Tablettes en Cunéiformes Alphabétiques Découvertes à Ras Shamra-Ugarit* I/II, Paris, 1963
CTM	*Concordia Theological Monthly,* St. Louis
CultBibl	*Cultura Bíblica,* Segovia
CW	*Die Christliche Welt*
DACL	F. Cabrol-H. Leclercq, *Dictionnaire d'Archéologie Chrétienne et Liturgie,* Paris, 1907ff.
DB	*Dictionnaire de la Bible*
DBS	*Dictionnaire de la Bible, Supplément,* ed. L. Pirot, A. Robert, H. Cazelles, and A. Feuillet, 1928ff.
DISO	Ch. F. Jean-J. Hoftijzer, *Dictionnaire des Inscriptions Sémitiques de l'Ouest,* Leiden, 1965
diss.	dissertation
DissAbs	*Dissertation Abstracts*
DJD	*Discoveries in the Judaean Desert,* 1955ff.
DLZ	*Deutsche Literaturzeitung*
DN	name of a deity
DTT	*Dansk Teologisk Tidsskrift,* Copenhagen
EA	Tell el-Amarna Tablets
EB	*Die Heilige Schrift in deutscher Übersetzung. Echter-Bibel,* Würzburg
EGA	R. M. Boehmer, *Die Entwicklung der Glyptik während der Akkad-Zeit,* Berlin, 1965
Egyp.	Egyptian

Einl.	Einleitung
EJ	*Encyclopaedia Judaica*
EKL	*Evangelisches Kirchenlexikon*, Göttingen, I 1956, II 1958
EMiqr	*Entsiqlopēdiä Miqrā'ît–Encyclopaedia Biblica*, Jerusalem
EnEl	Enuma Elish
Eng.	English
ErfThSt	*Erfurter Theologische Studien*
ErJb	*Eranos-Jahrbuch*
EstBíb	*Estudios Bíblicos*, Madrid
EstEcl	*Estudios Eclesiásticos*
Ethiop.	Ethiopic
ETL	*Ephemerides Theologicae Lovanienses*
EvQ	*The Evangelical Quarterly*
EvTh	*Evangelische Theologie*, Munich
ExpT	*The Expository Times*, London
FreibThSt	*Freiburger Theologische Studien*
FRLANT	*Forschungen zur Religion und Literatur des Alten und Neuen Testaments*, Göttingen
FzB	*Forschung zur Bibel*
gen.	genitive
GesB	W. Gesenius-F. Buhl, *Hebräisches und aramäisches Handwörterbuch*, [17]1921
GF	A. Alt, *The God of the Fathers*, trans. in *Essays on Old Testament History and Religion* (1966), 1-77
GGA	*Göttingische Gelehrte Anzeigen*
GHK	*Hand-Kommentar zum Alten Testament*, ed. W. Nowack, Göttingen
Gilg	Gilgamesh Epic
GK	W. Gesenius-E. Kautzsch, *Hebräische Grammatik*, [28]1909 (=Kautzsch-Cowley, *Gesenius' Hebrew Grammar*, [2]1910)
Gk.	Greek
Gl	Inscriptions in the E. Glaser collection (Old South Arabic)
GLECS	*Comptes Rendus du Groupe Linguistique d'Études Chamito-Sémitiques*, Paris
Greg	*Gregorianum*
GSAT	*Gesammelte Studien zum Alten Testament*
HAT	*Handbuch zum Alten Testament*, ed. O. Eissfeldt, 1st series
Ḫatt.	Ḫattic
HAW	*Handbuch der Altertumswissenschaft*, ed. W. Otto, Munich, 1929ff.
Heb.	Hebrew
Hitt.	Hittite
HNT	*Handbuch zum Neuen Testament*, ed. G. Bornkamm
HO	*Handbuch der Orientalistik*, ed. B. Spuler, Leiden, 1952ff.
HSAT	*Die Heilige Schrift des Alten Testaments*, ed. E. Kautsch-A. Bertholet, [4]1922/23
HThR	*Harvard Theological Review*
HUCA	*Hebrew Union College Annual*, Cincinnati
IB	*The Interpreter's Bible*, ed. G. A. Buttrick, 1951-57
ICC	*The International Critical Commentary*
IDB	*The Interpreter's Dictionary of the Bible*, ed. G. A. Buttrick, I-IV, 1962
IEJ	*Israel Exploration Journal*, Jerusalem
ILC	J. Pedersen, *Israel. Its Life and Culture*, 1926, [3]1953, 4 vols. in 2
impf.	imperfect
impv.	imperative
In	*Interpretation*
inf.	infinitive
in loc.	on this passage
Introd.	Introduction (to)
IPN	M. Noth, *Die israelitischen Personennamen. BWANT*, 3/10, 1928

IrishThQ	*Irish Theological Quarterly*, Maynooth
JA	*Journal Asiatique*, Paris
Ja	Enumeration according to A. Jamme (Old South Arabic)
JAOS	*Journal of the American Oriental Society*
JBL	*Journal of Biblical Literature*
JBR	*Journal of Bible and Religion*, Boston
JCS	*Journal of Cuneiform Studies*, New Haven
JEA	*Journal of Egyptian Archaeology*, London
JEOL	*Jaarbericht ... Ex Oriente Lux*, Leiden
JES	*Journal of Ecumenical Studies*
JJS	*Journal of Jewish Studies*, London
JNES	*Journal of Near Eastern Studies*, Chicago
JNWSL	*Journal of Northwest Semitic Languages*
JoPh	*The Journal of Philology*
JPOS	*Journal of the Palestine Oriental Society*, Jerusalem
JQR	*Jewish Quarterly Review*
JR	*Journal of Religion*, Chicago
JRAS	*Journal of the Royal Asiatic Society of Great Britain and Ireland*, London
JRH	*Journal of Religion and Health*
JSOR	*Journal of the Society of Oriental Research*, Toronto
JSS	*Journal of Semitic Studies*, Manchester
JThC	*Journal for Theology and the Church*
JTS	*Journal of Theological Studies*, Oxford
Jud	*Judaica*
K	Tablets in the Kouyunjik collection of the British Museum
KAI	H. Donner-W. Röllig, *Kanaanäische und aramäische Inschriften*, I ²1966, II ²1968, III ²1969
KAR	E. Ebeling, *Keilschrifttexte aus Assur religiösen Inhalts*, 1915-1919.
KAT	*Kommentar zum Alten Testament*, ed. E. Sellin, continued by J. Herrmann
KAV	O. Schroeder, *Keilinschriften aus Assur verschiedenen Inhalts*
KB	*Keilinschriftliche Bibliothek*, ed. B. Schrader
KBL	L. Koehler-W. Baumgartner, *Hebräisches und aramäisches Lexikon zum Alten Testament*, ²1958, ³1967ff.
KBo	*Keilschrifttexte aus Boghazköy*
KHC	*Kurzer Handcommentar zum Alten Testament*, ed. K. Marti
KlSchr	*Kleine Schriften* (A. Alt, 1953-59; O. Eissfeldt, 1962ff.)
KUB	*Keilschriftenurkunden aus Boghazköi*
KuD	*Kerygma und Dogma*, Göttingen
Lane	E. W. Lane, *An Arabic-English Lexicon*, London, 1863-1893
Lat.	Latin
LD	*Lectio Divina*
Leslau, *Con-tributions*	W. Leslau, *Ethiopic and South Arabic Contributions to the Hebrew Lexicon* (1958)
Levy, *WTM*	J. Levy, *Wörterbuch über die Talmudim und Midraschim*, ²1924=1963
LexSyr	C. Brockelmann, *Lexicon Syriacum*, ²1968
LidzEph	M. Lidzbarski, *Ephemeris für semitische Epigraphik*, 1900-1915
LidzNE	M. Lidzbarski, *Handbuch der nordsemitischen Epigraphik*, 1898
lit.	literally
LRSt	*Leipziger Rechtswissenschaftliche Studien*
LSS	*Leipziger Semitische Studien*
LThK	*Lexikon für Theologie und Kirche*, 1930-38, ²1957ff.
LUÅ	*Lunds Universitets Årsskrift*
LXX	Septuagint
MAOG	*Mitteilungen der Altorientalischen Gesellschaft*, Leipzig
MBPAR	*Münchener Beiträge zur Papyrusforschung und Antiken Rechtsgeschichte*
MDAI	*Mitteilungen des Deutschen Archäologischen Instituts in Kairo*, Wiesbaden

MdD	E. S. Drower-R. Macuch, *Mandaic Dictionary*, Oxford, 1963
MDOG	*Mitteilungen der Deutschen Orient-Gesellschaft*, Berlin
MeyerK	*Kritisch-exegetischer Kommentar über das Neue Testament*, initiated by H. A. W. Meyer, Göttingen
MIFAO	*Mémoires publiés par les membres de l'Institut Français d'Archéologie Orientale au Caire*, Cairo
MIO	*Mitteilungen des Instituts für Orientforschung*, Berlin
MKAW	*Mededelingen der Kon. Nederlandse Akademie van Wetenschappen*, Amsterdam
MKPAW	*Monatsberichte der Königlich-Preussischen Akademie der Wissenschaften*, Berlin
MPG	*Patrologia Graeca*, ed. J. P. Migne, Paris
MPL	*Patrologia Latina*, ed. J. P. Migne, Paris
ms.	manuscript
MT	Massoretic Text
MThS	*Münchener Theologische Studien*
MThZ	*Münchener Theologische Zeitschrift*
Mus	*Le Muséon, Revue d'Études Orientales*
MUSJ	*Mélanges de l'Université St. Joseph*, Beirut
MVÄG	*Mitteilungen der Vorderasiatisch-Ägyptischen Gesellschaft* (Berlin), Leipzig
n.d.	no date
NedGTT	*Nederduitse Gereformeerde Teologiese Tydskrif*
NedThT	*Nederlands Theologisch Tijdschrift*, Wageningen
NKZ	*Neue Kirchliche Zeitschrift*, Erlangen, Leipzig
n.n.	no name
NovT	*Novum Testamentum*, Leiden
NRTh	*Nouvelle Revue Théologique*, Paris
NSI	G. A. Cooke, *A Text-Book of North-Semitic Inscriptions*, Oxford, 1903
NTS	*New Testament Studies*, Cambridge
NTT	*Norsk Teologisk Tidsskrift*, Oslo
obj.	object
OECT	*Oxford Editions of Cuneiform Texts*, London, 1923ff.
OIP	*Oriental Institute Publications*, Chicago, 1924ff.
OLP	*Orientalia Lovaniensia Periodica*
OLZ	*Orientalistische Literaturzeitung* (Leipzig), Berlin
Or	*Orientalia. Commentarii periodici Pontificii Instituti Biblici*, Rome
OrAnt	*Oriens Antiquus*
OrNeer	*Orientalia Neerlandica*, Leiden
OTL	*The Old Testament Library*
OTS	*Oudtestamentische Studiën*, Leiden
OuTWP	*De Ou Testamentiese Werkgemeenskap in Suid-Afrika*, Pretoria
PAAJR	*Proceedings of the American Academy for Jewish Research*
par.	parallel/and parallel passages
pass.	passive
PBS	*Publications of the Babylonian Section of the University Museum*, Philadelphia
PEQ	*Palestine Exploration Quarterly*, London
perf.	perfect
Phoen.	Phoenician
PJ	*Palästinajahrbuch*, Berlin
PN	name of a person
PN	H. Ranke, *Die ägyptischen Personennamen*, 1935-1952
PNU	F. Gröndahl, *Personennamen der Texte aus Ugarit*, Rome, 1967
prep.	preposition
PRU	*Le Palais Royal d'Ugarit*, ed. Cl. Schaeffer, Paris
PSBA	*Proceedings of the Society of Biblical Archaeology*, Bloomsbury (London)

ptcp.	participle
Pun.	Punic
PV	*Parole di Vita*
PW	A. Pauly-G. Wissowa, *Real-Encyclopädie der classischen Altertums-wissenschaft*, 1894ff.
Pyr.	Pyramid Texts, ed. K. Sethe
QuaestDisp	*Quaestiones Disputatae*, ed. K. Rahner and H. Schlier, 1959ff.
R	H. C. Rawlinson, *The Cuneiform Inscriptions of Western Asia*, London, 1861-1909
RA	*Revue d'Assyriologie et d'Archéologie Orientale*, Paris
RAC	*Reallexikon für Antike und Christentum*, ed. Th. Klauser, 1941ff.
RÄR	H. Bonnet, *Reallexikon der ägyptischen Religionsgeschichte*
RB	*Revue Biblique*, Paris
RdM	*Die Religionen der Menschheit*, ed. C. M. Schröder
RE	*Real-Enzyklopädie für protestantische Theologie und Kirche*, ³1896-1913
REg	*Revue d'Égyptologie*
repr.	reprint, reprinted
RES	*Revue des Études Sémitiques*, Paris
RES (with number)	*Répertoire d'Épigraphie Sémitique*
RevQ	*Revue de Qumrân*, Paris
RevRéf	*La Revue Réformee*
RGG	*Die Religion in Geschichte und Gegenwart*, ³1957-1965
RHA	*Revue Hittite et Asianique*, Paris
RHJE	*Revue de l'Histoire Juive en Égypte*
RHPR	*Revue d'Histoire et de Philosophie Religieuses*, Strasbourg, Paris
RHR	*Revue de l'Histoire des Religions*, Paris
RivBibl	*Rivista Biblica*, Rome
RLA	*Reallexikon der Assyriologie*, ed. G. Ebeling and B. Meissner, Berlin, I 1932, II 1938, III 1, 2 1957/59
RLR	*Revue de Linguistique Romane*
RLV	*Reallexikon der Vorgeschichte*, ed. Max Ebert, Berlin, 1924-1932
RoB	*Religion och Bibel. Nathan Söderblom-Sällskapets Årsbok*
RS	Ras Shamra
RScR	*Revue des Sciences Religieuses*
RSO	*Rivista degli Studi Orientali*, Rome
RSPT	*Revue des Sciences Philosophiques et Théologiques*, Paris
RT	*Recueil de Travaux relatifs à la philologie et à l'archéologie égyptiennes et assyriennes*
RTP	*Revue de Théologie et de Philosophie*, Lausanne
Ry	Enumeration in G. Ryckmans, *Inscriptions sudarabes* I-XVII; *Le Muséon*, 40-72
SAHG	A. Falkenstein-W. von Soden, *Sumerische und akkadische Hymnen und Gebete*
SAK	*Die sumerischen und akkadischen Königsinschriften*, ed. F. Thureau-Dangin (=*VAB*, I)
SAT	*Die Schriften des Alten Testaments in Auswahl*, trans. and ed. H. Gunkel, *et al.*, Göttingen
SAW	*Sitzungsberichte der Österreichischen Akademie der Wissenschaften in Wien*
SBAW	*Sitzungsberichte der Bayerischen Akademie der Wissenschaften*, Munich
SBM	*Stuttgarter Biblische Monographien*
SBS	*Stuttgarter Bibel-Studien*
SBT	*Studies in Biblical Theology*
SchThU	*Schweizerische Theologische Umschau*, Bern
ScrHier	*Scripta Hierosolymitana. Publications of the Hebrew University*, Jerusalem
SDAW	*Sitzungsberichte der Deutschen Akademie der Wissenschaften zu Berlin*
SEÅ	*Svensk Exegetisk Årsbok*, Lund

Sem	*Semitica*
Seux	J. M. Seux, *Epithètes Royales Akkadiennes et Sumériennes*, Paris, 1968
SG	F. Delitzsch, *Sumerische Grammatik*
SgV	*Sammlung gemeinverständlicher Vorträge und Schriften aus dem Gebiet der Theologie und Religionsgeschichte*, Tübingen
SJT	*Scottish Journal of Theology*, Edinburgh
SL	A. Deimel, *Šumerisches Lexikon*, Rome, 1925-1937
SMSR	*Studi e Materiali di Storia delle Religioni* (Rome), Bologna
SNumen	*Supplements to Numen*
SNVAO	*Skrifter utgitt av Det Norske Videnskaps-Akademi i Oslo*
Soq.	Soqoṭri
SPAW	*Sitzungsberichte der Preussischen Akademie der Wissenschaften zu Berlin*
SSAW	*Sitzungsberichte der Sächsischen Akademie der Wissenschaften zu Leipzig*
SSN	*Studia Semitica Neerlandica*
StANT	*Studien zum Alten und Neuen Testament*, Munich
St.-B.	H. L. Strack-P. Billerbeck, *Kommentar zum Neuen Testament aus Talmud und Midrasch*, 1923-1961
StOr	*Studia Orientalia*, Helsinki
StSem	*Studi Semitici*
StTh	*Studia Theologica*, Lund, Aarhus
StudGen	*Studium Generale*, Heidelberg
subj.	subject
subst.	substantive
suf.	suffix
Sum.	Sumerian
SVT	*Supplements to Vetus Testamentum*, Leiden
Synt	C. Brockelmann, *Hebräische Syntax*
Syr.	Syriac
Syr	*Syria. Revue d'Art Oriental et d'Archéologie*, Paris
TAik	*Teologinen Aikakauskirja*
TCL	*Textes Cunéiformes du Musée du Louvre*
TDNT	*Theological Dictionary of the New Testament*, ed. G. Kittel and G. Friedrich, trans. G. Bromiley
TDOT	*Theological Dictionary of the Old Testament*
TGUOS	*Transactions of the Glasgow University Oriental Society*
Th.	Theologie
Theol.	Theology (of)
THAT	*Theologisches Handwörterbuch zum Alten Testament*, ed. E. Jenni and C. Westermann, Munich, 1971
ThB	*Theologische Bücherei*
Theol.Diss.	*Theologische Dissertationen*, Basel
ThLZ	*Theologische Literaturzeitung*, Leipzig, Berlin
ThR	*Theologische Rundschau*, Tübingen
ThSt	*Theologische Studien*, Zurich
ThStKr	*Theologische Studien und Kritiken*, Berlin
ThViat	*Theologia Viatorum*
ThZ	*Theologische Zeitschrift*, Basel
Tigr.	Tigrīnya (Tigriña)
trans.	translated
TrThSt	*Trierer Theologische Studien*
TrThZ	*Trierer Theologische Zeitschrift*
TS	*Theological Studies*
TüThQ	*Theologische Quartalschrift*, Tübingen, Stuttgart
TynB	*Tyndale Bulletin*
UET	*Ur Excavations. Texts*, London, 1928ff.
UF	*Ugarit-Forschungen*

Ugar.	Ugaritic
Urk.	*Urkunden des ägyptischen Altertums*, ed. G. Steindorff
UT	C. H. Gordon, *Ugaritic Textbook*, Rome, 1965
UUÅ	*Uppsala Universitets Årsskrift*
VAB	*Vorderasiatische Bibliothek*
VAS	*Vorderasiatische Schriftdenkmäler der königlichen Museen zu Berlin*
VD	*Verbum Domini*, Rome
VG	C. Brockelmann, *Grundriss der vergleichenden Grammatik der semitischen Sprachen*, 1908-1913
VT	*Vetus Testamentum*, Leiden
Vulg.	Vulgate
WbÄS	A. Erman-H. Grapow, *Wörterbuch der ägyptischen Sprache*, I-V
WbMyth	*Wörterbuch der Mythologie*, ed. H. W. Haussig
Whitaker	R. E. Whitaker, *A Concordance of the Ugaritic Literature*, 1972
WMANT	*Wissenschaftliche Monographien zum Alten und Neuen Testament*, Neukirchen
WO	*Die Welt des Orients*, Göttingen
WTM	J. Levy, *Wörterbuch über die Talmudim und Midraschim*, ²1924 = 1963
WUS	J. Aistleitner, *Wörterbuch der ugaritischen Sprache*, ³1967
WZ	*Wissenschaftliche Zeitschrift*
WZKM	*Wiener Zeitschrift für die Kunde des Morgenlandes*
ZA	*Zeitschrift für Assyriologie* (Leipzig), Berlin
ZÄS	*Zeitschrift für Ägyptische Sprache und Altertumskunde* (Leipzig), Berlin
ZAW	*Zeitschrift für die Alttestamentliche Wissenschaft* (Giessen), Berlin
ZDMG	*Zeitschrift der Deutschen Morgenländischen Gesellschaft* (Leipzig), Wiesbaden
ZDPV	*Zeitschrift des Deutschen Palästina-Vereins* (Leipzig, Stuttgart), Wiesbaden
ZE	*Zeitschrift für Ethnologie*
ZEE	*Zeitschrift für Evangelische Ethik*, Gütersloh
ZMR	*Zeitschrift für Missionskünde und Religionswissenschaft*, Berlin
ZNW	*Zeitschrift für die Neutestamentliche Wissenschaft* (Giessen), Berlin
ZRGG	*Zeitschrift für Religions- und Geistesgeschichte*, Cologne
ZS	*Zeitschrift für Semitistik und verwandte Gebiete*, Leipzig
ZST	*Zeitschrift für die Systematische Theologie* (Gütersloh), Berlin
ZThK	*Zeitschrift für Theologie und Kirche*, Tübingen
ZZ	*Die Zeichen der Zeit*
→	indicates cross-reference within this *Dictionary*

TRANSLITERATION OF HEBREW

CONSONANTS

Hebrew Consonant	Technical Usage	Nontechnical Usage
א	ʾ	ʾ
בּ	b	b
ב	bh	bh
גּ	g	g
ג	gh	gh
דּ	d	d
ד	dh	dh
ה	h	h
ו	v, w	v
ז	z	z
ח	ch, ḥ	ch
ט	ṭ	t
י	y	y
כּ	k	k
כ	kh	kh
ל	l	l
מ	m	m
נ	n	n
ס	s	s
ע	ʿ	ʿ
פּ	p	p
פ	ph	ph
צ	ts, ṣ	ts
ק	q	q
ר	r	r
שׂ	ś	s
שׁ	sh, š	sh
תּ	t	t
ת	th	th

VOWELS

Hebrew Vowel	Technical Usage	Nontechnical Usage
—	a	a
—:	a	a
—ָ	ā	a
—ֶ	e	e
—ֱ	e	e
׳—ֶ	ey	ey
—ֵ	ē	e
׳—ֵ	ê	e
—ְ	e	e
—ִ	i	i
׳—ִ	î	i
—ָ	o	o
—ֳ	o	o
—ֹ	ō	o
וֹ	ô	o
—ֻ	u	u
וּ	û	u
׳—ַ	ai	ai
יו—ָ	āv	av
׳—ָ	āi	ai
ה	h	h

אָב 'ābh

Contents: I. The Word. II. "Father" in the Ancient Near East Outside the OT: 1. Egypt; 2. Mesopotamia; 3. The West Semitic Region. III. The OT: 1. Linguistic Usage; 2. The Role of the Father (Including beth 'abh); 3. Theological: a. "Sleeping with One's Fathers"; b. The God of the Fathers; c. The Land Promise to the Fathers; d. God's Saving Deeds to the Fathers; e. Teaching and Example of the Fathers; f. The Sins of the Fathers; g. The Fathers in the Royal Dynasty; h. Community Identification with the Fathers; i. Acknowledgment of the Sins of the Fathers; 4. God As Father: a. Proper Names; b. Yahweh As Father of the People; c. Yahweh As Father of the King; d. Isa. 9:5(6).

I. **The Word.** The word 'ab(u) is found with slight variations in all Semitic languages. All attempts to trace the word back to a triliteral root must be regarded as failures. Instead it is to be understood, with Köhler,[1] as an onomatopoetic word imitating the babbling sounds of an infant, i.e., as a child's word.

'ābh. On "Father" in the OT: G. Ahlström, Psalm 89 (Lund, 1959); B. Alfrink, "L'expression šākab 'im 'abōtāw," OTS, 2 (1943), 106-118; Alt, GF; B. Colless, "Dio la Patro," Biblia Revuo, 4/4 (1968), 5-19; F. M. Cross, "Yahweh and the God of the Patriarchs," HThR, 55 (1962), 225-259; L. Dürr, Das Erziehungswesen im AT und im antiken alten Orient. MVÄG, 36/2 (1932); J. W. Gaspar, Social Ideas in the Wisdom Literature of the OT (Washington, 1947); J. Hempel, Gott und Mensch im AT. BWANT, 3/2 (²1936); J. P. Hyatt, "Yahweh as 'the God of my Father'," VT, 5 (1955), 130-36; R. Knierim, Die Hauptbegriffe für Sünde im AT (1965); M. J. Lagrange, "La paternité de Dieu dans l'AT," RB, 5 (1908), 481-499; H. G. May, "The God of my Father–a Study of Patriarchal Religion," JBR, 9 (1941), 155-58; Noth, IPN; Pedersen, ILC, I-II, III-IV; J. G. Plöger, Literarkritische, formgeschichtliche und stilkritische Untersuchungen zum Deuteronomium. BBB, 26 (1967); J. R. Porter, The Extended Family in the OT (London, 1967); J. Scharbert, Solidarität in Segen und Fluch im AT und in seiner Umwelt. BBB, 14 (1958); de Vaux, AncIsr; J. N. M. Wijngaards, The Dramatization of Salvific History in the Deuteronomic Schools. OTS, 16 (1969).

On II. "Father" in the Ancient Near East Outside the OT: A. Erman-H. Ranke, Ägypten und ägyptisches Leben im Altertum (1923); H. Grapow, Die bildlichen Ausdrücke des Ägyptischen (1924); Gröndahl, PNU; J. Klíma, Gesellschaft und Kultur des alten Mesopotamiens (Prague, 1964); R. Labat, Le caractère religieux de la royauté assyro-babylonienne (Paris, 1939); Ranke, PN, I-II; J. Sainte-Fare Garnot, L'hommage aux dieux ... d'apres les textes des pyramides (Paris, 1954); A. van Selms, Marriage and Family Life in Ugaritic Literature (London, 1954); Stamm, AN; K. Tallqvist, Akkadische Götterepitheta. StOr, 7 (1938); J. Zandee, De Hymnen aan Amon van Pap. Leiden I 350 (Leiden, 1947).

[1] ZAW, 55 (1937), 169ff.

II. "Father" in the Ancient Near East Outside the OT.

1. *Egypt.* The Egyptian word for "father" is *it*.[2] In most cases this word is used of an earthly father.[3] It is also used in the broader sense of "ancestor, forefather," often in the plural.

This word is used figuratively in expressions like "I was a father to the child," and he was "a father to orphans, a husband to widows." An official was said to be "a good father to his people." The king was referred to as "father of the two countries" or as "the good bearer of water, who keeps his army alive, father and mother to all men."[4] It is clear that these expressions contain above all comparisons based on the idea of a father providing for the needs of his children.

It is noteworthy that the Egyptian terms used for relatives are limited to the most intimate family relationships (father, mother, son, daughter, brother, sister). This indicates that only the small family unit was felt to play a crucial role in Egyptian social life. The same thing was true in the public administration, where originally the highest public offices were held by royal princes.[5]

An outstanding feature of Egyptian family life was the reverence the son showed to his father. He was responsible for his father's funeral, and for offering the sacrifice at his tomb. E.g., the provincial prince Khnumhotep boasts: "I have exalted the name of my father, and have supplied the place of the cult of the dead and the provisions which are necessary for it."[6] But also more generally, Egyptian literature often contains admonitions that a person show love, gratitude, and respect to his parents.

It was the father's duty to educate the children, as is clear in that many of the Egyptian books of wisdom claim to be a father's teaching for his son.[7] They emphasize that it is good when the son obeys his father.[8]

Since the families and genealogies of the gods have an important place in Egyptian mythology, "father" is often used as a divine epithet. Thus, Osiris above all is known as the father of Horus, e.g., in Pyr. 650b he is called "the father of Horus, who begat him";[9] and Horus is said to be "the one who acts in his father's behalf" (*nḏ it.f*).[10] Several gods are known as "father of the gods" (*it nṯr.w*), among them Atum, Re, Nun, Geb, Ptah.[11] The primal- and creator-god boasts that he was "without father and mother," or that he is "the bull of his mother" (Kamutef), i.e., he begat himself (above all, Amon and Min).[12] "Father of fathers, mother of mothers," i.e., primal-father and primal-

---

[2] *WbÄS*, I, 141f.
[3] It is used of animals as well as of people. *WbÄS*, I, 14/15.
[4] Grapow, 132f.
[5] Helck-Otto, *Kleines Wörterbuch der Aegyptologie* (1956), 96f.
[6] Erman-Ranke, 184.
[7] Dürr, 15.
[8] *Ibid.*, 32f.
[9] Sainte-Fare Garnot, 120ff.
[10] *Ibid.*, 135ff.
[11] Zandee, 93f.
[12] *RÄR*, 364.

mother, also occur as divine epithets. Strange as it may seem, one and the same God can appear as father and mother: thus Ptah, Osiris, Amon. [13] Amon is often called "father and mother (or merely father) of mankind," which in particular emphasizes his function as creator (cf. Aton, who is described as "mother and father of everything which has been made," and the sun-god, who is called "mother of the earth, father of mankind"). [14]

From the first Intermediate Period on, there are also proper names which characterize a given individual as son of a god. Such a designation was limited to kings in the Old Kingdom. The reason for this change is that the social unrest in the first Intermediate Period brought about a democratization. In the New Kingdom names like "Amon is my father," "Chons is my father," etc., appear. According to Ranke, this indicates a deepened piety. [15]

Finally, the king is designated as "father of the child, nurse of the infant." [16] The priestly title it nṯr, "divine father," which refers to a priest of the highest rank, has not been explained satisfactorily. [17]

2. *Mesopotamia.* a. As M. Lambert has demonstrated, [18] the Sumerian language has at least three different expressions for "father": (i) *a,* later *a-a,* "father" = "begetter"; (ii) *ab-ba,* "father" = "head of the family"; and (iii) *ad-da,* which is found only in texts from Nippur, and to which the Elamite word for "father" is related. The difference between the first two terms is evident, e.g., in two epithets of En-lil: he is called *ab-ba dingir-dingir-e-ne,* "father of all gods," i.e., the *Pater familias* of the world of the gods; and *a-a-kalam-ma,* "father of the land," i.e., begetter and creator of the world.

b. Like the other Semitic languages, Akkadian has only one word for "father," viz., *abu(m),* which is used to convey both of these nuances. When it means "father" in the physical sense, it often appears alongside or is used as a synonym for *bānû,* "begetter." Sometimes a distinction is made between *ālidānu,* "the physical father," and "step-father" or "foster-father." [19] But *abu* is also used with reference to other men: kings speak of their predecessors on the throne as "my father" (there are also instances in which the plural means "ancestors"); a king or a protector of the people is addressed as "my father and lord" (*abī bēlī,* or some similar expression); cf. *TCL,* 14, 13:27: "Thou art my father and my lord, I have no other father but thee." The sheiks of the semi-nomadic peoples

13 Zandee, 93; Kees, *Der Götterglaube im Alten Ägypten* (²1956), 162.
14 Grapow, 133.
15 Ranke, *PN,* II, 233f., 238; cf. 226, 243.
16 Grapow, 133. The royal title *ity* is also related to the word *it;* cf. Kees, *Totenglauben* (²1956), 217.
17 Was the original meaning "father of daughters," who lived in the harem of the god? *RÄR,* 256.
18 *GLECS,* 9 (1960-1963), 52f.
19 Driver-Miles, *Assyrian Laws* (1935), 223.

were called *abu,* particularly in Mari but also later. In some cases *abu* means "official," "administrator," or "master"; of particular interest is the expression *abu ummāni kalāma,* "a master of all trades." [20] The Mesopotamian family was essentially patriarchal, but the authority of the father over the children was not entirely absolute. It is true that he could expose a child, but he did not have the power of life and death over his child. According to Sumerian laws, a son who acted contrary to his father was sold into slavery. The Code of Hammurabi requires punishment for the son who smites his father (CH § 195), and states that the father may disown his son or give his children into servitude for debts he has incurred. [21]

As in Egypt, so in Mesopotamia the education of the child was considered to be the responsibility of the father. For example, we read in EnEl VII, 147: "Let the father tell about it (i.e., the creation) and teach it to his son." [22] It was the duty of the sons to maintain the ancestral cult, though this was not regulated by law, but was founded on ancient custom. And yet, in documents having to do with the distribution of the paternal inheritance, often the heirs must accept the responsibility of maintaining the ancestral cult. [23]

It is also the responsibility of the father to support and to protect his family. From comparisons and other types of expressions (for illustrations cf. *CAD*), we become acquainted with the characteristics that were considered essential for a man to be a good father in the view of Mesopotamian society. For example, we find such statements as these: "The king treated his servants as a father treats his sons"; "let me learn from this whether you love me as a father"; it is said to be abnormal for a "father and mother to abandon their son." [24] Conversely, something was considered to be wrong if "sons despised their father" or if "a son and a father were angry with each other."

There are several indications of a feeling of an intimate relationship between the generations in Mesopotamian literature. We find this description of calamity in the Erra Epic: "The son will not be concerned about the health of the father, nor the father about the health of the son"; in incantation texts there is also an allusion to "curse through father or mother," but it seems best not to understand this in the sense of a child being responsible for his parents' crimes; [25] indirect examples are the deprecatory references to a king's sons who raise up a revolt against their father or kill him. [26]

Frequently the gods are designated as *abu.* To some extent this is to be understood literally in connection with the idea of genealogies of the gods. But this title also appears without genealogical connections. Anu, Enlil, Sin, Assur, etc. are called *abu ilāni,* "father of the gods." Quite often Nanna-Sin is designated simply as "father," but he is also referred to as *abu kibrāti,* "father of the world

---

[20] *BWL,* 158/11.
[21] Klíma, 190f.
[22] Dürr, 67.
[23] Klíma, 191.
[24] *BWL,* 70/11, Theodicy.
[25] Scharbert, 53ff.
[26] *CAD, s.v.,* 1a, conclusion.

regions," and *abu ṣalmāt qaqqadi*, "father of the blackheaded ones" (i.e., men). Anu is called *abu ša ilāni bānū kalāma*, "father of the gods, creator of all," and *abu šamê ū erṣetim*, "father of the heaven and of the earth." [27] Here it is clear that the word "father" is synonymous with creator or originator, and also an expression for power and authority.

Occasionally, the relationship between god and man is characterized as a father-child relationship. Thus a certain god is said to show mercy as a father, or to forgive as a father. It has been said that "they spoke of Marduk as one would speak of a father and a mother." Such a statement refers primarily to the kindness and care of the deity. It was natural, then, for the tutelary god of some man to be addressed as *abī*, "my father." [28]

There is a particular problem connected with statements in which a king asserts that he has no other father or mother than a certain deity. [29] Scholars are divided as to whether such a statement is intended to convey the idea that the king was physically the product of a divine begettal, or merely that the deity gave the king special protection. [30]

Perhaps this question can be settled by referring to the use of *abu* in proper names. A few proper names, such as *ᵈAnum-ki-i-a-bi-ia*, "Anu is like my father," merely suggest that the deity's behavior is similar to a father's behavior. Others, like *Šamaš-abi*, "Shamash is my father," *Sin-Abūšu*, "Sin is his father," and the like, indicate unequivocally that the god who is named is considered to be the man's father. Stamm understands these names as "expressions of prospective trust"; they are analogous to the names which refer to a man as a son of the deity or as begotten by him. [31] It is certain that there is no mythology here, but rather a man is simply described as standing under special divine protection. [32] But we cannot be sure about names in which *abī*, or the like, seems to be a substitute for a divine name, as in *Abī-nāsir*, "my father protects," *Abī-iddina*, "my father has given," etc. Noth regards *abu* as a theophorous element, [33] which is certainly true in many cases (especially with reference to the tutelary god), [34] but there are other cases in which it seems to refer to the earthly father, as Stamm has argued.

3. *The West Semitic Region.* West Semitic literature is little different from Akkadian in the way it uses the word "father." [35] Most of the examples refer to the earthly father; thus, e.g., Mesha (line 2 of the Mesha Inscription), Aḥiram (*KAI*, 1.1), Barrakib (*KAI*, 215.18), and Panammuwa (*KAI*, 214.8f.) speak of their fathers in a literal sense. In the Ugaritic texts, Keret and Danel are men-

---

27 Tallqvist, 1f.
28 Stamm, 54f.
29 Labat, 57; Engnell, *Studies in Divine Kingship* (Uppsala, 1943), 16.
30 Sjöberg, *RoB*, 20 (1961), 14-29.
31 Stamm, 208f.; cf. 222.
32 Dhorme, *La religion assyro-babylonienne* (1910), 196f.
33 *IPN*, 66ff.
34 Stamm, 54f.
35 *DISO*.

tioned as fathers. The plural is used to refer to the forefathers, [36] and the expression *byt 'b* is used for the family or the dynasty. [37] In the Ugaritic texts, a certain *"Hrgb,* father of the eagle (vulture)" [38] is mentioned in conjunction with *"Sml,* the mother of the eagle." [39] It is obvious in this case that a mythological couple represent the (species) eagles. Ugaritic also has the word *ḥtk,* which (probably with different vocalizations) sometimes means "father" and sometimes "origin." [40]

There are numerous examples of the metaphorical use of *'b* in West Semitic literature. For example, Kilamuwa says: "I was a father to one person, and a mother to another, and a brother to yet a third." [41] And in the Karatepe Inscription we read, "Baal made me a father and a mother of the Danuna," [42] a statement which obviously is describing the king as protector and sustainer of his people. Ahikar is called "father of all Assyria" (55). This expression means that he was the counsellor, because the land was dependent on the counsellor as a child on his father.

In the Ugaritic texts, Danel calls El his father, as when he says: "O Bull El, my father." [43] It is not absolutely clear whether this means that the king is the son of the god, because the god Baal uses the same expression, [44] and the bull El is said to be Baal's father. [45] As a divine epithet, *'b* is applied to El: he is called *'b bn ʾl,* "father of the sons of the gods" (i.e., of the pantheon), [46] *'b 'dm,* "father of mankind" (i.e., of the human race), [47] and *'b šnm,* [48] an epithet which has not yet been explained satisfactorily. At first it was assumed that this expression meant "father of the years" (so still Driver); but now many scholars doubt this, and it is thought that *šnm* is a place name, or the son of El, [49] or El's celestial habitation. [50]

It is interesting that some Aramaic inscriptions state that some king was put on the throne because of the righteousness (or loyalty, *ṣdq*) [51] of his father. [52] The Aqhat Epic refers to certain responsibilities which a son has to his father. But these have to do with cultic assistance primarily. [53]

---

[36] *KAI,* 215.16; cf. *DISO,* 5.

[37] *DISO,* 3; *KAI,* 24.5; 214.9; 215.2f.

[38] *CTA,* 19 [I D], 121.

[39] *CTA,* 19 [I D], 135.

[40] Van Selms, 94; cf. also *UF,* 1 (1969), 179, n. 4.

[41] *KAI,* 24.10f.

[42] *KAI,* 26 I.3.

[43] *CTA,* 17 [II D], I, 24.

[44] *CTA,* 2 [III AB], III, 19.

[45] *CTA,* 2 [III AB], I, 16f.; 6 [I AB], VI, 27; etc.

[46] *CTA,* 32, 25.

[47] *CTA,* 14 [I K], I, 37, 43, etc.

[48] *CTA,* 6 [I AB], I, 8; 4 [II AB], IV, 24; 17 [II D], VI, 49.

[49] *UT,* Glossary.

[50] *WUS.*

[51] See *KAI,* 215.11.

[52] *KAI,* 215.19f.; 216.4f.; cf. 215.1f., where only the father is mentioned.

[53] *CTA,* 17 [II D], I, 27-34; Koch, *ZA,* N.F. 24 (1947), 214ff.; similarly already Engnell, 136f.

'b often appears as a theophorous element in proper names. Sometimes it is used as a substitute for a divine name, as in *'brm, abi-rāmi,* "the father is exalted," *'brpš, abi-rapi,* "the father heals" (or "'Rapi' is the father"?). Sometimes it explicitly refers to a god as father, e.g., *'bmlk, abimilku,* [54] *'bb'l,* [55] *'tr'b, aš-tar-a-bi,* [56] *rašap-abi, ršp'b 'bršp.* [57]

Noth has shown that names containing *'b* and *'ḥ* are phenomena that may be found generally in North Semitic literature, and therefore concludes that they originated at a time "in which the North Semitic territory was an entity complete within itself." [58] Gradually, this type of name becomes more and more infrequent among the individual peoples, although new names using *'b* and *'ḥ* appear. Further, it is to be observed that *'lyd'* occurs as well as *'byd'*, and *'lkrb* as well as *'bkrb,* which indicates that most probably *'b* is actually a theophorous element.[59] According to Noth, this is to be explained in that in the ancient Northwest Semitic tribal religion, the tribal god was regarded as father (or brother) of the tribe. This concept gradually disappeared, but a number of proper names reflecting it lingered on. "But as tribal ancestor, the deity was not only begetter of the tribe, but also head, leader, and protector." [60] It cannot be determined whether the main emphasis should be placed on the physical begetting or on the protection and care of the god. It is probable that the latter came more and more into the foreground.

III. The Old Testament.

1. *Linguistic Usage.* In addition to "earthly father," the Hebrew word *'abh* has a number of meanings in the OT. (a) It refers to a grandfather (Gen. 28:13; perhaps also 49:29). (b) It is used of the founding father or ancestral father (David, 1 K. 15:11; 2 K. 14:3; 18:3), especially of a tribe or people (Shem, Gen. 10:21; Abraham, Gen. 17:4f.; Isa. 51:2; Moab and Ben-Ammi, Gen. 19:37f.; Esau, Gen. 36:9,43; Jacob, Dt. 26:5; Isa. 43:27; the patriarchs, Dt. 1:8; 6:10; 9:5; 29:12 [Eng. v. 13]; 30:20; 1 Ch. 29:18). Often the term "the fathers" is used in the sense of the first or the former generations of the people, i.e., the forefathers (e.g., in Ex. 3:15; 20:5; Nu. 20:15; 1 K. 14:15; Isa. 51:2; Jer. 7:22; 16:11f.; Ps. 22:5[4]; 44:2[1]; 106:7). (c) *'abh* sometimes means the founder of an occupation or of a way of living (e.g., Jabal is called the father of those who dwell in tents and have cattle, Jubal is said to be the father of musicians, Gen. 4:20; Jonadab, the son of Rechab, is called father, i.e. founder, of the Rechabite movement, Jer. 35:6,8; cf. 1 Macc. 2:54). This is probably related to the way of thinking that motivated guilds of priests, singers, and prophets to trace their origin back to

---

[54] Gröndahl, 315, 360.
[55] *KAI,* 5.1; 184.4.
[56] Gröndahl, 323, 378.
[57] *Ibid.,* 349, 361, 408f.; Huffmon, *APNM,* 154.
[58] *IPN,* 66ff.
[59] Stamm, 53, expresses doubts about this interpretation of certain Akkadian names.
[60] Noth, *IPN,* 75.

some ancestral father. [61] (d) *'abh* is applied to a man who is considered worthy of special honor, e.g., an older man (1 S. 24:12[11]), a teacher or prophetic master (2 K. 2:12; 6:21; 13:14), a priest (Jgs. 17:10; 18:19; cf. *beni,* "my son," as a word used by a wisdom teacher to address his students). (e) *'abh* sometimes means a protector, who to some extent takes the place of a father (Ps. 68:6 [5], "father of the fatherless," so also Sir. 4:10; Job 29:16, "a father to the poor"; Isa. 22:21, "a father to the inhabitants of Jerusalem." (f) *'abh* is used to designate a counsellor (Gen. 45:8; 1 Macc. 2:65; 11:32). [62] (g) *'abh* also can mean creator (of the rain, Job 38:28).

The reason *'abh* has so many different meanings in the OT is probably that the Semitic languages originally referred to a distinction between the generations, and were not concerned to denote exact relationships between people. Consequently, each representative of the older generation was called *'abh,* and each representative of the younger generation was called a → בֵּן *bēn.* This explains how *'abh* can be used as a title of honor. In most cases, however, the Hebrew linguistic use of this word corresponds with our own.

2. *The Role of the Father (Including beth 'abh).* The social life of Israel was closer to that of the Semitic nomadic peoples than to the city culture of the ancient Near East. The dominant factors in her social structure were the tribe and the clan rather than the village, the city, and the district. As among the Bedouins, a well-rounded life was thought to be possible only within the fellowship of the tribe. [63] As a result, an individual's parentage and genealogy were considered to be of great importance. Thus the tribal father or original ancestor was very significant. In Deutero-Isaiah (51:2), "Abraham your father" is used as an example from which one may learn and take courage.

In the Israelite family, the father has almost unlimited authority. He is master of the house; the children are taught to honor and fear him (Mal. 1:6). He controls the other members of the family as a potter controls his clay (Isa. 64:7 [8]). Yet "he is not an isolated despot, but the centre from which strength and will emanate through the whole of the sphere which belongs to him and to which he belongs. When a man is called father, it really implies the same thing, kinship and authority also being expressed by the name of father. To the Israelite the name of father always spells authority. Naaman is called father by his servants (2 K. 5:13). The priest is called the father of the cultic community of which he is the head (Jgs. 18:19), and Elijah is called father by his disciples (2 K. 2:12). Round the man the house groups itself, forming a psychic community, which is

---

[61] Cf. A. Haldar, *Associations of Cult Prophets* (Uppsala, 1945), 36ff. Quell, *TDNT,* V, 961, n. 5: "patron," differs from this view. Scharbert, 61, writes: "The OT conveys a different idea here from the Phoenician mythology in Philo Byblius, where different gods are considered to be inventors of different occupations and skills."

[62] Cf. de Boer, *SVT,* 3 (1955), 57ff. According to Brunner, *ZÄS,* 86 (1961), 99, the Hebrew in Gen. 45:8 is the same as the Egyptian expression *ìt nṯr* in the sense of "tutor of the crown-prince."

[63] Scharbert, 76ff.

stamped by him. Wives, children, slaves, property are entirely merged in this unity." [64] "It is a terrible fate when one's father (and mother) forsakes him (Ps. 27:10); and for one to have no father is reason to lament (Lam. 5:3)." [65]

In light of this, it was natural for the "family" to be called "the father's house" (Heb. *beth 'abh,* which is analogous to Akk. *bīt abi*). Unfortunately, the terminology in the OT is not very consistent on this point. In addition to "family" (Ex. 12:3; 1 Ch. 7:2), *beth 'abh* can also be used to refer to a subdivision of a clan, which is composed of several families (Nu. 3:24; 34:14), or even to a tribe (17:17 [2]; Josh. 22:14), or to a different group (Ex. 6:14; Nu. 1:2). [66] As Elliger has shown, [67] Lev. 18 presupposes the situation which existed in a typical ancient Israelite household ("father's house"), "in which, under normal conditions, four generations lived together." [68]

Most examples of the expression *beth 'abh* occur in lists, or the like, and provide little information about family "consciousness." But Gen. 12 is quite clear. Here Abraham is commanded to leave his land, his kindred *(moledheth),* and his family *(beth 'abh)* in order to look for the promised land. This narrative shows clearly that the mandatory separation of Abraham from his kindred is unprecedented (cf. 20:13; 24:7). Similarly, in 2:24 leaving father and mother involves separating oneself from the old family and building a new one, in which the man becomes, in due course of time, the father of the family.

In the Legal material of the OT, the rights of the father appear only fragmentarily. From Ex. 21:7 we learn indirectly that a father could sell his daughter as a female slave. Older narratives show that the father could take away the birthright of his firstborn son (Gen. 49:4; 1 K. 1:11ff.), but the Deuteronomic law explicitly forbids such a practice (Dt. 21:15-17). Deuteronomy represents a later stage of development with regard to other laws as well. In Gen. 38:24, Judah himself pronounces the death penalty on his daughter-in-law, while in Dt. 21:18-21 the punishment of a rebellious son is left to the elders of the city.

Dt. 21:18 indicates indirectly that it was the duty of the children to obey their parents. The fifth (or fourth) commandment in the Decalog goes deeper: "Honor *(kabbedh)* your father and your mother" (the reason given here for obeying this commandment is a later addition). But this commandment is intended not only for the children, but also (and primarily) for the adults in the household; and what it emphasizes above all else is not obedience to parents, but an attitude of respect for them.

The Wisdom Literature has much more to say on this subject than does the Legal material of the OT. There the major emphasis is on the mutual responsibilities of parents and children. [69] The father's authority is undisputed: thus, it is a disgrace for a son to treat his parents wrong (Prov. 19:26) or to curse them

---

64 Pedersen, *ILC,* I, 63.
65 Hempel, 133.
66 Wolf, *JBL,* 65 (1946), 48.
67 *ZAW,* 67 (1955), 1-25.
68 *HAT,* 4 (1966), 239; cf. Porter, 6f.
69 Gaspar, 29ff.

(20:20; cf. also 28:24). But the responsibility of the father appears indirectly in Job 5:4, where the children of a foolish man have no protector. The first requirement of a father is to fear God; then he will be a refuge to his children (Prov. 14:26). There is a major emphasis in the Wisdom Literature on the importance of training children: a father must discipline his son, or else he will destroy him (19:18); he must train up a child in the way he should go (22:6); he must teach his son wisdom, if he wishes to be glad (10:1; 23:24). Several passages indicate that bodily punishment played an important role in the child's training (3:12; 4:3f.; 6:20-27; 13:1,24; 29:17f.). [70]

At the same time, it is the responsibility of the children to hearken to their father (Prov. 23:22) and in this way to make their parents glad (15:20; 23:22,25). [71]

3. *Theological.* In many expressions in which *'abh(oth)* occurs in the OT, there is a strong feeling of a bond between the generations.

a. *"Sleeping with One's Fathers."* Perhaps this feeling is reflected most clearly by the expression *shakhabh 'im 'abhothav,* "he lay down with his fathers" (Gen. 47:30; Dt. 31:16; 2 S. 7:12; and 35 times in 1-2 K. and 2 Ch.). As Alfrink has shown, this expression almost exclusively refers to kings, and only in cases in which a king died a natural death. The expression *ne'esaph 'el 'ammav,* "he was gathered to his people," has a similar meaning, but it is found only in the Pentateuch! However, the expression *ne'esaph 'el 'abhothav,* "he was gathered to his fathers," appears outside the Pentateuch (cf. Jgs. 2:10; 2 K. 22:20 = 2 Ch. 34:28). According to Pedersen, all these expressions grew out of the custom of burying a person at the family grave. [72] But the fact that the burial is usually mentioned separately seems to oppose this explanation. (And yet, 1 K. 11:21 makes it clear that *shakhabh,* etc., is synonymous with *muth;* David "sleeps with his fathers" and Joab "dies.") In agreement with this, the use of these expressions does not always correspond to actual burial places. [73] But in spite of this, the original idea must have been that the deceased is united in death with his fathers or relatives who died before him (→ שאול *she'ôl*). Later these formulas became stereotyped, and were not always used consistently.

b. *The God of the Fathers.* In the Exodus traditions, Yahweh is referred to several times as "the God of the fathers," e.g., in Ex. 3:15 (E): "Yahweh, the God of your fathers, the God of Abraham, the God of Isaac, and the God of Jacob, has sent me to you" (cf. 3:6, "I am the God of your father, the God of Abraham, the God of Isaac, and the God of Jacob"). Here the present form of the text emphasizes the continuity between the God who reveals himself to Moses and the God who guided the patriarchs. In the patriarchal narratives, the old

---

[70] Cf. Dürr, 114f.
[71] Gaspar, 102f.
[72] *ILC,* II, 480f.
[73] Alfrink, 118.

Pentateuch sources contain recollections that "God of the fathers" was an ancient divine name (Gen. 26:24–J; 28:13–J; 31:5,29,42–E), which originally referred to the personal protector-god and family-god of the patriarchal characters. Such personal gods are found among the Sumerians, where "the god of the man" appears as his special protector and personal advocate. [74] In Old Assyrian documents, there is an allusion to "Ashur and the god of thy father" as witnesses, and in Mari there is an oath "by the god of my father." [75] Finally, Alt has shown that about the beginning of the Christian Age, gods of an individual were coming to be identified with the major gods of the pantheon. [76]

In later literature of the OT, the formula "God of the fathers" plays a certain role. In Deuteronomy (1:11,21; 4:1; 6:3; 12:1; 26:7; 27:3; 29:24[25]), it is used to emphasize the continuity between the author's generation and the earlier generations in Israel. [77] In the Chronicler's work (1 Ch. 12:17; 2 Ch. 20:33; 24:18,24; 29:5; 30:7; 36:15; Ezr. 7:27), it is used consistently to emphasize the heinousness of apostasy ("to forsake the God of their fathers," or the like, e.g., 2 Ch. 34:33) or the efficacy of returning to God (2 Ch. 19:4; 30:22; 34:32). But on the whole this expression has become rather stereotyped, and is used interchangeably with "Yahweh your/our God" (13:12; 28:9; 29:5; 30:7; 34:33). This solemn formula emphasizes the intimate connection of the present with ancient history and with the faith of the forefathers. [78]

c. *The Land Promise to the Fathers.* Quite often the Deuteronomic preaching refers to God's saving deeds to the fathers. Yahweh loved and chose the fathers (Dt. 4:37; 10:15), but the covenant he made with them is in reality a covenant with the present generation, which now experiences again the sealing of the covenant in the cult (5:3). Generally, the fiction that those who are addressed in Deuteronomy experienced the exodus themselves is maintained, and interest is concentrated on the land promise. Without limiting himself to a stereotyped formula, the Deuteronomic preacher repeatedly asserts in different ways that Yahweh had sworn (*nishba‘*) to give the land of Canaan to the fathers: 1:8,35; 6:10,18,23; 7:13; 8:1; 9:5; 10:11; 11:9,21; 19:8; 26:3; 28:11; 30:20; 31:7; cf. also Josh. 1:6; 5:6; 21:43; Jgs. 2:1; 1 K. 8:40. [79] The different ways of expressing this idea by the frequent repetition of the theme but with the continual appearance of new words, emphasizes the importance of this assertion. The expression "Yahweh has sworn" has a counterpart in "the land which the Lord your God will give (*ntn*) you," which appears 23 times in Deuteronomy. [80] Here the divine promise that Israel will possess the land is considered to be fundamental to the existence of the people in the cultic Now (but this statement does not assume

---

74 S. N. Kramer, *The Sumerians* (Chicago, 1963), 126.
75 Hyatt, 131f.
76 Cf. Alt, May, Cross.
77 See below, c and d.
78 Scharbert, 201.
79 Plöger, 63ff.; Wijngaards, 73ff., 77ff.
80 Wijngaards, 77f.

the existence of a special Conquest Festival, as Wijngaards supposes). The expression *nishbaʻ laʼabhoth,* "he swore to the fathers," is also used with reference to the covenant (Dt. 4:31; 7:12) and other promises (7:8; 13:18[17]). It occurs also in Ex. 13:5,11 and Nu. 14:23, which are to be regarded as Deuteronomistic additions (Nu. 11:12b may also be an addition).

d. *God's Saving Deeds to the Fathers.* Two passages in the Deuteronomistic history refer repeatedly to God's deeds to the fathers: Josh. 24 (the amphictyonic assembly at Shechem) and 1 K. 8 (the consecration of the temple). In the first passage, Joshua recalls that the fathers once lived beyond the River (Euphrates) (24:2), that Yahweh brought them out of Egypt (24:6,17), but that they still served other (→ אחר *ʼachēr*) gods and were punished (24:14f.). In the second passage, Solomon first mentions the covenant Yahweh made with the fathers through the exodus (1 K. 8:21), then he prays that God might fulfil what he had promised to his father David (8:23-26), refers once more to the fact that Yahweh brought the fathers out of Egypt (8:53), and expresses this wish: "The Lord our God be with us, as he was with our fathers . . . that we may keep the commandments which he commanded our fathers" (8:57f.). The thought here is that the saving deeds of God in the past are a kind of guarantee of more saving deeds in the future: Yahweh will deal with the present generation as he dealt with the fathers. In the cultic celebration, that which happened to the fathers is present once again: "Not with our fathers, but with us" (Dt. 5:3).

The saving deeds of Yahweh to the fathers are treasured by the godly, and they receive courage and confidence from them. The author of a national Psalm of Lament uses what Yahweh did for the fathers and what the fathers related (Ps. 44:2[1]) as the point of departure for his prayer: just as Yahweh gave his people victory in the past, may he also help now. In Ps. 22, a (royal?) Psalm of Lament, the author says: "In thee our fathers trusted; they trusted, and thou didst deliver them" (v. 5[4]); in the final analysis, this is what gives the psalmist hope (cf. also Jgs. 6:13). Furthermore, the more didactic Ps. 78 draws instruction from the salvation history: the things our fathers have told us, we will tell to the coming generation (vv. 3f.), viz., that God gave a law to the fathers, which they were to teach to their children (v. 5), so that they could order their lives accordingly. This psalm also refers to the exodus miracle (v. 12) and condemns the disobedience of the people (cf. also 106:7). Thus the history of the fathers is a living heritage, from which one can receive courage and faith, or a warning.

e. *Teaching and Example of the Fathers.* The book of Deuteronomy emphasizes the responsibility of the fathers to instruct their children and to teach them to love God (6:7). Certain psalms put this teaching in a cultic context, e.g., Isa. 38:19 (the Psalm of Hezekiah): "the father makes known to the children thy faithfulness"; similarly also Ps. 22:31(30). In both passages, the worshipper is praying for deliverance from "death," which he promises to proclaim "in the great congregation" (Ps. 22:23,26[22,25]). [81] Josh. 4:21 also speaks of a cultic

---

[81] H. Ringgren, *Israelite Religion* (trans. 1966), 235.

tradition: When the children ask their fathers, "What do these stones mean?" the fathers will tell them the story of the crossing of the Jordan. In a similar way, the fathers were to tell their children the tradition of the exodus in the Passover festival (Ex. 12:24ff.; 13:8). The Deuteronomist emphasizes the father's duty to teach God's commandments to his children (6:7; cf. also 32:7,46). Ps. 78:5f. deals with God's saving deeds in general, which are to be handed down from generation to generation; and Gen. 18:19 refers to God's charge to Abraham as a father to teach his children and his household the righteous life. [82]

In this way there is formed a continuity between the generations, in which the fathers give instruction and provide an example. It may be good or it may be bad for children to follow the example of the fathers. There are many warnings in the OT against following the bad example of the fathers (Ps. 78:8,57; Ezk. 20:18; Zec. 1:4; 2 Ch. 30:7f.; cf. Jer. 9:13[14]; 23:27; implicitly also Am. 2:4). Dt. 32:17 mentions a violation of a good tradition: they sacrificed to gods whom their fathers had never feared.

f. *The Sins of the Fathers.* A special type of connection between the generations is reflected in an ancient confession formula. As a commentary on the commandment to worship one God alone, this has been inserted after the commandment forbidding the manufacture of graven images (Ex. 20:5f. = Dt. 5:9f.). It also occurs in the narrative that tells of Moses' interview with Yahweh on Sinai (Ex. 34:7) and in an intercessory prayer of Moses (Nu. 14:18). The formula affirms that Yahweh, the jealous God, "visits the sins of the fathers on the children, the grandchildren, and the great-grandchildren." [83] In the Decalog this statement stands in contrast to the promise that Yahweh will "show steadfast love to thousands (of generations?)," if one keeps his commandments. The basic idea this statement conveys is that the steadfast love and faithfulness of God are infinitely more powerful than the inevitable consequence of sinning against his jealous holiness (→ קנאה *qinʾāh*). But it also acknowledges and emphasizes the solidarity between the generations in deeds and their consequences. The retribution for sins is said to extend over a household for four generations, while God's grace is said to extend to a thousand generations. [84] In the final section of the Holiness Code, the same principle is applied to the case where the people continue in sin and must go into exile: then those who are left in the land "shall pine away... because of their (own) iniquity; and also because of the iniquities of their fathers they shall pine away like them" (Lev. 26:39–those who are left behind in Judah when the Babylonians have carried the Jews into exile lament in a similar way: "Our fathers sinned,... and we bear their iniquities,"

---

[82] On this see Dürr, 107f.

[83] Scharbert, 127f.; Knierim, 205.

[84] Using as the basis of his argument the ancient scheme of curse and blessing, Scharbert, 128, 180, explains this formula somewhat differently: the curse continues to be effective only into the fourth generation, while the blessing continues to be effective for an infinite period of time.

Lam. 5:7; cf. also Isa. 65:7). Here the sons are not without guilt. They have imitated their fathers. "Fathers and sons are regarded ... as being of one and the same mind, and destruction will come upon both of them alike." [85] Further-more, Lev. 26:40 contains the people's confession of their own sins along with the sins of their fathers, which was common in the postexilic period. [86]

A rigid interpretation of this same principle appears in the proverb quoted by Jeremiah (31:29) and Ezekiel (18:2): "The fathers have eaten sour grapes, and the children's teeth are set on edge." In both passages this proverb is reject-ed as false. The passage in Jeremiah looks forward to a new age, in which the old laws will no longer be valid. In Ezekiel this proverb is connected with the question of individual responsibility: it is not useless to return to God, for punish-ment is not finally determined by the sins of the fathers. Jer. 32:18f. contains a kind of dilemma between the concept of individual responsibility and the idea of a collective continuity from one generation to the next; actually, this dilemma is never reconciled in the OT: on one side stands the solidarity of the generations, and on the other the responsibility of the individual (when Dt. 24:16 states that the children shall not be put to death because of the sin of the fathers [this verse is quoted verbatim in 2 K. 14:6], it is dealing with civil penal law, not with divine retribution).

g. *The Fathers in the Royal Dynasty.* The writers of the Deuteronomic history also repeatedly state this dilemma in the relationship between the fathers and their descendants. In the narrative dealing with the Davidic dynasty, on the one hand, God remains faithful to his promise to David, so that a descendant of David will always sit on the throne; even when David's descendant was un-godly, Yahweh "gave him a lamp in Jerusalem..., because David did what was right in the eyes of the Lord" (1 K. 15:4f.). [87] On the other hand, the writers of the Deuteronomic history evaluate each individual king on the basis of his own religious attitude and behavior. If a king behaves "like his father (David)," his reign is considered to be a time of blessing (1 K. 15:11; 22:43; 2 K. 14:3; 15:3,34; 18:1-7; 22:2; 23:25). If, however, a king does that which is displeas-ing to Yahweh "like his father," "like his fathers," or the like (statements such as this must refer to wicked fathers), he is censured, and his reign is regarded as a time of disaster (1 K. 15:3; 2 K. 21:19ff.; 24:19; or 23:32,37). "By their religious behavior, the individual kings were thought to exhibit a certain solidarity either with David and the fathers who were loyal to the Yahweh covenant, or with the fathers who broke the covenant." [88]

h. *Community Identification with the Fathers.* The promises to the patriarchs are never mentioned in the preexilic prophets. And yet, from time to time they

---

[85] Scharbert, 202.
[86] See below, i.
[87] Scharbert, 197.
[88] *Ibid.*

mention a different kind of community identification with the fathers. The fathers sinned; even the patriarch Jacob was a deceiver (Hos. 12:4[3]), and the Israelites living today are like their fathers (9:10; Am. 2:4). The generations are alike in their apostasy: "a man and his father go in to the same maiden" (Am. 2:7). "The divine judgments come, not because of the sins of the fathers, but because the present generation has sinned like the fathers. Between fathers and sons stands a solidarity of attitude which is rebellion against God." [89]

Jeremiah also knows of this relationship of apostasy. The fathers have already forsaken Yahweh: "What wrong did your fathers find in me that they went far from me?" (Jer. 2:5). But the sons, i.e., the present generation, act the same way. They are stiffnecked, worse than their fathers (7:26); they go after the Baals like their fathers (9:12f.[13f.]; 23:27), they have turned back to the iniquities of their forefathers (11:10), and they sacrifice to the queen of heaven like their fathers (44:17). The example of the fathers is at work in the religious activities of the present generation and brings upon it a punishment that will destroy fathers and sons together (6:21; 13:14; 16:3f.; cf. 6:11,13). [90] Allusions to the promises to the fathers and the covenant which Yahweh made with them serve only to emphasize the apostasy (7:22; 11:3,7). In fact, according to 31:32, the covenant with the fathers will be transcended by a new covenant in which the inner renewal of the man guarantees covenant loyalty. It is in this context that the promise of the people's return to the land which was given to the fathers (30:3) belongs. Also, the promise that the people will remain in the land of their fathers (25:5) is given on the condition that they turn from their evil way. On the other hand, 3:18 and 16:15 (which contain the promise that the exiles will return to the land of Palestine) are probably later additions.

Ezekiel also declares this identification in apostasy, e.g., 2:3: "they and their fathers have transgressed against me"; 20:24: "their eyes were set on their fathers' idols"; cf. 16:44: "like mother, like daughter." All generations will suffer punishment (9:6); fathers and children will even eat one another (5:10). But at the same time, Ezekiel knows of a future restoration, in which the people shall dwell in the land where their fathers (the patriarchs) dwelled, with their children and their children's children (37:25). The return to the land which Yahweh gave to the fathers implies both the renewal of the covenant (36:28—note the covenant formula!) and the recognition of the power and nature of Yahweh (20:42). The land promised to the fathers will again become the inheritance of Israel (47:14). This restoration also means a return to the old relationship between Yahweh and the fathers.

Deutero-Isaiah knows the prophetic tradition that the fathers have sinned (Isa. 43:27; cf. 48:8). But at the same time he stands in the tradition of the poetry of the Psalms which reflects a positive attitude toward the fathers: "Look to Abraham our father" (51:2). In the other postexilic prophets, emphasis is placed on the idea that there is a solidarity between fathers and sons in sin (Zec.

---

[89] *Ibid.*, 211.
[90] Cf. *ibid.*, 214ff.

1:2f.; 8:14f.; Mal. 3:6f.): Therefore Yahweh will requite "your iniquities and your fathers' iniquities together" (Isa. 65:6f.).

i. *Acknowledgment of the Sins of the Fathers.* The feeling of solidarity between the generations in sin is also expressed positively in the confession of sins: "Both we and our fathers have sinned" (Ps. 106:6; so similarly Jer. 3:25; 14:20). 2 K. 22:13 affords a concrete example: "Great is the wrath of the Lord that is kindled against us, because our fathers have not obeyed the words of this book"– however, this verse does not speak of "our" sins. Lev. 26:40 (H; postexilic redaction?) predicts that the dispersed Israelites will confess their own sins and the sins of their fathers. We find this type of confession as a liturgical formula in the prayer of repentance of the postexilic community (Ezr. 9:6f.; Neh. 1:6; Dnl. 9:16; Tob. 3:3; cf. Bar. 1:16f.; 3:4ff.). [91] It is difficult to determine the extent to which this formula had already been formed in the preexilic period, because the date of most of the relevant passages is uncertain. Jer. 3:25 may be a liturgical expansion, but Jer. 14:20 shows that "the confession of the ʿavon of the fathers along with one's own was already practiced in the preexilic Jerusalemite cult." [92] It is worthy of note that the first certain evidence for this is to be found in Jeremiah, the great "individualist."

4. *God As Father.*

a. *Proper Names.* ʾabh appears as part of many proper names in the OT. In most such names the ʾabh serves as a theophorous element: ʾabhiʾasaph, "(my) father has gathered," ʾabhighayil, "(my) father has rejoiced (?)," ʾabhidhan, "my father has judged," ʾabhidhaʿ, "the father has taken knowledge (of me)," ʾabhihudh, "(my) father is majesty" (or "may he be praised"), ʾabhihayil, "(my) father is fear," ʾabhichayil, "(my) father is might," ʾabhitubh, "my father is goodness," ʾabhital, "my father is dew," ʾabhinadhabh, "my father has shown himself to be generous," ʾabh(i)ner, "my father is a lamp," ʾabhinoʿam, "my father is grace" (or a Tammuz epithet?), ʾabhisaph, "father has added," ʾabhiʿezer, "my father is help," ʾabhiram, "(my) father is exalted" (→ אברהם ʾabhrāhām), ʾabhishagh (meaning uncertain), ʾabhishuaʿ, "father is help," ʾabhishur, "(my) father is a (protecting) wall," ʾebhyathar, "father is/gives abundant(ly)." To some extent, all the names may be traced back to old names which reflect the idea that the tribal deity was the ancestor of the members of the tribe, but the extent to which this concept was still alive in biblical Israel is uncertain. It is possible that in some cases certain gods are called "father," as perhaps ʾabhiʾel, "(my) father is El" (1 S. 9:1; 14:51; Saul's grandfather); but cf. ʾeliʾabh, "my God is father"; and also ʾabhimelekh, "my father is Milk" (= Molech or Melekh) (or "king"), ʾabhshalom, which means either "the father is (the god) Shalom" or "the father is peace." ʾabhital and ʾabhinoʿam might also be included

---

91 *Ibid.,* 202, 247.
92 Knierim, 208.

in this group, if Tal is a god of the dew and if Noʻam, "the delightful one," is an epithet for Baal or Tammuz. Finally, in the names yoʼabh and ʼabhiyyahu, Yahweh is designated as father, probably in the sense of "protector." We cannot be sure about the significance of ʼabhiyyam, which, indeed, has been interpreted as ʼabhiyya(hu) (1 K. 14:31; 15:1-7), but probably should be understood differently ("my father is truly [mi] x"?). [93]

b. *Yahweh As Father of the People.* Other than in proper names, Yahweh is called father very rarely in the OT. [94] Occasionally he is compared with a father: as a father, he pities his children (Ps. 103:13); he reproves the man whom he loves as a father reproves the son in whom he delights (Prov. 3:12). These passages are particularly interesting because they show what characteristics of the father were considered to be the most important. The same thing is true *mutatis mutandis* of Nu. 11:12, where Moses asks reproachfully whether he had conceived and brought forth the people, and thereby intimates indirectly that Yahweh is the mother (!) of the people. The real point of this figure is that Yahweh cares for the people and is responsible for their existence.

Yahweh is also designated the father of the people of Israel. Already in Ex. 4:22(J) Yahweh calls Israel his firstborn son and demands his release from Egypt that he might serve him. Here, Yahweh makes his claim on the Israelites and confirms that he is acting in their behalf. Two more examples of this occur in the Song of Moses, Dt. 32. In v. 6, we read: "Is not he your father, who created (→ קנה qānāh) you, who made you and established you?" The reference to Yahweh as the creator and founder of his people establishes his claim to their gratitude. "To make" and "to establish" are part of the regular creation terminology. The meaning of qanah is disputed, and in any case can be used of creation (Prov. 8:22) as well as of child-bearing (Gen. 4:1). It cannot refer to physical begetting in Dt. 32:6. This is more probable in v. 18, which speaks of "the Rock that begot (yaladh) you" and of "the God who gave you birth (cholel)." But again, this verse is probably not speaking of a mythological begetting by a rock deity, because elsewhere in this song tsur is used figuratively in the sense of refuge (vv. 15,37), as it is ordinarily. Just as little can Jer. 2:27 be used to support the hypothesis of a myth of a birth from the rock, for this passage rebukes those "who say to a tree, 'You are my father,' and to a stone, 'You gave me birth.'" Both → עץ ʻēts and → אבן ʼebhen are a part of the regular terminology used in polemics against idols. Thus, Jer. 2:27 simply means that those whom the prophet rebukes turn to idols as creators and protectors.

Hosea uses the figure of the father in speaking of God in 11:1f., although the word ʼabh does not actually occur here: Yahweh called Israel out of Egypt as his son, trained him as a good father, and showered him with his care. Similarly, in Isa. 1:2 Yahweh says that he brought up children who have rebelled against him. Both of these passages refer to the disappointment of Yahweh's hope that his children would love him in return. The same thought is found in Jer. 3:19: "I

---

[93] So *KBL*[3].
[94] Lagrange; Hempel, 131ff.; Colless.

thought you would call me, My father, and would not turn from following me";
a child is loyal to his father, but Israel has forsaken his God. Another passage
in Jeremiah (31:9) emphasizes the paternal love and care of Yahweh: he will
protect those who are returning home, "for I am a father to Israel, and Ephraim
is my firstborn." This language has some affinities with that in Ex. 4:22.

The other relevant passages emphasize in particular the authority of the divine
father. Isa. 45:9-11 is especially characteristic. Here a father is compared with
a potter: as a father does not have to give an account for his actions to his children
and as a potter has the clay completely at his disposal, so Yahweh, the creator,
has his people at his disposal and deals with them according to his will, and they
have no right to question him. The same idea is expressed in Isa. 64:7(8): "Thou
art our Father; we are the clay, and thou art our potter; we are all the work of
thy hand"–here in a prayer for paternal compassion. The power of the heavenly
father to help and to redeem is emphasized in Isa. 63:16: Israel feels himself
separated from his earthly fathers; now Yahweh is the only father who can help;
he is "the Redeemer (→ גאל gōʾēl) from of old." Finally, once Malachi speaks
of God as father and creator: "Have we not all one father? Has not *one* God
created (→ ברא bārāʾ) us? Why then are we faithless to one another, profaning
the covenant of our fathers?" (Mal. 2:10); the fact that Israel is a son carries with
it the idea of accepting his responsibility as a son. In another passage, Malachi
emphasizes the authority of Yahweh which Israel had despised: a person honors
and fears his father, but Israel does not honor and fear his divine father (1:6).

It follows from all this that the idea of God as father of the people of his own
possession does not occupy a central place in the faith of Israel. This is only one
of many figures which the OT uses to describe the relationship between Yahweh
and Israel. These figures seem to have been created generally *ad hoc;* mythological roots are hardly to be ascertained.

c. *Yahweh As Father of the King.* The idea of the king as son of God is a
more firmly established characteristic of OT thought than that of Israel as
Yahweh's son, and yet it is not found very often. The classic example of this
concept occurs in Ps. 2:7: "You are my son, today I have begotten you," which
clearly is a type of adoption formula. This statement is complemented in the
Nathan prophecy, where we read: "I will be his father, and he shall be my son"
(2 S. 7:14; cf. 1 Ch. 28:6). In a little greater detail, Ps. 89:27f.(26f.) says that the
king will call Yahweh "Father, God, and Rock of his salvation," and Yahweh
will make him the firstborn and the highest of the kings of the earth.

The real significance of these statements is disputed. The idea that they refer
to a physical begetting hardly seems probable; it is more likely that they think
of the king's relationship to Yahweh in terms of adoption. [95] Ps. 2:7 can be understood as an adoption formula. It is worthy of note that the poets in Pss. 2 and 89
both call on God as father in a situation in which the authority of the king is
being threatened. Thus, the sonship of the king is considered to be a divine

---

[95] Ahlström, 111f.; Kraus, *BK,* XV, 19.

guarantee of his power and authority. It is divine power that gives the king his power.

d. *Isa. 9:5(6)*. Among the titles of the king whose coming is announced in Isa. 9 (in v. 5[6] he is called "son") is found the epithet *'abhi 'adh*. The meaning of this expression is obscure. *'adh* can mean "booty"; and if *'abhi 'adh* could be interpreted as "father of booty" in the sense of "one who takes booty," this would fit the context of the whole passage very well. But this translation is doubtful, since there are no other examples in which *'abh* is used in this way. If we take *'adh* in the sense of "eternity," this expression may be understood as a royal epithet meaning "father of eternity," i.e., father (protector, etc.) for all the future, which would agree well with *pele' yoets*, and in and of itself is not incompatible with the other royal titles that occur here. [96]

Ringgren

---

[96] Cf. O. Kaiser, *Isaiah 1-12*. OTL (trans. 1972), 129; on the connection of the idea "eternal" with the king, see Ps. 21:5,7(4,6).

אָבַד *'ābhadh;* אֲבֵדָה *'ᵃbhēdhāh;* אַבְדָן *'abhᵉdhān;* אֲבַדּוֹן *'ᵃbhaddôn*

Contents: I. Etymology, Occurrences. II. "Wander Off." III. 1. The Hiphil and the Piel with a Divine Subject; 2. The Qal of Divinely Willed Destruction. IV. 1. The Hiphil and the Piel in General Usage; 2. The Qal in General Usage. V. *'abhaddon* = The Underworld.

I. **Etymology, Occurrences.** In the Northwest Semitic languages, the primary meaning of *'abhadh* is "to perish."[1] Occasionally, the meaning "wander off, run away" also appears, especially with reference to animals, e.g., in 1 S. 9:3,20; the Sabbath Ostracon, line 3;[2] in Ugaritic perhaps of men,[3] and in the obscure Canaanite gloss in Papyrus Anastasi I, 23.[4] In the other Semitic languages this meaning is more widespread (Arabic, Ethiopic, etc.).

'ābhadh. M. A. Beek, "Das Problem des aramäischen Stammvaters (Deut. XXVI 5)," *OTS*, 8 (1951), 193-212; E. Jenni, "Faktitiv und Kausativ von אבד 'zugrunde gehen'," *Hebräische Wortforschung. Festschrift für W. Baumgartner. SVT*, 16 (1967), 143-157; J. Lewy, "Grammatical and Lexicographical Studies," *Or*, N.S. 29 (1960), 20-45, esp. 22-27; A. Oepke, "ἀπόλλυμι," etc., *TDNT*, I, 394-97; D. Yellin, "Some Fresh Meanings of Hebrew Roots," *JPOS*, 1 (1920). 10f.

[1] See *DISO*, the lexicons in Hebrew, Aramaic, Syriac, Ugaritic, etc.; cf. also Jenni, 151.
[2] A. Dupont-Sommer, *Sem*, 2 (1949), 31.
[3] *CTA*, 2 [III AB], IV, 3.
[4] But see *ANET*, 477.

This seems to indicate that the basic meaning "to run away" developed into the meaning "to perish," as an animal normally is lost when it wanders away from the herd. This same type of development is usually thought to apply also in Hebrew usage.[5]

In Akkadian the problem is more complicated. The more modern Akkadian lexicons assume that there are two roots *'bt:* I. "to destroy" (passive "to be destroyed, to fall to pieces"), and II. "to escape, run away" (only of men, e.g., slaves and warriors).[6] One must therefore seriously consider the possibility that in the other Semitic languages, also, two originally independent homonymous roots have coalesced.[7] However, no final answer to the etymological question can be given.

In the OT, the verb *'abhadh* occurs more than 100 times in the qal, about 40 times in the piel and about 25 times in the hiphil. In addition to this, we find the nouns *'abhedhah, 'abhedhan, 'obhedhan,* and *'abhaddon.* A root *'bd* II, "to endure," and the noun derived from it, *'obhedh,* "duration," is independent of *'bd* I.[8]

II. "Wander Off." Only in the qal do both principal meanings, "to perish" and "wander off," occur in the OT. In 1 S. 9:3,20, the verb is used in the concrete sense, referring to animals that have run away from the herd. But it appears more often in the figurative sense: Israel is like sheep whose shepherds (kings and others in positions of responsibility in the society) have forsaken and neglected them, and who consequently are wandering aimlessly (Jer. 50:6; Ezk. 34:4,16). Or they feel that their shepherd (Yahweh) has forsaken them (Ps. 119:176).

The use of *'abhadh* in Dt. 26:5 is significant: *'arammi 'obhedh 'abhi,* "a wandering (*'obhedh*) Aramean was my father," or (as many scholars render it) "an Aramean on the point of destruction."[9] Albright clearly prefers a third meaning which is close to Akk. *abātu* II: "a fugitive Aramean."[10] This interpretation of the word does not occur elsewhere in the OT; it refers specifically to the Jacob Story (Jacob flees from Esau). The rendering "wandering," which has parallels in Akkadian,[11] has more to recommend it, because it encompasses the entire patriarchal history and in this way emphasizes the relationship of the early Israelite tribes with the Arameans, who lived a nomadic life.

III. 1. *The Hiphil and the Piel with a Divine Subject.* The meaning "to perish" (qal) and "to cause to perish, to destroy, to annihilate" (piel and hiphil) is more frequent. In order to get a general view of the subject and object of this

---

[5] Jenni, 148f. with additional literature, and OT lexicons, esp. König.

[6] *CAD,* I/1, 41-47; *AHw,* I, 5 *abātu(m);* von Soden puts the second meaning under *nābutu(m),* since it appears only in the N-stem. *CAD* takes a different approach. Lewy, 22-29, adopts a transitive meaning "to leave," or the like, for *'bt* II.

[7] Concerning the original distinction in meaning see Brockelmann, *VG,* II, 137.

[8] See Yellin.

[9] Beek, 199-201, 211f., mentions other possible translations; see also König, *KAT,* III, *in loc.*

[10] *From the Stone Age to Christianity* (1957), 238.

[11] Taylor Prism, V, 22f.; see Mazar, *BA,* 25 (1962), 101.

verb and thus determine its meaning more exactly, it seems best first of all to investigate the causative forms, the piel and the hiphil. The question here is whether there is really a difference between the piel and the hiphil of 'abhadh. Jenni argues that the primary significance of the piel is factitive (producing a condition), while that of the hiphil is causative (producing an action). Therefore, the hiphil usually takes persons as an object, but the piel takes both persons and things. The hiphil more often refers to the future, while the piel is used of the present or in general statements. On the whole, these distinctions are valid; but Jenni himself emphasizes that there are a number of exceptions. These distinctions can hardly have theological significance.

When one examines the approximately 65 occurrences of the transitive forms of the verb 'abhadh, the piel and the hiphil, two things stand out: in almost half the passages Yahweh is the subject, [12] and more than half the passages deal with military and political situations. Thus it is not surprising that in many passages Yahweh is depicted as a "warrior," who destroys and overthrows the nations, e.g., Israel's enemies at the exodus and the conquest (Dt. 8:20; 11:4). In the prophets in particular, one often encounters the idea that Yahweh will destroy the heathen "at the end of the days." But it is noteworthy that 'abhadh is used only in the prophets of the seventh and sixth centuries B.C. (concerning Assyria, Babylon, Egypt, Ammon, etc.): Zeph. 2:5,13; Jer. 49:38; 51:55; Ezk. 25:7,16; 28:16; 30:13; Ob. 8. In more general terms, the book of Jeremiah speaks of the destructive power of Yahweh and his prophet (1:10; 12:17; 18:7), using the characteristic Jeremian words "to break down" and "to pluck up."

In the prophetic preaching, similar threats are also directed against Israel: Yahweh will use the nations to destroy Israel (Jer. 15:7; 25:10; cf. Dt. 28:63; Jer. 31:28). The image of Yahweh as the one who destroys in war probably has two roots: (1) the ancient Israelite figure of Yahweh as a war-god, [13] and (2) the cultic-mythical idea of "the revolt of the nations" in the New Year Festival. [14] But Yahweh acts as more than a warrior. All forces in the nation and society which oppose God must submit: Yahweh destroys transgressors of the Law (Lev. 23:30; Dt. 7:10), liars (Ps. 5:7 [Eng. v. 6]), and those who oppress the righteous (Ps. 143:12). This idea surely originated in the cultic sacral law, [15] and may be connected with the idea of Yahweh as the destroyer of the heathen cult (Ezk. 6:3; cf. Mic. 5:9ff.[10ff.]).

Sometimes in military contexts the verb 'abhadh is used in the piel and hiphil to describe how Israel destroys heathen nations, or heathen nations Israel. Actually, the difference between these passages and those already mentioned, in which Yahweh was the author of destruction, is not great. In any case, according to OT thought Yahweh is the one who guides historical events. When

---

[12] Jenni, 152.
[13] Cf. H. Fredriksson, *Jahwe als Krieger* (Lund, 1945); G. von Rad, *Der Heilige Krieg im alten Israel* (⁴1965).
[14] See esp. S. Mowinckel, *Psalmenstudien*, II (1922), 57-65, 254-276.
[15] See, e.g., G. von Rad, *GSAT* (1958), 225-247; H.-J. Kraus, *Die prophetische Verkündigung des Rechts* (1957).

Israel destroys its enemies (Dt. 7:24; 9:3; Nu. 24:19; Est. 9:6,12), or when the heathen, as Yahweh's instrument, destroy Israel (Josh. 7:7; 2 K. 13:7; 24:2; Dt. 28:51; Lam. 2:9; etc.), Yahweh is behind it.

2. *The Qal of Divinely Willed Destruction.* The intransitive form of the verb *ʾabhadh* (qal) complements what has just been said about the piel and the hiphil. Although it is not specifically stated, in many cases it is quite clear that Yahweh is the author of the described destruction, as that of Egypt (Ex.10:7), the Canaanites (Dt. 7:20), the Philistines (Am.1:8; Zec. 9:5), Moab (Nu. 21:29f.; Jer. 48:8, 46), Tyre (Ezk. 26:17), or all of Israel's enemies (Jgs. 5:31; Ps. 2:12; 9:4[3]; 10:16; 80:17[16]; 83:18[17]; Isa. 41:11; 60:12). They all will come under divine judgment and perish; the same thing will also happen to Israel because of her disobedience to the law (Lev. 26:38; Dt. 28:20,22; Jer. 9:11[12]) and her idolatry (Dt. 4:26; 8:19f.; 11:17; 30:18; Josh. 23:13,16). In most of these passages there recurs the typical expression *va'abhadhtem me'al ha'arets*, or the like, "and you shall perish from the land. . . . " Thus, in these texts, which deal with the acquisition of the land, the divine punishment consists in God's driving his people out of the land. Other passages state even more directly that the people shall perish in exile (Jer. 27:10,15; Ob. 12; cf. Isa. 27:13).

In Wisdom Literature and in the Psalms which are related to it, we encounter reminiscences of the sacral-legal use of *ʾabhadh* in the qal: anyone in the community who acts wickedly shall perish (Ps.1:6; 37:20; 73:27; Job 4:9; 18:17; 20:7; Prov.11:10; 28:28 [in these passages, the predominant subject is → רָשָׁע *rāshāʿ*, "the wicked, the criminal"]; cf. also the references in 4QpPs37 3:4,8). The same is true of the liar (Prov.19:9; 21:28). More concretely, the biblical text states that the house of Ahab and those who took part in Korah's revolt will perish (2 K. 9:8; Nu. 16:33; cf. Est. 4:14).

IV. 1. *The Hiphil and the Piel in General Usage.* The passages dealt with above refer more or less clearly to divinely willed destruction. In addition, *ʾabhadh* is used in a more general way for destruction of enemies in political and religious conflicts (2 K. 10:19; 11:1; 19:18; Jer. 46:8; cf. also Jer. 40:15 and the Mesha Stela, *KAI,* 181.7), for ill-treatment of the people by kings and princes (Jer. 23:1; Ezk. 22:27), and for removal of idols (Nu. 33:52; Dt. 12:2f.; 2 K. 21:3–all in the piel; cf. the qal in Jer. 10:15, and the Aramaic peal in Jer. 10:11). In Wisdom Literature this word often designates the destruction done by fools, by the wicked, or by human vice (always in the piel: Prov. 1:32; 29:3; Eccl. 7:7; 9:18; cf. Ps. 119:95; Eccl. 3:6[?] and 1QS 7:6). [16]

2. *The Qal in General Usage.* Finally *ʾabhadh* in the qal exhibits a variety of nuances: A dozen passages refer to things and persons who vanish or perish (weapons: 2 S. 1:27; property: Dt. 22:3; cf. CD 9:10; caravans: Job 6:18; etc.). Of greater theological interest is the use of this word in prophetic texts where

---

16 See Jenni, 152.

the verb describes how in critical times, when evil increases, good attributes and positive ideas vanish (truth: Jer. 7:28; knowledge of the law: Jer. 18:18; Ezk. 7:26; wisdom and good counsel: Isa. 29:14; Jer. 18:18; 49:7; Ezk. 7:26; cf. Ps. 146:4; Dt. 32:28 and CD A 5:17; righteousness: Mic. 7:2; courage: Jcr. 4:9; etc.). The two plainly stereotyped expressions "the place of refuge (*manos*) is lost," i.e., there is no place of escape (Am. 2:14; Jer. 25:35; cf. Ps. 142:5[4]; Job 11:20), and "hope (→ תקוה *tiqvāh*) is lost" (Ezk. 19:5; 37:11; cf. Ps. 9:19[18]; Job 8:13; Sir. 41:2; 11QPsᵃ 22:8; etc.) should also be included here. Quite understandably, idiomatic meanings of *'abhadh* developcd: thus the participle *'obhedh* often means "poor" (Job 29:13; 31:19; Prov. 31:6; cf. Sir. 11:12). But quite often the qal form means simply "to die" (e.g., Nu. 17:27[12]; Isa. 57:1; Ps. 41:6[5]; 49:11 [10]; Job 4:7,11,20; Eccl. 7:15; Jonah 1:6,14; cf. the Murabba'āt Letter 45.7 and 11QPsᵃ 22:9). This meaning, however, is also present in many of the passages mentioned earlier.[17]

V. **'abhaddon = The Underworld.** With this nuance of *'abhadh* we come to the most important noun from this root, *'abhaddon* (with its by-form *'abhaddoh*). Very rarely does this word mean "destruction" (Job 31:12; [18] perhaps also in 1QM fragm. 9:3). Much more often in the OT, and particularly in Wisdom Literature, it means the "place of destruction," i.e., the Underworld (in three passages it is parallel with → שׁאול *she'ôl:* Job 26:6; Prov. 15:11; 27:20; once with → קבר: *qebher:* Ps. 88:12[11]; and once with → מות *māveth:* Job 28:22). In Job 28:22, *'abhaddon* speaks as a personification of death (cf. Rev. 9:11).[19] This term also plays an important role in late Jewish apocalyptic texts (1QH 3:16,19,32 and the Aramaic 1QGenAp 12:17).[20]

Otzen

---

[17] See J. L. Palache, *Sinai en Paran* (1959), 108, and cf. the piel forms in Ps. 9:6(5); 21:11 [10]; Est. 3:9,13; 4:7; 7:4; 8:5; 9:24, and the Aramaic haphel form in Dnl. 2:12,18,24, which mean simply "to put to death," Jenni, 150f., 155. A similar meaning is found in Aramaic inscriptions; see *KAI,* 223 B.7; 225.11; 226.10; cf. Jenni, 151.

[18] But see Yellin, 11.

[19] Cf. *TDNT,* I, 4.

[20] Cf. P. Wernberg-Møller, *Textus,* 4 (1964), 153f. On the use of this term in Rabbinic literature, see Volz, *Die Eschatologie der jüdischen Gemeinde* (1934), 328f.; Ginzberg, *Legends of the Jews,* I (1909), 10, 15; St.-B., III, 8t0.

```
┌─────────────────┐
│  אָבָה  'ābhāh   │
└─────────────────┘
```

Contents: I. 1. Etymology, Occurrences; 2. Meaning. II. Usages in the OT: 1. General Observations; 2. With *shāmaʻ*. III. Specific Theological Considerations: 1. God As Subject; 2. Hardness of Heart; 3. *'abhah* As an Attitude Toward God.

I. 1. *Etymology, Occurrences.* The root *'abhah* appears in almost all Semitic languages–it is missing only in Akkadian, since ostensibly *abū/ītu*, "desire," does not exist. [1] It is worthy of note that *'abhah* in different languages has opposite meanings. The meaning "to be willing, to appear willing," in Hebrew, Egyptian Aramaic, Jewish Aramaic (the Targums), and Egyptian *(ꜣby)*, is opposite to Arab. *'abā* and Ethiop. *'abaya*, "to be unwilling," as well as to the ancient South Arab. *t'by*, "refusal." [2]

In the OT, the verb appears only in the qal. The texts in which it occurs belong to the classical language. It is found in the Pentateuch and especially in the Deuteronomistic history. Isaiah and Ezekiel also contain a number of examples. In addition, it occurs in Ps. 81:12 (Eng. v. 11); Job 39:9; Prov. 1:10,25,30; 6:35, and in Chronicles, where the examples are literal repetitions from Samuel-Kings, except that 1 Ch. 19:19 has *lo' 'abhah 'aram*, "the Syrians were not willing," where 2 S. 10:19 reads *vayyir'u 'aram*, "So the Syrians feared." But the reading in Chronicles may be earlier. This word occurs also in the Hebrew text of Sir. 6:33. In the Qumran texts, other synonyms appear in place of *'abhah*, especially *ratsah* (which is also the usual verb for "to be willing" in modern Hebrew).

2. *Meaning.* Honeyman thinks that *'abhah* and → אֶבְיוֹן *'ebhyôn* come from a common root which originally meant "to lack, to be in need"; but Barth and others argue that these words come from different roots. [3] → אוה *'āvāh* and the cognate words *ya'abh* and *ta'abh* in Ps. 119 also have similar meanings. [4] The original meaning of *'abhah* which fits best with all OT occurrences is "to show intention in a certain direction." The primary emphasis here is not on the intention as a psychological factor in the inner-man (cf. *'avah*, usually with *nephesh* as subject!), but on the main behavioral patterns and actions in which the intention is manifested.

In the OT, *'abhah* is almost always used with a negative, usually *lo'* (*'en* occurs in Ezk. 3:7, and *'al* in Prov. 1:10). The verb is used without the negative in Isa.

'ābhāh. J. Barth, *Wurzeluntersuchungen* (1902), 3f.; G. Garbini, "Note semitiche," *Ricerche Linguistiche*, 5 (1962), 179-181; F. Hesse, *Das Verstockungsproblem im AT. BZAW*, 74 (1955); A. M. Honeyman, "Some developments of the semitic root *'by*," *JAOS*, 64 (1944), 81f.; L. Köhler, "Ein verkannter hebräischer irrealer Bedingungssatz," *ZS*, 4 (1926), 196f.; Th. Nöldeke, *Beiträge zur semitischen Sprachwissenschaft* (1904).

[1] *AHw*, I, 89f.
[2] *KBL³*.
[3] Cf. the Literature under → אֶבְיוֹן *'ebhyôn*.
[4] See Garbini.

1:19; Job 39:9; Sir. 6:33. Since this verb has the negative meaning "to be unwilling" in Arabic and Ethiopic,[5] Nöldeke (66) considered this meaning to be original. If that were so, the negative in Hebrew might be interpreted as a strengthening of the negative sense. This hypothesis has rightly been rejected by Honeyman and Brockelmann.[6] It is easy to explain how the original meaning suggested above, "to show intention in a certain direction," was used in different languages predominantly for a positive or negative reaction.

II. Usages in the OT.

1. *General Observations.* In most cases, *'abhah* is followed by an infinitive, e.g., "he showed himself (did not show himself) willing to do this or that," as in Gen. 24:8, "but if the woman is not willing to follow you"; Jgs. 19:10, "but the man would not spend the night"; Job 39:9, "is the wild ox willing to serve you?" The verb whose infinitive occurs most often after *'abhah* is → שָׁמַע *shāmaʿ*, "to be unwilling to hear."[7]

Since *'abhah* is not an auxiliary verb in Hebrew, it is not appropriate to add, after the pattern of modern languages, an infinitive in cases where *'abhah* is used absolutely. In 1 S. 31:4, the armor-bearer does not want to kill king Saul. This is to be understood to mean that, because of fear and respect, the armor-bearer is not able to react positively to the king's command (cf. also 1 K. 22:50; Prov. 1:10).

The person or thing that does not receive a positive response is introduced in Hebrew by *le* (Dt. 13:9[8]; Prov. 1:30).

The terms → מָאֵן *māʾēn,* "to refuse" (Dt. 25:7), *paraʿ,* "to ignore" (Prov. 1:25), and → נָאַץ *nāʾats,* "to despise" (1:30), occur in parallelism with *loʾ 'abhah.*

2. *With shāmaʿ.* *'abhah* often occurs with *shamaʿ.* Several times the construction is *loʾ 'abhah (li)shemoaʿ,* "he was not willing to hear." *'abhah* is not to be regarded merely as an auxiliary verb here, as is shown by the cases in which *'abhah* appears in parallelism with *shamaʿ,* e.g., Jgs. 11:17: "The king of Edom would not listen *(shamaʿ),* ... also the king of Moab would not consent *('abhah)."* The meaning of *'abhah* and *shamaʿ* is not identical. The difference seems to be that *'abhah* denotes the first beginnings of a positive reaction, whereas *shamaʿ* indicates complete obedience. Thus the sequence of these two verbs expresses an intensification: Dt. 13:9(8): "You shall not yield *('abhah)* to him or listen *(shamaʿ)* to him, nor shall your eye pity him...." In 1 K. 20:8 we find the expression, "Do not heed *(shamaʿ)* or consent *('abhah)"* (cf. also Isa. 1:19; Ps. 81:12[11]).

In synonymous parallelism with the whole expression *(loʾ) 'abhah lishmoaʿ* we find the negative phrases *'im telekhu 'immi qeri,* "if you walk contrary to

---

[5] However, there are exceptions in Arabic, Brockelmann, *Synt.,* § 52b.
[6] See also § 165c.
[7] See below, II.2.

me" (Lev. 26:21), and *'im tema'anu umerithem*, "if you refuse and rebel" (Isa. 1:20), and the positive expression *'im tatteh 'oznekha*, "if you incline your ear" (Sir. 6:33).

III. Specific Theological Considerations.

1. *God As Subject.* God appears as the subject of *'abhah* in specifically Deuteronomic material: "the Lord was unwilling to destroy you" (Dt. 10:10; 2 K. 8:19; 13:23); "the Lord would not hearken to Balaam" (Dt. 23:6[5]; Josh. 24:10); "the Lord would not pardon" (Dt. 29:19[20]; 2 K. 24:4). Here also *'abhah* and *shama'* appear together and refer to the covenant relationship. [8] God's act is to be understood in light of the covenant. In the framework of the covenant, a "positive reaction" is demanded of the people.

2. *Hardness of Heart.* As lord of the covenant, God also controls the activities of the enemies of his people. God hardened Pharaoh's heart so that he would not let the people go (Ex. 10:27). He also hardened Sihon's heart (Dt. 2:30). But the covenant people themselves are often the ones who rebel. In this case, the *lo' 'abhah*, "unwillingness," of the people is a technical term for hardness of heart, and appears in parallelism with → מרה *mārāh* (Dt. 1:26; Isa. 30:9; Ezk. 20:8) and other typical expressions for hardness of heart (Lev. 26:21; Isa. 1:19f.; 30:9; Ezk. 3:7; cf. also the context of Isa. 28:12). The refusal of the people is summed up in the words: "but you would not" (Dt. 1:26; Isa. 30:15; cf. Mt. 23:37).

3. *'abhah As an Attitude Toward God.* *'abhah* is used to describe the positive reaction to God, the answer which man gives to his lord. Just as *shama'* means both "to hear" and "to obey," so *'abhah* means not only "to have an intention" but also "to show this intention." These two aspects cannot be separated from each other. Thus, *'abhah* stands alongside other expressions for faith, trust, and confidence as an expression for a personal commitment to God, which is the right attitude for man in covenant relationship with God. *'abhah* often occurs in a situation in which man is called on to make a choice, as in Isa. 30:15. Yahweh, the Holy One of Israel, offers salvation and deliverance: "In returning and rest you shall be saved; in quietness and in trust shall be your strength." But the people refuse *(lo' 'abhithem)* and trust in the power of horses rather than in God (30:16). In 1:19, the people are urged to show a positive intention toward God. The other possibility is expressed by characteristic terms for hardness of heart, *ma'en*, "to refuse," and *marah*, "to rebel" (1:20).

In the passages in the Wisdom Literature, *'abhah* is not directed specifically to God, but to Wisdom, its reproof (Prov. 1:25), its counsel (1:30), or quite generally in admonitions, to the son (Sir. 6:33).

B. Johnson

---

8 Wildberger, *BK*, X, on Isa. 1:19.

אֶבְיוֹן *’ebhyôn*

Contents: I. 1. Etymology; 2. Occurrences; 3. Semantic Field of "Poor" in the OT; 4. Relationships of the Words for "Poor"; 5. The LXX. II. Need for Material and Legal Assistance: 1. Sociological Change of the *’ebhyon* in the Sabbatical Year, the Year of Release, and the Year of Jubilee; 2. Prohibition Against Defeating the Ends of the Law in the Book of the Covenant; 3. Slavery As a Payment for Debts, and the Oppression of the *’ebhyon* and the *tsaddiq* in Amos; 4. *’ebhyon* As a Tribal Brother in Deuteronomy; 5. *din ‘ani ve’ebhyon* As "Knowledge of God" in Jeremiah; 6. Oppression of the *’ebhyon* As *’aven* and *to‘ebhah* in Ezekiel; 7. The King As Advocate of the *’ebhyon*. III. The *’ebhyon* in the Wise Order of Creation. IV. The *’ebhyon* in Expectation of Divine Help: 1. The Enemies of the *’ebhyon;* 2. Affliction, Illness, Loneliness, Nearness to Death; 3. Religious Classification of the *’ebhyon;* 4. Yahweh, Deliverer of the *’ebhyonim;* 5. *’ebhyon* in Late Prophetic Proclamations of Salvation. V. Qumran.

I. 1. *Etymology.* Now, as before, the etymology of *’ebhyon* is uncertain. Some scholars think it was derived from a Semitic root, while others argue that it was borrowed from Egyptian. (a) Usually, *’ebhyon* is thought to be derived from a

---

’ebhôn. S. W. Baron, *Histoire d'Israël,* I (Paris, 1956); C. Barth, *Die Errettung vom Tode in den individuellen Klage- und Dankliedern des AT* (Zollikon, 1947); W. Baudissin, "Die alttestamentliche Religion und die Armen," *Preussische Jahrbücher* (1912), 209-224; J. Begrich, "Die Vertrauensäusserungen im israelitischen Klagelied des Einzelnen und in seinem babylonischen Gegenstück," *ZAW,* 46 (1928), 221-260=*ThB,* 21 (1964), 168-216; P. van den Berghe, "'Ani et 'Anaw dans les Psaumes," *Le Psautier,* ed. R. de Langhe (Louvain, 1962), 273-295; W. Beyerlin, *Die Rettung der Bedrängten in den Feindpsalmen der Einzelnen auf institutionelle Zusammenhänge untersucht. FRLANT,* 99 (1970); H. Birkeland, *'Anī und 'ānāw in den Psalmen. SNVAO 1932,* 4 (1933); *idem, Die Feinde des Individuums in der israelitischen Psalmenliteratur* (Oslo, 1933); *idem, The Evildoers in the Book of Psalms. ANVAO 1955,* 2; H. Bruppacher, *Die Beurteilung der Armut im AT* (1924); F. Buhl, *Die socialen Verhältnisse der Israeliten* (1899); A. Causse, *Du groupe ethnique à la communauté religieuse* (Paris, 1937); *idem, Les 'pauvres' d'Israël* (Paris-Strasbourg, 1922); L. Delekat, *Asylie und Schutzorakel am Zionheiligtum. Eine Untersuchung zu den privaten Feindpsalmen* (Leiden, 1967); *idem,* "Zum hebräischen Wörterbuch," *VT,* 14 (1964), 7-66, esp. 35-49; J. Didiot, *Le pauvre dans la Bible* (Paris, 1903); F. C. Fensham, "Widow, Orphan and the Poor in Ancient Near Eastern Legal and Wisdom Literature," *JNES,* 21 (1962), 129-139; A. Gamper, *Gott als Richter in Mesopotamien und im AT. Zum Verständnis einer Gebetsbitte* (Innsbruck, 1966); R. A. Gauthier, *Magnanimité: L'idéal de l'humilité dans la philosophie païenne et dans la théologie chrétienne* (Paris, 1951), 375-404; A. Gelin, *The Poor of Yahweh* (trans. 1964); B. Gemser, "The RÎB- or Controversy-Pattern in Hebrew Mentality," *SVT,* 3 (1960), 120-137; A. George, "Pauvre," *DBS,* 7 (1966), 387-406; H. Graetz, *Kritischer Komm. zu den Psalmen,* I (1882), II (1883); H. Gunkel-J. Begrich, *Einl. in die Psalmen* (1933); E. Hammershaimb, "On the Ethics of the OT Prophets," *SVT,* 7 (1960), 75-101; F. Hauck, "πένης, πενιχρός," *TDNT,* VI (1968), 37-40; F. Hauck-E. Bammel, "πτωχός," *TDNT,* VI (1968), 885-915; C. Hauret, "Les ennemis-sorciers dans les supplications individuelles," *Rech. Bibliques,* 8 (Bruges-Paris, 1967), 129-138; P. Humbert, "Le mot biblique *’ebyôn,*" *RHPR,* 32 (1952), 1-6; A. S. Kapelrud, "New Ideas in Amos," *SVT,* 15 (1966), 193-206; O. Keel, *Feinde und Gottesleugner. Studien zum Image der Widersacher in den Individualpsalmen. SBM,* 7 (1969); R. Kittel, *Die Psalmen,* Exkurs 8: "Die Armen und Elenden" (⁶1929), 284-88; H.-J.

(continued on p. 28)

root → אבה ʾābhāh with a common original meaning "to lack, to be in need." Heb. ʾabhah, "to comply with, to be willing," [1] is opposite to Arab. ʾabā, Ethiop. and Tigr. ʾabaya, "to be unwilling, to refuse," [2] and the Old South Arab. tʾby, "refusal." [3] The absence of Akkadian examples is striking. Thus, an inner Semitic derivation is possible only by inferring a common original meaning: an ʾebhyon is a man who wants something which he does not have, and consequently a man who is needy and poor. Against this, Humbert (2) emphasizes that ʾebhyon has no exclusively privative or negative meaning. "Hence the meaning is both privative and positive: undoubtedly it means the poor, but to the extent that he manifests a desire, a wish, in other words to the extent that he begs.... The word expresses not only a deficiency, but also an expectation and a demand." Ugar. ʾbynt [4], "wretchedness, misery," [5] occurs in parallelism with ʾnḥ; people from the city of ʾll are called ʾbynm. [6] Baumgartner, Aistleitner, Gordon, Humbert, etc., connect Ugar. ʾbynt and ʾbynm with the Heb. ʾebhyon. W. von Soden [7] has called attention to the complaint made to King Zimri-lim in the Letters of Women from Mari, which says a-bi-ia-na-ku, "I am a poor woman"; [8] he takes abiyānum, "poor," with the related meaning "afflicted, wretched," like Ugar. ʾbyn and Heb. ʾebhyon, as an "old Amoritic" word, which developed from a root ʾbī, "poor, needy," with the suffix -n. (b) Again, Th. O. Lambdin is the primary advocate

---

Kraus, Psalmen, I, Exkurs 3: "ʿAnī und ʿAnāw," BK, XV/1 (³1966), 82f.; A. Kuschke, "Arm und reich im AT mit besonderer Berücksichtigung der nachexilischen Zeit," ZAW, 57 (1939), 31-57; E. Kutsch, ʿanāwāh ʿDemut', ein Beitrag zum Thema ʿGott und Mensch im AT' (unpubl. inaugural diss., 1960); C. van Leeuwen, Le développement du sens social en Israël avant l'ère chrétienne. Studia Semitica Neerlandica, 1 (1955); J. Loeb, La littérature des pauvres dans la Bible (Paris, 1892); J. Maier, Die Armenfrömmigkeit. Texte vom Toten Meer, II (1960), 83-87; G. Marschall, Die ʿGottlosen' des ersten Psalmenbuches (1929); S. Mowinckel, Psalmenstudien, I, Åwän und die individuellen Klagepsalmen (1921), 113-122; P. A. Munch, "Einige Bemerkungen zu den ʿanijjim und den rešaʿim in den Psalmen," Le Monde Oriental (1936), 13-26; idem, "Das Problem des Reichtums in den Psalmen 37, 49, 73," ZAW, 55 (1937), 36-45; J. van der Ploeg, "Les pauvres d'Israël et leur piété," OTS, 7 (1950), 236-270; A. Rahlfs, ʿAni und ʿanaw in den Psalmen (1892); E. Renan, History of the People of Israel, III (1891), 31-40; N. H. Ridderbos, De ʿwerkers der ongerechtigheid' in de individueele Psalmen (Kampen, 1939); H. Schmidt, Das Gebet der Angeklagten im AT. BZAW, 49 (1928); K. Schwarzwaller, Die Feinde des Individuums in den Psalmen (unpubl. diss., 1963); W. Staerk, "Die Gottlosen in den Psalmen. Ein Beitrag zur alttestamentlichen Religionsgeschichte," ThStKr, 70 (1897), 449-488; J. J. Stamm, Das Leiden der Unschuldigen in Babylon und Israel. AThANT, 10 (1946); H. Steiner, Die Gē'im in den Psalmen (unpubl. diss., Bern-Lausanne, 1925); de Vaux, AncIsr, 72-74; C. Westermann, The Praise of God in the Psalms (trans. 1965); idem, "Struktur und Geschichte der Klage im AT," ZAW, 66 (1954), 44-80=ThB, 24 (1964), 266-305; H. W. Wolff, Amos' geistige Heimat. WMANT, 18 (1964).

[1] KBL³.
[2] Leslau, Contributions, 9; Lexicon, 378b.
[3] W. W. Müller, Die Wurzeln Mediae und Tertiae Y/W im Altsüdarabischen (diss., Tübingen, 1962), 25.
[4] CTA, 17 [II D], I, 17.
[5] Gordon, UT, Glossary, No. 24.
[6] UT, 313, 6.
[7] "Zur Herkunft von hebr. ʾebjon ʿarm'," MIO, 15/2 (1969), 322-26.
[8] ARM, X = Theologisches Literaturblatt, 31 (1967), No. 37. 23; 44. 10.

of the view that *ʾebhyon* is derived from Egyptian. [9] According to Erman-Grapow, there are examples of occurrences of *byn* from the end of the Old Kingdom on: referring to persons, *byn* means "worthless, sluggish, to be in a wretched condition, evil," referring to harmful animals, "malicious, dangerous," referring to abstract things or ideas, "evil, bad, pernicious"; "the Evil One," "the Evil," plural "evil deeds," "calamity." According to Lambdin, Copt. *bōōn,* "wicked" (fem. *boone*), and *ebyēn,* "wretched, miserable," belong to the root *byn.* With W. F. Albright, [10] he accepts a phonetic development from *(e)būne(w)* to *ʾĕbyūne* (> Heb. *ʾebhyon*) to *ʾebyēn.* Because of the vowel change from *ū* to *ē* in Late Egyptian and because of the o-vowel in Heb. *ʾebhyon,* the borrowing cannot have been later than the twelfth century. *ʾebhyon* with a degrading meaning would have been transferred to a specific class of Semitic (Canaanite) workers, "very possibly in connection with shipping and shipping crews." [11] Other Coptologists, as W. Spiegelberg, [12] W. Westendorf, [13] separate *ebyēn* from *bōōn* etymologically and argue that *ebyēn* was borrowed from Heb. *ʾebhyon;* W. von Soden agrees with this view. [14]

2. *Occurrences.* *ʾebhyon* occurs 61 times in the Hebrew OT: Ex. 23:6,11 (the Book of the Covenant) twice; Dt. 7 times; 1 S. 2:8 (Hannah's Song of Praise); Est. 9:22; Am. 5 times; Isa. 5 times (14:30; 25:4; 29:19; 32:7; 41:17[?]); Jer. 4 times; Ezk. 3 times; Pss. 23 times (not 33 times); Prov. 4 times; Job 6 times. While *ʾebhyon* does indeed occur in the Book of the Covenant, it does not appear in the J and E traditions or in the Deuteronomistic history (except in Hannah's Song of Praise in 1 S. 2:8); it is also notably absent in the Priestly Code. The occasional use of this word in the prophets (17 times) in comparison with the 23 occurrences in the Psalms is also striking.

3. *Semantic Field of "Poor" in the OT.* Besides *ʾebhyon,* there are several words for "poor" in the OT: → דל *dāl* 48 times; *dalal* 6 times; *dallah/dallath* in conjunction with *ʿam* or *ʾerets* 5 times; *misken* 6 times (4 times in Eccl. and twice in Sir.); → עני *ʾanî* 74 times; *ʾanav* 20 times; *ʾani,* "distress, oppressed condition" 36 times; *ʾanavah,* "humility" 4 times; *ʾenuth* once; *rash* 21 times; *rush* 3 times; *rish* 8 times (7 times in Prov. and once in Sir.); *chaser,* "to decrease, lack" 23 times; *chaser,* "one who has too little" 17 times; → חסר *cheser* twice; *choser* 3 times; *chesron* once; *machsor* 13 times.

4. *Relationships of the Words for "Poor."* *ʾebhyon* often appears in the stereotyped formula *ʾani veʾebhyon,* "poor and needy": Dt. 24:14; Jer. 22:16; Ezk. 16:49; 18:12; 22:29; Ps. 35:10 (some conjecture that *ʾani* should be deleted

---

9 "Egyptian Loan Words in the OT," *JAOS,* 73 (1953), 145-155, here 145f.
10 *Vocalization of the Egyptian Syllabic Orthography* (1934), 18.
11 Lambdin, 146.
12 *Koptisches Handwörterbuch* (1921), 23, n. 12.
13 *Koptisches Handwörterbuch* (1965), 24f.
14 *MIO,* 15/2 (1969), 323.

here); 37:14; 40:18 (Eng. v. 17); 70:6(5); 74:21; 86:1; 109:16,22; Prov. 31:9; Job 24:14. The motif of the certainty of hearing should be emphasized, *(ki) va'ani 'ani ve'ebhyon,* Ps. 40:18(17); 70:6(5); 86:1; 109:22. In addition, *'ebhyon* stands in parallelism with *'ani:* Am. 8:4; Dt. 15:11; Isa. 29:19; 32:7; 41:17; Ps. 9:19(18); 12:6(5); 72:4,12; 140:13(12); Prov. 30:14; Job 24:4.

The combination *dal ve'ebhyon* is found in Ps. 72:13; 82:4. *dal* and *'ebhyon* appear in parallelism in Am. 4:1; 8:6; Isa. 14:30; 25:4; 1 S. 2:8; Ps. 72:12; 113:7; Prov. 14:31; Job 5:15.

rash occurs in the same context as *'ebhyon* only once, viz., Ps. 82:3f., "Give justice to the weak *(dal;* or should we read *dakh,* "the oppressed," because of v. 4a?) and the fatherless *(yathom);* maintain the right of the afflicted and the destitute (*'ani varash*). Rescue the weak and the needy *(dal ve'ebhyon);* deliver them from the hand of the wicked."

5. *The LXX.* In the LXX *'ebhyon* is translated as follows: *pénēs* 29 times; *ptōchós* 10 times; *endeēs* 5 times; *adýnatos* 4 times; *tapeinós* twice; *asthenēs* once; and *deísthai,* "to fear" 3 times.

II. Need for Material and Legal Assistance.

1. *Sociological Change of the 'ebhyon in the Sabbatical Year, the Year of Release, and the Year of Jubilee.* In the regulations of the Book of the Covenant concerning the Sabbatical Year, the *'ebhyon* is clearly contrasted with the land-owner: whereas the landowner can live off the produce of the foregoing years during the seventh year while the land lies fallow, the *'ebhyon* is forced to eat that which grows wild on the fallow ground in the Sabbatical Year (Ex. 23:11), because he has no property or produce. This characterization of the *'ebhyon* is not related to the question whether this social institution was intimately connected from the very first with the idea of a recurring restoration of the original state of affairs *(restitutio in integrum).*[15] As a result of a changed economic situation, then, by means of a legal interpretation Dt. 15:2 replaces the agricultural fallow ground with a "release" *(shemittah)* from debts, according to which each creditor must set his neighbor free from all obligations.[16] In the Year of Jubilee, moreover, the people are obliged to help an → אָח *'āch,* "brother," faced with economic difficulties by lending him money free of interest and giving him food without realizing a profit (Lev. 25:36f.); and if he sells himself into slavery to pay his debts, he shall serve as a hired servant *(sakhir)* or a sojourner (→ תּוֹשָׁב *tôshābh*) and not as an → עֶבֶד *'ebhedh,* "slave," until he is set free in the Year of Jubilee (vv. 39-43). According to Dt. 24:14, one may not oppress a hired servant who is poor and needy *(lo' tha'ashoq sakhir 'ani ve'ebhyon);* instead, he must give him his hire on the day he earns it, since he is poor (*'ani*) and thus sets his heart on it (v. 15).

---

[15] Jepsen, Cazelles.
[16] Cf. H. M. Weil, "Gage et cautionnement dans la Bible," *AHDO,* 2 (1938), 171-240, here 189; de Vaux, 173-75.

2. *Prohibition Against Defeating the Ends of the Law in the Book of the Covenant.* The Book of the Covenant explicitly forbids perverting the justice due to the poor (*lo' thatteh mishpat 'ebhyonekha beribho,* Ex. 23:6). It is possible that a series of prohibitions (23:1,6,8,9) lies behind the series of laws in Ex. 23:1-9 having to do with the behavior of the judge and the leading circles in the judicial organization;[17] if so, the short form, "you shall not pervert justice" (v. 6), was given a social application by the addition of *'ebhyonekha,* and was later expanded by a prohibition against showing partiality to the mighty (v. 3; read *gadhol*). Along with the law protecting the *'ebhyon* from the perversion of justice, in this context there are also prohibitions against slaying the innocent and righteous (*naqi vetsaddiq,* v. 7b) or against oppressing a stranger (→ גר *gēr,* v. 9a).

3. *Slavery As a Payment for Debts, and the Oppression of the 'ebhyon and the tsaddiq in Amos.* The protection of the "poor" from the perversion of justice and from exploitation is a major theme in the prophecy of Amos; he uses *'ebhyon* (2:6; 4:1; 5:12; 8:4,6), *dal* (2:7; 4:1; 5:11; 8:6), and *'anavim* (2:7; 8:4). Of particular significance is the parallelism of *'ebhyon* and *tsaddiq* (2:6; 5:12); *tsaddiq* and *'ebhyon* are victims of the disappearance of justice (5:12). People afflict the righteous *(tsaddiq),* take a bribe or hush-money, and oppress the needy (*'ebhyonim)* in the judicial process in the gate (5:12); because of the corruption of the judges, the innocent are pronounced guilty and the needy are deprived of their rights. Kapelrud says: "They who should represent justice and righteousness, who should be [*tsaddiqim*] par excellence, did so no more.... Others had taken their place: ['*anavim, 'ebhyonim, dallim*], the poor, needy people, who were trampled down by the mighty, they were the real [*tsaddiqim*]. They were entitled to have their rights in the Israelite society ... their condition and their position in society were an integrated part of their [*tsedhaqah*]."[18] This parallelism of *tsaddiq* and *'ebhyon* also appears in the invective against Israel: because of a trifling debt, Israel sells the righteous into slavery for silver and the *'ebhyon* for a pair of shoes as a payment for debts (2:6b). Many scholars attribute the selling of the *tsaddiq* for silver to the corruption of the judges, but the selling of the *'ebhyon* for a pair of shoes because of a minimal debt to the avarice of the creditor.[19] Here, the prophet is not renouncing the casuistic law which enjoins slavery as a payment for debts,[20] but unjust and unscrupulous slavery as a payment for debts which are not real or serious. In connection with selling the *tsaddiq* and *'ebhyon* into slavery as a payment for debts in 2:6b, v. 7a mentions the affliction of the *dallim* and the *'anavim* as another crime of Israel. The protection of the innocent and of the poor in society is of the very warp and woof of the Israelite way of life. Accordingly, the social and ethical implications of this system are expressed in precepts, prohibitions, and wise admonitions to

---

17 Cf. also W. Richter, *Recht und Ethos* (1966), 123.
18 Kapelrud, 203f.
19 Cripps, Sellin, Robinson.
20 Contra R. Bach, "Gottesrecht und weltliches Recht in der Verkündigung des Propheten Amos," *Festschrift G. Dehn* (1957), 23-34, here 28f.

tribal brothers, especially to the influential and wealthy classes. The parallelism of *tsaddiq* and *'ebhyon* here is rooted in the unjustified selling of the poor into slavery as a payment for debts. Am. 8:6 contains a reproach against profiteers who deal the poor *(dallim)* into slavery for silver and the needy *('ebhyon)* for a pair of shoes as a payment for debts; here the *tsaddiq* of 2:6b is replaced by *dallim*, while *'ebhyon* appears in both passages. Am. 4:1 records an accusation against the pleasure-seeking women of Samaria for oppressing the poor *(ha'osheqoth dallim)* and crushing the needy *(harotsetsoth 'ebhyonim)*, while they ask their husbands to bring drinks for carousing. Cf. also 8:4, "trample upon the needy" *(sha'aph 'ebhyon)*, and "bring the poor of the land to an end" *(hishbith 'aniyye 'arets)*.

4. *'ebhyon As a Tribal Brother in Deuteronomy*. In conjunction with the social regulations of the Book of the Covenant and as a continuation of the social criticism of the prophets, the Deuteronomist, in his reform and restoration of Israel, attempts to establish an ideal community of tribal brothers *('ach)* in which, among other things, a special participation of the *'ebhyon* in the *nachalah*, "inheritance," is guaranteed by numerous regulations. In light of this, E. Renan saw in Deuteronomy a system of guarantees for the poor at the expense of the rich.[21] The sermon in the Year of Release, Dt. 15:3-11, enjoins the wealthy to provide for the poor: they must not harden their heart against the *'ebhyon* (v. 7), but must open their hand to him and lend him sufficient for his need, whatever it may be (v. 8); avarice toward a poor tribal brother is sin *(chet')* before Yahweh (v. 9); Yahweh blesses the one who gives freely and without grudging *(velo' yera' lebhabhekha*–v. 10). The realistic concluding remark that the *'ebhyon* will never cease out of the land (v. 11) is significant; it is on the basis of this that Yahweh commands his people to open wide their hand to the needy *('ani)* and poor *('ebhyon)* tribal brother.

In the reinterpretation in Dt. 15:4-6, the end of poverty is connected with the promised divine blessing: the prerequisite for Yahweh's blessing, for the inheritance, and for the absence of the poor *('ebhyon)* is obedience to his voice. V. 6 shows how literally this blessing was understood: Israel may "lend to many nations, but may not borrow; and may rule over many nations, but they may not rule" over Israel. In light of this real and materialistic understanding of the blessing, the *'ebhyon* must be understood as a man without these material possibilities. If we go back to the legal interpretation in v. 2 which places these statutes in the context of the law concerning the Year of Release, the *'ebhyon* is a debtor in the "hand" of the creditor, who oppresses him by demanding or exacting the debt by force *(naghash;* cf. *lo' yiggosh)*. Worthy of note is the "negative and entirely unascetic evaluation of poverty . . . , as was typical of ancient Israel. It is an evil from which one can gain no value."[22]

---

21 *History*, III, 186.
22 G. von Rad, *Deuteronomy. OTL* (trans. 1966), 107.

5. *din ʿani veʾebhyon As "Knowledge of God" in Jeremiah.* As in Amos, so in Jeremiah *ʾebhyon* means the socially poor, who, according to 5:28, has to suffer under the fat and sleek rich, because they do not judge with justice the cause of the fatherless and do not defend the rights of the needy. By way of contrast, King Josiah is praised in 22:16 because "he judged the cause of the poor and needy" *(dan din ʿani veʾebhyon);* the prophet calls this just and socially righteous behavior a true knowledge of God *(daʿath ʾothi).* [23] Cf. also the dubious expression *dam naphshoth ʾebhyonim neqiyyim* in Jer. 2:34.

When the prophet in Jer. 20:13, at the end of a lament over his personal struggles, confesses his confidence that Yahweh delivers *(hitstsil)* the life of the needy *(ʾebhyon)* from the hand of the evildoers, thereby designating himself as an *ʾebhyon,* then *ʾebhyon* here has a religious sense as in the Individual Laments. George says: "This is the way he speaks of his weakness in contrast to the terrible power of his enemies, but also of the absolute ease with which he has been saved (I 17-19; XV 19-21; XXVI 20-24)." [24] The genuineness of the praise in v. 13 is disputed. [25]

6. *Oppression of the ʾebhyon As ʾaven and toʿebhah in Ezekiel.* In Ezk. 18:12, the oppression of the poor and needy *(ʾani veʾebhyon honah)* is listed among the abominable things *(toʿebhoth)* of a violent son *(ben parits)* which are punishable by death. This list also includes robbery (cf. Lev. 19:13), refusing to restore the garment taken in pledge (Ex. 22:25f.[26f.]; Dt. 24:10-13,17), lending at interest, and taking increase (cf. Ezk. 22:12; Ex. 22:24[25]; Dt. 23:20f.; Lev. 25:36f.). The social catalog of the works of the righteous in Ezk. 18:6-8 includes, in addition, giving bread to the hungry, covering the naked with a garment, and executing true justice between man and man (cf. Ex. 23:6-8; Dt. 16:18-20). According to the sermon against the ruling classes in 22:25-30 (from the period after 587 [26]), the landed gentry in Judah committed extortion *(ʿosheq),* robbery, oppression *(honu)* of the poor and needy, and extortion *(ʿashaq)* of the sojourner without redress. Cf. also the guilt *(ʿavon)* of Sodom in 16:49: pride, surfeit of food, prosperous ease, and failing to aid the poor and needy. Also in Ezekiel, the *ʾebhyon* (as also the *ʾani*) is a socially and legally deprived person, whose economic or legal oppression the prophet denounces as *ʾavon* (16:49) or *toʿebhah* (18:12; 16:49?).

7. *The King As the Advocate of the ʾebhyon.* According to Ps. 72, the ideal king is given Yahweh's righteousness in order that he may judge Yahweh's people with righteousness (vv. 1f.). As advocate and last court of appeal, "he shall defend the cause of the poor of the people *(ʿaniyye ʿam),* give deliverance to the needy *(yoshiaʿ libhne ʾebhyon),* and crush the oppressor" (v. 4). The king's world dominion (vv. 8-11) is the reward for his just and social rule (vv. 13f.). The verbs

---

23 Cf. G. J. Botterweck, *Gott erkennen. BBB,* 2 (1951); *idem,* in J. B. Bauer *Bibeltheologisches Wörterbuch,* I (³1967), 320ff.

24 George, 393.

25 Cf. W. Rudolph, *HAT,* 12 (³1968), *in loc.*

26 W. Zimmerli, *BK,* XIII/1, 523.

hitstsil, chus, hoshia' and *ga'al* are used in this psalm to express the king's intervention in behalf of the *'ebhyon, 'ani,* and *dal.* Cf. Isa. 11:4f.; Prov. 29:4.

III. The 'ebhyon in the Wise Order of Creation. In Proverbs, *'ebhyon*
occurs only in the second (14:31), sixth (30:14), and seventh (31:9,20) collections. *dal* (15 times) and *rash* (14 times), as well as *'ani* and *'anav* (9 times) are
much more prevalent in Proverbs than *'ebhyon.* Of the 42 passages in Proverbs
referring to the poor, 33 come from the second and fifth collections, which are
certainly preexilic. In the second collection (10:1–22:16), the evaluation of
poverty and riches is not altogether "neutral," [27] but "divided," [28] or better,
differentiated: poverty is a person's own fault, and is attributed to idleness or
negligence (10:4a; 14:23b; 14:4a; 19:15; 20:4b,13a; 21:17,20b) or to subor-
dination (13:18a, cf. 18b). The poor is despised (10:15b; 14:20a; 15:15a;
19:7a) and ruled by the rich (19:7a). On the other hand, the admonition in
14:31 [29] regards the oppression of the poor (*'osheq dal;* according to 17:5, the
mocking of the *rash*) as an insult to the Creator, and kindness toward the needy
(*chonen 'ebhyon;* cf. 19:17, *chonen dal*) as honoring the Creator. Obviously,
the "innocent poor" (*'ebhyon*) are under Yahweh's protection. [30] Showing bene-
volence to the *'ebhyon* and *'ani* is also commanded in the praise of the good
woman (31:20). In this second collection, the wise in Israel stand beside the
poor and needy (14:21 – *'anayim;* 21:13 – *dal;* 22:16 – *dal*), and give them
religious motivation (14:31 – *'ebhyon;* 17:5 – *rash;* 19:17 – *dal*). [31] The person
who shows kindness to the poor receives kindness from Yahweh (19:17) and will
be blessed (22:9).

The words of Agur refer to the devouring (→ אכל *'ākhal)* of the poor and
needy (*'aniyyim ve'ebhyonim),* along with slander, cursing parents, pride, etc.,
as accursed sins (30:14). Lemuel is admonished to maintain the rights of the poor
and needy (*'ani ve'ebhyon*) (Prov. 31:9). The dumb and desolate children in
v. 8 correspond to the poor and needy here. According to vv. 6ff., strong drink
is for him who is perishing (→ אבד *'ābhadh)* and for those in bitter distress (*mare
naphesh),* so that they may forget their poverty (*rish*) and misery (→ עמל *'āmal).*

In his discussion of the difficult problem of the relationship between one's
actions and his lot in life, Job presses to the very limits of "wisdom"; he cannot
accept the idea "no suffering without sin" either for himself or as a correct evaluation of what takes place in the world in general. Among other things, he defends
his position by calling attention to the plight of the *'ebhyonim* and the *'anavim*
(Job 24:1–24; these words occur in vv. 4,14): they are cheated out of their lands
and flocks, and even out of just one ass and ox; thrust off the road, they hide
themselves. As day-laborers, hungry and thirsty, they gather fodder, glean the
vineyard, etc. Naked or clothed scantily, they are exposed to cold and rain, and

---

[27] B. Gemser, *HAT,* 16 (²1963), 61f.
[28] U. Skladny, *Die ältesten Spruchsammlungen* (1962), 20.
[29] Cf. W. Richter, *Recht und Ethos,* 118, 149, 151.
[30] Cf. Skladny, 20, 38f.
[31] Cf. Gemser, *loc. cit.*

suffer hunger. Furthermore, the *'ebhyonim* and *'anavim* appear alongside the widow (→ אלמנה *'almānāh*) and the orphan (→ יתום *yāthôm*). N. Peters speaks of the miserable lot of the working classes enslaved by the ungodly rich. [32] Job 24:14 speaks of the murderer *(rotseach),* who kills the poor *('ebhyon)* and needy *('ani).*

Job emphasizes that he has helped the poor and needy (Job 29:12ff.): he delivered *(malat)* the poor *('ani)* and the fatherless, caused him who was about to perish *('obhedh)* and the widow to rejoice, helped the blind and lame, and was a father to the poor *('ebhyonim)* (v. 16); he scrupulously searched out the cause of people whom he did not know, and snatched away the prey, i.e., the possessions of the poor, from the unrighteous *('avval).* In an oath of purification, he emphasizes that he helped the perishing *('obhedh)* and the poor *('ebhyon)* (31:19). Since he wept for him whose day was hard *(qesheh yom)* and grieved for the poor *('ebhyon)* (30:25), he believes he has a right to a favorable hearing and compassion. The *'ebhyon* appears in the same group as the *'ani, yathom, 'almanah, 'ul, pisseach, 'obhedh,* and *dal.* Eliphaz solves the problem of theodicy according to the traditional view and tries to overcome its unsolved problems by trust and confidence: God saves the needy *('ebhyon)* from the hand of the mighty *(chazaq)* and gives to the poor *(dal)* new hope (5:15f.; cf. also 34:19,28; 36:6,15). Ps. 37, an acrostic from the late Wisdom Literature, deals with the lot of the righteous and the wicked: in times of distress, the *tsaddiq, tammim, 'ani,* and *'ebhyon* receive Yahweh's help and deliverance *(samakh, teshu'ah, ma'oz, 'azar, palat),* while the *resha'im* are withered, faded, destroyed, and cut off. In 37:14, the *'ani* and *'ebhyon* stand in parallelism with those who walk uprightly *(yishre dharekh).* The wicked try to bring down the poor and needy and to slay those who walk uprightly. The *'ebhyon* and *'ani* are put in the same category as the *tsaddiq, tammim, yashar derekh,* and *chasidh.* In harmony with the concept in the Wisdom Literature of the relationship between one's actions and his lot in life, it is significant that in the final analysis the *rasha'* can have no stability, while in the Psalms of Petition and Lament, God is invoked against the wicked. In the didactic poem, Ps. 49, the *'ebhyon* of v. 3(2) appears as an antithesis to the *'ashir,* "rich"; since this passage does not affirm that riches are vain in view of death, either ethically or religiously, and since it does not identify the *'ashir* with the wicked, the *'ebhyon* must also be understood in the economic sense of "poor, needy." The Wisdom Song, Ps. 112, mentions generous kindnesses shown to the *'ebhyonim* as being among the virtues of a godfearing man (v. 9; cf. also vv. 4b,5a).

IV. The 'ebhyon in Expectation of Divine Help.

1. *The Enemies of the 'ebhyon.* The enemies (→ איב *'ōyēbh*) of the *'ebhyon* present a special problem. [33] The "destitution" of the *'ebhyon* in the Individual Psalms of Lament is characterized essentially as being caused by enemies,

---

[32] *Das Buch Job. Exegetisches Handbuch zum AT,* 21 (1928), 260.
[33] Cf. H. Birkeland, *Feinde,* 87-94; *idem, Evildoers,* 59-87; Keel, 95-230.

'oyebh (Ps. 9:4,7[3,6]; 35:19; 69:5,19[4,18]), tsorer (69:20[19]), evildoers or wicked (→ רָשָׁע rāshā' – 9:6,17f.[5,16f.]; 10:4; 12:9[8]; 140:5,9[4,8]), those who hate (sone' – 9:14[13]; 35:19; 69:5,15[4,14]; 86:17; sone' tsaddiq – 34:22[21]; cf. 37:12,32; 112:10), persecutors (rodheph – 35:3; 109:16), ruthless men ('arits – 86:14; cf. 37:35), violent men ('ish chamasim – 140:2,5[1,4]), despoilers (gozel – 35:10), plunderers (bazaz – 109:11), and creditors (nosheh – 109:11). They fight against (lacham – 35:1) the poor or seek after his life (mebhaqqesh nephesh – 35:4; cf. 70:3[2]; 86:14) with a net (10:9; 35:7f.; 140:6[5]), a pit (35:7f.), or a snare (140:6[5]). They are dangerous like lions ('ari – 35:17), serpents (nachash), and vipers ('akhshubh – 140:4[3]). Against the 'ebhyon, they behave themselves arrogantly (ge'eh – 140:6[5]), magnify themselves (maghdil 'alai – 35:26), and are strong (chazaq – 35:10). As evil men ('adham ra' – 140:2[1]), they devise evil (choshebh ra'athi – 35:4; cf. 35:20) against the 'ebhyon, rejoice (sameach) at their calamity (35:26), and desire (chaphets) their hurt (40:15[14]). They insult (choreph – 69:10[9]; cf. 69:3,10f.,20f.[2,9f.,19f.]; 109:25; cf. also 74:10,18,22) and make great boasts ('ish lashon – 12:4[3]) with sharp (140:4[3]) or flattering tongue (12:3[2]), under which are mischief and iniquity (10:7), and which they make sharp as a serpent (140:4[3]); their mouth is filled with cursing (10:7). Finally, they seek deceitful witnesses ('edh chamas – 35:11), those who contend (ribh – 35:1) and those who condemn (shophet – 109:31), to convict the innocent 'ebhyon. This characterization of the "enemies" is derived from the sphere of one's fellow men, from the judicial system, from practices in war and hunting, and from chaos and the Underworld.

The references to the 'ebhyonim in the Individual Psalms of Lament are not sufficient to solve the old and new controversies concerning the "enemies": the shades of meaning inherent in these descriptions of the enemies are too varied to determine whether they are to be interpreted generally as external or internal enemies who pose a danger to the state, [34] or as a specific group or faction who oppose the godly, [35] or as sorcerers, demons, etc. [36] The question of whether the persecution of the enemies is the real cause of the miserable condition of the complaining worshipper, or only the result of some other deeper distress which appears to the worshipper as a sign that God is angry with him and has forsaken him, while giving occasion to the adversary to assault him with persecution, scorn, insults, slander, etc., is just as difficult and insoluble. The worshipper attributes his distress as well as his deliverance to God: cf. Ps. 69:27(26): "they persecute him whom thou hast smitten, and him whom thou hast wounded, they afflict still more."

2. *Affliction, Illness, Loneliness, Nearness to Death.* The destitution of the 'ebhyon is to be inferred from the whole tenor of the appropriate psalms: it manifests itself in affliction, illness, loneliness, and nearness to death: thus, the

---

[34] Birkeland.

[35] Hupfeld, Graetz, Causse, R. Smend, Duhm.

[36] Mowinckel, Pedersen, Nikolski, Brock-Utne. This uncertainty is shared by Schwarzwäller, Keel, H. Goeke.

godly is in anxiety and distress (69:18[17]); in the day of trouble *(yom tsarathi)* he calls on God (86:7; cf. 10:1), as Israel did when their enemies afflicted them. The prophetic idea of the day of judgment (Am. 5:18-20; Isa. 2:12; 13:6-9; etc.) is also related to this day of distress *(tsar)*, so that the godly man who is in distress *(tsar)* and trouble *('amal)* believes that he is under the judgment of God. Evils *(ra'oth)* without number (Ps. 40:13[12]) encompass the worshipper. *ra'ah, 'amal,* and *tsarah* break in upon him as a hostile power; he experiences them as illness and indisposition. His heart is stricken within him (109:22); he supposes that he is gone like a shadow at evening, and shaken off like a locust (109:23); he feels he is at his end (69:4,21[3,20]). Supplication *(tachanunah–86:6)*, groaning *('anaqah–12:6[5])*, calling out *(qara'–69:4[3])*, and crying *(tse'aqah–9:13[12])* characterize his miserable and helpless situation. The description of the poor in 69:2f.(1f.) is particularly impressive: the waters come up to his neck, he sinks in deep mire and comes into deep waters, the flood sweeps over him (cf. 69:15f.[14f.]). Torrential downpours and chaotic floods bring him to the brink of destruction, he supposes he is in the Underworld *(sha'are maveth–9:14[13])* or in Sheol (86:13), from which Yahweh alone can deliver him. Friends and foes overwhelm him with insults, reproaches, and scorn (35:16,21; 40:16[15]; 69:10f.,20f.,34[9f.,19f.,33]; 109:25). In vain, he looks for pity and consolation (69:21[20]). Lonely *(yachidh–25:16)* and a stranger and alien *(muzar, nokhri)* to his own brothers (69:9[8]), he is excluded from the community of the living, and therefore from a happy life. But the sufferer interprets all this in the final analysis as suffering ordained by God, as "the disruption of a happy existence or of a whole existence." [37]

3. *Religious Classification of the 'ebhyon.* In order to classify the *'ebhyon* religiously, it is helpful to examine the motif of the plea for a favorable hearing by God ("and [for] I am poor and needy," *[ki] va'ani 'ani ve'ebhyon*–40:18 [17] = 70:6[5]; 86:1; 109:22) in answer to the prayer for divine help; in context, it is illuminated further: 40:17(16) = 70:5(4) refer to "those who seek thee" *(mebhaqeshekha)* and "those who love thy salvation" *('ohabhe teshu'athekha).* 86:1, "for I am poor and needy" *('ani 'ani ve'ebhyon)* is followed by the statement, "for I am godly" *(ki chasidh 'ani);* cf. the servant *('ebhedh–vv. 2,4,16;* cf. also 109:28) who "trusts" (v. 2). A related motif of the plea for a favorable hearing appears in 69:30(29): "I am afflicted and in pain" *(va'ani 'ani vekho'ebh);* cf. in addition "those who hope in thee" *(qovekha)*, "those who seek thee" *(mebhaqeshekha–v. 7[6])*, and "those who love his name" *('ohabhe shemo–v. 37* [36]); according to the expression of trust in v. 34(33), Yahweh "hears" the *'ebhyon*, and "does not despise his own that are in bonds" *('asirav).* In the expression of certainty that Yahweh will hear his prayer in 35:10, the psalmist declares that Yahweh will deliver the weak *('ani)* from him who is "strong" *(chazaq)*, and the needy *('ebhyon)* from "him who despoils him" *(miggozelo);* according to v. 20, "those who are quiet in the land" suffer because of the words of those who hate them. In the lament over the end of the godly *(chasidh)* and the faithful *('emunim–12:4[3])*, Yahweh gives his promise of salvation "because

---

[37] C. Westermann, *Der Psalter* (1967), 53.

the poor are despoiled" *(mishshodh 'aniyyim)*, "because the needy groan" *(me'eneqath 'ebhyonim*–12:6[5]). In the expression of certainty that Yahweh will hear in 140:13(12), Yahweh maintains "the cause of the afflicted" *(din 'ani)* and "executes justice for the needy" *(mishpat 'ebhyonim)*, and then the "righteous" *(tsaddiqim)* give thanks for the righteous help and the "upright" *(yesharim)* dwell in his presence (v. 14[13]). In 9:19(18), the worshipper declares his confidence that the *'ebhyon* shall not always be forgotten and the "hope of the poor" *(tiqvath 'anavim)* shall not perish for ever; according to v. 11(10), "they put their trust in thee" *(yibhtechu bhekha)*, "they know thy name," for thou hast not forsaken "those who seek thee" *(doreshekha)*; Yahweh's favorable hearing of the "meek" *('anavim*–10:17) is connected with doing justice to the "fatherless and the oppressed" *(yathom vadhakh*–v. 18).

On the basis of *parallelismus membrorum* and of usage in other contexts, we find that the *'ebhyon* of the Individual Psalms of Lament is connected not only with the *'ani* or *'anav* ("the poor"), but also with those who are designated as *'ebhedh*, "servant" (86:2; 109:28), *chasidh*, "godly" (12:2[1]; 86:2), *'emunim*, "faithful" (12:2[1]), *tsaddiqim*, "righteous" (140:14[13]), *yesharim*, "upright" (140:14[13]), or "the quiet in the land" *(righ'e 'erets*–35:20). They seek Yahweh *(biqqesh*–40:17[16] = 70:5[4]; 69:7[6]; *darash*–9:11[10]), love *('ahabh)* his salvation (40:17[16] = 70:5[4]), trust in him (9:11[10]; 86:2), hope *(qavah)* in him (69:7[6]), know his name (9:11[10]) or love his name (69:37[36]).

4. *Yahweh, Deliverer of the 'ebhyonim.* Yahweh is the deliverer of the *'ebhyonim*. In the Individual Psalms of Lament, the believing hope and the certainty that Yahweh will give a favorable hearing is expressed by referring to the divine deliverance: Yahweh is the hope of the afflicted *('anayim)*, who does not forget the needy *('ebhyonim)* (9:13,19[12,18]); he is a stronghold for the oppressed *(misgabh laddakh*–9:10[9]) and a strong deliverer *('oz yeshu'athi*–140:8[7]). Cf. also *ma'oz laddal*, "a stronghold to the poor," or *la'ebhyon*, "to the needy," in Isa. 25:4. In cries for help and statements expressing a feeling of the certainty of deliverance, the following verbs describing the activity of the divine deliverer appear[38]: *ga'al*, "redeem" (69:19[18]); *yasha'* in the hiphil, "save" (12:2[1]; 69:36[35]; 86:2,16; 109:26,31) from evildoers or judges, or *yasha', yeshu'ah*, "deliver, deliverance" (12:6[5]; 35:3,9; 69:30[29]; 140:8[7]); *natsal* in the hiphil, "deliver" (35:10; 69:15[14]; 70:2[1]; 40:14[13]; 86:13; 140:2[1]); *palat* in the piel, "deliver" (70:6[5]; 40:18[17]). Cf. also Ps. 82:4. The oppressed worshipper asks for protection: *saghabh*, "set on high" (69:30[29]); *shamar*, "preserve" (86:2; 140:5[4]); *natsar*, "preserve" (140:5[4]). Yahweh is helper and help *('ezer* or *'ezrah*–10:14; 35:2; 70:2,6[1,5]; 40:14,18[13,17]; 86:17; 109:26); he stands at the right hand of the needy *('amadh limin*–109:31), gives him strength *(nathan 'oz*–86:16), strengthens his heart *(kun*–10:17), covers his head *(sakhah*–140:8[7]), saves his life *(hashibh*–35:17), and gives him life (86:17). This hope and confidence is based on the *'ebhyon*'s faith in God: Yahweh is good (86:5),

---

[38] Cf. J. J. Stamm, *Erlösen und Vergeben* (1940); Chr. Barth, *Die Errettung vom Tode*, 124-146.

gracious (chanan–9:14[13]; 86:3,15,16), abundant in steadfast love (chesedh–69:14,17[13,16]; 86:5,13,15) and faithfulness (86:15), slow to anger (86:15), and full of mercy (rachamim–69:17[16]; 86:15), and in spite of folly and wrongs (69:6[5]) is ready to forgive (salach–86:5) and to comfort (nicham–86:17). Yahweh delights in the welfare of his servant (35:27) and blesses the righteous (109:26).

In his distress, again and again the ʼebhyon emphatically calls on Yahweh as "my God" (ʼelohai–35:23; 70:6[5]; 40:18[17]). The "poor" relies on Yahweh to hear his prayer (haʼazin–86:6; 140:7[6]; hiqshibh ʼozen–10:17; ʻanah–69:14, 17,18[13,16,17]; 86:7; shamaʻ–10:17; 69:34[33]) and to turn to him (peneh ʼelai–69:17[16]). Thus he prays that Yahweh might not be silent or far away (35:22; cf. 10:1; 70:6[5]; 40:18[17]), and that he might not hide his face (69:18 [17]) and forsake those who seek him (9:11[10]), but because of the oppression or the groaning of the poor and oppressed that he might arise (haʻirah, qumah–10:12; 12:6[5]; 35:2,23), as a warrior contends or fights (ribh, lacham–35:1f.) and destroys the enemies (cf. 9:4-6[3-5]; 10:14; 70:3[2]; 40:15[14]; 35:4-8; 69:23-29[22-28]; 109:6-19; 140:11f.[10f.]; cf. also 74:19-21).

Yahweh has established his throne for judgment (9:8[7]) and rules as a righteous judge (9:5[4]); he judges the world with righteousness (9:9[8]), executes judgment (9:17[16]), and avenges the blood of the peoples (doresh damim–9:13[12]), so that they stumble and perish (9:4,6[3,5]). Thus the ʼebhyon prays that Yahweh might be vigilant in his defense and vindicate him according to his divine righteousness (35:23f.), and maintain the cause of the afflicted (din ʻani) and execute justice for the needy (mishpat ʼebhyonim–140:13[12]; cf. 10:18).

Various hypotheses of a cultic-sacral legal aid have been proposed for the statements pertaining to deliverance in the Individual Psalms concerning enemies. H. Schmidt envisions a sacral judicial proceeding during a detention for investigation in the temple, which ended in acquitting and liberating an innocent person who had been accused. [39] Perhaps such an investigation procedure is to be assumed in Pss. 35 and 69. [40] L. Delekat has offered another explanation, which is based on a supposed institution of asylum: oppressed worshippers seek refuge from their creditors and personal enemies in the sanctuary. [41] Thus, according to him, 86:14-17 and 86:1-3, e.g., are prayers in expectation of an oracle of protection against the violence of the creditor; Pss. 9-10, 35, and 40 are prayers for an oracle of protection by those suspected of robbery; with the verdict of protection, which represents a kind of security against the creditor, one could leave the sanctuary once more. It is possible that in the terms machseh, "refuge," misgabh, "stronghold," and ʻoz or maʻoz, "protection," there are reminiscences of sanctuaries for asylum, which were later spiritualized in the idea of a spiritual communion with Yahweh at the Zion sanctuary. For statements that have to do with deliverance, recently W. Beyerlin has postulated a juridical institution employing the ordeal or execration as evidence. In the statements pertaining

---

[39] Gebet der Angeklagten; idem, HAT, 15 (1934).
[40] Thus O. Eissfeldt, The OT (trans. 1965), 119.
[41] Asylie und Schutzorakel am Zionheiligtum.

to deliverance which refer to this supposed institution, Pss. 3, 4, 5, 7, 11, 17, 23, 26, 27, 57 and 63, 'ebhyon does not occur; according to Beyerlin, there is no reference, or at least no sure reference, to the sacral-legal institution in Pss. 9-10, 12, 86, 140. But even if one is not able to show clearly any specific legal institution for our Individual Psalms of Lament, still it can be established that they were spoken in the Yahweh sanctuary on Zion. Here the oppressed begged for divine gifts, help, and deliverance, as well as legal aid and a righteous judgment (cf. 9:6-9,16f.,18-21[5-8,15f.,17-20]; 10:12-15,16-18; 35:23f.; 140:13[12]).

In the Psalm of Praise (Ps. 113) and Hannah's Song of Praise (1 S. 2:1-10), [42] the psalmist declares that Yahweh raises the poor (dal) from the dust and lifts the needy ('ebhyon) from the ash heap to make them sit with princes and inherit a seat of honor (kisse' khabhodh). According to the context, the dal and the 'ebhyon belong to the same group as the feeble, hungry, poor, and godly; Yahweh has exalted them. Cf. Lk. 1:46-55 par.

5. 'ebhyon in Late Prophetic Proclamations of Salvation. The proclamation of salvation for the 'aniyyim (and 'ebhyonim–Isa. 41:17-20), who have to seek water in vain during a drought and suffer thirst, contains Yahweh's promise that he will answer them and not forsake them; vv. 18f. connect the situation with the miraculous exodus, in which Yahweh will give the wilderness abundant water (cf. also Isa. 43:20; 48:21; 49:10; Ex. 17:1-7; Nu. 20:2-13). Here also the 'aniyyim and the 'ebhyonim are in need of divine help and salvation. According to the oracle concerning the Philistines in Isa. 14:28-32, which with Duhm is probably to be dated after the battle of Issus and before the conquest of Tyre and Gaza by Alexander, after the downfall of the enemies in Philistia, the dallim, "poor," will feed on Yahweh's pasture (read bekhari, "in my pasture," instead of bekhore, "first-born") and the 'ebhyonim, "needy," will lie down in safety; according to 14:32b, the "afflicted of his people" feel that they have found refuge in Zion which the Lord has founded. Here the people of Yahweh are designated as dallim and 'ebhyonim, or 'aniyye 'ammo. The dallim, 'ebhyonim, and 'aniyyim receive Yahweh's special attention; they enjoy his special care.

In the (secondary) promise in Isa. 29:17-24, according to v. 19 the 'anavim and the 'ebhyonim shall obtain fresh joy and exult, for with the cosmic transformation the ruthless ('arits), the scoffer, and those who watch to do evil (shoqedhe 'aven) shall be no more; according to v. 21, the latter are described as those who by a word make a man out to be an offender, lay a snare for the arbitrator in the gate, and with an empty plea turn aside him who is in the right (tsaddiq). The 'anavim and the 'ebhyonim will rejoice because they are redeemed from ruthlessness, calamity, faultfinding, and legal obstacles. But these passages pertain not merely to those who are oppressed materially and legally; rather, they are oriented (still under the promise) entirely to the fulfilment of the promise of Yahweh, to his salvation.

---

42 Cf. Westermann, Praise, 124f.

V. Qumran. In the Qumran literature, the OT ideas of the ʿani and the ʾebhyon are taken up and continued. In the War Scroll the ʿanavim and the ʾebhyonim seem similar to the poor and needy in the Psalms and Deutero-Isaiah. While in 1QM 14:2ff. the Sons of Light carry out the divine vengeance as "the poor in spirit" (ʿanve ruach–cf. Isa. 66:2) and "the perfect of way" (temime dherekh), and "all the nations of wickedness have come to an end" (1QM 14:7), according to 1QM 11:9 the hordes of Belial fall by the oppressed that Yahweh had redeemed (ʾebhyone phedhuthe[khah]); according to 11:13 God delivers the enemies "into the hands of the poor (ʾebhyonim) and into the hand of those bent to the dust" (koreʿe ʿaphar). In the Hodayoth, God delivers the soul of the poor (nephesh ʿani–1QH 5:13), the soul of the poor and needy (nephesh ʿani varash– 5:14), the soul of the poor (nephesh ʾebhyon–5:18; cf. 2:32; 3:25). According to 1QH 5:22, God causes all the poor of grace (ʾebhyone chasedh) to arise from the tumult together. This poverty is a poverty of compassionate grace and of gracious communion; cf. the allusion of J. Maier [43] to the paradox of servitude and election. In 1QpHab 12:3,6,10, the ʾebhyonim, who are overthrown and plundered by the Wicked Priest, are identified with the elect (bachurim). In 4QpPs37 2:5, on v. 9, the MT qove (or qoveʾ) yhvh, "those who wait for the Lord," is replaced by ʿadhath bechirav, "the Congregation of his elect." It is significant that Ps. 37:21f. is interpreted as the Congregation of the Poor in 4QpPs37 3:10, and that ʿanavim in Ps. 37:11 is replaced by ʾebhyonim in 4QpPs37 2:9.

Although a conditional or unconditional community of goods is prescribed in the canon of the Qumran sect, [44] in 1QS the terms ʿani, ʿanavim, and ʾebhyonim are completely missing; ʿanavah, "humility," occurs eight times. Apparently, the terms ʿanavim and ʾebhyonim have no economic or social dimension at Qumran, so they have no relevance for the form of its corporate economy and life. It is impossible to determine whether the community of goods pertains to a cultic-ritualistic effort to gain purity, i.e., freedom from corrupting possessions, or to a "picture of the form of life ... which God will establish in the coming age." [45] Cf. → עני ʿānî, with the excursus on "Poverty."

Botterweck

---

[43] *Armenfrömmigkeit*, 68, 86f.
[44] Cf. Bammel, *TDNT*, IV, 898.
[45] *Ibid*. Cf. also Maier, 13, on 1QS 1:11.

אָבִיר   'ābhîr;   אַבִּיר   'abbîr

Contents: I. 1. Etymology, Occurrences; 2. Meaning. II. Secular Usages. III. Derived, Religious Meaning: 1. God's Hosts; 2. Designation for God.

I. 1. *Etymology, Occurrences.* The root *'abhar* appears in Akkadian, Ugaritic, and Aramaic. In Akkadian we find *abāru*, "power, strength," e.g., *abāru u dunnu*, "strength and might"; *CAD* supposes that the original meaning was "strength," while *AHw* thinks it was "clamp." The adjective *abru*, "strong" *(AHw)*, is uncertain. [1] Persons and buildings can "be strong," but the word is generally not used of bulls. Thus, *abāru* means strength, but not necessarily that signified by a bull. In Ugaritic, on the other hand, *ʾbr* means a strong animal, and is translated by "bull" or "wild ox," which follows from the context; "as a wild bull in the midst of a trap." [2] Various peoples lived in ancient Ugarit; and Aistleitner sees, in particular proper names having *ʾbr* as one component, remains of an old stratum; [3] and he interprets Ugar. *ʾbr* as the Hurrian *ʾwr*, "lord." [4]

In the OT we find two forms of *'byr*, one with the daghesh in the second radical, and one without it. According to a widespread interpretation, this is an artificial distinction which the Massoretes invented to avoid any suspicion that Yahweh was to be identified with the bull in the phrases "the Mighty One of Jacob" *('abhir ya'aqobh)* and "the Mighty One of Israel" *('abhir yisrael)*. The form without the daghesh occurs only 5 times: in the phrase "the Mighty One of Jacob" in Gen. 49:24; Isa. 49:26; 60:16; and Ps. 132:2,5; and in the phrase "the Mighty One of Israel" in Isa. 1:24. It is significant that the form with daghesh only rarely–perhaps only three or four times–means "bull," and that in these cases the word is used poetically. Altogether the form with daghesh occurs about 17 times, and, to be sure, with different meanings. From the way in which the Massoretes distinguished between the form of the word with a daghesh and without a daghesh in pointing a purely consonantal text, it may be concluded that they clearly heard in the word *'byr* the idea of "bull."

'ābhîr. Alt, *GF;* W. Caspari, "Hebr. *abīr* als dynamistischer Ausdruck," *ZS,* 6 (1928), 71-75; J. Debus, *Die Sünde Jerobeams* (1967); O. Eissfeldt, "Lade und Stierbild," *ZAW,* 58 (1940/41), 190-215; E. Otto, *Beiträge zur Geschichte der Stierkulte in Ägypten. Untersuchungen zur Geschichte und Altertumskunde Ägyptens,* 13 (1938); J. A. Soggin, "Der offiziell geförderte Synkretismus in Israel während des 10. Jahrhunderts," *ZAW,* 78 (1966), 179-204; H. Torczyner, "אביר kein Stierbild," *ZAW,* 39 (1921), 296-300; M. Weippert, "Gott und Stier," *ZDPV,* 77 (1961), 93-117.

[1] *CAD,* I/1, 63a.
[2] *CTA,* 12 [BH], II, 56.
[3] *WUS,* 5.
[4] See also *OLZ,* 62 (1967), 535.

2. *Meaning*. The use of the word in Akkadian and Ugaritic indicates a double application, but perhaps it suggests a common denominator. *’abbir* is used in the OT of strong animals, not only of bulls and wild oxen but also of stallions and war-horses. In the Song of Deborah, *’abbir* is used in parallelism with *sus*, "horse," and therefore could mean "stallion" (Jgs. 5:22). But here *’abbir* probably means "strong, powerful," and thus is used to modify stallions. Ps. 68, which is probably very ancient, refers to *’adhath ’abbirim* in v. 31 (Eng. v. 30), which probably means "host of strong ones." Since we cannot determine whether *’abbir* here means a specific animal or a host of enemies, the translation "strong" is to be preferred. In Ps. 22:13(12), the parallelism with *parim* shows that *’abbire bhashan* means "the bulls of Bashan"; here, however, as in Jgs. 5:22 the parallel expression is used figuratively of the enemies. Also in Ps. 50:13, a comparison with v. 9 suggests the meaning "bulls," although *’abbirim* here can mean all kinds of strong animals. In Jer. 8:16; 47:3; 50:11, as in the Song of Deborah, the context suggests the meaning "stallions." This shows clearly that the idea of "bull" was not connected with *’abbir* unconditionally. And yet, while *’abbirim* means quite generally "strong one" in Jer. 46:15, still it contains a reference to oxen (the Apis of the Egyptians).

II. Secular Usages. In addition, *’abbir* can be used of strong men: "chief of the herdsmen" (1 S. 21:8[7]), "hero" or "tyrant" (Isa. 10:13), "the mighty" (Job 24:22; 34:20). Similarly, *kol ’abbirai* in Lam. 1:15 means the mighty ones in Judah. In this sixth-century B.C. song the word clearly does not have the additional meaning "bull." The same is probably true of the expression *’abbire lebh*, "the stouthearted, the stubborn of heart" (Ps. 76:6[5]; Isa. 46:12).

III. Derived, Religious Meaning.

1. *God's Hosts*. In the sense of "the strong, the mighty," *’abbirim* refers to "heavenly powers." Gunkel proposed the meaning "host of the gods" or "host of angels" in Ps. 68:31(30), but this is not likely. Such a meaning is evident, however, in Ps. 78:25, where the *lechem ’abbirim*, "bread of the strong ones" or "bread of the angels," means manna; cf. the LXX. In conjunction with the *lechem ’abbirim*, manna is called *deghan shamayim*, "the grain of heaven," in v. 24b; cf. Ps. 105:40, *lechem shamayim*, "bread of heaven."

2. *Designation for God*. As noted above, only in five passages, where *’byr* is used of God, did the Massoretes feel it necessary to write this word without a daghesh; by so doing they intended to exclude the meaning "bull." Perhaps they were thinking in particular of the conditions that existed during the time of Jeroboam I, when this North Israelite king established the worship of the two golden calves in Bethel and Dan (1 K. 12:25-33). It is not possible to determine whether they also were thinking of the Canaanite Baal cult, but probably they were not.

It is evident from Gen. 49:24 that *’abbir ya‘aqobh* is an ancient North Israelite expression which is connected with Joseph in the so-called Blessing of Jacob. "The Mighty One of Jacob" is also mentioned in the ancient Temple Psalm

(Ps. 132:2,5), where David and his successors are closely connected with the ark and the covenant, and where statements from the realm of the ancient North Israelite cult are preserved. This psalm bears witness to the amalgamation of the North Israelite and Judean cult traditions which David undertook.

If this divine name was taken over from a pre-literary tradition (Alt) as a designation of the God of the fathers, it follows that "Jacob" was understood to be synonymous with "Israel," as is the case so often in poetry, and thus "the Mighty One of Jacob" was considered to be a designation of the God of Israel. In Isa. 1:24, the expression "the Mighty One of Israel" ('abbir yisrael) actually occurs (Alt).

In Isa. 49:26 and 60:16 (which is dependent on 49:26), 'abbir ya'aqobh is used in apposition to go'el, "redeemer," and here, like go'el, it is used as a divine epithet. Here the original designation of the God of the fathers has become an epithet for Yahweh understood in the universal sense. For further information on "bull" and bull deities, cf. → עֵגֶל 'ēghel, and → שׁוּר shôr.

Kapelrud

אָבַל 'ābhal; אָבֵל 'ābhēl; אֵבֶל 'ēbhel

Contents: I. 1. Etymology, Cognates in the Ancient Near East; 2. Synonyms, Meaning, Occurrences. II. Usage in Connection with Mourning for the Dead. III. Usage in Connection with Announcements of Judgment: 1. General Usage or Usage with Reference to People; 2. Usage with Reference to Nature and Vegetation.

I. 1. *Etymology, Cognates in the Ancient Near East.* The root 'bl occurs in several Semitic languages, but from time to time with different meanings: in contrast to Akk. *abalu*, "to dry (up)" *(AHw)*, in Arabic and its kindred languages there are words from this root which are connected with "mourning" and "illness," while the meaning "to dry" does not occur here.[1] There is no

---

'ābhal. R. Bultmann, "πένθος, πενθέω," *TDNT*, VI (1968), 40-43; G. R. Driver, "Confused Hebrew Roots," *Gaster Anniversary Volume* (London, 1936), 73-75; A. Guillaume, "Hebrew and Arabic Lexicography," *Abr-Nahrain*, 1 (1959/60), 6, 17f.; A. S. Kapelrud, *Joel Studies. UUÅ* (1948); E. Kutsch, "'Trauerbräuche' und 'Selbstminderungsriten' im AT," *ThSt*, 78 (1965); Leslau, *Contributions*, 9; N. Lohfink, "Enthielten die im AT bezeugten Klageriten eine Phase des Schweigens?" *VT*, 12 (1962), 267f., 275; V. Maag, *Text, Wortschatz und Begriffswelt des Buches Amos* (1951), 115-17; H. Graf Reventlow, *Liturgie und prophetischen Ich bei Jeremia* (1963), 154ff.; J. Scharbert, *Der Schmerz im AT. BBB*, 8 (1955); de Vaux, *AncIsr*, 56-61; M. Weiss, "Methodologisches über die Behandlung der Metapher, dargelegt an Am I, 2," *ThZ*, 23 (1967), 16ff.

[1] Leslau, Guillaume; Guillaume has shown that Driver's translation of 'abalatun by "dried figs" is incorrect.

clear example in Ugaritic. Examples in Syriac, Aramaic, and Late Hebrew were influenced by the OT. Under these circumstances, it is extremely difficult to determine a common Semitic original meaning of this root; one must begin with the linguistic usage in the Bible: → ילל *yālal;* → ספד *sāphadh.*

2. *Synonyms, Meaning, Occurrences.* *'abhal* is used in parallelism with or as a synonym of *yabhesh,* "to be dry, dry up" (e.g., Jer. 12:4; 23:10; Joel 1:10; Am. 1:2), *'umlal,* "to be feeble, languish" (Isa. 19:8; 24:4,7; 33:9; Jer. 14:2; Lam. 2:8; Hos. 4:3; Joel 1:10), *qadhar,* "to be dark" (Ps. 35:14; Jer. 4:28; 14:2; Ezk. 31:15), → בכה *bākhāh,* "to weep, bewail" (2 S. 19:2 [Eng. v. 1]; Neh. 1:4; 8:9; Est. 4:3), → ספד *sāphadh,* "to weep, lament" (e.g., Am. 5:16; Mic. 1:8). Thus, both principal meanings which occur in the Semitic world around Israel also appear in the OT. Since Driver, this had led to the division of the occurrences into two homonymous roots: *'abhal* I, "to mourn," and *'abhal* II, "to dry up, wither." [2] But it is strange that in this division the hithpael participle and the substantive should occur only in I, while the qal and hiphil (in completely different ways [3]) are assigned to both roots. It is more likely, then, that we are dealing with different meanings of the same root, although it is true that their inner connection is difficult to discern. [4]

II. **Usage in Connection with Mourning for the Dead.** One clearly distinguishable realm in which *'abhal* is used is that of mourning for the dead. The word does not (in any case not primarily) describe the inner feelings of the mourner, but his outward behavior. This is clear from the ancient mourning customs [5] which are explicitly mentioned in some passages where *'abhal* occurs (cf. Gen. 37:34; 2 S. 13:31-37). Above all, these customs include putting on sackcloth *(saq),* sprinkling dust and ashes on the head, lying on the ground, and shaving the beard and the hair of the head. *'abhal* is clearly a technical term for all of these customs together that might be observed in case of a death. It is distinguished from → ספד *sāphadh* and → בכה *bākhāh* in that it refers less directly to the funeral dirge during the burial and more to the entire period of mourning, even that which takes place after the funeral. This is demonstrated by the fact that *'abhal* often appears in connection with statements concerning periods of time: the mourning continues seven days (Gen. 50:10), thirty days (Dt. 34:8), many days *(yamim rabbim* or *yamim–*Gen. 37:34; 2 S. 13:37; 14:2; 1 Ch. 7:22; cf. Gen. 27:41; according to 2 S. 13:38 the mourning can continue for three years, and according to Gen. 37:35, until the death of the mourners). The cessation of the mourning is clearly marked *(vayyittemu yeme bhekhi 'ebhel,* "then the days of weeping and mourning were ended," Dt. 34:8; *vayya'abhor ha'ebhel,* "and when the mourning was over," 2 S. 11:27; *shalemu yeme 'ebhlekh,* "your

---

[2] *KBL,* Maag.
[3] Cf. *KBL[1], KBL[3],* and Kutsch, 35.
[4] The proposal of a root *'abhal* III, "to shut, close," to account for Ezk. 31:15 *(GesB* in later editions) has rightly found scarcely any followers.
[5] Cf. de Vaux.

days of mourning shall be ended," Isa. 60:20), the mourning is said to be "made" (*'asah 'ebhel*–Gen. 50:10; Jer. 6:26; Ezk. 24:17). The external character of mourning also appears in expressions like "mourning garments" (*bighedhe 'ebhel*–2 S. 14:2; *'ebhel ma'ateh*–Isa. 61:3), "mourning bread" (*lechem 'al 'ebhel*–Jer. 16:7?), "house of mourning" (*beth 'ebhel*–Eccl. 7:2,4). Special intensity in observing mourning customs is designated by adding descriptive statements like "great" (*'ebhel gadhol*–Est. 4:3), "grievous" (*'ebhel kabhedh*–Gen. 50:11), "as for an only son" (*'ebhel yachidh*–Jer. 6:26; Am. 8:10), "as one who laments his mother" (*'abhel 'em*–Ps. 35:14?); intensity is also expressed by the number of those who are perplexed: usually individuals, but also the entire people (e.g., 1 S. 6:19; 2 S. 19:3[2]; 2 Ch. 35:24). Now, whereas *'abhal* ordinarily refers to the observance of external mourning customs, in 2 S. 14:2 it is used to designate feigned mourning. Thus, it is best to translate *'abhal* "to be in mourning," i.e., to observe the period of mourning with its attendant customs, when it is connected with mourning for the dead. In no way does this exclude the inner feeling; Job 29:25 speaks of comforting mourners.

III. Usage in Connection with Announcements of Judgment.

1. *General Usage or Usage with Reference to People.* When *'abhal* is used in connection with calamities (1 S. 6:19), it can be understood as mourning over those who have perished. This does not apply where there are no dead to be mourned in the calamity (Neh. 1:4), when a passage is dealing with an event affecting nature (Isa. 33:9), or when a calamity is announced for the future (Est. 4:3). This use of *'abhal* is clearly distinguished from mourning for the dead. Here again, the word refers not so much to the feeling of sorrow, but to the external behavior; and again the customs connected with mourning for the dead are mentioned in connection with *'abhal* (sackcloth and fasting–Joel. 1:10ff.; sitting on the ground–Isa. 3:26; baldness–Am. 8:10; in addition Ezr. 10:6; Neh. 1:4; Est. 4:3; Ps. 35:13f.; Jer. 6:26; and Mic. 1:8 contain more or less complete descriptions of mourning customs), and statements concerning periods of time occur (Neh. 1:4; three weeks: Dnl. 10:2). Here *'abhal* occurs in passages which contain announcements of judgment, as a reaction to judgments which had already been executed or were about to be executed (1 S. 6:19; Neh. 1:4; Isa. 3:26; 19:8; 24:4,7; 33:9; Jer. 4:28; 14:2; Lam. 1:4; 2:8; Hos. 10:5; Joel 1:9f.), or to the threat of judgment (Ex. 33:4; Nu. 14:39; 1 S. 15:35; 16:1; Ezr. 10:6; Est. 4:3; 6:12; Job 14:22; Ps. 35:14; Jer. 6:26; 12:4,11; 23:10; Ezk. 7:12,27; 31:15; Am. 1:2; 5:16; 8:8; 9:5; Mic. 1:8). That this represents a reaction is emphasized by introductory formulas like "when I heard" (*keshom'i*–Neh. 1:4; 8:9; cf. Ex. 33:4) or "for this" (*'al zoth*–Jer. 4:28; Am. 8:8; Mic. 1:8; cf. Hos. 4:3).

The difference between this usage and that pertaining to mourning for the dead can be seen in 2 S. 12:15ff., although *'abhal* does not appear in this passage: as long as the child is sick, David engages in all customs which are connected with *'abhal* in other passages; but after the child is dead, he stops. He defends his behavior by reasoning that as long as the child was alive, perhaps God could be moved to be gracious, but not after the child was dead (vv. 22f.). In a judgment or a threat of judgment, *’abhal* always takes place with reference to a possible change of things. Rarely is this so clearly expressed as in 2 S. 12:22f.– however, the statements made in Ps. 35:13f. remind one greatly of David's behavior during the child's illness. Often mourning is emphasized so much that no hope seems to be in sight (e.g., Jer. 4:28; 14:2; Lam. 1:4; 2:8; Joel 1:9f.); but in many passages it is obvious that behind the mourning lies the silent expectation that a change will follow observance of the mourning customs (Nu. 14:39–in vain, to be sure; Ezr. 10:6; Neh. 1:4; Est. 4:3–1 S. 15:35 and 16:1 are also to be understood on the basis of this concept). In Dnl. 10:2, *’abhal* is clearly the preparation for receiving a revelation, in which the coming of a new age is announced. Thus, a change for the better can often be described simply as a change from *’abhal* to joy, to festive joy (Neh. 8:9; Est. 9:22; Isa. 57:18f.; 60:20; 61:2f.; 66:10; Jer. 31:13), and conversely the coming of calamity can be described as a change from joy to *’abhal* (Job 30:31; Lam. 5:15; Am. 8:10; cf. Isa. 24:7f.). Here, *’abhal* designates in general a time of judgment or calamity. It is obvious that in announcements of judgment, *’abhal* cannot be rendered simply "to mourn." It expresses not only the idea that the afflicted are bowed down and humbled under the judgment which they have experienced or which has been threatened, but also that they have humbled themselves in anticipation of an expected change. This latter idea is particularly prominent in later texts in connection with the concept of repentance and returning to God (cf. the passages in Ezr., Neh., and Est., but also 1 Macc. 3:47-51; 4:38-40; etc.).

2. *Usage with Reference to Nature and Vegetation.* The passages where *’abhal* is used not with reference to people, but referring to nature and vegetation ("the earth," *ha’arets*–Isa. 24:4; 33:9; Jer. 4:28; 12:4,11; 23:10; Hos. 4:3; "the ground," *’adhamah*–Joel. 1:10; "the pastures," *ne’oth*–Am. 1:2; Judah–Jer. 14:2; gates–Isa. 3:26; wine–24:7), pose a special problem. It was because *’abhal* often appears in parallelism with *yabhesh* and *’umlal* in these passages that some scholars postulated a special root *’abhal* II, "to dry up, wither." But this explanation is not convincing: the overlapping between the usage of *’abhal* for men and for vegetation is fluid (cf. the parallelism of *ha’arets* and *yoshebh bah* in Hos. 4:3; Am. 8:8; 9:5, or of *’abhal* and *’umlal* with reference to people in Isa. 19:8; Jer. 14:2; Lam. 2:8). Of course, it is conceivable that "to dry up, wither," is the proper meaning of *’abhal* when it is used with reference to nature, since there is hardly any allusion to individual customs in the passages pertaining to "nature" (but cf. Joel 1:13f. with 1:9ff.); but this is not a sufficient reason for accepting a second root *’abhal*. It is important to recognize first of all that these passages pertaining to nature belong to announcements of judgment, and usually have to do with a calamity which has come upon the land. This is the way in which the totality or extensiveness of the judgment of calamity is expressed: even nature participates in the humiliation, the "diminution" [6] of the people struck with the calamity.

---

[6] Kutsch.

Attempts to show the inner connection of different meanings of 'abhal are not lacking; Driver thinks that two roots form the basis for the same word. [7] Scharbert believes that the concept which all the meanings have in common is that of a loss of vitality which is expressed in external degeneration. [8] However, since the idea of a person humbling himself is not included in this explanation, Kutsch suggests that the main idea is that of "diminution," which embraces not only "being diminished" by death, misfortune, or drought, but also "self-diminution" with reference to the realization of desires or in the sense of conversion and repentance. [9] As far as the origin of the application of 'abhal to nature is concerned, Kapelrud (following Hvidberg) traces this back to the vegetation lament in the Canaanite cult, which is conceivable as an instance in which Israel adopted the form of Canaanite ritual. [10]

Baumann

---

[7] Driver, 75.
[8] Scharbert, 51, 54.
[9] Cf. esp. 35ff.
[10] Reventlow, 158.

אֶבֶן 'ebhen

Contents: I. 1. Occurrences; 2. Meaning. II. Derived, Religious Meaning.

I. 1. *Occurrences.* The root *'bn* occurs in all Semitic languages except Arabic with the meaning "stone" (Akk. *abnu;* Ugar. *'bn;* Syr. *'abnā;* Ethiop. *'ĕbn*). In the OT, *'ebhen* has different meanings, but all of them include the element "stone."

In earliest times people knew stone as a building material, and the idea expressed in Gen. 11:3 indicates that the author was astonished that in Mesopotamia other building materials were used for large buildings. In the Holy Land, stones were so abundant that it was natural for them to be used for many purposes, and not for building purposes alone. Stones were rolled over the mouths of wells in order to protect them (Gen. 29:2ff.). The weary wanderer used a stone as a pillow (28:11). He could set up the same stone as a pillar and pour oil on it (28:18;

'ebhen. G. Beer, *Steinverehrung bei den Israeliten* (1921); M. Dahood, "Is *'Eben Yiśrā'ēl* a Divine Title (Gn 49,24)?" *Bibl,* 40 (1959), 1002-1007; K. Galling, "Serubbabel und der Wiederaufbau des Tempels in Jerusalem," *Festschrift W. Rudolph* (1961), 67-96; J. Jeremias, *Golgotha* (1926); G. van der Leeuw, *Phänomenologie der Religon* ([2]1955), 5, 2 (trans. *Religion in Essence and Manifestation,* 1938); H. Ringgren, *Israelite Religion* (trans. 1966), 19-25; A. W. Schwarzenbach, *Die geographische Terminologie im Hebräischen des AT* (1954), 118-122; W. Robertson Smith, *The Religion of the Semites* (London, [3]1927); R. de Vaux, *AncIsr.*

35:14; cf. below; → מצבה *matstsēbhāh*). Because of its permanence, a stone could serve as a memorial and witness (31:45f.; 1 S. 7:12). The Israelites used stones and earth (unbaked brick) for building altars, and great boulders could simply serve as altars (1 S. 6:14; 14:33). It seems to have been normal to heap up stones in the form of a cube. The number of stones used for this is uncertain. 1 K. 18:31-32a speaks of twelve stones, which symbolize the twelve tribes of Israel, but this is probably a gloss influenced by Ex. 24:4 and Josh. 4:1-9.

The law concerning the altar in Ex. 20:25 (Dt. 27:5; Josh. 8:30f.: observance of this law) forbids the building of an altar of stone with a chisel, since this would involve the risk of profaning the altar. In other words, in divine worship only things in their natural state are to be used. It is also possible that this prohibition goes back to an idea that the numina resided in the stone.

The OT refers to people throwing stones (Ex. 21:18; 2 S. 16:6). It also mentions those who used stones in slings (1 S. 17:40; 1 Ch. 12:2). It often alludes to stoning as a death penalty (*ragham ba'ebhen*–Lev. 20:2,27; 24:23; Dt. 21:21; *saqal ba'abhanim*–Dt. 13:11 [Eng. v. 10]; 17:5; 22:21).[1] The majority of the offenses which are to be punished by stoning according to OT laws are theological in nature. They include apostasy from Yahweh (Dt. 13:11[10] = 17:5), blaspheming God (Lev. 24:14,16,23; 1 K. 21:10-14; cf. 2 Ch. 24:21), profaning the Sabbath (Nu. 15:35f.), sacrificing to Molech (Lev. 20:2), witchcraft and soothsaying (20:27), and transgressing a taboo commandment (Ex. 19:13; Josh. 7:25). A second, smaller group of offenses which are to be punished by stoning are sins in the sexual sphere, especially adultery (Dt. 22:21; Ezk. 16:40; 23:47). To this group also belongs the stoning of a betrothed virgin who was raped in the city and did not cry for help (Dt. 22:23f.). From the realm of tribal ethics, we encounter the law that a stubborn and rebellious son who does not obey in spite of repeated warnings and chastisements is to be stoned (21:18-21). An ox who gores someone and kills him is to be stoned (Ex. 21:28-32). Finally, in the political realm, we read of the stoning of Rehoboam's taskmaster (1 K. 12:18 = 2 Ch. 10:18).

The stones of the field were all known (Job 5:23). Also, hail was regarded as stones hurled by Yahweh.

Job 5:23 seems to mean that the peasant lives in peace with the pests of his field, but it is possible that the text is corrupt. *'adhone hassadheh*, "masters of the field" or "males of the field," or *bene hassadheh*, "sons of the field," are readings that have been proposed.[2]

'ebhen sometimes appears in the OT as a metallic stone (Job 28:2; Dt. 8:9),[3] and in many contexts dealing with precious stones, e.g., onyx stone (*'ebhen hashshoham*–Gen. 2:12; Ex. 28:9ff.; 35:27; Ezk. 1:26). Collectively, precious stones are designated as *'ebhen yeqarah* (2 S. 12:30; 1 K. 10:2; Ezk. 28:13), but this designation is not clear, since it can be used of precious building stones (1 K. 5:31[17]; 7:9-11; 2 Ch. 3:6; cf. Isa. 28:16; Jer. 51:26).

---

1 De Vaux, 159.
2 *ZAW*, 35 (1915), 63f.; *HUCA*, 24 (1952), 102.
3 Glueck, *AASOR*, 15 (1935), 47ff.

Stones also played an important role in the system of weights and measures in the ancient Near East, since the weights were often made of stone. [4] "The stones in the bag" (Prov. 16:11) are stone weights. The royal standard weight is called "the king's stone" ('ebhen hammelekh–2 S. 14:26). Correct weights are called 'abhne tsedheq, "just stones" (Lev. 19:36; cf. Dt. 25:15–'ebhen shelemah vatsedheq, "a full and just stone"; Prov. 11:1–'ebhen shelemah, "a just stone"); the opposite are called 'abhne mirmah, "deceitful stones," i.e., false weights (Mic. 6:11). Diverse weights are an abomination to Yahweh (Prov. 20:10,23; Dt. 25:13). Moreover, crude stones were probably used as a calculating device. Eissfeldt finds an allusion to this in 1 S. 25:29 ("the bundle of the living"). [5] According to Galling, Eccl. 3:5 ("casting away stones and gathering stones together") is also a reference to this. [6] According to Ex. 4:25 and Josh. 5:2f., a stone knife or flint *(tsor)* was used for circumcision, which indicates the archaic character of that rite.

The plumb bob in ancient Israel was not lead but stone. Thus Isaiah could speak of 'abhne bhohu, "stones of destruction" (RSV "plummet of chaos") (Isa. 34:11; the measuring line and the stones of the level were also used in the destruction of buildings; cf. positively Zec. 4:10, but Galling interprets 'ebhen habbedhil in this verse as "stone of judgment"). [7] 'ebhen is also directly connected with 'ophereth, "lead" (Zec. 5:8, which speaks of a heavy leaden cover; "stone" is probably identical with "cover" here).

2. *Meaning.* 'ebhen is used almost always of actual stone. However, it must be observed that the concept of stone was more comprehensive in Hebrew than it is in modern languages. The examples cited under I.1 above show the varieties in its usage. When the OT uses 'ebhen for hail, weights, or precious stones, it is easy to see the close connection with actual stone. All of these share the qualities of hardness and firmness (cf. Job 6:12–"strength like the strength of stone"). Stone is dumb (Hab. 2:19); because of fear, man is like stone (Ex. 15:16). A stony heart (Ezk. 11:19; 36:26) is a hard, insensitive, and rebellious heart, which only God can change.

II. **Derived, Religious Meaning.** As was mentioned above, stones could serve as memorials, symbols, and witnesses (Gen. 31:45f.; Josh. 4:6f.; etc.; 1 S. 7:12–'ebhen ha'azer, "Ebenezer"). The narrative dealing with Jacob at Bethel, where he poured oil on the stone (Gen. 28:18; 35:14), shows that the stone had a central place in the religious cult. Behind the narrative in Gen. 28 stands the ancient idea that the stone which was erected at a cult place was a symbol of the God. How a God El-Bethel, or actually → בית אל *bêth 'ēl,* was related to this stone is not easy to explain. But perhaps the divine epithet 'ebhen yisra'el, "Stone (Rock) of Israel," sheds light on these terms. This expression is used of Yahweh

---

[4] De Vaux, 203; cf. Dahood, *Bibl,* 44 (1963), 291.
[5] *BSAW,* 105/6 (1960).
[6] *ZThK,* 58 (1961), 7ff.
[7] Galling, 89f.

in Gen. 49:24 together with the old term אביר → יעקב *'ābhîr ya'aqobh,* "the Mighty One of Jacob." As the ancient narratives show, a stone could serve as a symbol for God. But later, the conflict of the prophets with the old gods of Canaan and with other gods of neighboring peoples made this idea impossible in Israel. The prophetic polemic against idolatry occasionally inveighs against the worship of stone and tree (Jer. 2:27; 3:9; Ezk. 20:32; Dnl. 5:4,23; cf. Isa. 37:19 and the prohibition against cultic stones in Lev. 26:1). The later allusion to "holy stones" (*'abhne qodhesh*–Lam. 4:1) has reference to stones of the sanctuary on Zion which had been destroyed.

The divine epithet *'ebhen yisra'el,* "Stone (Rock) of Israel," is usually explained by taking *tsor,* "rock," as a designation for God. But Dahood does not find any exact parallel to this epithet and completely eliminates it from the text by emendation.

According to Isa. 8:14f., Yahweh will become a stone of offense and a rock of stumbling to Israel. In spite of the figures based on hunting in these verses, the two statements have to do with the likelihood that one who is travelling at night might stumble over stones and fall (cf. Ps. 91:12). Zec. 12:3 figuratively refers to a heavy stone which young people used to test their strength. It is likely that a proverbial expression lies behind Ps. 118:22, "The stone which the builders rejected has become the head of the corner," i.e., the person who was despised has gained respect through humiliation and insult. Isa. 28:16 speaks of a cornerstone, which is called → אבן בחן *'ebhen bōchan,* "a tested stone," which gives confidence to the believer. This verse, like Ps. 118:22, is explained in the NT as referring to the Messiah.

In Isa. 28:16, Galling finds a figurative use of the technical building term "cornerstone" or "angle joint," [8] while Jeremias thinks the idea here is based on the cornerstone of the temple (*'ebhen shethiyyah,* "stone of drinking"), which holds back the water of the flood. [9] The problem is that we do not know whether this idea, which appears for the first time in Rabbinic literature, was known in the time of Isaiah. In any case, this passage corresponds very well with Isaiah's emphasis on the Zion traditions.

Kapelrud

---

[8] *Ibid.,* 72f.
[9] Jeremias, 73.

אַבְרָהָם *'abhrāhām*

Contents: I. The Meaning of the Name. II. History: 1. General Considerations; 2. Patriarch; 3. Founder of a Cult; 4. Covenant Partner. III. Theological Development: 1. JE; 2. Deuteronomy; 3. The Psalms and the Prophets; 4. The P Document and the Chronicler.

I. **The Meaning of the Name.** In Gen. 17:5, *'abhraham* is explained from the perspective of popular etymology as being from *'abh* + *hamon*, "father of a multitude." Moreover, this is connected with the change of his name from *'abhram* to *'abhraham*. However, none of the scholarly interpretations of this word justifies such a linguistic history. The introduction of the consonant *he* into the name *'abhram* simply amounts to another legitimate way of writing it under the influence of a different dialect. [1] Etymologically, there are three possible explanations for the name *'abhraham*. (1) If it is connected with Akk. *Abam-rāmā*, [2] "love the father," it is a summons to the newborn child and his brothers and sisters. (2) But it is more likely that *rām* is to be understood in the

---

'abhrāhām. W. F. Albright, "The Names Shaddai and Abram," *JBL*, 54 (1935), 173-204; *idem, Yahweh and the Gods of Canaan* (London, 1968), 47-95; Alt, *GF;* K. T. Andersen, "Der Gott meines Vaters," *StTh*, 16 (1962), 170-188; H. Cazelles, "Patriarches," *DBS*, 7 (1966), 31-156; R. E. Clements, *Abraham and David. Genesis XV and its Meaning for Israelite Tradition. SBT*, N.S. 5 (1967); G. Cornfeld, ed., *Pictorial Biblical Encyclopedia* (1964), 559-568; German ed. G. J. Botterweck, *Die Bibel und ihre Welt* (1969), 1135-1153; F. M. Cross, "Yahweh and the God of the Patriarchs," *HThR*, 55 (1962), 225-259; O. Eissfeldt, "El und Jahwe," *JSS*, 1 (1956), 25-37 = *KlSchr*, III (1966), 386-397; *idem*, "Jahwe, der Gott der Väter," *ThLZ*, 88 (1963), 481-490 = *KlSchr*, IV (1968), 79-91; K. Galling, *Die Erwählungstraditionen Israels. BZAW*, 48 (1928); C. H. Gordon, "Abraham and the Merchants of Ura," *JNES*, 17 (1958), 28-31; *idem, The World of the OT* (1958), 117-124; *idem*, "Hebrew Origins in the Light of Recent Discovery," in A. Altmann, ed., *Biblical and Other Studies* (London, 1963), 3-14; H. Gunkel, "Abraham," *RGG²*, I, 65-68; M. Haran, "The Religion of the Patriarchs," *ASTI*, 4 (1965), 30-55; J. Hoftijzer, *Die Verheissungen an die drei Erzväter* (Leiden, 1956); J. M. Holt, *The Patriarchs of Israel* (Nashville, 1964); A. Jepsen, "Zur Überlieferungsgeschichte der Vätergestalten," *WZ* Leipzig, 3 (1953/1954), 265-281; A. S. Kapelrud, "Hvem var Abraham?" *NTT*, 64 (1963), 163-174; R. Kilian, *Die vorpriesterlichen Abrahamsüberlieferungen. BBB*, 24 (1966); N. Lohfink, *Die Landverheissung als Eid. SBS*, 28 (1967); *idem*, "Die Religion der Patriarchen und die Konsequenzen für eine Theologie der nichtchristlichen Religionen," *Bibelauslegung im Wandel* (1967), 107-128; L. Rost, "Die Gottesverehrung der Patriarchen im Lichte der Pentateuchquellen," *SVT*, 7 (1960), 346-359; H. H. Rowley, "Recent Discovery and the Patriarchal Age," *The Servant of the Lord* (Oxford, ²1965), 281-318; R. de Vaux, *Die hebräischen Patriarchen und die modernen Entdeckungen* (1961); *idem, Die Patriarchenerzählungen und die Geschichte. SBS*, 3 (1965); M. Weidmann, *Die Patriarchen und ihre Religion. FRLANT*, 94 (1968); A. Weiser, "Abraham," *RGG³*, I, 68-71; W. Zimmerli, "Sinaibund und Abrahambund, Gottes Offenbarung," *Gesammelte Aufsätze* (1963), 205-216.

[1] H. Bauer, *ZAW*, 48 (1930), 75; J. A. Montgomery, *JBL*, 46 (1927), 144.
[2] Stamm, *AN*, 103, 291f.

sense of "is exalted"; however, this indicates not Akkadian, but West Semitic origin. Accordingly, Albright interprets 'abhraham to mean "he is exalted (stative) as far as his father is concerned" (adverbial accusative), i.e., "he is of good ancestry." [3] (3) It is more probable, however, that 'abhraham is to be interpreted as a theophorous name meaning, "the (divine) father is exalted," as Noth thinks. [4] Ugar. 'brm (two examples; cf. a-bi-ra-mi [5]) supports this view. If it is to be explained as a theophorous name, the relationship of the deity to the one who bears the name is presented in the form of a human relationship (→ אב 'ābh), which would be significant for the type of religion that was characteristic of the patriarchal period.

II. History.

1. *General Considerations*. The historical nucleus of the Abraham traditions was and is the subject of lively debate because of the efforts to explain and interpret the biblical traditions in the light of contemporary or nearly contemporary archeological sources. [6] Scholars have cited the Nuzi documents, the West Semitic proper names from Mari, and the Amorite relations and movements between Canaan and Mesopotamia in reconstructing Abraham's historical and cultural background in Mesopotamian Ur during the first half of the second millennium B.C. (de Vaux–1850 B.C.; Albright and Moscati–1700; Rasco–1650; Bright–20th-16th centuries). C. H. Gordon advocated a later date in the third quarter of the second millennium B.C., because he assumed a connection between Abraham and the Hittite Ura in Asia Minor and conceived of Abraham as a caravan trader. [7] H. Cazelles assumes that in the patriarchal period first there was "more a Semitic-Amoritic" movement, and then "more an Aramaic" movement. [8] Many scholars take the view that since Abraham was called a Hebrew (Gen. 14:13), he must have belonged to the Hapiru (→ עברי 'ibhrî). [9] Such archeological evidence can aid in an attempt to reach a solution to this problem only when it is connected with a strong traditio-historical investigation of the patriarchal narratives.

2. *Patriarch*. The patriarchal narratives represent Abraham as the father of Isaac and the grandfather of Jacob-Israel. Consequently, he is the great ancestor of all Israel. This artificial scheme appears for the first time in J, but it was certainly already an element in the tradition when the J narrative was compiled. In this J tradition, we can perceive a close connection between Abraham and Hebron (Gen. 13:18–J; 18:1-15–J; cf. 23:1-10–P) and especially the sanctuary at Mamre. This territorial connection indicates that Abraham was an ancestor of

---

[3] Albright, *JBL*, 193ff. Cf. also de Vaux, *Patriarchen*, 3.
[4] *IPN*, 67ff., 145; cf. also the *Festschrift Alt* (1953), 143f.
[5] Gröndahl, *PNU*, 44, 46, 315, 360; but differently explained in *OLZ*, 62 (1967), 535, where the word is divided 'br-m.
[6] Albright, Gordon, de Vaux, Rowley, *et al.*
[7] Cf. W. F. Albright, *Yahweh*, 56ff.
[8] Cazelles, 141.
[9] Cf. the survey in Cazelles, 142-156; and Weidmann, *passim*.

the Judean tribes which settled in the neighborhood of Hebron, especially the Calebites (cf. Josh. 15:13ff.). Abraham's elevation to ancestor of all Israel could not have taken place until a time when Judah and Israel were more closely connected and Judah was the dominant portion. This points to the Davidic kingdom and to the period of the Davidic-Solomonic empire.

As the ancestor of all Israel, Abraham appears as a military leader (Gen. 14:14), a priestly intercessor for his people (18:22f.–J), a prophet (20:7–E), and an example of human piety and human obedience to God (Gen. 22–J). It is worthy of note that the figure of Abraham dominates the patriarchal traditions and has partly displaced the figure of Isaac.

3. *Founder of a Cult.* In connection with his role as the great ancestor of the people of Israel, Abraham is represented in particular as the founder of a cult. We are told that he built altars at Shechem (Gen. 12:6–J), Bethel (12:8–J), and Beer-sheba (21:33–J), in addition to the altar at Mamre (13:18; 18:1ff.–J). The establishment of the altar at Beer-sheba was actually a part of the Isaac tradition (cf. 26:25–J), which was transferred to Abraham. [10] The traditions of the establishment of the altars at Shechem and Bethel were originally connected with Jacob (28:19–E; 33:19f.–E) and were attributed to Abraham later when he began to be regarded as the great ancestor of all Israel. [11] Therefore, Abraham's role as founder of a cult must be connected primarily with Hebron-Mamre.

The question of the nature of patriarchal religion is still a subject of scholarly discussion. Alt interpreted the patriarchal religion as primarily a tribal religion, in which the deities were designated by the eponym by which they were first revealed. Thus, "the God (or "Shield," Gen. 15:1) of Abraham" was the deity that was worshipped by the Abraham tribe. Essentially, this was the religion of a nomadic family without any direct connection with a definite, permanent sanctuary. It belonged to the nomadic sphere outside the cultivated land. The tradition that Abraham built the altar at Mamre arose first among Abraham's descendants when they came into the cultivated land. With a minor modification of Alt's well-known view, H. G. May and K. T. Andersen have proposed a cult of "the God of my Father." On the whole, this cult contains the same characteristics as that suggested by Alt, except that the name of the patriarch is not specifically mentioned in the divine name. O. Eissfeldt strongly emphasizes the contrast between the gods worshipped by the patriarchs in Mesopotamia (Gen. 35:1-7; Josh. 24:2,14f.) and the El-deities which are always connected with the land of Canaan. The differences between the religio-cultic and the tribal-popular interests among the patriarchs that immigrated into Canaan are worthy of note. While great importance is placed on the Mesopotamian or Aramaic origin of the wives of the patriarchs, in religio-cultic matters Israel's attitude toward Canaan is completely positive. In the cult traditions of the patriarchal narratives, the El-deities are manifest everywhere. E and P clearly affirm that Abraham first came into contact in Canaan with the God who later revealed himself to Moses as

---

[10] Alt, 54; Jepsen, 276ff.
[11] Jepsen.

Yahweh. According to L and P, the first promise of this deity to Abraham took place at Hebron, but according to E it was at Beer-sheba. Eissfeldt agrees with Alt on the type of that patriarchal deity, but in his opinion the different El-deities are to be thought of as hypostases or revelatory forms of the one El. The combining of these into the one God of the Fathers, who again was merged with Yahweh, would have to be dated during the period of the conquest. The identification of Yahweh with the God of the Fathers would have taken place much more easily when the promise of deliverance from Egypt and the land promise came into contact with the content of belief in the patriarchal deity (Gen. 15:18-21; 12:1-3,7; 18:18; etc.). M. Haran also emphasizes in particular the connection of the conquest and possession of the land with the promises to the patriarchs; he views the heritage of the Proto-Israelite religion as the persistence of the divine designations as well as certain institutions and customs from the Mosaic period.

In opposition to these reconstructions of a nomadic tribal religion, Cross, in harmony with the earlier view of Gressmann, defends the idea that Abraham's work as founder of a cult points to a connection with the religion of El in Canaan. This is supported by Abraham's connection with Mamre, where at one time an El-deity (El-Shaddai?) was worshipped, and agrees with the biblical testimony that Abraham had a direct connection with it as the leader of a tribal migration into the settled land. Cazelles emphasizes primarily the initiating activity of the personal God, who speaks to man, gives him commandments, makes promises, foretells the destiny of his descendants, etc. In the second place, this God of the Fathers is primarily a tribal god, and he does not exhibit the characteristics of a fertility-god or a storm-god. But this idea of a personal god was also not completely foreign to the Mesopotamians in the first half of the second millennium B.C., as prayers to Shamash, Ea, Ishtar, or Marduk, and also the Ugaritic texts of Keret and the Danel Epic, show, although of course this is not the dominant characteristic of their concepts of deity.

4. *Covenant Partner.* A third characteristic of the Abraham narratives is the tradition of a divine covenant with Abraham (Gen. 15–JE). Since it is not connected with any locality, Alt understands this event as a legend of the founding of a cult which belonged to the religion of the tribes who descended from Abraham. However, it is more likely that this event is to be connected with Hebron (13:18–J) and with Abraham's leadership in the settlement of that region. The primary content of the covenant is a divine oath, in which the possession of the land is promised to Abraham and his descendants (15:18-21). The promise that Abraham's descendants would be numerous (15:5) was added to this later. Thus the covenant tradition shows that, together with his role as patriarch and founder of a cult, Abraham was also the leader of the Amoritic seminomads who settled in the region of Hebron. Here, once again, he founded the cult which he had formerly promoted at Mamre, and as a justification for this appealed to a divine oath or covenant which the El of the sanctuary had made with him that he and his descendants would be given the land. There is no clear indication as to the date of this migration of Abraham into the region of Hebron, but we may

suggest that it was either shortly before or about the same time as the Amarna period of the fourteenth century B.C. [12]

III. Theological Development.

1. *JE*. Several Abraham traditions had already been arranged in a cycle before J incorporated them into his epic history concerning Israel's origin. In a previous stage in the development of this cycle, Abraham must have already been connected with Isaac and Jacob to form a continuous family history. This earlier stage reflects a strong Judean influence, and originated when the old Abraham traditions were brought from Hebron-Mamre to Judah by Calebite settlers. These Calebites were worshippers of Yahweh, and as such are the ones responsible for the identification of the God of Abraham with Yahweh. In the J history, the figure of Abraham becomes a part of a theological system of promise and fulfilment, which forms the basic theme of the work. Yahweh has given Abraham a threefold promise: that his descendants will become a nation, that they will possess the land of Canaan, and that they will become a blessing to the nations (Gen. 12:1-3; 15:7-12,17,18abc). This oath is reaffirmed to the subsequent patriarchs, Isaac and Jacob (26:2-5; 28:13-15). The threefold promise has its center in the divine covenant with Abraham (15:5,7), and undoubtedly came from an earlier tradition of such a covenant with originally more local significance. The divine author of the covenant is now introduced clearly as Yahweh, and the land which is promised to Abraham's descendants for a possession extends "from the river of Egypt to the great river, the river Euphrates" (15:18b). The J account of this covenant was later expanded (15:13-16,18bβ,20f.), and was combined with a divergent tradition (15:1f.,4-6) which is often attributed (though today this is frequently doubted as well) to E. J saw the fufilment of the covenant in the Davidic-Solomonic kingdom with the Davidic monarch at the head as the source of its blessing (Gen. 12:3; cf. Ps. 72:17). Yahweh's covenant with Abraham was an anticipation and a promise of his later covenant with David (2 S. 7). In contrast with this, Cazelles places the promise to Abraham in J in the framework of the ancient Near Eastern world during the first half of the second millennium B.C., and emphasizes that the J tradition does not depend on the king as such, but on the heirs of the divine promise. According to the faith of Abraham, which developed between Egypt and Mesopotamia, his God would give, if not to him at least to his descendants, something comparable to that which Marduk gave Hammurabi. A religious hope in protection and salvation would be significant, then, only if it attributed to the protecting deity analogous universal power. The deity is present in the tribe and guarantees the cohesion of its descendants. Against this view is the fact that promises of other gods of Mesopotamia to their worshippers, e.g., to Gudea, Ishme Dagan of Isin, Lipit Ishtar, and Sin-Iqisham of Larsa, and perhaps also to the Ugaritic king Keret and to the hero Danel, aroused hopes which pertained to the individual's glory and success.

---

[12] Albright, de Vaux, Cazelles, Bright, *et al.*, hold otherwise.

No clear theological development of the figure of Abraham can be found in the E tradition. The promise of the land is mentioned in Gen. 50:24, a passage which perhaps comes from E (cf. also Dt. 31:23–E?).

2. *Deuteronomy.* The figure of Abraham plays an important role in the introductory parenesis of Deuteronomy. Yahweh's covenant with Abraham holds a central position in the whole complex of the patriarchal traditions. It is interpreted throughout as an oath sworn by God, although the word *berith* also occurs (Dt. 7:12; 8:18; cf. 4:31). The covenant with Abraham is extended to the three patriarchs (1:8; 6:10; 7:12; 8:18; 9:5; 11:9). Furthermore, there are no longer allusions to the Davidic kingdom, and the covenant has to do with a promise of the future choice of Israel, which is connected with the covenant at Horeb (5:3ff.). In the face of Israel's disobedience (9:27) the covenant with Abraham justifies the appeal to Yahweh's grace, and in a later exilic addition it is used to establish the permanence of the divine choice of Israel in spite of the loss of the land and of national unity (4:30f.). This use of the figure of Abraham to establish the enduring nature of the covenant made with Israel through him also appears in the Deuteronomistic history in 2 K. 13:23, a passage influenced by the situation that resulted from Judah's overthrow and the experience of the exiles (cf. also 1 K. 18:36).

3. *The Psalms and the Prophets.* It is striking that in the Psalms Abraham is seldom mentioned. In Ps. 47:10 (Eng. v. 9), an Enthronement Psalm of pre-exilic origin, Israel is called "the people of the God of Abraham," which indicates that the Abraham tradition was used in the Jerusalem royal cult. This agrees with the suggestion which has already been made that there was a connection between the covenant of Abraham and the covenant of David, which may have been the case in the J tradition. In Ps. 105:6, Israel is addressed as "the offspring of Abraham," and in vv. 8ff. (= 1 Ch. 16:15ff.), the psalmist appeals to the covenant with Abraham as an "everlasting covenant." This covenant, extended to Isaac and Jacob, includes the promise of possession of the land of Canaan. This psalm is certainly dependent on the postexilic form of the Abraham tradition in P.

In the preexilic prophets, there is no authentic reference to the Abraham traditions. Mic. 7:20 is a postexilic oracle, as is also probably Isa. 29:22. In the prophets of the exile, Ezekiel and Deutero-Isaiah, a new theological evaluation of Abraham appears. Ezk. 33:24 shows that those who remained in Judah after 586 B.C. used the tradition of the divine oath that Abraham would possess the land to establish their claim that they were the divinely chosen remnant of Israel. Ezekiel rejected this claim (Ezk. 33:27ff.). In contrast, Deutero-Isaiah appeals to the figure of Abraham (Isa. 41:8; 51:2) because he finds in him a guarantee of the divine intention to restore Israel. That interest in Abraham was reawakened in the exilic and postexilic periods indicates the critical condition caused by the loss of the land and the downfall of the Davidic monarchy. It was natural for one to appeal to the covenant tradition guaranteeing Israel possession of the land by a divine oath. Since the Abraham tradition was particularly important to the court circle in Jerusalem, the failure of the monarchy occasioned a fresh re-examination and a fresh return to Abraham as the recipient of the oath which had established the royal authority and power in Israel. While the covenant at Sinai-Horeb raised a question about Israel's future deliverance, since Israel had indeed transgressed the commandments (cf. Jer. 31:31-34; Ezk. 36:26-28), the Abraham covenant took on new significance as a unilateral divine oath, promising the growth of a national consciousness and possession of the land.

4. *The P Document and the Chronicler.* The most significant development in the priestly Abraham tradition is the new interpretation of the divine covenant with Abraham in Gen. 17. In this passage, the deity who makes the covenant bears the name El Shaddai; for it is part of the constant scheme of P that El Shaddai was the divine name which was used consistently from Abraham to Moses. The covenant is described as a *berith 'olam* ("an everlasting covenant"), a term used earlier for the tradition of the Davidic covenant (2 S. 23:5; cf. Isa. 55:3). This intensifies even more the description in J where the covenant is a unilateral divine oath. Now, the establishment of the monarchy is expressly included in the terms of the covenant, whereas earlier it was included only by implication. Also the threefold promise is changed somewhat: Abraham will become the father of a multitude of nations, his descendants will receive all the land of Canaan as an everlasting possession, and El Shaddai will be their God (Gen. 17:4-8). This last promise must be understood cultically, viz., as a reference to the divine *kabhodh* (glory) which dwells in the midst of Israel. P declares that this promise became a reality when the tabernacle was built after the revelation at Sinai. For P, the covenant with Abraham is the ever abiding covenant by which Israel lives. The Sinai event does not result in the establishment of a new covenant, but initiates the fulfilment of the promises which were made to Abraham.

The sign of this covenant is the rite of circumcision, which clearly is a religious rather than a social rite (Gen. 17:10-14). The importance of the making of this covenant is further emphasized by its connection with the changes of name from Abram to Abraham and from Sarai to Sarah (17:5,15). In P, the figure of Abraham is the historical beginning for the doctrine that the Jewish people are the subject of an eternal choice of God. This choice was verified by the rite of circumcision, and it could not be annulled by transgressing the laws given at Sinai.

In the Chronicler's work, the figure of Abraham is presented as an indication that Yahweh had chosen Israel and had given them the land, in harmony with the P tradition. The promise of the land is central (2 Ch. 20:7). In a psalm taken over by the Chronicler, this promise is considered to have been confirmed to the other two patriarchs, Isaac and Jacob (1 Ch. 16:15ff.). The reference to Yahweh as the "God of Abraham, Isaac, and Jacob" (29:18; 2 Ch. 30:6) is undoubtedly a reflection of this promise. Ezra's prayer in Neh. 9:6-37 alludes to the Abraham covenant, and in a way that indicates familiarity with the J and P accounts (note the allusions to the change of Abraham's name, Gen. 17:5[P], and the list of the inhabitants of Canaan which were added to the J account, 15:20f.).

Clements

אָדוֹן ’ādhôn; אֲדֹנָי ’ᵃdhōnāi

Contents: I. '*adhon:* 1. Etymology; 2. Extrabiblical Material; 3. The OT. II. '*adhonāi:* 1. Usage; 2. The Ending -āi; 3. Dalman's Interpretation; 4. Baudissin's View; 5. Ugaritic Parallels; 6. Time of Origin; 7. Summary.

I. 'adhon.

1. *Etymology.* '*adhon* or '*adhan,* "lord," and its feminine cognate '*adhath* are not common Semitic words; outside the Hebrew of the OT, they occur only in "Amoritic," Canaanite, Phoenician, Punic, and (at least '*adhath*) Palmyrenian, while '*adhonāi* is found only in the OT and in literature influenced by it. Further, like his cult, the name of the Greek god Adonis certainly had a Semitic predecessor (probably Phoenician) '*adhon,* as brought to light unexpectedly through an inscription, just as an excavation of an Adonis temple at Dura-Europus in 1922-1923 corrected earlier ideas of this god as merely an ideological figure, and made it necessary to regard him as a genuine cult figure. As is evident in the literature cited below, quite a number of etymological explanations have been proposed. Thus, Albright has revived the suggestion that the word '*adhon* is derived from Egyp. *idnw,* "administrator, steward," earlier proposed by S. Yeivin in 1936.[1] He dated this Egyptian loanword in the third millennium B.C., in a period when the mutual interchange between Egypt and Canaan was very lively. But H. Bauer and P. Leander think that '*adhon,* or more accurately '*adhonāi* (since they consider '*adhon* to be a later abbreviated form of '*adhonāi*), originated in the pre-Semitic substratum which is to be assumed for Syria-Palestine.[2] The most probable explanation is that '*adh ('adhan)* and '*adhath* are onomatopoetic words for "father" and "mother." This has been proposed by Ginsberg[3] and also by Herdner,[4] and is supported by the Ugaritic texts *CTA,* 23[SS] and 24[NK]. The first text has in lines 32-33: *hlh tṣḥ 'd 'd whlh tṣḥ ỉm ỉm,* "behold, she cries, 'Father, father,' and behold, she cries, 'Mother, mother'"; and the second text has in lines 33-35: '*dnh yšt mṣb mznm ỉmh kp mznm,* "her father prepares the frame for the scales, her mother the pan of the

---

'*ādhôn.* W. W. Graf Baudissin, *Kyrios als Gottesname im Judentum und seine Stelle in der Religionsgeschichte,* I-IV (1929); L. Cerfaux, "Le nom divin Kyrios dans la Bible grecque," *RSPT* (1931), 27-51; idem, "Adonai et Kyrios," *RSPT* (1931), 415-452; G. H. Dalman, *Studien zur Biblischen Theologie. Der Gottesname Adonaj und seine Geschichte* (1889); O. Eissfeldt, *Adonis und Adonaj. SSAW,* 115/4 (1970); W. Foerster and G. Quell, "κύριος," *TDNT,* III, 1039-1098.

[1] *JBL,* 69 (1950), 385-393, a review of C. H. Gordon, *Ugaritic Handbook.*
[2] *BLe,* § 28t, 61iα.
[3] H. L. Ginsberg, *OLZ,* 37 (1934), 473-75.
[4] Andrée Herdner, "Les noms de parenté en ugaritique," *GLECS,* 6 (1951-1954), 67f.

scales." The development of the meaning from *'adh, 'adhan,* "father," to "lord," and from *'adhath,* "mother," to "lady," is readily understandable. As for the linguistic relationship of *'adhāth* to *'adh* and *'adhān* (> *'ādhôn*), perhaps two possibilities are worthy of consideration. Either the feminine *'ath* is the counterpart to the masculine *'adh* or a *-th* has been added to the masculine *'adhān* to form the feminine. In the latter case, it is assumed that the final *-n* of *'adhān* has been assimilated to the feminine ending *-th.* [5]

2. *Extrabiblical Material.* In extrabiblical literature, *'adhan* or *'adhon* is used of human and divine lords, just as it is in the OT. The oldest occurrences of our word, which appear in the Akkadian letters from Mari *(Aduna-Adad),* [6] which have been influenced by Amorite and Canaanite, and from Amarna *(Aduna),* [7] are found in proper names which declare concerning some god or other that he is the lord of the person bearing his name, or represent a shortened form of such theophorous proper names. The Ugaritic texts (both those written in syllables and those written in the cuneiform alphabet) also show that *'dn* is a part or a shortened form of a part of theophorous proper names. *'dn* is applied to a god in *CTA,* 1 [VI AB], IV, 17, where the head of the Ugaritic pantheon, the god El, says to another (evidently younger) god: *'t 'dn tpʻr,* "you shall be called 'lord!'" Unfortunately the context of this statement is so fragmentary that it cannot be determined with certainty which young god is here given the name *'dn,* "lord." Quite probably it is Alʾiyan Baʿal, the god of the quick-blooming, but also quick-withering, spring vegetation. If so, we would have here a trace of the Semitic youthful god who must be the predecessor of the Greek god Adonis (but strangely this has not been authenticated anywhere up to this time), a trace that is confirmed by the statement preserved by the Alexandrian lexicographer of the sixth century A.D., Hesychius *(s.v. "Αδωνις): Adōnis despótēs hypó phoiníkōn kaí bólou ónoma,* "Adonis means 'lord' to the Phoenicians and is the name of Baal." In Ugarit, *'dn* is used for men as well as for gods, which is also the case with *'dth,* "lady." Thus, in *CTA,* 6 [I AB], VI, 56, Niqmad is called not only *mlk ʾgrt,* "king of Ugarit," and *bʻl trmn,* "possessor of trmn," but also *'dn yrgb,* "lord of yrgb"; and in *CTA,* 56, Tlmyn addresses the queen-mother as *'dty,* "my lady," while Tlmyn calls himself her servant *('bd).*

In the Phoenician inscriptions there are many examples of *'adhon* and *'adhath,* and these words are used of deities and of men. In an inscription from Umm el-ʿAwāmīd from the year 132 B.C., *'adhon* occurs several times, once in the expression *la'adhon lebhaʿal shamem,* "to the lord, to Baʿal-shamem," and again in the combination *la'adhon melakhim,* "lord of the kings," where the "kings" intended are those of the Seleucid dynasty who were ruling at that time. But with regard to *'adhath,* from the tenth century B.C. on, the *Baʿalat Gebal,* the main goddess of Byblos, is often referred to by the authors of the inscriptions or by

---

[5] For further discussion on etymology, see Gröndahl, *PNU,* 89; Huffmon, *APNM,* 159; cf. also *KBL*[3].

[6] Huffmon, *APNM,* 20, 159.

[7] Knudtzon, EA 1556.

her devotees, who refer to her as *'adhto,* "his lady." A Palmyrenian inscription dating from A.D. 142-143, published by Cantineau, seems to refer to a woman as *'adath,* "lady." [8] In this inscription, a man by the name of Māle states that he has made his grave "for himself, his wife *(la'adhtah),* for his sons, for his daughters, and for his grandchildren."

Thousands of Punic inscriptions begin with the phrase *lerabbath lethinith pan ba'al vela'adhon lebha'al chammon,* and thus are dedicated not only to Ba'al Hammon, who usually appears in the second part of the phrase, but also to the "lady Tinit, the face of Ba'al," whose dignity as lady is not expressed by *'adhath* here, but by *rabbath.* Transcriptions of the Punic *'adhon* into Greek and Latin have also been preserved for us. In a Punic inscription from the hill El-Hofra in the Algerian Constantine dating from the second century B.C., written in Greek letters, we find *l-adoun,* which is the Greek transliteration of the Punic *la'adhon.* [9] Also, in verses 998-1001 of the "Poenulus" written by Plautus *ca.* 200 B.C., we find *donni,* which corresponds to the Punic *adoni,* "my lord," being shortened by the deletion of the initial *a.* But in these texts *adoun* refers to a god, viz., to *Bal Amoun,* which here is placed after "our lady Tinit, the face of Ba'al" *(rhubathōn thinith phane bal),* while the address *donni='adhoni,* "my lord," is directed to a man.

3. *The OT.* In the OT, *'adhon* is used in reference to an earthly lord over 300 times and to a divine lord about 30 times, if we leave *'adhonāi* out of consideration. 2 S. 3:4, where David's son born to Haggith is named *'adhoniyyah* or (as his name is spelled in other passages) *'adhoniyyahu,* "my lord is Yahweh," is the oldest example that can be dated with certainty where Israel employed the concept of *'adhon.* It is possible that Israel had already called its heavenly lord or a human lord *'adhon* earlier than this. But the passages which assume that this title was used at an earlier time, like Gen. 42:10, where the brothers of Joseph, not knowing who he was, address him as "my lord" *('adhoni)* and refer to themselves as "your servants" *('abhadhekha)* in relationship to him, or like Ex. 23:17, where God at Sinai commands all the males of Israel to appear "before the Lord Yahweh" *('el pene ha'adhon yhvh)* three times a year, may have transferred a later usage of this word back into an earlier time. The OT speaks of the earthly lord over such things as wives (Gen. 18:12), lands (42:30), houses (45:8), districts (1 K. 16:24), and many similar things. Frequently the king is called *'adhon;* and in Jer. 22:18; 34:5, *hoy 'adhon,* "Ah, lord," appears as a lament over the dead king. The plural of our word, *'adhonim,* does occur as a genuine plural, but often it has reference to an individual earthly lord as a *pluralis majestaticus* (plural of majesty). This may be the case in 1 K. 16:24, which speaks of "the owner of the hill" *('adhone hahar),* and in Isa. 19:4, where the prophet warns the land of Egypt that it will fall into the hand of a "hard master" *('adhonim qasheh).* In this latter case, then, the substantive is in the plural, whereas the singular is used for the appositional adjective. Generally speaking, *'adhon* seems

---

8 J. Cantineau, *Syr,* 17 (1936), 354f.

9 J. Friedrich, *ZDMG,* 107 (1957), 282-290.

to mean "the lord as the master," [10] while → בעל baʿal means the owner (cf. Ps. 105:21, where Joseph is called lord, ʾadhon, of Pharaoh's house, and "ruler [moshel] of all his possessions").

When "my lord" (ʾadhoni, occasionally ʾadhonāi) is said to or about a man, frequently it is merely an expression of courtesy, viz., a substitution for the "You" of an address, or for a reference to a person as "He." Here we may cite two examples: in Gen. 31:35, Rachel makes this request of her father Laban, "Let not my lord be angry" (ʾal yichar beʿene ʾadhoni); and in 24:27, the chief servant of Abraham utters this prayer, "Blessed be Yahweh, the God of my master (ʾadhoni) Abraham, who has not forsaken his steadfast love and his faithfulness toward my master (ʾadhoni)." Leaving aside for the moment the term ʾadhonāi, here we call attention to the terms for "lord" (ʾadhon, haʾadhon, or ʾadhonim [as a pluralis majestaticus]) as they are applied to Yahweh. We will follow the sequence of books as they appear in the Hebrew Bible, and note those passages where terms for Yahweh are used in addition to ʾadhon, which emphasize his power and lay greater emphasis on ʾadhon. They are the following: Ex. 34:23, haʾadhon yhvh ʾelohe yisraʾel, "the Lord Yahweh, the God of Israel"; Dt. 10:17, yhvh ʾelohekhem huʾ ʾelohe haʾelohim vaʾadhone haʾadhonim, "Yahweh your God is God of gods and Lord of lords"; [11] Josh. 3:13, yhvh ʾadhon kol haʾarets, "Yahweh, the Lord of all the earth"; Isa. 1:24, neʾum haʾadhon yhvh tsebhaʾoth ʾabhir yisraʾel, "the Lord says, Yahweh of hosts, the Mighty One of Israel"; Isa. 3:1; 10:16; and 10:33, haʾadhon yhvh tsebhaʾoth, "the Lord, Yahweh of hosts"; 19:4, neʾum haʾadhon yhvh tsebhaʾoth, "says the Lord, Yahweh of hosts"; Mic. 4:13, layhvh bitsʿam vechelam laʾadhon kol haʾarets, "their gain to Yahweh, their wealth to the Lord of the whole earth"; Zec. 6:5 and Ps. 97:5, ʾadhon kol haʾarets, "the Lord of all the earth"; Ps. 114:7, milliphne ʾadhon chuli ʾarets milliphne ʾeloah yaʿaqobh, "Tremble, O earth, at the presence of the Lord, at the presence of the God of Jacob"; 135:5, gadhol yhvh vaʾadhonenu mikkol ʾelohim, "Yahweh is great, and our Lord is above all gods"; and 136:1-3, hodhu layhvh... leʾlohe haʾelohim... laʾadhone haʾadhonim, "O give thanks to Yahweh,... to the God of gods,... to the Lord of lords." These passages are very important in determining the meaning of ʾadhonāi, inasmuch as they confirm emphatically the impression made by ʾadhonāi that it is used to emphasize Yahweh's rule over all the world, as we shall see, and thus suggest a similar concept for ʾadhonāi.

II. ʾadhonāi.

1. *Usage.* In the OT, ʾadhonāi appears 449 times, of which it occurs alone 134 times and in connection with yhvh (Yahweh) 315 times. When it is used with Yahweh, the order is ʾadhonāi yhvh 310 times and yhvh ʾadhonāi 5 times. In the earlier historical books (Gen.-2 K.) ʾadhonai is found only 21 times. In the

---

[10] Köhler, *OT Theol* (trans. 1957), 31.

[11] Cf. the Egyptian expression nb nbw with the same meaning; cf. further under → בעל baʿal.

prophetic books the use of *'adhonāi* (alone or in connection with *yhvh*) increases to 320 occurrences, of which the book of Ezekiel alone furnishes 217 examples. In the great majority of these passages *'adhonāi* is used in introductions, *koh 'amar,* and in concluding formulas, *ne'um,* of prophetic oracles, e.g., Isa. 10:24, *koh 'amar 'adhonāi yhvh tsebha'oth,* "Thus says the Lord, Yahweh of hosts"; and 3:15, *ne'um 'adhonāi yhvh tsebha'oth,* "says the Lord, Yahweh of hosts." In the Psalms, *'adhonāi* occurs 55 times, and in Lamentations, 14. Thus it is clear that *'adhonāi* and *'adhonāi yhvh* or *yhvh 'adhonāi* are better adapted to speeches and prayers than they are to narratives, laws, and wisdom sayings.

2. *The Ending -āi.* In the word *'adhonāi,* everything depends on the explanation of its ending *-āi.* Some scholars interpret this ending as a substantive-afformative, regardless of the function it serves. Others think that it is the possessive pronominal suffix, first person singular, attached to the plural *'adhonim.* Under the assumption that the afformative *-āi* implies an intensification of the root word, it is argued that *'adhonāi* should be translated either "Lord of all" or "my lord." In the latter case, in view of the abundance of similar parallels such as Monsieur, Madame, Madonna, the possibility must always be left open that in *'adhonāi* there is a solidification of a vocative into a predicate nominative form. While Dalman could still say, "it is now generally accepted that in Old Testament literature *'adhonāi* was an independent name for God (like *'elohim* or *ha'elohim*) meaning 'the Lord,' 'the Lord of all',"[12] at the present time the opposite view enjoys virtually general recognition. This is due in particular to Dalman's *Studien,* and to Baudissin's work on *Kyrios* which was influenced by it. In fact, Baudissin said that this work was to be read in connection with Dalman's *Studien.*[13] More recent studies of this problem make it clear that at the present time the interpretation of the ending of *'adhonāi* as a possessive suffix dominates the field. Quell, after he has declared himself in favor of the pronominal nature of the suffix *-āi* in *'adhonāi,* says: "On the other hand, *'adhonāi* also occurs in we-texts (e.g., Ps. 44:24), so that it is impossible to take it as a possessive form 'my lord' in biblical texts unless one assumes that an original vocative has ossified as a nominative. Granted this assumption, one may assume... that *'adhonāi* as a divine name had its origin as an address in private prayer.... The lengthening of the ā may be traced to the concern of the Massoretes to mark the word as sacred by a small external sign."[14] In support of his contention that the vocative *'adhonāi* was used to function as other cases, he appeals to Baudissin, who cited the late Heb. *rabbi,* Syr. *mari,* and Akk. *bēlti* as parallels to *'adhonāi.*[15] Köhler writes: "The divine name Yahweh occurs more than 6700 times in the OT. In speech, Judaism uses instead the word *'adhonāi,* the *pluralis excellentiae,* 'my Lord,' in the sense of 'my dominion,' and this expression has become such a fixed usage that it is best and most correctly translated 'the Lord.' This is the *kýrios* of

12 Dalman, 13.
13 Baudissin, II, 18.
14 *TDNT,* III, 1060f., n. 109.
15 Baudissin, II, 35ff.

the Septuagint. God is called in the OT 'Lord'."[16] Ringgren says: "The real proper name of the Israelite God, however, is Yahweh.... The Septuagint simply translates it with *Kyrios*, 'Lord,' because at the time of translation motives of reverence prevented people from pronouncing the name of God; they replaced it instead with *ʾadhonāi*, 'the Lord (lit. 'my lord').'"[17] Vriezen, again referring to Baudissin, writes: "The expression ʾAdonai Yahweh, 'my Lord Yahweh,'... also occurs, often as a vocative, but also generally as a divine name; in Ezekiel this expression appears most of the time, although Yahweh alone is also used."[18] Finally, van Dijk compares the *bath ʿammi*, "daughter of my people," which appears in Jeremiah and Lamentations, with *ʾadhonāi*, and concludes: "Still, it is equally possible that the suffix of *ʿammî* in *bat ʿammî* has lost its proper character as in the case of *ʾᵃdōnāy* in 1 Kg 3,10 and Ez 13,9, 'the Lord', as noted by [*GesB*, 9], and the LXX already renders *ʾᵃdōnāy* as *Kyrios*. The same possibility obtains in the Ugaritic proper name *bn adty*, 'Son of the Lady' (= a goddess). See *UT* 2039:4 and 2097:7"[19] (= *PRU*, V, p. 53 or 120). In order to get a better understanding of the problem of whether the ending *-āi* in *ʾadhonāi* is a pronominal suffix or an afformative reinforcing the meaning of the root word, a more detailed analysis of the books of Dalman and Baudissin, paying particular attention to their differences, is in order.

3. *Dalman's Interpretation.* According to Dalman, the substitution of *ʾadhonāi* for the address forms *ʾadhonai* and *ʾadhoni*, which up until that time were also used for God without offense, was first undertaken by scribes living after OT times. But the ending *-āi* retained the same meaning as *-i* and *-ai*, and thus remained the pronominal suffix first person singular, and assumed a personal relationship of the speaker to God. Dalman frequently finds this personal relationship in passages where such an interpretation is artificial and unnatural. Thus, speaking of *ʾadhonāi* in Ex. 15:17, *makhon leshibhtekha paʿalta yhvh miqqedhash ʾadhonāi konenu yadhekha*, "the place, O Yahweh, which thou hast made for thy abode, the sanctuary, O Adonai, which thy hands have established," he contends that it "is to be explained from the point of view of the singer who calls God *ʾeli*, 'my God,' in v. 2, or is to be deleted on the basis of the testimony of the Samaritan Pentateuch and the Targum."[20] But on the prophets' use of *ʾadhonāi*, he says: "It is a remarkable fact that the prophets who relate a commission or call of God which they received personally, i.e., Proto-Isaiah (6:9), Amos (7:15), Jeremiah (1:10), Ezekiel (2:3), and Deutero-Isaiah (48:16; 50:4), have a special preference for *ʾadhonāi*. No reason can be given for this other than that their relationship to Yahweh in the role of his servant was a particularly personal one. But then, the suffix on *ʾadhonāi* was certainly *not*

---

[16] Köhler, *OT Theol*, 30.
[17] H. Ringgren, *Israelite Religion* (trans. 1966), 67f.
[18] Th. C. Vriezen, *Outline of OT Theology* (1958), 196.
[19] H. J. van Dijk, *Ezekiel's Prophecy on Tyre* (1968), 8f.
[20] Dalman, 26.

without meaning." [21] In relation to the "introductions to the prophetic oracle" in particular, Dalman says further concerning the use of *'adhonāi* by the prophets: "'*adhonāi*, therefore, is completely in place; for the prophet speaks in the name of the one who sent him and who is thus his Lord in a particular sense. Moreover, *ha'adhon* by itself is familiar enough to Isaiah, who uses it five times. The same is true of the use of *'adhonāi* in the prophetic oracle," viz., it expresses the special relationship of the prophet to Yahweh, his Lord. "More special emphasis seems to be placed on the suffix particularly in 50:4,5,7,9; if so, the compounding of the divine name in this context is explained very well. The prophet refers to the fact that his God, who inspired him to speak, will also defend him against his enemies." [22] Dalman attempts to justify the deletion of Ezk. 13:9; 23:49; 24:24; 28:24; Job 28:28 on the one hand, and of 1 K. 2:26; 22:6; 2 K. 19:23 on the other. He reasons this way: "On the basis of the extant written material, one can hardly speak of a real history of the use of *'adhonāi* in the period covered by the OT books (leaving Daniel out of consideration), least of all of a transition from a conscious use of the suffix to a use of the suffix which has no significance. If we may assume, then, that the usage which is prevalent now was also the original usage, then we are justified in deleting those few passages where *'adhonāi* occurs in the mouth of God (4 times in Ezekiel and once in Job) and in ordinary historical narratives (3 times in the books of Kings). And if we disregard the book of Daniel, we find that *'adhonāi* is used in speeches of men to God or about God, which agrees with the usage of the profane *'adhoni*, and in certain instances emphasis may fall on the suffix to a greater or lesser degree." [23] Later in his work, Dalman again takes up this admission that the suffix on *'adhonāi* is weakened in significance when he writes: "'*adhonāi* was a natural substitute for *yhvh* because it often appears in the OT as an introduction to Yahweh.... At the same time, it must be assumed that the significance of the suffix was on the verge of disappearing, not because it was unknown, but because people were no longer concerned to express their own personal relationship to God, but rather their belief in his position as Lord. A man did not desire to call on *his* Lord, but on 'the *Lord*'." [24]

Dalman believed that these quotations from his *Studien* supported his thesis that the ending *-āi* was a possessive suffix and that the *'adhonāi* which had this suffix always assumed a personal relationship between the speaker and Yahweh. But the deletions or emendations of Ex. 15:17; Ezk. 13:9; 23:49; 24:24; 28:24; and Job 28:28 on the one hand, and of 1 K. 2:26; 22:6; and 2 K. 19:23 on the other, are arbitrary, which would not be necessary if *'adhonāi* were interpreted as a name meaning "the Lord of all" with *-āi* as the substantival afformative. With regard to the special relationship of service which the prophets Proto-Isaiah, Amos, Jeremiah, Ezekiel, and Deutero-Isaiah had to Yahweh and the explanation of their frequent use of *'adhonāi,* we have just as much, if not

---

[21] *Ibid.,* 34.
[22] *Ibid.,* 30.
[23] *Ibid.,* 33.
[24] *Ibid.,* 74.

more, right to maintain that most of these prophets emphasize the majesty of Yahweh more than others, and that their use of *'adhonāi* in the sense of "the Lord of all" would fit very well with this emphasis. The reference in the second quotation to Isaiah's use of *ha'adhon* by itself five times (along with *'adhonāi*),[25] and the remark that *ha'adhon* by itself could probably have served the same purpose as *'adhonāi*,[26] remarkably suggests the idea that *'adhonāi* means approximately the same thing as *ha'adhon*, viz., the Lord in the sense of Lord of all. Finally, the last quotation clearly states that the significance of the suffix on *'adhonāi* was on the verge of disappearing and that a man did not desire to call on his Lord when he used *'adhonāi*, but on "the Lord." Undoubtedly, Dalman is correct when he sees the meaning "the Lord of all" for *'adhonāi* in some of the passages he examines. But he dates the origin of this meaning of *'adhonāi* much too late. The truth is that it did not take place at the end of the history of this word, but at the beginning.

4. *Baudissin's View*. Like Dalman, Baudissin also denies the form *'adhonāi* to the authors of the OT books, and attributes it to later scribes, who introduced this form in order to distinguish between the sacral and secular spheres. To accomplish this, they restricted the forms *'adhoni* and *'adhonai* (which up to that time had been applied to God) to the secular sphere, and introduced a special word form, *'adhonāi*, to designate Yahweh as "Lord" or "Lord of all," and added it to many passages, especially in the book of Ezekiel. But Baudissin differs from Dalman in that he considers *'adhonāi* (which has been corrected from *'adhoni* or *'adhonai*) to be "original" when it appears in an address to God and thus is vocative, while in the other cases of the use of *'adhonāi* he rejects the idea that the ending *-āi* in *'adhonāi* is still a possessive suffix and consequently that *'adhonāi* can be understood to mean "my Lord," and attributes these occurrences of *'adhonāi* wholly to late text traditionists. He says: "The questions as to whether the word *'adhonāi* is original and as to how the ending *-āi* in *'adhonāi* is to be understood must for the most part be left unanswered. We will show later [II, ch. 3,2] that it is likely that this form is very late and assumes an earlier form *'adhoni*.... Perhaps the ending *-āi* can only be either a pronominal suffix first person singular or a nominal ending, which later (at least in part by the Septuagint) apparently came to be understood as a pronominal suffix."[27] In another place, he emphasizes this with these words: "Since we find the divine epithet *'adhon* used clearly with pronominal suffixes, at least in part, in Hebrew and Phoenician, and also since the ending *-āi* can be a pronominal suffix, it seems to me that everything favors the position that the ending *-āi* on *'adhonāi* is nothing other than a pronominal suffix. But above all, *one thing* is established, viz., that there has been a change in the meaning of the form *'adhonāi*. It is impossible to apply this to all cases in the OT uniformly, as Dalman has tried to do. Either the ending is a nominal ending which was later understood as a

---

25 *Ibid.*, 30.
26 *Ibid.*, 74.
27 Baudissin, I, 482f.

pronominal suffix, or vice versa." [28] Accordingly, he examines the attempts of
Dalman to force the meaning "my Lord" on 'adhonāi or, where this is absolutely
impossible, to delete these occurrences of 'adhonāi as being late, and emphatically
rejects them. Thus he writes: "Outside the Pentateuch, which uses it only in
address with perhaps one exception, the meaning 'my Lord' does not fit in most
cases, at any rate not in all. Only in address is it evident that the meaning 'my
Lord' is a suitable translation throughout. In only a minority of other instances
is the use of this divine designation intended to express the personal relationship
of the speaker to Yahweh. ... Beginning with the assumption that the ending in
'adhonāi could not be anything but the pronominal suffix, Dalman tries to show
that it is possible to interpret this word as 'my Lord' in almost all passages." [29]
Again he says: "In the prophets, 'adhonāi in the sense of 'my Lord' fits only in
individual passages, but in the sense of a proper name with the meaning 'the
Lord' it fits everywhere. The same is true of its usage in the Psalms." [30] And
further he writes: "Dalman's distinctions are not remotely sufficient to justify
the interpretation of this name which he considers to be the only possible one.
In my opinion, in the great majority of passages it is necessary to interpret
'adhonāi as a proper name meaning 'the Lord,' viz., the Lord absolutely, so that
either the ending is not a pronominal suffix, or its meaning as a pronominal
suffix has been lost. ... In 2 K. 19:23 (= Isa. 37:24), by the 'adhonāi of the
present text Isaiah hardly wants to emphasize that the Assyrians have mocked
his, i.e., Isaiah's, Lord, but rather after the solemn reference of the foregoing
text to the 'Holy One of Israel' as the one whom Sennacherib had mocked, he
means to emphasize that he has insulted the Lord of all." [31]

5. *Ugaritic Parallels.* As the Ugaritic texts have shed new light on other
lexicographical and grammatical phenomena of the OT, so this also appears to
be the case with regard to the Ugaritic ending -āi, which is a reinforcement of
the basic word to which it is added. This Ugaritic ending -āi may be compared
with the ending of 'adhonāi and promises to make an important contribution to
the explanation of 'adhonāi. Only two examples will be mentioned. In the text
dealing with a bitter battle between the gods Ba'al and Yam, *CTA*, 2 [III AB],
IV, we read in line 5: *l'rṣ ypl ỉlny wl'pr 'ẓmny,* "The all-powerful one falls to
the earth, and the all-mighty one to the dust." The second Ugaritic text, *CTA*, 51,
which contains words with the ending -āi, is a letter made up of 18 lines, written
by Tlmyn and Aḫtmlk to their mother, their lady *(lỉmy 'dtny),* which, after the
usual formulas used to express devotion and good wishes (lines 1-9), continues
in lines 10-18: *hnny 'mny kll mỉd šlm w'p 'nk nḫt ṯmny 'm 'dtny mnm šlm
rgm ṯṯb l'bdk,* "Everything here with us is very well, and I am enjoying peace.
Is everything there well with our lady? Answer your servant!" Both texts show
the ending -āi as a reinforcement of a basic word, the first text in *ỉlny* and *'ẓmny,*

---

[28] *Ibid.,* II, 31.
[29] *Ibid.,* II, 18.
[30] *Ibid.,* II, 22.
[31] *Ibid.,* II, 19f.

which clearly mean something like "full of power" and "full of might," the second in *hnny* and *ṯmny*, which describe the situation in which the authors of the letter assume that their readers have an interest, and the group of persons concerning whose condition they inquire, in the broadest possible terms, and thus probably they are to be rendered by "everything here" or "in this place," and "everything there" or "in that place." [32]

Just as the afformative -*āi* in these Ugaritic texts reinforces the meaning of a basic word and has nothing at all to do with a possessive suffix, so also with the ending of *'adhonāi*: basically it is a nominal afformative, which reinforces the meaning of the basic word *'adhon*, and the meanings "Lord" and "Lord of all" come from this. But we should probably reckon with the possibility advocated by Dalman, Baudissin, and others that in many passages that now have *'adhonāi* as an address to Yahweh, originally the reading was *'adhoni* or the *pluralis majestaticus 'adhonai*. This seems to be the case, e.g., in Gen. 15:2, where Abraham asks Yahweh, "My Lord Yahweh, what wilt thou give me?" *('adhonāi yhvh mah titten li)*, or in Ex. 4:10, where Moses explains to Yahweh, "Oh, my Lord, I am not eloquent" *(bi 'adhonāi lo' 'ish debharim 'anokhi)*. If so, then the forms *'adhoni* and *'adhonai*, "my Lord," which refer to God, were changed later to *'adhonāi* in the course of the tendency to use them only in the secular sphere and to use *'adhonāi*, "the Lord of all," exclusively for Yahweh. For even the expression *'adhonāi 'elohai* in Ps. 38:16 (Eng. v. 15), where *'elohai*, "my God," comes immediately after *'adhonāi*, "Lord of all," and seems to suggest that the ending -*āi* should be interpreted as a possessive suffix and that this expression should be translated "my Lord," still can readily be understood as "my Lord of all." Thus, the special relationship of the worshipper to God need not be lost by adopting this explanation of *'adhonāi*. When a man addressed God as "Lord of all," he expressed his close relationship to God, for the LXX translators often render *'adhonāi* not by *kýriós mou*, "my Lord," but simply by *kýrios*, "Lord," indicating that by addressing God as "Lord" they felt a man was expressing the idea that God is the Lord of the worshipper. Nevertheless, inasmuch as *'adhonāi* in the Hebrew text often seems to have to mean "my Lord" because of the relationship between the worshipper and God demanded by the context, we are forced to interpret this as a late scribal alteration of the text from an original *'adhoni* or *'adhonai* to *'adhonāi*. But in spite of all this, it is still true that the overwhelming number of occurrences of this word demand that it be understood as a proper name, "Lord of all." Thus, in his above-quoted statements Baudissin is correct or *'adhonai*, "my Lord," to *'adhonāi*, the meaning of *'adhonāi* was changed to "Lord of all," [33] which, as we have already seen, [34] Dalman accepts for a later, but too late a time.
but which he dates much too late, as his own position suggests.

Still another phenomenon in the Ugaritic texts can make a contribution toward answering the question of the meaning and time of origin of the divine name

---

[32] Similarly, L. Delekat, *Asylie und Schutzorakel am Zionheiligtum* (1967), 369, n. 6.
[33] Baudissin, II, 31.
[34] See above, II.3.

’adhonāi: viz., just as the names Yahweh and Adonai usually appear together in the order Adonai Yahweh or (much more rarely) Yahweh Adonai (although occasionally they appear in parallel stichoi), so Ugaritic deities also have double names. Two examples may be cited here. The two parts of the double name of "Hephaistos of Ugarit," *ktr wḫss*, "Able and Intelligent," usually appear together in this order, as in *CTA*, 17 [II D], V, 25f., where we read: *’ḫr ymgy ktr wḫss*, "afterwards came *ktr wḫss*"; while in lines 10f. of the same column of this text *ktr* and *wḫss* appear in two parallel stichoi, so that here it is said of Dan’el: *hlk ktr ky‘n wy‘n tdrq ḫss*, "he truly sees the coming of the *ktr*, and he sees the speedy arrival of the *ḫss*." In a similar way, the moon-goddess of Ugarit has a double name. In *CTA*, 166, 47f., her two names stand together in the order *ȝb nkl*, and in *CTA*, 24 [NK], 1, they are reversed as *nkl wȝb*; but in lines 17f. of this latter text, where it says: *tn nkl yrḫ ytrḫ ȝb*, "Give, O *nkl*, *yrḫ* wants to buy the *ȝb*," the two names of the goddess appear as members of two parallel stichoi. The division of the two names of this goddess into two stichoi corresponds to what has already been pointed out above with regard to the separation of *yhvh* and ’adhonāi into two parallel stichoi in Ex. 15:17. [35]

The Song of Moses after the downfall of the Egyptians at the Sea, in 15:1-19, is certainly one of the oldest passages in the OT. Even if it cannot be dated in the thirteenth century B.C., as Albright thinks, [36] but is to be put in the first half of the tenth century, still it shows that the designation of Yahweh as ’adhonāi, "Lord of all" ("my Lord" would be out of place here) is very old. Neither the indication in many Hebrew manuscripts and the Samaritan Pentateuch of an original *yhvh* instead of ’adhonāi, which Dalman uses in support of this view, nor his contention that in our passage ’adhonāi is not original, are able to call its genuineness into question. Its genuineness in this passage is much more certain than in the two passages, Ex. 23:17 and 34:23 (which Dalman also considers to be very old, perhaps contemporary with 15:17), which require all Israelite males to appear three times a year before the Lord Yahweh *(ha’adhon yhvh)*. These passages apply the epithet *ha’adhon*, "the Lord," to Yahweh, an epithet that is on the same level as ’adhonāi as a designation of Yahweh, except that *ha’adhon* has the definite article *ha-* before it, while ’adhonāi has the ending *-āi* after it expressing a *status emphaticus* (the emphatic state). Other than Ex. 15:17, the following passages show ’adhonāi in parallelism with *yhvh*: Isa. 3:17, *sippach ’adhonāi qodhqodh benoth tsiyyon vayhvh pathehen ye‘areh*, "Adonai will smite with a scab the heads of the daughters of Zion, and Yahweh will lay bare their secret parts"; Isa. 49:14, *vatto’mer tsiyyon ‘azabhani yhvh va’dhonāi shekhechani*, "But Zion said, Yahweh has forsaken me, and Adonai has forgotten me"; Mic. 1:2, where perhaps the first ’adhonāi is to be deleted, *vihi yhvh bakhem le‘edh ’adhonāi mehekhal qodhsho*, "and let Yahweh be a witness against you, Adonai from his holy temple"; Ps. 30:9(8), *’elekha yhvh ’eqra’ ve’el ’adhonāi ’ethchannan*, "To thee, O Yahweh, I cried; and to Adonai I made supplication"; 35:22, *ra’ithah yhvh ’al techerash ’adhonāi ’al tirchaq mimmenni*, "Thou hast seen, O

---

[35] See above, II. 3.
[36] W. F. Albright, *Yahweh and the Gods of Canaan* (1968), 10, 23, 29, 38.

Yahweh, be not silent!" "O Adonai, be not far from me!" 38:16(15) (where *'adhonāi* is neither to be deleted nor emended to *yhvh*) *ki lekha yhvh hochalti 'attah tha'aneh 'adhonāi 'elohai,* "But for thee, O Yahweh, do I wait; it is thou, O Adonai my God, who wilt answer"; 130:1f., *mimma'amaqqim qera'thikha yhvh 'adhonāi shim'ah bheqoli,* "Out of the depths I cry to thee, O Yahweh! O Adonai, hear my voice!" 130:3, *'im 'avonoth tishmor yah 'adhonāi mi ya'amodh,* "If thou, O Yah, shouldst mark iniquities, Adonai, who could stand?"

It is obvious that the *'adhonāi* that appears in these passages is genuine because its presence is necessitated by the *parallelismus membrorum.* But it should also be equally as evident that in at least most of these passages *'adhonāi* does not mean "my Lord," but "the Lord of all." Thus, in these passages we have a fairly early confirmation for our conclusion drawn from Ex. 15:17 that *'adhonāi =* "the Lord of all," because the passages from the prophetic books go back into the eighth century B.C., and those from the Psalms, at least in part, can be contemporary with these prophetic passages or even older.

6. *Time of Origin.* Dalman and Baudissin admit that the ending of *'adhonāi,* which in their opinion originally meant "my Lord," gradually lost its function as a pronominal suffix. Only, as we have seen, they date the change from *'adhoni* and *'adhonai* to *'adhonāi,* and consequently the transition from "my Lord" to "the Lord of all," very late, as a matter of fact in the period after the OT books were already completed, when later "scribes" or "Massoretes" could undertake only minor alterations, as the correction from *'adhoni* or *'adhonai* to *'adhonāi.* But actually the *-āi* of *'adhonāi* was never a pronominal suffix. Rather, from the very beginning it was a nominal afformative, which elevated the basic form *'adhon* to a *status emphaticus* and gave *'adhonāi* the meaning "the Lord of all." Thus, no insurmountable obstacle stands in the way of assuming that *'adhonāi* is as old as Israel's adoption of the Yahweh cult. Now as far as subject matter is concerned, Yahweh's command to the people of Israel to worship no other god, and the reason given for this, viz., that Yahweh is a jealous God, are completely conceivable in the time of Moses. Furthermore, *'adhonāi,* "the Lord of all," may have been used first toward the end of the thirteenth century B.C. when the sanctuary at Shiloh was of very great cultic and religious significance and the designation of Yahweh (perhaps meaning the same thing as *'adhonāi*) as *yhvh tsebha'oth yoshebh 'al hakkerubhim,* "Yahweh Sebaoth (→צבאות *ts^ebhā'ôth*), who is enthroned on the cherubim," was first coined there. Or, it may have originated with the appearance of Elijah three or four centuries later, when, according to 1 K. 18:21, this prophet gave Israel the alternative: "If Yahweh is God, follow him; but if Baal, then follow him," and thus again demanded of his people conduct corresponding to the conception of Yahweh as "Lord of all." Just as many literary prophets beginning with Amos emphasized that Yahweh was "the Lord of all" in their preaching in the name of Yahweh, so also earlier cultic reforms could have called people back to Adonai.

7. *Summary.* The attempt to give a brief history of the use of the divine name Adonai would look something like this: The Song of Moses, Ex. 15:1-19, and

other examples attest to the usage of Adonai in the first half of the tenth century B.C. or earlier. The next time *'adhonāi* appears in passages which can be dated with certainty is in the last third of the eighth century B.C. in parallelism with Yahweh in Isa. 3:1 and Mic. 1:2 as well as in the Psalms mentioned above, which at least partly are contemporary with Isaiah and Micah or earlier. Some of the writing prophets use Adonai frequently, especially in introductions to divine oracles, as "Thus says Adonai Yahweh" (Am. 3:11, *koh 'amar 'adhonāi yhvh*), or in concluding formulas of divine oracles, as Isa. 3:15, "says Adonai Yahweh Sebaoth" *(ne'um 'adhonāi yhvh tsebha'oth)*. It is worthy of note that this Adonai is often accompanied by expressions like "Sebaoth," which further emphasize in particular the excelling majesty of this Lord of all and stress it in this way. Furthermore, it should be pointed out that Amos, Isaiah, and Ezekiel, whose preaching particularly emphasizes the majestic exaltation of their God, use Adonai in conjunction with such expressions depicting his omnipotence more often than other prophets.

Notwithstanding the vast difference in the number of occurrences of Yahweh and Adonai in the OT as it now stands (over 6700 occurrences of Yahweh, and approximately 450 of Adonai), up until *ca.* 300 B.C. the divine names of Yahweh and Adonai, at least to a great extent, were on equal footing and appear side by side. But beginning *ca.* 300, Adonai gradually came to be used more than Yahweh until finally it completely displaced it, in any case in spoken language. The consonants of the Tetragrammaton יהוה came to be pronounced *'adhonāi,* or if *yhvh* was preceded by *'adhonāi,* it was pronounced *'elohim,* and in the Massoretic Text it is written יְהֹוָה or יֱהֹוִה. In this period, the book of Chronicles often replaces the *yhvh* of the book of Kings, which was its earlier model, by *'elohim,* and a similar change takes place in Pss. 42–87. The book of Esther contains no divine name, but refers to God indirectly in 4:14 as "another quarter" *(maqom 'acher).* Ecclesiastes uses *'elohim* exclusively, while the book of Daniel (apart from *'adhonāi* in 1:2 and several occurrences of *yhvh* and *'adhonāi* in chap. 9, which for the most part is spurious) uses only *'elohim* and its Aramaic counterpart *'elaha'.* According to Dalman, the suppression of the name Yahweh began *ca.* 300 B.C., and the change from *yhvh* to *'adhonāi* or *'elohim* was complete by the second century B.C., while Baudissin thinks that the grandson of Jesus ben Sira, *ca.* 132 B.C., did not yet know of the replacement of Yahweh by Adonai. If, as we have tried to show above, the use of the divine name Adonai *('adhonāi)* for Yahweh is very old, since there is evidence for its existence with this sense at least as early as the tenth century B.C., then the much discussed question whether the *kýriós (mou)* of the LXX translators indicates an original Adonai *('adhonāi)* or represents the prototype for audibly speaking the Tetragrammaton *yhvh* by Adonai with the meaning Yahweh, may be partially resolved by noting that the choice of *kýrios* may also have been encouraged and facilitated by the fact that in Hellenism in general and in Oriental Hellenism in particular *kýrios* was a widespread designation for deities. It is certain that Dominus, Lord, Seigneur, Herr, and other similar names of the God of the Bible are directly or indirectly dependent on Adonai. Therefore, there is no justification whatsoever for the idea that the occurrences of *'adhonāi* or of the plural suffix *-āi* attached to *'adhon* did not originate with the authors of the biblical books, but must be attributed entirely to late scribes. On the contrary, the use of the plural suffix goes back to the origin of the biblical books, and only in a minority of instances (apart from cases in which *'adhonāi* was added to other terms for Yahweh which already stood in the text), particularly in those which contained an address to Yahweh and in which he was addressed originally by *'adhoni* or *'adhonai,* "my Lord," can it be considered possible that they originated with later text traditionists who wished to avoid any connection of the forms *'adhoni* and *'adhonai* with Yahweh and to replace them with *'adhonāi,* which they knew quite well in the sense of "Lord of all" from many ancient biblical passages. The inclination to distinguish *nomina sacra* from secular names by a particular pronunciation or manner of writing is indeed also to be observed elsewhere, even up to our own time.

It cannot be determined when the change took place from *'adhoni* and *'adho-nai,* "my Lord," as addresses directed to Yahweh, to *'adhonāi,* "Lord of all," nor when *'adhonāi* began to be inserted into contexts which seemed to be appropriate (if indeed this possibility is to be considered at all in preference to the view that *'adhonāi* must be regarded as original in such passages), especially since the LXX and the other ancient translations are not able to contribute anything to the solution of this problem. But it may be conjectured that the changes are connected with the displacement of the pronunciation of the Tetragrammaton *yhvh* by *'adhonāi* beginning *ca.* 300 B.C. In any case, the disinclination to pronounce the divine name Yahweh or to use it at all, and the combination of the consonants of *yhvh* with the vowels of *'adhonāi* [37] which originated at that time, caused *'adhonāi* to be held in high esteem and to be used more frequently as a divine name. It is no wonder that the name Adonai began to enjoy greater popularity at the expense of Yahweh. Thus, it is possible that it was added to biblical passages which already contained statements showing the majesty of God, as the introductory and concluding formulas in the prophets, *koh 'amar* and *ne'um.* Likewise, we must reckon with the possibility that *'adhoni* and *'adhonai,* "my Lord," which had been commonly used as addresses to Yahweh, were abandoned in favor of *'adhonāi,* "Lord of all," especially since there was an inclination at that time to make a strong distinction between the sacral and the secular spheres. One can hardly do more than conjecture about these issues, but inasmuch as the divine epithet or divine name *'adhonāi* may be considered genuine and ancient to a much greater extent than was formerly assumed, such questions lose much of the significance that was attributed to them earlier. We should at least have learned from their ardent discussion, which has yielded no convincing result, that one must not confuse the designation of Yahweh as *'adhonāi,* "Lord of all," with the displacement of Yahweh by Adonai, for Adonai was being used as a divine name at least five hundred years before its displacement of Yahweh, which did not begin until *ca.* 300 B.C. or even later.

Eissfeldt †

---

[37] There is a slight difference between the vowel pointing of the first letters of *yhvh* and *'adhonāi,* because the *yodh* in *yhvh* can take a simple *sheva,* but the *aleph* in *'adhonāi* must take the *chateph-pathach.*

אַדִּיר 'addîr; אַדֶּרֶת 'addereth

Contents: I. General Usage. II. The OT.

I. General Usage. As far as we can tell, the root *'dr* is of West Semitic origin and originally meant "to be broad, large, powerful." In Phoenician inscriptions, the verb occurs with the meaning "to be great, powerful" (subject "people") or "to rule" (with *'al*); in the piel it means "to make great, glorify" (of the king, of gods).[1] The adjective appears in both Phoenician and Punic inscriptions with the meaning "great, powerful," sometimes referring to gods, kings, lands, power, rain, etc., or as a technical term for different rulers. The root also appears in Ugaritic as an adjective, referring to the different materials in Aqhat's bow,[2] to a large territory,[3] and once to those in power.[4] In the feminine, *'drt* is used of a "noble" wife (i.e., not a concubine) and perhaps once of Astarte.

II. The Old Testament. In Hebrew, the root *'dr* rarely occurs as a verb. In Ex. 15:11 Yahweh is designated as *ne'dar baqqodhesh*, "mighty, glorified in holiness (or in the sanctuary)"; the context shows that here Yahweh is described as the incomparable, omnipotent God. Yahweh's arm is "glorious in power" *(ne'dari bakkoach,* Ex. 15:6), evidently referring to his might and strength in general. God is glorious *(ne'dar)* in splendor (Sir. 43:11; said in connection with the rainbow created by him). But also it can be said of the memory of someone that it is "glorious" or "in honor" *(ye'edhar,* Sir. 49:13). The hiphil form occurs twice, in Isa. 42:21: Yahweh will "magnify" *(yaghdil)* and "glorify"[5] his law; and in Sir. 36:6, where it is in parallelism with "strong" and refers to Yahweh's hand and arm, thus designating Yahweh's mighty works.

The substantive *'addereth* may be rendered on the one hand "might, glory, honor": Ezk. 17:8 (of the grape vine as a symbol of Israel); Zec. 11:3 (parallel to → גָּאוֹן *gā'ôn,* of the glorious vegetation which is despoiled); but it can also designate a mantle (Josh. 7:21,24), especially an expensive or royal mantle, as in Jonah 3:6, or a prophet's mantle (1 K. 19:13,19; 2 K. 2:8,13; Zec. 13:4). Behind this usage is perhaps not only the idea of the mighty and the powerful, but also the fact that the mantle is large and wide.

'addîr. G. Ahlström, " אדר," *VT,* 17 (1967), 1-7.

[1] *DISO; KAI.*

[2] *CTA,* 17 [II D], VI, 20-22.

[3] *CTA,* 16 [II K], I, 8; II, 108.

[4] *CTA,* 17 [II D], V, 7, "the *'drm* at the threshing-floor"; so Greenfield, *ZAW,* 73 (1961), 227f.; according to others, "haystacks or cedars."

[5] "Demonstrate as glorious"; according to Westermann, *Isaiah 40-66. OTL* (trans. 1969), 111, this is an addition.

The adjective *'addîr* is not connected with any particular sphere. The water of the Red Sea in which the Egyptians perished is *'addîr,* "mighty" (Ex. 15:10); the same is true of the sea with its waves which is subdued by the king Yahweh (Ps. 93:4). Both of these passages allude to the power of the chaos sea. Similar associations are suggested by Isa. 33:21 (the great ships which sail the sea). In other passages, the idea of splendor and glory is prevalent in this word, as when a great cedar is called *'addîr* (Ezk. 17:23; cf. also Zec. 11:2 of glorious trees). Ezk. 32:18 seems to use *'addirim* with reference to "nations," if one follows the Massoretic vocalization; the powerful nations must go into the nether world.

But power and splendor also belong to men who have gained a certain position. Thus, e.g., the kings slain by Yahweh are said to be *'addirim,* "famous" (Ps. 136:18), and "their mighty one" (*'addîr*) in Jer. 30:21 is a designation for the coming savior king (used in parallelism with *moshel,* "ruler"). Further, princes or nobles are designated as *'addîr,* Jer. 14:3; 25:34ff.; cf. Jgs. 5:13,25; Nah. 2:6 (Eng. v. 5); Neh. 3:5; 10:30(29); 2 Ch. 23:20. In this connection *'addîr* may stand in parallelism with *gibbor,* "hero" (Jgs. 5:13).

But power and splendor are primarily characteristics of the gods. Thus *'addîr* also occurs primarily with reference to God. Ps. 16:3 refers to the "holy ones"; but it is disputed whether this refers to human nature. If it refers to deities (other than Yahweh), then the text must be emended so that the psalmist has not "delight," but "no delight" in them. But since *qadhosh,* "holy," is usually connected with God, this interpretation is very probable. [6] Furthermore, *'addîr* appears as an attribute in 1 S. 4:8, where the Philistines cry out in fear: "Who can deliver us from the power of these mighty gods (*'elohim 'addirim*)?" According to the polytheistic understanding of the Philistines, the plural form expresses the "unknown" in the terrifying divine world of Israel. Yahweh is the mighty one (*'addîr*), mightier than "the mountains of prey" (Ps. 76:5[4]), [7] or mightier than the powerful waves of the sea (93:4). He can subdue the life-threatening might of the sea with his breath (Ex. 15:10). Here *'addîr* is closely connected with creation and deliverance (the chaos sea). Similar motifs appear in Isa. 33:21, where the saving power of Yahweh is compared with broad streams. Furthermore, Yahweh is the powerful one (*'addîr*), who cuts down the forests of Lebanon (10:34). What is true of Yahweh is also true of his name, which according to Ps. 8:2,10(1,9) is majestic in all the earth, which again in context refers to his creative power.

Usually, then, *'addîr* appears in contexts having to do with Yahweh's cosmological or other superhuman acts. This explains the secondary meaning "splendid, brilliant" (in parallelism with *na'or,* "glorious," Ps. 76:5[4]).

Ahlström

---

[6] See the comms.
[7] See the comms.

אָדָם ’ādhām

Contents: I. Meaning, The Ancient Near East, Etymology. II. Usage in the OT. III. Anthropological and Theological Considerations.

I. Meaning, The Ancient Near East, Etymology.

1. *’adham*, meaning "man" or the proper name "Adam" (Gen. 4:25; 5:1-5; 1 Ch. 1:1),[1] usually appears in prose texts with the article, and in poetic texts without the article.[2] Predominantly, this word occurs as a collective singular designating a class (as "man" in English),[3] and therefore can be translated by "mankind" or as a plural "men." At the same time, it is often used of individuals (e.g., in passages using "blessed" like Ps. 32:2, or in Ezk. 27:13; Prov. 28:17; Eccl. 5:18 [Eng. v. 19]), and functions adjectivally ("human") or indefinitely ("someone"),[4] but never appears in the plural or in the construct.

2. This word does not occur in Akkadian with the meaning "man, mankind," but the Akkadian words *adamātu*, "dark, red soil," and *adamu*, "red blood" (cf. Heb. *dam*, postbiblical *’adham*) or "red garment," seem to be equivalent to Heb. *’adhamah* and *’adhom*.[5] The Akkadian word corresponding to Heb. *’adham*

’ādhām. On "Man" in the OT: M. Bič, "The Theology of the Biblical Creation Epic," *SEÅ*, 28-29 (1963/64), 9-38; N. P. Bratsiotis, "נפש-ψυχή, ein Beitrag zur Erforschung der Sprache und Theologie der Septuaginta," *SVT*, 15 (1966), 58-89; *idem*, Άνθρωπολογία τῆς Παλ. Διαθήκης, I (Athens, 1967); J. S. Croatto, *Revista Bíblica* (Argentina), 25 (1963), 29-30; W. Eichrodt, *Das Menschenverständnis des AT. AThANT*, 4 (1947); J. de Fraine, *Adam und seine Nachkommen* (1962); K. Galling, *Das Bild vom Menschen in biblischer Sicht* (1947); A. Gelin, *L'homme selon la Bible* (Paris, 1962; London, 1968); H. Goeke, *Das Menschenbild der individuellen Klagelieder. Ein Beitrag zur alttestamentlichen Anthropologie* (diss., Bonn, 1970); F. C. Grant, "Psychological Study of the Bible," *SNumen*, 14 (1968), 107-124; J. Hempel, *Gott und Mensch im AT. BWANT*, 3/2 (1926, ²1936); *idem*, *Das Ethos des AT* (²1964); A. R. Johnson, *The Vitality of the Individual in the Thought of Ancient Israel* (Cardiff, ²1964); C. Keller, "Leib, Seele, Geist: eine Skizze der bibl. Psychologie," *Beiträge zur Psychiatrie und Seelsorge*, 9 (1968), 2-7; L. Köhler, *Hebrew Man* (trans. 1956); H. Lamparter, *Das biblische Menschenbild* (1956); C. Lattey, "Vicarious Solidarity in the OT," *VT*, 1 (1951), 267-274; O. Loretz, *Die Gottebenbildlichkeit des Menschen* (1967), Appendix: E. Hornung, "Der Mensch als 'Bild Gottes' in Ägypten," 123-156; O. Loretz, *Schöpfung und Mythos . . .* (1968); E. Lussier, "Adam in Gen 1,1–4,24," *CBQ*, 18 (1956), 137-39; H.-P. Müller, "Mann und Frau im Wandel der Wirklichkeitserfahrung Israels," *ZRGG*, 17 (1965), 1-19; H. van Oyen, *Ethik des ATs* (1967); Pedersen, *ILC;* N. Perrin, "The Son of

(continued on p. 76)

1 *GK,* § 125f.
2 *GK,* § 126h.
3 *GK,* § 126m.
4 *GK,* § 139d.
5 *CAD,* I/1, 94f.; *AHw*, 10.

is *awīlum* or *amī(ē)lu,* which also occurs in Hittite (alongside Hitt. *antuḫša*) as a foreign word. [6] In Akkadian the word designates the individual man as the representative of the class (alongside *awīlūtum, amī(ē)lūtu,* "mankind"), man in contrast to deities and animals, the citizen or resident of a region, the king ("man of Eshnunna," particularly in Mari) as well as the slave (particularly in Nuzi). A shift in meaning from "nobleman" to "full citizen" to "man," even "slave," can be ascertained. [7] The indefinite is used more often in Akkadian than it is in Biblical Hebrew. [8] The ancient poetic word for "man," *ṣalmāt qaqqadi,* "black-headed," is used almost exclusively as a designation for the natives of a land. [9]

The Akkadian traditions about the origin of man are not entirely uniform. The most widespread version says that man was created from the blood of a slain god. [10] According to the Old Babylonian myth of Atraḫasīs, the blood of a god "who has understanding" is mixed with clay. [11] It is remarkable that there is hardly any reference elsewhere in Akkadian literature to this half-divine origin of man. [12] Other statements mention only the creation out of clay. [13] Life or breath *(šaru)* is given by the gods. [14]

Man in Ancient Judaism and Primitive Christianity," *BiblRes,* 11 (1966), 17-28; G. Pidoux, *L'homme dans l'AT* (Neuchâtel, Paris, 1953); J. R. Porter, "The Legal Aspects of the Concept of 'Corporate Personality' in the OT," *VT,* 15 (1965), 361-380; H. W. Robinson, "The Hebrew Conception of Corporate Personality," *BZAW,* 66 (1936), 49-62; A. Safran, "La conception juive de l'homme," *RTP,* 98 (1964), 193-207; O. Sander, "Leib-Seele-Dualismus im AT?" *ZAW,* 77 (1965), 329-332; J. Scharbert, *Solidarität in Segen und Fluch im AT und in seiner Umwelt. BBB,* 14 (1958); W. Schmidt, "Anthropologische Begriffe im AT," *EvTh,* 24 (1964), 374-388; idem, "Gott und Mensch in Psalm 130," *ThZ,* 22 (1966), 241-253; idem, "Gott und Mensch in Psalm 8," *ThZ,* 25 (1969), 1-15; F. J. Stendebach, *Theologische Anthropologie des Jahwisten* (diss., Bonn, 1970); F. Stier, "Adam," *Hdb. theol. Grundbegriffe,* ed. H. Fries, I (1962), 13-25; F. Vattioni, "L'albero della vita," *Aug,* 7 (1967), 133-144; L. Wächter, *Der Tod im AT* (1967); idem, "Erfüllung des Lebens nach dem AT," *ZZ,* 22 (1968), 284-292; G. Whitfield, *God and Man in the OT* (London, 1949); H. Wildberger, "Das Abbild Gottes, Gen 1,26-30," *ThZ,* 21 (1965), 245-259, 481-501; W. Zimmerli, *Das Menschenbild des AT* (1949); idem, *Was ist der Mensch? Gött. Univ. reden,* 44 (1964); idem, "Der Mensch und seine Hoffnung nach den Aussagen des AT," *Studia Biblica et Semitica. Festschrift für Th. C. Vriezen* (1966), 389-403; idem, *Man and His Hope in the OT* (trans. 1971).

On Sections I.2-4: F. M. Th. de Liagre Böhl, "Das Menschenbild in babylonischer Schau," *SNumen,* 2 (1955), 28-48; P. Dhorme, *La religion assyro-babylonienne* (Paris, 1910), 180-206; S. Morenz, *Egyptian Religion* (trans. 1973), 47-49, 183; idem, *Gott und Mensch im alten Ägypten* (1964); E. Otto, *Gott und Mensch. AHAW,* 1 (1964); J. Sainte-Fare Garnot, "L'anthropologie de l'Egypte ancienne," *SNumen,* 2 (1955), 14-27.

For special literature on man's being made in the image of God, see nn. 60-68.

   [6] J. *Friedrich, Hethitisches Elementarbuch* (1940ff., ²1960ff.), II, 82, 112.
   [7] Böhl, 29f.
   [8] *CAD,* I/2, 48-62; *AHw,* 90f.
   [9] *CAD,* 16, 75f.
   [10] Of Lamga, *KAR,* 4=*AOT,* 135; of "the rebel" Kingu in EnEl VI, 10-27.
   [11] Lambert-Millard, *Atra-ḫasīs* (1969), 56ff.
   [12] Böhl, 34f.
   [13] E.g., the so-called Theodicy, § 26, *AOT,* 291.
   [14] Dhorme, 186f.

There is complete unity in the Akkadian texts as to man's duty: he must serve the gods and work for them. [15]

There is no reference to a first man by name in the Akkadian texts. Adapa, who has often been compared with Adam because of the similarity in name, is the "son of Ea" and a wise king; but he is not said to be the first man. On the contrary, he is "the typical man" [16] insofar as he loses immortality. The same is true of Gilgamesh. The idea that the gods have (eternal) life, while man is mortal, is axiomatic. [17]

The superiority of man over the animal world is made clear in the figure of Enkidu. [18] An obscure passage in the Theodicy speaks of the gift of (ambiguous) speech. [19] On the other hand, the insufficiency of man in contrast to the gods is also expressed. The gods determine the destiny of man, and "the counsel of the god of the watery abyss, who knows it?" [20]

3. In Northwest Semitic 'adham is already used in the sense that it has in Biblical Hebrew, and here it also occurs in the construct state. [21] According to Dahood, 'dm occurs more often in Phoenician than 'š, "man," which is considered to be a typical northern idiom. [22]

In the Ras Shamra texts, El is 'b 'dm, "the father of mankind." [23] CTA, 3 [V AB], B, 8, speaks of 'dm ṣ't špš, "people of the East." [24] The place of man is made clear from a passage in the Aqhat Epic, where Aqhat refuses the offer of 'Anat, with the remark that men and gods are different because men are mortal. [25]

In Arabic only the proper name 'ādama, "Adam," occurs (banū 'ādama, "the people"); besides, 'adam(a) means "skin," as also in Hos. 11:4, according to some scholars. [26]

4. Egyptian has several words for "man," "mankind," [27] e.g., p'.t, "mankind," originally the primitive inhabitants of Egypt; rḫy.t, "people," which is often used of peoples in subordinate positions; and especially rmṯ, which at first designated only the Egyptians as "genuine people," but from the Middle Kingdom on serves as a designation for the class "man." [28] rmṯ and p'.t mean people in contrast to deities and animals.

From the Middle Kingdom on, we often encounter the statement that people

---

15 EnEl VI, 27f.; AOT, 135; Atraḫasis Epic, I, 1ff.

16 Böhl, 33.

17 Gilgamesh Fragment, XI, 202ff., AOT, 194; Etana Myth.

18 Gilg. II; clothes, culture, lines 102-107.

19 § 26, AOT, 291.

20 Ludlul bēl nēmēqi, II, 37; AOT, 275; MDOG, 96 (1965), 51.

21 DISO, 4.

22 M. Dahood, Qoheleth and Northwest Semitic Philology (1962), 34f.

23 CTA, 14 [I K], 36, 136, etc.

24 WUS, 7.

25 CTA, 19 [I D], VI, 35f.

26 KBL, אדם, III; Blachère-Chouémi, I, 63f.; H. Wehr, A Dictionary of Modern Written Arabic (1961), 10.

27 See A. Gardiner, Ancient Egyptian Onomastica, I (1947), 98ff.

28 Morenz, Egyptian Religion, 47ff.; idem, Gott und Mensch, 17.

were generated from the tears of the creator-god, which clearly is based on a wordplay on *rmt,* "man," and *rmy.t,* "tears." Thus, since people were generated before the procreation of the gods, they are also mentioned before them in lists. [29] However, a First Man or Primal Man is unknown in Egyptian literature. There is no place for another "First" beside the Primal (First) God as creator (→ אחד *'echādh*).

Man is a compound that cannot exist without the body; therefore, one tries to preserve the body by embalming. People have the "soul" elements Ka, Ba, and Ach in common with the gods. In this regard there is no fundamental difference between gods and men; the gods are simply more powerful. [30] In Merikare, 132, it even says that people "came forth from his (the god's) limbs." [31]

Both gods and men are subject to the highest god. Er (Re, Amun) gives them light (→ אור *'ôr)* and life; he is concerned for people, who are designated as "cattle of God," i.e., provided for by the divine herdsman, in the well-known passage in Merikare, 130f. [32] Heaven and earth along with everything that lives have been made for people. On the other hand, we read in Amenemope, 18, "God is in his excellence, man in his imperfection"; man "does not know how things will be on the morrow." [33] Proper names emphasize the help of the gods or designate the person wearing the name as "man" of the god, i.e., belonging to him. In the eighteenth dynasty there is even a reference to a "brother of (the goddess) Mut." [34]

5. Etymologically, *'adham* cannot be explained with certainty. F. Delitzsch thought it came from a Semitic root *adāmu,* "to build," to which he traced *admānu,* "building," and *admu,* "child"; [35] but according to contemporary scholars these words should be read *watmānu* and *watmu.* Dillmann enumerates a number of other early attempts to explain the origin of this word. [36] Sayce tried to trace *'adham* back to *Adapa,* [37] and Nöldeke to Arab. *'anām.* [38] Walker cites the Sum. *addamu* and translates "father of man," "father of mankind"; [39] however, the word for "my father" is *a-a-mu.* H. Bauer assumes that the original meaning was "skin." [40] The connection of *'adham* with *'adhom,* "to be red," seems plausible; this has been suggested by C. Brockelmann [41] and J. Pedersen ("... the normal human color which is prominent after washing, thus reddish-

---

[29] So already in Pyr. 1466 b/d, "before heaven, earth, men, gods were generated"; cf. S. Sauneron - J. Yoyotte, *Naissance du monde* (Paris, 1959), 74f.

[30] Sainte-Fare Garnot, 24.

[31] *AOT,* 35.

[32] *AOT,* 35.

[33] *AOT,* 43f.

[34] Sainte-Fare Garnot, 24.

[35] F. Delitzsch, *Prolegomena eines neuen hebr.-aram. Wörterbuchs zum AT* (1886), 103f.

[36] A. Dillmann, *Genesis* (⁶1892), 53f.

[37] A. H. Sayce, *ExpT,* 17 (1906), 416f.; but cf. above, I.2.

[38] *ZDMG,* 40 (1886), 722.

[39] *ZAW,* 74 (1962), 66-68.

[40] *ZA,* 28 (1913), 310f.

[41] *Synt.,* § 11.

brown ... "). [42] The connection with *'adhamah,* "ground, dust," is also clear and is certainly assumed in Gen. 2:7; 3:19. But the fact that in Akkadian this word appears with the meanings "red" and "red soil," but not with the meaning "man," argues against these etymological derivations of *'adham.*

II. Usage in the OT.

1. *'adham* occurs 562 times in the OT. In the earliest traditions of the Pentateuch (J, E) it occurs 48 times, 24 of which are in Genesis 2f. alone (always with the article except in 2:5; we must emend 2:20b; 3:17,21): Yahweh forms the man from dust, makes him a living being *(nephesh chayyah)* by breathing into him the breath of life *(nishmath chayyim),* gives him command and prohibition, has him name the animals, creates the woman from his rib, and punishes him according to his transgression. Gen. 6:3 assumes that Yahweh's *ruach,* "spirit," abides in man; 6:5 and 8:21 call the "imaginations and thoughts" of man's heart evil, and Nu. 16:29 refers to the common death of all men. Ex. 33:20 (no man can see Yahweh and remain alive) and Nu. 23:19 (in his truthfulness and steadfastness God is different from all human nature) mention the divine-human confrontation.

Several times *'adham* appears in construct expressions (sons of men or daughters of men; heart, malice, firstborn of men; and in *pere' 'adham,* "a wild ass of a man," Gen. 16:12). [43]

2. In P (with H), *'adham* appears as a proper name in Gen. 5:1-5, and in addition to this occurs 49 times, 14 of which have to do with the relationship between man and animals.

The universal aspect is clear in Gen. 1:26f., the Flood Narrative, and the Noachic commandments of 9:5f. (cf. Lev. 24:17,21) as well as in Nu. 19:11,13 (contamination by touching a dead body).

P uses the word repeatedly as an indefinite pronoun in the construction *'adham ki,* "when any man" (Lev. 1:2; 13:2).

3. In Deuteronomy and the Deuteronomistic history, the theological emphasis is quite clear in the use of *'adham* (20 times). Dt. 4:32 and 32:8 refer to the creation and separation of men by God; 5:24 to the experience at the mountain of God, according to which God can speak to man without man dying; 8:3 declares that man does not live by bread alone, but by the word of God; 1 S. 16:7, that man looks on the outward appearance, but Yahweh looks on the heart; 1 K. 8:38f., that God knows man and hears his prayer, and according to the parenthesis in 1 K. 8:46, there is no man who does not sin; 1 S. 15:29 repeats the thought of Nu. 23:19.

This literature also uses *'adham* in the law of the devoted thing (killing men,

---

[42] *Berytus,* 6 (1939/1941), 72.
[43] *GK,* § 128 1.

Josh. 11:14); in the polemic against foreign cults, whose gods are the work of men's hands (Dt. 4:28; cf. 2 K. 19:18; Isa. 37:19); and in passages that deal with the removal of human bones (1 K. 13:2; 2 K. 23:14,20).

ha'adham in Dt. 20:19 ("for the men are the trees of the field") is problematic; in any event an interrogative *he* has been misread as an article (see the LXX and Syriac), so that what is affirmed in the present text was originally meant to be negated.

4. The non-Deuteronomistic portions of the Historical Books Joshua, Judges, Samuel, and Kings, contain no statements that are important for a theological understanding of *'adham*. Arba was the greatest man among the Anakim (Josh. 14:15); after the loss of his hair Samson becomes weak like all other men or like anyone else (Jgs. 16:7,11,17; cf. 1 S. 25:29); the inhabitants of Laish had no dealings with men (Jgs. 18:7,28; perhaps *'adham* should here be emended to *'aram,* "the Arameans"; see the LXX I and Syriac). David does not want to fall into the hand of man (2 S. 24:14), and Solomon was wiser than all men (1 K. 5:11[4:31]). "Human strokes" are threatened in 2 S. 7:14; the intrigues and rumors of men are denounced in 1 S. 24:10(9) and 26:19.

"Heart (courage) of man" (1 S. 17:32) and the scarcely intelligible *torath ha'adham,* "human instruction" (2 S. 7:19), should probably be emended. [44]

5. In Isa. 1–39 the word *'adham* occurs 17 times. In 31:3 the difference between God and man is stated quite clearly: "the Egyptians are men, and not God; and their horses are flesh, and not spirit"; in the same pericope it is predicted that Assyria will fall by a "non-man," *lo'-'adham* (31:8). In the other passages threats are predominant: the humiliation of man on the day of Yahweh (2:9,11,17,20,22; 5:15; cf. 13:12; 17:7) and the desertion of the land by man (6:11f.); only the "poor among men" shall exult (29:19). In his prayer, Hezekiah laments that in the underworld he will look upon man no more (38:11).

6. *'adham* occurs ten times in Deutero-Isaiah, three times in the polemic against idolatry in 44:11-15. The creation motif is taken up in 45:12. Israel is not to be afraid of mortal man (51:12); the *'ebhedh* is more unattractive than other men (52:14). 56:2 praises the man who keeps the Sabbath and does no evil, and 58:6 demands the self-humbling of man as true fasting.

The text and meaning of 43:4 ("I give men in return for you...," perhaps to be emended to *'adhamoth;* Volz reads *'alaphim*) and 47:3 (to be emended to *'amar?*) [45] are uncertain.

7. Jeremiah's assessment of man is concentrated in the wisdom saying in 17:5 ("Cursed is the man who trusts in man...") [46] and in the prayer in 10:23 ("the way of man is not in himself...."). [47]

---

44 See H. W. Hertzberg, *I & II Samuel. OTL* (trans. 1964), 144 and 282, on these two passages.
45 See Volz, *KAT,* IX, 36, 82.
46 On the genuineness of this passage, see Rudolph, *HAT,* 12 (³1968), 115.
47 *Ibid.,* 77.

In Jeremiah 'adham occurs 29 times in all. Nine times (usually in threats) it is coupled with → בהמה beḥēmāh, "beast" (7:20; 21:6; 27:5; 31:27; 33:10,12; 36:29; 50:3; 51:62); seven times it is used in oracles concerning regions deserted by men (2:6; 4:25; 32:43; 49:18,33; 50:40; 51:43; of filling Babylon with men: 51:14); three times of making idols (10:14; 16:20; 51:17); twice of the dead bodies of men which will fill the land (9:21[22]; 33:5); and twice in oracles concerning other disastrous fates of men (47:2; 49:15). According to the general scholarly opinion, the statements concerning a man's responsibility for his own sins (31:30) and the Deuteronomistic phrases in 32:19f. are not from Jeremiah himself.

8. The book of Ezekiel contains approximately one fourth of all the occurrences of 'adham in the OT. The prophet, as representative of the creature, is addressed by ben 'adham, "son of man," 93 times: this is correct Hebrew and is not to be explained by linguistic usage in Babylonian or Aramaic.[48] The affinity with H appears in 20:11,13,21: by the observance of Yahweh's ordinances man shall live (cf. Lev. 18:5). The difference between man and God is emphasized in the poem concerning Tyre (28:2,9–'adham in 34:31 is probably a later addition).[49] Mostly eschatological texts announce that men will fill the land (23:42; 36:10,11,12,37,38; cf. 31:14) or that the land will be deserted by men (29:11; 32:13). The vision which Ezekiel saw at his call describes animals in the form of men (1:5,26) with human hands (1:8; cf. 10:8,21) and human faces (1:10; cf. 10:14; 41:19); 19:3,6 speak of man-eating lions (cf. 36:13f.), and 4:12,15 of human dung. Slaves who are sold are called nephesh 'adham (27:13), dead bodies, 'etsem 'adham (39:15), and corpses, meth 'adham (44:25). The expression 'adham ubhehemah, "man and beast," is used seven times, usually in threats of destruction (14:13,17,19,21; 25:13; 29:8; 36:11; cf. 38:20).

9. 'adham occurs in the Minor Prophets 28 times. In Amos it occurs only in the doxology in 4:13: "... who declares to man what is his thought."[50]
In Hosea, the problematic ke-'adham in 6:7 is usually interpreted today as a place name;[51] however, the meanings "like man" or "like Adam" are not excluded. 13:2 (against idolatry) is also disputed.[52] 9:12 (childlessness) and 11:4 ("human cords" or "leather cords") are connected with the Exodus tradition.
Mic. 6:8 states the duty of all mankind. 'adham also occurs in the following passages in Micah: 2:12; 5:6(7) (future abundance of men); 5:4(5) (fighters against Assyria); and 7:2 (none upright among men).
Habakkuk laments the human misery caused by the Chaldeans (subjugation, bloodshed–1:14; 2:8,17). In Zephaniah 'adham appears in threats (1:3,17); in Joel in a call to lament (1:12); in Jonah it occurs in the description of the repentance of men and animals (3:7,8) and in the conclusion concerning the great

[48] Zimmerli, BK, XIII, 70f. → בן bēn.
[49] Ibid., 832.
[50] (?) See H. W. Wolff, BK, XIV/2, 249, 254-56, 264.
[51] Wolff, Hosea (trans. 1974), 105, 121; Rudolph, KAT, XIII, 141f.
[52] Wolff, Hosea, 219, 225; Rudolph, 237f., 242.

number of young innocents in Nineveh (4:11). For Haggai and Zechariah, the distresses that men and beasts suffer are caused by the delay in the work of rebuilding the temple (Hag. 1:11; Zec. 8:10 [twice]); the third night vision of Zechariah announces that in the future there will be a multitude of men and cattle in Jerusalem (Zec. 2:8[4]). In Zec. 11:6 'adham appears in parallelism with "inhabitants of the land"; the doxology in 12:1 praises the One who founded the earth and formed the spirit of man ('adham in 9:1 and 13:5 should probably be emended.)[53]

10. 'adham occurs 62 times in the Psalms. The recurring universalistic expression bene 'adham, "sons of men," is significant[54]: God has created all men (89:48 [47]), given them the earth (115:16), looks down from heaven upon them (14:2; 33:13; 53:3[2]), is terrible in his deeds among them (66:5), must be praised for his wonderful works to men (107 passim; 145:12); he shows his goodness in the sight of men (31:20[19]); they take refuge in the shadow of his wings (36:8 [7]); men are instructed concerning their mortality (49:8[7]);[55] God turns man back to the dust (90:3). 'adham (usually without the article) or ben 'adham (→ בֵּן bēn), "son of man," is used in a similar sense: Yahweh provides man with food (104:14), teaches men knowledge and knows their thoughts (94:10f.); but: What is man? (8:5[4]–ben 'adham; 144:3); only a breath (39:6,12[5,11]), mortal (49:13,21[12,20]; 82:7); his help is vain (56:12[11]; 60:13[11]; 108:13[12]); he is not trustworthy (118:8; 146:3), a liar (116:11). Three times in the Psalms 'adham is connected with → אַשְׁרֵי 'ashrê, "blessed" (32:2; 84:6,13[5,12]), which in other passages is connected with → אִישׁ 'îsh, "man," → גֶּבֶר gebher, "man," or other substantives and statements. Idols are the work of men's hands (115:4; 135:15). Ps. 105:14 uses 'adham as an indefinite pronoun.

11. 'adham appears 27 times in Job. In all these instances, it is connected with man's encounter with God and the universal fate of man (ben 'adham does not occur in Job). God is the watcher of men (7:20), pays attention to people and man(kind), requites man according to his work (34:11,29f.), leads him to knowledge (37:7; 28:28), decides between men (16:21; 21:4), and shows all men his work (36:25); man is born of a woman (14:1) and to trouble (5:7); he can have no recollection of prehistoric time (15:7; 20:4), is like a maggot and a worm (25:6), hides his iniquity (31:33); but the wicked man's portion is misery (20:29; 27:13). 'adham occurs in parallelism with → אֱנוֹשׁ 'enôsh, "man," in 25:6; 36:25 (and probably also in 37:7).[56]

12. The 44 occurrences of 'adham in Proverbs are distributed proportionately throughout the individual collections. Usually 'adham occurs in admonitions or maxims concerning the wise and the foolish, concerning their true and false behavior (concerning the wise in 3:13; 8:34; 12:23,27; 19:11,22; 28:2,14,23;

---

[53] See Horst, HAT, 14 (³1964), 244, 256.
[54] See Kraus, BK, XV, 106f., 264.
[55] On this, see ibid., 366.
[56] See Fohrer, KAT, XVI, 481.

and concerning the wicked in 6:12; 11:7; 15:20; 17:18; 19:3; 20:25; 21:16, 20; 24:30; 27:20; 28:17; 29:23,25). The reputation one has with his fellow men is important (3:4). Proverbs never speaks of Israel or the Israelites. But man's relationship to God is emphasized in this book: man plans his way, but Yahweh controls destiny, which is often incomprehensible to man, and requites him according to his work (12:14; 16:1,9; 20:24,27; 24:12).[57] 'adham occurs three times in makarisms ("Blessed are") (3:13; 8:34; 28:14), twice in the verdict *kesil 'adham,* "foolish man" (15:20; 21:20; see Gen. 16:12).

13. In the 49 occurrences of 'adham (among which *bene 'adham,* "sons of men," occurs 10 times) in Ecclesiastes, the author declares especially the total dependence of man[58]: his fate is determined in advance, he has no opportunity to dispute about it (6:10; 3:19). Diligence and prudence are commendable, but cannot guarantee success and therefore are vanity (1:3; 2:21f.; 6:11; 10:14). Death is the end of everything (7:2,14; 12:5). Life is beyond man's comprehension (3:11; 6:12; 8:17; 9:1,12) and laborious (1:13; 6:7; 8:6; 9:12); the heart of man is full of evil (9:3; cf. 8:9,11). And yet man should enjoy life and delight in everything which God has given (3:13,22; 11:8). The "end" of the whole is: it is proper for each man to fear God and keep his commandments (12:13).

14. In the book of Daniel (where 'adham occurs 4 times), the angel having the appearance of a man (10:16,18), who speaks to the seer with a man's voice (8:16), addresses him as *ben 'adham,* "son of man" (8:17); see under → אֱנוֹשׁ *'enôsh.*

15. 'adham occurs twice in Lamentations: God regards the cause of the oppressed (3:36, where 'adham is in parallelism with *gebher*); his constant sigh is unjustified (3:39).

16. Nehemiah uses 'adham three times as an indefinite (2:10,12; 9:29). In the books of Chronicles (where 'adham appears 10 times), 1 Ch. 29:1 and 2 Ch. 19:6 direct attention away from man to God. 2 Ch. 6:18 contains the words *'eth ha'adham,* "with man" ("will God dwell indeed with man on the earth?"), which are missing in the parallel passage in 1 K. 8:27. 1 Ch. 21:13 repeats 2 S. 24:14, and 2 Ch. 6:36,29,30 repeat 1 K. 8:46,38,39. In 1 Ch. 5:21, the *nephesh 'adham,* "men alive," are captives. In 2 Ch. 32:19 the gods of the heathen are called the work of men's hands, and 1 Ch. 17:17 (like 2 S. 7:19) has an uncertain text (perhaps: "Thou hast been able to find me out better than men").[59]

III. Anthropological and Theological Considerations. The use of the word 'adham in the OT presents one of the strongest evidences for ancient Israelite universalism. In most passages using 'adham, including the earliest texts, it is

---

[57] Cf. Ringgren, *ATD,* XVI/1, 10f.

[58] Cf. Zimmerli, *ATD,* XVI/1, 134-142.

[59] So Rudolph, *HAT,* 21 (1955), 130f.

clear that this word is not intended to refer particularly to Israelites, but to all men. Taking into consideration the number of passages and the most important statements, the most prominent concern with regard to 'adham in the OT is the relationship between God and man; and nowhere is there any reason to doubt that the OT author has the God of Israel in mind; but this is no indication of a particularistic narrowness: it is the Lord and Keeper of all men whom alone and exclusively Israel wishes to confess. Essentially, what the OT says about man is determined by an encounter with and a relationship to God. That this God speaks and acts like a person brings about the living response and action of man. That there is only one God, that he stands behind all events of life and destiny, leads to a constant confrontation between man and God, and prevents all excuses that could be used in the world of polytheism and natural religion. But this does not mean that the Israelite appraisal of man results from mystical speculation about the afterlife. Israel's testimony concerning man was gained from life's experiences and reason and was authenticated in life. Even that which the OT affirms objectively about God and his dealings with man is to be advanced and defined as a phenomenon of the human sphere. Even where mythical traditions about the surrounding world enter into the presentation, as in the pre-history of Genesis, they are made to serve the intention of the Israelite view of man.

The oft repeated assertions that the OT did not intend to give general teachings concerning man, and that the various OT statements about man are inconsistent and should not be placed on the same level, need to be examined and clarified. It is clear that the purpose of the Wisdom Literature is to give instruction concerning the potentialities and limitations of man. But also the Psalms, the Prophets, P, and Deuteronomy intend to give instruction and teaching concerning the true nature of man. When they give this instruction, they want to be understood to say that it was applicable to all men for all time. The OT ideas that the way of man is not in his own power, that he does not live by bread alone but by the word of God, that God requires love and humility, are not limited to a single situation or to a single moment in time. We must reject any suggestion that the witness of a believer in Yahweh would have been essentially different from this at another time and in another situation. The OT writings agree on fundamental ideas concerning man. Of course, it is axiomatic that the language of a literature which came into being during the course of a thousand years was subject to change and did not always remain constant. That the earliest and latest writings of the OT agree so much in their anthropology is unique in the history of ideas.

The following individual characteristics of the OT view of man are most prominent.

(a) Man has a unique position among created beings. The divine breath of life is breathed into him alone; the command and prohibition of God is given to him alone; he has to name the animals, i.e., he is their lord (Gen. 2). He almost has divine position; the earth with all its creatures is subject to him (Ps. 8). God created him in his image (→ צֶלֶם tselem), and gave him dominion (Gen. 1:26-28).

The meaning of the statement that God created man in his image is not absolutely certain. At present, the predominant view is that it refers to man's dominion over the nonhuman world. [60] Like Engnell, [61] Wildberger derives his understanding from the royal ideology. Hornung shows that in Egypt the idea that all men were made in the image of God is found before that of Pharaoh. [62] Stamm [63] and Loretz [64] emphasize the close kindred relationship between God and man, which is comparable to the relationship between a father and his son (Gen. 5:3). In recent years Humbert [65] and Köhler [66] in particular have defended the position that this indicates that God and man are similar in external form. However, a study of the nature of God in P shows that such an interpretation is not admissible. The statement that God created man in his image is reinterpreted theologically when it is declared that man is a creature who "hears the word of God, speaks to God in prayer and obeys him in service." [67] The only certainty here is that the statement ascribes to man an exceptional position. He is the "great exception" among the living creatures; his special position lies in that he has a relationship to God which is peculiar to him alone.

However, the concept of the exceptional position of man is to be derived less certainly from the "principal passages" which are emphasized again and again, often only on the basis of traditional arguments, than from the overall impression made by the entire OT, where God's precepts and commands apply only to man, where the divine revelation is given only to man, where man alone is responsible for his decisions, and where man alone can be sinner or "righteous." [68]

---

[60] Zimmerli, *Menschenbild*, 20; *idem*, *Was ist der Mensch?* 11; Galling, 12; H. Gross, "Die Gottebenbildlichkeit des Menschen," *Lex tua veritas. Festschrift Junker* (1961), 89-111, 98; Wildberger, 259; Safran, 195.

[61] I. Engnell, *SVT*, 3 (1955), 103-119.

[62] Hornung, 136, 147.

[63] J. J. Stamm, "Die Imago-Lehre von K. Barth u. d. at.liche Wissenschaft: 'Antwort'," *Festschrift K. Barth* (1956), 84-98, esp. 96-98.

[64] Loretz, *Gottebenbildlichkeit*, 92.

[65] P. Humbert, *Études sur le récit du paradis . . .* (1940), 153-175.

[66] L. Köhler, *ThZ*, 4 (1948), 16-22; *idem*, *OT Theol* (trans. 1957), n. 114; *idem*, *Hebrew Man*, 31, "upright stature."

[67] F. Horst, "Der Mensch als Ebenbild Gottes," *Gottes Recht* (1961), 222, 234; cf. *In*, 4 (1950), 259-270.

[68] On the idea of man's being made in the image of God, cf. further: D. Barthélemy, *God and His Image. An Outline of Biblical Theology* (trans. 1966); J. Jervell, *Imago Dei. Gen 1, 26f. im Spätjudentum, in der Gnosis und in den paulinischen Briefen. FRLANT*, 76 (1960); F. Michaeli, *Dieu à l'image de l'homme. Étude de la notion anthropomorphique de Dieu dans l'AT* (1950); E. Osterloh, "Die Gottebenbildlichkeit des Menschen. Eine exegetisch-systematische Untersuchung zu Gen 1,27," *ThViat* (1939), 9-32; M. Rehm, *Das Bild Gottes im AT* (1951); L. Scheffczyk, *Der Mensch als Bild Gottes* (1969); E. Schlink, "Die biblische Lehre vom Ebenbild Gottes," *Pro Veritate. Festgabe für L. Jaeger und W. Stählin*, ed. E. Schlink and H. Volk (1963), 1-23; W. H. Schmidt, *Die Schöpfungsgeschichte der Priesterschrift. Zur Überlieferungsgeschichte von Gen 1,1–2,4a. WMANT*, 17 (1964), 127ff.; J. Schreiner, "Die Gottebenbildlichkeit des Menschen in der alttestamentlichen Exegese," *Das Personenverständnis in der Pädagogik und ihren Nachbarwissenschaften*, ed. J. Speck (1967), 50-65; R. Smith, *The Bible Doctrine of Man* (London, 1951); G. Söhngen, "Die biblische Lehre von der Gottebenbildlichkeit des Menschen," *MThZ*, 2 (1951), 52-76.

(b) The OT recognizes man's total dependence with great clarity. Man is a creature of God composed of flesh, soul, and spirit (→ בשׂר *bāśār;* → נפשׁ *nephesh;* → רוח *rûach*). [69] In contrast to man in our day, to the ancient Israelite it was a matter of astonishing reflection that he was brought into being through a mysterious embryonic process separate and apart from his own volition and help, and under conditions which were ordained by a Being wholly other than himself, in which he had no right to participate and against which he had no right of veto. The OT emphasizes throughout that life comes within the limits of birth and death. But man knows that he is dependent not only with regard to the basic structure of human existence, but also with regard to the possibilities which life offers and denies; he is weak and helpless. There is no guarantee that he can determine his own destiny or think that his life will be prosperous by his own efforts and accomplishments. Life has its own laws and an irreversible deterioration. For the believer, however, it is not a series of meaningless accidents, but a divinely determined sequence of events which are full of meaning.

(c) In the OT, man's awareness of his dependence is not to be separated from his consciousness of responsibility. The Creator has a claim on his creatures including or excluding any other claim. The affirmation that man is Yahweh's *'ebhedh,* "servant," involves assuming complete responsibility before him, and not merely partial responsibility before tribe and people. It is true that the ancient Israelite regarded himself as a member of the whole group; [70] but this did not mean that he ceased to be conscious of his own individual personality. The statement, "one man is no man . . . " [71] must be rejected. We need to revise such statements as these which for all practical purposes deny the individualism that existed in ancient Israel, at least in the judicial realm. [72] The life of the individual is a test. God knows and judges each decision of man. For the Israelite, this examination is an essential part of life; in this understanding he arrives at the ultimate goal and fulfilment of life. He knows that he is under obligation to obey, and is prepared to submit to the judgment of the one who sees his thoughts and feelings from every angle and who can call him to give a complete account of his deeds. It is remarkable to see how the different OT texts dealing with this subject witness universally to this way of thinking and acting. The sources which come from the earliest period do not differ from the late legal writings here; the prophets, who denounce the sacrificial cult, are no different from the psalmists or the Chronicler, who lives within the cultic order; the Israelite Wisdom Literature is not at variance with the Apocalyptic.

(d) Man is "sinful"; he does not meet the total requirement but constantly fails. The passages using *'adham,* especially in J and D, are unmistakable on this point. Sin is of irrational power and depth. Thus, when man is said to be → צדיק *tsaddîq,*

---

[69] Cf. esp. D. Lys, *Nephesh* (1959); *Ruach* (1962); *Bâsâr* (1967).
[70] Cf. the works on the concept of "corporate personality," esp. J. de Fraine.
[71] Köhler, *OTTheol,* 129.
[72] See Porter.

"righteous," as in Psalms, Proverbs, and Job, this does not mean that he is sinless, for these books also witness clearly to universal sinfulness (Ps. 51:7[5]; 130:3; 143:2; Prov. 20:9; Job 14:4; 15:15f.; 25:4-6). Calamity is attributed to a person's own guilt, as in the Paradise story the loss of Paradise is attributed to transgression. What J meant by the symbol of eating the fruit is still an open question; but the text makes it plain that he explains the difficulty of man's lot on earth as the direct result of man's guilt. Thus, he has detected in man a fundamental evil, which in his judgment alienates him from God. The change which took place in the time of Solomon (assimilation to the religious environment, adoption of Canaanite techniques and civilization) must have influenced this judgment: the "Fall of Man" is the movement away from the ancient relation to Yahweh, i.e., that of obedience and sonship. [73]

(e) Even after he is driven out of Paradise, man still remains under divine protection. God acts toward man as a father toward his child. [74] This involves a conscious affirmation of life and destiny. It should be observed that this affirmation reflects Israel's understanding of her own destiny: he who ordained it is "gracious, compassionate, and of great goodness." Israel's historical experiences from the ninth century B.C. on, and particularly in the exilic age, were not assimilated to strengthen this confession; on the contrary, they were centuries of immeasurable suffering. Nevertheless, Israel persisted in the belief that the will of the compassionate God would be carried out in the history of the people and in the life of each individual.

Maass

---

[73] Among the more recent works on this subject, cf. U. Bianchi, "Péché original et péché 'antécédent'," *RHR*, 170 (1966), 117-126; A. M. Dubarle, *Le péché original dans l'Écriture* (²1967); M. Guerra Gómez, "La narración del pecado original ... ," *Burgense*, 8 (1967), 9-64; K. Condon, "The Biblical Doctrine of Original Sin," *IrishThQ*, 34 (1967), 20-36; P. Grelot, "Reflexions sur le problème du péché original," *NRTh*, 89 (1967), 337-375, 449-484; J. Gross, *Entstehungsgeschichte des Erbsündendogmas* (1960/1963), 2 vols.; H. Haag, *Biblische Schöpfungslehre und kirchliche Erbsündenlehre. SBS*, 10 (³1967); K. R. Joines, *The Serpent in the OT* (diss., Southern Baptist Theological Seminary, 1967); L. Ligier, *Péché d'Adam et péché du monde* (1960/61), 2 vols.; N. Lohfink, "Genesis iif. als 'Geschichtliche Ätiologie'," *Scholastik*, 38 (1963), 321-334; S. Lyonnet, "Péché Original," *DBS*, 7 (1966), 509-563; G. Quell, "Sin in the OT," *TDNT*, I, 267-286; J. Scharbert, *Prolegomena eines Alttestamentlers zur Erbsündenlehre. QuaestDisp*, 37 (1968); W. Vollborn, "Das Problem des Todes in Genesis 2 und 3," *ThLZ*, 77 (1952), 709-714.

[74] See esp. II.10 above. → אב 'ābh.

┌────────────────┐
│ אֲדָמָה *ʾadhāmāh* │
└────────────────┘

Contents: I. 1. Etymology; 2. Occurrences. II. Usages in the OT Text. *ʾadhamah* As:
1. A Substance; 2. Cultivated Land; 3. Property; 4. Dwelling Place. III. Specific Theological Considerations: 1. Cultic Aspects; 2. Theological-Anthropological Significance;
3. The Land of Israel.

I. 1. *Etymology.* *ʾadhamah* (Syr. *ʾadamtā*, Arab. *ʾadamat*, Nabatean *ʾadhmatah*)
is derived from the root *ʾdm*, "to be red," which also appears in Ugar. *ʾdm*, [1]
Arab. *ʾadima*, Ethiop. *ʾadma*, Akk. *adammu*, and Egyp. *idmy* ("red linen"), [2]
so that *ʾadhamah* is said to mean "red, plowed land," [3] "red earth," [4] or "reddish
gleaming cultivated land containing iron," [5] depending on the impression that it
makes on the eye. [6] Rocks also were "differentiated by color rather than material formation." [7] König suggested that *ʾadhamah* might be derived from Arab.
ʾádama, iunxit, "he has joined," addidit, "he has added." [8] In this case, *ʾadhamah*
would be a covering layer. [9] In the LXX it is translated almost always by *gē,* in
the Targum by *ʾarʿā* and *ʾadhmᵉthā* (5 times), in the Syriac usually by *ʾarʿā,*
but also by *ʾatrā,* "place," and by *ʾadamtā* and *qeṭmā,* "ashes." [10]

───────────────

ʾadhāmāh. A. Amsler, "Adam le terreux dans Genèse 2-4," *RTP,* 38 (1958), 107-112;
Dalman, *AuS,* II; A. Dietrich, *Mutter Erde* (³1925); R. Gradwohl, *Die Farben im AT. Eine
terminologische Studie. BZAW,* 83 (1963); A. de Guglielmo, "The Fertility of the Land in
the Messianic Prophecies," *CBQ,* 19 (1957), 306-311; J. Kelso, *The Ceramic Vocabulary of
the OT* (New Haven, 1948); A. Lefèvre, "Genèse 2,4b-3,24 est-il composite?" *RScR,* 36 (1949),
465-480; J. G. Plöger, *Literarkritische, formgeschichtliche und stilkritische Untersuchungen
zum Deuteronomium. BBB,* 26 (1967), 60-129; G. von Rad, "Verheissenes Land und Jahwes
Land im Hexateuch," *ZDPV,* 66 (1943), 191-204; repr. *ThB,* 8 (²1961), 87-100; L. Rost, "Die
Bezeichnungen für Land und Volk im AT," *Festschrift O. Procksch* (1934), 125-148; repr.
Das kleine Credo und andere Studien zum AT (1965), 76-101; A. W. Schwarzenbach, *Die
geographische Terminologie im Hebräischen des AT* (Leiden, 1954); H. Wildberger, "Israel
und sein Land," *EvTh,* 16 (1956), 404-422.

[1] ? thus *WUS,* Gordon, Driver.
[2] The possible etymological origin of *dam,* "blood," in this root cannot be demonstrated
with certainty; Gradwohl, 4f.
[3] *KBL³,* 15.
[4] Schwarzenbach, 133.
[5] Galling, *BRL,* 151; Levy, *WTM,* I, 29.
[6] *AuS,* I, 233; II, 26-28.
[7] Philby, *Heart of Arabia,* I (1922), 26; cf. Josephus *Ant.* i.1.2; *ʾodhem,* "ruby," Ex.
28:17; Ezk. 28:13.
[8] E. König, *Hebräisches und aramäisches Wörterbuch zum AT* (1910), 5.
[9] Similarly ("Haut") *BLe,* § 61n III.
[10] Schwarzenbach, 136.

2. *Occurrences.* '*adhamah* occurs 221 times in the OT.[11] The plural '*adhamoth* is found only in Ps. 49:12 (Eng. v. 11). We also call attention to six conjectural readings, some of which are uncertain: in Isa. 43:4; Ps. 76:11(10); Prov. 30:14 read '*adhamah* or '*adhamoth*, "land, lands," instead of '*adham*, "man"; in Mic. 5:4(5) read *be'adhmathenu*, "on our land," instead of *be'armenothenu*, "in our palaces"; in Zec. 13:5 read '*adhamah qinyani*, "the land has been my possession," instead of '*adham hiqnani*, "(the) man possessed me"; and in Jer. 32:20 read with the LXX *kaí en toís gēgenési(n)*, "and in the earth-born ones," instead of *ubha'adham*, "and among men." The text of Isa. 15:9 is obscure; read with Driver '*emah*, "terror." [12]

In Josh. 19:36, '*adhamah* is the name of a place belonging to the tribe of Naphtali, and is probably identical with the modern Ḥaǧar ed-Damm, "bloodstone." But it is not very likely that '*adhmah* in 1 K. 7:46; 2 Ch. 4:17 is to be identified with '*adham* (the modern Tell ed-Dâmiyeh; cf. Josh. 3:16), and thus that the original meaning of '*adhamah* is preserved here as "in (the) earth pit" or "in (the) earthen mold." [13]

We may define '*adhamah* more precisely by studying its etymology, the various contexts in which it appears, and words or phrases which have the same meaning in synonymous parallelism or the opposite meaning in antithetical parallelism. We may also study adjectives which are used with '*adhamah: tobhah*, "good" (Josh. 23:13,15; 1 K. 14:15), *teme'ah*, "unclean" (Am. 7:17), *shemenah*, "rich" (Neh. 9:25); demonstrative pronouns (Gen. 28:15; Josh. 23:13,15; 1 K. 14:15), pronominal suffixes, genitival combinations, in which '*adhamah* functions as a *nomen regens* for Egypt (Gen. 47:20,26), Israel (only in Ezk.–17 times), Judah (Isa. 19:17), *qodhesh*, "holiness" (Ex. 3:5), *haqqodhesh*, "holy" (Zec. 2:16[12]), Yahweh (Isa. 14:2), '*ammi*, "my people" (Isa. 32:13), *hakkohanim*, "priests" (Gen. 47:22,26), *nekhar*, "foreign" (Ps. 137:4), and '*aphar*, "dust" (Dnl. 12:2), or as a *nomen rectum* of '*obhedhe*, "till" (Isa. 30:24), *peri*, "fruit" (Gen. 4:3; Dt. 7:13; etc.), *pene*, "face" (Gen. 4:14; 6:1,7; etc.), *remes*, "creeping thing" (Gen. 6:20; Hos. 2:20[18]), '*ish*, "man" (Gen. 9:20), *ma'sar*, "tithes" (Neh. 10:38[37]), '*abhodhath*, "till" (1 Ch. 27:26), *kol mishpechoth*, "all the families" (Gen. 12:3; 28:14; Am. 3:2), *tsemach*, "that which grows" (Gen. 19:25), *mizbach*, "altar" (Ex. 20:24), *bikkure*, "firstfruits" (Ex. 23:19; 34:26; Neh. 10:36[35]), *she'erith*, "remnant" (Isa. 15:9), *malkhe*, "kings" (Isa. 24:21), *tebhu'ath*, "produce" (Isa. 30:23), *charse*, "vessels" (Isa. 45:9), and relative clauses, which are particularly numerous in Deuteronomy and D (Dt. 4:40; 5:16; 7:13; 11:9,21; 21:1,23; etc.).

'*adhamah* is often connected with the prepositions '*al* (48 times), '*el* (19 times), and *me'al* (17 times) (cf. also '*al pene ha-* 18 times, and *me'al pene ha-* 13 times), but seldom with *min* (9 times), *le* (4 times), *be* (twice), and *ba'abhur* (once).

---

[11] G. Lisowsky, *Kondordanz zum hebräischen AT* ([2]1966), 24f.
[12] *Festschrift W. Rudolph* (1961), 135.
[13] Noth, *BK*, IX, 164. Cf. *BRL*, 379-381; *BHHW*, I, 570f.; Ottosson, *Gilead* (Lund, 1969), 209f.

II. Usages in the OT Text. Beginning with its original meaning (I.1), *'adhamah* has taken on various nuances of meaning.

1. *'adhamah As a Substance.* (a) As a substance, *'adhamah* means reddish-brown *loose earth* (humus), which from time to time is dry, but is capable of absorbing water, as distinct from "stones" *('abhanim,* Ex. 20:24f.; cf. 2 K. 3:19-25; Isa. 5:2) and conceptually from → עפר *'āphār,* "dust" (which occurs 108 times in the OT, of which it is in parallelism with *'adhamah* in Gen. 3:19; Job 5:6; cf. Isa. 29:4; Job 14:8).[14]

Like dust (Josh. 7:6; Ezk. 27:30; Lam. 2:10; cf. Job 2:12; 16:15) and ashes (2 S. 13:19; Est. 4:1), *'adhamah* was sprinkled on the head (1 S. 4:12; 2 S. 1:2; 15:32; Neh. 9:1) as a sign of mourning, self-abasement, and humility.[15] The original apotropaic (protection from demons by disfigurement) and magical (union with the lot of the dead) rite is adopted, preserved, and at the same time eliminated in traditional usage. It could remind the Israelite of his own nothingness (dust and ashes! Gen. 2:7; 3:19; 18:27; Sir. 10:9; Isa. 26:19; Job 20:11; 21:26; Ps. 22:30[29]), and be a sign of humble submission to divine providence.[16]

(b) Without distinguishing it in meaning from clay as a raw material (cf. Isa. 30:14; Ps. 22:16[15]; Prov. 26:23; Job 2:8; 41:22[30]), *'adhamah* as dry soil[17] is used in the manufacture of earthen vessels (Isa. 45:9) and as molds in the manufacture of metals (1 K. 7:46; 2 Ch. 4:17).[18]

(c) The *'adhamah* forms a cohesive, durable surface area. From it the snare springs up (Am. 3:5), upon it stand the waters of the flood (Gen. 8:8,13). It opens its mouth (Gen. 4:11; Nu. 16:30) like a wild animal, "is split asunder" *(baqa'),* "swallows" (→ בלע *bāla')* the company of Korah, and closes over them again (Nu. 16:30-34; par. *'erets).*

The blood of the innocent who is slain cries out from the ground (Gen. 4:10) until it is covered with dirt (Gen. 37:26; Isa. 26:21; Ezk. 24:7f.; Job 16:18), or until the vengeance is executed.[19]

(d) On *'adhamah* as matter in the creation, see III.2.

2. *'adhamah As Cultivated Land.* (a) As productive humus, *'adhamah* is arable land that is to be cultivated by → אדם *'ādham,* "man" (→ עבד *'ābhadh,* "to till," Gen. 2:5; 3:23; 4:2,12; 9:20; 47:23; 2 S. 9:10; Zec. 13:5; 1 Ch. 27:26), and

---

[14] Essentially *'aphar* is often the same as *'adhamah,* G. Fohrer, *KAT,* XVI (1963), 319f.

[15] E. Kutsch, "'Trauerbräuche' und 'Selbstminderungsriten' im AT," *ThSt,* 78 (1965), 25-42.

[16] P. Heinisch, *Die Trauergebräuche bei den Israeliten. BZfr,* 13/7-8 (1931), esp. § 3, 33-39.

[17] Kelso, § 2.

[18] On Ex. 20:24, the altar made out of *'adhamah,* see III.1.c.

[19] Cf. E. Merz, *Die Blutrache bei den Israeliten. BWAT,* 20 (1916), 50.

is synonymous with *sadheh*, "field" (Gen. 47:20-24; Dt. 21:1; cf. Joel 1:10 with
2:21). It is to be distinguished from → מדבר *midhbār*, "wilderness, desert," and
→ שממה *sheّmāmāh*, "devastation, waste," as land without seed and inhabitant
(Isa. 1:7; 6:11; Jer. 2:2,6). It yields *(nathan)* or brings forth *(yatsa'* in the hiphil,
Hag. 1:11; cf. *tsamach*, "sprout," Job 5:6), → כח *kōach*, "strength" (Gen. 4:12),
tsemach, "growth" (Gen. 19:25), *peri*, "fruit" (Gen. 4:3; Dt. 7:13; 26:2,10; 28:4,
11,18,33,42,51; 30:9; Jer. 7:20; Mal. 3:11; Ps. 105:35), *yebhul*, "produce, increase" (Lev. 26:4,20; Dt. 11:17), and *tebhu'ah*, "produce" (Isa. 30:23), which
the Deuteronomist indicates by the formula "grain, wine, and oil." According
to Gen. 2:9, the *'adhamah*, activated by Yahweh, has the potential power to
make *kol 'ets*, "every tree," grow. It is certainly true that individual elements
of the older and more widespread chthonic myths concerning "Mother Earth"
have been preserved here by tradition, but they have also been reinterpreted in
light of Yahwistic faith.

(b) In contrast with the shepherd *(ro'eh)*, the peasant farmer *('obhedh 'a-
dhamah*, "tiller of the ground," Gen. 4:2; *'ish ha'adhamah*, "tiller of the soil,"
lit. "man of the ground," 9:20; *'ish 'obhedh 'adhamah*, "tiller of the soil," lit.
"a man tilling the ground," Zec. 13:5) is connected with the cultivated land in
the closest possible way.

(c) The cultivation of the grapevine is also a part of the cultivation of the
land (Gen. 9:20). [20] Isa. 28:24 gives a detailed description of how the field was
cultivated (see further Gen. 47:23; Isa. 30:23). Fertilizing with manure was not
unknown (Jer. 8:2; 9:21[22]; 16:4; 25:33; Ps. 83:11[10]). Foreign and domestic
workers (Gen. 5:29; 2 S. 9:10), oxen and asses (Isa. 30:24), helped with the work
in the field.

(d) Practical experience teaches that diligence leads to prosperity. "He who
tills his land will have plenty of bread" (Prov. 12:11; 28:19; cf. 24:27,30-34).
But to diligence and to the richness of the land *(shemenah*, "rich," Neh. 9:25;
cf. *tobhah*, "good," Josh. 23:13,15; 1 K. 14:15) water must be added at the right
time and in sufficient amounts in the form of dew (cf. 2 S. 17:12) and rain (1 K.
17:14; 18:1; Isa. 30:23), and Yahweh must add his blessing (Dt. 7:13; 11:17;
28:4,11; 30:9), in order for the crops to grow and increase. If no rain falls, the
peasant farmer is anxious because of the *'adhamah* (Jer. 14:4).

(e) Earthquakes *(haphakh*, "overthrow," Gen. 19:25), "droughts" (Hag. 1:11),
enemy conquerors (Isa. 1:7; Dt. 28:33,51), locusts (Dt. 28:42; Ps. 105:35; cf.
Mal. 3:11), Yahweh's curse (Dt. 28:18) and wrath (Jer. 7:20) destroy the fruit
of the *'adhamah*, and thus the land lies waste like a wilderness (Isa. 6:11) and
yields only thorns and thistles (32:13; cf. Gen. 3:18). Dried up, the *'adhamah*
"mourns" (→ אבל *'ābhal*, Joel 1:10; cf. Isa. 24:4; 33:9; Jer. 12:4; 23:10; Hos.
4:3; Am. 1:2), i.e., the land lies neglected and devastated. There is no reminis-

---

[20] *AuS*, II, 130-218; J. Aro, "Gemeinsemitische Ackerbauterminologie," *ZDMG*, 113
(1963/64), 471-480.

cence of a personification of the land here.[21] Conversely, the *ʾadhamah* "rejoices" (→ שמח *śāmach*, → גיל *gîl*, Joel 2:21) because of the rich harvest which God has given.

3. *ʾadhamah As Property.* Although the cultivated land which assures a means of livelihood is to be understood as "a unity extending across the borders of the nations"[22] (cf. the expressions *kol mishpechoth haʾadhamah*, "all the families of the earth," Gen. 12:3; 28:14; and *kol haʿam* [read *haʿammim*] *ʾasher ʿal pene haʾadhamah*, "all the people [peoples] that are upon the face of the earth," Ex. 33:16; Dt. 7:6; 14:2; similarly Isa. 23:17; 24:21; Jer. 25:26), *ʾadhamah* can be used for some portion of this unity and refer to individuals, to groups, or to one nation in a particular relation.[23] For a large portion of the population, possession of property is the basis of economic existence. As the possession of livestock is essential to the nomad (Gen. 13:2; 30:43; 46:32; Dt. 3:19; Job 1:3), so property is essential to the agriculturalist (cf. → נחלה *nachᵃlāh*, "inheritance," Nu. 35:2; 1 K. 21:3; *chelqath hassadheh*, "parcel of land," Ruth 4:3).

ʾadhamah is property that could be "sold" (*makhar*, Gen. 47:20) in hard times and "bought" (→קנה *qānāh*, 47:19,20,23) by Joseph from the "people of Egypt" (→ עם *ʿam* in the sense of "owner," 47:21,23; cf. 23:7,11,13; 2 S. 16:18; 2 K. 11:18-20; 14:21; 23:30-35) for the Pharaoh, while the priestly property was excluded (Gen. 47:22,26; cf. Diodorus i.73; Herodotus ii.168). We know that property was taken away from some and given to others in the time of Antiochus IV Epiphanes, who "divided" (→חלק *chalaq*, "divide," Dnl. 11:39, cf. v. 24) *ʾadhamah* to his favorites. One way a person could legally become the owner of a piece of property was by calling that property by his name (Ps. 49:12[11]; cf. 2 S. 12:28; Isa. 4:1).[24] Am. 7:17 speaks of parcelling the land by line. 1 Ch. 27:26,31 mentions stewards of the royal property in the time of David.[25] By way of contrast, the Rechabites, as foreigners, owned no property in the *ʾadhamah* (Jer. 35:7; on this idea cf. 1 Ch. 29:15; Ps. 39:13[12]; 119:19).

As *property*, *ʾadhamah* is the available, defined (cf. the warnings against removing the landmark, i.e., changing the property line, Dt. 19:14; 27:17; Prov. 22:28; Job 24:2; Hos. 5:10) portion of the entire cultivated land (as distinguished from the wilderness), which could be acquired by purchase, donation, or military conquest (inheritance, redemption, latifundium economics, the Year of Jubilee, the Sabbatical Year, etc., are not expressly mentioned in connection with *ʾadhamah*) or could be claimed legally by one calling his name over it. → ארץ *ʾerets*, → חבל *chebhel*, → חלק *chēleq*, → נחלה *nachᵃlāh*, → ירש *yārash*, → סגלה *sᵉghullāh*, → קנין *qinyān*.

The meaning of Job 31:38, where the *ʾadhamah* bursts out with accusing cries for help, is disputed. Many commentators think that the lament of the land is

---

[21] J. Scharbert, *Der Schmerz im AT. BBB,* 8 (1955), 50.

[22] Rost, 78.

[23] *Ibid.,* 94, notes 27-29.

[24] K. Galling, "Die Ausrufung des Namens als Rechtsakt in Israel," *ThLZ,* 81 (1956), 65-70.

[25] De Vaux, *AncIsr,* 125ff. Cf. also the conjecture on Zec. 13:5.

connected with a crime adhering to the property, as e.g., exploiting farm laborers, making profits by illegal means, or even killing the previous owner. Fohrer thinks it refers to "exhaustion of the soil and exploiting the land in one's own interest." If one accepts this interpretation, "the term *'adhamah* would indicate that all of his (Job's) cultivated land is meant, and not just a portion of it." [26]

4. *'adhamah As Dwelling Place.* (a) The productive cultivated land is the *dwelling place of man.* While the wilderness, "where no man dwells" (Jer. 2:6; Job 38:26; cf. Isa. 6:11; Jer. 9:1,11[2,12]), is a place where people only march through, and the pastureland is changed according to a fixed temporal rhythm, [27] the *'adhamah* presents a basis for permanent residence.

On it dwell "all men" (Gen. 6:1,7; Nu. 12:3), "all peoples" (*kol ha'ammim,* Dt. 7:6; 14:2; Ex. 33:16–singular with the meaning "each people, all people"; the LXX, Syriac, and Vulgate also read *'ammim*), "all families" (*kol mishpechoth,* Gen. 12:3; 28:14; Am. 3:2), "all kings" (Isa. 24:21) and "kingdoms" (Isa 23:17; Jer. 25:26), and all Israel's neighbors (Jer. 12:14). The dwelling place of "all peoples" does not mean the whole world here, but the land on Israel's horizon. [28]

(b) Although *'adhamah* is connected more intimately with a people or with several tribes by genitival combinations, pronominal suffixes, or relative clauses (see I.2), it never has a *political meaning,* because the territories of a state can include portions of the wilderness and of the *'adhamah,* but *'adhamah* means only the productive cultivated land of a state. Often, *'adhamah* probably comes close to the emotion-filled idea of "home." [29]

As we analyze specific texts, we find that in Gen. 47:20,26 "the land of Egypt" is property. *'adhmath yisra'el,* "the land of Israel," which like *hare yisra'el,* "the mountains of Israel," occurs only in Ezekiel (17 times; *'adhmath yehudhah,* "the land of Judah," occurs in Isa. 19:17), means more than a geographical, political territory. Ezekiel's picture of the future is "not that of a political kingdom, but of a religious community." [30] "Land of Israel" sums up in a single expression the qualification of the incomparable land given by Yahweh, which is laid down especially in Deuteronomy (→ אֶרֶץ *'erets*). [31] "The soil of my people" in Isa. 32:13 is the farming land. When *'adhamah* appears with suffixes in the Pentateuch (Ex. 23:19; 34:26; Dt. 7:13; 28:4,11,18,33,42,51; 30:9; cf. also Neh. 10:36[35]; Ps. 105:35), it is always connected with the "fruit of the ground" except in Dt. 12:19; 29:27(28); 32:43. The passages in which the *'adhamah* has pronominal suffixes, referring to all Israel (Dt. 12:19; 29:27[28]; 32:43), Judah

---

[26] G. Fohrer, *KAT,* XVI, 411.

[27] L. Rost, "Weidewechsel und altisraelitischer Festkalendar," *ZDPV,* 66 (1943), 205-215; Dalman, *AuS,* VI (1939), 204-213.

[28] H. Wildberger, *JHWHs Eigentumsvolk. AThANT,* 37 (1960), 77.

[29] Rost, 78-80.

[30] *Ibid.,* 78.

[31] Cf. Zimmerli, *BK,* XIII, 146-48, 168f.

(2 K.25:21=Jer. 52:27; Isa. 1:7; Jer. 27:10; 42:12; Ezk. 36:24; 37:14; Jonah 4:2), Northern Israel (2 K. 17:23; Am. 5:2; 7:11,17; 9:15), Israel=Judah (Isa. 14:1; Jer. 16:15; 23:8; Ezk. 28:25; 34:13,27; 36:17; 37:21; 39:26,28), the community after the exile (Neh. 10:36,38[35,37]), Egypt (Ps. 105:35), the Canaanites (Lev. 20:24), the nations who were Israel's neighbors (Jer. 12:14), the Seleucid kingdom (Dnl. 11:9), or any subject people (Jer. 27:11), are to be understood as referring to one's own land (one's fatherland). The passages in which 'adhamah is defined more precisely by relative clauses, all of which refer to all Israel except for Ex. 8:17(22) (the land of Egypt), Isa. 7:16 (the land of the kings of Aram and Northern Israel), [32] and Jer. 35:7 (the Rechabites), describe the land as the basis for subsistence, not as a territory of the state.

(c) To be "cursed" (→ ארר 'ārar, Gen. 4:11) and "driven away" (→ גרשׁ gārash, Gen. 4:14) from one's dwelling place (the ground) is equivalent to being separated from the human community. Gunkel points out "that he who goes away from the land thereby separates himself from Yahweh's presence," [33] because outside Canaan other powers rule (1 S. 26:19; Jonah 1:3; 1 K. 20:23; 2 K. 17:26; and esp. Lev. 16:7-10; 2 K. 5:17f.).

To be blotted out (machah, Gen. 6:7; 7:4,23; hishmidh, 1 S. 20:15; 2 S. 14:7; 1 K. 13:34; shalach, Jer. 28:16; 'asaph, Zeph. 1:2; karath, Zeph. 1:3) from (me'al) the 'adhamah means death and complete destruction. On the other hand, "life" means to be on the 'adhamah (Ex. 20:12; Dt. 4:40; 30:20).

(d) Just as it is the dwelling place of man, the 'adhamah is also the *domain in which animals live*.

The following are mentioned in connection with 'adhamah: small fauna (remes, Gen. 1:25; 6:20; 7:8; 9:2; Lev. 20:25; Dt. 4:18; Ezk. 38:20; Hos. 2:20[18]), flies (Ex. 8:17[22]; 10:6), locusts (Dt. 28:42; Mal. 3:11; Ps. 105:35), small (Dt. 7:13) and large livestock (Jer. 7:20), oxen and asses (Isa. 30:24), and mules (2 K. 5:17).

(e) The dead sleep in the 'adhmath → עפר 'āphār, "the dust of the earth" (Dnl. 12:2; Bab. bīt epri), [34] which denotes either the "Underworld" [35] or the earth as the substance in which the dead are bedded down. [36]

III. Specific Theological Considerations.

1. *Cultic Aspects.* (a) Cultically, "the holy land" ('adhmath [haq]qodhesh, Ex. 3:5; Zec. 2:16[12]; cf. Josh. 5:15) is distinguished from "unclean land" ('adhamah teme'ah, Am. 7:17). Cultic purity is threatened by not burying a

---

[32] According to R. Kilian (*Die Verheissung Immanuels Jes 7,14. SBS,* 35 [1968], 41-46) Isa. 7:16 is a later addition.

[33] *GHK,* I/1 (⁷1966), 45.

[34] K. Tallqvist, *Sum.-akk. Namen der Totenwelt* (1934), 37.

[35] N. H. Ridderbos, *OTS,* 5 (1948), 177.

[36] Fohrer, *KAT,* XVI, 319f.

slain person properly (Dt. 21:1-8), [37] and is destroyed by sinful conduct (Ezk. 36:17; cf. Lev. 18:28). A foreign land ('adhmath → נכר nēkhār, Ps. 137:4) is the same as an unclean land. In it no native cultic songs will be sung. Only "Yahweh's land" is holy (Isa. 14:2).

(b) Naaman asks for 'adhamah from Israel in order that he might sacrifice to Yahweh on it in his own native land (2 K. 5:17), because in his view the influence of a god is limited to his land (cf. 1 S. 26:19; 1 K. 20:23; 2 K. 17:26), and thus Yahweh could be worshipped only on Israelite soil. But cf. Jer. 29:7-14.

(c) In Ex. 20:24, 'adhamah (air-dried lumps of earth) is the material used for making an altar (in contrast to mizbach 'abhanim, "an altar of stone," Ex. 20:25). No explanation of this ancient law handed down in the Book of the Covenant, which assumes a seminomadic or (because of 'adhamah) settled way of life, is ever given in biblical texts, and therefore it remains hypothetical. E. Robertson sees here a reference to the brief durability of the altar, [38] I. Oppelt to the author's high regard for the land, [39] and H. Holzinger to the relationship of joint responsibility between the deity and the land on which he was worshipped. [40] There may be a connection with the cult of chthonic numina here, but this cannot be proved. [41]

(d) In harmony with the relationship between cult and culture, the farmer brings an offering of the fruit of the ground (Gen. 4:3).
Grateful appreciation for the fertility given by Yahweh, not by Baal, through the offering of the → ראשית rē'shîth, "first," the → בכורים bikkûrîm, "firstfruits," or the re'shith bikkurim, "first of the firstfruits" (Ex. 23:19; 34:26; Dt. 26:1-15; cf. Lev. 19:24; 23:9-14,15-20; Nu. 15:17-21; 18:12f.; Neh. 10:36[37])—exchanging the presumably original magical concept of the sacrifice of the firstborn for the new concept of gratitude [42]—and prayer for Yahweh to bless the ground (Dt. 26:15), along with strict obedience to the law, guarantee the reward for all labor.

2. *Theological-Anthropological Significance.* (a) Men and animals (Gen. 2:7,19; cf. Isa. 64:7[8]; Job 4:19; 10:9; 33:6), which together are called *kol hayequm*, "every living thing" (Gen. 7:4,23; cf. Dt. 11:6), are formed *(yatsar)* concretely by Yahweh from the 'adhamah. From a literary historical point of view, the fact that 'aphar and 'adhamah are parallel in Gen. 2:7 indicates origi-

---

[37] Plöger, 97-100.
[38] *JJS*, 1 (1948), 12-21.
[39] *RAC*, V, 1116.
[40] *KHC*, II, 80.
[41] On the altar of earth at Shechem, see Galling, *BRL*, 14; *RAC*, I, 331. On altars of earth that have been found outside Israel (the *arae gramineae* or *cespitiae* of the Italians, which were preserved by the Romans esp. in the service of rural deities), see Reisch, *PW*, I/2 (1894), 1670f.; Ziehen, *RAC*, I, 310f.
[42] Wildberger, 411.

nally different strata of the Paradise narrative [43] pertaining to the way in which the weakness of man was depicted (Gen. 3:19; 18:27; Ps. 103:14; Job 30:19).

(b) Origin, life, and destiny connect the → אדם 'ādhām, "man," [44] with the 'adhamah. However, the 'adhamah is cursed because of the sin of man (Gen. 3:17-19), so that the original solidarity gives way to an alienation between man and the elementary basis of his existence. [45] According to the Yahwistic version, man's originally easy work for food is replaced by hard labor (cf. Gen. 2:7,15 with 3:23). The land lost its "original fertility." [46] Thorns and thistles impede the productivity of the land (3:18). After the toil of life, the 'adham returns (shubh) to 'adhamah out of which he was taken (laqach), for he is → עפר 'aphār (3:19; Ps. 104:29; cf. Dnl. 12:2). The same fate also awaits the most powerful of men (Ps. 146:4; Eccl. 3:20).

(c) Gen. 4 describes a punishment even more severe than that imposed in 3:17-19. One who kills his own brother is banished from the ground, which opens its mouth to drink his brother's (→ אח 'ach) blood (4:11f.). The 'adhamah completely refuses to yield its strength to him (4:12). The growing wickedness of man (see 2:4b–3:24; 4:1-16,17-24; 6:1-4) leads to the decision of Yahweh (stated anthropopathically) to destroy everything which he created from the 'adhamah except Noah (6:5-8). However, in the new period of salvation history, Yahweh, because of his compassion on man in his moral weakness, restricts his punitive holiness (8:21). The toil of work is relieved by Noah (5:29), because as an 'ish ha'adhamah, "man of the ground" (RSV, "tiller of the soil"), he is the first to plant a vineyard (9:20).

3. *The Land of Israel.* (a) Outside the Primitive History, the 'adhamah motif is quite relevant for the Deuteronomistic conception of a pragmatic theological history connected with the tradition of Israel's election. Israel does not possess the 'adhamah as a natural gift by virtue of a sequence of historical events. While other nations may boast of their permanent possession of land (Mesha Inscription, *KAI,* 181.10: "The people of Gad have lived in the land of Ataroth since the beginning of time"), Israel owes its land to Yahweh, whose guidance in salvation history reaches its climax in the gift of the land (Am. 2:10; 3:2). Deuteronomy and the Deuteronomistic history never tire of repeating this idea. [47] Before they were settled in Canaan, the clans and tribes of Israel had no land (Dt. 26:5); but Yahweh "swore" (→ נשבע nishba', Nu. 11:12; 32:11; Dt. 11:9,21; 28:11; 31:7)[48] to the fathers that he would give them the 'adhamah as a place to live and as a basis for existence. At the time of the conquest, as the only possessor ("Yahweh's

---

[43] Gunkel, *GHK,* I/1, 6, 26; J. Begrich, *ThB,* 21 (1964), 19; W. Fuss, *Die sog. Paradieserzählung* (1968), 25; etc.

[44] Amsler, 108f.; E. Lussier, "Adam in Gen. 1,1-4,24," *CBQ,* 18 (1956), 137-39.

[45] G. von Rad, *Genesis. OTL* (trans. 1961), 91.

[46] Guglielmo, 308.

[47] On the Deuteronomistic redaction of Am. 2:10-12, see W. H. Schmidt, *ZAW,* 77 (1965), 178-183.

[48] Plöger, 63-79; N. Lohfink, *Die Landverheissung als Eid. SBS,* 28 (1967).

land" occurs only in Isa. 14:2; cf. 2 Ch. 7:20; the obscure text in Dt. 32:43 suggests a similar interpretation; cf. Lev. 25:23) Yahweh "gives" (→ נתן nāthan– Ex. 20:12; Lev. 20:24; Dt. 11:9; 21:1; 26:15; 1 K. 9:7 = 2 Ch. 7:20; 1 K. 14:15; 2 K. 21:8; Jer. 24:10; 25:5; 35:15; Ezk. 28:25; cf. 2 Ch. 33:8) the land in guileless, free grace. Thus, Israel takes possession of it (→ ירש yārash, Lev. 20:23-25; Dt. 30:18; 31:13; 32:47) as its land (Dt. 7:13; 21:23) and as an inheritance (→ נחלה nachªlāh) after the divinely effected expulsion of its inhabitants. The OT describes the conquest as a united effort of Yahweh and Israel: Yahweh brings Israel into the land (Dt. 31:20), and Israel goes over the Jordan (31:13; 32:47). There Israel is said to enjoy the blessings of the rich (Neh. 9:25) and good (Josh. 23:13,15; 1 K. 14:15) land, so that Dt. 31:20 can even speak of the 'adhamah flowing with milk and honey.[49] Israel experiences Yahweh's faithfulness to a word which he gave under oath when they receive the land which he swore to their fathers (Josh. 21:45). The eschatological gift of salvation is actualized for each new generation by the proclamation in the cult and the family; cf. especially the prayer offered when the firstfruits are offered: "I declare *this day* to the Lord your God that *I* have come into the land."

(b) The land promise, which originally was given unconditionally, is understood conditionally in the theology of the Deuteronomistic history. The Deuteronomist had to interpret this promise in light of the fact that after it had been fulfilled temporarily, Yahweh's people lost the land when they were carried into exile. They kept Israel's hope alive in the integrity of this promise by maintaining from a historico-theological perspective that the land would be restored to God's people if they would return to him. The promise of the land and the gift of the land are inseparably related to obedience or disobedience to Yahweh's righteous will. Therefore, none who has not obeyed Yahweh completely during the march through the wilderness is allowed to see the land (Nu. 32:11). Although Yahweh intends to give the land to Israel "for ever" (*kol hayyamim*, Dt. 4:40; cf. Jer. 25:5), they can actually live a long and happy life on the 'adhamah ('arakh yamim, Dt. 4:40; 5:16; 11:9; 25:15; 30:18,20; 32:47; *rabhah yamim*, 11:21) only if all of them ("even their children," 31:13) continually obey ("all the days that they live upon the 'adhamah," 4:10; 12:1; 31:13; similarly 12:19; cf. 1 K. 8:40; 2 Ch. 6:31) all the commandments (Lev. 26). In the parenetic expansions of Deuteronomy, the promise of the 'adhamah appears specifically in the commandment concerning honoring one's parents (Ex. 20:12; Dt. 5:16) and in the law concerning just measures and weights (Dt. 25:13-16) as a motivation for complete obedience to Yahweh (see also 21:22f.; 26:1-11). The choosing of "life" means that God's people will continue to dwell in the land (30:20). In a specific historical situation, surrender to a foreign conqueror may mean that Israel will be allowed to stay in their native land, while rebellion against this conqueror may mean that they will lose their 'adhamah (Jer. 27:10f.).

---

[49] In all other passages where this expression occurs, 'erets alone is used; even some mss. of Dt. 31:20 have 'erets; on this stereotyped formula with 'erets and 'adhamah, see Plöger, 124-26.

The many admonitions to keep the law and the urgent warnings against transgressing any form of it originate out of a concern to preserve the land as the
greatest possession in salvation (which indicates that the hope of a resurrection
was yet to be fully developed).

When the Israelites were unfaithful or disobedient, i.e., when they went after
foreign gods, Yahweh reacted by destroying them from off the ʾadhamah (→ אבד
ʾābhadh, "perish," Josh. 23:13; → גלה gālāh, "remove, go into exile," 2 K. 17:23;
25:21; Jer. 52:27; Am. 7:11,17; hishmidh, "destroy," Dt. 6:15; Josh. 23:15; 1 K.
13:34; Am. 9:8; → כלה kālāh, "consume," Ex. 32:12; Dt. 28:21; → כרת kārath,
"cut off," 1 K. 9:7; → נוד nûdh, "wander," 2 K. 21:8; nasach, "pluck off," Dt.
28:63; Sir. 48:15; nathash, "uproot," Dt. 29:27[28]; 1 K. 14:15; Jer. 12:14f.;
2 Ch. 7:20; → סור sûr, "remove," 2 Ch. 33:8; → תמם tāmam, "utterly destroy,"
Jer. 24:10).

The threats of calamity are fulfilled by devastating the land (Isa. 6:11; Joel
1:10) and by carrying a portion of the people into exile (Am. 7:11,17; Jer. 35:15-
17), who are separated from the legitimate Yahweh cult because they have lost
their native land and their property (Ps. 137:4).

Still, the land promise which was confirmed by an oath remains in effect and
is fulfilled again in the New Exodus. Yahweh will "bring" his people "back"
(boʾ in the hiphil, Jer. 23:8; Ezk. 20:42; 34:13; 36:24; 37:12,21; cf. Jer. 16:15;
31:23-28) into the ʾadhamah, "place" them on their own land (hinniach ʿal, Ezk.
37:14), plant them again on their land (Am. 9:15; cf. Jer. 24:6; 32:41; 42:10),
and "gather" them into their own land (kanas, Ezk. 39:28; cf. Ps. 147:2). There
they will dwell on their own land securely (Ezk. 28:25f.; 34:27; 39:26) and in
paradisiacal abundance (Am. 9:13-15), and will receive a rich abundance of seed
and fruit of the ground (Isa. 30:23-26; Dt. 30:9). Yahweh grants the penitent
prayer of the people to return to the land (1 K. 8:34 = 2 Ch. 6:25). He gives them
peace (Isa. 14:1, → ארץ ʾerets, menuchah) on the ʾadhamah, which they inherit
as their portion "in the holy land" (Zec. 2:16[12]).

J. G. Plöger

אָהַב ʾāhabh; אֲהָבָה ʾahᵃbhāh; אַהַב ʾahabh; אֹהַב ʾōhabh

Contents: I. Love Outside the Bible: 1. Egypt; 2. Mesopotamia. II. 1. Occurrences, Etymology; 2. Meaning; 3. The Scope of the Concept of Love in the OT. III. Secular Uses: 1. Sexual Love; 2. Partiality (of Parents), Affection (among Friends); 3. Socio-Ethical Behavior (of the Community); 4. Love for Neighbors, Love for Enemies. IV. Theological Uses; 1. The Theological Critical Message of the Prophets; 2. Pareneses of the Deuteronomist; 3. Love for God in the Cult; 4. Qumran.

I. Love Outside the Bible.

1. *Egypt*. The usual Egyptian word for "love" is *mry*.[1] It often appears in the forms of the passive participle, *mry* and *mrr*, "one who is loved (by . . .)." The substantive *mrw.t* means both "love" and "favor." *mry* is the opposite of *mśdy*, "to hate," e.g., in expressions like: "one who loves life (or the good) and hates death (or the evil)." In parallel statements, especially in tomb formulas, *mry* often occurs with *ḥsy*, which is usually translated "to praise." These two verbs are interchangeable and designate both the internal attitude and the corresponding external behavior. Love is usually localized in the "heart" (*ib*) (or, more vaguely, in the "body," *ḥ.t*) as the seat of motivation for personal living.

mry can be construed with an infinitive as an object, and thus perhaps can

---

ʾāhabh. F. Buck, *Die Liebe Gottes beim Propheten Osee* (1953); J. Deák, *Die Gottesliebe in den alten semitischen Religionen* (diss., Basel, 1914), 81-83; F. Hesse and H. W. Huppenbauer, "Liebe," *BHHW*, II, 1083-85; E. Kalt, *Biblisches Reallexikon* (²1938), II, 56-71; F. Maass, "Die Selbstliebe nach Leviticus 19,18," *Friedrich Baumgärtel zum 70. Geburtstag. Erlanger Forschungen, R.A.: Geisteswissenschaften*, X (1959), 109-113; O. Michel, "Das Gebot der Nächstenliebe in der Verkündigung Jesu," *Zur sozialen Entscheidung* (1947), 53-101; W. L. Moran, "The Ancient Near Eastern Background of the Love of God in Deuteronomy," *CBQ*, 25 (1963), 77-87; G. Nagel, "Crainte et amour de Dieu dans l'AT," *RTP*, 33 (1945), 175-186; J. Nikel, *Das AT und die Nächstenliebe. BZfr*, 6/11-12 (1913); A. Nygren, *Agape and Eros* (trans. 1953); Pedersen, *ILC;* G. Quell and E. Stauffer, "ἀγαπάω," *TDNT*, I, 21-55; O. Schilling, "Die alttestamentliche Auffassung von Gerechtigkeit und Liebe," *Worte des Lebens. Festschrift für M. Meinertz* (1951), 9-27; C. Spicq, *Agapé dans le NT, Analyse des Textes* (3 vols., Paris, 1957/59); D. W. Thomas, "The root אהב 'love' in Hebrew," *ZAW*, 57 (1939), 57-64; V. Warnach, *Agape. Die Liebe als Grundmotiv der neutestamentlichen Theologie* (1951); idem, "Liebe," *Bibeltheologisches Wörterbuch*, ed. J. B. Bauer (³1967), 927-965; C. Wiéner, *Recherches sur l'amour pour Dieu dans l'AT* (1957); J. Ziegler, *Die Liebe Gottes bei den Propheten. ATA*, 11/3 (1930); W. Zimmerli, "Liebe," II. Im AT, *RGG*³, IV, 363f.

On I: E. Drioton, *Pages d'égyptologie* (Cairo, 1957); idem, *Maximes relatives à l'amour pour les dieux. AnBibl*, 12 (1959), 57-68; A. Hermann, *Altäg. Liebesdichtung* (1959); S. Morenz, "Die Erwählung zwischen Gott und König in Ägypten," *Festschrift für Wedemeyer* (1956), 118-137; E. Otto, *Die biographischen Inschriften der äg. Spätzeit* (1954); idem, *Gott und Mensch. AHAW*, 1 (1964).

[1] *WbÄS*, II, 98ff.

serve as an auxiliary verb in the sense of "to want, to wish." But much more often it appears with a personal object, and is used primarily of the affectionate relationships between married couples and different members of the family, between king and subjects or master and servants, and between God and man.

When *mry* is used of marital love, it is obvious that usually it has reference to sexual love. In a great number of portrayals at tombs, beside the owner is depicted "his beloved wife," "his beloved son," etc. From the earliest period (cf. Pyr. 2192) to the Magical Papyri of the Late Period, the love of Isis for her brother-husband Osiris in her dual role as sister-wife is regarded as typical.

Several proper names of the type *Mr.t it.ś (mwt.ś)*, "one beloved by her father (her mother)," testify to the love between parents and children. [2] Autobiographical texts like to talk about affectionate relationships between members of the family, and contain formulas like "one loved by his father, one praised *(ḥsy)* by his mother, one loved by his brothers and sisters, etc." [3] Particularly in the tomb context, "the beloved" son appears as the ideal person to offer the sacrifices of his father.

Love describes the ideal relationship between a king and his subjects. Some kings state proudly, "Men love me." Sinuhe praises the new king with these words: "He is a lord of favor, great in sweetness, he is one who conquers by love *(mrw.t)*. The inhabitants of the city love him more than they love themselves..." (Sinuhe B, 66). But even more important is the divine love which is promised to the Pharaoh by virtue of his unique position as "the beloved one" and "the chosen one." A whole series of royal names proclaims the one who possessed these names as "the beloved one of Re." Often the divine activity in the Pharaoh's behalf is said to have been done "as a result of my love for you" (e.g., *Urk.*, IV, 579). But it should be noted that here often such a text has in mind a mutual love (selection) between God and king. [4] The formula *mrr nṯr mrr św*, "God exalts the one who loves him," which appears very early as a proper name, probably was derived from the royal ideology, [5] but is also used of private citizens, and appears quite often on scarabs. [6] On the other hand, the late temple inscriptions emphasize primarily the electing divine love. [7] According to the scarabs, God gives love, life, etc., to the one who loves him, but according to the temple inscriptions to the one whom he loves.

Bergman

2. *Mesopotamia.* The usual Sumerian word for "love" is *ki-ág*, a compound word whose original meaning is unknown. The king is designated as the one beloved by the deity, and the selection of a man for the kingship is the result of this divine love. E.g., Eannatum says that Inanna, who loves him, has given him

---

2 Ranke, *PN*, I, 135ff.
3 Otto, *Biogr. Inschr.*, 168, 172, 174, etc.
4 Morenz.
5 So Morenz.
6 Drioton, *Pages*, 121ff.; *AnBibl*, 57ff.
7 Otto, *Gott und Mensch*, 46f.

the *ensi*-ship of Lagash and the kingship of Kish. [8] Also marital love and love between friends are designated as *ki-ág*, e.g., *dam-ki-ág*, "the beloved husband," *ku-li-ki-ág*, "the beloved friend." [9] The temple is the place that is beloved by the deity; expressions like "his beloved temple" occur frequently.

Accordingly, Akk. *rāmu* (→ רחם *rācham*) is used, which designates the relationship between parents and children. Ashurbanipal says that his father loved him in a special way. [10] According to CH, the mother will give her inheritance to her son whom she loves (§ 150). *rāmu* is also used of marital love. Ishtar's invitation to Gilgamesh to become her husband, which he refuses because of all the others who have loved her (Tammuz, etc.; Gilg. VI, 46ff.), is worthy of note.

The use of this idea in political life is especially interesting. The Amarna letters state that princes "love" each other, that the vassals "love" the pharaoh and that the pharaoh "loves" them, and that the subjects should "love" their king. This "love" includes primarily loyalty, fidelity, and obedience. [11]

The normal attitude of man toward the gods is fear: the king often says that he is "afraid of *(pāliḫ)* one of the gods," while there are hardly any examples where it is said that he loves the gods. At the same time, the king (or man) is the "beloved" *(narāmu)* [12] of the gods. The gods love the sanctuaries: Hammurabi says that he loves the Esagila, and Nebuchadrezzar speaks of "Babylon, which I love." It is said that the gods love the cultic activities of the king (e.g., *niš qātīya*, "lifting up the hands"); likewise a man can love the cult of the gods. [13] Furthermore, the statement that the gods [14] or the kings love "justice" and "righteousness" *(kettu, mēšaru)* [15] is almost stereotyped.

Haldar

II. 1. *Occurrences, Etymology.* The root *'ahabh* and its derivatives are found not only in the OT and in Hebrew texts outside of and later than the OT books, but also in related Semitic dialects, although admittedly not in as large numbers in the latter. [16]

In the OT, the root *'ahabh* occurs in all types of literature and was in use in all periods, even if special meanings changed under different circumstances. That the OT quite frequently uses this root, which appears infrequently in other Semitic dialects, but never as a part of a proper name as is possible in these dialects,

---

[8] *VAB*, I/1, 23.

[9] *SAK*, 18, VI.8 and 6.

[10] *VAB*, VII/2, 259.

[11] Moran, 79f.; also in Mari, cf. *ARM*, X, 7. 13.

[12] Seux, 189ff.

[13] See W. Muss-Arnolt, *A Concise Dictionary of the Assyrian Language* (1905), 966f.

[14] Tallqvist, *Akk. Götterepitheta* (1938), 167.

[15] Seux, 236f.

[16] For examples in Ugaritic, see *WUS*, 9, and III.1 below. In the Aramaic papyri from Elephantine, *'ahabh* appears only as part of a proper name: A. E. Cowley, *AP*, I, line 4; XXII, line 107; Noth, *IPN*, 223, 251; Nos. 924, 937. The appearance of *'ahabh* in Cowley, *AP*, LXXV, line 3, is uncertain; cf. *DISO*, 6. *'ahabh* occurs only once in extant Punic material, *DISO*, 6. On occurrences in Samaritan, see D. W. Thomas, 59, No. 5.

may indicate that the idiomatic use of 'ahabh in Biblical Hebrew developed independently from these dialects for linguistic and theological reasons. In the OT, the verb form of 'ahabh occurs 140 times in the qal, 36 times as a qal active participle usually with the meaning "friend," once as a niphal participle, and 16 times as a piel participle in the sense of "paramour." As far as substantival forms are concerned, 'ahabhah occurs 50 times, 'ahabh twice, and 'ohabh twice.

The etymology of 'ahabh cannot be regarded as certain, and thus it provides only insufficient information as to the original meaning of this root. Under the assumption that 'ahabh is to be traced back to a biliteral root hb, D. W. Thomas has revived the suggestion made by A. Schultens in 1748 that this root is related to Arab. habba, "to breathe heavily, to be excited." [17] The OT examples which are cited in favor of this explanation (Prov. 30:15; [18] Ps. 55:23 [Eng. v. 22]; Hos. 8:13) are textually disputed, and the way in which the ancient versions translate these passages can hardly be used as proof of a lost root hb. [19] On the other hand, G. R. Driver [20] and (obviously independently of him) H. H. Hirschberg [21] have connected the root 'ahabh with Arab. 'ihāb, "skin, leather" (cf. Cant. 3:10). [22] Accordingly, an affectionate feeling in the physical realm was applied to the emotional stimulation which produced it. If this supposition is correct, then the emotional experience is the germ cell for the development of the concept of 'ahabh.

2. *Meaning.* This last statement seems to be supported at least by the fact that this emotional feeling which flows out of one's perceptions is contrasted with hate, → שׂנא śānē' (Dt. 5:9,10; 21:15; Jgs. 14:16; 2 S. 19:7[6]; Isa. 61:8; Am. 5:15; Mic. 3:2; Mal. 1:2; Ps. 45:8[7]; 97:10; 109:5; Prov. 9:8; 10:12; 12:1; 13:24; 14:20; 15:17; 15:9, in antithesis with → תועבה tô'ēbhāh; see also 1 QS 1:3-9; 9:16, 21; 1 QH 14:10,19, in antithesis with → מאס mā'as); indeed, love can suddenly be turned into hate (2 S. 13:15). Ps. 109:4 renounces the ingratitude by which one who receives love rewards it with its opposite, enmity (→ שׂטן śāṭān).

The parallel expressions or ideas in Hebrew help us in determining the various corresponding gradations of meaning of 'ahabh(ah). He who loves someone or something cleaves to him (→ דבק dābhaq, Dt. 11:22; 30:20; Prov. 18:24; cf. 1 K. 11:2), runs after him (radhaph, Isa. 1:23), goes after him (→ הלך אחרי hālakh 'achªrê, Jer. 2:25b), seeks him (shachar, Prov. 8:17 [qere]; → בקשׁ biqqēsh, Ps. 4:3[2]; 40:17[16]=70:5[4]), gains faithfulness (→ משׁך בחסר māshakh bᵉchesedh, Jer. 31:3; cf. Hos. 11:4). Behind this yearning to be near someone physically lie internal emotions: one is knit to another with his soul (niqsherah benephesh, 1 S. 18:1), is occupied with affectionate desire (→ חפץ chāphēts, Ps. 34:13[12]; → רצון rātsôn, Prov. 16:13), chooses (→ בחר bāchar) the one he loves (Dt. 7:7f.;

---

[17] D. W. Thomas, 61; cf. J. J. Glück, *VT,* 14 (1964), 367f.

[18] See Glück.

[19] Cf. H. S. Nyberg, *ZAW,* 52 (1934), 252; E. W. Nicholson, *VT,* 16 (1966), 355ff.

[20] *JBL,* 55 (1936), 111; *JTS,* 39 (1938), 160f.

[21] *VT,* 11 (1961), 373.

[22] Hos. 11:4 cannot be cited as opposed to the view of Driver and Hirschberg.

10:15; Isa. 41:8; Ps. 78:68); the one chosen is lovely (→ נעם *nāʿēm*, 2 S. 1:23), precious (→ יקר *yāqar*, Isa. 43:4), or honored (→ נכבד *nikhbādh*, Isa. 43:4; Ps. 87:2f.). According to these interpretative parallels, love is the passionate desire to be intimately united with a person (in all of life's relationships, not only inwardly, but also outwardly) with whom one feels himself united in his affections (Gen. 2:23f.).

It is interesting that the root → רחם *richam* (Akk. *remu*), "to love with compassion," which often appears in proper names as an indication of God's love to the person bearing the name (or giving the name), never appears as a parallel to *'ahabh*, while the root → דוד *dôdh*, significantly, occurs with *'ahabh* only in Cant. 1:3f. If we have not overestimated the implications of these facts, they seem to show that the root *'ahabh* in the OT has a basic meaning which is to be sharply distinguished from that of *racham*, and perhaps also from that of *dodh*, which prevents it from being used in connection with a divine name or from functioning as divine appellative in proper names. Consequently, the Hebrew of the OT has filled the concept of *'ahabh(ah)* with an entirely special meaning.

That the LXX uses the verb *agapáō* as a translation for *'ahabh* in an overwhelming majority of cases also favors this assumption. In prebiblical Greek the difference between the meaning of *eráō*, *philéō*, and *agapáō* is pale and fluid. [23] Strictly speaking *agapáō* means simply "to be content with something." The LXX uses the word *agápē* (2 S. 13:15; Jer. 2:2; Cant. 2:4,5,7; 3:5,10[?]; 5:8; 7:7; 8:4,7; Eccl. 9:1) or *agápēsis* (2 S. 1:26; Ps. 109:5; Jer. 2:33; 31:3 [LXX 38:3]; Hos. 11:4; Zeph. 3:17) to translate the noun *'ahabhah*. As the LXX translators prefer to render Hebrew words built from the root *'hb* by forms of *agapáō*, a Greek word which originally was not characteristic, quite clearly *agapáō* acquired its classical meaning initially through translation from the Hebrew. This also indicates that the Hebrew root *'hb* could not be readily expressed either by *eráō* or by *philéō* because its fundamental meaning did not correspond to that of these words. Thus, the root *philéō* could be used to translate *'ahabh* only in very special cases, e.g., when a text described an inner affection for a thing, but not for a person: Gen. 27:9 (cf. v. 14), referring to savory food; Isa. 56:10, referring to sleep; Prov. 8:17; 29:3, referring to Wisdom (admittedly personified). In this sense, the LXX uses the denominative form of *philía*, viz., *philiázō*: to be a friend of unrighteousness in judgment (2 Ch. 19:2). The compounds using *philéō* and its cognates also indicate that this Greek word was used in the LXX to describe affection for things or conditions: *philamartḗmōn*, "loving sin" (Prov. 17:19), *philogýnaios*, "giving oneself over to polygamy" (1 K. 11:1), *philogeōrgos*, "loving agriculture" (2 Ch. 26:10), *philoneikeín*, "loving strife" (Prov. 10:12). The qal active participle of *'ahabh* is translated by *phílos* whenever the text is describing friendly relationships between men (Jer. 20:4,6; Ps. 38:12[11]; 88:19 [18]; Prov. 14:20; 17:17; 21:17; 27:6; Est. 5:10,14; 6:13). Also *'ahabhah* is translated by *philía* when the text is referring to affection for things (Prov. 15:17; 17:9; 27:5). In individual cases *'ahabh* is translated in the LXX by *antéchesthai*,

---

[23] See Stauffer, *TDNT*, I, 36.

"to cling to someone" (4:6), *epithymētēs einai,* "to be eager for" (1:22), *zēteō,* "to seek" (Mic. 3:2), *eráō,* "to love" (Est. 2:17), *erōtís,* "passion" (Prov. 7:18 for *'ohabh*). It should be mentioned that *eráō* and *erōtís* were used only once apiece, as a translation of *'ahabhah* and *'ohabh,* and in a text that had to do with sexual love, which is the basic concept expressed by these words. Therefore, *agapáō* may be regarded as the classical equivalent to *'ahabh,* even though it is also used to translate Heb. *ratsah, richam,* and *chaphets.*[24]

3. *The Scope of the Concept of Love in the OT.* The scope of the concept *to love/love* in the OT idiom is very broad. It extends from the affection of members of the opposite sex for one other (Isaac and Rebekah, Gen. 24:67; Jacob and Rachel, 29:18,30; Leah and Jacob, 29:32; Shechem and Dinah, 34:3; Samson and one of the daughters of the Philistines, Jgs. 14:16; Samson and Delilah, 16:4,15; Elkanah and Hannah, 1. S. 1:5; Michal and David, 18:20; Amnon and Tamar, 2 S. 13:1,4) or even conjugal intercourse itself (Hos. 3:1); to the intimate bonds between father and (favorite) son (Gen. 22:2; 25:28; 37:3; 44:20; Prov. 13:24) or between mother and her favorite child (Gen. 25:28) or between daughter-in-law and mother-in-law (Ruth 4:15); to friendly relationships between men, like Saul and David (1 S. 16:21), Jonathan and David (18:1-3; 20:17; 2 S. 1:26), teacher and disciple (Prov. 9:8), servant and master (Ex. 21:5; Dt. 15:16); even to the intimate relationship between a people and their military leader (1 S. 18:16,22). Both love for one's fellow men as a kind, friendly, helpful attitude toward one's countrymen (Lev. 19:18) and the pouring out of one's heart to the stranger (19:34; Dt. 10:18,19) are to be understood in the latter sense. Pedersen correctly emphasizes the community-related character of the concept of love and friendship in the OT.[25]

But finally, the root *'ahabh* is also used for the relationship between Yahweh and Israel or his godly ones (Dt. 10:12; 11:13,22; 19:9; 30:6; Josh. 22:5; 23:11; Jer. 2:2), and thus indicates total love which demands all of one's energies. To some extent this attitude of man toward God is manifested in one's love for Jerusalem, Yahweh's sanctuary, Zion (Isa. 66:10; Lam. 1:2; Ps. 122:6), or for God's name (Ps. 5:12[11]; 69:37[36]; 119:132). But all this is based on Yahweh's love for Israel, which motivates him to punish and to save them (Hos. 11:4[9:15]; Jer. 31:3; Isa. 43:4; 63:9; Zeph. 3:17; Mal. 1:2; Dt. 7:8,13; 10:15; 23:6[5]; 2 Ch. 2:10[11]; 9:8).

However, this survey does not warrant any hasty conclusions concerning the specific character of the concept of love, since the different historical periods or especially the literary forms connected with the types of literature found in the OT characteristically have filled this root with stereotyped content, and accordingly are interested in entirely different aspects of the concept of love. Thus the narrative sources are more concerned with the relationship of men to each other, while the didactic socio-ethical interests of the Wisdom Literature see the same

---

24 Quell, 20f., 21, n. 2.
25 Pedersen, *ILC,* II, 309f., 341f., 353, 414. For further discussion, see below.

subject under symbols which correspond to this type of literature. The meditative expressions of faith in the Psalms or the strains in the Song of Solomon expressly devoted to the theme of love are of a different character from the prophetic oracles which criticize Israelite cultic and social beliefs and practices. Prophetic oracles lay greater emphasis on Yahweh's love for his people, which motivated him to perform mighty acts to save them, and on Israel's failure to reciprocate this love, which is expressed in the figure of unfaithfulness and disaffection. Deuteronomy and the literature dependent on it employ very specialized uniform phrases to express the relationship of love between God and his people. Undoubtedly the concept of love in the various types of OT literature was expanded and deepened as time went on, especially by including the concept of God's love for man and man's love for God.

The word 'ahabh and its derivatives in the OT have a strikingly pragmatic character. Not only does love presuppose a concrete inner disposition which is based on experiences and events, but it includes a conscious act in behalf of the person who is loved or the thing that is preferred. In this sense love ultimately has a sociological (indeed, a socio-ethical) basis. [26] Perhaps the most impressive statement of this pragmatic character of 'ahabh is found in 1 S. 18:1-4: "Jonathan made a covenant with David, because he loved him as his own soul (be'ahabhatho 'otho kenaphsho), and Jonathan stripped himself of the robe that was upon him, and gave it to David, and his armor, and even his sword and his bow and his girdle." Thus, the friendship which was established between these two valiant warriors was sealed by → ברית berîth, "covenant," which was the bond of a friendly relationship. Later Jonathan confirmed his friendly relationship with David once again by his oath that he would help him against the pursuits of his father Saul (20:17ff.). In this way Jonathan demonstrated to his bosom friend his fidelity to this oath. At an earlier time Saul also had bestowed his affection on David by making him his armorbearer (16:21), but in the meantime David's military successes and popularity transformed this feeling into the exact opposite (18:8).

The Pentateuchal sources also depict the attitude indicated by love: "Jacob loved Rachel, and he said, 'I will serve you (Laban) seven years for your younger daughter Rachel'" (Gen. 29:18). "And he loved Rachel more than Leah, and served Laban for another seven years" (29:30). "Now Israel loved Joseph more than any other of his children, . . . and he made him a long robe with sleeves" (37:3f.). The Book of the Covenant also makes this meaning of the concept of love clear: "But if the slave plainly says, 'I love my master, my wife, and my children; I will not go out free . . . '" (Ex. 21:5; cf. Dt. 15:16). Inner affection for his master and love for his wife and children are the attitudes that motivate the slave to refuse to accept his personal freedom. Several of the biblical Proverbs sum up this practical consequence of love, e.g.: "Hatred stirs up strife, but love covers all offenses" (Prov. 10:12); "He who forgives an offense seeks love, but he who repeats a matter alienates a friend" (17:9). Indeed, love that does not manifest itself in appropriate behavior is condemned: "Better is open rebuke than silent

---

[26] Cf. *ibid.*

love" (27:5). Cant. 8:6b perhaps also has in mind the way in which love expressed itself: "Love is strong as death." Love is not passive, but is active in the highest, most passionate degree.

Anyone who sets his heart on something wicked is naturally motivated to do wickedness: "Your chiefs are rebels and companions of thieves. Every one loves a bribe and runs after gifts. They do not defend the fatherless, and the widow's cause does not come to them" (Isa. 1:23f.). According to Trito-Isaiah, even non-Israelites who energetically follow Yahweh are to be preferred to such leaders, so e.g.: "And the foreigners who join themselves to Yahweh, to minister to him, to love the name of Yahweh, and to be his servants... and every one who holds fast my covenant" (56:6). Thus it is quite clear that one's love to Yahweh must be expressed in activity. The Israel that loves Yahweh follows him in obedience: "I remember the devotion of your youth, your love as a bride, how you followed me in the wilderness, in a land not sown" (Jer. 2:2). Similarly, the deeds Yahweh does in behalf of his people are to be explained out of his love for them: "I have loved you with an everlasting love; therefore I have continued my faithfulness (→ חסד chesedh) to you" (31:3; cf. Hos. 11:4). It was because of his love and compassion alone that Yahweh saved them, lifted them up, and sustained them in the past; and this is especially the theme of the Deuteronomic preaching: "It is because Yahweh loves you, and is keeping the oath which he swore to your fathers, that Yahweh has brought you out with a mighty hand, and redeemed you from the house of bondage, from the hand of Pharaoh king of Egypt" (Dt. 7:8). "Yet Yahweh set his heart in love upon your fathers and chose their descendants after them, you above all peoples, as at this day" (10:15).

An OT text can be speaking of love even when the word 'ahabh is not actually used, but the attitude of love is clearly described or demanded in the context. The OT enjoins people to love their enemies in this sort of passage: "If your enemy is hungry, give him bread to eat; and if he is thirsty, give him water to drink" (Prov. 25:21). "If you meet your enemy's ox or his ass (which has) gone astray, you shall bring (it) back to him. If you see the ass of one who hates you lying under his burden, you shall refrain from leaving him with it, you shall help him to lift it up" (Ex. 23:4f.).

It is precisely in such deeds of love that the command to love can be seen in a proper perspective, viz., the attitude of love is itself made the norm. Therefore, love is not merely a demand which a humanitarian spirit makes on a man, but it is rooted in the divine command to love. At the same time, the feeling of love for God and the prayer, "I love Yahweh, because he has heard my fervent cries" (Ps. 116:1, emended text), are based on man's faith in the active love of God for him.

By a stylistic device, then, the action produced by an inner motivation can be indicated by the object that is desired. The biblical author describes not the process, but the goal toward which the action is directed; i.e., grammatically speaking, he connects the verb 'ahabh with a real object which signifies an ethico-religious value or a definite type of behavior. Love for agriculture is characteristic of the king who rules prudently and sensibly (2 Ch. 26:10). He who strives for knowledge loves discipline (Prov. 12:1), but he who does not love reproof does not want to be wise (15:12). He who wants to prosper loves wisdom (19:8); he who seeks a genuine treasure loves wisdom (8:17); he serves God actively who loves his commandments, precepts, and instructions (Ps. 119 *passim*). However, he who loves a bribe necessarily manifests an unrighteous judgment (Isa. 1:23f.); he who seeks gain to his own shame loves only money and wealth (Eccl. 5:9[10]); he who has followed pernicious gluttony loves wine and oil (Prov. 21:17). He who does nothing at all and is very slothful loves sleep (Isa. 56:10; Prov. 20:13), and he who intends to stir up wickedness loves strife (Prov. 17:19). In this manner, appropriate conduct expresses desire for an object. Love and action are two sides of the same coin.

III. Secular Uses.

1. *Sexual Love.* Quell's assertion [27] that the original use of the concept of ’*ahabh* belongs to the realm of sexual love, of physical desire, of lust, and even of sensual pleasure, [28] may be supported, among other ways, by the use of this root in Ugaritic: [29] *CTA,* 4 [II AB], IV-V, 38f.: "Truly, the male organ of King El will have intercourse with thee, the love of the bull will stimulate thee." *CTA,* 3 [V AB], C 3f.: "(The object of the) affection of Pdry, the daughter of the goddess of light, the love of Ṭly, the daughter of the goddess of rain...." *CTA,* 5 [I* AB], V, 18: "Aliyan Ba‘al became fond of a heifer in the pasture, and a cow in the field of the lion Mametu." [30] Even if we cannot explain the entire breadth of the concept of this root in this idiom from its usage in the extant Ugaritic texts, still it is quite clear that in these Canaanite mythological statements ’*hb* is used of sexual behavior.

In the OT this root is also used when referring to sexual love, to the marital relationship as something given at creation in a positive sense, although a different root (→ ידע *yādhaʻ*) [31] is used for the act of sexual intercourse itself. Thus the emphasis suggested by the word ’*ahabh* is not really on sexual love, but more on experiencing and desiring love. [32] Isaac is fond of Rebekah (Gen. 24:67), Jacob of Rachel (29:18,20,30), Samson of a Philistine woman (Jgs. 14:16) and of Delilah (16:4,15). Accordingly, Eccl. 9:9 knows nothing better to recommend than the time which a man enjoys with the wife whom he loves. Prov. 5:18f. even praises the feeling of marital devotion with the words: "Let your fountain be blessed, and rejoice in the wife of your youth, a lovely (’*ahabh*) hind, a graceful doe. Let her affection fill you at all times with delight, be infatuated always with her love." The strength aroused by love is regarded as fundamentally a marvel: "Three things are too wonderful for me; four I do not understand: the way of an eagle in the sky, the way of a serpent on a rock, the way of a ship on the high

---

27 Quell, 22.
28 Cf. Kalt, 56.
29 Cf. H. H. Hirschberg, *VT,* 11 (1961), 373; A. D. Tushingham, *JNES,* 12 (1953), 151.
30 Gordon, *UT,* 1002 (*PRU,* II, 8-11), 46, is uncertain.
31 See E. Baumann, *ZAW,* 28 (1908), 22ff.
32 Cf. Tushingham, *loc. cit.*

seas, and the way of a man with a maiden" (Prov. 30:18f.). As a matter of fact, without reservation the Song of Solomon praises the rapturous experience of sexual love as a motivating power that is plainly supernatural. Indeed, a man can almost be sick from insatiable longing (Cant. 2:5; 5:8). Love is stronger than floods, stronger even than death (8:6f.). This love is holy, taboo: "Stir not up nor awaken love until it please" (2:7; 3:5; 8:4). Thus Canticles is able to praise love in full and stirring tones. What it means is not really sexuality, but eroticism, sensual experience. This love is based on complete reciprocity. The young maiden also loves her chosen one intimately and passionately (1:3), wants to be near him (1:7), seeks him on her bed by night, but does not find him (3:1), wants to rise to seek him at once in the streets and squares of the city (3:2), in order after lengthy asking and searching at last to find him and bring him into her mother's house (3:4). The love experience is a joy produced by fulfilled yearning, and is to be experienced to the greatest depth. Although we meet this view for the first time in Canticles, which was written at a late date, there can be little doubt that in all ages this common human emotion of love gave rise to similar literary gems.

These statements are altered very little by the cultic interpretation of Canticles. [33] In either case, Canticles is referring to sexual love. The only difference is that according to the cultic interpretation this assumes a figurative, symbolic meaning.

It is disastrous when one does not control his love emotion, but in unbridled passion acts in a way contrary to genuine love, thus hurting the one he loves and transgressing the law of chastity. Amnon, filled with passionate sensual desire, overpowers his unsuspecting half-sister Tamar as she cares for him with all good intentions and concern, and after he has disgraced her he drives her away and refuses to marry her (2 S.13:1-19). In this act, he transgresses the moral law in Israel (vv. 12f.). An order preserved by society also lies behind these human relationships. Such unrestrained behavior, the intention of which is not active mutual affection, but self-gratification, will ultimately change into the opposite emotions, anger and hate. Therefore, Amnon's crime was also destined to cause a disastrous development in the history of David's family—in this case, in determining who would be David's successor to the throne. It was perhaps also for this reason that the record of this event was taken up into the tradition. David himself was not free from the guilt of a similar sin. His sensual desire for Bathsheba (2 S. 11) leads him into adultery and later into the malicious murder of one of his bravest officers who was deeply devoted to him, the Hittite Uriah, who was married to Bathsheba. The court prophet Nathan reproved him severely for this act (2 S. 12). Ultimately this transgression also played an important role in determining David's successor to the throne, although this may not have been desired by David himself (1 K. 1:11-40). Love that is not consciously aware of the importance of behavior, but strives only to enjoy life without any self-restraint, must inevitably lead to complications and is to be rejected. Even where it is not explicitly stated, this ethical dimension of love in the OT is quite clear, as in the man's marital love

---

[33] W. Wittekindt, *Das Hohelied und seine Beziehungen zum Ištarkult* (1926); M. Haller, *HAT*, 18; H. Schmökel, *Heilige Hochzeit und das Hohelied* (1956); H. Ringgren, *ATD*, XVI.

for and fidelity to his barren wife.[34] Finally, Prov. 5–7 gives a clear and instructive description of the opposite of genuine love and of unchaste relationships with the prostitute.[35]

Love is destined to lead to grief when several rival wives belong to one man, and when he prefers one above the others (2 Ch. 11:21). The husband's preference would not necessarily be because a particular wife was blessed with a greater number of children. In fact, much more often the OT emphasizes the cases in which husbands love their wives sincerely in spite of their childlessness. Elkanah, for example, was sincerely devoted to his wife Hannah (1 S. 1:5) even though she had not yet borne him a son. He prefers her to his other wife Peninnah and puts forth great effort to comfort her in her distress. We may also call to mind the relationship between Leah and Rachel, who was barren. In spite of her barrenness, Jacob loved Rachel more deeply than Leah, who had several children (Gen. 30:1). The tension between Sarah and Hagar which arose after Ishmael's birth, when Hagar looked challengingly on her mistress (Gen. 16; 21:9-14), is also significant.

Ancient Near Eastern and OT lawgivers considered it necessary to establish specific laws to protect the children of the wife who is less loved (Dt. 21:15-17). It is obvious here that harsh treatment of innocent children necessitated the creation of such laws. The way in which Joseph was treated by his father Jacob also affords an example of a father's preference for a son of the wife he loves the best (Gen. 37:3f.).

2. *Partiality (of Parents), Affection (among Friends)*. This strongly emotional characteristic of the concept of love is quite clear in descriptions of the relationship between the generations, between master and servant, and of the friendship between men. These feelings may, indeed, belong completely to the realm of the original emotions of love and friendship; there is also a danger here of a sudden change into the opposite, hate. Saul takes pleasure in David and makes him his armorbearer (1 S. 16:21). However, his preference for David decreases as David becomes successful and gains popularity with the troops (18:8f.), and changes into jealous anger. However, Jonathan's friendship with David is of greater stability; in this situation he is ready to help him who is being pursued by his suspicious father (20:17, cf. 18:3). David himself memorialized this friendship in his lament over Saul and Jonathan (2 S. 1:26). The personal relationship between master and servant (Ex. 21:5; Dt. 15:16) may be because the servant obtained from his master a wife, who was also a maidservant. In a case like this, if a servant chose to accept his freedom, he would have to give up his wife and children. Thus a servant's fidelity to his master is at least supported by his love for his wife and children.

Love between the generations was sometimes occasioned because children of the favorite wife enjoyed greater paternal affection. But other motivations are

---

[34] See below.
[35] According to Ringgren, *ATD*, XVI, 27ff., → זר *zār*, "stranger" or "foreigner," is probably to be interpreted allegorically.

also at work here. Abraham has a particularly deep love for Isaac, who is his only son and one born late in his life, and who is also his heir and the bearer of the promise God gave to him. Jacob also loves the son who is born to him in his old age (Gen. 37:3). Isaac's partiality to Esau is based more naturally on his special fondness for the tasty morsels of game which Esau killed, whereas Rebekah had greater affinity with the well-bred Jacob (25:27f.). However, the OT says nothing directly about the mutual love of sons. But it does state that Ruth loved her mother-in-law (Ruth 4:15).

3. *Socio-Ethical Behavior (of the Community).* Like the love between the generations, relations between friends can also be problematic. Favoritism and jealousy are the hostile brothers of love. And love does not enjoy constancy in all cases. The Preacher has clearly recognized this ambivalence: "a time to love, and a time to hate; a time for war, and a time for peace" (Eccl. 3:8). Indeed, generally speaking the Preacher considers the character of love and hate to be relative: "whether it is love or hate man does not know. Everything before them 'is vanity'" (9:1b). No one knows whether love really edifies and hate really debases. Emotions are subjective and vacillating; one can hardly estimate what they accomplish. The action may run counter to the intention. The Wise Men of Israel were grievously concerned about the lack of love's domination and sovereignty in life. Thus they urged the parent to discipline the son he loves (Prov. 13:24), and a man to reprove a wise man in order to gain his friendship (9:8). Thus a wise king loves him who speaks what is right (16:13) even if he criticizes the ruler. Genuine love and friendship remain true especially in times of adversity (17:17) because of their unselfishness. Thus true fellowship is not something that is expressed in outward appearance, but something that has real substance. "Better is a dinner of herbs where love is than a fatted ox and hatred with it" (15:17). So one must have a clear head and a sharp eye in order to be able to distinguish between genuine, unselfish love and selfish, false, pretended love. Love can be shallow and insincere. Love and behavior motivated by love are not to be separated from emotion, and yet they are not dependent on emotion, but require wise consideration.

In light of this, it should be clear that love cannot be determined on the basis of one's emotions, but on the basis of ethical responsibility for one's actions, which sets severe limits on one subjectively living as he feels and desires. In such relationships, *'ahabh* designates a positive relationship to a specific kind of behavior, whether it be good or bad. Thus, the wise man loves discipline (Prov. 12:1). He who loves wisdom makes his father glad (29:3; cf. 19:8). But the scoffer does not love discipline and wisdom (15:12), he prefers strife or scorn (1:22; 17:19). He who "loves" his tongue will eat its fruits, i.e., reap the evil consequences of his excessive talking (18:21; cf. Ps. 34:13f.[12f.]). Wisdom guards the one who "loves" it (Prov. 4:6; 8:17 [*qere*]), but he who hates wisdom loves death (8:36). Above everything else, essentially the wise man loves wisdom itself, which guides him rightly in other areas of love. Consequently, ethical actions which promote fellowship transcend ethical and legal categories, and culminate in love of justice, which has its basis in God (Ps. 33:5; 37:28), and which is to be expected of him as king (99:4; of the earthly king, 45:8[7]). On the other hand, the tyrant (*gibbor*) loves evil and lying (52:5f.[3f.]), which, however, God will punish. He who loves violence hates Yahweh, who tests the righteous and the wicked (11:5). These psalms place love among men in the realm of theology and ethics. Earthly communion is no human convention, but an arrangement established and designed by God.

4. *Love for Neighbors, Love for Enemies.* In this sense, an act which grows out of love for one's fellow man is not humanitarianism, but a deed prompted by divine arrangement (Lev. 19:18). Love for one's fellow man is also to be extended to the stranger (→ גר *gēr*) who sojourns in one's own native land (19:34; Dt. 10:18f.), but not to the *nokhri,* "foreigner." However, Schilling correctly points out that love for enemies as it is expressed in the Wisdom Literature [36] suffers because of religious tensions with heathen non-Israelites. [37] "Old Testament man had not yet seen the compatibility of dogmatic intolerance and civic or international tolerance." [38] The enemy and the adversary was a man from Israel itself. Thus David spared the Lord's anointed, Saul, although he fought against him (1 S. 24:7[6]; 26:11). Therefore, love for enemies is to be understood in a civic legal sense, not in a national sense. If an adversary is smitten with calamity, one shall not refrain from helping him. As a result of the offer of divine love for the accomplishment of the duty to love one's fellow man, this command takes on a pedagogical, parenetic character: "You shall love your neighbor as yourself" (Lev. 19:18). Buber translates: "Love your neighbor and yourself alike," i.e., "behave toward your neighbor as you do toward yourself." [39] Hillel interpreted the "golden rule" this way: "You shall not do to your neighbor that which is unpleasant to you." [40] It is true that both of these interpreters give this command a negative form, but they have correctly understood its meaning. The OT quite clearly considered the "care" [41] of one's own life and possessions to include maintaining the existence of one's own family and tribe; and although this is not specifically commended, neither is it specifically condemned. [42] Therefore, it used this effort to preserve oneself as a standard for measuring one's love for his fellow men. If the feeling of love expresses a genuine deep-rooted bond with mankind in general, then naturally it must have a concrete connection with a person's own interests. Consequently, even if the OT does not explicitly demand self-denial and altruism, it advocates the kind of behavior which equates concern for the well-being of one's neighbor with the assertion of one's own will. In no case should one allow his own selfish interests to prevail when this would be harmful to his neighbor.

---

[36] See above.
[37] Schilling, 21f.
[38] *Ibid.*
[39] M. Buber, *Two Types of Faith* (trans. 1951), 69.
[40] *Sab.* 31a, similarly Targum Jerushalmi I; cf. Michel, 62f.; Buber, 73f.
[41] H. von Oyen, *Ethik des AT* (1967), 101f.
[42] But see Maass.

The call for actions that reflect genuine love has also motivated the prophets, and understandably so. To be sure, they did not use the term 'ahabh(ah) explicitly in this connection, but continually called for a benevolent attitude toward *personae miserae* (widows, orphans, and strangers) as such. Here again 'ahabh is used with a certain mode of action as its object. One must love good, hate evil, and establish justice in the gate (Am. 5:15). Accordingly, the prophets characterized unjust actions as love of evil (Hos. 12:8[7]; Mic. 3:2 [*qere*]). One must not take false oaths because Yahweh hates these things (Zec. 8:17), while love of truth, kindness, and peace is to be preferred to engaging in religious rites (8:19; Isa. 58:6f.). Thus, even if it cannot be said that the prophets were literally advocates of love for one's fellow man, still they were all opposed to egotism and selfishness, and aggressively defended the cause of the poor and oppressed. But above all, their oracles make it quite clear that helping the poor is fundamental to an enduring relationship between God and his people and between the people and their God, a relationship that compels one to action.

It was not until a rather late period that the OT expanded the concept of love to include the communion between the people and God. This was probably because 'ahabh primarily conveyed the idea of a purely sentimental love, which to some extent had erotic overtones. Such a concept could not be used to designate the relationship between God and his people, since they stand over against each other as Creator and creature. God is the Lord of history and his people are created by him in this history.

IV. Theological Uses.

1. *The Theological Critical Message of the Prophets.* Thus it is not evident from the beginning that the concept of love was based on God's acts in behalf of his people. Yet, perhaps a clear distinction needs to be made between God's acts in behalf of individuals and God's acts in behalf of his people as a whole. It could be that originally the relationship between God and his people was founded on a different principle than God's love for the individual. First of all, the covenant, which was initiated by God himself, unites him with his people. But by the very nature of things, they remain distinct from one another. After the covenant is sealed, they are united with one another by → חסד *chesedh,* "steadfast love." Likewise, the OT does not seem to feel that the relationship of God to the individual was motivated by the bond of love. This should already be clear from the fact that in the formation of Hebrew proper names, one who wore the name (or one who gave it) did not use the verb 'ahabh as a testimony to such an attitude on God's part. Nevertheless, the feeling of security in Yahweh's guidance of the individual may be understandable by a consciousness of his fatherly love (Ps. 103:13, *richam;* 2 S. 7:14). But the affirmation that God surrounds the pious or the righteous with love is also evidently late. It is primarily the Deuteronomist who has considered Yahweh's deeds in behalf of the patriarchs a work of love (Dt. 4:37) (cf. Isa. 41:8, where the verb *bachar,* "choose," is linked with Abraham as God's 'ohebh, "friend"). Thus this idea also occurs in writings which were revised in the Deuteronomistic spirit (2 S. 12:24, Yahweh

loves Solomon; cf. on the other hand Jedidiah, → ידיד yādhîdh). Yahweh's love for the Patriarchs also includes his love for their descendants, Israel. But Yahweh's attitude toward Cyrus (Isa. 48:14) shows that this electing love is not limited to Israel. The intention here is to emphasize that Cyrus is the submissive executor of Yahweh's will and the chosen mediator of the divine decision. But the statements found in Ps. 146:8; Prov. 3:12; 8:17,21; and Neh. 13:26 also come from a later period. The statement in Prov. 15:9, "But he loves him who pursues righteousness," may indeed be preexilic, but this proves little when it comes to arguing for an early origin of the idea of Yahweh's love for the righteous or pious individual.

Against this background, we can see quite clearly why Hosea's attempts to present Yahweh's relationship to his people under the figure of his own marriage must have struck his contemporaries as daring and even scandalous. We cannot go into the problem of Hos. 1 and 3 in detail here,[43] but it should be clear that the prophet Hosea manifested a new understanding of God's relationship to his people and of their response to his deeds. We cannot know for certain whether some of Hosea's predecessors held this same interpretation.[44] Perhaps the concept of Yahweh's covenant with the people of Israel[45] provided the impetus for the idea of a marital bond between Yahweh and his people. However, marriage is also understood as a covenant (→ ברית berîth, Mal. 2:14). Here, this concept is not understood as sacral, but as civil.[46] It is worthy of note that Hosea's use of the concept of love to express his understanding of God's nature reflects the original meaning of the word ’ahabh as love between husband and wife. It is hardly likely that Hosea derived this figure from the Canaanite understanding of the cult and of God. On the contrary, Hosea probably speaks apologetically against Canaanite practices, because he (like Jeremiah later) is committed to the concept of marital fidelity, but strongly opposes a mere gratification of sexual lust. Thus it is clear that for Hosea love is expressed in a loving attitude toward the person loved. Yahweh instructs Hosea to marry a harlot, and even commands him to love his wife who went after another man. Both of these events are to be interpreted as symbolic statements concerning Yahweh's love for his unfaithful people. The reason that there was discord in this marriage is that the wife did not remain faithful to her husband. She did not act in a manner consistent with love, but went after her lovers (piel ptcp. me’ahabh, 2:7,9,12, 14,15[5,7,10,12,13]). At Peor, Israel had already shown her infidelity (9:10, ’ohabh). After the settlement in the land of Canaan, she looked on the gifts of the soil not as gifts of Yahweh, but of Baal (2:10[8]), and worshipped him. Israel's refusal to reciprocate God's love or her misdirected love is an expression of her inner alienation from God (8:9). Israel lowered herself to the level of a harlot, she gave herself over to foreigners. Understandably, this provoked her

---

[43] Cf. on this T. H. Robinson, *HAT*, 14 (³1964), 2f.; H. W. Wolff, *Hosea* (trans. 1974); W. Rudolph, *Hosea. KAT*, XIII/1; and other comms. *in loc.*

[44] Cf. Ziegler, 64f.

[45] *Ibid.*, 73-77.

[46] De Vaux, *AncIsr*, 33.

husband to wrath. His love changed to antipathy. He divorced his wife. This reaction is wholly in keeping with the OT concept of love and marriage. And yet, Yahweh's love ultimately overcomes his wrath against his people (14:5[4]; cf. 11:9a), and once again he draws them unto him with bands of love (11:4). [47]

Among the prophets that came after Hosea's time, Jeremiah in particular took up this figure of marital love. But he distinguishes between Israel's first love when she was a bride (Jer. 2:2) and followed her husband faithfully in the wilderness, and her behavior after the settlement in the land of Canaan. At that time Israel yielded herself to other enticements, which the prophet Jeremiah characterizes as marital infidelity. In doing so, he uses in particular the figure of the hierodule, which was probably very widespread in his day and designates a love-affair with the god of fertility. Israel goes after lovers (2:20,23,25; 30:14). But genuine love for and fidelity to Yahweh excludes a sacral sexual pleasure. The prophet presents this behavior in an abundance of figures, from bowing down as a harlot upon every high hill and under every green tree (2:20; 3:6,13), to a female camel in heat (2:23f.). Sensual desire for the world of the god of fertility replaced grateful obedience to and love for Yahweh. Israel's false love also manifested itself in her adoption of the star cult (8:2), the worship of the queen of heaven (7:18; 19:13; 44:17). Thus Israel brought catastrophe upon herself. But Yahweh cannot be angry with his people forever. Thus he draws Ephraim unto him again in love. Faithfulness causes him to let mercy prevail over justice (31:3f.).

Ezekiel took over from Hosea and Jeremiah the figure of marriage to describe the relationship between Yahweh and his unfaithful people, and developed it in ways that are harsh, even crass (Ezk. 16; 23). He focusses not only on the people of Judah and Israel, but in a special way on the cities of Jerusalem and Samaria as their capitals. Yahweh chose Jerusalem, or Jerusalem and Samaria, from Egypt, saved them, and provided for them abundantly. But they turned away from him, failed to practice pure marital love to their Lord Yahweh, joined themselves to lovers (16:33,36,37; 23:5,9,22), and thus became harlots. Therefore Yahweh will punish them.

Finally, the figure of marriage also appears in Deutero-Isaiah (Isa. 43:4; 49:14ff.; 51:17ff., maternal love). Here, however, as in Trito-Isaiah (62:4f.; 63:9), Yahweh is at work to bring back all the lost and to restore a right relationship between himself and his people, or the city of Jerusalem, based on love and compassion. In later prophecy we encounter this figure of love occasionally, but without any clear reference to the character of love expressed by the *marital* relationship. Yahweh will rejoice again over his people (Zeph. 3:17). Yahweh loves Jacob, but hates Edom (Mal. 1:2; 2:11). The Chronicler's history regards the giving of a king to Israel as a work of God's love (2 Ch. 2:10[11]; 9:8). Perhaps 1 K. 10:9 should be interpreted in the same way.

2. *Pareneses of the Deuteronomist.* The Deuteronomic pareneses use the concept of genuine love, apart from the figure of marriage, extensively, and

---

[47] See above, II.1.

enlarge on its theological and ethical significance (Dt. 7:8,13; 23:6[5]; 30:16,20). That which Israel has is Yahweh's gift. Yahweh gave it to Israel because of his love for them. He saved the forefathers from the time of the patriarchs, i.e., for the sake of his oath he led the people out of Egypt, promised them the land, and caused them to multiply. Yahweh's love expressed itself in action in behalf of his chosen people. Here the concept of love has been separated from the realm of the original idea of sensuality, and theologically has become the original basis for Yahweh's benevolent deeds in his people's behalf, even though the love reciprocated to him by his people has proved to be weak and powerless. Yahweh's love is the prototype for love in general. He gives out of his own initiative, but he desires that the people he loves unite themselves unto him alone. In light of the recognizable connections between Hosea and Deuteronomy, it is quite possible that Deuteronomy took over this figure from the prophet Hosea. The Deuteronomist's concept of love differs from that of Hosea, which was derived from the background of sexual love and marriage, and here he has made a notable advancement in the OT concept of the knowledge of God.

Perhaps the intention of Deuteronomy was to teach Israel pedagogically her duty to reciprocate God's love, not in the original sense of emotion, but in the form of genuine obedience and pure devotion (cf. Jer. 2:2). Since the Deuteronomist defines God's relationship to his people and their fathers according to his own theological concept of love, he can hardly give any advice other than that the only possible way for Israel to live is in a love, fidelity, and devotion to Yahweh which reciprocates this love: "you shall love the Lord your God with all your heart, and with all your soul, and with all your might" (Dt. 6:5). The question has been raised as to how such love as this can be commanded. However, if love is not merely an emotional feeling for a person or a thing, but also involves a behavior that is becoming to love, then it is possible for Deuteronomy to elevate this behavior to the level of a commandment. The Deuteronomist is not a prophet who at God's bidding must criticize the people's behavior in a specific situation, but he is a teacher who wishes to immortalize such criticism in binding, timeless teachings in order that Israel might live in Yahweh's land a life which he blesses and with which he alone is pleased. It is in this sense that Yahweh tells his people to love, to keep his commandments out of love, and to subject themselves to him in obedience. [48] He calls on them to keep his *mitsvoth*, "commandments" (5:10; 7:9; cf. Ps. 119:47,48,97,113,119,127,140,159,163,165, 167), to serve him (Dt. 10:12; 11:13), to obey his voice (30:20), to walk in his ways and to cleave to him (11:22; 19:9). This love of just and obedient behavior constrains man even more when he is convicted that Yahweh himself loves justice and righteousness (cf. also Ps. 33:5; 37:28). Thus the Israelite is forced to make a decision: "See, I have set before you this day life and good, death and evil. If you obey the commandments of the Lord your God which I command you this day, by loving the Lord your God, by walking in his ways, and by keeping his commandments and his statutes and his ordinances, then you shall live and multiply, and the Lord your God will bless you in the land which you are entering to

---

[48] On the political concept of love, cf. above, I.2.

take possession of it" (Dt. 30:15f.). Thus parenetically the Deuteronomist has attempted to connect the idea of God's love for his people, which had been attained by the prophets, with the concept of their responsibility, which he presents under the figure of the obedience of a vassal king to the lord of the covenant. [49] But the Deuteronomist is also working under the disconcerting pressure of the deterioration of his people. Would the divine promise of help fail to materialize now that his people had apostatized? To be sure, the downfall of the kingdom of Israel and the acute crisis facing the kingdom of Judah were the result of disobedience on the part of kings of both kingdoms. But Yahweh is prepared for a new beginning. Because of his kindness he will forgive his people once again: "And the Lord your God will circumcise your heart and the heart of your offspring, so that you will love the Lord your God with all your heart and with all your soul, that you may live" (30:6). Here Yahweh's love for his people and Israel's love for her God are interwoven. But Yahweh is always the one who takes the first step in love, and Israel must actively respond to this love. Israel feels a great responsibility because Yahweh has taken the first step. A failure to love and obey Yahweh brings a curse on Israel. Perhaps it is against this background that the expansion in the prohibition against making graven images in the decalog (Ex. 20:5; Dt. 5:9f.) is to be understood, when it states that Yahweh's steadfast love will extend to the thousandth member of the children of those who love him and keep his commandments. But if Israel turns to other nations and joins them, then this bond of love will be broken (Josh. 23:11-13) and Israel will be given over to these nations. But on the other hand, for the Deuteronomist this means that commandments and laws are not really burdens to Israel, but are to be kept for the sake of love, and if this is the case Yahweh will give his people a reward. Yahweh is not a somber lawgiver, but a loving God who wants to take care of his people, but who also (for this very reason) expects their fidelity and devotion. This must be manifested in their whole manner of life; thus the other nations must be able to see it and acknowledge it. According to Jgs. 5:31aβ, which is probably Deuteronomistic, "the friends (of Yahweh) must be like the sun as he rises in his might." Thus the Deuteronomist and his school have developed a doctrine of the love of God for his people, and the love of Israel for her God. From his perspective, Nehemiah (1:5) applies this doctrine to Israel's history: Yahweh "keeps covenant and steadfast love with those who love him and keep his commandments." In their interest, Yahweh is against the enemies of his people, but also very severe on those who break the covenant. It is against this background again that love is contrasted with the wrath (→ אנף 'ānaph) and the fear (→ ירא yārē') of God. [50]

3. *Love for God in the Cult.* Life in Yahweh's love and the attempt to reciprocate this gracious gift in an appropriate manner has naturally also found expression in the cult. It was in Yahweh's sanctuary that man became aware of his love, and it was only in his sanctuary at Jerusalem that man could manifest love to

---

[49] See above, I.2.
[50] Cf. Nagel.

him in return. Not only does this give rise to the demand for cult centralization and cult purity, but also it is made concrete by joy in Yahweh's public worship (Ps. 27:4), by love for his sanctuary in Jerusalem (Lam. 1:2; Isa. 66:10; Ps. 26:8; 122:6), or by love for his name (Ps. 5:12[11]; 69:37[36]; Isa. 56:6). In the sanctuary, where men call on Yahweh's name together, they concentrate on his presence and his love. This love for the sanctuary is in harmony with Yahweh's love for the gates of Jerusalem (Ps. 51:21[19]; 87:2[1]). In this way, Israel's love for Yahweh has been made objective. This love for Yahweh in the cult was not considered to contradict one's love for neighbor, brother, stranger, or even enemy. The unity of the godly or of the godly community was effected chiefly by the worship of Yahweh, and in conjunction with this one's own personal behavior tended to be neglected. In light of this one-sided understanding of godliness, the prophetic criticism of the cult and the love of God practiced in the cult is completely understandable and necessary. In the cult God is present through his sanctuary and the ritual. Consequently, this form of love for God is always in danger of forgetting genuine brotherly love. This sort of divine service induces one to limit love for neighbor to the narrow circle of his fellow believers (cf. 1QS 1:9f.: "that they may love all the sons of light, ... and that they may hate all the sons of darkness"). In truth, this kind of piety is so close to the attitude of the introvert and the self-centered that it constantly threatens a genuine relationship of love between God and man, and man and God.

4. *Qumran*. This concept of the love of God bore fruit later in the Qumran community. According to the Damascus Document, God is merciful to them that love for him (CD B 2:20f.), indeed he had already loved Israel's ancestors (CD A 8:15f.; B 1:28-30), because Abraham had not gone astray like the other sons of Noah and was made a friend of God (CD A 3:2), and so his sons also were inscribed as friends of God (CD A 3:3). God loves not only those who had gone before, but also those who followed after (CD A 8:17; B 1:29f.) for the sake of the covenant (cf. Dt. 7:8; 10:15). In other words, he loves the Spirit (of Light) (1QS 3:26) and takes pleasure in its works.

Thus those who belong to the community will also love him out of free will (1QH 14:26) and act according to his will, because they love what he has chosen (1QS 1:3), what he loves (1QH 14:10[?]; 15:9f.), and hate what he abhors. In this love the members of the community are united to one another (1QS 1:9). In faithful love they belong to one another, they think justly and preserve the holy community (1QS 2:24; cf. 5:4,25; 8:2), and they love one another according to the abundance of their portion (1QH 14:19).

In general, the principal factor determining admission into the community is insight into the revelation according to which one can (1QS 9:16) and must (1QS 9:21) love the one and hate the other. Only the person who loves God's correction is admitted into the community (1QH 2:14).

This idea of God's love for his community is appropriately based on the concept of his love for the patriarchs in Deuteronomy. It demands a reciprocal love on the part of those who are chosen as well as love for one's fellow man. But this is binding only in the circle of the community itself; those who are rejected as

members are hated. In the Qumran literature we do not find concrete commandments to act in a manner becoming of love in the theological and ethico-social
sense. Rather, love has become a comprehensive term for the feeling of the relationship between God, the community, and the individual members of the
community, a way of designating the self-understanding of the conventicle. The
idea of love as an expression of human association has in the Qumran community
lost contact with its original concept and dynamic. [51]

Wallis

---

[51] *TDNT,* I, 38-55, goes into the ways in which the Rabbis, Hellenistic Judaism, and the
NT interpret love.

אֹהֶל 'ōhel; אָהַל 'āhal

Contents: I. Grammar and Etymology: 1. Word Formation and Frequency of Occur-
rence; 2. Meaning in Other Semitic Languages. II. The Tent in Daily Use and During
Festivals: 1. The Nomadic Tent; 2. Use by the Inhabitants of the Land; 3. 'ohel As a
Solemn Expression; 4. 'ohel with Ethical Predicates. III. The Heavenly Tent. IV. Tent
Sanctuaries: 1. Ancient Near Eastern; 2. Arabic; 3. 'ohel (mo'edh) in Pentateuchal Strata
Before the Priestly Code; 4. Tent Sanctuary and Tent Tradition After the Settlement; 5. The
Tent of Yahweh in Jerusalem; 6. The 'ohel mo'edh of the Priestly Code; 7. The Postexilic
Tent.

I. Grammar and Etymology.

1. *Word Formation and Frequency of Occurrence.* The segholate noun 'ohel
occurs 340 times in the OT. [1] A (denominative?) verb is derived from the root
'hl, which appears twice in the qal, once in the piel in the sense "to tabernacle,"

'ōhel. A. Alt, "Zelte und Hütten," *Alttestamentliche Studien F. Nötscher ... gewidmet. BBB,*
1 (1950), 16-25 = *KlSchr,* III, 233-242, cited hereafter; G. Cornfeld, *Pictorial Biblical Encyclopedia* (1964), 673-77; German ed. G. J. Botterweck, *Die Bibel und ihre Welt,* II (1969), 1381-89;
F. M. Cross, "The Tabernacle," *BA,* 10 (1947), 45-68; Dalman, *AuS,* VI, 1-145; G. H. Davies,
"Tabernacle," *IDB,* IV, 498-506; J. Dus, "Gibeon–eine Kultstätte des Šmš und die Stadt des
benjaminitischen Schicksals," *VT,* 10 (1960), 353-374; *idem,* "Der Brauch der Ladewanderung im alten Israel," *ThZ,* 17 (1961), 1-16; *idem,* "Noch zum Brauch der 'Ladewanderung',"
VT, 13 (1963), 126-132; *idem,* "Die Erzählung über den Verlust der Lade 1 Sam 4," *VT,* 13
(1963), 333-37; *idem,* "Die Thron- und Bundeslade," *ThZ,* 20 (1964), 241-251; D. W. Gooding,
The Account of the Tabernacle (1959); M. Görg, *Das Zelt der Begegnung. Untersuchungen
zur Gestalt der sakralen Zelttraditionen Altisraels. BBB,* 27 (1967); M. Haran, "'Otfe, maḥmal
and ḳubbe. Notes on the Study of the Origins of Biblical Cult Forms: The Problem of Arabic
Parallels," *D. Neiger Memorial Volume* (1959), 215-221; *idem,* "The Nature of the ''Ōhel
Mô'ēdh' in Pentateuchal Sources," *JSS,* 5 (1960), 50-65; *idem,* "The Complex of Ritual Acts

[1] *KBL.*

(continued on p. 119)

and perhaps also in Ugaritic.[2] However, Rabin thinks this verb comes from an Arabic root meaning "to get back, recover."[3] In Mishnaic Hebrew the piel and hiphil forms get the meaning "to spread out like a tent" in describing defilement one incurs when he touches a dead body.[4]

2. *Meaning in Other Semitic Languages.* The root *'hl* appears in almost all Semitic languages, and means (probably from the beginning on) both the tent as a dwelling place and the aggregate of tent dwellers. This double sense also occurs in Hebrew ("tent dwellers," e.g., in 1 Ch. 4:41) and perhaps also in Ugaritic.[5] In harmony with the different type of civilization, Akk. *ālu(m)* < **ahlum,* means "city" and "city authorities."[6] On the other hand, the Egyptian loanword *įhr* denotes only the dwelling place of nomads,[7] and Syr. *yahlā*[8] and Arab. *'ahl* mean only "people, family,"[9] a meaning taken over into Akkadian as the loanword *a'lu.*[10]

II. The Tent in Daily Use and During Festivals.

1. *The Nomadic Tent.* As it appears in the OT, the nomadic tent is composed of several curtains *(yeri'oth)* of goatskin and therefore is dark (Cant. 1:5). It is fastened down to pegs *(yathedh)* with cords *(metharim, chabhalim, yetharim).* Unlike the long wall tent which is common among Arabian nomads in modern times,[11] we are probably to assume that Syrian-Arabian nomads of antiquity used a bell tent supported in the middle by a wooden pole *('ammudh).* The door

---

Performed Inside the Tabernacle," *ScrHier,* 8 (1961), 272-302; *idem,* "Shiloh and Jerusalem," *JBL,* 81 (1962), 14-24; R. Hartmann, "Zelt und Lade," *ZAW,* 37 (1917/18), 209-244; K. Koch, *Die Priesterschrift.... FRLANT,* 71 (1959); *idem,* "Die Eigenart der priesterschriftlichen Sinaigesetzgebung," *ZThK,* 55 (1958), 36-51; *idem,* "Stiftshütte," *BHHW,* III, 1871-75; A. Kuschke, "Die Lagervorstellung der priesterschriftlichen Erzählung," *ZAW,* 63 (1951), 74-105; E. Kutsch, "Zelt," *RGG*[3], VI, 1893f.; S. Lehming, "Erwägungen zur Zelttradition," *Gottes Wort und Gottes Land. H. W. Hertzberg... dargebracht* (1965), 110-132; W. Michaelis, "σκηνή," *TDNT,* VII, 370-74; J. Morgenstern, "The Ark, the Ephod and the 'Tent of Meeting'," *HUCA,* 17 (1942/43), 153-266; 18 (1944), 1-52; 1945 ed., published independently, cited hereafter; M. Noth, *Exodus. OTL* (trans. 1962), 254-56; V. W. Rabe, "The Identity of the Priestly Tabernacle," *JNES,* 25 (1966), 132-34; G. von Rad, "Zelt und Lade," *NKZ,* 42 (1931), 478-498=*GSAT,* 109-129; L. Randellini, "La tenda e l'arca nella tradizione del VT," *Studii Bibl. Franciscani,* L.A. 13 (1962/63), 163-189; L. Rost, "Die Wohnstätte des Zeugnisses," *Festschrift F. Baumgärtel* (1959), 158-165; de Vaux, *AncIsr,* 294-97.

2 Driver, *CML,* 133.
3 *ScrHier,* 8 (1961), 384-86.
4 Levy, *WTM,* I, 35; M. Jastrow, *Dictionary of the Targumim* (1903, repr. 1950), I, 20.
5 *CTA,* 17 [II D], V, 30f.; cf. further *CTA,* 19 [I D], IV, 59f.
6 *AHw,* 39.
7 *WbÄS,* I, 119.
8 Brockelmann, cf. *VG,* I, 242.
9 *Ibid.,* 194.
10 *AHw,* 39.
11 Dalman, *AuS,* VI, 1-59.

(pethach) covered with a curtain supports this view (Gen. 18:9f.). One who puts up a tent stretches it out (usually the qal or hiphil of *natah*, but also *parash*, *mathach*) or pitches it *(taqa')*. When he gets ready to move to another location, he pulls it up (qal and piel of *nasa'*) and packs it *(tsa'an)*. Usually several tents are set up together. If the nomads intend to stay only temporarily, they form the tents into a camp *(machaneh)*; but if they intend to stay a long time, they set up a village of tents *(tirah)* protected by a stone wall. Wealthy wives have their own tents (Gen. 24:67; 31:33; Jgs. 4:17).

Migratory tribes of the east and south are well-known tent dwellers (Jgs. 6:3,5; Jer. 49:28f.; Hab. 3:7; Ps. 120:5). Each Israelite knows that the forefathers of mankind in general (Gen. 4:20; 9:21,27) and the patriarchs of Israel (12:8; 13:3; etc.) lived only in tents. The tent is the essence of the nomadic way of life. Where people continue that life out of fidelity to the customs of their ancestors, as among the Rechabites, the tent remains the traditional dwelling place (Jer. 35:7-10).

2. *Use by the Inhabitants of the Land.* Occasionally the inhabitants of the land also use tents as stables for cattle (2 Ch. 14:14 [Eng. v. 15]), or as dwellings for themselves on special occasions (2 S. 16:22) on the roof of the house. But as temporary dwellings, booths (→ סכה *sukkāh;* → חפה *chuppāh*) made of leafy branches or matting seem to have been more common. [12]

Tents and booths also play a role in military expeditions. Whereas David carries a tent with him (1 S. 17:54), the ark, Israel, and Judah dwell in booths (2 S. 11:11). Syrian soldiers spend the night in *'ohalim*, "tents" (2 K. 7:8,10); their kings in *sukkoth*, "booths" (1 K. 20:12,16). Chaldean troops also use tents (Jer. 37:10). We should probably assume that the later Assyrian custom of the commander-in-chief camping in a booth [13] and his soldiers in tents [14] was the practice in vogue earlier in wars during the monarchical period. [15] In the Hellenistic period the king has a palatial tent (Dnl. 11:45; cf. Jth. 10:17-22; 14:14f.).

3. *'ohel As a Solemn Expression.* The tent, as the kind of dwelling used in primitive times (which are acknowledged to be nomadic), is used as a solemn expression for one's "hearth and home." A battle is concluded by the soldiers fleeing to their own "tents" or by the prearranged cry, "every man to his tents" (Jgs. 7:8; 20:8; 1 S. 4:10; 13:2; 2 S. 18:17; 19:9[8]; 20:1,22; 1 K. 12:16; 2 K. 8:21; 13:5; 14:12; 2 Ch. 10:16; 25:22). After receiving the blessing at the cult place, the cult worshippers return to their own *'ohel*, "tent" (Dt. 16:7; Josh. 22:4,6-8; 1 K. 8:66; 2 Ch. 7:10). The host dismisses the (Levite) guest to his tent (Jgs. 19:9); is this merely a formula for dismissing a guest, or did the Levites still live in tents at this time?

Apart from this formal usage, the dwelling of an individual is seldom called

---

[12] These correspond to the Egyp. *imȝw/iȝmw;* Alt, 238f.; cf. *WbÄS, s.v.*
[13] *ANEP,* 374.
[14] *ANEP,* 170f.
[15] Alt, 237.

'ohel, "tent," and then only when 'ohel has reference to a group of tents. In Ps. 52:7(5), the writer describes Yahweh bringing death on man by saying that he tears him from his 'ohel, "tent." Job 19:12 says that God brings many troops against the tent of a man with whom he is angry (cf. Job 20:26). The idea of putting the tent sanctuary of Yahweh in its own place may have arisen from the fact that man's dwelling place was called a tent. According to Ps. 132:2-5, David returned to the 'ohel of his house after he had found a dwelling place (mishkanoth–a popular expression, which is parallel to 'ohel) for the God of Jacob (cf. Isa. 16:5). In Ps. 84:2(1), the mishkanoth, "dwelling place," of Yahweh is praised. It is much better to be a doorkeeper in the house of Yahweh than to dwell in the tents of the wicked (resha') (v. 11[10]).

More often, the dwelling places of a whole people are summed up as their 'ohalim, "tents." This is the case not only with nomadic peoples like Kedar (Cant. 1:5) and Edom (Ps. 83:7[6]), but also of Jacob (Jer. 30:18; Mal. 2:12) and Judah (Zec. 12:7; cf. Jer. 4:20; Hos. 9:6; Ps. 78:55; Lam. 2:4).

4. 'ohel with Ethical Predicates. Since a tent and its inhabitants form a unit, a tent can be filled with good or evil forces; and within the sphere of activity affecting one's destiny, it can impart to anyone who enters it a condition corresponding to the respective forces that control it. Statements like "the light (of the wicked) is dark in his tent" (Job 18:6) or "there are those who are incredibly negligent in their tents" (12:6) provide a transition to such ideas. In times of prosperity God "protects" one's tent (Job 29:4, LXX). This idea is even clearer where the tents of the righteous, tsaddiqim (Ps. 118:15) or yesharim (Prov. 14:11), are extolled, while those of the wicked (resha'im) are deplored (Job 8:22; 21:28). A tent can actually embody safety or peace (shalom) within it (Job 5:24). But wickedness ('avlah) can also dwell in it (Job 11:14; 22:23), as is the case with the tents of the wicked ('ohole resha', Ps. 84:11[10]) or the tents of bribery (shochadh, Job 15:34). Since a man's deed as the source of his future destiny is localized in his dwelling place, the 'ohel, "tent," becomes his trust and confidence (mibhtach, Job 18:14).

Since the ethically colored use of 'ohel is evident particularly in Job, we should not make generalizations about this use. The frequent use of this word in Job is probably to be explained by the inclusion of Job and his friends among the children of the East (→ קֶדֶם qedhem), who ordinarily dwell in tents, although the rich Job and his family have houses (1:4,13f.,18).

Thus, the use of 'ohel in the general sense of "dwelling" is limited to a few linguistic areas. 'ohel is by no means used for "dwelling of any kind."[16]

III. The Heavenly Tent. The only preexilic example of the use of 'ohel for the heavenly tent is Ps. 104:2. Yahweh, who covers himself with light as with a garment, is extolled hymnically: "who hast stretched out (natah) the heavens like a tent, / who hast laid the beams of thy chambers on the waters (above), /

---

[16] AuS, VI, 9; cf. Michaelis, 371, n. 10.

who makest the clouds thy chariot, / who ridest on the wings of the wind *(ruach)*."

Unfortunately the idea intended here is no longer clear. Is the psalmist merely expressing figuratively his awe that God had easily stretched out the firmament like a tent cloth? [17] Or is he comparing two different views derived from two different ways of life: a Bedouin tent as immense as heaven, and a massive, two-storied rural building having within it waters on which vessels (or beams) float? [18] The concept in v. 5 of the earth being set *(yasadh)* on its foundations supports this latter concept of heaven.

Heaven plays an important role as *'ohel* in Deutero-Isaiah, especially in the hymnic passages where the vocabulary is firmly established. The solidly established *(raqa', yasadh, 'asah)* earth always stands as a tent dwelling for mankind over against heaven, which is spread out *(natah)* with a substance light as *doq* (veil? gauze?) [19] (Isa. 40:21f.; cf. 42:5; 44:24; 45:12; 51:13; cf. 51:16 in the Syriac). Apparently Deutero-Isaiah knows nothing about the idea of a vault of heaven (→ רָקִיעַ *rāqîa'*), which is so dominant elsewhere in the OT. In connection with the heavenly tent, Deutero-Isaiah speaks of divine actions toward kings and princes of the nations (40:23; 42:5; 44:24-28; 45:13), of giving authentic oracles (40:21f.; 42:9; 45:11; 51:16), or of destroying heathen oracles (44:25). This connection of the tent with oracles reminds one of the tent sanctuary in the period before the Priestly Code; [20] cf. also the gift of the *ruach*, "spirit," in 42:5 with Nu. 11:16ff.

The later passages, Jer. 10:12 = 51:15; Zec. 12:1; Job 9:8, move in the same realm of ideas. They also contrast the solidly established earth with the expanded heaven (Job 9:6), and it is probably no accident that they refer to the *ruach* in their larger context (Jer. 10:13f.; 51:16f.; Zec. 12:1).

IV. Tent Sanctuaries.

1. *Ancient Near Eastern.* The nomads of the ancient Near East must have hidden their holy objects under a canvas (tent) roof because they especially wanted to protect them. Unfortunately no direct accounts of this have yet been found. However, among Semites who had become settled down, we still find the idea that deities (at appointed times) live in tents. This is expressed most clearly in Ugaritic myths and epics where deities are said to go out of their *'hl*, which is also called *mšknt (miškanatu)*. [21] According to Diodorus (xx. 65.1), the Carthaginians carried a holy tent with them into battle. [22] Other examples are less certain. A demi-relief from the temple of Bel at Palmyra depicts something like a red tent on a camel, and behind this three female figures, perhaps goddesses. [23]

---

[17] Duhm, *KHC*.
[18] Gunkel, *GHK*.
[19] *KBL*.
[20] See below.
[21] *CTA*, 17 [II D], V, 30f.; *CTA*, 15 [III K], III, 18.
[22] Smith-Stübe, *Religion*, 25.
[23] *Syr*, 15 (1934), Plate XIX.

A similar motif appears on a Syrian terra cotta. [24] Certainly the round booths for the god Min at Koptos do not belong here. [25]

Proper names from the Syriac-Arabic region give us indirect information concerning the role of the tent as a holy place. In the Israelite sphere, Oholiab is a legendary overseer of the "tabernacle" from the tribe of Dan (Ex. 31:6; 35:34; 38:23). The shortened form of this name, Ohel, occurs as the name of a son of Zerubbabel (1 Ch. 3:20). Further, we find the Edomitic Oholibamah as a female and tribal name (Gen. 36:2,5,14,18,25,41; 1 Ch. 1:52), the Phoenician 'hlb'l [26] and 'hlmlk, [27] the Thamudic 'hln, the Lihyanic 'hlbn, [28] and the Sabean 'hl'l. [29] The meaning of the name Oholiab is disputed. BDB, 14, assume a construct relationship here: "tent of X." [30] But Noth finds difficulty with this explanation because 'abh never occurs elsewhere in a name as the last element in a construct relationship, and he prefers to interpret this name as a sentence, "the deity X is a tent (a figurative term meaning protection)." [31] Of course, this conflicts with the usual name which is to be interpreted as a sentence, in which the predicative element comes *after* the subject.

2. *Arabic.* As the *qubbah* mentioned in Nu. 25:8 seems to have been a ritual tent, [32] so the pre-Islamic Arabs used the *qubbe,* a small tent made out of red leather (cf. Ex. 26:14) containing two stone idols. It was carried on a camel in processions, on searches for pastureland, and in battles. A seer *(kāhin)* was responsible for taking care of it, and maidens were associated with it (cf. 1 S. 2:22). It came to serve as a place of refuge (cf. 1 K. 2:28ff.). The *qubbe* is a genuine parallel to the OT *'ohel mo'edh.* [33]

Other material derived from the Arabic region has little in common with the Israelite tent sanctuary. This is the case with the *mahmal,* a pavilion made out of black silk, under which the Koran was brought to Medina, [34] or with the *'otfe* or the *merkeb* of the more recent past, a stationary sedan chair which is placed on the back of a camel and indicates the direction that should be taken in travels and in battles. [35]

3. *'ohel (mo'edh) in Pentateuchal Strata Before the Priestly Code.* More than half of the occurrences of *'ohel* in the OT, viz., 182 (of which, indeed, 140 belong to the P stratum) denote a holy tent consecrated to Yahweh. 133 passages (of

---

24 F. Cumont, *Études syriennes* (1917), 273-76.
25 *RÄR,* 462, 467; Lacau, *ChrÉg,* 28 (1953), 13-22.
26 *CIS,* I, 54.
27 *CIS,* I, 50, 2.
28 On both of these, cf. Moritz, *ZAW,* 44 (1926), 87.
29 J. Halévy, *Inscriptions sabéennes* (1872), 46,2.
30 So similarly Kerber, *Die rel.-gesch. Bedeutung der hebräischen Eigennamen des AT* (1897): "tent partner of (the god) X."
31 Noth, *IPN,* 159.
32 "Wedding tent," Morgenstern, 260.
33 See below. Further details are given in Morgenstern, 208-221.
34 *Ibid.,* 196f.
35 *Ibid.,* 157-193; pictures in *BHHW,* III, 1871.

which 120 appear in P, and 6 in Ch.) call it the *'ohel mo'edh*, [36] which is usually translated "tent of meeting" (between Yahweh and Moses, or Yahweh and Israel). But some scholars have suggested that it be translated "tent of assembly" of divine beings,[37] or "tent of assembly for a festival."[38] Luther translated "Stiftshütte" because of the medieval distinction between parish churches and collegiate churches. Ex. 33:7-11; Nu. 11:16-29; 12; Dt. 31:14f., speak of the *'ohel (mo'edh)* in passages which have been loosely inserted into the context, and which are characterized by their being "loaded with problems," unlike most other Pentateuchal legends. The term *mo'edh* is suspect in all passages of later origin, since in surrounding passages we find simply *ha'ohel*. (The combination *'ohel mo'edh* cannot be demonstrated with certainty earlier than in P.)

Ex. 33:7-11 belongs to the Sinai complex. In a series of sentences using *vav* with the perfect, [39] Moses is instructed [40] to pitch a tent outside the Israelite camp and to call it *'ohel (mo'edh)*. [41] Yahweh appears there in a pillar of cloud when necessity requires, and speaks to Moses "face to face" about problems that are vital to the people. In the present context, the intention of this paragraph is to indicate the place where God reveals himself in order that communication with the God of Sinai might continue after the people leave this region.

According to Nu. 11:16-29, Yahweh appears shortly after the departure from Sinai. After the people murmur at the *'ohel (mo'edh)*, he takes 70 portions of the *ruach*, "spirit," of Moses, and distributes them to the elders of Israel, who then begin to prophesy. In connection with this story, Nu. 12 tells how Miriam and Aaron murmur against Moses' foreign wife and his special position before Yahweh. Yahweh, who appears at the tent, teaches them the difference between a prophet and God's servant, Moses, and punishes Miriam with leprosy. It is only through Moses' intercession that her illness is taken away.

Dt. 31:14f. deals with the end of Israel's wandering in the wilderness just before Moses' death. Yahweh commissions Moses to appoint Joshua as his successor at the *(mo'edh-)*tent, by which the Israelites had been led up to that time.

The similarity of ideas and choice of words in these four paragraphs is striking. Admittedly, they say nothing about the design of the tent. But they do make a number of things clear: (a) Moses had the unique privilege of an intimate relationship with God at the tent; Yahweh spoke with him "face to face" (Ex. 33:11), "mouth to mouth," and Moses beheld his → תמונה *temûnāh* (an image of God?) (Nu. 12:8). (b) The tent was located outside the camp, and one had to go out (*yatsa'*, Ex. 33:7f.; Nu. 11:26; 12:4) to it, while all the tents where the people lived had doors which faced toward the holy tent (Ex. 33:8). (c) When a person came near the tent or went into it, he presented himself in a specified way

---

[36] Kuschke, 82.

[37] H. Gressmann, *Mose und seine Zeit* (1913), and G. Beer, *HAT*, 3 (1939), on Ex. 33:7ff.; cf. Isa. 14:13 and Ugar. *m'd*.

[38] Wilson, *JNES*, 4 (1945), 245; cf. Cross, 65.

[39] This is ritual style; see K. Koch, *Die Priesterschrift . . .* , 96f.

[40] So Baentsch, *GHK*, in contradistinction from more recent commentaries which find here an iterative narrative.

[41] According to the LXX and Syriac, the reference is to Moses' own tent, which now receives sacral consecration; cf. Görg, 155.

(hithyatstsebh, Nu. 11:16; Dt. 31:14 [twice]; cf. Ex. 33:8). (d) Yahweh came down (yaradh, Ex. 33:9; Nu. 11:17,25; 12:5) in the pillar of cloud and appeared to the people (Dt. 31:15; Ex. 33:10), whereas the pillar stood (ʿamadh, Ex. 33:9f.; Nu. 12:5; Dt. 31:15) at the door of the tent. (e) Aside from Moses, only Joshua, as servant, is connected with the tent (Ex. 33:11; Nu. 11:28; Dt. 31:14f.). These points of agreement suggest that the four passages originated in the same circle of authors. Often scholars assign them to E because they refer to prophets, and E is the only Pentateuchal source that mentions prophets. [42] Noth thinks that three of these passages were late insertions in J, [43] and that Dt. 31:14f. was a late insertion by a Deuteronomistic hand. [44]

Nothing is said about sacrifices and rites in these passages except for the two references to the people rising up and worshipping (Ex. 33:8,10) when Moses officiated at the sanctuary. Only Ex. 33:7 states that any one who sought (mebhaqqesh) Yahweh would go out to the tent. Thus the tent seems to have been chiefly a place where oracles were given, which is also suggested by its connection with the prophetic task in Nu. 11f. However, biqqesh, "seek," can also mean the pilgrimage to the "epiphany of Yahweh" at the festival. [45]

It is disputed whether we are to assume a connection between the moʿedh-tent and the ark in these passages. The only basis for making such a connection is the statement in Ex. 33:7, venatah lo michuts lammachaneh, "and (Moses used to) pitch ... outside the camp." The point at issue here is how one is to interpret the little word lo. (a) Some scholars delete it with the LXX, (b) others apply it to Moses ("for himself"), [46] (c) others apply it to Yahweh ("for him"), [47] (d) and still others apply it to the ark, which originally had been mentioned in the foregoing text, but had subsequently been omitted. [48]

Viewed historically, if this tent actually goes back to the period before Israel's conquest of Canaan, there is no reason to disconnect it from the person of Moses.

4. *Tent Sanctuary and Tent Tradition After the Settlement.* Usually it is assumed that the narratives concerning the ʾohel (moʿedh) may be traced back to a roving sanctuary of nomadic peoples who later became Israelite tribes, a sanctuary which became unnecessary soon after the conquest and vanished. There is uncertainty, however, as to the region and tribal league in which it was used before it vanished. (a) According to de Vaux, the last place it was located historically was Baal-peor in Transjordan (Nu. 25:6). [49] (b) Since the Jerusalemite prophet Nathan opposed king David's plans to build a temple with the argument that since the exodus from Egypt Yahweh had moved about in Israel "in a tent and a dwelling" (2 S. 7:1-6), some scholars have concluded that he is refer-

---

[42] So recently Haran, *JSS*, 52; Görg, 138-170.
[43] *OTL* on Ex. 33:7ff.; Nu. 11:16ff.; chap. 12.
[44] *A History of Pentateuchal Traditions* (trans. 1971), 32f., n. 126.
[45] W. Beyerlin, *Origins and History of the Oldest Sinaitic Traditions* (trans. 1965), 122f.
[46] Baentsch, *GHK;* Noth, *OTL;* Haran, *JSS,* 53.
[47] Gressmann, *SAT;* Beer, *HAT,* 3.
[48] Holzinger, *KHC;* Eissfeldt, *Hexateuchsynopse* (1922), 274*; Beyerlin, 114.
[49] De Vaux, 297.

ring to an ancient Judean theology concerning Yahweh's appearances to his people "which could not be reconciled with the idea of connecting Yahweh with one place." [50] We may conclude from this that the tent was native to Judah. Could it have served as the sanctuary of the ancient six-tribe league at or near Hebron? [51] Referring to a Moslem tent festival near Joppa, Kraus goes a step further and suggests that the reference here is to a great Harvest Festival in the southern (or eastern) wilderness, where the Israelite amphictyony gathered together in a tent camp around the nomadic sanctuary of the 'ohel mo'edh. [52] He considers Hos. 12:10(9) to be an important proof of this interpretation: "I am the Lord your God from the land of Egypt; I will again make you dwell in tents, as in the days of the appointed feast." [53] He also cites Nu. 24:1f., where Balaam set his face toward the wilderness and saw Israel "encamping tribe by tribe." Dt. 33:18 is also of interest, because it refers to the tents of Issachar and Zebulun in connection with a sacrificial feast. However, these references take us far beyond the Judean sphere. (c) Other scholars suggest that the tent sanctuary should be connected with one of the great cult places in central Palestine. One possible location is Shiloh, because according to Josh. 18:1; 19:51 (which, to be sure, are late passages) the tribes assembled there at (the door of) the 'ohel mo'edh; according to 1 S. 2:22, the sons of Eli lay with the women who served at the entrance of the tent of meeting there; and according to Ps. 78:60, Yahweh dwelt among men in his residence and tent there. [54] But the reference in 1 S. 1:24 to a permanent house or temple at Shiloh opposes the localization of the tent there. (d) Another possibility is that the tent was located at Gibeon, since 1 Ch. 16:39; 21:29; 2 Ch. 1:3, state that it was there. [55] Görg connects Nob with the sanctuary at Gibeon, and also thinks that the tent stayed at Nob for a long time. [56]

It is hardly possible to determine with certainty where the tent was located, because there are so few references to its location in the OT. The best that we can do is to go on to the outstanding points of contact between the different tent traditions through traditio-historical investigations. Thus we must seek for circles which have a close continuity with Moses and Joshua, and which have a high regard for the institution of the 70 elders and a specific form of prophetism, a prophetism which has nothing in common with the great literary prophets, and which knows of a unique servant of God over the nabis. [57] This problem obviously does not exist whenever one uses the tent of David in Jerusalem as his point of departure for the tradition of the mo'edh-tent in general. [58]

---

[50] Von Rad, *OT Theol,* I (trans. 1962), 238, n. 114; Kuschke, 103.
[51] Von Rad, *Studies in Deuteronomy* (trans. 1953), 43.
[52] *Worship in Israel* (trans. 1966), 130.
[53] This interpretation is rejected by H. W. Wolff, *Hosea* (trans. 1974), 215.
[54] So Beyerlin, 119; Haran, *JBL,* 20.
[55] So E. Auerbach, *Moses* (1953), 159.
[56] Görg, 127-136.
[57] On the basis of Nu. 12, Kraus, 105ff., postulates an office, "which included all the functions of mediation and direction laid down in the divine law concerning intercession and sacrifice which were required as between Yahweh and his people" (p. 110).
[58] So Rabe, 132-34.

5. *The Tent of Yahweh in Jerusalem.* According to the (redactional) note in
1 K. 8:4, when Solomon dedicated the temple, he transferred not only the ark of
Yahweh, but also the *'ohel mo'edh,* to the newly erected sanctuary. In 2 Ch. 5:5,
the Chronicler assumes that Solomon brought the tent to the temple from Gibeon,
while the context of the books of Samuel and Kings suggests that the tent Solomon
brought to the temple was the one David had erected some ten years earlier in his
capital as a protection for the ark which he transferred to Jerusalem at that time
(2 S. 6:17). Furthermore, it is certain that the ark and the tent were connected
from the time that David brought the ark to Jerusalem.

The tent David erected in Jerusalem is not called *'ohel mo'edh,* but *'ohel yhvh,*
"tent of Yahweh." It must have been relatively large, because not only was the
anointing oil kept there, which the priest Zadok had to have in order to anoint
Solomon (1 K. 1:39), but also inside this tent there was an altar with horns where
the commander-in-chief Joab sought protection (1 K. 2:28-34), although he was
unable to escape from his rival Benaiah. This is the first passage in which the
concept of asylum appears along with the tent, but it seems to be connected with
the altar more strongly than with the tent.

If there is a historical nucleus in the conversation between David and Nathan
in 2 S. 7:1-7, then it indicates that Nathan looked on the Jerusalem tent as a
successor to the earlier *(mo'edh-)*tent. [59] He assumes that it was moved from
tribe to tribe by a decree of Yahweh in order to impart the role of leadership
to the tribe in question: "I have been moving about in a tent and a dwelling. /
In all places where I have moved among all the Israelites, / did I speak a word
with any of the tribes of Israel, / whom I commanded to shepherd my people Israel,
saying, / 'Why have you not built me a house of cedar?'" (2 S. 7:6f.). Regardless
of whether or not the Davidic tent of Yahweh was brought into the Solomonic
temple and kept (folded up) in one of its chambers, terminology accruing to the
tent became a part of the language of the temple. The Psalms extol the temple
as a tent, especially in connection with the concept of asylum (Ps. 27:5; 61:5[4];
cf. 15:1; 78:60; and Isa. 33:20f.). The idea of the tent as a symbol of leadership
(presumably with regard to the Jerusalem tradition) seems to lie behind the
allegorical historical presentation in Ezk. 23, where the two wives of Yahweh,
'oholah = Samaria, [60] and *'oholibhah* = Jerusalem, "(my) cult tent is in her," are
described in their degradation. [61] In both cases the idea seems to be that the tent
was supposed to be Yahweh's possession, but his two wives were maintaining
their own tents, i.e., their own separate realms of authority.

6. *The 'ohel mo'edh of the Priestly Code.* Nowhere in the OT is so much
importance attributed to the holy tent as in the P account of the giving of the law
at Sinai in Ex. 25–Nu. 10. On Mt. Sinai, Moses was shown a pattern (→ תבנית
tabhnîth) of the *mo'edh*-tent (Ex. 25:9), which P prefers to call → מִשְׁכָּן *mishkān,*
and he built it according to that pattern, and used it during the wilderness wander-

---

59 Von Rad, see above; Kuschke, 95f.
60 A feminine form? Or should we read *'oholah,* "who has a tent sanctuary," *GesB, KBL?*
61 On the interpretation of these names, cf. Zimmerli, *BK,* XIII/1, 541f.

ings as the only sanctuary. In the description of the tent in P, there are striking
similarities with the account of the building of the Solomonic temple (1 K. 6f.).
There was a time, of course, when biblical scholars attributed the priority to the
wilderness sanctuary. However, the unrealistic and formal style of P as compared
with the realistic account of the building of the temple led Wellhausen to conclude that the "tabernacle" in P was "the copy, not the prototype, of the temple
at Jerusalem." [62] Further research since Wellhausen has shown that this conclusion is one-sided. It is true that there are points of agreement between the
P description of the tent and the Solomonic temple, including the ark with the
cherubim (Ex. 25:1-22; cf. 1 K. 8:6-8, arranged differently to be sure, → כפרת
kappōreth), the bread of the Presence (Ex. 25:23-30; cf. Ezk. 41:22), the altar of
burnt-offering (Ex. 27:1-8; cf. Ezk. 43:18-27), the bronze sea (Ex. 30:17-21; cf.
1 K. 7:23-26), and perhaps also the altar of incense (Ex. 31:1-10; cf. 1 K. 7:48). But
in addition to this, there are other features of the tent which do not fit the material
used for a permanent stone building, but rather are more suitable to a movable
structure for wandering in the wilderness, such as wooden partitions instead of
stone walls (Ex. 26:15-30), and curtains instead of doors (26:31-37) and instead
of outer walls (27:9ff.). But there are even more differences than these. This is
particularly clear in the huge coverings which are spread out on top of each
other in four thicknesses over the sanctuary, the largest of which was made out
of eleven curtains of goatskins (each measuring 30 cubits long and 4 cubits wide),
bearing the name ʾohel. There is nothing in the Solomonic temple to compare
with this portion of the tabernacle and with the two half curtains that hang over
the back of the tabernacle made out of reddish rams' skins and fish skins (26:7-
14). Furthermore, the all-surpassing position of Moses as the only person commissioned by God to maintain the sanctuary and to watch over the services there
is foreign to Jerusalemite custom. The wilderness sanctuary described by P would
have been well organized and able to function without curtains, while conversely
the ʾohel curtains (with the wooden frames to support them) were adequate for
a holy room without a block house. This leads us to conclude that in addition to
the Solomonic temple, there was another pattern for the tent sanctuary which
had its origin outside Jerusalem.

The way in which these two patterns have been merged may be explained
either by a literary-critical approach or by a traditio-historical approach. Galling
conjectures that there are two independent P sources behind Ex. 25ff. [63] The
earlier source, P^A, has in mind a genuine long tent. [64] The later source, P^B, has a
second set of expensive tapestry hanging underneath the curtains of goatskins,
and tries to transform the tent which was made like the temple into a narrowly
enclosed cult room. But this leaves many unsolved problems.

A better way to deal with all the strata found in the text is to begin with a style
analysis, and to consider the sentences with the *vav* and the perfect which can
be easily recognized in Ex. 25ff. as the older nucleus of a (quasi-)ritual presum-

---

[62] Wellhausen, *Prolegomena to the History of Ancient Israel* (trans. ed. 1957), 37.
[63] Galling, *HAT*, 3.
[64] Cf. the illustration in *ibid.*, 135.

ably from P, as Koch (Priesterschrift) and Görg have attempted. According to this approach, the early stratum referred to a tent sanctuary without vertical walls, but with the ark, the table of the Presence, a lampstand and an Aaronic priesthood. In this stratum, the tent sanctuary was not yet called ('ohel) mo'edh. Unfortunately, it is not possible to determine the time or the place in which these cultic elements originated.

In the period after the destruction of the Solomonic temple, P describes the "tabernacle" of the Mosaic period as the program for the anticipated reconstruction in Jerusalem. For this purpose, P transformed the cult tent, which was considered to be Mosaic, into a miniature pattern of the temple that was yet to be built. In order to preserve the length of the tent sanctuary, the dimensions of the Jerusalem temple were reduced to half their actual size, and the entrance halls of the temple were eliminated. In the ancient tent, a wooden substructure was made out of planks which were set up vertically and fastened to each other. It was made in the form of a block house 30 cubits long, 10 cubits wide, and 10 cubits high. It had no permanent covering. In place of this there was a magnificent covering adorned with cherubim, which hung down on the outside of the wooden partitions and was called a mishkan (26:1-6). The curtains of the traditional tent sanctuary and the two protective coverings probably were not simply laid over the wooden partitions, but were stretched out on the side with tent-pegs. [65]

P took over from Jerusalem the separation of the Holy Place from the (cubical) holy of holies as its design, as well as the theophany of the divine → כבוד kābhôdh, "glory." However, in P the "glory" is no longer connected with the great New Year Festival, but appears unexpectedly at times of severe calamity (Nu. 14:10; 16:19; 17:7[16:42]; 20:6). P also took over observance of the great sacrifices from Jerusalem, but they are made to serve P's viewpoint, especially with regard to atonement (→ כפר kipper) and remission of sins. Nothing is said in P about the tent being a place where oracles were given. Instead of this, the longing for cultic holiness in the midst of the people is emphasized. Presumably the ark (like the altar of burnt offering in the outer court) [66] is located in the holy of holies and is a center of the holy region. From the holy of holies outward, holiness streams in concentric circles and on a gradually descending scale the further one is removed from the center. [67] This explains the careful and deliberate use of gold, silver, or bronze, or violet purple, reddish purple, crimson red, or white materials, and the offices of the high priest (=Aaron), priests, and Levites in connection with the tent sanctuary. In order to promote holiness, the tent sanctuary is moved into the center of the camp, where the individual tribes can camp around it according to a specific plan (Nu. 2).

The sanctuary arranged thus, providing blessing and atonement, is the goal of God's way with Israel, indeed with creation. With its completion, Israel is really a people and Yahweh is truly God. In the sanctuary, the static idea of holiness is united with a dynamic concept of the always unexpected irruptive

---

[65] Cf. the illustrations in BHHW, III, 1873f.
[66] "Lageplan," BHHW, III, 1875.
[67] Koch, ZThK, 41-45.

meeting of God with his people, which gave rise to the expression "tent of mo'edh (meeting)." As in the old narratives, the door of the tent also plays an important role here: "I will meet with you there, to speak there to you (Moses). / There I will meet the people of Israel, / and it shall be sanctified by my glory; / I will consecrate the mo'edh-tent and the altar; / Aaron also and his sons I will consecrate, to serve me as priests. / And I will dwell among the people of Israel, / and will be their God. / And they shall know that I am the Lord their God, / who brought them forth out of the land of Egypt / that I might dwell among them; / I am the Lord their God" (Ex. 29:42-46).

7. *The Postexilic Tent.* The disappearance of the holy tent in the Solomonic temple gave rise to the legend in the postexilic period that Jeremiah dragged the 'ohel out of the temple before it was destroyed and hid it in an unknown place, where it will be discovered in the eschaton (2 Macc. 2:4-8). The Samaritans state that Joshua hid the tent in the synagogue on Gerizim. [68] Such speculations concerning the tent of God help to explain why the LXX attributes to the tent much greater importance than the NT does. [69]

Koch

---

[68] J. Bowman, "Samaritanische Probleme," *F. Delitzsch–Vorlesung* [1957] (1967), 23.
[69] See *TDNT*.

אוֹב 'ôbh

Contents: I. 1. Orthography; 2. Etymology. II. The Ancient Near Eastern Background. III. Use in the OT.

I. 1. *Orthography.* In the singular this word is written in the *plene* form (אוֹב 'ôbh), but in the plural it is written defectively (אֹבוֹח 'ōbhôth). [1] The *scriptio defectiva* in the plural makes it possible to confuse 'obhoth with 'abhoth, "fathers," even if the suggested emendation of 'abhotham to 'obhoth in Job 8:8 is more clever than convincing. [2]

'ôbh. W. F. Albright, *Yahweh and the Gods of Canaan* (London, 1968); C. J. Gadd, *Ideas of Divine Rule in the Ancient East* (London, 1948); H. A. Hoffner, "Second Millennium Antecedents to the Hebrew 'ōb," *JBL,* 86 (1967), 385-401; H. Schmidt, "אוב," *Festschrift K. Marti.* *BZAW,* 41 (1925), 253-261; F. Schmidtke, "Träume, Orakel und Totengeister als Künder der Zukunft in Israel und Babylonien," *BZ,* 11 (1967), 240-46; M. Vieyra, "Les noms du 'mundus' en hittite et en assyrien et la pythonisse d'Endor," *RHA,* 69 (1961), 47-55.

[1] *GK,* § 81.
[2] Albright, 142, n. 85.

2. *Etymology*. At least three views of the etymology of *'obh* have been suggested. According to one view, *'obh* is the same word that means a "bottle made out of skins" which holds wine, in Job 32:19. [3] This would mean that the technique of necromancy was labelled ventriloquism. The LXX uses *engastrímythos*, "ventriloquist," in all passages except Isa. 29:4, where *'obh me'erets* is rendered by *hoi phōnoúntes ek tês gês*, "the ones calling out of the earth." Sometimes the Vulgate reads *magus*, "sorcerer" (1 S. 28:3; Lev. 19:31; 20:6), and sometimes *python*, "diviner" (Isa. 8:19; 29:4; 2 K. 21:6; 23:24; Dt. 18:11; Lev. 20:27). According to a second view, *'obh* is derived from the same Semitic verbal root from which the Arabic verb *'āba*, "to return," is derived. [4] This theory is opposed by the fact that this verbal root is not used in the older Semitic languages such as Akkadian, Ugaritic, Hebrew, Phoenician, and Aramaic. According to a third view, *'obh* is a non-Semitic cultural loanword, which is found in Sumerian (*ab*, "opening"), Akkadian (*aptu*, Neo-Assyrian *apu*), Hurrian and Hittite (*a-a-bi*, normalized *ayabi*), Ugaritic (*'ēb* < *'ayb*) and Hebrew (*'obh*), and in all these languages means *mundus*, "sacrificial pit." [5] The word is old; it was in use earlier than the second millennium B.C. It is also found in the name of the wilderness station Oboth (Nu. 21:10f.; 33:43f.), and indicates that waterholes were nearby. Albright [6] compares the Upper Mesopotamian tribal name *Ubrapi'* with the proper names found at Byblos from the early second millennium B.C., *Ibdâdî* and *Ib-addî*. [7] But because of the similar name of the male moon-god *'Ib/'Eb* in the Ugaritic texts, this suggestion must be treated with caution. [8] The divine name *Ub* can also be found in a Luwian proper name *mÚ-ba-LÚ-iš;* [9] cf. other Luwian names of the type "divine name + *zitiš*" ("man of the God . . . "): *mdIŠTAR-LÚ*, *mYarra-zitiš*, *mŠanta-zitiš*, *mTarḫunda-zitiš*. For an example of connection with a dead ancestor in such a name, cf. *mḪuḫḫa-zitiš*. [10]

II. The Ancient Near Eastern Background. The oldest references to *ab*, "pit," in connection with sacrifice are to be found in the Sumerian version of the Gilgamesh Epic, [11] where we learn that Gilgamesh dug a pit in the ground (*ab-làl-kur-ri gál-mu-na-ab-tag₄*), and out of it he called forth the spirit (*líl*) of his dead companion Enkidu. The Akkadian version [12] uses the expression *takkap erṣeti* ("hole in the ground") for such a pit, and the word *zaqīqu* for the spirit. [13]

---

[3] Nöldeke, *ZDMG*, 28 (1874), 667; Zimmern, *GGA* (1898), 817; Tur-Sinai, *EMiqr*, I, 135-37.

[4] Gesenius, *Thesaurus*, s.v.; Hitzig and König, *Offenbarungsbegriff*, 2, 150.

[5] Hoffner, 385ff.

[6] Albright, 122f., 146, n. 43.

[7] *AfO*, 19 (1959/60), 120.

[8] *UT*, 348, No. 10.

[9] *KUB*, XXII, 70, rev. 82.

[10] *KBo*, V, 7, rev. 9; ḫuḫḫa-"ancestor."

[11] BE XXI, No. 35, obv. 16f.

[12] Gilg. XII, 83f.

[13] *CAD*, XXI, 60; Hoffner, 398.

The entire episode reminds us of 1 S. 28. [14] From the fifteenth to the end of the thirteenth centuries B.C. examples of this sort appear in the Hittite ritual. [15] In this ritual, sacrificial pits (ḫatteššar, patteššar, a-a-bi; Akk. asru; Sumerogram TÚL, BÙR) were dug (kinu-, padda-) in the ground at a place which had been determined by interrogating the gods. In this pit, oblations (loaves, cheese, butter, honey mixed with milk, oil, honey, wine, beer, and sacrificial blood), expensive gifts of silver (models of the human ear, breast ornaments, a miniature ladder), and often even the sacrificial animal, were lowered into the pit. After the sacrificial animal was lowered, someone below in the pit slaughtered it. Two of the objects lowered into the pit symbolized the twofold intention of the entire procedure. The silver model of an ear indicated the wish of the offerer to "hear" and to learn from the inhabitant of the Underworld. The silver ladder or staircase expressed the desire that the spirit might ascend to the world above. The wholly chthonic orientation of the procedure and of the accessories used is quite clear in the preference for night as the time for carrying out the ritual, for silver (instead of gold, copper, etc.) as the kind of metal to be used for the gifts, and for black sacrificial animals (especially hogs and dogs).

Of particular interest is the personification of the pit as the deity ^DA-a-bi, who is the object of a particular exorcism ritual. [16] He is the god of the Underworld, and presides there over a court of justice in which scales (Sum. giš.rín zi.ba.na) are used. [17] ^DA-a-bi belongs to the same class of Underworld deities as the chthonic spirit tarpiš. [18] It is very probable that tarpiš represents the same ancient migratory word as Heb. teraphim. [19] Thus, both 'obh and teraphim are to be identified as mantic properties of the Underworld, in which it was thought that the source of true knowledge was to be found (→ יִדְּעֹנִי yiddeʿōnî). Also the expression → רְפָאִים rephāʾîm, "spirits of the dead," is connected with 'obh in the second millennium B.C., if the tribal name Ub-rapiʾ in the Mari texts is really to be interpreted in this way. Also in the alphabetic text from ancient Ugarit a form of this ancient migratory word is found: 'ēb (from *'ayb), in combination with 'il in ảlảb, "ancestral spirit." [20] Albright emends Isa. 14:19 and finds 'lʾb there. [21] Again, it must be emphasized that 'lʾb itself is not a monument or a stele. [22] In the expression skn ảlảb, it is skn which designates the monument; ảlảb is the spirit or soul of the dead who is remembered by the skn (monument). Also the word spelled syllabically as il-abi[23] should not be interpreted erroneously as "God of the father," because abu/apu appears commonly in later Assyrian

---

[14] Cf. Gadd, 88f.

[15] Hoffner, 385ff.; Vieyra, 47ff.

[16] KUB, VII, 41; ZA, 54 (1961), 131f.; ^DA-a-bi also occurs in KUB, X, 63, I, 18, 20, 24, 26; XXXIV, 96, 6; XXIV, 49, III, 31; KBo, X, 45; II, 19; III, 22; Bo 2072, III, 13, 16, 19.

[17] KUB, VII, 41, III, 19f.

[18] See H. Hoffner, JNES, 27 (1968), 61-68; with regard to the Babylonian šēdu as "external soul," cf. A. L. Oppenheim, Ancient Mesopotamia (1964), 198-201.

[19] See Hoffner, loc. cit.

[20] UT, 358, No. 165; Hoffner, JBL, 386f.; Astour, JAOS, 86 (1966), 279, 281.

[21] Albright, 141, n. 80.

[22] Cf. Hoffner, JBL, 387.

[23] Astour, 279, n. 25.

texts as a word for the pit in the ground. [24] That this deity is known both as *ʒb* and as *ʒlʒb* corresponds exactly with the two ways of writing a divine name in Hittite texts: ᴰ*Kunirša* (Canaanite *qn 'rṣ*) and ᴰ*Elkunirša* (Canaanite *'l qn 'rṣ*). [25]

III. Use in the OT. The OT uses this expression in three different senses: (1) the pit which has been digged out, by means of which the spirits of the dead are called up (1 S. 28:7f.); (2) the spirit or spirits of the dead which are troubled (Isa. 29:4); [26] and (3) the necromancer who calls forth the spirits to get information (Lev. 19:31; 20:6,27; Dt. 18:11; 1 S. 28:3,9; 2 K. 21:6 [= 2 Ch. 33:6]; 23:24; Isa. 8:19). The OT does not describe how the pit was prepared. But this is no objection to this interpretation. The spirit ascends (*'alah,* 1 S. 28:8,11,13f.) from the ground and undoubtedly comes forth from a prepared opening. Although the language of Isa. 29:4 is perhaps somewhat figurative, still in the scornful words found there we can get some impression of the way in which the spirits were called: "Then deep from the earth you shall speak, from low in the dust your words shall come; your voice shall come from the ground like the voice of a ghost, and your speech shall whisper out of the dust." The prophets of Yahweh describe the audible manifestations of the *'obh* as "whispering" or "chirping" (*tsaphtseph*), an expression which denotes the cry of certain birds (Isa. 10:14) or the rustling of the leaves of the willow tree (cf. the name of a tree *tsaphtsaphah,* Ezk. 17:5). The different verbs connected with *'obh* indicate only that here was the source of secret information: a person "turned to" (*tiphnu 'el,* Lev. 19:31), "sought" (*darash 'el,* Isa. 8:19; *darash be,* 1 S. 28:7), "used" (*'asah*) or "consulted" (*sha'al be,* 1 Ch. 10:13) the necromancer, who asked advice of (*sha'al 'el,* Dt. 18:11) the spirit or spirits who came up out of the pit, or "divined by" (*qasam be,* 1 S. 28:8) them.

1 S. 28 is the most fruitful and probably also the oldest witness in the OT for the understanding of *'obh.* In this passage we learn that the crisis which gave rise to the consultation of the necromancer was a serious military threat (vv. 4f.). Naturally, the approved ways of seeking advice (*nebhi'im,* "prophets"; *'urim,* "Urim"; *chalomoth,* "dreams") were exhausted first, but Yahweh did not answer (*'anah,* v. 6). When this happened, out of desperation Saul commanded his officers to seek out for him a woman who had access to an *'obh.* Saul went to her at night partly to conceal his identity, and partly because necromancers of this sort preferred to do their work at night. [27] He made a twofold request: (1) "Divine (*qasam*) for me by a spirit (*'obh*)," and (2) "Bring up for me (*ha'ali*) whomever I shall name to you" (v. 8). After the woman had obtained a promise of protection from her client (v. 10), the name of the dead person who should be brought up was given to her (v. 11). This passage gives no information as to the procedure the woman used to entice the spirit of Samuel to come forth. When it appeared, she alone had a visionary experience (vv. 12f.), because Saul had to ask her:

---

[24] *CAD,* I/2, 201a.

[25] Otten, *MIO,* 1 (1953), 125ff.; Hoffner, *RHA,* 76 (1965), 5ff.

[26] Robertson-Smith, *JoPh,* 14, 127f.

[27] See above, II.

"What do you see?" This visionary experience gave the woman greater potential for comprehension, for suddenly she knew the true identity of her disguised client (v.12). She described that which appeared to her in the vision as "spirits (→ אלהים 'elōhîm, "gods") coming up out of the (opening in the) earth" (v.13), and as "an old man ('ish zaqen)..., who is wrapped in a robe (me'il)" (v.14). The account of Saul's nocturnal visit to the ba'alath 'obh is told in artistic literary style. But still there can be no doubt that this document accurately reflects the practice of necromancy in ancient Israel.

Schmidtke compares the 'obh with Bab. eṭemmu, "spirit of the dead," and gives a somewhat different explanation. He alludes to the calling forth of Enkidu by Gilgamesh and emphasizes the role of the Babylon spirits of the dead in the giving of oracles.

Hoffner

אָוָה 'āvāh; אַוָּה (הַוָּה) 'avvāh (havvāh); תַּאֲוָה ta'avāh; מַאֲוַיִּים ma'aviyyîm

---

Contents: I. 1. Etymology, Occurrences; 2. Meaning. II. Secular Use: 1. General; 2. The Wisdom Literature; 3. Formula of Authority. III. Religious Meanings: 1. God's Desire; 2. The Doctrine of Retribution; 3. The Tenth Commandment; 4. In J.

I. 1. *Etymology, Occurrences.* It is clear that the root 'vh belongs only to West Semitic languages. Outside of Hebrew, it is found in Arabic ('awā), Jewish Aramaic ('vy), Syriac ('wā), and Mandean (awa I). Palache takes as his starting-point the meaning "to agree," [1] but the only support for this is the peal participle in Syriac. All other extant forms can be connected with two spheres of meaning: (a) "to devote oneself to," (b) "to stay, dwell." [2] The verb appears in the piel and hithpael. In addition, Palache interprets na'avah and na'vu in Isa. 52:7; Cant. 1:10; Ps. 93:5, as the *niphal* of 'avah. [3] The substantives ta'avah (cf. also the place name Kibroth-hattaavah, Nu. 11:34f.; 33:16f.; Dt. 9:22), 'avvah, and

---

'āvāh. F. Büchsel, "ἐπιθυμία, ἐπιθυμέω," *TDNT,* III, 168-172; J. Herrmann, "Das zehnte Gebot," *Festschrift E. Sellin* (1927), 69-82; E. Nielsen, *The Ten Commandments in New Perspective* (trans. 1965); J. L. Palache, *Semantic Notes on the Hebrew Lexicon* (Leiden, 1959); J. Reider, "Etymological Studies in Biblical Hebrew," *VT,* 2 (1952), 113-130; H. Graf Reventlow, *Gebot und Predigt im Dekalog* (1962); J. J. Stamm with M. E. Andrew, *The Ten Commandments in Recent Research* (trans. 1967).

[1] Palache, 2.
[2] Cf. Lane and Blachère-Chouémi; Brockelmann, *LexSyr; MdD.*
[3] Palache, 2; so also *KBL.*

ma'aviyyim are derived from *'avah*. The substantive *havvah* (Mic. 7:3; Prov. 10:3; 11:6), which cannot be separated from *'avah* semantically, perhaps also belongs to this group. On the interchangeability of *aleph* and *he*, cf. *'ekh* and *hekh*. Of course, an etymological connection of *havvah* with Arab. *hawiya*, "to love," cannot be rejected. Cf. also Arab. *'wy*, "to give up to, renounce." [4] In Hos. 10:10, *ba'thi*, "I have (will) come," is to be read instead of *be'avvathi*, "in my desire"; [5] and in Prov. 18:1, *to'anah*, "pretext(s)," is to be read instead of *ta'avah*, "desire." [6]

2. *Meaning*. *'avah* is synonymous with *chamadh*, "to desire." This is supported by more than simply the parallelism in Gen. 3:6. Even more convincing are Prov. 6:25 and Ps. 68:17 (Eng. v. 16), where *chamadh* appears in the same connection as *'avah* does in Ps. 45:12(11) and 132:13f. Also the linguistic usage of the Tannaites, who use these two verbs in parallelism (*Aboth* vi.5), seems to lead to the conclusion that these two ideas were understood as synonyms. The meaning "to desire" is not exhausted by a mere regulation of the will. The aspiration is rooted deep in human existence. Apart from Ps. 132:13f., *'avah* in the piel is always connected with *nephesh*, "soul," as its subject: *'avvah* and *havvah* also appear only in connection with *nephesh*. *ta'avah* is used in connection with *nephesh* (Isa. 26:8; Ps. 10:3), *lebh*, "heart" (Ps. 21:3[2]), and *'adham*, "man" (Prov. 19:22). The ascription of "desire" to God (Ps. 132:13f.; Job 23:13) and to an animal (Jer. 2:24) is figurative language. In Gen. 49:26; Nu. 34:7f.,10, *ta'avah* and *'avah* (or *ta'ah*) mean "residence" and "to reside" respectively. [7]

II. Secular Use.

1. *General*. Just as desire belongs to human existence, so also does its goal: it is directed toward fundamental necessities, such as eating (Mic. 7:1; Job 33:20) and drinking (2 S. 23:15 = 1 Ch. 11:17), and toward the opposite sex (Ps. 45:12 [11]; cf. Jer. 2:24).

2. *The Wisdom Literature*. The connection between human existence and the aspiration designated by the word *'avah* (a connection suggested by the language itself) is described in an instructive way in the Wisdom Literature. Fulfilled desire increases self-confidence (Prov. 13:12,19; 19:22), while a man who has everything he desires, but cannot enjoy it, has an empty life (Eccl. 6:2). The Wisdom Literature warns against a desire which would lead one to injure himself (Prov. 23:3,6; 24:1). The principle of retribution depends on the success or failure of the personal quality of the desire (Prov. 13:4; 21:25f.).

3. *Formula of Authority*. While Micah laments that the mighty do and permit what they desire (7:3), in the Deuteronomistic material it is clear that no

---

[4] *KBL*[3].
[5] See *BHK*.
[6] *BHK*.
[7] Reider, 113.

real limits are placed by law on the office of the king in the execution of his purposes. The reference to the unlimited power of the king is an important element in the formula which was used when the authority of the kingship was offered to a man (2 S. 3:21; 1 K. 11:37). When the royal court offers to serve the king, it uses the ceremonial formula, "according to all your heart's desire" (1 S. 23:20). This formal use of *'avvah* and *'ivvah* appears in those portions of Deuteronomy which deal with centralization of the cult, and always in connection with an appeal to the individual to take advantage of his freedom to choose life (Dt. 12:13-19, 20-28; 14:22-27; 18:1-8). There is a reminiscence of this usage in 1 S. 2:16.

III. Religious Meanings.

1. *God's Desire.* When God is the subject of *'ivvah,* this verb is in parallelism with *bachar,* "to choose" (Ps. 132:13f.; Job 23:13, where *bachar* is to be read instead of *be'echadh,* "in one," cf. *BHK*). Consequently, this word describes God's all-encompassing freedom of choice, not in the sense that it is open to him as a possibility, but that he actually claims it for himself.

2. *The Doctrine of Retribution.* The transition from secular to religious usage may be best observed in the doctrine of retribution; however, in the OT the antonyms "lazy" and "industrious" are replaced by "the righteous" and "the wicked" (Prov. 10:24; 11:23; Ps. 112:10). The words used in petitions and laments are typical of the doctrine of retribution. The evil which the wicked desires (Prov. 21:10) is the downfall of the righteous (Ps. 140:9[8]). On the other hand, the desire of the meek is dependent on God's help (10:17), which does justice (10:18; 140:13[12]; Isa. 26:8f.). It is in the mouth of the righteous that *ta'avah* assumes the meaning "supplication," which is characterized by the "certainty of hearing" on the part of the righteous (Ps. 10:17; 38:16[15]; 140:13 [12]; cf. 21:3[2]). Help comes on a specific day, for which the person in distress yearns in prayer (Isa. 26:8f.; Jer. 17:16; Am. 5:18). But of course, God's intervention can overturn prevailing standards (Am. 5:18-20).

3. *The Tenth Commandment.* It follows from what has already been said that the Deuteronomic expansion of the Decalog (Dt. 5:21[18]) is to be understood neither as a "watering down"[8] nor as a spiritualization. Rather, it is the result of the Deuteronomist's appropriation of the Decalog, the result of preaching.[9] The formal relationship between *velo thith'avvah beth re'akha,* "and you shall not desire your neighbor's house" (Dt. 5:21[18]), and *'al tith'av lemat'ammothav,* "do not desire his delicacies" (Prov. 23:3,6), is due presumably to the influence of Wisdom, especially since it has didactic interests and preference for the root *'vh* in common with Deuteronomy. If this conjecture is

---

[8] Nielsen, 42.
[9] Reventlow, 87. Cf. Stamm-Andrew, 107ff.

correct, it means that the apodictic legal maxim of Deuteronomy has been recast in the form of a rule to govern conduct.

4. In J. Essentially, the understanding of 'avvah in the hithpael and of ta'avah in J is to be distinguished from this. The etiology in Nu. 11:4-35 is fundamental for determining J's usage. The people of Israel distrusted the leadership of God and attempted to do what they desired. And when they were given the quail, it seemed to them that what they had intended was successful. But "while the meat was yet between their teeth, before it was consumed, the anger of the Lord was kindled against the people, and the Lord smote the people with a very great plague" (11:33). The ta'avah is an expression of man's self-assertiveness. It manifests itself as guilty rebellion against God, which must be punished. The same connection of disobedience, guilt, and punishment is found in Gen. 3:6. Because Eve yields to the "delight to the eyes"[10] presented to her, she becomes disobedient to God. Ps. 78:29f.; 106:14 take up Nu. 11.

Mayer

---

[10] G. von Rad, *Genesis. OTL* (trans. 1961), 87.

אוֹי 'ôy → הוֹי *hôy*

┌─────────────────────────────────────┐
│ אֱוִיל ʼᵉvîl; אִוֶּלֶת ʼivveleth   │
└─────────────────────────────────────┘

Contents: I. Etymology. II. Occurrences in Prebiblical Wisdom Literature. III. Theological Significance.

I. Etymology. The word 'evil is rendered by "Tor" in German,[1] by "fool" in English,[2] and by "fou," "sot," or "insensé" in French.[3] In the OT Books of Wisdom (19 times in Prov., in addition to which 'ivveleth occurs 22 times; 5 times in the Prophets, and 3 times in the Psalms), it stands in antithesis to chakham, "wise" (9 times), and to other expressions like yashar, "upright," or sekhel, "prudence." Its etymology is uncertain. Its relationship to the South Arabian word 'wl, "to lead back," is not at all clear.[4] Leslau, who finds examples of 'evil only

---

'evil. T. Donald, "The Semantic Field of 'Folly'," *VT*, 13 (1963), 285-292; W. O. E. Oesterley, *The Book of Proverbs* (London, 1929), LXXXVIf.

[1] Gemser, Zimmerli.
[2] Toy, Scott.
[3] Barucq, Duessberg.
[4] Jamme, *Sabaean Inscriptions* (Baltimore, 1962), Index, 427ff.

in Ethiopic,[5] surmises that the Ethiopic was infiltrated by the biblical language. In Biblical Hebrew, an adjective *'evili* (Zec. 11:15) is derived from *'evil;* however, *'evil* is actually a substantive and sometimes is used in the plural, but never in the feminine. *'ivveleth,* which exhibits the rather rare *qitteleth* form,[6] is also derived from *'evil.* This word is used to describe defects of the body and of the spirit,[7] and assumes a root *'vl.* However, it is hardly possible to connect this root with Aram. *'vlt,* "slave" (*CIS,* II, 64, 1), since the latter comes from Akk. *awē-lū(tu);*[8] cf. Evil-merodach (for Awēl Marduk, "man of Marduk") in 2 K. 25:27, which is written in Hebrew with anti-Babylonian vocalization. *'evil* is connected with *kesil,* "fool," in the OT, indicating a great similarity in meaning; *'ivveleth* is a characteristic of the *kesil* (Prov. 12:23; 26:5; etc.).

The first OT passage using *'evil* that can be dated with certainty is Hos. 9:7. Thus this word is not part of the earlier elements of the Hebrew language. Its frequent occurrence in the oldest collections of proverbs (in Prov. 10–22 *'evil* is found 12 times and *'ivveleth* 16 times; in Prov. 25–29 *'evil* appears twice and *'ivveleth* 4 times) leads to the assumption that this word was being used in circles of Wisdom teachers before the prophets started using it.

The related root *ya'al,* which occurs only in the niphal and means "to behave foolishly," "to prove oneself to be a fool," points to earlier occurrences. Nu. 12:11, where it is used in connection with *chata',* "to sin," is probably from E. In Isa. 19:13, it stands in parallelism with *nasha',* "to be deluded," and is connected with *hith'ah,* "to lead astray." Jer. 5:4 says that the poor (*dal*) are foolish because they do not know the way of the Lord. Further examples appear in Jer. 50:36 and Sir. 47:23.

II. Occurrences in Prebiblical Wisdom Literature. The old collections in Prov. 10–22 and 25–29 imply a connection between a "fool" and unfruitful speech (*'evil* in Prov. 10:8,14,21; 12:16; 14:3,9; 17:28; 20:3; 24:7; 29:9; *'ivveleth* in 12:23; 13:16; 15:2,14; 24:9). In Egyptian Wisdom Literature extending from Ptahhotep (e.g., lines 37, 148, 152) through Ani (VII, 7) and especially Amenemope (whose only goal was to learn the correct answer to a speech, cf. Prov. 18:13), down to Ankhsheshonk (e.g., 8, 3), the common themes are self-control in speech and praise of silence. Accordingly Prov. 17:28 is clear: "Even an *'evil* who keeps silent is considered wise." The fool of Prov. 14:29 and 17:12 is quick-tempered, just as in Amenemope. Babylonian Wisdom Literature gives similar advice.[9]

None of these extrabiblical texts has an exact equivalent to the OT *'evil.* However, Prov. 10:8 may help us here, because Isa. 19:11 states that "the princes of Zoan are utterly foolish (*'evilim*)." Prov. 10:8 speaks of the one who is "*'evil* (a fool, foolish) of lips," a compound expression of the Egyptian type, in which

---

[5] Leslau, *Contributions,* 10.
[6] *GK,* § 84a,o; *BLe,* 477z.
[7] *GK,* § 84b,c,d.
[8] Baumgartner, *BiOr,* 19 (1962), 134.
[9] W. Lambert, *BWL,* 99, 101, in order to avoid strife; p. 105, lines 127-134.

a talkative person is called '*šɜ r* or '*šɜ ḥrw*, "rich in mouth," or "in words," i.e., garrulous;[10] there are also compounds with *ḥry*, "chiefs" or "leaders." The Hebrew *'vl* means "first" or "strong." It is possible that in the monarchical period a scornful term was created from this root to describe the pretentious or untactful babbler of the Wisdom School. At this point, the "folly" of the *'evil* had no religious connections and presuppositions other than those of international Wisdom, which during this time found their way into the Jerusalem court. As a matter of fact, apart from the parallelism in Prov. 19:3, *'evil/'vl* is never used in connection with Yahweh or the law in the Solomonic collections. The fool does not act at the right time (13:16), and thus he is a failure in life and in his word (10:14,21; 14:17; 16:22). He is a servant to the wise (11:29). He is a young, unreasonable man (22:15), who does not hearken to his father (15:5), returns to his "vomit" (26:11), and clings to his "folly" tenaciously in his behavior (27:22).

III. Theological Significance. Hosea exalts *chokhmah*, "wisdom," and reproves Israel for being a child who lacks it (13:13). It is not surprising that he uses the vocabulary of the Wise against the calculating alliances of the kings of the northern kingdom. In 9:6 he foresees a deterioration in Israel, and in 9:7 her punishment: Israel shall experience ("know") it, because "the prophet is an *'evil* and a man under the spirit of madness" (*meshugga'*, cf. Dt. 28:34).[11] The root *'vl* still refers to manner of speech here, in fact in a degrading sense. Similarly Isa. 19:11 says, "the princes of Tanis (Zoan) are utterly *'evilim*, the wise counselors of Pharaoh give stupid counsel." The same thing is found in Jeremiah, the disciple of Hosea, who preserves this vocabulary of Wisdom in 4:22. But Israel's "knowledge" here is theological in nature: the Judeans are *'evilim*, "foolish," because they do not "know" Yahweh. In Jeremiah (22:16), for a king to "know Yahweh" means to take up the cause of the widow and the orphan.

This theological meaning, according to which someone is *'evil*, "a fool," if he does not want to know Yahweh's righteousness, appears in the sayings of the Wise. According to Prov. 24:9 the *'evil* commits sin; according to 14:8 his *'ivveleth* is for treachery *(mirmah)*. This is even clearer in the first (postexilic) collection of proverbs. According to 22:15, the evil to which one clings because of his sin is bound up with his *'ivveleth*, "folly," because of a lack of discipline *(musar)*. The solemn prologue in the first collection ultimately says that *'evilim*, "fools," despise discipline, while the fear of God is a fundamental principle of Wisdom. Three times the Psalms (in fact, all from the postexilic period) reflect this theological viewpoint. God knows the *'ivveleth*, "folly," of the psalmist, because his wrongs are not hidden from him (Ps. 69:6 [Eng. v. 5]). Because of their sins, *'evilim*, "fools," are humbled (107:17), and folly explains their lamentable condition (38:6[5]). Eliphaz reminds Job of this doctrine (Job 5:2f.): "The wrath (of God)[12] kills the *'evil* (fool)." Finally, this theological meaning is to

---

10 *WbÄS*, I, 228, 17 and 18.
11 On this cf. H. W. Wolff, *Hosea* (trans. 1974), 156f.
12 Horst, *BK*, XVI, *in loc.*, interprets this line differently.

be found in two later prophetic texts: "In this holy way of return, *ʾevilim* shall not pass" (Isa. 35:8; text uncertain). The "worthless shepherd" of Deutero-Zechariah (Zec. 11:15) is a shepherd to whom God, in his displeasure, commits the care of his sheep, after he has broken the bond between Judah and Israel.

However, the term *ʾevil*, which served to identify true human wisdom with the fear of God and obedience to his laws, was gradually forgotten, since it was no longer appropriate to new problems which had arisen. Ecclesiastes never uses it. Ben Sira, who is very traditional, uses it four times in a very general sense. The foolish son of the wise Solomon is a fool (Sir. 47:23). Ben Sira considers it more important for a man to hide his *ʾivveleth*, "folly," than to hide his wisdom (41:15; see also 8:15 and 20:24 in sections that are extant in Hebrew). The term was weakened so much that the LXX translated *ʾevil* by 13 different Greek words, and *ʾivveleth* by 11; add to this *ápeiros*, "unacquainted with," in Zec. 11:15. But on the whole, *áphrōn*, "fool," enjoys a certain preference. The term *ʾevil* is also missing in the language of the Mishnah and the Midrashim. It was nothing more than the echo of the inheritance of Wisdom.

Cazelles

אָוֶן ʾāven; פֹּעֲלֵי אָוֶן pōʿᵃlê ʾāven

Contents: I. Etymology, Original Meaning. II. Passages in the OT: 1. Occurrences; 2. Parallel and Contrasting Ideas. III. 1. Linguistic Use in the Preexilic Prophets; 2. Later Use Outside the Psalter; 3. *ʾaven* and *poʿale ʾaven* in the Psalter.

I. Etymology, Original Meaning. The noun *ʾaven* and the root *ʾvn* which is to be deduced from it (although the verbal form does not occur in the OT) have no cognate in other ancient Near Eastern languages. Ugar. *ʾn* should not be connected with Heb. *ʾaven*.[1] Instead, this Ugaritic root is a cognate of the

ʾāven. H. Birkeland, *Die Feinde des Individuums in der israelitischen Psalmenliteratur* (Oslo, 1933); *idem, The Evildoers in the Book of Psalms. ANVAO 1955,* 2; H. Cazelles, "Sur un rituel du Deuteronome XXVI 14," *RB,* 55 (1948), 54-71; J. Hempel, "Die israelitischen Anschauungen von Segen und Fluch im Lichte altorientalischer Parallelen," *ZDMG,* 79 (1925), 20-110; cf. esp. 82-85; H.-J. Kraus, *BK,* XV, 40-43; G. Marschall, *Die 'Gottlosen' des ersten Psalmenbuches* (1929); S. Mowinckel, *Psalmenstudien,* I (1921), VI (1924); *idem,* "Fiendene i de individuelle klagesalmer," *NTT,* 35 (1934), 1-39; *idem, The Psalms in Israel's Worship* (Oxford, 1962), II, 1ff.; *idem, Religion und Kultus* (1953), 26f.; N. Nicolsky, *Spuren magischer Formeln in den Psalmen. BZAW,* 46 (1927); Pedersen, *ILC,* I/2, 431; A. F. Puukko, "Der Feind in den alttestamentlichen Psalmen," *OTS,* 8 (1950), 47-65; N. H. Ridderbos, *De 'werkers der ongerechtigheid' in de individueele Psalmen* (Kampen, 1939).

1 Contra *WUS,* 295.

OT *'oni*, "mourning," which is to be derived from a root *'nh*. Of course, *KBL¹* (1953), 20, made no distinction between *'vn* and *'nh;*[2] but now *KBL³* (1967), 22 and 67, accurately distinguishes between the two nouns and the two roots.

In individual cases, difficulties in exegesis can arise when no external distinction is made between *'aven* and *'on* ("power," "riches") in an unpointed consonantal text. However, any confusion is rendered impossible by proper Massoretic vocalization using a *qamets* and a *seghol* in the singular of the absolute state (90 % of the examples). On the other hand, in the plural (which is used rarely) and in certain forms using the pronominal suffix, both nouns sound the same even in a pointed text (*'onim*, etc.). In these cases, the two nouns can be distinguished only by their meaning in the context.

Presumably *'aven* and *'on* go back to the same root (perhaps originally *'aun*). The possibility of two different roots, which was often discussed in former generations, is little likely.[3] If we assume that the same root lies behind both nouns, then it is logical to assign to this root a relatively neutral original meaning such as "power," which could then take on a positive or a negative aspect.[4] In fact, those examples of *'aven* in which it is possible to determine precisely the situation assumed in the context can be combined under the aspect of "power used in relation to a community or an individual with a negative effect or intention."

II. Passages in the OT.

1. *Occurrences*. As a result of this double meaning of *'vn*, at least two of the (at most) 80 OT occurrences of *'aven* (leaving out *'aven* in place names) are disputed. If we put aside these dubious occurrences (Job 18:7,12) as well as those which are to be deleted by essential emendations or which appear in obscure contexts (Isa. 41:29; Ezk. 30:17; Hos. 12:12 [Eng. v. 11]; Hab. 3:7; Ps. 56:8[7]; Prov. 11:7), a total of eight, this leaves 72 passages all together. These occurrences are found exclusively in prophetic, cultic, and sapiental texts. Most frequently *'aven* appears in the Psalter (39 %), Job (18 %), I, II, and III Isaiah (15 %), and Proverbs (12.5 %). *'aven* occurs only twice in the OT narrative traditions, once in the context of a prophetic saying (Nu. 23:21), and once as a late interpolation from the prophetic tradition (1 S. 15:23). It is worthy of note that *'aven* does not appear at all in the OT legal texts. It is not a part of the language of P, nor can it be traced in the Deuteronomistic history. Only a small percentage of the examples comes from the preexilic period. Disregarding passages in the Psalms whose dates are disputed, the following examples, which certainly come from the eighth century B.C., are to be regarded as the oldest in the OT: Isa. 10:1; 31:2; Hos. 6:8; 10:8; Am. 5:5; and Mic. 2:1. We may add to this from the late preexilic period Jer. 4:14,15 and Hab. 1:3.

---

[2] Cf. also Cazelles, 54ff.

[3] Cf. E. König, *Hebräisches und Aramäisches Wörterbuch* (1910), 16.

[4] So Mowinckel, *Psalmenstudien,* VI (1924), 17, n. 3; *Psalms,* I, 193ff.; II, 1ff.; *Religion,* 26f.

2. *Parallel and Contrasting Ideas.* Because of their variety, parallel ideas which are closely associated with '*aven* especially in metrically structured texts help only to a limited extent in obtaining a more precise understanding of the meaning of this word. The use of → חמס *chāmās,* "violence," in parallelism with '*aven* (Isa. 59:6; Hab. 1:3; cf. further Ps. 55:10f.[9f.]) brings out the negative aspect of '*aven* as an action intended to hurt other persons. Among similiar parallels to '*aven* we may mention *tokh,* "oppression" (Ps. 10:7), *shodh,* "destruction" (Hab. 1:3), and '*ish damim,* "bloodthirsty men" for *po'ale 'aven,* "evildoers" (Ps. 5:6f.[5f.]; 59:3[2]). → אלה '*ālāh,* "curse," may also be mentioned in this connection (10:7). These ideas correspond fully with the fundamental meaning of '*aven* suggested above.

But we also encounter ideas which are closely associated with '*aven* that mean "deception" or "lying." This is true of → שוא *shāv',* "emptiness, vanity, lie" (Isa. 59:4; Zec. 10:2; cf. Ps. 41:7[6]; Job 11:11 speaks of *methe shav',* "worthless men," who bring forth '*aven*), → שקר *sheqer,* "deception, falsehood" (Zec. 10:2; Ps. 7:15[14]; cf. Prov. 17:4), and → מרמה *mirmāh,* "deceit, treachery" (Ps. 10:7; 36:4[3]; Job 15:35; cf. Ps. 5:6f.[5f.]). The equating of *po'ale 'aven* with '*adham beliyya'al,* "worthless person" (Prov. 6:12), also points in this direction. The majority of these examples have in mind "deception" actively practiced by evildoers with the purpose of hurting others. However, in some cases the context causes one to expect this word to be used in the sense of "self-deception" or "vanity" (Zec. 10:2; perhaps also Ps. 7:15[14]; Job 15:35). This forms a transition to parallel ideas appearing less frequently, which suggest that '*aven* conveys the concept of "nothingness, vanity": → הבל *hebhel,* "vanity" (Zec.10:2), → שוא *shāv',* "emptiness, vanity" (Isa. 1:13), and → תהו *tōhû,* "emptiness" (Isa. 59:4). Finally, as a term which often appears in connection with '*aven,* → עמל '*āmāl* (Nu. 23:21; Isa. 10:1; 59:4; Hab. 1:3; Ps. 7:15[14]; 10:7; 55:11[10]; 90:10; Job 4:8; 5:6; 15:35) exhibits the two major semantic aspects of '*aven:* on the one hand the afflictions or calamities brought on a third party, and on the other hand the "nothingness of sin." [5] The close connection between '*amal* and '*aven* is particularly clear in the figurative expression "they conceive '*amal* (mischief) and bring forth '*aven* (iniquity)" (Isa. 59:4; Job 15:35; similarly Ps. 7:15[14]; cf. further Job 4:8: "plow '*aven* [iniquity]" and "sow '*amal* [trouble]").

Thus it appears that, in conformity with parallel ideas, '*aven* not only means the abuse of power which brings harm and destruction, but also can denote the nothingness of such wickedness. When "deception" or "lying" appear as parallels to '*aven* or are used in especially close connection with '*aven* in some other way, then this also refers either to the nothingness of the deeds of '*aven* or to the particular way in which the *po'ale 'aven* behave.

There is no term or expression which is used characteristically as a contrast to '*aven* or to *po'ale 'aven* in the OT. Most often we encounter *tsaddiq* (according to Ps. 92:8ff.[7ff.], the *po'ale 'aven* ["evildoers"] are like grass, but the *tsaddiq* is like a palm tree or a cedar in Lebanon; other examples of this contrast occur

---

[5] E. Sellin, *ThAT* ([2]1936), 70.

in Ps. 94; Job 34:36; 36:10; Prov. 21:15). Frequently, we also find *'ani*, "poor, affliction" (Ps. 14:4-6; but 53:6[5] has a different reading; Job 36:21) and *mishpat*, "justice" (Isa. 59:7ff.; Hab. 1:3f.; Prov. 19:28; 21:15), and these examples are sufficient to show that the use of *'aven* is not connected with a special category of wicked activity, but (like the terms which are used in contrast to it) denotes a fundamental religio-ethical condition which collectively influences man.

III. 1. *Linguistic Use in the Preexilic Prophets.* Even in the linguistic use of the early prophets of the eighth century B.C., *'aven* has a rather wide meaning: according to Isa. 10:1, decrees which are destined to harm honest helpless people are called "*'aven* (iniquitous) decrees." Similarly, Mic. 2:1 calls the attempt of the rich to increase their wealth by unjust means *'aven*. Thus, *'aven* is used in this material to designate unlawful legal manipulations and, in general, social injustice. Hab. 1:3 contains a third example of this use of the word from the late preexilic period.

The eighth century prophets also use this word to characterize wrong cultic acts of various sorts: Hos. 10:8 speaks polemically of "the high places of Aven," thus using *'aven* to inveigh against Canaanite cultic practices which had been adopted in Israel. Am. 5:5 refers to the *'aven* character of the cult of Bethel.

Hos. 6:8 uses this word to apply to still a third realm. The context suggests that here also *po'ale 'aven* is to be understood of men who are guilty of cultic wrongs. But v. 8b ("tracked with blood") does not agree with this interpretation very well. Thus perhaps this passage has in mind a rebellion which originated at Gilead (2 K. 15:10,14,25).[6] The continuity of vv. 5-11, which describe different cultic and noncultic wrongs, especially of the priests, would be preserved if we assumed that the Gilead priesthood participated in that political overthrow. It is clear that *po'ale 'aven* in Isa. 31:2 refers to evildoers in the political sphere. It has reference to representatives of the pro-Egyptian party whom the prophet opposed.

These occurrences of *'aven*, which certainly belong to the eighth century B.C., paint the following picture.

(a) *'aven* describes a concept which involves evaluation. Therefore, it can be used in various realms in the condemnation of human deeds or attitudes.

(b) The above-mentioned prophetic texts, which call certain deeds and attitudes *'aven*, encompass the most important areas of prophetic criticism: social injustice, cultic wrongs, corrupt politics. Thus, it is clear that *'aven* denotes a deed or an attitude which in the view of the prophets is opposed to the will of God.

(c) In all cases, the accusation of the prophets is levelled against persons who from time to time in their sphere of life or in their profession have special power at their disposal, but misuse it. Yet, we must not think primarily of deeds of violence committed brutally and openly, but of more or less unobtrusive wickedness, accomplished with cunning and deceit by unjust legal interpretation or

---

[6] So W. Rudolph, *KAT*, XIII/1, 145f.; similarly H. W. Wolff, *Hosea* (trans. 1974), 122, although he does not exclude a cultic interpretation—" 'traces of blood' might refer to child sacrifice."

deceptive cultic or political propaganda, and which the severe prophetic criticism (at first in part generalized) considered to be ultimately wickedness against Yahweh. In this connection, it is important to observe that the doers of 'aven use this word mainly as a means of carrying out their plans.

The prophetic texts express the firm conviction that deeds of 'aven against Yahweh's will are always futile, "empty," even if the main harm they do lies in the realm of human relations. The divine punishment follows unconditionally. As early as Am. 5:5 we encounter the thought that Yahweh's judgment also brings 'aven on the evildoer now. This aspect is expressed more clearly in the essentially later text Jer. 4:14f. Here 'aven is used as a comprehensive term for the crimes which Jerusalem had committed against Yahweh; but it also refers to the punishment God was about to bring upon Judah in the form of a military invasion from the north.

2. *Later Use Outside the Psalter.* In prophetic and sapiential texts that originated at a later time, in the main this framework is not exceeded, and yet we must not fail to recognize a growing tendency to generalize. Antisocial behavior, especially injustice in legal affairs, is called 'aven in Isa. 58:9; 59:4; Ezk. 11:2; Prov. 17:4f.; 19:28; 21:15; and perhaps also in Job 34:22 (note the context) and Prov. 6:18. In the later prophetic criticism of the cult, 'aven is generally used to characterize the sacrificial cult as lying and deceit (1 S. 15:22f.; Isa. 1:13; 66:3), referring to illegitimate cult practices which mediate false instruction (Zec. 10:2) or are otherwise detrimental (Isa. 32:6; cf. Prov. 6:18; "pointing the finger" in Isa. 58:9 and Prov. 6:12f. is probably not to be interpreted as a magical act).[7] As in the earlier texts, in the exilic period 'aven is also used to characterize the opponent of the politico-historical will of Yahweh proclaimed by the prophets (Isa. 41:29). A particular theme of the Wisdom Literature is that Yahweh's punishment is an inevitable consequence for all who have committed 'aven in any respect (Job 21:19; 31:3). The po'ale 'aven cannot hide themselves from God (11:11; 34:22); suddenly they will be destroyed (Prov. 6:12-15). Anyone who practices deeds of 'aven will reap what he has sown (Job 4:8). Conversely, he who obviously is not "righteous" must suffer 'aven (understood as Yahweh's punishment, Prov. 12:21; 30:20). Therefore, the Wisdom Literature does not lack admonitions to avoid everything which is reproved by Yahweh as 'aven, and which could be punished with 'aven (Job 34:8; 36:10). Only the prophetic statements in Isa. 55:7; 58:9; and 59:4ff. speak of a possible conversion of the doers of 'aven, viewed in an eschatological frame of thought. Here, of course, what is at stake is not an individual evildoer or a group, but the people of God as a whole.

3. *'aven and po'ale 'aven in the Psalter.* The use of 'aven or po'ale 'aven in the postexilic hymns and didactic poems of the Psalter does not differ from

---

[7] Cf. G. Fohrer, *Jesaja,* III (1964), 211.

the use of these terms in the Wisdom Literature. Thus, in general Ps. 92 deals
with the fate of certain evildoers who must perish as Yahweh's enemies, in comparison with the secure existence of the righteous. Similar connections may be
found in Ps. 66:18; 119:133; and 125:5, to some extent in connection with moral
admonitions. (According to the preexilic Ps. 101:8, it is the king's responsibility
to destroy the po'ale 'aven.) Finally, Ps. 90:10 sees in 'aven the ultimately vain
toil of life, determined by God for man in general.

A specialized use of 'aven, which seems to stand out in bold relief from its
linguistic use elsewhere, appears in certain Individual Psalms of Lament, in which
the enemies of the worshipper are characterized as po'ale 'aven (Pss. 5, 28, 36,
59, 64, 94, 141; in 59:6[5] as boghedhe 'aven, "those who treacherously plot iniquity"). We also encounter this designation in earlier prophetic texts (Isa. 31:2;
Hos. 6:8); but in the psalms mentioned here the corrupting work of the po'ale
'aven is described more precisely: as a rule in these passages the evildoers appear
in groups. They band together, scheme together, and boast together (Ps. 59:4[3];
64:3[2]; 94:4). They prowl through the streets and howl in the evening twilight
in a sinister way like hungry dogs (59:7, 15f. [6, 14f.]). They attempt to kill the
righteous worshipper (59:4[3]; 94:21). They are also described as mischief-
makers, who devise their plots in seclusion on their beds (36:5[4]), hide carefully
(64:7[6]) and use friendly words, but have mischief in their hearts (28:3; cf. also
the Royal Song, 101:4). From ambush they suddenly shoot their poisonous words
at the godly like an arrow (64:4[3]). Usually words are the weapons which they
use. They whet their tongues like a sword (64:4[3]); their throat is compared
with an open sepulchre (5:10[9]). They speak lying words (5:6f.[5f.]; 36:4f.[3f.];
59:13[12]; cf. 101:5-7) and slanders (59:8[7]). Since the deeds of these enemies
are directed against the godly, they are also enemies of Yahweh (59:6[5]). Inevitably the punishment of divine judgment will come upon them (94:16f.,23),
often with the same weapons which they use against the godly (64:8[7]). They
fall into the very nets which they themselves made (141:10).

To be sure, this reaction of Yahweh to the works of the po'ale 'aven in the
Individual Psalms of Lament is identical to the descriptions of the divine punishment of the doers of 'aven in prophetic and sapiential texts. Accordingly, Ps. 14:4
and 53:5(4) do not have in mind some sort of mysterious enemies who wish to
destroy the godly with curses or lies, but here the po'ale 'aven (as often in the
prophetic tradition) are people who harm innocent persons in precarious situations for their own advantage. Also, some of the psalms which have typical
descriptions of enemies reveal that a specific social stratum or professional group
is intended, as was the case with the use of 'aven by the earlier prophets. Thus,
the po'ale 'aven in Ps. 94 belong to the body of judges, who oppress the widow,
the orphan, and the sojourner, and pervert the right of the poor.

But there are also similarities between the special description of the po'ale
'aven as malicious enemies of the worshipper in the Individual Psalms of Lament
and the use of 'aven in the prophetic tradition. The motif of evildoers devising
devices of 'aven on their beds at night and performing their evil plans early in
the morning is already found in Mic. 2:1; the same motif appears in Jer. 4:14
and especially in exilic and postexilic texts (Isa. 59:7; Ezk. 11:2; and also Isa.

32:6; 55:7).[8] The motif of waiting in ambush (Isa. 29:20) and of mischievous speech (Isa. 58:9; 59:4) also appears; indeed, the examples in the earlier prophets assume that the doer of *ʾaven* uses words in order to carry out his evil.[9]

Thus, the use of *ʾaven* or of *poʿale ʾaven* in the Individual Psalms of Lament does not differ fundamentally from the use of these terms outside the Psalter. Also, it is clear that in the Individual Psalms of Lament the *poʿale ʾaven* are not a homogeneous group in Israelite society. Therefore, the interpretation that identifies them specifically as "sorcerers" who use magical means to achieve their evil objectives[10] is feasible only in some cases.

In an attempt to define *poʿale ʾaven* more precisely, the following points should also be taken into consideration. (a) The typical description of the works of the enemies of the worshipper outlined above is by no means always connected with the application of the term *poʿale ʾaven* to the person doing these works. To be sure, there are some individual laments that speak of deeds that qualify as *ʾaven*, but those who perform these deeds are called → רשע *rāshāʿ*, "wicked" (Pss. 7, 10, 55), → אויב *ʾôyēbh*, "enemy" (Pss. 7, 41, 55), → צורר *tsôrēr*, "vexer, adversary, enemy" (Ps. 7), or → רע *rāʿ*, "evildoer" (Ps. 10). The appearance of these enemies who are not called *poʿale ʾaven* is characterized wholly as *poʿale ʾaven:* they roam about in groups (55:4,11f.[3,10f.]), do evil by means of speaking, cursing, and lying (10:7; 41:6,8[5,7]; 55:22[21]), and pretend deceitfully that they are intimate friends of the worshipper (41:10[9]; 55:13f., 21ff.[12f., 20ff.]).

(b) The majority of the Individual Psalms of Lament that contain descriptions of the enemies (29 out of 40) mention neither the *poʿale ʾaven* nor *ʾaven*. But to some extent these psalms contain essentially more detailed and more extensive descriptions of the works of the enemies than the eleven psalms that actually use *ʾaven* (cf. esp. Pss. 31, 35, 37, 69, 73, 109, 140). Thus, there is no reason to assume that the picture of the enemy who waits in ambush, curses, slanders, and usually appears in a group has an especially close connection with the idea of *poʿale ʾaven*.

These observations show that the *poʿale ʾaven* are not one group among the enemies in the Individual Psalms of Lament which can be narrowly defined. A closer analysis of the way they are described indicates that they cannot be distinguished from the *ʾoyebhim,* the *mereʿim,* the *reshaʿim,* and other enemies which have been designated in these psalms, which to some extent also appear outside the Psalter as parallels to *poʿale ʾaven* (cf. Isa. 31:2; 55:7; etc.). Because of this, scholars have also tried to interpret the enemies in the Individual Psalms of Lament (along with the ideas used to designate these enemies) collectively and homogeneously as the essence of complete "evil power,"[11] specifically as sorcerers and demons,[12] as foreign enemies of the king,[13] or as personal opponents

---

[8] V. Maag, *Text, Wortschatz und Begriffswelt des Buches Amos* (1951), 64, finds the "sinister, horrifying" aspect of *ʾaven* expressed already in Am. 5:5.

[9] Cf. above, III.1(c).

[10] Mowinckel, *Psalmenstudien,* I; Nicolsky, Pedersen.

[11] Mowinckel, *Religion,* 26.

[12] Mowinckel, *Psalmenstudien,* I, 121; "Fiendene," 3; G. Widengren, *The Accadian and Hebrew Psalms of Lamentation* (1936), 197ff.

[13] Birkeland.

of an individual who is being persecuted or is suffering because he has been falsely accused or for other reasons.[14] It must be admitted that these interpretations apply only to a certain (rather large) portion of the passages involved. This is particularly true of the interpretation that makes the enemies foreign enemies of the king, for the descriptions of the enemies and the statements concerning the situation of the worshipper in the individual lament fit very poorly with this view (even in Ps. 59:6[5], where → גוים *gôyim* stands in parallelism with *boghedhe 'aven*, we are not to think of foreign enemies). The view that these psalms have in mind personal enemies of a "private" worshipper, who want to harm him by misusing their power, especially by slander, cursing, false accusations, and other "sins of the tongue," is much more likely. This would also explain why their works would be called *'aven*, and the like, in striking agreement with the linguistic use of *'aven* by the prophets. The reason for the differences between the description of the activities of the *po'ale 'aven* in the individual laments and in the prophetic oracles is that the psalmists and the prophets speak from different perspectives: as Yahweh's spokesman the prophet criticizes a deed or a type of behavior as *'aven*, as evil caused by the misuse of power, while in the psalms of lament the person who has been wronged describes his suffering, and in so doing puts forth special effort to emphasize the deceitful actions of his enemies by using typical figures.

Bernhardt

---

[14] Gunkel/Begrich, *Einl. in die Psalmen* (1933), 176ff.; Marschall; Puukko, 56ff.; Ridderbos; H. Schmidt, *HAT*, 15 (1934), VIf.

 אוֹר *'ôr*

Contents: I. 1. Etymology, Occurrences, Synonyms; 2. Religio-Historical Background. II. Natural Light: 1. The Physical Basis: a. Light of Day and Light of the Heavenly Bodies; b. Dawn; c. Dusk; d. Darkening of the Stars; e. The Paths of the Heavenly Bodies; Months; Years; f. Light and Darkness As Cosmic Substances; 2. Light and Darkness in Human Existence: a. Position of Darkness; b. Light and Life; Light of the Eyes; c. Darkness in the Underworld; d. The Night; e. Morning As Salvation; f. Eschatological Elimination of Darkness; 3. Lamps. III. Figurative Use: 1. Light As Prosperity, Salvation: a. General Considerations; b. God, the Light of Man; c. God's Light As Salvation, Success; d. Light of the Countenance of God; 2. Walking and Way: a. Success and Failure; b. The Light of the Law and of Wisdom; 3. Light and Darkness in Ethical Contexts: a. Sinners and Light; b. Instances of an Ethical Dualism; c. Light and Justice; the Servant of the Lord. IV. God and Light in Theophanic Texts: 1. Fundamental Considerations; 2. Terminology; 3. Ps. 104:2; 4. Man's Participation in the Divine Light; 5. Solar Elements in the OT Picture of God? 6. Theophany and the Coming of Salvation; Isa. 60:1-3, etc. V. The Qumran Texts.

I. 1. *Etymology, Occurrences, Synonyms.* The Hebrew root *'wr* (substantive and verb) corresponds to Ugar. *'r*, "to be bright, to illumine," and Akk. *urru*, "day." There is a rare cognate form of *'wr*, the substantive *'orah* (Ps. 139:12 [Eng. v. 11]), pl. *'oroth* (Isa. 26:19). *ma'or*, pls. *me'orim* and *me'oroth*, "light-bearer, lamp, light," is a derivative of *'wr*. When it is pronounced *'ur* in the OT, *'wr* means "fire"; accordingly, the verb in the hiphil can have the meaning "to kindle, set on fire." Originally the fire of the hearth was also the source of light.

In the OT, the verb appears in the qal and niphal only rarely, but in the hiphil it occurs more frequently, in all about 45 times. The basic meaning is "to be bright," in the hiphil "to disseminate light, illuminate." The substantive *'or* appears about 150 times and means "brightness, brilliance, daylight." *ma'or* occurs about 20 times, usually with the meaning "lamp," and occasionally "light."

The Hebrew root → נור *nûr* is closely related to *'wr*. In the OT it is represented by the derivative *nir/ner*, "lamp," and *menorah*, "lampstand." It corresponds to Ugar. *nyr/nr*, "to illumine, light, lamp";[1] cf. Akk. *nūru*, "light."[2] From the Aramaic root *nhr*, the verb *nahar*, "to shine," and the substantive *neharah*, "daylight," are found occasionally in the Hebrew OT, while *nehor/nehir*, "light," and *nahiru*, "illumination," appear in the Aramaic parts of the OT. Other important synonyms of *'wr* treated in the present article are → נגה *nāghah*, "to shine," *noghah*, "brightness," and יפע *yāpha'* in the hiphil, "to shine forth, shine out." *shachar*, "dawn," is also important for this study. Cf. also → חשׁך *chōshekh*, "darkness"; → יום *yôm*, "day"; → הלל *hālal*, "to shine"; → זהר *zāhar*, "to be light, shining"; → שׁמשׁ *shemesh*, "sun"; → ירח *yarēach*, "moon"; and → כוכב *kôkhābh*, "star."

'ôr. S. Aalen, *Die Begriffe 'Licht' und 'Finsternis' im AT, im Spätjudentum und im Rabbinismus. SNVAO* (1951); F. Asensio, *El Dios de la Luz* (1958); R. Bultmann, *Zur Geschichte der Lichtsymbolik im Altertum* (1948)=*Exegetica* (1967), 323-355; C. Colpe, "Lichtsymbolik im alten Iran und antiken Judentum," *StudGen*, 18 (1965), 116-133; A. M. Gierlich, *Der Lichtgedanke in den Psalmen. FreibThSt,* 56 (1940); J. Hempel, "Die Lichtsymbolik im AT," *StudGen,* 13 (1960), 352-368; E. Hornung, "Licht und Finsternis in der Vorstellungswelt Altägyptens," *StudGen,* 18 (1965), 73-83; P. Humbert, "Le thème vétérotestamentaire de la lumière," *RTP,* 99 (1966), 1-6; L. Koehler, "Die Morgenröte im AT," *ZAW,* 44 (1926), 56-59; S. N. Kramer, *The Sumerians, Their History, Culture, and Character* (1963); H. Lesètre, "Lumière," *DB,* IV (1908), 415ff.; H. G. May, "Some Aspects of Solar Worship at Jerusalem," *ZAW,* 55 (1937), 269-281; idem, "The Creation of Light in Gen. 1,3-5," *JBL,* 58 (1939), 203-211; G. Nagel, "Le culte du soleil dans l'ancienne Egypte," *ErJb,* 10 (1943), 9-55, other articles also appear here; Fr. Nötscher, *"Das Angesicht Gottes schauen" nach bibl. und babylon. Auffassung* (1924); idem, *Zur theol. Terminologie der Qumran-Texte. BBB,* 10 (1956), 92-148; A. Oepke, "λάμπω," *TDNT,* IV, 17-28; H. Ringgren, "Light and Darkness in Ancient Egyptian Religion," *Liber Amicorum. Festschrift C. J. Bleeker* (1969), 140-150; W. H. Schmidt, *Die Schöpfungsgeschichte der Priesterschrift, WMANT,* 17 (²1967); W. von Soden, "Licht und Finsternis in der sumer. und babylon. Religion," *StudGen,* 13 (1960), 647-653; P. Wernberg-Møller, "A Reconsideration of the Two Spirits in the Rule of the Community," *RevQ,* 3 (1961/62), 413-441.

[1] *WUS,* 214.
[2] *AHw,* 805.

2. *Religio-Historical Background*. (a) In the Ugaritic texts, the concepts
of light and darkness do not play an important role. There the emphasis is on
the fertility cult and the changes in the seasons. Dawn and Dusk are the first
sons of the creator-god, and consequently the alternation of day and night is a
primitive date for the creation of the world. The sun is less important than the
moon, the "luminary of heaven." The moon is connected with the fertility of the
ground. Light is associated with dew and rain, and is perhaps thought of as
a consort of the god of the atmosphere. [3] The sun's function is to uncover or
expose; it is the "luminary" of the gods and the witness of truth. The scorching
summer sun is typical for the dry season and is connected with the god of the
Underworld. The expression *pn špš nr by*, [4] "the countenance of the sun shines
upon me" = "I enjoy the favor of the (Hittite) king," is of special interest. [5]

The astral deities also have a subordinate role among the Sumerians. The main
gods are the gods of the atmosphere, of heaven, of the underground ocean, and
the goddess of the earth. The bright-eyed god of the air, father of the gods and
creator-god, separated heaven and earth in creation. He causes the day to appear. [6]
His light "rises up," he "makes his emblems bright." [7] Thus, outside the group
of astral gods, the god of the air has connections with light, and is above the
astral gods in rank. As father of the sun-god, the moon-god, son of the god of the
air, has preeminence over the sun-god. The moon is the greatest of the heavenly
lights. His light represents wisdom. The sun-god is the one who exposes man's
deeds, the judge who is responsible for the moral order of the world. The gods
live in the bright and blessed land where the sun rises. As an example of the
figurative use of light and darkness, we may cite the following: "my god, the day
shines brightly over the land, for me the day is dark." [8]

Among the Babylonians the picture is different in essential points. Marduk
("calf of the sun, child of the sun"), originally a god of the spring sun, has taken
the place of the Sumerian god of the air in the pantheon, and as a result the
triangular scheme of the ancient nature religion (heaven, atmosphere, earth or
the deep) falls apart and is replaced by the astral deities, especially by the triad
sun, moon, and Venus. Through their orbits, these deities regulate fate and
history. It is now understood that the sun sheds light upon the world, makes the
days shorter and the nights longer, and regulates the seasons. Its importance
is extensive. The sun-god is overseer of the cosmos, and thus protector of law
and patron of the weak, and is connected with didactic and moral characteristics.
Naturally, the light of the astral gods is mentioned often. The ruler of the dark
Underworld is Nergal, who is responsible for the horrors of fever, pestilence,
and death, but who is also interpreted as a representative of the scorching midday
sun. Demons wreak havoc during the night. There is no dualism between light

---

3 *WUS*.
4 *UT*, 1015, 9f.
5 Cf. *CRAI* (1952), 232.
6 Kramer, 119.
7 Von Soden, 648.
8 Man and His God, 68; *ANET Suppl.*, 154.

and darkness in the Babylonian view of the creation of the world. A darkening
of the stars is an indication of a time of curse.

In the Egyptian religion, the sun gained an important position very early. The
first gods came out of primitive water. The egg out of which the sun (and thus
light) emerges is hatched by the eight primitive deities, two of which are person-
ifications of darkness (Hermopolis). The identification of the sun-god Rē‘ with
the primitive god Atum (Heliopolis) is perhaps secondary. In Heliopolis there
was a cosmogony, according to which the sun was brought forth by the goddess
of heaven, whose husband was the earth. Besides these two gods there is the god
of the air, who in the creation separates earth and heaven from each other. Thus,
here air, earth, and the firmament form a stage between primitive water/primitive
god and sun. This little monistic concept, which is very close to an empirical
observation, is very ancient, and we can see in it a "pre-solar" religious scheme
similar to that which we found among the Sumerians.

With the increasing significance of the sun, among the Egyptians the sun-god
becomes the creator, and is the origin of all life and well-being. Life is a gift of
the sun. Light and life belong together. When the sun goes down, men "die" as
it were, they sleep like the dead. But the night, which also belongs to the world
of creation and is an emanation of primitive darkness, also conceals renewing
powers within it. Each sunrise is a repetition of the creation of the world, but in
a very particular way on the morning of the New Year's Day. The sun determines
the seasons; a solar calendar is well known. The power of the sun extends to the
realm of knowledge and to the moral and political order of the world. There is
a dualistic motif in the idea of the matutinal battle of the sun-god with the serpent
Apophis, which probably personifies the darkness of night. However, primitive
water and primitive darkness are not represented as opponents of the creation of
the world. The darkening of the sun and of the earth are mythical figures for
political revolution and interregnum. The Egyptians also use the concepts of light
and darkness figuratively: "The sun of him that knew thee not hath set, O Amūn.
But he that knoweth thee, he shineth. The forecourt of him that assailed thee is
in darkness, while the whole earth is in sunlight." [9]

(b) The religio-historical background of the OT concept of light is to be
sought in the "pre-solar" stage, which may be seen in the Ugaritic texts, among
the Sumerians, and in an ancient stratum of the Egyptian religion (cf. also the
Babylonian account of creation from Berossos). The subordinate role of the
heavenly bodies and presumably a combination of the cosmic light with the air
is characteristic of this scheme. Light is primarily daylight. A further characteristic is the superiority of the moon over the sun. This scheme is helpful in illu-
minating important aspects of the OT concept of light, e.g., the sequence of the
creation of the world in Gen. 1, the inferior evaluation of the sun in comparison
with the moon, and the predominant role of the day-night complex (in contradistinction to the solar year) in the Israelite consciousness of time and in the
metaphorical use of light.

---

[9] Erman, *Literature of the Ancient Egyptians* (trans. 1927), 310.

On the other hand, the uniqueness of the OT concept of light stands out in contrast to that of surrounding nations. According to OT thought, natural light is distinctly separated from the person of God, which is impossible in nature religions. In the OT, light is an emanation of the plan of divine creation. Therefore, it does not come forth from darkness, as in cosmogonic thought.

II. Natural Light.

1. *The Physical Basis.*

a. *Light of Day and Light of the Heavenly Bodies.* In the OT, the view that the brightness of the day comes from the sun is not expressed. For a correct understanding of the OT idea of light, the distinction between light and sun is important.[10] Of course, the sun shines during the day, but the moon and the stars do the same thing at night, and in spite of this the night is not really bright. Thus, by itself a shining body in heaven does not cause brightness. In the OT the sun is understood essentially as one of the several lights of the firmament. Both the sun and the nocturnal luminaries are called '*orim* (Ps. 136:7), or *me'orim* (Ezk. 32:8) or *me'oroth* (Gen. 1:14-16) (perhaps also '*oroth*, Isa. 26:19). Every passage that speaks of the shining ('*wr* in the hiphil) or the light ('*or*) of the sun (Gen. 1:14-16; Isa. 30:26; 60:19; Jer. 31:35; Ezk. 32:8; Ps. 136:7-9) also refers to the light of the moon and sometimes also to the stars.[11] In descriptions of the darkening of the cosmos, which includes the sun and the nocturnal luminaries,[12] it is worthy of note that the shining of the sun is not mentioned, only that of the moon and the stars (Isa. 13:10; Ezk. 32:7f.). In texts devoting special attention to the sun, it is remarkable that there is no reference to its shining (Ps. 19:2-7[1-6]; 104:19-23; Jgs. 5:31; in 2 S. 23:4 '*or* refers to the morning, not to the sun). The word → נגה *nōghah*, "brightness," is nowhere used with reference to the sun (not even unequivocally in 2 S. 23:4; Prov. 4:18 refers to the dawn, not to the rising sun), but is used in connection with the moon (Isa. 60:19; cf. the verb *naghah* in the hiphil in 13:10) and the stars (Joel 2:10; 4:15[3:15]). Thus the moon is also called *lebhanah*, "the shining white one," while the sun has no corresponding name, although admittedly it is a "greater light" than the moon (Gen. 1:16). In the verb → זרח *zārach*, which (along with *yatsa'*) is the technical term for the rising of the sun (it is not used in connection with the moon or the stars), the idea of light seems to be very obscure, if indeed it really exists at all.[13] Any rendering of this word other than the traditional rendering ("to rise"; cf. the LXX *anatéllō*) would not be appropriate, not even in 2 K. 3:22.

Of course, a closer relationship between light and the sun in the OT would be established if it could be shown that '*or* should be rendered "sun" or "sunshine" in certain passages.[14] But Hab. 3:4 cannot be included in such a list of passages, because a few verses later (v. 11) the sun appears in another context.

---

[10] Aalen, 14.
[11] *Ibid.,* 19f.
[12] See below, II.1.d; 2.f.
[13] Aalen, 39f.
[14] See the lexicons.

In Job 37:21, the light is the light of the bright sky, i.e., of the day, or even the lightning. Even in Isa. 18:4 it is sufficient to think of the bright daylight, although a day with sunshine is undoubtedly assumed. In Job 31:26, the rendering of 'or by "sun" is suggested because it stands in parallelism with the moon. But here again, this is not necessary. We must keep in mind that the light of day is considered to be separate from the light of the sun everywhere in OT thought.

It is not its light, but its heat that distinguishes the sun from the nocturnal luminaries (Ex. 16:21; 1 S. 11:9; Isa. 49:10; Jonah 4:8; Ps. 121:6).[15] When the sun is described as light, it is just as one light among others in the firmament of heaven—analogous to the moon and the stars. In fact, the stars are not independent, but are coordinated in and subordinated to the rhythm of day and night.[16]

Thus, empirical observation apart from cognitive reflection did not lead men to conclude from the first that the light of day originates from the sun. Indeed, in cloudy weather the sun is not visible, and yet the day is bright. Furthermore, men observed that it began to get bright in the morning long before sunrise.[17] Thus, they understood the light of the day or of the morning as something independent of the sun.

This view is clearly presupposed in the account of creation in Gen. 1. Here the light is explicitly called the light of the day (v. 5); it already exists before the lights of heaven are formed (vv. 14ff.).[18] The same is true of the darkness and of the regular alternation of day and night (vv. 5ff.). The sun and the moon are both called "great lights," and their function is to give light upon the earth (v. 15). They do not constitute day and night, but are attributes and characteristics of the day and of the night. They "separate the day from the night" (v. 14), i.e., they separate the time of light in the day-and-night unity from the time of darkness, by their shining (vv. 14ff.). The same view appears in Jer. 31:35 and Ps. 136:7-9.

As is evident from other creation texts in the OT, this thought pattern is characteristic for the OT. According to Ps. 74:13-17, the result of God's clash with the powers of chaos is the establishment of the rhythmic alternation of day and night. In connection with this, the moon (ma'or) and the sun are described as attributes of day and night: "thine is the day, thine also the night; thou hast established luminary and sun" (v. 16). A similar view is found in Ps. 65:7-9 (6-8), without mentioning the heavenly bodies. In Job 38:4ff., the primeval morning is represented as the beginning of the creation of the world (v. 12; cf. the morning stars in v. 7). The sun is not mentioned here, which is intelligible only if it is not regarded as the source of light (cf. also Am. 5:8).[19]

In keeping with this independence of daylight from the sun, light ('or) is explicitly used in connection with morning, dawn, and day in several passages in which no reference is made to the sun (Gen. 44:3; Jgs. 16:2; 19:26; 1 S. 14:36;

---

[15] Cf. II.1.e, and the word chammah for sun.
[16] Aalen, 19f.
[17] See below, II.1.b.
[18] Aalen, 14f.
[19] Ibid., 17.

25:34,36; 29:10; 2 S. 17:22; 2 K. 7:9; Isa. 58:8; Hos. 6:3,5; Am. 5:20; Mic. 2:1; Zeph. 3:5; Zec. 14:6f.; Ps. 139:11f.; Job 3:3-8 [v. 4: *neharah*]; 17:12; 38:19; Neh. 8:3). Sometimes it is possible to observe an explicit or a supposed distinction between the light of the day and the light of the sun. In Isa. 30:26, the light of the sun is compared with the light of the day. In Eccl. 12:2, *'or,* probably meaning daylight, stands alongside the sun, the moon, and the stars. In 2 S. 23:4, the rising sun and the "morning light" are named side by side (cf. also Am. 8:9). [20]

b. *Dawn.* This whole concept is confirmed by an investigation of the process of daybreak. The dawn (→ שַׁחַר *shachar,* which traditionally, but erroneously, is rendered "sunrise") appears a good hour before sunrise in Palestine. Even earlier, about $1^1/_2$ to 2 hours before sunrise, a faint gleam may be seen on the eastern horizon, and gradually this grows into a light which sweeps over the whole horizon. This swath of light is the *shachar,* "the dawn." [21] This idea is in harmony with the practice of comparing the dawn with eyelids (Job 3:9; cf. 41:10 [18]) or with wings (Ps. 139:9). The idea lying behind *shachar,* "dawn," is that of still distant light (Ps. 139:9), of light looking forth (Cant. 6:10) as out of an eye (Job 3:9; 41:10[18]; Cant. 6:10) or coming out of a crevice (Isa. 58:8). Furthermore, the phenomenon of gradually becoming brighter (Prov. 4:18), from a state of darkness (Joel 2:2) to a complete "establishment" of light (Hos. 6:3,5), is characteristic of the *shachar,* "dawn." Still, twilight (which assumes the dawn), or better dusk, *nesheph* (1 S. 30:17; 2 K. 7:5,7; Job 7:4; Ps. 119:147), when the stars can still be seen (Job 3:9; 38:7), belongs to the night. While the dawn is causing the stars to disappear, only the morning star, Venus, remains visible (Isa.14:12).

It is clear from Job 38:12-15 that the morning is the predominant concept, while the dawn is a part of the more detailed description of the breaking of the morning. The dawn is represented as a gigantic claw which takes hold of the earth on the horizon from north to south. During the period of dawn, the earth is changed by the growing light; it assumes a character which is comparable with the impression made by a seal (v. 14): its features "stand out" (*hithyatstsebh,* v. 14b). Jgs. 19:25ff. provides a similar picture of this sequence. The night ends with the rising of the dawn, and the morning breaks (v. 25). The "turn of the morning" soon follows, and then the full brightness begins (v. 26). Here, as in Job 38:4-15, the sun is not mentioned. It is evident from Gen. 19:15,23 that a considerable period of time elapses between dawn and sunrise (cf. 32:25,27, 32[24,26,31]). The night ends with the rising *shachar,* "dawn" (Gen. 32:25,27 [24,26]; Josh. 6:15). Now it is bright enough to set out on a journey (Gen. 19:15, 23; 44:3; 1 S. 9:26; 29:10).

Perhaps it is not always possible to determine the exact time of the oft mentioned "morning light." However, the night is at an end with the morning light, and during the morning light the accomplishments or crimes of the preceding night are surveyed (1 S. 14:36; 25:34,36; 2 S. 17:22). Now that which has been

---

[20] On this see below, II.1.b.
[21] Dalman, *AuS,* I, 600; Koehler; Aalen, 37, n. 3.

planned for the new day is begun (Jgs. 16:2; 1 S. 25:36; 2 K. 7:9; Mic. 2:1; cf. Job 24:14). Only exceptionally is there a reference to the rising of the sun in such texts and situations (Jgs. 9:33). Usually they speak only of the morning light or just light (Jgs. 19:26; Job 24:14; Neh. 8:3), or simply mention that it is getting bright (1 S. 29:10; 2 S. 2:32).

On the whole, it follows from this that in the consciousness of the Israelites the sunrise is by no means decisive for the concept of the morning light. Rather, the Israelites connect light with the morning and the dawn.

c. *Dusk.* Thus, according to Israelite thought the boundary line between night and day does not coincide with the sunrise. However, as far as sundown and evening are concerned, the picture is not so clear. When the sun goes down, the day ends (Jgs. 14:18; 2 S. 3:35; Dnl. 6:14; Ps. 104:19f.). But the OT nowhere states that the setting of the sun brings about the beginning of night and darkness (not even Ps. 104:19f.). The expression "between the two evenings" (*ben ha'arbayim*) favors the idea that a distinction was made between sundown and nightfall. The most probable interpretation of this expression (see esp. Ex. 12:6; Nu. 9:11; cf. Dt. 16:6) is that the evening includes the time between sundown and complete darkness.

One can hardly appeal to passages like Am. 8:9; Mic. 3:6; Jer. 15:9 to prove that there was no distinction between sundown and the end of the day. Exact parallels to these passages in Sumerian and Egyptian texts [22] seem to show that the "going in" of the sun does not bring the day as such to an end. Cf. especially Jer. 15:9 and also Job 5:14. Possibly a solar eclipse (thus perhaps Am. 8:9) or simply the clouding of the sky (cf. the word *qadhar*, Mic. 3:6, in this sense in Ezk. 32:7; 1 K. 18:45) forms the background.

d. *Darkening of the Stars.* From the passages which have been mentioned (Am. 8:9; Mic. 3:6; Jer. 15:9), the most that can be deduced is that, according to the Israelite view, when the sun shines it is a cooperating light source of the day (cf. 2 S. 23:4). The distinction between daylight and sun advocated above does not oppose this idea. But immediately it must be added that in a similar way the moon and the stars are sources of nocturnal light. The day as such is bright, just as the night as such is dark. But both are provided with a cosmic light body. It is significant that the motif of the cosmic darkening of the heavenly bodies regularly has to do both with the sun and the nocturnal luminaries. The light of the heavenly bodies may go out, but this does not mean that day and night come to an end. As a result of the darkening, of course, darkness spreads over the land (Am. 8:9; Isa. 5:30; Ezk. 32:8; cf. Joel 2:2). But according to Isa. 5:30; Ezk. 32:7; Zeph. 1:15; Joel 2:2, this is caused by the clouds. These passages are in fact referring to the coming of a day, of the day of the Lord, which is a day of darkness (Am. 5:18; Zeph. 1:15; Joel 2:2). Thus these passages do not conflict with a distinction between daylight and sun: the sun does not constitute or effect the day

---

[22] See above, I.2.a.

any more than the moon and the stars effect the night. The relationship of the sun to the day is not different from the relationship of the moon and the stars to the night. The day is the framework in which the sun functions, just as the night is the framework in which the moon and the stars function.

e. *The Paths of the Heavenly Bodies; Months; Years.* That, however, according to the OT view the sun and the moon are attributes of the day and the night does not mean they should be understood merely as random accidents. Their regular and rhythmically alternating movements connect them rather firmly with the structure of the world and with the course of time. The paths of the heavenly lights are an integral part of the order of the world and have their foundation in laws which are prescribed for them by the Creator (Jer. 31:35f.; Ps. 148:3-6; Job 38:33; Ps. 104:19; 19:6f.[5f.]). This raises no question about the priority of day and night over against the luminaries, since the covenant that God has made concerns day and night primarily (Jer. 31:35; 33:25; Gen. 8:22; Ps. 19:3[2]; 74:16). However, the movements of the sun and of the luminaries of the night have their place in the rhythmic alternation of day and night, but without effecting this alternation.

The paths and movements of the heavenly bodies are more important than their light-giving function. In fact, in the OT the light of the sun, moon, and stars is explicitly mentioned only in passages where they appear together, and this means in the framework of the day-night unity (Gen. 1:14-16; Jer. 31:35; Ps. 136:7; 148:3; Isa. 13:10; 30:26; 60:19; Ezk. 32:7f.; Joel 2:10; 4:15[3:15]). Except when it is connected with the sun or the sun and the stars, the moon is almost never mentioned (the exceptions are Ps. 8:4[3]; Job 25:5). As far as the relationship of the paths of the luminaries to the month and the year is concerned, the phases of the moon naturally played a basic role in the organization of the calendar (which was in fact a lunar calendar), and consequently in appointing the festivals (Gen. 1:14; Ps. 104:19). It is true that the actual phases of the moon are mentioned almost not at all in the OT, if we mean by this the increase and decrease of the light of the moon (Isa. 60:20). OT man was not interested primarily in the light of the moon, but in the beginning or middle of the new month. The movements of the moon served to mark the course of time, the alternation of day and night, and also the succession of the months (see Gen. 1:14; Ps. 72:5,7; 89:37f.[36f.]).

Even more important than this is that the OT texts know no distinction between a bright time of the year and a dark time connected with the path of the sun. According to Eccl. 12:2, the (relative) darkness of the winter is due to the cloudy sky, not to the low path of the sun. Actually, the Israelites had no clear idea about the influence of the sun on the change of seasons.[23] Naturally they were conscious of the great heat of the sun during the summer (Ex. 16:21; Isa. 49:10; Jonah 4:8; Ps. 32:4; Neh. 7:3), but this was explained by the fact that summer was a time when the sky was not cloudy. Also OT man connected the ripening of the

---

23 See Dalman, *AuS*, I, 42f.

early fruit with the sun (Dt. 33:14; cf. Isa. 18:4f.). But nowhere in the OT is the annual path of the sun an object of interest. The context in which the sun was thought to function was consistently day and night. Only rarely is it placed within the context of the seasons, and then usually with reference to the summer heat.

Thus it seems impossible to assume that in ancient Israel there were cult practices or festivals which were related to the increase and decrease of sunlight in the framework of the seasons. This would presuppose that a solar interpretation of the world and of time was prevalent, as for example in Babylon. But this view had not been adopted in Israel. [24] Under these circumstances, there is no justification for the supposed connection between the Autumn Festival and the solar equinox, [25] or for explaining the fact that the Jerusalem temple faces east from the autumnal equinox. [26] Judging from the probable orientation of the second temple, which must have been parallel to the southern wall of the Herodian temple area, the temple did not face directly east, but was turned somewhat northward. This fits an orientation to the dawn rather than to the sunrise. [27]

f. *Light and Darkness As Cosmic Substances.* If light as light of the day is independent of the sun, this raises the question of whether light and darkness were understood in the OT as substances existing in the cosmic sphere. There are statements in the book of Job that may support this idea. Here the question is asked: "Where is the way to the dwelling of light, and where is the place of darkness?" (38:19f.). It is assumed that, like snow and hail (v. 22), light and darkness also were kept in "storehouses" somewhere in the cosmos. There are gates leading to the place where darkness is kept (v. 17). The dawn also has a "place" where it stays when it is not functioning (v. 12). The idea in 26:10 seems to be that the horizon is the boundary line between light and darkness, which would mean that light and darkness cross over this boundary alternately each morning and each evening.

The idea of substance is not obvious in Gen. 1. It is hardly the intention of the writer to give an account of the "origin of light" in v. 3. As a matter of fact, the substantive *'or,* "light," in connection with *hayah,* "to be," may have an adjectival meaning; so in Ex. 10:23; Zec. 14:7; perhaps also (without *hayah*) in Gen. 44:3; 1 S. 29:10 (where, admittedly, it can also be understood as a verb). If this adjectival interpretation of Gen. 1:3 is correct, then we may translate: "let it become light (bright)!" Then the "creation of light" would be nothing more than making the first morning or day bright, which corresponds to the representation of creation in Job 38:7,12. It would be easier to understand the darkness in Gen. 1:2 as a kind of substance, because it already existed before the first night. It is likely, though, that the narrator is thinking existentially and theologically rather than physically.

---

[24] See above, I.2.

[25] J. Morgenstern, *HUCA,* 22 (1949), 388.

[26] F. S. Hollis in *Myth and Ritual,* ed. S. H. Hooke (London, 1933), 91ff., and before him C. V. L. Charlier, *ZDMG,* 58 (1904), 386ff.

[27] Aalen, 83, n. 23.

2. *Light and Darkness in Human Existence.*

a. *Position of Darkness.* In spite of the relationship of darkness to chaos in Gen. 1:2, darkness is not thought of as a power hostile to God. The OT does not speak of a battle or a dualism between light and darkness. Here, neither the primeval ocean nor the darkness is considered to be a power of chaos in the sense of mythical adversaries of God. God acts on the ocean not for the purpose of destroying it, but only for the purpose of confining it to certain fixed limits, where it has a positive task in the household of the world. The role of darkness is to be understood as analogous to this. It is true that it is associated with the state of chaos (Gen. 1:2; Jer. 4:23), and is sporadically connected with sea monsters or with the sea (Job 3:8f.; 26:13; Isa. 5:30; Job 22:11). But in these cases the biblical writers are thinking of darkness as becoming too powerful and as overstepping its bounds. When the world was created, the limits of darkness were established. Although its rank is inferior to that of light, by creation it was built into the world order, viz., in the rhythmic alternation of day and night ordained by God. It is an "organized power of chaos." [28] God is the creator of both light and darkness (Isa. 45:7). His power and goodness transcend the antithesis of light and darkness (Ps. 139:12). He "turns deep darkness into the morning, and darkens the day into night" (Am. 5:8). In the creation he set this alternation of day and night in motion. This alternation constitutes time and establishes the world (Gen. 8:22; Ps. 74:13-16; 65:7-9[6-8]; Jer. 33:25; Job 38:4-15). [29]

However, this position of darkness in the world order, and consequently in the life of man, is full of tension. The good will of God is connected with light. Only light is described as "good" (Gen. 1:4), not darkness. There is as little room here for the idea that light was derived from darkness (as advocated by a monistic cosmogony or system [30]) as there is for the view that light and darkness had a common origin out of the divine *Urgrund,* the primeval foundation of all things.

The inferiority of darkness is shown in different ways: in the association of light and life, [31] of darkness and the Underworld, [32] of darkness and evil men; [33] in the figurative use of light in the sense of success and salvation and of darkness in the sense of failure and destruction; [34] in the idea that darkness is a potential power of chaos; [35] and finally in the expectation that darkness will be eliminated in the eschatological state of salvation. [36]

Until the final state of perfection comes, darkness represents a latent possibility of chaos, in fact an instrument in the hand of God. Darkness points to the tension

---

[28] *Ibid.,* 10ff.; the Egyptian view is similar; Hornung, 74, 78ff.
[29] See further H. Ringgren, *The Faith of the Psalmists* (1963), 119ff., on Ps. 104:19-23.
[30] See above, I.2.
[31] See below, 2.b.
[32] See below, 2.c.
[33] See below, III.3.a.
[34] See below, III.1.
[35] See below.
[36] See below, II.2.f.

and interim character of this world and world order. Like the other "powers of chaos" (Sea, Wilderness), darkness makes man aware of the instability of the world, and represents the possibility that it can return to chaos. As creator of the world, God holds in his hand the possibility of putting an end to creation through the powers of chaos. An abnormal and comprehensive irruption of darkness would return the world to the state of chaos (Jer. 4:23f.). [37] But as long as darkness continues to operate within the limits prescribed for it in creation, it is not a power of chaos.

Earlier research was inclined to find a dualistic conflict between light and darkness in Genesis as an imitation of the prototype of Marduk's battle with the chaos monster in the Babylonian creation myth. [38]

b. *Light and Life; Light of the Eyes.* The superiority of light over darkness is expressed, among other ways, in the relationship which the OT makes between light and life. Here we must think primarily of natural light. Only in the light of creation can one have life. "To see the light" means "to live" (Job 33:28; 3:16). Children who are born dead have not seen the light (3:16) or the sun (Ps. 58:9[8]; Eccl. 6:4f.). The dead see the light no more (Ps.49:20[19]; Job 33:28). This synonymous meaning of light and life is evident in the pregnant expression *'or hachayyim* (Ps. 56:14[13]; Job 33:30), whether we translate it with Symmachus at Ps. 56:14(13) "the light of life," or with the LXX "the light of the living." [39] Light and life also appear together in Ps. 36:10(9): "For with thee is the fountain of life; in thy light do we see light." But it is probable that light here means "salvation, way, orientation." [40]

The light of the day is reflected in the light of the eyes (Prov. 29:13). An increase of this light means increased vitality and joy (Ezr. 9:8; Prov. 15:30; 1 S. 14:27,29). [41] The verb form *ha'ir* (hiphil) is also used in this sense (Ezr. 9:8; Prov. 29:13; Ps. 13:4[3]; 19:9[8]; cf. Eccl. 8:1). When the light of the eyes fails, a person is approaching death (Ps. 38:11[10]; 13:4[3]).

c. *Darkness in the Underworld.* In the Underworld (→ שְׁאוֹל *she'ôl,* "Sheol"), there is no alternation of day and night; it is a land "without order, and when it is bright (i.e., morning), it is as darkness" (Job 10:22).

d. *The Night.* The OT appraisal of night (→ חשֶׁךְ *chōshekh,* → לֵילָה *laylāh*) is ambiguous. Night is the time when God intervenes and punishes the wicked (Ex. 11:4; 12:29f.; 2 K. 19:35; Job 34:20; cf. Gen. 32:25ff.[24ff.]), but it is also a time regulated and standardized by the cult (Isa. 30:29; Ps.134:1), and a time of meditation and thanksgiving (Ps. 16:7; 63:7[6]; 92:3[2]; 119:55,62).

---

[37] See below, 2.f.

[38] See H. Gunkel, *Schöpfung und Chaos* (1895; ²1921); A. Jeremias, *The OT in the Light of the Ancient East* (trans. 1911), 39. Pedersen, *ILC,* I-II, 464ff., argues on the other hand that the antithesis between light and darkness has many nuances in the OT.

[39] Aalen, 64.

[40] See below, III.2.

[41] Aalen, 64.

e. *Morning As Salvation.* In spite of these positive characteristics, the night lacks the most crucial characteristic, viz., God's intervention to save man. This belongs to the morning (Ps. 5:4[3]; 46:6[5]; 88:14[13]; 119:147; 130:6; 143:8; Isa. 8:20; 58:8; Hos. 6:3; → בקר *bōqer*). God's merciful deeds are "new every morning" (Lam. 3:22f.). According to Ps. 46:3ff.(2ff.), the coming of salvation in the morning means a restitution of creation, which is threatened by the powers of chaos. We should probably understand Job 38:4-15 to mean that not only the primeval morning, but every morning, signifies a renewal of creation. The fashion of the earth becomes visible (v. 14), and the wicked are removed from the earth (vv. 13,15). This daily renewal of creation is not connected with the sunrise[42] as it is in Egyptian literature,[43] but with the morning. This appraisal of the morning may be connected with experiences which the Israelites had had in the distress of battle (2 K. 7:5ff.; 19:34ff.; Ps. 46:6ff.[5ff.]). Furthermore, the custom of holding court trials and of giving the righteous the efficacious help of the law in the morning (Ps. 101:8; 2 S. 15:2; Jer. 21:12; Job 7:18; cf. Ps. 73:14) certainly contributed to this. The statements in Hos. 6:3b,5 are understandable against this background: "his (God's) going forth is sure as the dawn; he will come to us..." (v. 3b). "And thy (God's) judgment goes forth as a light" (v. 5b). These verses seem to presuppose that judgment was given at dawn (cf. 2 S. 15:2). Zeph. 3:5 and Ps. 37:6 provide important parallels.[44]

f. *Eschatological Elimination of Darkness.* The darkening of the heavenly bodies is an element in the prophetic preaching concerning the future.[45] We also encounter the idea in the OT that darkness itself will come to an end and that God's light alone will shine. Prophetic threats are directed generally against the light of heaven (Jer. 4:23; cf. Isa. 5:30) or explicitly against the luminaries, in fact against sun, moon, and stars together (Isa. 13:10; Ezk. 32:7f.; Joel 2:10; 3:4 [2:31]; 4:15 [3:15]). They will become black and will no longer give light. Only in Am. 8:9 is the sun mentioned alone. The earth will quake and even be returned to a state of chaos (Isa. 5:30; 13:9; Zeph. 1:15; Joel 2:10), but only for sinners (Isa. 13:9; Zeph. 1:16f.; Joel 2:11ff.). The basic theme is the coming of the day of the Lord (Am. 5:18,20; Isa. 13:9; Zeph. 1:14f.; Joel 2:1; 3:4[2:31]; 4:14[3:14]; → יום *yôm*). For the sinner, this day is a day of darkness (Am. 5:18,20; Zeph. 1:15; Joel 2:2).

The shaking of the luminaries refers to their light, but in particular to their ordered paths. When God appears, the "host of heaven" will be punished (Isa. 24:21-23). The old world order is about to be dissolved. According to Isa. 60:19, the sun and the moon will be superseded by God's eternal light. Conversely, it can be said that the light of the sun and of the moon will be abundantly increased in the time of salvation (30:26). It is likely that here, more or less clearly, we have the idea that an eternal day will dawn. This thought is clearly expressed in Zec.

---

[42] Ringgren, *Festschrift Bleeker,* 144f.
[43] See above, I.2.
[44] See below, III.3.c.
[45] See above, II.1.d.

14:7. In the time of salvation, there is "neither day nor night, for at evening time there shall be light." The rhythm of day and night has ceased, i.e., the present world time is at an end. The "ordered dualism" of light and darkness, which was given along with the rhythm of day and night and the movement of the heavenly bodies and is a part of the character of the present creation, is abolished by a state in which only day and light rule.

3. *Lamps*. Artificial light was usually provided by lamps (*nir* or *ner*, Job 18:5f.; Jer. 25:10; etc.). Lamps were set up in the sanctuary, but it is not clear whether they burned during the day·(Ex. 25:31ff.; Lev. 24:2; 1 K. 7:49; 2 Ch. 13:11). A comparison of 1 S. 3:3 with 4:21 seems to suggest that the lamp of the sanctuary was understood as a kind of representation of God (cf. the lamps mentioned in Zec. 4:2).

Some scholars have attempted to date the illuminations which, according to Jewish sources, occurred in the temple grounds during the Feast of Tabernacles back into OT times. They identify them with the vigils which they suppose to be assumed in passages such as Ps. 134:1 and Isa. 30:29. Of course, for practical reasons we must assume that artificial light was used in any nocturnal festival in the sanctuary. Any symbolic interpretation is late, and the numerous suggestions of scholars remain uncertain. [46]

III. Figurative Use.

1. *Light As Prosperity, Salvation.*

a. *General Considerations*. The figurative use of light and darkness in the OT displays a richly varied picture. As a figure for success and well-being, light embraces a broad sphere (Am. 5:18,20; Job 17:12; 18:5f.; 22:28; Prov. 13:9; Lam. 3:2; Est. 8:16). Conversely, darkness stands for suffering and failure (Isa. 8:22; Jer. 23:12; Am. 5:18,20; Ps. 23:4; Job 17:12; 29:3; Lam. 3:2). In religiously oriented texts, light is a symbol for the salvation given by God (Isa. 9:1[2]; 58:8; Ps. 18:29[28]; 36:10[9]; 43:3; 97:11; Job 29:3). Also a verb meaning "to shine" with God as its subject can have a similar meaning (Ps. 18:29[28]; 118:27; Job 33:30). Less frequently the sun serves as a symbol of well-being and salvation (Jgs. 5:31; Jer. 15:9; Mal. 3:20[4:2]; → שֶׁמֶשׁ *shemesh*). Sometimes "light" is replaced by "lamp," which is also a figure for success and salvation (Ps. 18:29[28]; 2 S. 22:29; Prov. 13:9; 24:20; Job 18:6; 21:17; 29:3; → גר *nēr*). A lamp set up in the house was a symbol for the prosperity and wealth of the family (Jer. 25:10; Prov. 31:18).

It is probable that this was the starting-point for the symbolic use of the lamp as a figure for the permanence of the royal house (1 K. 11:36; 15:4; 2 K. 8:19; Ps. 132:17; cf. 2 S. 21:17). Others want to see in the lamp ordered for the "anointed one" in Jerusalem (Ps. 132:17; 1 K. 11:36) the idea of a cultic symbol, or to identify the light of the "sacral kingship" directly with the light of the sanctuary. [47]

---

[46] Aalen, 58, n. 3.
[47] See above, II.3.

b. *God, the Light of Man.* In some passages, God himself is characterized as the light or lamp of man or of Israel (Ps. 27:1: "my light"; 2 S. 22:29: "my lamp"; Isa. 10:17: "the light of Israel"; 60:1: "your light"; Mic. 7:8: "a light to me"). It would be a mistake to see in such expressions a designation for the metaphysical nature of God. All that they indicate is the importance God has in man's life to provide him salvation and help. There is no essential difference between Ps. 18:29(28), which says that God "lights my lamp," and 2 S. 22:29, which states that God himself "lightens my darkness." [48]

c. *God's Light As Salvation, Success.* The situation is the same when the OT speaks of "the light of Yahweh" (Isa. 2:5), "his (God's) light" or "lamp" (Job 29:3), or in the same sense, of "thy light" (Ps. 36:10[9]; 43:3). Here too light is to be understood as a symbol not of God's person, but of the salvation which God gives. The reference to seeing the light in Ps. 36:10(9) is therefore not to be understood in a mystical sense. "To see the light" simply means to experience salvation or deliverance (Isa. 9:1[2]; 53:11 in the LXX and 1QIsᵃ).

d. *Light of the Countenance of God.* The expression "light of the countenance" of God, which probably means "God's favor and grace" (Ps. 4:7[6]; 44:4[3]), stands somewhat by itself. This idiom appears in the secular sphere as well (Prov. 16:15; Job 29:24), and also in Ugaritic and Babylonian texts. [49] The same idea can be expressed verbally: God "makes his face to shine" (Nu. 6:25; Ps. 31:17[16]; 67:2[1]; 80:4,8,20[3,7,19]; 119:135; Dnl. 9:17). A "mystical" interpretation is also out of place for this expression; a word for "to see" is missing here.

2. *Walking and Way.*

a. *Success and Failure.* The figure of walking or of the way originated in OT thought from the conviction that the crucial point in life does not lie in theoretical observations, but in practical living. This symbolism is implied in the passages already mentioned above which speak of "the light of God." [50] "To walk in God's light" seems in Isa. 2:5 to mean "to walk in his paths" (v. 3), i.e., to live according to his instructions. However, the general idea is that man finds a way of well-being and salvation. Therefore, the light which God gives represents his protecting and preserving guidance (Ps. 43:3; Prov. 4:18; Job 22:28; 29:2f.; Isa. 9:1[2]; 42:16).

Conversely, in a similar connection darkness designates the way of the ungodly which leads to stumbling, i.e., destruction (Dt. 28:28f.; Jer. 13:16; 23:12; Job 12:24f.; 5:13f.; Prov. 4:19). But this does not mean that the godly person (or Israel) is spared from walking (or sitting, Mic. 7:8) in darkness, in order that he might subsequently see the light (Isa. 9:1[2]; 50:10; 53:11 in 1QIsᵃ and the LXX), or if need be that he might have God's light in the darkness (Job 29:3).

---

48 On Isa. 60:1, see below, IV.6.
49 See above, I.2.
50 See above, 1.c.

Walking in the light can become a comprehensive goal for human existence. To "walk before God's countenance in the light of life" is the goal and destiny of life, while stumbling in the darkness means death (Ps. 56:14[13]; cf. also 89:16 [15]). This symbolism was sometimes transferred to the people, as in the case of the wilderness wanderings, when Israel was led by the light of the pillar of fire (Ex. 13:21f.; Ps. 78:14; 105:39; Isa. 42:16; 58:8; Neh. 9:12,19). But one day the light of the morning will rise over Israel (Isa. 60:1f.). [51]

b. *The Light of the Law and of Wisdom.* The idea of the law or of wisdom being a guide which gives light is very close to the motif of walking in the light. Without this light on the way, man gropes in darkness (Prov. 6:23; Ps. 119:105; Eccl. 2:13f.). It is worthy of note that gradually a more abstract way of thinking is evident here. The understanding and interpretation of the law is regarded as instruction and wisdom. One indication of this is that the word "enlighten" (*ha'ir,* hiphil), which means "to shine, to make bright" everywhere else, assumes the meaning "to instruct, to impart understanding" (Ps. 119:130, where admittedly the meaning "to give light on the way" is also possible). Light is used in parallelism with wisdom or understanding, and darkness with folly (Eccl. 2:13f.; Dnl. 5:11,14; cf. also Job 37:19,21; 38:2; 22:11-14; Mic. 3:6). In this sense, light is actually the privilege of God (Job 12:22; 28:11; Dnl. 2:22), but God reveals to man "deep and mysterious things" (Dnl. 2:21f.). The idea that the law or wisdom "enlightens" the eyes or the countenance (*ha'ir,* hiphil, Ps. 19:9[8]; Eccl. 8:1) belongs in a different context. Here the enlightening goes back to the concept of strengthening a person's vitality.

3. *Light and Darkness in Ethical Contexts.*

a. *Sinners and Light.* There is a contrast in the OT between light and sinners. In the ancient Near Eastern world around Israel, the sun was the point of departure for this concept [52] (perhaps 2 S. 12:11f. indicates a step in this direction in the OT; cf. also Nu. 25:4). But the OT uses the word light to convey this thought. Sinners, night, and darkness belong together. They "do not know the light," i.e., they avoid the day (Job 24:16), and "rebel against the light" (v. 13). At night they devise their plans (v. 14; Mic. 2:1) or carry out their deeds; the darkness is their morning; for "they are friends with the terrors of deep darkness" (Job 24:17). They make their headquarters in dark places, from which they direct their attacks against the righteous (Ps. 11:2; 74:20).

In order to understand these passages, it is important to realize that sinners think that no one sees them (Job 24:15), not even God (22:13f.; Ps. 10:8,11). But for God "there is no gloom or deep darkness where evildoers may hide themselves" (Job 34:21f.; cf. Zeph. 1:12; Ps. 139:11f.). "Thou hast set ... our secret sins in the light of thy countenance" (Ps. 90:8).

---

[51] See below, IV.6.
[52] See above, I.2.

b. *Instances of an Ethical Dualism.* The symbolic application of darkness to the deeds of the wicked, which occurs so often in Judaism, is found in the OT only by way of implication. Prov. 2:13, where "the ways of darkness" in which the wicked walk symbolizes their behavior, comes closest to this idea in the OT. Light occurs just as infrequently as a symbol of personal ethical purity (however, see Job 25:5). Only in Isa. 5:20 do light and darkness seem to be understood abstractly in the sense of good and evil. In the OT as a whole the ideas of light and darkness are not used in a figurative sense as religio-ethical qualities which describe the nature or behavior of people. Of course, the idea that night and darkness are the elements in which sinners operate (cf. Ps. 10:8f.; Prov. 7:9f.; Isa. 29:15)[53] is related to this way of thinking. The prevailing idea in the OT, however, is that darkness is a hiding-place for the wicked and a covering for their sins, while light exposes and convicts the wicked of their evil deeds in the daytime. That the "ethical dualism" of Judaism,[54] by a certain shift in emphasis, should have developed from this is easily understandable.

c. *Light and Justice; the Servant of the Lord.* The connection of justice (*mishpat*) with light and morning (cf. Zeph. 3:5; Mic. 7:9; Ps. 37:6)[55] also belongs here. The idea is that justice is brought to light or that it goes forth as light. The verb used here is *yatsa'*, hiphil *hotsi'*. The exegesis of Isa. 42:1-3 and 51:4f., where this terminology also occurs, is important, but it is disputed. The verb *yotsi'* (or *tetse'*) here can hardly be understood to mean "to lead or bring forth (to the nations)."[56] Instead, the idea is that the servant will cause justice to appear, to the best of the nations. If the verb *yatsa'* does have an object, it is light, i.e., the idea is that of bringing to light or making manifest (see, e.g., Job 12:22; 28:11). The construction in Mic. 7:9 and Zeph. 3:5 is to be understood in the same way.

According to Mic. 7:8f., man finds himself in darkness and God brings him to the light. This is similar to the situation described in Isa. 42:6f. (cf. 49:9). Thus, in these texts light represents not only the manifestation of justice, but also the salvation of the oppressed which is attained through justice. Light is salvation which manifests itself (cf. the use of "salvation" in Isa. 49:6; 51:5) and which is brought about by justice. Now inasmuch as justice has its source in the Torah (42:4; 51:4), the Torah is also, as it were, a light for those who are saved. Further, when the servant of the Lord himself is represented as a "light to the nations" (42:6; 49:6; cf. 51:4), this is because he mediates light, i.e., the justice which brings salvation (and perhaps also the Torah). The genitival construction here is an objective genitive, somewhat analogous to the expression "the light of Israel" (Isa. 10:17).[57]

---

53 See above, 3.a.
54 Cf. Qumran, see below, V.
55 See above, II.2.e. on Hos. 6:3,5.
56 So also Aalen, 90.
57 See above, III.1.b.

IV. God and Light in Theophanic Texts.

1. *Fundamental Considerations.* In the texts studied thus far, light is never a personal attribute of God, but generally speaking is the natural light of the created world or artificial light kindled by man. This rigorous distinction between natural light and the person of God (which is not retained in Judaism) is significant for the OT concept of creation. A theogonic origin of light is excluded here.

2. *Terminology.* In the main, the connection of light and darkness with the person of God is limited to the idea of theophany, and consequently lies on a dynamic plane. It is hardly necessary to analyze the concept of → כבוד *kābhôdh*, "glory," whose original meaning is probably not "brightness," but "weight," [58] in order to sustain this thesis. As a matter of fact, there is no clear connection between *kabhodh*, "glory," and the concept of light before Ezekiel (1:26-28; 10:4: *noghah;* 43:2), which indicates a late stage of development. In earlier texts, fire is used characteristically in connection with the concept of *kabhodh* (e.g., Ex. 24:16f.; Lev. 9:23f.). In the Pentateuch, the only circumstance in which light appears as a divine attribute is in connection with the bright pillar of fire in the wilderness (Ex. 13:21; 14:20).

One technical term used with light in theophanic texts is the verb → הופיע *hôphîa'* hiphil, "to shine forth" (Dt. 33:2; Ps. 50:2; cf. Ps. 80:2[1]; 94:1). The word → נגה *nāghah,* "to shine," which has already been mentioned, appears in the same role (so in Hab. 3:4 in connection with *'or;* Ps. 18:13[12] = 2 S. 22:13). These passages are not speaking of a heavenly light (the first descriptions of God in heaven appear in Judaism). All these OT passages refer to God in his theophany. This principle applies even to Ex. 24:10, where, however, the concept of light is present only very slightly. Ezekiel is the only one who even approaches the idea of God dwelling in heaven in the OT when he uses attributes of light to describe, not only God, but also other beings (angels) coming from heaven (8:2).

3. *Ps. 104:2.* Of course, Ps. 104:2, a passage which states that God "covers himself with light as with a garment," presents difficulties. Since a theophany cannot be assumed here, it is natural to think of a continuing attribute of God. If so, this passage represents an exception in the OT. It also raises the question of whether the light with which God covers himself is a cosmic light (as it is interpreted by the Rabbis). The garment recalls the idea of heaven as a garment of the deity, which is familiar from the history of religion. [59] The Rabbis found in this passage a proof for their theory that the natural light of creation had its origin in heaven. However, v. 2a must be interpreted in view of that which precedes: light here appears in parallelism with "honor and majesty." God transcends the physical heaven (cf. Ps. 102:26f.[25f.]).

4. *Man's Participation in the Divine Light.* In the OT, men are not usually represented as participating in the divine light. Moses, whose skin shines (verb

---

[58] Aalen, 73ff.

[59] R. Eisler, *Weltenmantel und Himmelszelt* (1910), I, 51ff.

qaran) after his meeting with the Lord (Ex. 34:29f., 35), is an exception. It is not explicitly stated that this shining originated with God, but it is probably assumed (cf. *kabhodh* in 33:18).[60]

5. *Solar Elements in the OT Picture of God?* An earlier generation of scholars was greatly concerned with the question of the extent to which OT terms for light which were associated with God might indicate a solar influence. However, a figurative use of the sun to designate God or his saving intervention is conspicuously rare in the OT. The only passage that can be mentioned is Mal. 3:20(4:2). (In Ps. 84:12[11], *shemesh* does not mean "sun," but "stronghold, defense"; cf. the parallelism and see Isa. 54:12.) → זרח *zārach*, "to rise," is not to be understood as referring to the sun in Isa. 60:1f.; Dt. 33:2.[61] The connection of the sun with justice and ethics, which is so familiar in the religious world around Israel, can hardly be demonstrated with certainty in the OT.[62] However, the comparison of the king with the sun, which is so popular in the ancient Near East, has left its traces in the OT (2 S. 23:4; cf. Prov. 16:15; Jgs. 5:31).

Scholars have often supposed that the chariot vision in Ezk. 1 is derived from Babylonian descriptions of the sun-god.[63] At Ugarit, the expression "light of the countenance of God"[64] has a solar background to the extent that the king is called "sun" in connection with this expression.[65] This background does not seem to be present in Babylonian texts,[66] and it does not appear in the OT. The background for the theophanic term *hophia'* is to be sought in the dawn rather than in the rising of the sun (cf. Job 3:4,9; 10:22). However, Schnutenhaus wants to explain the theophanic terms *yatsa'*, *hophia'*, and *zarach* as applying characteristics of the Babylonian sun-god to Yahweh.[67]

6. *Theophany and the Coming of Salvation; Isa. 60:1-3, etc.* The primary purpose of the theophany of God is the deliverance and salvation of the nation and of the individual. This thought must lead to the connection of the concept of theophany with the light symbolism of salvation. One indication of this connection is the use of the word "come" (→ בוא *bô'*, or synonymous terms) to describe God's manifestation in connection with the light symbolism of the theophany and the light symbols of salvation. These three elements are present in Dt. 33:2, but especially in Isa. 60:1-3. In this important eschatological passage, "the *kabhodh* (glory) of God" and perhaps also the word *zarach* (vv. 1-2; cf. Dt. 33:2) point to

---

[60] On the question of Israel's participation in God's light according to Isa. 60:1,3; 62:2, see below, 6.

[61] See below, 6.

[62] See above, III.3.a.

[63] E.g., A. Jeremias, *Handbuch der altorientalischen Geisteskultur* (²1929), 363; Aalen, 82, n. 6. On the problem connected with the Jerusalem temple facing east, and on the question of the temple and the solar equinox, see above, II.1.e.

[64] See above, II.1.d.

[65] See above, I.2.

[66] See Nötscher, *Angesicht,* 140ff.

[67] F. Schnutenhaus, "Das Kommen und Erscheinen Gottes," *ZAW,* 76 (1964), 9.

a theophany, while *zarach* also indicates the motif of salvation in the morning. This latter motif is suggested also by the expression "your light": the "light of Jerusalem" means the salvation that is imparted to Jerusalem,[68] or if "your light" is interpreted as "God's light," this means that God is the one who brings salvation.[69]

It is not the rising of the sun that provides a background for this figure, but the dawn, as is clear from the reference to the dawn in Isa. 58:8 (cf. *zarach* in 58:10) and to the twilight in 59:10. In 62:1, the verb *yatsa'* is used in connection with the acquittal which takes place at dawn (Hos. 6:3,5; Ps. 37:6; Mic. 7:9; Isa. 42:1,3; 51:4f.).[70] The torch mentioned in 62:1 also refers to the dawn (in distinction from the sunrise) (cf. Job 41:10f.[18f.]).

Furthermore, the reminiscence of the nocturnal wilderness wandering stands behind the whole section (cf. Isa. 42:16; 52:12).[71] The idea that Israel shares in the light itself (60:1,3), indeed, according to 62:2, even in the *kabhodh*, "glory," through the manifestation of God's light, is, however, distinctive in our verses. This hardly means that Israel shares in the divine nature.[72] The thing that is emphasized is not the nature of God, but what God gives to his people, viz., the whole condition of deliverance and victory (62:2), which, to be sure, is due to the nearness of God.

Therefore, the darkness described in Isa. 60:2, which covers the earth and the peoples, denotes the negation both of salvation and the nearness of God. The light is present only in Israel, and only as Israel experiences the coming age of salvation, thus causing the heathen to realize the nearness of God (60:3; 62:2). From this fact, later Judaism derived the theory that Jerusalem would be the cultic center of the whole world even in the eschatological age. The Jewish and NT idea of the eschatological "glorification" of the world and of the righteous can also be traced back to Isa. 60:1-3 and 62:1f. One parallel to these verses in Isaiah appears in Ezk. 43:2,5, where the east represents the salvation which comes in the morning, and the word *kabhodh*, "glory," represents the theophany. The following chapters in Ezekiel describe the age of salvation which has its cultic center in the new temple.

V. The Qumran Texts. In the Qumran literature, *'or, ma'or, ha'ir, hophia'*, and (once) *noghah* appear as terms for light. In the liturgical tradition of Judaism, the light of the day retains its independence from the sun, just as it does in the OT (1QS 10:1-3,10; 1QH 12:4-7; 1QM 14:13f.).[73] On the other hand, the sun is considered to be the "regulating principle of the world" (1QM 17:6f.), which represents something new in comparison with what we find in the OT (cf. the solar calendar). The Qumran literature states that the light of the stars is of

---

[68] See above, III.1.a.
[69] See above, III.1.b.
[70] See above, II.2.e; III.3.c.
[71] See above, III.2.a.
[72] Cf. above, IV.4.
[73] Aalen, 106f., 237ff.

heavenly origin (1QS 10:2f.), which corresponds to the thought of Judaism. The use of light to convey the idea of success, and of darkness to convey the idea of failure, is associated with the concepts of salvation (as glorification) in the eternal light of the hereafter (1QS 4:7f.) and of eternal destruction (1QS 2:8; 4:13) respectively. An ethical dualism of light and darkness, which is expressed in the view that two camps (the sons and spirits of light and the sons and spirits of darkness) stand in opposition to each other, is predominant (1QS 1:9f.; 3:3-26; 1QM 1:1-17; 13:2-16). The source of the light that brings salvation is God (1QS 11:3-5; 1QH 7:25; 9:26f.; 18:1-6), who has made the light shine on man (1QH 9:26f.), and thereby has given him salvation (1QH 9:26-29) and above all enlightenment (1QS 2:3; 4:2; 11:5). This enlightenment does not mean a substantial change in man (the passage that comes closest to this idea is 1QH 7:24). This participation in the realm of light has to do with new understanding and right conduct. The role light plays in trying and accusing man is not important. However, God's light or brightness is understood as a fire which consumes sinners (1QH 6:18f.; 1QM 14:17f.).

Light is not used in connection with God's person in the sense of a divine attribute.

Aalen

אוּרִים *'ûrîm* → גּוֹרָל *gôrāl*

אוֹת *'ôth*

Contents: I. 1. Etymology; 2. Statistical Survey; 3. Synonyms. II. Secular Use. III. Theological Use: 1. The Substance and Settings of Signs; 2. The Functions of Signs: a. Epistemic Signs; b. Signs of Protection; c. Faith Signs; d. Mnemonic Signs; e. Covenant Signs; f. Confirmation Signs; g. Sign-Acts (Symbolic Acts); 3. Conclusions.

I. 1. *Etymology.* The etymology of *'oth* is wholly uncertain.[1] If the *tav* may be regarded as an original feminine ending,[2] it may derive from the root *'vh*, which, however, means, "to wish, to desire."[3] Associating this word with Akk. *ittu*,[4] which sometimes denotes the sign of the oracle, does not lead to any helpful results.[5]

'ôth. (Besides the commentaries): O. Bächli, *Israel und die Völker. AThANT*, 41 (1962); K. Baltzer, *Covenant Formulary* (trans. 1970); W. Eichrodt, "Der Sabbat bei Hesekiel. Ein Beitrag zur Nachgeschichte des Prophetentextes," *Lex tua veritas. Festschrift H. Junker*

(continued on p. 168)

[1] Keller, 146; Rengstorf, *TDNT*, VII, 209.
[2] Keller, 146.
[3] *KBL*³, 20f.; but cf. J. L. Palache, *Semantic Notes on the Hebrew Lexicon* (Leiden, 1959), 3f.; *TDNT*, VII, 209, n. 51, "to establish, to mark(?)."
[4] *CAD*, VII, 304-310; *AHw*, 405f.
[5] *TDNT*, VII, 209; Keller, 148f.

2. *Statistical Survey*. The word *'oth* occurs 78 times in the OT; in 75 cases the LXX translates it by *sēmeíon*. [6] Since *sēmeíon* appears in the LXX only 125 times in all, it is clear that its major use is as a translation of *'oth*.

3. *Synonyms*. Alongside *'oth* there appear in the OT many synonyms which characterize the function of the sign or its exact nature. The most frequently used synonym of *'oth* is → מוֹפת *môphēth*, "wonder" (in connection with *'oth:* Ex. 7:3; Dt. 4:34; 6:22; 7:19; 13:2,3 [Eng. vv. 1,2]; 26:8; 28:46; 29:2[3]; 34:11; Isa. 8:18; 20:3; Jer. 32:20,21; Ps. 78:43; 105:27; 135:9; Neh. 9:10); it appears in this connection almost exclusively in the Deuteronomic and Deuteronomistic literature and denotes (even when it is used without *'oth*) signs that confirm, warn, inspire fear, or prognosticate. *mopheth* is used in particular to describe the events connected with the exodus. It is impossible to prove that this word has "apocalyptic overtones." [7]

The synonym → זכרון *zikkārôn*, "memorial, remembrance" (which is used in connection with *'oth* in Ex. 13:9; on Josh. 4:6, cf. v. 7), sheds light on the function of *'oth*, inasmuch as it alludes to the mnemonic use of a sign. The purpose of a *zikkaron* is "to prevent something from being forgotten which deserves to be handed down, and to make it real over and over again"; [8] therefore, it is natural to translate this word "remembrance, actualization." [9] The element of "public-

---

(1961), 65-74; O. Eissfeldt, *Hexateuchsynopse* (1922); *idem, The OT* (trans. 1965); V. Hamp, "Genus litterarium in Wunderberichten," *EstEcl,* 34 (1960), 361-66; J. Haspecker, "Wunder im AT," *Theologische Akademie,* II (1965), 29-56; F. J. Helfmeyer, *Die Nachfolge Gottes im AT. BBB,* 29 (1968); A. R. Johnson, *The Cultic Prophet in Ancient Israel* (Cardiff, ²1962); C. A. Keller, *Das Wort OTH als "Offenbarungszeichen Gottes". Eine philologisch-theologische Begriffsuntersuchung zum AT* (1946); R. Kilian, *Die Verheissung Immanuels Jes 7,14. SBS,* 35 (1968); H.-J. Kraus, *Worship in Israel* (trans. 1966); N. Lohfink, "Der Bundesschluss im Land Moab. Redaktionsgeschichtliches zu Dtn 28,69-32,47," *BZ,* N.F. 6 (1962), 32-56; D. J. McCarthy, *Treaty and Covenant. A Study in Form in the Ancient Oriental Documents and in the OT. AnBibl,* 21 (1963); M. Noth, *History of Pentateuchal Traditions* (trans. 1971); H. D. Preuss, " . . . ich will mit dir sein!" *ZAW,* 80 (1968), 139-173; G. Quell, "Das Phänomen des Wunders im AT," *Verbannung und Heimkehr. Festschrift W. Rudolph* (1961), 253-300; G. von Rad, *Problem of the Hexateuch and Other Essays* (trans. 1966); K. H. Rengstorf, "σημεῖον," *TDNT,* VII (1964), 200-269; W. Richter, *Traditionsgeschichtliche Untersuchungen zum Richterbuch. BBB,* 18 (²1966); *idem, Die sogenannten vorprophetischen Berufungsberichte. FRLANT,* 101 (1970); L. Rost, "Weidewechsel und altisraelitischer Festkalender," *Das kleine Credo und andere Studien zum AT* (1965), 101-112; J. Scharbert, "Was versteht das AT unter Wunder?" *BuK,* 22 (1967), 37-42; G. Schmitt, *Der Landtag von Sichem. ArbT,* ser. 1, 15 (1964); C. Westermann, *Praise of God in the Psalms* (trans. 1965); *idem, Basic Forms of Prophetic Speech* (trans. 1967); W. Zimmerli, "Erkenntnis Gottes nach dem Buche Ezechiel," *ThB,* 19 (1963), 41-119; *idem,* "Ich bin Jahwe," *ThB,* 19 (1963), 11-40; *idem, ThZ,* 5 (1949), 374-76.

6 Hatch-Redpath, *Concordance,* II (1954), 1263f.

7 Keller, 61.

8 *Ibid.,* 64.

9 *Ibid.,* 65; cf. P. A. H. de Boer, *Gedenken und Gedächtnis in der Welt des ATs* (1962), 19, 38f.; W. Schottroff, *"Gedenken" im Alten Orient und im AT. Die Wurzel zākar im semitischen Sprachkreis. WMANT,* 15 (1964), 299-328.

ity" in *zakhar* can be seen from its use in legal genres, where it has the meaning "publish, introduce as evidence."[10]

The word → טוֹטָפוֹת *ṭôṭāphôth*, "frontlets" (used in connection with '*oth* in Ex. 13:16; Dt. 11:18), which emphasizes the function of '*oth* as a mnemonic sign, presumably means something similar to *zikkaron*.[11]

The synonym '*edh* indicates another function of '*oth*, viz., that of witnessing ('*edh* is used in connection with '*oth* in Isa. 19:20; cf. Ex. 4:8).

→ מסוֹת *massôth*, "trials" (which is used in connection with '*oth* in Dt. 4:34; 7:19; 29:2[3]) has reference to the signs with which Yahweh "tried" Pharaoh. Yahweh put Pharaoh and perhaps also the Israelites to the test in order to find out whether they knew and acknowledged him.[12] The synonym *musar*, "discipline, education" (which is used in connection with '*oth* in Dt. 11:2, cf. v. 3), seems to attribute a similar function to the word '*oth*.

Other synonyms of '*oth* emphasize the divine power and might which are manifested in the "signs," especially in connection with the exodus. This is the case with *gedholah*, "great thing" (Josh. 24:17), *yadh chazaqah*, "mighty hand" (Dt. 4:34; on 6:22, cf. v. 21; 7:19; on 11:3, cf. v. 2; 26:8; on 34:11, cf. v. 12; Jer. 32:21), *zeroa' netuyah*, "outstretched arm" (Dt. 4:34; 7:19; on 11:3, cf. v. 2; 26:8; Jer. 32:21), *mora' gadhol*, "great terror" (Dt. 4:34; 26:8; on 34:11, cf. v. 12; Jer. 32:21), *milchamah*, "war" (Dt. 4:34), *kabhodh*, "glory" (Nu. 14:22), *shephatim gedholim*, "great acts of judgment" (on Ex. 7:3, cf. v. 4), *ma'asim*, "deeds" (Dt. 11:3). "The synonymity of '*oth* with *deghel*, 'standard,' that which may be seen and observed, is particularly instructive"[13] (*deghel* appears in conjunction with '*oth* in Nu. 2:2).

II. Secular Use. A "sign" by its very nature points to something. This simple observation makes it unlikely at best that the word '*oth* belongs primarily to the theological sphere.[14] There is no theological implication whatsoever in its use in the fourth Lachish letter, line 10,[15] which mentions fire signals (*mashsha'ath*) in conjunction with '*oth* in line 11, where they were being used to convey military information. A similar military context is suggested by the use of '*oth* for the signs of families (Nu. 2:2 [P]; similarly Ps. 74:4), by means of which the Israelite camp was arranged. This camp order is based on the "idea of a military camp,"[16] and the signs of families are flags or standards, which can hardly be assigned a theological function on the basis of their relationship to the tent of meeting, and thus be interpreted as a "sign of security which guarantees the divine order."[17] Josh. 2:12,18, where the sign requested as a pledge by Rahab and given by the spies is a scarlet cord bound in the window, also points to a war

---

[10] H. W. Wolff, *Hosea* (trans. 1974), 145, with further literature.
[11] Cf. Keller, 65f.
[12] Cf. Quell, 288.
[13] *Ibid.*, 292.
[14] As Keller, 14, and others assert.
[15] Cf. *KAI,* 194.10; *TDNT,* VII, 209f.
[16] Cf. A. Kuschke, *ZAW,* 63 (1951), 74-105; M. Noth, *Numbers. OTL* (trans. 1968), 24.
[17] Keller, 144.

setting, although reflecting a legal situation in which the sign functions as an agreement or a guarantee. Job (21:29) refers to signs in the sense of "evidence" or "examples"[18] refuting the doctrine of retribution, thus appealing to the wisdom of experience, to which *'oth* as a sign of revelation is foreign.[19]

The secular use of the word *'oth*—in the military sphere as a designation for signs and for signals giving information, in the legal sphere as a designation for signs of a contract or a guarantee, in the sphere of experiential wisdom as a designation for evidence and examples, the kinds of signs which also appear in theological usage—makes it clear that this word was used originally in secular language,[20] whence it was probably borrowed concurrently or secondarily by theological usage.

III. Theological Use.

1. *The Substance and Settings of Signs.* "*'oth,* 'sign,' is an object, an occurrence, an event through which a person is to recognize, learn, remember, or perceive the credibility of something." In my opinion, this definition suggested by Gunkel[21] correctly emphasizes the functional character of a sign, for that which is crucial in a sign is not the sign itself or its execution, but its function and its meaning. The substances of signs are as protean as the world in which they occur.

An *'oth* may occur in different settings: creation, history, and cultic institutions. In harmony with the Israelite tendency to historicize, signs in creation and cultic institutions are often connected with historical events.

Signs in the order of creation or in nature include the lights in the firmament of the heavens (Gen. 1:14), the rainbow (9:12,13,17), second growth, wild growth, sowing and reaping (Isa. 37:30), an unexpected crop (Isa. 55:13), astral phenomena (Jer. 10:2), the permanence of the mountains and the stilling of the raging sea (on Ps. 65:9[8], cf. vv. 7f.[6f.]). Signs in history include above all the plagues in Egypt in particular and the events connected with the exodus in general (Ex. 7:3; Dt. 4:34; 6:22; 7:19; etc.). Signs connected with cultic institutions include circumcision (Gen. 17:11), the blood of the Passover lamb (Ex. 12:13), eating the *matstsoth,* "unleavened bread" (13:9), the consecration of the firstborn (13:16), the Sabbath (31:13,17; Ezk. 20:12,20), the stars (Gen. 1:14), and the covering of the altar (Nu. 17:3[16:38]).

2. *The Functions of Signs.* By assigning to these phenomena which exist or take place in creation, history, and cultic institutions the character of signs, these passages indicate that they have a significance beyond their outward form. Their meaning needs interpretation before it can be understood. This raises the question of the *function* of a sign.

---

18 *TDNT,* VII, 213.
19 Contra Keller, 47.
20 So also Quell, 292; *TDNT,* VII, 213, n. 78; Zimmerli, *ThZ,* 374-76.
21 H. Gunkel, *Genesis*[7], 150.

The function of a sign, like its outward form or substance, shows that its miraculous or striking nature is not what matters, for the intention of a sign is not to terrify the onlooker, but to mediate an understanding or to motivate a kind of behavior. When Moses works signs at God's command (Ex. 3:12; 4:8, 9,28,30), they serve to demonstrate his legitimacy to the people; the Israelites are not simply to respond to them in astonishment. If they had, these signs would have failed to accomplish their purpose. Moreover, Moses does not work signs for "his own greater glory," although they do establish his legitimacy. They establish his legitimacy as one sent from God, and also guarantee the reliability of the message with which he is sent to the Israelites. Similarly, the signs which God worked in Egypt were not designed primarily to terrify Pharaoh and his people, but to cause him to acknowledge "that I am Yahweh" (Ex. 7:3, cf. v. 5), or "that I, Yahweh, rule in the midst of the land" (Ex. 8:19[23], cf. v. 18[22]). The signs which God worked in connection with the exodus are meant to bring about the same result among the Israelites: the recognition and acknowledgment of Yahweh as the only God (on Dt. 4:34, cf. v. 35; cf. Ex. 10:2). The accusation that Israel has no mind to understand, no eyes to see, and no ears to hear, in spite of having experienced these signs (Dt. 29:2[3], cf. v. 3[4]), grows out of this concept. Behind this idea lies the expectation implicit in giving signs that they will arouse faith when they are recognized (Nu. 14:11), and promote readiness to hearken to Yahweh's voice (14:22), to take his words seriously (Jer. 44:29), to recognize the work of God in the fate of idolaters (Ezk. 14:8), and to acknowledge the intervention of God on behalf of his own (Ps. 86:17).

a. *Epistemic Signs.* This summary, which in essence is merely descriptive, makes it possible to categorize signs in the OT on the basis of their various functions. First of all, we will deal with epistemic signs, which must be placed in a larger context if their backgrounds are to be made clear.

Like all of God's works, his signs are intended to impart knowledge, and thus there are "imperative components in the knowledge formula." [22] There is such a close connection between knowledge and signs that, in the context of the knowledge formula, "to know" means virtually "to accept the certainty of something on the basis of a sign." [23] The knowledge formula belongs "by nature to the realm of symbolic events," [24] or, more specifically, to the realm of demonstrative signs. [25]

That the knowledge formula appears in the pre-priestly tradition concerning Moses (J) [26] raises the question of the source to which the "signs" belong, especially as it pertains to explicitly epistemic signs. Zimmerli's view concerning the knowledge formula [27] is supported by Eissfeldt's view that Ex. 7:3,5 belong to

[22] Zimmerli, "Erkenntnis," 67.
[23] *Ibid.,* 93; cf. *TDNT,* VII, 213-16.
[24] *Ibid.,* 95.
[25] *Ibid.,* 98.
[26] *Ibid.,* 66.
[27] *Ibid.,* 58, 61 on Ex. 7:5; 8:18(22); 10:2.

P [28] and that Ex. 8:18f.(22f.); 10:2 belong to J. [29] Consequently, the use of 'oth in the sense of an epistemic sign can be traced back to the early monarchical period. The use of 'oth to convey this meaning corresponds to the emphasis in J on "the victory of God's dominion in the face of the nation's enemies and Israel itself." [30] The universalism characteristic of J [31] is expressed in Ex. 8:18f. (22f.), which states that Pharaoh will know by the sign that Yahweh rules in the midst of the land. If the theocentric interpretation of history is typical of J, and with it the idea that "God is the one who really shapes all history," [32] then we must consider the possibility that this peculiarity might be found in the Yahwistic use of 'oth to mean an epistemic sign. This possibility is in fact confirmed: knowledge follows upon the deed of Yahweh, which is to be regarded as a necessary prerequisite of knowledge. [33]

From a traditio-historical perspective, the story of the plagues, which includes Ex. 7:3, (also 5); 8:19(23), (also 18[22]); 10:2, represents nothing but an expansion of the main theme, "the exodus from Egypt," in the historicization of the Passover ritual and of the death of the Egyptian firstborn sons, with narratives characterized by their "later 'discursive' legend-style." [34] Consequently, the story of the plagues and the use it makes of 'oth as epistemic signs do not belong to the old themes of the Pentateuch, according to the traditio-historical view. However, this does not alter their relation to the main theme as a narrative elaboration of the statement that those who participated in the exodus experienced the help of their God at the Red Sea, while the attempts of the Egyptians to pursue and overthrow them were thwarted. This event, and not the Passover ritual, [35] may have occasioned the expansion of the main theme by the story of the plagues. [36]

In this context, the plagues appear as signs by which Israel, in her weakness before the mighty of this world, can "know" the power and help of her God. There were many situations in the history of Israel when she found it necessary to remember Yahweh's help in the past, as in the period of the military conquest of Canaan, and during the Philistine and Assyrian oppressions. That the signs which Yahweh did in Egypt are given special emphasis in Deuteronomy would seem to indicate that the period of the Assyrian oppression in particular was a time when Yahweh's signs in Egypt were constantly being called to remembrance. Of course, this says nothing about the possible date of the story of the plagues and the signs it mentions. On the contrary, this story must have originated at a time when Yahweh proved himself more powerful than the powerful of the world. Israelite tribes during the period of the military conquest of Canaan experienced this in the framework of the War of Yahweh, [37] and the tribes united

---

28 O. Eissfeldt, *Hexateuchsynopse,* 119*.
29 *Ibid.,* 122*, 126*.
30 Sellin-Fohrer, *IntrodOT* (trans. 1968), 149.
31 *Ibid.,* 150.
32 Weiser, *The OT* (trans. 1961), 100.
33 Cf. Zimmerli, "Erkenntnis," 80; see later on 1 S. 10:9.
34 Noth, *Pentateuchal Traditions,* 65; cf. 65-71.
35 So Noth, 67, 190.
36 Cf. Haspecker, 53.
37 Cf. Quell, 261.

under David had the same experience in their successful exploits against the neighboring peoples. This coincides roughly with the time of the origin of J. Therefore, J is to be credited with the development of the plague signs, as is also clear from traditio-historical and historical considerations. The generally assumed localization of J in the southern kingdom (Judah) also favors this view. This would be the easiest way to explain the local Egyptian color which appears in the plague signs. [38]

The form-critical investigation of this material begins appropriately with the question of the *Sitz im Leben* of the knowledge formula, which appears in "prayers, in narrative accounts, in supplementary confessional statements, but also in parenetic speeches." [39] We may conjecture that its original setting was in the framework of discourse oracles. [40] But since the knowledge formula is itself a composite speech form in which the formula of divine introduction, "I am Yahweh," has been amalgamated, [41] this also raises the question about the setting of the formula of divine introduction. Zimmerli thinks it originated in connection with legal statements uttered in the context of worship and in the theophanic statements which were made in conjunction with the form of the oracle that certified that Yahweh had heard or would hear the petitioner. [42] Zimmerli supposes that the expansion of the formula of divine introduction to the knowledge formula took place in a context of worship or in the framework of the proclamation of the divine law. [43] Now it is in this context that the question of the setting of epistemic signs must be resolved. This question can be answered most easily for Ex. 10:2, a text that assumes so-called "children's curiosity," which is also implicit in 13:8, and explicit in 13:14 and Dt. 6:20. In all these passages, the "signs" are connected with the exodus from Egypt. The response to this "curiosity" corresponds to what Zimmerli calls supplementary confessional statements. [44]

In Dt. 1:1–4:40 we find traces of the so-called covenant formulary. [45] Here the theology developed in 4:32-39 follows "in its structure... the pattern of an antecedent history." [46] But the discovery of certain elements of the covenant formulary does not mean that we have arrived at the formula itself. Therefore, it is more natural to assume that the setting for Dt. 4:32-38, (40) is the legal sermon, which is concerned with explaining why Yahweh is acknowledged as the only God. [47] This would explain the use of the knowledge formula in the context of

---

[38] Cf. Noth, 69f.

[39] Zimmerli, "Erkenntnis," 79.

[40] Cf. *ibid.*, 98, with reference to 1 S. 6.

[41] Cf. *ibid.*, 103.

[42] Zimmerli, "Ich bin Jahwe," 18, 24, 25-27.

[43] Zimmerli, "Erkenntnis," 103.

[44] *Ibid.*, 79.

[45] Cf. Baltzer, 31-34.

[46] *Ibid.*, 34.

[47] Von Rad, *Deuteronomy. OTL* (trans. 1966), 50f., interprets this differently as preaching designed to encourage those in exile.

parenetic historical retrospects. [48] The same setting is to be assumed for Dt. 29:2, 3(3,4). Here again, in 29:1-7(2-8), we are dealing with a parenetic historical retrospect which is intended to motivate the hearers to keep the covenant and to carry out the demands of the covenant, and not with the antecedent history of the covenant formula, [49] which is not even formally homogeneous. [50] Possibly 29:1-6a(2-7a) was originally a cultic text [51] with its locus in the proclamation of the law.

The fourth story of the plagues (Ex. 8:16-28[20-32]) takes on a parenetic function through the knowledge formula (v. 18[22]), even though this passage is not a parenetic text, but a narrative account [52] whose setting can no longer be determined. Here the plague of flies as such is not called a sign, but rather the protection of the people of God from this plague. This is a motif which appears in other plague stories (Ex. 9:4,26; 10:23; 11:7), and it is possible that this motif was the theme around which the plague stories were originally combined. The main emphasis here is on the protection or "redemption" (Ex. 8:19[23]) of Israel. Thus, in spite of the narrative framework in which this plague is presented, it is clear that at least Ex. 8:18f.(22f.) is a parenesis.

The same thing applies to Ex. 7:3,5. Here, the connection of the sign with the knowledge formula indicates a clear theological emphasis, and even though it is set in a narrative context it is a parenesis.

Jer. 44:29 is part of an announcement of judgment. [53] V. 25 states the transgression, v. 27 the announcement of judgment, and vv. 28f. the consequences of divine intervention: recognition of the potency of the divine word. [54] If the announcement of punishment to an individual in its pre-literary form is still closely connected with the "elements of the regular judicial procedure" from which it probably arose, [55] then the function of the sign in Jer. 44:29 as a witness (Isa. 19:20; cf. Ex. 4:8) is comprehensible. The preceding context, especially vv. 15-20, makes it clear that the announcement of judgment is connected with a disputation. But this would seem to indicate that the announcement of the sign was preceded by a corresponding question from the prophet's audience concerning the validity of the divine announcement of judgment.

In Ezk. 14:1-11 we find a hybrid form involving invective and legal style; [56] the legal style appears especially in v. 8, where the threats that God will set his face against one of his people and that he will cut him off from the midst of his people are derived from legal terminology. [57] By the addition of the knowledge

---

[48] Zimmerli, "Erkenntnis," 66.
[49] Contra Baltzer, 35; McCarthy, *Treaty*, 138; von Rad, 179.
[50] So also Baltzer, 35.
[51] So Lohfink, 38.
[52] See above, Zimmerli, "Erkenntnis," 79.
[53] On this form cf. Westermann, *Basic Forms*, 169ff.
[54] Cf. the schema in *ibid.*, 171.
[55] *Ibid.*, 172.
[56] Zimmerli, *BK*, XIII/1, 302.
[57] *Ibid.*, 311.

formula, the "legal oracle is changed into a prophetic oracle of demonstra-tion"[58] But, of course, this is not to deny that the two forms "and you shall know that . . ." and "I am Yahweh" were originally combined in a legal con-text.[59] The sign in this context includes the function of a sign as evidence and truth in the legal sense.

Ps. 86 is usually designated as a lament of the individual,[60] in which the worshipper asks for "a sign of salvation" (v. 17). Even if this song has its setting in the cult, the idea that this sign is an oracle announcing that God had heard or would hear is not the only possible interpretation.[61]

We may draw certain conclusions about the function of signs mentioned in these passages from the different types or genres that texts containing epistemic signs represent, of which parenesis is predominant. The primary purpose of parenesis is not to relate historical events, but to motivate people and to arouse them to action. Within the framework of the parenetic reflections on history, the signs are mentioned in order to motivate the hearers to acknowledge and to revere Yahweh as the only God (Dt. 4:34f.), or to be faithful to the covenant (29:2f.[3f.]). The sign is intended to help one see the seriousness of the divine announcement of judgment; therefore, it functions as evidence, which has its setting in the legal realm (cf. Jer. 44:29; Ezk. 14:8). Here, too, the sign serves to motivate the hearer to believe. The purpose of Ex. 8:18f.(22f.) is also parenetic, as is indicated, among other ways, by the knowledge formula. The emphasis in this sign is on the protection of the people of God from the plague; therefore, the purpose of this sign is also to motivate people: in this case, to motivate Israel to trust in Yahweh. On the other hand, the signs mentioned in Ex. 7:3 bring the Egyptians to a knowledge of Yahweh (7:5), not in the sense of faith and trust, but in the sense of acknowledging the superior power of Yahweh; thus, the func-tion of signs to motivate people is present here also. Finally, the function of the sign in Ps. 86 (cf. v. 17), an individual lament, calls attention to the situation of the sign. Lament assumes need, in which a man reaches a limit of his own pos-sibilities, beyond which only God can pass with a sign.[62] Here also, the purpose of the sign is to confirm something: the worshipper's faith that God will intervene and help, but also the psalmist's enemies' abashed realization that "thou, Lord, hast helped me and comforted me" (Ps. 86:17).

Therefore, a sign has different aspects: on the one hand, the God who provides it regards man, and on the other hand, man acknowledges the presence and the activity of God. To this extent the alternation between divine word and human response, between divine deed and human reaction, is evident in the epistemic sign.

---

[58] *Ibid.*, 312.
[59] Cf. *ibid.*, 56f.
[60] Kraus, *BK*, XV³, 596.
[61] Cf. *ibid.*, 599.
[62] On the relationship between signs and situations of crisis, cf. Scharbert, 40-42.

b. *Signs of Protection.* Signs are meant to impart knowledge; thus those who meet Cain know by the sign (mark) that he bears that he is not to be killed (Gen. 4:15–J). This sign serves to protect Cain, and probably is to be understood as a tattoo, perhaps as a tribal sign, [63] although the further suggestion that it was a sign that the Kenites belonged to the tribes that worshipped Yahweh [64] is highly questionable. In any case, here we are dealing with a particular type of epistemic sign, viz., a sign of protection, but not a "revelatory sign of protection," [65] since the sign here does not impart knowledge about God, but about Cain. [66] The sign mentioned in Ex. 12:13 (P) is also a sign of protection, by means of which Yahweh or the "destroyer" recognizes the houses of the Israelites and thus "passes over" them. This sign, given in the form of a blood ritual, serves as a "safeguard," [67] originally (as an apotropaic ritual performed prior to moving flocks to new pastures) probably against the "destroyer." [68]

c. *Faith Signs.* Closely related to epistemic signs are signs that do not explicitly impart knowledge about Yahweh, but motivate people to believe in Yahweh and to worship him. Therefore, these may be called faith signs in the sense that they are signs that confirm faith.

This function of signs seems to have its primary locus in the Deuteronomic and Deuteronomistic literature. Nu. 14:11bff. is "strongly permeated by Deuteronomistic conceptions and turns of phrase," and seems to be a later addition to the story of the spies, the nucleus of which is Yahwistic. [69] Similarly, Yahweh's judgment in Nu. 14:22,23a is expressed in Deuteronomistic terminology. [70] The two references to signs in the story of the spies or of Caleb (Nu. 14:11b,22) appear in the context as reasons for punishment, and serve the parenetic purpose of warning the people against unbelief in spite of the signs they had experienced, or of motivating the people to believe. In this case, the purpose of these signs was to lead Israel to "an unconditional trust in her God." [71] The same thing may be said about the story of Caleb in Dt. 1:22-46, a passage which also refers to Yahweh's deeds in Egypt and in the wilderness (1:30f.), and to Israel's lack of trust in Yahweh (1:32). Beyond its momentary display and effect, the sign acquires a lasting effect through its function of confirming faith. In the context of the story of Caleb, which from a traditio-historical point of view is a part of the expansion of the main themes of the Pentateuch and in the compilation of the Pentateuch was added to the main theme of "Guidance in the Wilderness," [72]

---

63 Gunkel, *Genesis*[7], 46f.; von Rad, *Genesis. OTL* (trans. 1961), 103f.
64 Von Rad, 104.
65 Keller, 75.
66 *TDNT,* VII, 214f.
67 Rost, 104.
68 Cf. also Noth, *Exodus. OTL* (trans. 1962), 91f., 96.
69 Noth, *Numbers*, 108.
70 *Ibid.,* 109.
71 *Ibid., 108.*

the signs mentioned in Nu. 14:11,22 seem to have had their desired effect on Caleb; he follows after Yahweh (Nu. 14:24; 32:12; Dt. 1:36; Josh. 14:8,9,14; Sir. 46:10). [73]

The reference in Dt. 11:3 to the signs which Yahweh did in Egypt, which were intended to motivate Israel to love God and to keep his commandments (cf. v. 1), also has a parenetic purpose. Even though Dt. 10:12–11:31 contains the formal elements of the covenant formulary and 11:2-7 resembles the antecedent history of this formulary, [74] still it is worthy of note that the fundamental features of this formula do not appear here in their traditional order and that they are found in parenetic style. [75] We are not dealing with the covenant formulary here, but with a parenesis, which in its historical retrospect reveals a certain dependence on the hymn in its style and wording. [76] Dt. 13:2f.(1f.) is part of casuistic legislation, the nucleus of which is to be sought in vv. 2,3,6a(1,2,5a). [77] By combining this nucleus with parenetic additions in vv. 4b,5,6b(3b,4,5b), the original legal text was transformed into a legal parenesis, the purpose of which was to warn the people against anti-Yahwistic prophets. By the signs which they announced and which sometimes came to pass, these prophets were trying to motivate the people to follow other gods. They used signs to establish the credibility of their summons. The signs intended here can be perceived by the senses as confirmations of the prophetic teaching effected by the deity. [78] Such signs are very similar to confirmation signs, which cannot be clearly distinguished from faith signs. However, the primary purpose of the signs mentioned in Dt. 13:2f.(1f.) is more to motivate the people to follow other gods than to confirm the correctness of the prophetic word. This passage, by considering the possibility that these signs might be fulfilled (v. 3[2]), throws light on the Israelite view of signs. A sign in itself must not motivate people to believe; crucial instead is the word that accompanies the sign. This word declares in what or whom the sign is intended to motivate a person to believe. Therefore, there is no sign revelation without a corresponding word revelation interpreting the sign. [79]

This explanatory word revelation is presupposed in the signs mentioned in Dt. 26:8 in connection with the exodus from Egypt. These signs precede the entrance into the land of Canaan, and together with the entrance into the land they motivate the people to offer their firstfruits to the Lord. By bringing this offering and reciting the historical events connected with it (26:5b-9), using the so-called Little Historical Credo, [80] the Israelite confesses his faith in Yahweh,

---

[72] Noth, *Pentateuchal Traditions*, 122-130.
[73] On the terminology, cf. Helfmeyer, 95-103; → אחרי 'acharê.
[74] Von Rad, *Deuteronomy*, 83.
[75] *Ibid.*
[76] So in my opinion von Rad, 84.
[77] Cf. Helfmeyer, 77-79.
[78] Von Rad, 96.
[79] Cf. Quell, 283.
[80] Von Rad, *ThB*, 38, 11.

who has brought him out of Egypt into this land. The reference to the signs of
the exodus occurs here in a liturgical formula,[81] which is "clothed in that
hortatory style typical of Deuteronomy"[82] and is perhaps based on the schema
of the Thanksgiving Song of the Individual.[83] The description of the situation
in which Yahweh performed his sign, which was clearly a situation of
affliction (vv.6f.), favors this latter suggestion.

This same situation is assumed in Josh. 24:17. The signs of the exodus motivate those whom Joshua addresses to determine to worship Yahweh (v. 16). Even
if Josh. 24 can be considered pre-Deuteronomistic, [84] still, among other things,
the connections of vv. 16,17b with the Deuteronomistic literature [85] and the fact
that the form, at least, of this chapter derives from preaching [86] indicate that it
is related to the Deuteronomistic literature. Schmitt takes this into consideration, for stylistic reasons considering Josh. 24 in part to be "a preliminary stage
of Deuteronomistic preaching and literature." [87] Vv.17f. contain a confession
which possibly originated in the cult. [88]

The sign Isaiah offers Ahaz is also designed to arouse faith (Isa. 7:11). [89] Its
purpose is to persuade Ahaz not to fear (v. 4), but to believe (v. 9). [90] It is closely
connected with the preceding context, because it is intended to assure the one
addressed that he would receive the divine help that had been promised, thus
making it easier for him to base his decision on faith. [91] Thus, this offer of a sign
has its setting in an announcement of salvation, which, however, Ahaz rejects
with the argument that he will not demand of Yahweh and put him to the test
(v. 12). This statement assumes that one "puts Yahweh to the test" by asking
him for a sign (cf. Dt. 6:16; Ex. 17:2). Even though in the context of Isa. 7 Ahaz'
argument must be considered an excuse based on supposed political considerations, [92] the assumption on which his argument rests expresses an opinion about
asking for signs native to Israel and decidedly negative in nature, since it reveals
a lack of trust. Since there is sufficient evidence that God was at work in history
and in his promises (through the preservation of the Davidic dynasty), asking
for a sign would be putting Yahweh to the test. Ahaz argues that it is possible
to believe in God in a critical situation without a sign. But this situation is not
concerned with a *request* for a sign, but with an *offer* of a sign which would
make it easier for Ahaz and his people to believe. It is wrong for Ahaz to reject
the divine offer, and therefore Isaiah gives Ahaz another sign (v. 14), which

---

[81] *Ibid.*
[82] Von Rad, *Deuteronomy*, 157.
[83] Von Rad, *ThB*, [38], 12; *Deuteronomy*, 158.
[84] Schmitt, 23.
[85] *Ibid.*, 16f.
[86] *Ibid.*, 17, 20.
[87] *Ibid.*, 21.
[88] *Ibid.*, 64.
[89] Scharbert, 37: "to confirm the prophetic word."
[90] Cf. O. Kaiser, *Isaiah 1-12. OTL* (trans. 1972), 91ff.; Kilian, 32.
[91] Kilian, 31.
[92] *Ibid.*, 33f.

means disaster for Ahaz. The prophet introduces this sign with *lakhen*, "therefore," which is the usual introduction for a prophetic threat. [93] This sign is not intended to arouse faith in Ahaz, but to reveal his unbelief. In contrast, the signs mentioned in Ps. 65:9(8) motivate fear and rejoicing, the proper "reactions of the inhabitants of the world to the great deeds of the creator and conqueror of chaos." [94] The signs of creation (establishment of the mountains) and of the preservation of the world (the stilling of the roaring seas) are not merely "great deeds" of Yahweh, but reveal his power and lead men to "do obeisance (bow themselves) before the creator and king of the world," [95] which is expressed here in the strikingly hymnic [96] National Song of Thanksgiving. [97] The setting for this song may be the cult. [98]

We cannot determine whether Ps. 78, which mentions God's signs in Egypt in v. 43, also belongs to the cult because of the "amalgamation of types or genres" in this psalm. [99] The parenetic, didactic purpose of this psalm is clear. [100] It evaluates history on the basis of the "principles of the Deuteronomistic history" [101] with its sequence of divine acts of salvation, Israel's sin, divine punishment, conversion, and forgiveness. In this context, vv. 43,42 represent the first two stages of this sequence. God expected his signs in Egypt to motivate Israel to believe and to be faithful to him, but just the opposite happened: "they did not keep in mind his power (lit. hand)," i.e., they did not draw the right conclusions from God's signs, did not recognize their continuing function of establishing and guaranteeing the "memory of his power (hand)." Thus, "in light of the miracles of Yahweh..., the sin of the people was evident." [102]

d. *Mnemonic Signs*. Mnemonic signs are closely related to faith signs, as the last-mentioned text shows, in that they maintain Israel in faith and give expression to this faith.

The custom of eating the *matstsoth* (unleavened bread) is for Israel a sign on the hand and a memorial (*zikkaron*) between the eyes, for it points to the exodus from Egypt (Ex. 13:9). The same thing applies to the consecration of the firstborn (13:16). The connection with the exodus assumes the historicization of the original agricultural festival. [103] This connection alone gives the cus-

---

93 *Ibid.,* 35.
94 Kraus, *BK,* XV³, 452.
95 *Ibid.,* 450.
96 Gunkel, *Psalmen⁵,* 272; Kraus, *BK,* XV³, 449.
97 Gunkel, 272. Kraus, 449, holds a different view.
98 Kraus, 450.
99 Gunkel, 342.
100 Kraus, 539.
101 *Ibid.*
102 *Ibid.,* 548.
103 Cf. Noth, *Pentateuchal Traditions,* 48; Kraus, *Worship in Israel,* 61ff.; cf. Schottroff, *WMANT,* 15, 95, 299, 313, 317.

tom the character of a mnemonic sign or of a "memento of the day of the exodus."[104] If the expressions "a sign on the hand" and "a memorial between the eyes" originally meant tattoos and ornaments that were hung on the head, which are to be regarded as signs of belonging to certain cults,[105] then the custom of eating the *matstsoth* can be understood as "a sign indicating that the Israelites belonged to Yahweh."[106]

Deuteronomy is particularly concerned with recalling vividly the events in salvation history.[107] Therefore it is not surprising that there is a Deuteronomistic section in Ex. 13:1-16.[108] This is clear from the style and from the parenetic character of the text, which is evident in the structure of the passage in the form of a question asked by the children (13:8,14).

Just as the consecration of the firstborn in Ex. 13:16 is intended to serve as a sign and a mark (*totaphoth,* "frontlets") to remind Israel of the exodus from Egypt, so also the affirmation of Yahweh's uniqueness together with the demand that the people love God (Dt. 6:4f.) and the admonition to obey him (11:13,22) are intended to serve as a sign and a mark (6:8; 11:18). These words, in 6:4-9 "a chain of very forceful imperatives,"[109] in 11:18-21 (perhaps not original in this context) an admonition,[110] remind Israel of the uniqueness of Yahweh and of the people's obligation to love God and to obey him. The summons to this sign has its setting in the proclamation of the law, perhaps (if 6:8 was originally connected with 6:4) in the cult, since the summons "Hear, O Israel!" opened the cultic assembly in ancient times.[111] Therefore, it is doubtful whether these words are called a sign and a mark only "in a figurative sense."[112] The senses must be able to perceive a sign, or else it is not a sign. The mute existence of these words cannot be the sign. These words must be proclaimed in preaching or pronounced in confession in order to be a sign.

The senses are also able to perceive the sign which Joshua sets up after the miraculous crossing of the Jordan at Gilgal (Josh. 4:3,8,20). The twelve stones are to be a sign (v. 6) and a memorial (v. 7, *zikkaron*) "that the waters of the Jordan were cut off before the ark of the covenant of the Lord when it passed over the Jordan" (v. 7). That the interpretation of the sign is clothed in the form of an answer to a question asked by the children (v. 6b) reveals the parenetic purpose of the text, which also furnishes, among other things, an etiological explanation of the twelve stones.[113] It is impossible to determine with certainty whether the Jordan version (v. 9) or the Gilgal version of this event is primary from a traditio-historical point of view.[114] The most likely setting for it

---

[104] Beer, *HAT,* 3, 72.
[105] Noth, *Exodus,* 101.
[106] Beer, 73.
[107] Bächli, 70-74.
[108] Noth, *Pentateuchal Traditions,* 30, n. 106; 49; *Exodus,* 92f., 101.
[109] Von Rad, *Deuteronomy,* 63.
[110] *Ibid.,* 85.
[111] *Ibid.,* 63.
[112] *Ibid.*
[113] Noth, *HAT,* 7 (²1953), 31.
[114] Noth, 27, thinks the Jordan version is primary.

would be the Gilgal sanctuary, where this tradition may have been preserved as
a "festival legend."[115] Noth thinks that vv. 6f. of this tradition are Deuteronomistic because they contain expressions that are identical with Dt. 6:20f.[116] All
these considerations make it clear that the sign recalling the crossing of the Jordan, which may have been preserved in the framework of a "festival legend"
which was read over and over again, had a parenetic function. Here too the sign
is accompanied by a verbal interpretation.

Just as stones have no value as a sign apart from the interpretation and the
historical event to which it refers, so also the covering for the altar made out
of censers cannot serve as a sign without reference to a historical event and a
verbal interpretation (Nu. 17:3 [16:38]). But since we are dealing with censers
"of these men who have sinned at the cost of their lives" (17:3 [16:38]), because
they rebelled against Moses and Aaron (16:1-3), and thus against Yahweh
(16:11), the covering for the altar can be a sign (17:3 [16:38]) and a memorial
(reminder) (17:5 [16:40], zikkaron); for they sinned with the censers, as is clear
from 17:5 (16:40).[117]

In this context, which supports the claims of the Aaronides, the story of
Aaron's rod belongs thematically (Nu. 17:16-26 [1-11]); in conjunction with
Nu. 17:1-6 (16:36-41) it is to be understood as an appendix to the Levitical
recension of P.[118] Like the covering of the altar, Aaron's rod serves as a sign
of warning designed to remind the "rebels" (17:25 [10]) of the God-given prerogatives of the Aaronides. It is obvious that these traditions were preserved or
even originated in priestly circles. Their purpose is to remind the people of the
inviolability of the priestly claims as a warning. To this extent, mnemonic signs
here come close to being signs of warning.

e. *Covenant Signs.* A special category of mnemonic signs consists of covenant signs, of which the rainbow (Gen. 9:12f.,17), circumcision (17:11), and the
Sabbath (Ex. 31:13,17; Ezk. 20:12,20) are named as examples in the OT. These
signs are related to the covenant in different ways. While the rainbow reminds
(Gen. 9:15f. → זכר zākhar) God himself of the covenant, or more exactly of his
covenant promise (9:11, etc.), circumcision and the Sabbath seem at first glance
to be covenant obligations which are to be performed by those who are participants in the covenant between Yahweh and Israel. To the extent that these signs
recall the covenant between Yahweh and Israel, the signs of the covenant are
related to mnemonic signs.

P goes beyond J in its delineation of the covenant idea (Gen. 9:1-17).[119]
Approaching this subject from the viewpoint of salvation history, P divides
the sealing of the covenant between Yahweh and man into three stages, and
attaches a specific sign to each stage: the Noachic covenant with the rainbow,

---

115 So Hertzberg, *ATD*, IX², 31.
116 Noth, 37.
117 Cf. Noth, *Numbers,* 129f.
118 *Ibid.,* 122.
119 Von Rad, *Genesis,* 129.

the Abrahamic covenant with circumcision, and the Mosaic covenant with the Sabbath. In light of this Procksch characterizes the theology of P as a *"theologia foederis"* (a covenant theology).[120] Now, since it is customary, especially in pre-literary eras, "to establish a 'sign' on the occasion of solemn vows, promises, and other 'covenant ceremonies,' which is designed to remind the participants of the covenant at the proper time,"[121] the Noachic covenant also has a mnemonic sign, viz., the rainbow. It serves as "a sign for Yahweh himself ..., so that he will not forget the promise which he has given."[122] Other passages in the OT refer to the bow which Yahweh uses in battle (Lam. 2:4; 3:12); lightning flashes are his arrows (Ps. 77:18f. [17f.]; cf. Hab. 3:9-11). Thus, the appearance of the rainbow may mean that God has laid his bow aside.[123]

According to the schematization of salvation history in P, Yahweh's covenant with Abraham follows in Gen. 17. Vv. 1-8 contain promises, while vv. 9-14 state the covenant obligation, which is identical with the sign of the covenant (v. 11). Wherever it is practiced, circumcision is regarded as "a tribal and cultic sign";[124] in Israel, "those who bear this sign... are participants in the divine covenant."[125] He who accepts this sign and bears it appropriates the covenant established by Yahweh and confesses his faith in him;[126] thus the covenant sign of circumcision became a sign of confession, and during the exile (along with the Sabbath) a unique *"status confessionis"* (state of confession).[127] Inasmuch as the uncircumcised are considered to be foreigners and unclean (Isa. 52:1), this covenant sign serves as a sign of distinction; any male in Israel who is not circumcised is subject to excommunication (Gen. 17:4). The text does not go on to affirm that this sign has the function of "covenant security."[128] As the sequence of the passage (beginning with v. 10) is obligation (vv. 10f.), the circle of persons involved in the obligation (vv. 12f.), and sanctions (v. 14), it is cast in "'legal' style."[129]

The regulation concerning the keeping of the Sabbath (Ex. 31:12-17), in the sequence of obligation (vv. 13, 14aα) and sanction (vv. 14aβ, bβ), also follows the structure of a legal text (vv. 15-17 are to be regarded as a later addition).[130] It is true that the Sabbath (→ שַׁבָּת *shabbāth*) is not explicitly called a "covenant" sign. However, there can be no doubt that this is its function because it is called a "sign between me and you" (v. 13), or a "sign between me and the people of Israel" (v. 17), and because, according to the way in which P divides history into

---

[120] Procksch, *KAT*, I[2,3], 483.
[121] Gunkel, *Genesis*[7], 150.
[122] *Ibid.*
[123] Procksch, 481; von Rad, *Genesis*, 130.
[124] Gunkel, 269.
[125] Procksch, 519.
[126] Cf. von Rad, *Genesis*, 195f.
[127] *Ibid.*, 196.
[128] Procksch, 519.
[129] Gunkel, 270.
[130] Noth, *Exodus*, 241.

periods, the Mosaic covenant follows the Abrahamic covenant, and, like that
covenant, must have a covenant sign. Through the expression "that you may
know that I, the Lord, sanctify you" (v. 13), which, probably is based on Ezk.
20:12, this covenant sign also takes on the character of a mnemonic sign.[131] By
this sign, which, like circumcision, is also a sign of confession and a mark of
distinction, Israel and all the world know that Yahweh "sanctifies" Israel (v. 13),
i.e., that he has separated them from the nations, taken them unto himself for a
possession, and placed them under his protection.

Ezk. 20:12 is similar to Ex. 31:13 in form and content. This similarity argues
less for a later priestly redaction of this prophetic text[132] than for the "roots
of Ezk. in the priestly legal tradition,"[133] since the Sabbath seems to be firmly
established in the text of Ezk. 20 (vv. 12,13,16,20,21,24). In the context of a
historico-theological invective, the Sabbath appears as an epistemic sign (vv. 12,
20) of the divine election of Israel (v. 12) and of the covenant between Yahweh
and Israel (v. 20). For Israel, the Sabbath was a "sign of confession of the Yahweh
covenant"[134] more than a "sign securing Yahweh's relationship to his people,"[135]
since, as the context shows (vv. 14,17,22), the existence of the covenant does not
depend on fulfilling the Sabbath law. But by celebrating the Sabbath, Israel does
recall her relationship to Yahweh based on Yahweh's election and the covenant. To that extent, this sign of the covenant acquires the significance of a sacra-
mental sign.[136] In this context, the observance of the Sabbath is the "outward
sign," Yahweh's election and the covenant are the "inward grace" to which the
sign points and which it makes present.

f. *Confirmation Signs.* The significant thing about a sign is not the sign itself,
but its function. Therefore, a sign has an auxiliary function, since it calls attention to, confirms, or corroborates something beyond itself, as is the case with the
confirmation signs, which sometimes overlap with epistemic and faith signs.

In Ex. 3:12 (E), God gives Moses a sign as a corroboration of his mission and
its success (cf. a parallel incident in Jgs. 6:17). Strangely, the sign does not take
place at once, but is postponed to a future date: God promises Moses that he will
appear to the Israelites at the same place where he is now appearing to Moses.[137]
The future character of this sign has led Noth to assert that v. 12 "has obviously been transmitted in a fragmentary state," since the text does not
mention the sign promised to Moses.[138] But there are other passages in the
OT where a sign designed to confirm or corroborate a divine message does

---

[131] Cf. Botterweck, *Gott erkennen. BBB,* 2 (1951), 87f., "Gotteserkenntnis und Sabbat-
heiligung"; *idem TüThQ,* 134 (1954), 134-147, 448-457, esp. 144f.
[132] So Eichrodt, "Sabbat," 71; *idem, Ezekiel. OTL* (trans. 1970), 268.
[133] Zimmerli, *BK,* XIII, 447.
[134] *Ibid.*
[135] Eichrodt, "Sabbat," 65.
[136] *Ibid.,* 66, 69.
[137] Beer, *HAT,* 3, 29.

not take place until some time in the future, as in 1 S. 2:34 (where the sign is that the sons of Eli will die *on the same day*); 10:2-9 (where the sign is Saul's encounters with different people after he leaves Samuel); and Jer. 44:29,30 (where the sign is the deliverance of Pharaoh Hophra to his enemies). Thus, there is no valid reason for supposing there is a lacuna in Ex. 3:12 because the sign to Moses is not mentioned. A sign announced for some future time obviously calls for a greater measure of faith (in this case faith in the divine nature of Moses' call and Yahweh's promise of help) than one that takes place on the spot.

On the other hand, the signs mentioned in Ex. 4:8f. (and the context; J), which are faith signs, as the text makes clear (v. 1), take place then and there. Here (vv. 2-5,6f.,9) we are dealing with miracles, or more precisely "transformation miracles,"[139] which serve to authenticate Moses and his message. Since Moses actually did "signs" in the sight of the Israelites (vv. 30f.), and since vv. 27,28, 30,31 are not to be considered entirely late just because Aaron was inserted into this section at a later time,[140] there is no reason to give a positive answer to Noth's question: "Can J then in 4.1ff. be said merely to have rounded off the picture of Moses as divine messenger which was present in his mind?"[141] The legitimation of Moses and his message naturally follows from the situation described here.

Just as in Ex. 3f., a confirmation sign[142] occurs in Jgs. 6:17 in the framework of the call schema.[143] Gideon asks for a sign so that he can know whether Yahweh has spoken with him. But this sign confirms also *what* the *mal'akh,* "angel," said, that Yahweh had sent him (v. 14), and that he had promised to be with him (v. 16; cf. v. 12).[144] Since the execution of this sign (vv. 19-21) is connected with an altar tradition (v. 24), it must be asked whether the author of the story of the call knew the story of the fulfilment of the sign as it is reported in Jgs. 6:11-24.[145] Richter has shown that the call of Gideon is important to the author of Jgs. 6:11-24,[146] but not the establishment of a Yahweh sanctuary.[147] Since confirmation signs are a vital part of the call schemes cited by Richter (Ex. 3f.; 1 S. 9:1-10:16),[148] while nothing is said about signs in altar traditions, it is natural to locate the confirmation sign which Gideon requested in the call story.

The same applies to the call story in 1 S. 9:1-10:16. 10:1 (LXX and Vulg.), 7,9 explicitly refer to signs. We are told the nature of these signs in 10:2 (Saul

---

[138] Noth, *Exodus,* 42.
[139] Beer, 34.
[140] Noth, *Pentateuchal Traditions,* 30; *Exodus,* 51.
[141] Noth, *Exodus,* 45.
[142] Hertzberg, *ATD,* IX², 192: a sign of testing.
[143] Richter, *BBB,* 153.
[144] Cf. Preuss, *ZAW,* 139-173.
[145] Cf. Richter, 154.
[146] *Ibid.,* 153-55.
[147] So Hertzberg, 191.
[148] Richter, 153.

will meet two men by Rachel's tomb), 3f. (Saul will meet three men at the oak
of Tabor), and 5f. (Saul will meet an ecstatic band of prophets at Gibeath-
elohim). The realization of these signs which Samuel announced is intended to
confirm to Saul that Yahweh had anointed him to be prince over his heritage
(10:1, LXX and Vulg.). These commonplace events become signs "whereby
Saul can see the reality of the event"[149] by the context in which they occur. But
neither Samuel nor Saul has anything to do with these signs fulfilling their
intended function. This is God's work, for "God gave him (i.e., Saul) another
heart; and all these signs came to pass that day" (10:9). The connection between
these two statements is hard to determine. Hertzberg connects the "change of
heart" with Saul's ecstasy, and transfers this line to the end of v. 10.[150] However, this transposition is not necessary if we compare this text, e.g., with Dt.
29:2f.(3f.) and Ex. 7:3. Then it becomes clear that the proper function of a
sign is guaranteed only when Yahweh gives an "understanding heart" to those
who experience the signs (Dt. 29:2f.[3f.]). To be sure, signs take place when this
is not the case, but they do not fulfil their proper and lasting purpose of leading
people to a knowledge of Yahweh and to faith in him. Accordingly, Pharaoh
does not know the signs in their essential function because Yahweh hardens
his heart (Ex. 7:3), just as a God-given "new heart" is necessary to obedience
(Ezk. 36:26f.; cf. Jer. 31:33f.). Not only the establishment of the sign, but also
the mediation of its correct understanding has its origin with God. Therefore,
in our passage (1 S. 10:9), the meaning is that God gives Saul another heart, "and
thus these signs come to pass" as God intended, i.e., with the function of confirming Saul's faith. They do not fail to be effective as confirmation signs, because God "gives Saul another heart."

1 S. 2:34 also speaks of a confirmation sign. Like the sign announced in Ex.
3:12, this sign is put off into the future. By the death of his two sons on the
same day, Eli can know the accuracy of the prophetic announcement of judgment (the nucleus of which appears in vv. 31f.). Therefore, the expression "and
this shall be the sign to you" means the same thing as "and this is the way in
which you shall know the truthfulness of my word." This sign is mentioned in
a context that describes the sinful practices of the sons of Eli (2:12-17, 22-25),
and then judges it from a theological point of view (in the prophetic announcement of judgment), a feature of Deuteronomistic texts.[151]

Confirmation signs may be commonplace or miraculous. The sign Hezekiah
requests (2 K. 20:8) to confirm Yahweh's promise that he would be healed (v. 5)
is miraculous. Isaiah gives Hezekiah the choice of asking that the shadow go
forward or backward ten steps (v. 9), and understandably he decides to ask
that the shadow go backward (v. 10). The sign takes place after Isaiah cries to
Yahweh (v. 11; par. Isa. 38:22,7 and context). The possibility of a magical
interpretation is eliminated from the miraculous execution of the sign through
Isaiah's appeal to Yahweh.

---

[149] Hertzberg, *ATD*, IX², 66.
[150] *Ibid.*, 60, n. 5; cf. p. 67.
[151] *Ibid.*, 26.

g. *Sign-Acts (Symbolic Acts).* Very closely related to confirmation signs are signs that prophets perform in the framework of their so-called symbolic acts or sign-acts (Isa. 8:18; 20:3; Ezk. 4:3). These signs do not attract attention because they are miraculous, but because they are peculiar. [152] Without an appropriate interpretation, they remain largely unintelligible. A sign-act and verbal interpretation belong together; and it is erroneous to infer from the sequence in the texts under consideration, where execution of the sign is followed by interpretation, that a temporal and material distinction should be made between them, and then to conclude from this that these signs did not have the function of clarifying a prophetic oracle. [153]

Thus, the names of Isaiah's sons, "A remnant shall return" (cf. Isa. 7:3) and "The spoil speeds, the prey hastes" (cf. 8:1-3), are intended to clarify or confirm the prophetic oracles with which they were associated (on 7:3, cf. 10:21f.; on 8:1-3, cf. 8:4 and 7:7-9). Their names and the name of Isaiah himself, which means "Yahweh is (works) salvation," are signs and portents in Israel (Isa. 8:18). Also, the name of the prophet himself confirms the oracles associated with it, especially the oracle handed down in Isa. 12:2f., which speaks of God's "salvation." [154]

Isaiah's going about naked and barefoot is also an *'oth,* and a *mopheth,* "portent" (Isa. 20:3), to confirm and clarify the fate of the Egyptians and the Ethiopians as it is announced in v. 4. This sign-act also stands in a larger context and serves to confirm the calamity threatened against Egypt in 19:1-25 (cf. esp. 19:4).

Just as the prophetic oracles threatening calamity (Ezk. 5:5-15) anticipate verbally the events that they announce, so the sign-acts that accompany them describe the event symbolically (4:1–5:4). [155] Such signs intensify the oracle with which they are associated, perhaps even provoke it, since their striking execution awakens in those who witness the sign the question of its meaning, and thus they are in no sense "independent means of preaching," [156] since they reveal a clearly discernible relationship to the word. The sign-act of the siege of the city (4:1-3) represents that which is stated in the interpretation given in 5:5-15. Whether the sign-act with the plate, which is explicitly called a "sign for the house of Israel" (4:3), is an original part of the context or a "later expansion," [157] does not alter the sign character of the act at all, which probably goes back to Ezekiel, even if it may have been added by him later. [158]

3. *Conclusions.* It is impossible to limit the use of *'oth* to a specific literary stratum or to a specific traditio-historical stage, but predominantly it is found

---

[152] Quell, 293: "The peculiar characteristic of these signs is that they seek to gain sympathy for the absurd and the challenging."
[153] Contra Keller, 99.
[154] Cf. Kaiser, *Isaiah 1-12,* 169.
[155] Cf. Zimmerli, *BK,* XIII, 103.
[156] Eichrodt, *Ezekiel,* 81; similarly *TDNT,* VII, 217, but cf. the restriction placed on this point here.
[157] So Zimmerli, 113; cf. the evidence he gives for this on pp. 101f.
[158] *Ibid.*

in a specific genre, viz., parenetic texts, although not exclusively. It may be that those responsible for parenetic literature depend on the baroque description of "signs and wonders," etc. (cf. the synonyms of *'oth*), in the hymn,[159] but the didactic intention is the fundamental characteristic of their words, and it is expressed in legal sermons, parenetic reflections on history, and confessional statements. Most likely, the setting in which signs were used is the cult.

We may conclude from this analysis of the history of the genre in which signs are found that in such a parenetic context the emphasis is less on the event and more on the function of the sign, as is evident in the description of *'oth* as signs imparting knowledge, signs of protection, signs producing faith, signs that bring remembrance, signs of the covenant, signs of confirmation, and sign-acts. This functional character of a sign also makes it clear that *'oth,* independent of the context in which it appears and independent of its function, is a "formal idea."[160]

The word *'oth* plays a vital role in the call stories (cf. Ex. 3:12; 4:8f.; 1 S. 10:[1],7,9), where, especially after the commission, the protest, and the divine promise of help, it serves to authenticate the one called before others (Ex. 3:12; 4:8f.) or to assure the one called himself (Jgs. 6:17; 1 S. 10:1,7,9).[161] Since this word alone is used in the call stories that have been mentioned, in this context its significance as a sign of confirmation or as a sign of authentication is clear. But we should also pay attention to the kind of situation in which these "signs" belong. As is often the case, we are dealing here with situations of crisis, which result in the divine commission of "saviors." Divine commission and promise of help result in the protest of the one called, "which Yahweh overcomes... through signs."[162] While it is almost impossible to determine the setting of Ex. 3f. outside the literature in which it has been placed,[163] it seems quite likely that the setting for 1 S. 9:1–10:16 is a prophetic circle.[164]

Now if it is true that prophetic circles, in addition to (or in conjunction with) circles of parenetic teachers, are also a setting in which the word *'oth* was used, then faith in the divine commission and in the promise of help connected with it in the framework of the call story also follows from the functional character of a "sign," the ultimate purpose of which is to confirm faith, as we have emphasized.

Rahab's request for a sign of guarantee (Josh. 2:12, 18) provides a possible beginning for the use of *'oth* in call stories in the secular realm.

It is possible to determine the setting of the word *'oth* in a specific literary stratum only in the case of "covenant signs," which are to be found wholly in the Priestly Code and in Ezekiel, which is closely connected with it. In my opinion, this enables us to demonstrate a historical development of this word, at least for P and Ezekiel. Since *'oth* in the secular realm means a sign guarantee-

---

159 Quell, 289; *TDNT,* VII, 213.
160 *TDNT,* VII, 210, 216.
161 Cf. the summary in Richter, *FRLANT,* 91, 139.
162 *Ibid.,* 95.
163 Cf. *ibid.,* 100, 117.
164 *Ibid.,* 56.

ing an oath or an agreement (Josh. 2:13,18), it seems logical to believe that P and Ezekiel begin with this use of the word, and transfer it to the theological realm as a designation for covenant signs.

We may conjecture that a similar development of the use of 'oth took place especially in the Deuteronomic and Deuteronomistic literature, but this cannot be proved. The parenetic function of 'oth is particularly striking in this literature, which declares the mighty acts of God to those who see the signs and to their audiences. *God* performs the signs; *he* also causes his signs to be understood in their function of confirming man's knowledge of God and faith in him, because he "gives him another heart" (1 S. 10:9). This does not mean, however, that the biblical authors are concerned exclusively with "the action of God and the passiveness of man." [165] It is true that man does not participate in the performance of a sign (except when he is the subject of the divine commission), but he takes part in the function of that sign when he comes to understand its meaning, or else he could not be held guilty for refusing to know, to believe, and to obey.

Helfmeyer

---

[165] Quell, 256.

אָח 'ach; אָחוֹת 'āchôth

Contents: I. Use in the Ancient Near East. II. Occurrences, Meaning. III. Legal Use. IV. Theological Use. V. Use in Proper Names.

I. Use in the Ancient Near East. The root 'ach is a common Semitic root; it signifies first of all a person's own blood brother, but it also has the broader meaning of kinsman, fellow countryman, companion, etc. Thus, e.g., Akk. *aḫu* is used as an address to persons of equal rank (esp. in letters, and also among kings), and further to refer to professional colleagues, covenant partners, and fellow tribesmen (in the Mari tablets). Sometimes, the gods also are designated collectively as "brothers." In Akkadian proper names, *aḫu* usually means a person's own blood brother, e.g., *Sin-aḫa-iddinam,* "Sin has given a brother"; [1]

'ach. C. H. Gordon, "Fratriarchy in the O.T.," *JBL,* 54 (1935), 223-231; A. Hermann, *Altägyptische Liebesdichtung* (1959), 59, 75ff.; H. Jahnow, *Das hebr. Leichenlied. BZAW,* 36 (1923), 61ff.; P. Koschaker, "Fratriarchat, Hausgemeinschaft und Mutterrecht in Keilschriftrechten," *ZA,* N.F. 7 (1933), 1-89; Pedersen, *ILC,* I-II, 57ff.; G. Ryckmans, "Les noms de parenté en Safaitique," *RB,* 58 (1951), 377-392; *'ḫ,* 382-384; A. van Selms, *Marriage and Family Life in Ugaritic Literature* (London, 1954); A. Skaist, "The Authority of the Brother at Arrapha and Nuzi," *JAOS,* 89 (1969), 10-17; E. A. Speiser, "The Wife-Sister Motif in the Patriarchal Narratives," in A. Altmann, ed., *Biblical and Other Studies* (1963), 15-28; de Vaux, *AncIsr,* 19ff., 41ff., 53ff.

[1] Stamm, *AN,* 43ff.

but a god also is called a brother, e.g., *Aḫu-dūr-enši*, "the brother is a wall for the weak,"[2] *Aḫu-ilum*, "the brother is God,"[3] and in names expressing trust, as *Ilī-aḫī*, "my God is my brother," and *Ilī-kī-aḫ*, "my God is like a brother."[4] Basically, the use in proper names is similar to that of → אב *'ābh*, "father."

The Ugar. *'ḫ* is used both of human brothers, e.g., *CTA*, 14 [I K], 9 ("the king had seven brothers"), and of divine beings, e.g., 'Anat-Luṭpan, *CTA*, 18 [III D], IV, 24, 'Anat-Ba'al, *CTA*, 2 [III AB], II, 11.[5] Moreover, there is a typical Ugaritic word *'ry*, "relative."[6] On love between brothers and sisters, cf. van Selms, 119f. In West Semitic inscriptions the same situation exists as in Akkadian. Indeed, the word *'ach* is used in this material of kinsmen,[7] in letter style between persons of equal rank, of professional colleagues,[8] and of a king who protects his subjects.[9] In Nabatean, *'ḥ mlk'*, "brother of the king," is the title of a distinguished minister, and *'ḥth mlk'*, "sister of the king," is the queen.[10]

The situation is similar in Egyptian with the use of *śn*. This word, the root of which is related to *śnw*, "two," means both a person's own blood brother (often in a broader sense, a kinsman) and companion (cf. also *śn.k im*, "your brother here"="I" in letters), and sweetheart (in love poetry, which is not to be traced back to the practice of marrying one's own sister)[11]—a meaning that is unique to Egyptian. This latter use corresponds to the frequent designation of one's sweetheart and of one's wife as *śn.t*, "sister." The word *śnw*, "second, companion, partner," often found in the expression *nn śnw.f*, "there is no one like him," should also be considered. Particularly numerous are the cases in which Osiris is called the brother of Isis and Nephthys, in which Horus and Seth or Seth and Thoth are called "the two brothers," and in which Isis and Nephthys are called "the two sisters."[12]

II. Occurrences, Meaning. In Hebrew, *'ach* means chiefly a person's own blood brother, e.g., Gen. 4:8-11 (Cain and Abel); 25:26 (Esau and Jacob, cf. Hos. 12:4 [Eng. v. 3]); 37:2,4ff.; 42:3f.,7 (Joseph and his brothers); Ex. 4:14 (Aaron, the brother of Moses); Jgs. 9:5 (Abimelech kills his brothers). It is evident from Ex. 4:14 that the OT does not make a sharp distinction between brother and half brother; 2 S. 13:4 also indicates this. Sometimes, the relationship of full brothers is emphasized by adding the words, "son of (the same) mother" (Dt. 13:7[6]; Jgs. 8:19; Ps. 50:20; metaphorically, Gen. 27:29).

---

2 *Ibid.*, 55f.
3 *Ibid.*, 297f.
4 *Ibid.*, 400.
5 *WUS*, 11f.
6 *WUS*, 35.
7 *KAI*, 214.27ff., written *'yḥ*.
8 Cf. *'achay malkhayya'*, "my brothers, the kings," *KAI*, 216.14.
9 *KAI*, 24.11.
10 *DISO*, 8f.
11 Hermann, 75f.
12 *WbÄS*, IV, 151, 15.

'ach also means one's kinsman, e.g., Gen. 14:14, 16 (Abraham's nephew, Lot; cf. 13:8, "we are brothers"), and in a broader sense a fellow tribesman or a fellow countryman, e.g., Gen. 31:32 (Jacob and Laban: "in the presence of our brothers," i.e., kinsmen); Ex. 2:11; 4:18 (the Hebrews are the "brothers" of Moses); Lev. 10:4 (the sons of a cousin); 25:25 (the one responsible as go'el, "redeemer"); Nu. 20:3 ("our brethren" = the Israelites); Josh. 1:14f. (the other Israelites in relation to the Reubenites and the Gadites); Jgs. 9:18 (Abimelech is the brother, i.e., the fellow tribesman of the citizens of Shechem). Basic to this latter use of the word is the idea that the tribes and the nation descended from a common father. [13] Thus, "thy (our, etc.) brothers" and "the children of Israel" often appear side by side in apposition to each other (Lev. 25:46; Dt. 3:18; 24:7; Jgs. 20:13; cf. Nu. 25:6). In several passages, this genealogical concept of history is expressed by making individuals representatives of a tribe or of a nation, and by describing relationships between tribes in categories normally used for family relationships: Canaan shall become a slave to his brothers (i.e., the Israelites) (Gen. 9:25); Ishmael will be an enemy to his brothers (i.e., to other tribes) (16:12; 25:18); in the Blessing of Jacob, Simeon and Levi are addressed as brothers (49:5); in the account of the conquest of the land, the tribes of Judah and Simeon are referred to as brothers (Jgs. 1:3,17), who even speak to each other; the Israelites ask the oracle: "Shall we again draw near to battle against our brethren the Benjaminites (i.e., the tribe of Benjamin)?" (20:23,28). This type of expression occurs quite often when reference is made to Jacob and Esau or Israel and Edom: Isaac blesses his sons and promises that Esau will serve his brother (Gen. 27:29,40); toward the end of the wilderness wandering the Israelites send messengers to Edom, saying, "Thus says your brother Israel" (Nu. 20:14); similarly, in Dt. 2:4,8, the Edomites are called "your brethren the sons of Esau." Dt. 23:8(7) refers to this brotherly relationship when it says: "You shall not abhor an Edomite, for he is your brother"; Amos reproves Edom because he "pursued his brother with the sword" (Am. 1:11); in Ob. 10,12; Mal. 1:2ff., there are references to Edom's shameful treatment of their Israelite brothers.

Quite often 'ach is used of compatriots or members of the same nation. The law of the king in Deuteronomy forbids the Israelites to make a foreigner (→ נכרי nokhrî) king ("one from among your brethren you shall set as king over you," 17:15). With the same emphasis against foreigners, prophets are to be raised up "from your brethren" (18:15). In Dt. 23:20f.(19f.), the Jews are indeed allowed to take interest from a nokhri, but they are forbidden to demand interest from an 'ach. Dt. 24:14 makes a distinction between an 'ach, "a brother," and a → גר gēr, "a sojourner," although the Israelites have the same responsibility to both in this passage (cf. Dt. 23:8[7], where the Israelites are said to have the relationship of a ger to the Egyptians). Neh. 5:8 speaks of "our Jewish brethren." Isa. 66:20; Mic. 5:2(3) (cf. Jer. 29:16) speak of the Israelite brethren in the Diaspora and of their return.

---

[13] ILC, 57f.

As a rule, only a fellow countryman is considered to be a → רֵעַ *rēa'*, "neighbor." *'ach* appears in parallelism with or is used synonymously with *rea'* (or *merea'*) in Lev. 19:17; 2 S. 3:8; Jer. 9:3(4); Ps. 35:14; 122:8; Job 6:15 (cf. also 30:29); Prov. 17:17; 19:7. *'ach* is used in place of *rea'* (neighbor) in the Holiness Code (Lev. 19:17; 25:25,46) in Deuteronomy (15:7,9,12; 19:18f.; 22:1-4), and possibly also in Job 22:6. The laws in P prefer *rea'*. *'ach* is used of neighbors in a general sense in Ps. 49:8(7), "no man can ransom his brother" (perhaps also in Prov. 18:19). In Ps. 22:23(22), "my brethren" is clearly identical with → קָהָל *qāhāl*, "congregation," i.e., the cult community; perhaps the same is true of 122:8.

Furthermore, sometimes *'ach* is used as a polite address to strangers (Gen. 19:7; 29:4; Jgs. 19:23), and also in diplomatic correspondence between allies, as perhaps in Nu. 20:14 and certainly in 1 K. 9:13 (Solomon speaking to Hiram); 20:32 (Ahab speaking of Ben-hadad). Perhaps the "covenant of brotherhood" (*berith 'achim*) in Am. 1:9 (an expression which occurs only once in the OT) also points to a similar meaning. Several scholars think this expression refers to the relationship between Tyre and Israel, but others think it refers to the tribal relationship between Israel and Edom.

'ach is used of general acquaintance in Job 30:29 ("a brother of jackals, and a companion [*rea'*] of ostriches": someone who spends his life in the desert). Similarly, a "brother of thieves" (Prov. 18:9) is one who is engaged in a common cause with thieves.

The use of the word *'achoth*, "sister," follows quite similar lines. This word means chiefly a person's own blood sister (Gen. 4:22; 20:12; Lev. 18:9,11; etc.), and then a female relative (Gen. 24:60). In a broader sense, it is used of nations and cities (Jer. 3:7: Israel is Judah's sister; Ezk. 16:46: Jerusalem and Samaria are sisters). Like *'ach*, *'achoth* also refers to an acquaintance (Job 17:14, of a worm; cf. Prov. 7:4, of wisdom, see below). In the Song of Solomon, the beloved or sweetheart (following an Egyptian prototype?) is often called "sister" (4:9-12; 5:1f.; cf. 8:8). This same love motif is also applied to Wisdom (Prov. 7:4).[14]

Finally, both *'ach* and *'achoth* are used in the funeral dirge (1 K. 13:30; Jer. 22:18).[15] These terms are probably used in this setting in order to express the intimate relationship between the mourners and the deceased. Sometimes in the lament over Tammuz, this god is also called "brother."

III. Legal Use. No particular rights of brothers are mentioned in the OT legal material. As a rule, sons have hereditary rights; the oldest son was given a double portion (Dt. 21:17). When the daughters of Job are given an inheritance "among their brothers," this is to be understood as something quite special (Job 42:15; cf. Prov. 17:2). A man's sister and the wife of his brother are numbered among his closest relatives, with whom he is forbidden to have sexual intercourse (Lev. 18:9,16; 20:17,21; Dt. 27:22). Likewise, brothers and sisters are among the relatives of a priest with whose corpses he is allowed to defile himself (Lev. 21:2f.–P; Ezk. 44:25). According to Dt. 25:5-9 (cf. Gen. 38:8ff. → יבם *yābhām*),

---

[14] Cf. Ringgren, *Word and Wisdom* (1947), 106, 111f.
[15] Jahnow, 61ff.

the brother of a dead man is obligated to marry his sister-in-law. The duty of *ge'ullah*, redemption, is also the duty of a brother, Lev. 25:25 (→ גאל *gōʾēl*).

Some scholars have tried to prove that there are remnants of a family system which was controlled by the authority of brothers among the Hittites, the Hurrians, and the Elamites: the brother gives the sister to her husband "for sisterhood," [16] one can adopt another as his brother, [17] etc. But according to Skaist this is true only in exceptional cases, as e.g., when the father is dead. The attempts to demonstrate similar conditions in Israel [18] are precarious. [19]

IV. Theological Use. The strong family solidarity of the Israelites also includes the relationship between brothers and sisters. He who has neither a brother nor a *reaʿ*, "friend," is defenseless (2 S. 13:3,6; cf. Eccl. 4:8). The story of Cain is typical (Gen. 4). Cain violates the simplest duty which he has to Abel, and then passes off the accusation of God with the words, "am I my brother's keeper?" (4:9); in saying this, he disavows an otherwise obvious responsibility. Thus, the text also emphasizes in particular that the blood of his brother cries out (→ צעק *tsāʿaq*) to God for revenge. On the other hand, it is considered to be a special tribute to the Levites that they killed even their own sons and brothers who were guilty of idolatry (Ex. 32:29): by doing this they set loyalty to God above family solidarity.

With the extension of the idea of brotherhood to all fellow tribesmen and fellow countrymen came also the increased demand for solidarity. In the Holiness Code and Deuteronomy there are numerous references to duties toward a brother. Since all Israelites are brothers, one should help everyone who becomes poor (Lev. 25:35f.). Deuteronomy especially emphasizes this duty (15:7,9,11f.), and even applies it to the way one treats his brother's domestic animals (22:1-4). One is forbidden to bear false witness against a brother (19:18f.—in the similar law in Ex. 20:16, the word *reaʿ*, "neighbor," is used).

Jeremiah's brothers and the house of his father dealt treacherously with him (Jer. 12:6); therefore, he warns his hearers not to trust in a brother or a neighbor because they are all deceivers (9:3[4]). Similarly, Job laments that his brothers and friends (*reaʿ*) have dealt treacherously with him (6:15). One who robs his "brother" (missing in the LXX) and does evil to one of his fellow countrymen deserves to die (Ezk. 18:18). Isa. 66:5 contains this promise to those who are faithful to Yahweh: "your brethren who hate you ... shall be put to shame." In the descriptions of suffering in the Psalms of Lament where the worshipper says that he has been forsaken by his brothers and his friends (companions) (Ps. 69:9[8]; 88:9[8] speak only of "companions," while Job 19:13 refers to both *ʾach*, "brethren," and *yodheaʿ*, "acquaintances"), what is being depicted is a disruption of the normal social relationship.

---

[16] Koschaker, 14, 28f.
[17] *Ibid.*, 37ff.
[18] Gordon.
[19] However, cf. Speiser.

Sayings in the Wisdom Literature express the same view of brotherly solidarity; and yet, they declare that good friends can be better than brothers (Prov. 18:24; 27:10; cf. 17:17, where "friend" and "brother" are used synonymously). Prov. 18:19 and 19:7 have in mind a schism in the brotherly community; 6:19 counts the one "who sows discord among brothers" as one of the seven abominations, and Ps. 133:1 emphasizes how pleasant it is "when brothers dwell in unity."

V. Use in Proper Names. Finally, *'ach* appears as a component in certain proper names. In obvious theophoric names like *'achiyyah,* "Ahijah," and *yo'ach,* "Joah," "Yahweh is (my) brother," or *'achi'el,* "Ahiel," "my brother is El," the deity is characterized as a relative in typical ancient West Semitic fashion (→ אב *'ābh*). [20] In the name *'achimelekh,* "Ahimelech," *melekh,* "king," must be a designation for God. In other names like *'achiram,* "Ahiram," "my brother is exalted," a person's own blood brother could be meant. But even here it is likely that originally the divine brother was meant, although this idea was soon forgotten.

Ringgren

---

[20] Noth, *IPN,* 66ff.; cf. Huffmon, *APNM,* 160f.; Gröndahl, *PNU,* 91.

אֶחָד *'echādh*

Contents: I. General Observations. II. One God: 1. In the Ancient Near East; 2. One Yahweh; 3. One Creator; 4. Eccl. 12:11. III. Use in the Created Realm: 1. Uniqueness Through Election; 2. Original or Future Unity of Those Presently Divided; 3. Solitude As a Negative Factor; 4. Equality of Fate. IV. Theologically Relevant Expressions Using *'echādh.*

I. General Observations. The numeral *'echadh,* "one," begins the series of ordinary numbers. It is an adjective. It can be used as a cardinal, ordinal, and distributive number. In prose literature from the time of Solomon, it already

---

'echādh. P. R. Ackroyd, "Two Hebrew Notes," *ASTI,* 5 (1966/67), 82-86; W. F. Bade, "Der Monojahwismus des Dtn," *ZAW,* 30 (1910), 81-90; E. Jacob, "Ce que la Bible dit de l'unité et diversité des peuples," *Revue de Psychologie des Peuples,* 16 (1961), 118-133; G. A. F. Knight, "The Lord is One," *ExpT,* 79 (1967/68), 8-10; C. A. Labuschagne, *The Incomparability of Yahweh in the OT* (1966), 137f.; B. Otzen, *Studien über Deuterosacharja* (1964), 205-208; F. Perles, "Was bedeutet יהוה אחד Deut. 6, 4?" *OLZ,* 2 (1899), 537f.; G. Quell, "κύριος," *TDNT,* III, 1079-1081.

On II.1.a.: J. Bergman, *Ich bin Isis. Studien zum memphitischen Hintergrund der griechischen Isisaretalogien* (1968); R. O. Faulkner, "Some Notes on the God Shu," *JEOL,* 18 (1964), 266-270; E. Otto, *Gott und Mensch nach den äg. Tempelinschriften der griech.-röm. Zeit* (1964); T. Säve-Söderbergh, "The Solitary Victory," *Pharaohs and Mortals* (1961), 159-170; K. Sethe, *Amun und die acht Urgötter von Hermopolis* (1929); J. Zandee, *De hymnen aan Amon van Papyrus Leiden I 350* (Leiden, 1947).

appears as an indefinite article. As a numerical adjective and adverb it takes on meanings such as "only," "unique," "prominent," "alone," "same, uniform," "entire, undivided." As an element in various expressions, its use is even wider (cf. English "as one man," "all one," "one with"). There are other Hebrew words which are closely related to 'echadh, and partially used interchangeably with it: → בדד bādhādh, "alone," yachadh, "union, all together," → יחיד yāchîdh, "only, alone, solitary," lebhadh, "alone," ri'shon, "the first." In the Hebrew OT, 'echadh had not yet come to be used in a theological program. Therefore, we cannot deal with *monotheism* in this article. However, 'echadh is found in religious and theological statements of varying importance and with meanings which do not wholly agree.

II. One God.

1. *In the Ancient Near East.* In spite of its polytheism, the world around Israel could speak of "one" God.

a. *Egypt.* The word w' appears several times with a substantival meaning as a divine epithet, "The One, The Only." [1] It is important to a correct understanding of the Egyptian idea of God that a whole series of gods is given this title. E.g., it can be shown that w' was applied to Atum, Re, Amun, Ptah, Aton, Thoth, Geb, Horus, Haroëris, Khnum, and Khonsu. [2] In this sense, frequently a $w'w$ is added to this word to reinforce it after the manner of an etymological figure, [3] perhaps meaning "The Most Unique One." *ḥr ḥw.f*, "after his kind," serves as a more precise designation of uniqueness. But even more frequently w' is emphasized by means of a negative supplement, especially *nn kyy ḥr ḥw.f*, "there is none other after his kind"; *nn śnnw.f*, "he has no second." [4]

When one considers more closely the contexts in which this uniqueness of God is emphasized, it is striking that the creation, "the first time" (*sp tpy*), is mentioned quite often. The solitariness of the Primal God before the creation is a favorite theme (cf., e.g., The Book of the Dead 17 = *Urk.*, V, 6ff.). Thus, Amun is the Only One in Primeval Time, "the Great and Oldest One, who belongs to Prehistoric Time" (*Urk.*, IV, 111, 9). The solitariness of his being is naturally confirmed by his being the first originator, who set in motion the beginning. This aspect is often expressed in a long formula, which is called to mind by Jn. 1:2. [5] As creator of all, he is also called *nb w'*, "One Lord," and is *w' ir nt.t kmỉ wn.t*, "the Only One, who has made what is and has created what exists" (*Urk.*, IV, 495, 4). The common expression *ntr w' ir św m ḥḥw*, "the only God, who has splintered himself into millions," emphasizes the extremely close connection between the greatly variegated world and the "One

---

[1] *WbÄS*, I, 275, 10.

[2] Zandee, 70, gives some references.

[3] *WbÄS*, I, 275, 15-16; 277, 9; cf. the less frequent combination w' $w'ty$, 279,1.

[4] Otto, 11ff., mentions several variants; his large collection of examples deals with some thirty gods and goddesses.

[5] So perhaps Zandee, 72ff.

Lord of creation," and points to an extremely pantheistic understanding. [6] In general, expressions using wʿ and ḥḥw occur frequently, so that the connection of the god Ḥḥ with Shu, the first emanation of the Primal God Atum, results in several significant constructions. Goddesses also appear frequently as wʿ.t(t), sometimes interpreted as "the Solitary Eye" or the Royal Uraeus. [7] This term is applied to Hathor (Dendera is "the house of 'the Only One'") [8] and Isis (Θιουιν < tꜣ wʿ.t as a genuine name of Isis in a hymn from Medinet Madi) [9] in particular.

It is significant that the king often appears as "the Only One," which is characteristic of the Egyptian royal ideology. Apparently he is given this title because of his role as the representative of the creator-god on earth (thus, Thutmose I is called "the perfect God of the First Time," Urk., IV, 83, 11). [10] This uniqueness of the king is emphasized quite often in contexts of war in documents from the New Kingdom. The king defeats the hostile, chaotic powers and maintains order. The designation of Hatshepsut as wʿ.t.t Ḥr (Urk., IV, 390) is parallel to the title of the goddesses mentioned above.

b. *Mesopotamia.* In Sumerian there are several words for "one," the different usages of which have never been investigated. Deities are often designated as "unique" or "solitary." In Akkadian we find ištēn, "one" (cf. Heb. ʿashte ʿasar, "eleven") and (w)ēdu, "only," "alone" (→ יחד yachadh); see CAD, VII, 275ff., or IV, 36ff. In many expressions ištēn and ēdu are used alternately without any distinction in meaning, e.g., pâ ištēn/ēda iššaknū, "they came to an agreement." Also, there is no detailed investigation of the theological implications of these words.

Among divine beings and kings, ištēn, "one, a person," can have the meaning "solitary, separate" (CAD, VII, 287a). This is the case in an ancient Assyrian incantation text for the female demon Lamashtum [11] and in the Song of Agushaya for the warlike goddess Ishtar. [12]

c. *Ugarit.* In a mythological text, after the completion of the building of his palace, the god Baal declares that he alone (ʾḥdy) is king over the gods (CTA, 4 [II AB], VII, 49-52). The emphasis on the word "alone" causes one to suspect that the situation was that Baal's rule was under constant threat by Mut, the god of drought. Baal's royal rule is coexistent with the peaceful kingship of the creator-god Ilu. [13]

---

[6] Otto, 58f., 106.

[7] WbÄS, I, 278, 6; 279, 11.

[8] WbÄS, I, 278, 7.

[9] Bergman, 225, 280ff.

[10] Säve-Söderbergh, 159ff.

[11] BIN, IV, 126, 1; von Soden, Or, n.s. 25 (1956), 141ff.

[12] VAS, 10, 214, III, 4; r. VI, 21; RA, 15 (1918), 178, r. VI, 8; on the song: H. Ringgren, Word and Wisdom, 69ff.

[13] W. H. Schmidt, BZAW, 80 (²1966), 64ff.

2. *One Yahweh*. There are many keywords in the Deuteronomic/Deuteronomistic vocabulary which are often repeated in this material, but *yhvh 'elohenu yhvh 'echadh*, "Yahweh our God, Yahweh is Unique," is not one of these. In contrast to this, the command to love God in 6:5 is often repeated. It seems to be vital to Deuteronomic/Deuteronomistic theology, while the statements about Yahweh which are connected with it are never the same (cf. Dt. 5:9; 7:9; 10:14f., 17f., 21f.; 11:2-7; 13:6 [Eng. v. 5]; 30:20; Josh. 23:3). The demand for love is itself one of many formulations of the fundamental demand made on Israel to worship Yahweh alone and not any of the other gods (→ אהב *'āhabh*). [14] Here, there is probably a connection with the love motif in ancient Near Eastern treaties and royal letters. [15] Dt. 6, up to about v. 19, is an annotated rewriting of the beginning of the Decalog. In light of this, it seems that Dt. 6:4f. is to be regarded as a reiteration of the love motif in 5:10. Thus, the meaning of *'echadh* in 6:4 must be determined by the fundamental demand of Deuteronomy in general, and by the beginning of the Decalog in particular. On this basis, it affirms that Yahweh is the *one* and *only* God for *Israel*. The closest parallel to this in subject matter is Dt. 32:12: "Yahweh alone (*badhadh*) did lead him (Israel in the wilderness), and there was no foreign god with him." This does not deny the existence of other gods. Yahweh is *'echadh*, "one," with regard to the one who is addressed, viz., "Israel." In the ears of the contemporaries of the ones responsible for this statement, because of its direct connection with the love motif here, *'echadh* probably suggested emotional connotations, which this word can have in love lyrics when one refers to his sweetheart as the "only one": cf. Cant. 6:8f. [16] As the God whom Israel loves, Yahweh is Israel's *only one* and *unique one*. The late eschatological text, Zec. 14, which draws on diverse traditions, uses Dt. 6:4 in the middle (14:9). After the eschatological battle, Yahweh will be enthroned in Jerusalem as king of creation, and then "Yahweh will be unique and his name unique." Thus the statement in Dt. 6:4 is now given a universal application (cf. 14:16). *'echadh* is connected with the God-King motif (cf. Pss. 93, 97, 99; but also Dt. 10:17f.), as it is also once in Ugaritic literature. [17] Yahweh's "name" is to be understood in the sense of the Deuteronomistic theory of the presence of Yahweh in the Jerusalem temple (1 K. 8:27-29). [18]

Job 23:13 must be rejected as a proof for "one" God in the OT. The context demands a verb, cf. 9:12. Read *be'echodh* (infinitive from *'ḥz* I, as a dialectical variant of *'ḥd*, in which the *zayin* and the *daleth* are interchanged): "when he snatches away, who can hinder him?" In Dt. 6:4, *yhvh 'elohenu yhvh 'echadh* can be interpreted as two nominative sentences in sequence or as one nominative sentence with three different possibilities as to subject and predicate. In the Deuteronomic/Deuteronomistic material, *'elohenu*, "our God," is to be understood as in apposition to *yhvh*, "Yahweh," because when *'elohim* is used predi-

---

14 N. Lohfink, *Das Hauptgebot* (1963), 73ff.
15 W. L. Moran, *CBQ*, 25 (1963), 77ff.
16 On this, see G. Gerleman, *BK*, XVIII.
17 See II.1.c.
18 Further on Zec. 14, see III.2.c.

catively after *yhvh,* it is always preceded by *hu'* (Dt. 4:35; 7:9; Josh. 24:18; 1 K. 8:60). The Nash Papyrus also, which adds *hu'* at the end, has understood it in this way, and so has the LXX. Whether the second *yhvh* is a repetition of the subject after the apposition or whether it is part of the predicate must remain an open question. The interpretation given above is possible with either syntactical explanation. It has often been suggested that Dt. 6:4 contains a "mono-yahwistic" statement: a statement made in opposition to dividing Yahweh into many local individual Yahwehs. In support of this, scholars have appealed to the large number of Baals and to the Deuteronomistic emphasis on the centralization of the cult (Dt. 12). But the analogy to the large number of Baals can no longer be maintained to the extent that it once was; there is no opposition to a "poly-Yahwism" anywhere else in Deuteronomy. Also 6:4f. may be older than the relatively late demand for centralization of the cult in Deuteronomy. Of course, the idea that 6:4 can be interpreted in the sense of theoretical monotheism is out of the question. Until late strata in the book (e.g., 4:19), Deuteronomy does consider the existence of other gods. Similarly, the view of Labuschagne that here Yahweh is being described as "the One Detached," as a God without a female companion and without a household, is remote from the Deuteronomic context. It is possible that 6:4f. was already a unit before the composition of Dt. 6, for 6:3 fits awkwardly before it, and 6:6ff. plunges into another theme without any transition from vv. 4f. Furthermore, the structure of 6:4f. follows the pattern of a brief literary form (summons to the hearers–address to "Israel"–statement intended to motivate the hearers–statement of Yahweh's demand of Israel), which is also found in 20:2ff. and 27:9f. It seems likely that the assembly of Israel for war or in the cult was the setting for this form. The speakers are priests. Thus, 6:4 may contain an ancient cultic formula. But what it affirmed will have been the same as that which we find in the Deuteronomic context.

3. *One Creator.* In Job 31:15 and Mal. 2:10, in connection with statements concerning the equality of all men, the creator (in Mal. also the father; cf. Mal. 1:6) is said to be *one.* This means that *one and the same* God has created all. It is hard to determine whether these passages have taken over an ancient attribute of the creator. [19]

4. *Eccl. 12:11.* In Eccl. 12:11, the editor of this teaching says that the "sayings of the wise" and the "(sayings of the) members of the assembly" derive from "one shepherd." This verse is difficult and disputed. Some commentators think that the "one shepherd" is God as the source of all wisdom teaching.

III. Use in the Created Realm.

1. *Uniqueness Through Election.* Election by Yahweh gives uniqueness and magnificence to the one elected.

---

[19] Cf. II.1.a.

a. According to 2 S. 7:23 = 1 Ch. 17:21, Israel is a *"unique* nation on earth" because of her deliverance from Egypt and because of her covenant relationship to Yahweh. According to one interpretation [20] which has recently been called in question, [21] 2 S. 7:22-24 is a Deuteronomistic addition to the ancient narrative of the Nathan oracle. [22]

'echadh in 2 S. 7:23 should not be corrected to *'acher,* "other," following the LXX. A phrase *goy 'acher ba'arets,* "other nation on the earth," would have to stand immediately after *umi,* "and who (what)," because in *mi* (who, what)-questions with comparisons, the words that come after *mi* and words that come after the comparison introduced by *ke* ("like, as") have different functions (cf. Mic. 7:18, where both positions are occupied).

b. The survivors of the fall of Jerusalem in 587 B.C. wrongly interpreted the idea that Abraham was *'echadh,* "one," as a guarantee of their security, and therefore this idea was rejected in Ezk. 33:24. But Deutero-Isaiah takes up this idea again in Isa. 51:2 as a motif of the hope of salvation.

c. Not earlier than in Chronicles, *'echadh* also appears in statements concerning the choice of the Davidides and of Jerusalem: 1 Ch. 29:1 (original in Chronicles–of Solomon) and 2 Ch. 32:12 (which is different from 2 K. 18:22, where *'echadh* does not occur–of the altar in Jerusalem).

d. A fugitive who was given to the service of the sanctuary [23] relates his prayer of asylum in Ps. 27:4: *"One thing* have I asked 'a hundred times' (read *me'ath*), [24] O Yahweh, that will I seek after: / that I may dwell in the house of Yahweh / all the days of my life...."

2. *Original or Future Unity of Those Presently Divided.* In the OT, the picture of *unity and wholeness* either for the origin of history or for the future is drawn as contrast to the experience of disunity.

a. The *Yahwist* thinks of an original unity. In Gen. 2:21-24, he reproduces an etiology intended to explain the attraction of the sexes to each other, an etiology which had been handed down to him. It ends with the expression *basar 'echadh,* "one flesh," in 2:24, which appears again with its pre-Yahwistic meaning in Mal. 2:15 and Sir. 25:26. By adding Gen. 2:25 ("and the man and his wife were both naked, and were not ashamed"), J gives this narrative, with its affirmation of the original unity of mankind, a new function in the larger narrative framework. This unity is disrupted in 3:7, when the man and his wife realized that they were naked. The motif of "unity-division" is repeated after

---

[20] Based on L. Rost, *Die Überlieferung von der Thronnachfolge Davids* (1926), 49.
[21] By Noth, Labuschagne, Kutsch, Seybold.
[22] On the use of the motif in Ezk. 37:22, see below, III.2.b.
[23] L. Delekat, *Asylie und Schutzorakel am Zionheiligtum* (1967), 198.
[24] M. Dahood, *AB, in loc.*

the flood at the beginning of real history in Gen. 11:1-9. Mankind, which up to this time had been monadic and had had "one language and the same words" (11:1; this may be compared with the idea of a Primitive Age in which all praise Enlil "with one tongue," which appears in the Sumerian Enmerkar Epic, 146),[25] sets out to build a city with a temple tower or a city stronghold[26] and aspires to organize a kingdom ("a name," to avoid being "scattered abroad," "one people": 11:4,6). Since this seems to be anarchy, Yahweh confuses their language and scatters mankind over the earth. The statement of J which indicates a possibility of restoring unity out of this division in the future is found in 12:1-3. Abraham will become a great people and will get a great name. To be sure, the unity of all men will not be forced, but in the division which continues to exist all the tribes of the fertile land will be given a blessing "in Abraham." The patriarchal narratives show that this blessing will be mediated to mankind by intercessory prayer, readiness for peace, and help. J seems to be quite critical of the great political empire of David and Solomon which strives for greater unity through the use of power.[27] If recent traditio-historical theories[28] are correct, in contrast to the earlier method of dividing this material into sources, then J inherited the problem of the unity between the Israelites and the Canaanites in the narrative of the attack of the sons of Jacob on Shechem (Gen. 34) which was handed down to him. In the transactions concerning a possible marriage which are described in this chapter, the intention of the Shechemites, with whom the sons of Jacob enter into discussion, is that the two groups become "one people" through the marriage (34:16,22). The ancient narrative by allusion called attention to the fact that in Israel such a marriage was forbidden (cf. Gen. 34:9 with Ex. 34:16–J). The attack on Shechem was morally justified both by this and by the fact that Dinah was defiled. However, for J this view of the relationship of the Israelites to the Canaanites was not satisfactory. He incorporated this narrative into his work: it affirmed that Yahweh had prevented the marriage by the attack of Jacob's sons on Shechem. But drawing from Gen. 49:5-7, J inserted additions in 34:25,30: in this way, he made the act of Jacob's sons sinful and the reason for their punishment. Accordingly, this day could no longer be understood as an exemplary one by the reader of J.

b. The motif of the new unity of the northern and southern kingdoms is a part of the *prophetic* proclamation of salvation after the judgment. In this context, the prophets can speak of one ruler and one people in the future. The oldest example appears in Hos. 2:2 (1:11) (*qabhats*, "gather together"; *ro'sh 'echadh*, "one head"). In Ezk. 37:15-28, *'echadh* is used as a literary leitmotiv (it occurs 11 times in 37:15-24). After the two exiles took place, *qabhats* must be understood as a gathering up of all the Israelites out of all the nations and their returning home out of exile. Then there will be "one people in the land"

---

[25] See Å. Sjöberg, *Der Mondgott Nanna-Suen* (Uppsala, 1960), 144-46.
[26] Thus O. E. Ravn, *ZDMG*, 91 (1937), 358ff.
[27] H. W. Wolff, *EvTh*, 24 (1964), 73ff.
[28] S. Lehming, *ZAW*, 70 (1958), 228ff.; A. de Pury, *RB*, 76 (1969), 5ff.

(an allusion to 2 S. 7:23) [29] with one king, "my servant David," "one shepherd for all of them." The *ro'eh 'echadh,* "one shepherd," of Ezk. 34:23 (again, "my servant David") is to be understood as a reflection of the theme of unity in Ezk. 37:15-28 (cf. the plural in the prototype in Jer. 23:4). [30] This external unity will be matched by an internal unity: Jer. 32:39, *lebh 'echadh vedherekh 'echadh,* "one heart and one way" (on the other hand, we must read *'acher* with the LXX in Ezk. 11:19). The Chronicler puts these statements about the future back into the idealized past: 1 Ch. 12:38f.; 2 Ch. 30:12.

c. Out of the *Jerusalem cult tradition* of the rule of the God of Zion was also developed the motif of the unity of creation which originated in Zion: Zeph. 3:9–the peoples (this should not be emended to *'ammi,* "my people") [31] serve Yahweh *shekhem 'echadh,* "shoulder to shoulder" = "with one accord"; Isa. 65:25–the wolf and the lamb feed *ke'echadh,* "together" (cf. Isa. 11:6, *yachdav,* "together"); Zec. 14:7–in the eschatological age, there will no longer be the differences of day and night as in this world, but there will be *yom 'echadh,* "one day" = "continuous day." [32] Zeph. 3:9 alludes to Gen. 11:1-9 (J) and Zec. 14:6-8 to Gen. 8:22 (J): thus, the End Time will be a restoration of the Primitive Age.

3. *Solitude As a Negative Factor.* When *'echadh* is used of the *individual* in contrast to several people or a group, it usually has a negative ring. In certain legal suits, the statement of one witness is not considered to be sufficient evidence: Nu. 35:30; Dt. 17:6; 19:15. Only one of the twelve tribes remains to the house of David (1 K. 11:13,32,36). Eccl. 4:7-12 deals with the theme of "the solitary man," partly in typical Koheleth wording and partly in traditional sayings. [33]

4. *Equality of Fate.* In Ex. 12:49; Nu. 9:14; 15:15; 16:22; Est. 4:11, *'echadh* is used to express the *equality of everyone* before the law in certain areas. Ezk. 48 uses this word as a leitmotiv to speak of the equality of all the tribes of Israel in the hereditary portion which they could expect to receive after the return from the exile. Negatively, the theme of the equality of everyone is found as a statement on human existence in Ecclesiastes. All men have *miqreh 'echadh,* "one fate," and *ruach 'echadh,* "the same breath" (3:19-21), for they all go to "one place" (3:20; 6:6), i.e., the Underworld. Ultimately, all the toil of man is for its mouth (6:7). [34] Therefore, everything is *hebhel,* "vanity" (2:15,17; 3:19; 6:4,9). Only one thing remains for man to do: to enjoy life now (2:24; 3:22; 9:7-10). This line of reasoning is also well documented from Egyptian and Mesopotamian literature.

---

[29] See III.1.a.
[30] W. Zimmerli, *BK,* XIII, 841, 917.
[31] Cf. G. Gerleman, *Zephanja* (1942), 58.
[32] See II.2 on Zec. 14:9.
[33] On parallels to Eccl. 4:12 in the Gilgamesh Epic, cf. B. Landsberger, *RA,* 62 (1968), 109.
[34] Cf. Ackroyd.

IV. Theologically Relevant Expressions Using 'echadh.   'echadh is one
element in certain *idioms* which are used in the OT in the context of theological
statements.

a. "As one man" can express the unity of Israel: Nu. 14:15 (of a united
effort to destroy a common foe); Jgs. 6:16; 20:1,8,11; 1 S. 11:7; 2 S. 19:15(14);
Ezr. 3:1; Neh. 8:1.

b. "With one voice" in Ex. 24:3 expresses the idea that all Israel was involved in making the covenant with Yahweh (cf. Ex. 19:8, *yachdav*, "together").

c. "Not one" is used to emphasize that a certain work which God has done
is complete: Ex. 8:27(31); 9:6,7; 10:19; 14:28; Josh. 23:14; Jgs. 4:16; 1 K. 8:56;
Ps. 34:21(20); 106:11.

d. "In one day" expresses the swiftness of Yahweh's acts: Isa. 9:13(14);
10:17; 47:9; 66:8; Zec. 3:9; 2 Ch. 28:6.

Lohfink/Bergman (II.1.a)

אַחֵר   *'achēr*

Contents: I. Occurrences, Meaning. II. The Expression "Other Gods."

I. Occurrences, Meaning. The word *'acher* occurs 161 times in the OT. Out
of these, it occurs 62 times in the expression *'elohim 'acherim,* "other gods,"
mainly in Deuteronomy and Jeremiah.
   'acher is a word which expresses relationship, and means "other, another"
in relationship to something that is mentioned earlier in the text or is assumed.
The type of relationship determines the exact meaning of the word. (a) The
relationship can be such that *'acher* adds something to what is mentioned
previously; here it can best be translated by "in addition, further, still," e.g.,
zera' 'acher, "another son" = "an additional son" (Gen. 4:25); *shibh'ath yamim
'acherim,* "seven additional days" (8:10,12); *'ohel 'acher,* "another tent" = "an
additional tent" (2 K. 7:8); *keli 'acher,* "an additional vessel" (Jer. 18:4); *megil-
lah 'achereth,* "an additional scroll, a further scroll" (36:28,32). This meaning
can be made emphatic by the addition of *'odh,* "yet, again, besides," or *yasaph,*
"to add," e.g., in Gen. 29:27,30; 30:24; 37:9. (b) *'acher* is also used when something mentioned or used earlier is replaced. Thus e.g., *beghadhim 'acherim*
(Lev. 6:4 [Eng. v. 11]; 1 S. 28:8; Ezk. 42:14; 44:19) means "other garments,"

'achēr. Fr. J. Helfmeyer, *Die Nachfolge Gottes im AT. BBB,* 29 (1968), 130-182; C. Lind-
hagen, *The Servant Motif in the OT* (Uppsala, 1950), 120-142.

i.e., "different" from those used earlier; *keseph 'acher* (Gen. 43:22) means "other (different) money," as a substitute for that which had been mentioned previously. (c) With the definite article, *'acher* expresses a direct relationship to the first, and then "other" is to be taken in the sense of "second": *chatser ha'achereth*, "the second outer court" (1 K. 7:8); *hakkanaph ha'achereth*, "the other, second wing" (2 Ch. 3:12); in expressions of time, it assumes the meaning of "following, next," e.g., *bashshanah ha'achereth*, "in the following, next year" (Gen. 17:21); *bayyom ha'acher*, "on the following day" (2 K. 6:29). In expressions of time without the definite article, it means "future, coming," e.g., *dor 'acher*, "a future, coming generation" (Jgs. 2:10; Joel 1:3). (d) In some cases, *'acher* is used of something that is different: *ruach 'achereth*, "another (i.e., different) spirit" (Nu. 14:24); *'ish 'acher* is a man who is different and who behaves differently (1 S. 10:6); *lebh 'acher* means "a different heart" (10:9). When the difference is viewed negatively, *'acher* is synonymous with "foreign": *belashon 'achereth*, "with another tongue," i.e., in a foreign language (Isa. 28:11); *le'am 'acher*, "to a foreign people" (Dt. 28:32); *ben 'ishshah 'achereth*, "the son of a foreign woman (wife)" (Jgs. 11:2).

II. The Expression "Other Gods." The expression *'elohim 'acherim*, "other gods," is found in texts that are dominated by the idea of the covenant, especially in Deuteronomy (18 times), Jeremiah (18 times), and in texts like Josh. 23f. (3 times) and 2 K. 17 (4 times).

In this expression, *'acher* means first of all "additional," as is also indicated by the basic commandment: "You shall have no other (additional) gods besides me" (Ex. 20:3; Dt. 5:7). Thus, *'elohim 'acherim* includes all imaginable gods which Israel might possibly worship. But sometimes the nuances "different" and "foreign" are also present when a text speaks of "other gods," in other words, of gods which are foreign to Israel's covenant relationship with Yahweh. In three passages (Dt. 31:18,16; Josh. 24:2,23; Jgs. 10:13,16), *'elohim 'acherim* is clearly synonymous with *'elohe hannekhar*, "the foreign gods"; here "foreign" is not to be understood in an exclusively national (=alien) sense. In 1 S. 7:3f., the *be'alim* and the *'ashtaroth* ("the Baals and the Ashtaroth") are mentioned as examples of the *'elohe hannekhar*, "foreign gods." On the other hand, *'el zar* (Ps. 44:21[20]; 81:10[9]) seems to mean only "alien" gods.

'abhadh 'elohim 'acherim, "to serve other gods," is the most common expression in the OT for the idolatry of the nations. It occurs 34 times in the OT with Israel as the subject of "serve." Frequently the illegitimate *'ebhedh*, "service," of Israel is connected with *hishtachavah le*, "to bow down to (before)," which designates bowing down before the image of a god in the cult. [1] We also often find *halakh 'achare*, "to go (walk) after," with the foreign gods as the object. Originally, this expression could have referred to the worshippers actually going or walking after the image of the god in a cultic procession, but in the OT it is used as a more general term for the worship of idols. [2]

---

[1] Cf. Zimmerli, *ThB*, 19 (1963), 237ff.

[2] Cf. Helfmeyer, 130-151; → אחרי *achⁿrê*.

Other verbs which are used with 'elohim 'acherim, "other gods," are panah, "to turn to other gods" (Dt. 30:17; 31:18,20); hizkir beshem, "to mention the names of other gods in the cult" (Ex. 23:13; Josh. 23:7); yare', "to fear other gods" (2 K. 17:35,37f.); zanah, "to play the harlot after other gods" (Jgs. 2:17; cf. Ex. 34:15f.; Dt. 31:16). In this connection, the last verb assumes the marriage symbolism used for the covenant: the worship of other gods indicates that Israel has not been true to the marital fidelity which is demanded by the jealous God ('el qanna'), and therefore is harlotry.

Parallel to expressions which are used for the worship of other gods, frequently there are expressions which describe the consequences of idolatry for a person's relationship to Yahweh and his covenant. When someone serves other gods, he forgets (shakhach) Yahweh (Dt. 8:19; Jgs. 3:7), turns aside from following him (shubh me'achare, 1 K. 9:6; Josh. 22:16), forsakes ('azabh, Dt. 29:24f.[25f.]; Jer. 22:9), transgresses ('abhar, Dt. 17:2f.; Josh. 23:16), breaks (hephar, hiphil of parar, Gen. 17:14; Dt. 31:16,20; Jer. 11:10), or despises (ma'as, 2 K. 17:15f.) the covenant. [3]

All these expressions belong to the covenant concept. The prohibition against serving other gods assumes the covenant: Yahweh delivered Israel out of Egypt and by making the covenant with them made them a people for his own possession ('am seghullah) and a people holy to him ('am ... qadhosh leyhvh) (Ex. 19:5f.; Dt. 7:6). The existence of the people wholly depends on Yahweh; thus he has an exclusive claim on their loyalty and worship.

When Israel serves other gods, they break this covenant which was made after the deliverance from Egypt (Dt. 29:25ff.[26ff.]; 31:20). The consequence they must suffer is a curse and death (Dt. 30:19); therefore, the non-Yahwistic cult must be destroyed with all its symbols (Dt. 7:5), and anyone who gives himself to idolatry must be punished by stoning him to death (Dt. 13:6ff.[5ff.]; 17:2ff.). It is also consistent with this concept when 2 K. 17 interprets the fall of the northern kingdom as being because the people of Israel feared other gods (v. 7), lived according to the customs of the Canaanites, and served idols (vv. 8,12). The one covenant God excludes the "other gods"; they are incompatible with him and with his covenant.

Erlandsson

---

[3] Cf. the synonyms of "following gods" in Helfmeyer, 152-182.

אַחֲרֵי 'achᵃrê

Contents: I. Secular Use: 1. Temporal Meaning; 2. Exclusively Local Meaning; 3. Local Meaning Indicating a Relationship; 4. Origin. II. Theological Use: 1. Scope; 2. Other Idioms Synonymous with *halakh 'achare;* 3. Following Other Gods; 4. Origin; 5. Following and Imitating.

I. Secular Use.

1. *Temporal Meaning.* The preposition *'achar* is used to express a temporal succession without implying any concrete relationship between what comes first and what follows (Gen. 9:28; 10:1,32; Lev. 14:43; Nu. 6:19; Jer. 40:1; Hos. 3:5; etc.). One exception to this is the phrase *zeraʿ 'achare,* which expresses a relationship between an ancestor of a tribe or clan and his descendants which goes beyond the exclusively natural and temporal succession. This phrase appears predominantly in covenantal texts which deal with the divine covenant with Noah, Abraham, and David (Gen. 9:9; 17:7,9,10,19; 35:12; 48:4; Dt. 1:8; 2 S. 7:12 = 1 Ch. 17:11). Here, temporal succession establishes not only a blood relationship, but a sort of shared destiny, in which the rights and obligations of the predecessor are transmitted to his successors.

2. *Exclusively Local Meaning.* Without a more precise statement of the relationship between what precedes and what follows, *'achare* refers to spatial sequence (Gen. 37:17; 1 S. 17:35; 2 K. 4:30; 2 Ch. 26:17; Ezk. 9:5; Ruth 2:9; etc.). In military contexts, one army follows after another (Ex. 14:23,28; 1 K. 20:19); in a round dance (Ex. 15:20), a religious procession (Neh. 12:38; Ps. 68:26 [Eng. v. 25]), and a funeral procession (2 S. 3:31), the participants follow "after" one another.

3. *Local Meaning Indicating a Relationship.* Various relationships are indicated by *'achare* in conjunction with *halakh,* "to go, walk," etc.: the relationship between a servant and his master (Isa. 45:14; Ps. 45:15 [14]; 49:18 [17]), between an army and its commander-in-chief (Jgs. 3:28; 4:14; 9:4; 1 S. 11:7; 17:13f.; 25:13), between a supporter and the cause or person he supports (Ex. 23:2; 2 S. 2:10; 15:13; 20:2,11,13,14; 1 K. 1:35,40; 2:28; 12:20; 16:21f.;

'achᵃrê. M. Buber, "Nachahmung Gottes," *Werke,* II (1964), 1053-1065; E. G. Gulin, "Die Nachfolge Gottes," *Festschrift K. Tallquist. StOr,* 1 (1925), 34-50; F. J. Helfmeyer, *Die Nachfolge Gottes im AT. BBB,* 29 (1968); *idem,* "'Gott nachfolgen' in den Qumrantexten," *RevQ,* 7 (1969), 81-104; G. Kittel, "ἀκολουθέω," *TDNT,* I, 210-16; H. Kosmala, "Nachfolge und Nachahmung Gottes II: im jüdischen Denken," *ASTI,* 3 (1964), 65-110; J. M. Nielen, "Die Kultsprache (Nachfolge und Nachahmung) im neutestamentlichen Schrifttum," *BiLe,* 6 (1965), 1-16; H. J. Schoeps, "Von der imitatio Dei zur Nachfolge Christi," *Aus früh-christlicher Zeit* (1950), 286-301; A. Schulz, *Nachfolgen und Nachahmen. StANT,* 6 (1962).

2 K. 9:18f.; 11:15; 2 Ch. 11:16; Ps. 94:15), between a disciple and his master (1 K. 19:20f.), and between a wife and her husband (Gen. 24:5,8,39,61; 1 S. 25:42; Ruth 3:10; Cant. 1:4). What is involved in all these instances is a relationship involving dependence or possession, in which those who follow owe obedience to those whom they follow. This meaning of 'achare can also be ascertained in pertinent ancient Near Eastern texts which use alāku (w)arki[1] to designate the same relationships.[2]

4. *Origin.* The concept of "following" appears in the "army-commander-in-chief" relationship especially in war sermons, whose setting is in the institution of the Yahweh war.[3] The elements which may be observed in these sermons, viz., the formula for commanding the army to set forth (Jgs. 3:28; 4:7,14), the statement that Yahweh goes out before the tribes in battle (4:14), and that the fear of Yahweh falls on the enemy (4:15), reappear in texts dealing with the idea of "following" in the wars of Yahweh.

(*halakh*) '*achare,* "to go (walk) after," is used in historical narratives which are based on court annals, in the sense of aligning oneself with a certain party, political loyalty, and political affiliation. This comports with the use of corresponding expressions in the Amarna Letters, the annals of Mursilis,[4] and Hittite international treaties.[5] In this context, the notion takes on an official character. Therefore, its setting is official language, where it was used to describe clearly defined political events and to designate relationships involved in international law.

II. Theological Use.

1. *Scope.* The nature of the relationships designated by '*achare,* especially those between an army and its commander-in-chief and between a supporter and the person he supports, provides the foundation for transferring this term to the theological realm.

Dt. 13:5(4); 1 K. 14:8; 18:21; 2 K. 23:3; 2 Ch. 34:31; Jer. 2:2; and Hos. 11:10 speak of following after Yahweh (*halakh* '*achare yhvh*). The idea of following Yahweh is in harmony with Yahweh's possession of Israel, which is based on or expressed by the election of Israel (Dt. 13:5[4]; on Jer. 2:2, cf. 2:3), the exodus from Egypt (Dt. 13:5[4]), the covenant (2 K. 23:3 = 2 Ch. 34:31; Jer. 2:2), and the fulfilment of a sign which had been announced (1 K. 18:21). The exclusive-

---

[1] *AHw,* 32, sub. 12; *CAD,* I, 320.

[2] CH § 135, Lex Ešnunna in A. Götze, *AASOR,* 31 (1956), § 59; EA 136, 11; 191, 15f.; cf. Ugar. '*ḥr mġy 'lȝyn b'l,* "afterward came Aliyan Baal," in the Baal-'Anat Myth, *CTA,* 4 [II AB], III, 23f., etc.

[3] G. von Rad, *Der Heilige Krieg im alten Israel* (⁴1965); R. Smend, *Yahweh War and Tribal Confederation* (trans. 1970).

[4] A. Götze, *MVÄG,* 38/6 (1933), 58:28f.; 68:16-18.

[5] J. Friedrich, *MVÄG,* 31/1 (1926), 122:8.

ness of this following after Yahweh is expressed by describing it as following "with undivided heart" (1 K. 14:8), by contrasting it with the worship of other gods (1 K. 14:8; 18:21; context of 2 K. 23:3; context of Hos. 11:10), and by its opposition to any form of syncretism (esp. in 1 K. 18:21). Thus, a certain polemical, militant emphasis characterizes this term.

2. *Other Idioms Synonymous with halakh 'achare.* The meaning which we have ascertained for *halakh 'achare* also attaches to the expressions *hayah 'achare* (1 S. 12:14: exclusive worship of Yahweh based on the reference to the *tsidhqoth yhvh,* 12:7ff.), *mille' 'achare* ("to perform or carry out something while following Yahweh," Nu. 14:24; 32:12; Dt. 1:36; Josh. 14:8f.,14; Sir. 46:6,10: "following" here expresses the trust of Caleb and Joshua in Yahweh's promise; 1 K. 11:6: here "following" expresses the exclusive recognition of Yahweh), and *dabhaq 'achare* (Ps. 63:9[8]: "following" here means recognition of Yahweh's proprietary rights over Israel on the basis of Israel's election).

3. *Following Other Gods.* In contrast to the concept of "following" Yahweh, the OT speaks of "following" other gods (Dt. 4:3; 6:14; etc.),[6] expressed primarily through the cultic worship. This amounts to a violation of the demand to worship Yahweh alone which is connected with the first commandment, and to a violation of Yahweh's proprietary rights over Israel by virtue of the covenant. In this light, we can understand the polemic against following other gods in which the terminology and jurisdiction connected with the Yahweh war has been transferred to the battle against the other gods and their worship (→ אחר *'achēr*).

4. *Origin.* The elements of the Yahweh war in the context of the terminology of "following" in particular suggest that the theological use of this idea originated in the relationship between an army and its commander-in-chief. If so, this term is related to the divine titles *yhvh tsebhaoth,* "the Lord (Yahweh) of hosts," and *melekh,* "king," which in turn are closely connected with the ark of the covenant. Thus, originally to "follow" Yahweh may have meant to follow the ark as a symbol of leadership, palladium of war, Yahweh's throne, and processional shrine. That the tables of the law were kept in the ark may have been the reason that following Yahweh became linked with fulfilling the law, although here the focus is on Yahweh's proprietary relationship toward Israel.

It is most likely that Levitical circles are responsible for the terminology of following Yahweh, because it is quite prominent in Deuteronomic/Deuteronomistic literature, a warlike spirit is typical of these circles, and they prefer to use the parenetic diction to which this idiom belongs.

---

[6] For an exhaustive list of the passages, cf. Helfmeyer, 131-152.

5. *Following and Imitating.* Only scanty connections between following and imitating can be established in the OT. They are to be sought in particular in terminology of the "way," to which the concept of following also belongs. "To go (walk) in the way of someone" means "to imitate that person's actions," "to act like him." [7]

The meaning of "following" in the sense of "imitating" (albeit merely cultic "imitating," in the framework of worshipping other gods) is suggested by Lev. 20:2ff. (*zanah 'achare,* "to play the harlot after"); Dt. 4:3 together with Hos. 9:10; Dt. 12:30; 2 K. 17:15a; Jer. 2:5; and Isa. 66:17. There is no passage in the OT that speaks of imitating Yahweh.

It is true that the demand for holiness (Lev. 19:2), and the motivation of commandments that deal primarily with social ethics and refer to the corresponding "exemplary" acts of God (Dt. 10:18f.; 15:15; etc.), supply substantial (but not terminological) points of contact with "imitating" Yahweh, but they are not connected with the concept of following him.

Helfmeyer

---

[7] F. Nötscher, *Gotteswege und Menschenwege in der Bibel und in Qumran. BBB,* 15 (1958), 43.

אַחֲרִית 'achªrîth

Contents: I. The Word. II. 1. Temporal "After"; 2. Logical "After"; 3. Future; 4. Posterity, Remnant; 5. End. III. "End of the Days": 1. Some Future Time; 2. The End Time.

I. The Word. *'acharith* is derived from *'achar,* "later, afterwards" (as *she'erith* is derived from *she'ar,* and *re'shith* from *ro'sh*).[1] It is an abstract noun, which it is best to translate neutrally by "that which comes after,"[2] and not by "end, result,"[3] which can be shown to be derived meanings. Without further modification, *'acharith* is what makes up that which comes after, as well as what results from a thing, a way, etc. From this general meaning come such modified meanings as "future, posterity, remnant, end," and "the last" (but not "back part").[4] Sometimes the context has to determine the meaning of *'acharith;* by itself its meaning cannot be defined precisely. It has many shades of meaning, and occasionally scholars cannot agree on its exact meaning in a certain passage. Since there is nothing with which to compare this word and its usage in ancient Near Eastern literature, it is best to begin with those occurrences in the OT where its meaning is clear.

---

[1] *BLe,* § 61m'.
[2] Cf. W. Zimmerli, *BK,* XIII, on Ezk. 23:25.
[3] So recently *KBL³*.
[4] See below, 4.

II. 1. *Temporal "After."* Passages like Dt. 8:16; Job 42:12; Prov. 29:21; and Sir. 38:20 demonstrate the original meaning of *'acharith*. Dt. 8:16 speaks of Yahweh, "who fed you in the wilderness with manna ... that he might humble you and test you, to do you good in that which came after." *'acharith* is the time after the wilderness period, not the end (result). Similarly, Job 42:12 states: "The Lord blessed that which came after for Job more than his beginning ... (v. 16) and after this Job lived a hundred and forty years, and saw his sons, and his sons' sons, four generations." *'acharith* is the (long) period after the testing. As in Dt. 8, it assumes a decisive change of relationship. So also Sir. 38:20: "Do not give your heart to it (i.e., death); drive it away, remembering that which comes after." Prov. 29:21 shows the transition to that which comes after as a logical consequence of earlier conditions: "He who pampers his servant from childhood will afterwards be miserable because of him." At the moment when the master needs his servant, he is not there to serve him.

2. *Logical "After."* Often *'acharith* means "after" in the logical sense.[5] Prov. 23:32 says that the after-effects (*'acharith*) of wine bite like a serpent. The after-effects of sleeping with a loose (strange) woman are bitter as wormwood (5:4). Afterwards, a man will groan because she consumed all of his possessions. Similarly, Prov. 20:21 says: "An inheritance gotten hastily in the beginning will *'acharith* (afterwards, in the end) not be blessed." Thus it is considered to be axiomatic that (14:12 = 16:25): "there is a way which seems right to a man, but its *'acharith* are ways of death." Jer. 5:31 says concerning the fate of the people: "the prophets prophesy falsely, and the priests rule at their direction; my people love to have it so, but what will you do in view of the consequences (*le'acharithah*)?"

Lam. 1:9 and Isa. 47:7 use *'acharith* in a similar sense. These texts shed light on the meaning of the debated passage, Jer. 12:4. With Baumgartner,[6] I would leave v. 4a as it is, but read v. 4b as a continuation of v. 4a (we should not read *'orchothenu,* "our ways," with the LXX, for in this case v. 4b would have to be transferred to another place). This gives the following meaning: during a drought (v. 4a), Jeremiah complains to Yahweh that he has made the wicked prosper (vv. 1,2). The people should despise this, but they do not—herein lies their wickedness (v. 4a). But the reason for their wickedness is that they think: Yahweh does not care what happens to us (*'acharithenu*), while the wicked increase (v. 4b). Thus to be sure, the drought comes because of the wickedness of the inhabitants of the land; but Yahweh could prevent this wickedness by not blessing the wicked.[7]

3. *Future.* In some texts, *'acharith* means the same thing as future. "Let not your heart envy sinners, but continue in the fear of the Lord all the day.

---

[5] See also 5!
[6] W. Baumgartner, *Die Klagegedichte Jer.* (1917), *in loc.*
[7] Contra Reventlow, *Liturgie* (1963), 241ff.

Surely there is a *future,* and your hope will not be cut off" (Prov. 23:17f.); so similarly 24:14. We may add to this Isa. 46:9f.: "remember the former things of old; for ... there is none like me, declaring the future (end) from the beginning and from ancient times things not yet done..." (in Isa. 41:22, *'acharonoth,* "the last things" [?], with 1QIsᵃ). Jer. 29:11 says clearly: "I know the plans I have for you ..., plans for *shalom* (welfare) and not for evil, to give you a future and a hope." But here again (as in 2. above), the uncertainty of the original meaning is made clear by the different shades of meaning which *'acharith* reflects. Thus, it cannot be determined with certainty whether it is better to translate it by "future" or "posterity" in Ps. 37:37; and even more perplexing is the use of *'acharith* in v. 38 (future, posterity, remnant?): "But transgressors (against Yahweh) shall be altogether destroyed; the *'acharith* of the wicked shall be cut off."

4. *Posterity, Remnant.* Thus "after(wards)" contains two other nuances: posterity and remnant. Clear examples of the meaning "posterity" are probably to be found in Ps. 109:13; Dnl. 11:4; Sir. 16:3. [8]

Ps. 109:13 says, "May his *'acharith* be cut off; may his (!) name be blotted out in the second generation." The context (vv. 9-12) speaks of the gradual rooting out of the sons of the accursed, but not of their death, so that presuppositions for the meaning "remnant" are not present, while the meaning "future" is excluded by the plural suffix in v. 13b. According to the reconstructed LXX prototype, Sir. 16:3 says: "Better is one (god-fearer) than a thousand, and to die childless than an *'acharith* of arrogance" (Heb., "than one who has many sons 'in contemptuousness' [read *bzlh*], and than an *'acharith* of arrogance"). Here *'acharith* cannot mean "end," but only "posterity," because an "end of arrogance" would be too subjective and insignificant in contrast to childlessness, which was a terrible condition for an Israelite. In light of this, the meaning of Dnl. 11:4 is probably also clear: "and when he has arisen, his kingdom shall be broken and divided toward the four winds of heaven, but not to his *'acharith.* ...." Finally, Ezk. 23:25a should be mentioned here. While the captive Oholibah will have her nose and ears cut off, "your *'acharith* shall fall by the sword." This parable is speaking of Oholibah and her children. [9]

Clear examples for the meaning "remnant" are to be found in Am. 9:1; Nu. 24:20; Am. 4:2; and Ezk. 23:25b. [10]

In a supplement to the Balaam Sagas, we read in Nu. 24:20: "Amalek was the first of the nations, but his *'acharith* shall come to destruction." [11] Since this saying is based on the contrast between *re'shith,* "first," and *'acharith, 'acharith* can only mean the scanty remnant that is left after the splendid beginning. Am. 4:2b says: "... they shall take you (cows of Bashan) away with hooks, and your

---

[8] Contra Rudolph, see below.
[9] Cf. Zimmerli, *BK, in loc.*
[10] On Am. 9:1, cf. H. Gese, *VT,* 12 (1962), 236f.
[11] Do not read *'abhodh* with M. Noth, *Numbers. OTL* (trans. 1968), *in loc.*

remnant with fishhooks." [12] The meaning "posterity," which Rudolph fundamentally opposes, does not fit here, since this saying is addressed exclusively
to the cows of Bashan. The translation "back part" is without any basis in the
text, [13] and cannot be derived from the original meaning of 'acharith. According
to Gese, [14] the remnant consisted of those who remained after the taking away.
Ezk. 23:25b (material survivors) is unique: "they shall seize your sons and your
daughters, but your 'acharith shall be devoured by fire." The meaning of 'acharith in Jer. 31:17 stands on the borderline between remnant and posterity: "there
is hope for your (Rachel's) 'acharith..., and your children shall come back to
their own country."

5. *End.* Finally, the "after(wards)" can end a transaction or an event. [15] In
this case, the reference is not to the chronological end, but to the outcome. [16]
Thus Prov. 25:8 warns: "do not hastily bring into court; for what will you do in
the end, when your neighbor puts you to shame?" The 'acharith of the four
world kingdoms of Dnl. 8 will be that evildoers prevail (v. 23). But of special
significance are sayings like: "a hard heart makes evil its end" (Sir. 3:26); "call
no one happy before his death; for in his *end* one understands man" (11:28);
"let me die the death of the righteous, and let my *end* be like his" (Nu.23:10).
'acharith has a similar meaning in Jer. 17:11; Job 8:13 (conjectural reading);
Prov. 1:19 (conjectural reading); cf. also Ps. 73:17f. and the text of Sir. 11:25
in the Hebrew: "the good of the day causes the evil to be forgotten and the
evil the good, and the *end* of a man comes over him." Dt. 32:20 transfers this
to the people: "I (Yahweh) will hide my face from them, I will see what their
end will be." 'acharith here is not the temporal end, but the judicial outcome
of the sin of the people (see also v. 29). Am. 8:10 conveys a similar thought:
when Yahweh turns feasts into mourning and songs into lamentation, *this* is
like the mourning for an only son, and its *outcome* like a gloomy day. Accordingly, the 'acharith of a year is its outcome (Dt. 11:12). In Dnl. 12:8, the seer
asks about the outcome of all the miracles which had been mentioned previously.
Eccl. 7:8 exalts the outcome of a thing above its beginning; cf. 10:13. Finally,
Ps. 139:9 is especially noteworthy: "if I take the wings of the morning and dwell
in the end of the sea...." The end of the sea is the west, i.e., not the edge of
the world, but that which belongs to it as its outermost (or uttermost) part.

III. "End of the Days."

1. *Some Future Time.* In the OT, 'acharith hayyamim, "end of the days,"
is common only in close connection with the preposition *be*, "at, in" (the situation is different in the Qumran literature). Translated literally, this expression

---

[12] For a detailed discussion of the arguments favoring this translation, cf. W. Rudolph,
KAT, XIII/2, comm. and textual criticism *in loc.*

[13] Rudolph: "pure imagination."

[14] Gese, *loc. cit.*

[15] See also 2.

[16] Cf. T. Boman, *Hebrew Thought Compared with Greek* (trans. 1960), 149.

means, "in the after(wards) of the days, in the following time"; cf. Akk. *ina aḫrāt ūmi*. [17] In Nu. 24:14 in particular it can be shown that the reference is to a limited future time. [18] Then, there is no reason to diverge from this meaning in Gen. 49:1; Dt. 4:30; and 31:29. [19] But in Jer. 49:39 also, the eschatological interpretation is not natural. [20] The best explanation of this verse seems to be that in the Persian Empire from the time of Darius I on, Elam blossomed forth again and thus its fate was changed. [21] Jer. 48:47 is missing in the LXX, perhaps because at the time this translation was made Moab no longer existed and its fate could no longer be changed. Although nothing is known with certainty about the postexilic history of Moab, it is better to interpret this passage in a noneschatological way with Rudolph than as an expectation of the end time, since there is hardly any evidence for this idea in Jeremiah. Jer. 23:20b = 30:24b stands on the borderline between future and eschaton. *be'acharith hayyamim*, "in the end of the days" ("in the latter days"), the people will understand that Yahweh's wrath has not turned back from bursting upon the head of the wicked. In my opinion, the noneschatological interpretation is more natural here.

2. *The End Time.* However, there are six passages which should be interpreted differently. Among them Isa. 2:2 = Mic. 4:1 are distinguished by their still not using the expression *be'acharith hayyamim* as an entirely technical term. On the other hand, it seems that the way it is used in Hos. 3:5 and Ezk. 38:16 opens the way for its development into a technical term, and in Dnl. 2:28 and 10:14 this development is complete. Thus, *be'acharith hayyamim* at the end of Hos. 3:5 is an obvious addition which locates the anticipated return of North Israel to Yahweh at the end of the days. This expression also clearly stands in an addition to Ezk. 38:16, which in turn is itself an addition to the original text: [22] "therefore, son of man, prophesy, and say to Gog (v. 14): ... you will come up against my people Israel, like a cloud covering the land. In the latter days I will bring you against my land, that the nations may know me, when through you, O Gog, I vindicate my holiness before their eyes" (v. 16). This expression is clearly used as a technical term in Dnl. 2:28 (Aramaic) and 10:14. In both passages the translation "future times" is possible, but it is not what the author intended. "(God in heaven) has made known to King Nebuchadnezzar what will be in the *'acharith* of the days" (2:28). The point of the vision does not lie in the course of future events, but in the destruction of the colossus and in the coming of an indestructible kingdom (v. 44). Thus the outcome of the future is what is intended, and not the future in general. Similarly, 10:14 says: "I (the angel that had appeared) came to make you understand what

---

[17] *AHw*, 21.

[18] M. Noth, *Numbers*, 192.; similarly on Ezk. 38:8, W. Zimmerli, *BK*, for the expression *'acharith hashshanim*.

[19] So correctly G. von Rad, *Genesis. OTL* (trans. 1961), 417.

[20] Rudolph, *HAT*, 12 (³1968), *in loc.*

[21] Cf. C. Rietzschel, *Problem der Urrolle* (1966), 77f., on the assumption that this passage is not genuine.

[22] Zimmerli, *BK, in loc.*

is to befall your people in (at) the 'acharith of the days. For the vision is for days yet to come." Since the following material deals with the stages of history from Cyrus to Antiochus IV, the meaning "future" cannot be excluded here; but the real purpose of the vision is to show how history will culminate, thus its outcome. Therefore, this passage has in mind the end, and not merely the future.

Seebass

אָיַב 'āyabh; אוֹיֵב 'ôyēbh; אֵיבָה 'ēbhāh

Contents: I. Use in the Ancient Near East: 1. Ugarit; 2. Mesopotamia; 3. Egypt. II. Use in the OT in General: 1. The Words; 2. 'oyebh, Meaning and Synonyms; 3. Theological Use; 4. Personal Enemies; 5. God As Enemy. III. The Problem of Enemies in the Psalms: 1. National Psalms and Royal Psalms; 2. Individual Psalms; 3. Present Status of the Debate.

I. Use in the Ancient Near East.

1. *Ugarit*. Outside of Hebrew, the root 'yb occurs in Ugarit (ʒb) and Akkadian (ayyābu); it also appears as a Canaanite gloss (ibi) in the Amarna Tablets (EA 129, 96; 252, 28). The Ugar. ʒb occurs sometimes in letters with reference to warlike situations,[1] and sometimes in mythological texts. The latter speak of the enemies of Baal: *CTA*, 2 [III AB], I, 8; *CTA*, 3 [V AB], III, 52, parallel to ṣrt, "enemy"; *CTA*, 4 [II AB], VII, 36, parallel to šnʒ, "hater"; *CTA*, 10 [IV AB], II, 24, parallel to qm, "foe." It is worthy of note that in this literature we find exactly the same synonyms of the root 'yb as we find in Hebrew.

2. *Mesopotamia*. The Akk. ayyābu appears in historical and religious texts as well as in letters, and designates personal and national foes. Frequently it is modified by *lemnu*, "evil," or connected with this word in the sense of "adversary": ayyābu ū lemnu. nakru, "enemy, hostile" (of persons as well as of lands

---

'āyabh. G. W. Anderson, "Enemies and Evildoers in the Book of Psalms," *BJRL*, 48 (1965/66), 18-29; E. Balla, *Das Ich der Psalmen. FRLANT*, 16 (1912); H. Birkeland, *Die Feinde des Individuums in der israelitischen Psalmenliteratur* (Oslo, 1933); *idem, The Evildoers in the Psalms. ANVAO 1955*, 2; H. Gunkel-J. Begrich, *Einl. in die Psalmen. GHK,* suppl. vol. (1933); S. Mowinckel, *Psalmenstudien*, I, *Åwän und die individuellen Klagepsalmen. SNVAO* (1921), 4; *idem, The Psalms in Israel's Worship* (Oxford, 1962); H. Ringgren, *The Faith of the Psalmists* (Philadelphia, 1963); G. Widengren, *The Accadian and Hebrew Psalms of Lamentation as Religious Documents* (Uppsala, 1936); further literature in O. Keel, *Feinde und Gottesleugner. SBM*, 7 (1969), 234-245.

On I: E. Hornung, *Geschichte als Fest* (1966); R. Labat, *Le caractère religieux de la royauté assyro-babylonienne* (Paris, 1939); E. Otto, *Gott und Mensch nach den äg. Tempelinschriften der griech.-röm. Zeit. AHAW*, 1 (1964); Seux; J. Zandee, *Death as an Enemy. SNumen*, 5 (Leiden, 1960).

[1] *UT*, 1012, 10,17,29; 2060, 31.

and nations) or *zā'iru,* "enemy," in particular are used as synonyms of *ayyābu.* *raggu,* "evil," is used like *lemnu,* while adjectives like *damqu, ṭābu,* "good," occur frequently as antitheses to these.

Of theological interest are instances in which the king boasts of having destroyed the enemies of the land in obedience to the command of the gods.[2] In these instances, either a general word or the name of the hostile nation may be used. A group of royal epithets refers to this function of the king,[3] e.g., *kāšid ayyābēšu,* "the one who conquers his enemies";[4] *mukabbis kišād ayyābēšu,* "the one who tramples upon the neck of his enemies";[5] *mušamqit māt nakiriši,* "the one who overcomes the land of his enemies";[6] etc. In the Psalms of Lament, the enemies could be national foes, personal adversaries, sorcerers, or demons; but their work is often described in such general terms that it is difficult or even impossible to determine their identity exactly.[7]

3. *Egypt.* In Egyptian, the most common word for "enemy," both personal and national, is *ḫfty,* literally, "the one who is against one"; but especially in late texts a whole group of synonymous expressions also appears. Of religious interest here also are references to the king as conqueror of enemies, especially because in this role he acts as a god and like the creator god casts down his enemies alone (the battle at Kadesh).[8] As representative of the god, he maintains the order of the world (*ma'at*) in this way.[9] The destruction of the enemies is also carried out cultically.[10] "The Egyptians make no fundamental distinction between mythical enemies of the gods and earthly enemies, i.e., political and criminal evildoers; both are simply 'enemies' in their language."[11] In temple inscriptions of the late period, more emphasis is placed on religion and ethics, so that the enemies are mainly "the evildoers," "the violent ones," etc.[12] The king is above all destroyer of *isf.t,* "sin, falsehood."[13] "Also quite often the old designations for 'enemies' of God or of the king are present—*bṯnw, ḫ3kw-ib, rkyw* ... the extent to which they have been transferred from a mythical plane to a genuinely religious one remains an open question."[14]

The numerous passages in the funerary texts that speak of the enemies of the dead are of an entirely different type.[15] Here in the main the enemies are demons

---

2 Labat, 253ff.
3 Seux, 24.
4 *Ibid.,* 137f.
5 *Ibid.,* 123.
6 *Ibid.,* 158.
7 Widengren, 233ff.; cf. Mowinckel, 81ff.; Birkeland, *Feinde,* 350ff.
8 Erman, *Literature of the Ancient Egyptians* (trans. 1927), 261-270; Hornung, 146.
→ אֶחָד *'echadh.*
9 Hornung, 18.
10 *Ibid.,* 17.
11 *Ibid.*
12 Otto, 24f., 36f.
13 *Ibid.,* 83ff.
14 *Ibid.,* 45.
15 Zandee, 217ff.

or hostile gods which are also enemies of Osiris or of the sun god, and want to inflict injury on the dead in different ways.

II. Use in the OT in General.

1. *The Words.* In Hebrew the verb *'ayabh,* "to be an enemy to," occurs once (Ex. 23:22, "I will be an enemy to your enemies and an adversary to your adversaries"); also the participle has a verbal function in 1 S. 18:29: "Saul was David's enemy (*vayehi sha'ul 'oyebh 'eth davidh*) continually." In all other cases *'oyebh* is a substantive, "enemy." Besides, the noun *'ebhah,* "enmity," occurs five times: Gen. 3:15 (between the woman and the serpent); Ezk. 25:15; 35:5 (the Philistines or the Edomites against Israel); Nu. 35:21f. (deathblow with or without hostile intent).

2. *'oyebh, Meaning and Synonyms.* *'oyebh* is either a personal enemy (as e.g., Saul and David, 1 S. 18:29; 19:17; 24:5,20 [Eng. vv. 4,19]; Elijah in the opinion of Ahab, 1 K. 21:20; Ish-bosheth and David, 2 S. 4:8) or an enemy nation which shows aggression against God's chosen people, as in the vast majority of cases. In this latter instance, an individual as leader of the enemy nation can also be designated as *'oyebh* of the whole nation ("Samson our enemy," Jgs. 16:23f.; Haman, Est. 7:6). One's own people, or the hero of the narrative, are never called *'oyebh;* the enemy is always the assailant coming from without. Thus, the OT often says that Israel fights against her enemies, but never refers to Israel herself as an *'oyebh.* Naturally, in historical texts the enemies of Israel are usually mentioned by name; the indefinite use of *'oyebh* usually appears in sections which have general formulas, as in parenetic passages of Deuteronomy, in the concluding section of H, in Solomon's prayer at the dedication of the temple (1 K. 8:33,44), and in Lamentations and Psalms. Sometimes God appears as enemy of his people. [16] Men are also called enemies of God in 1 S. 30:26; 2 S. 12:14; Nah. 1:2. The first two of these verses also have in mind Israel's enemies. Job says in 13:24 and 33:10 (quoted by Elihu) that God treats him like an enemy.

The following words are to a greater or lesser degree synonymous parallels to *'oyebh: ṣrr* (*tsorer, tsar*), literally "oppressor" (or simply "enemy") [17] (Ex. 23:22; Nu. 10:9; Dt. 32:27; Isa. 1:24; 9:10[11]; 59:18; Mic. 5:8[9]; Ps. 27:2; 74:10; 81:15[14]; 89:23f.,43[22f.,42]; Lam. 1:5; 2:4; 4:12; Est. 7:6); *śn'* (*sone', mesanne'*), "one who hates" (Ex. 23:4f.; Dt. 30:7 [with *rdp,* "persecutor"]; Ps. 18:18,41[17,40]; 21:9[8]; 35:19; 38:20[19]; 69:5[4]; 83:3[2]; 89:23f.[22f.]; 106:10); forms of *qwm,* "to rise up against": *qam,* Ps. 18:49(48); *mithqomem,* Job 27:7; Ps. 59:2(1); *qum 'al,* Dt. 28:7; 2 S. 18:31 (cf. v. 19); *mithnaqqem,* "avenger," Ps. 8:3(2); 44:17(16). *bene nekhar,* "foreigners," in Isa. 62:8 is also interesting. The parallel expressions *nilcham be,* "to fight against" (Isa. 63:10, of God), and *mebhaqqesh ra'ah,* "to seek someone's harm" (Nu. 35:23; cf.

---

[16] See below, II.5.
[17] *KBL*².

yachshebu ra'ah li, "to imagine the worst for someone," Ps. 41:6,8[5,7]), sound almost like a definition of *'oyebh*. *'ohebh*, "friend" (Jgs. 5:31), *'alluph meyudda'*, "familiar (intimate) friend" (Ps. 55:14[13]), and *rea'*, "neighbor" (Lam. 1:2), appear in antithesis to *'oyebh*.

The meaning of *'oyebh* can be determined further by analyzing the verbs which describe the work of the *'oyebh*, e.g., *hetsiq*, "to oppress" (Dt. 28:53,55,57), *tsarar*, "to oppress" or "be hostile to" (1 K. 8:37, etc.), *naghaph*, "to smite, strike" (Lev. 26:17; Nu. 14:42; Dt. 1:42; 1 K. 8:33 = 2 Ch. 6:24), *nakhah*, hiphil "to smite" (Jer. 30:14), *radhaph*, "to pursue, persecute" (Hos. 8:3; Ps. 31:16[15]; 143:3), *baghadh*, "to deal treacherously with, deceive" (Lam. 1:2). Furthermore, the proud behavior of the enemies is often mentioned: they exalt themselves (Ps. 13:3[2]), make themselves great (Lam. 1:9), scoff and revile (Ps. 74:10,18; Lam. 1:21; Ezk. 36:2), they rejoice (Lam. 2:17), open wide their mouths, i.e., rail (2:16; 3:46), gnash with their teeth (2:16), etc.

3. *Theological Use*. From a theological point of view (esp. in the Deuteronomistic history) the attacks of enemies on Israel are manifestations of divine punishment for Israel's apostasy. God gives the Israelites into the hand of their enemies (Jer. 21:7; 34:20f.); they will be smitten by their enemies (Dt. 1:42; 1 K. 8:33); they must even go into the land of their enemies (1 K. 8:46), and serve their enemy in his land (Jer. 17:4).

On the other hand, Yahweh can fight for Israel and thrust out her enemies (Dt. 6:19; 33:27). The passage concerning the ark in Nu. 10:35 states that when God arises, his enemies are scattered (cf. Ps. 68:2[1]). Several passages in the OT speak of the vengeance of Israel or of God on their enemies (Josh. 10:13; Jgs. 11:36; 1 S. 14:24; 18:25; Isa. 1:24). God saves (*yasha'*, *hitstsil*) his people from their enemies (Jgs. 2:18; 8:34; 1 S. 12:10; 2 S. 3:18; 22:1; 2 K. 17:39; cf. also Nu. 10:9). At some future time, he will bring back the scattered Israelites from the land of their enemies (Jer. 31:16; Ezk. 39:27). According to the Deuteronomistic point of view, the ideal is for Israel to have rest (→ מנוחה *menûchāh*) from her enemies (Dt. 12:10; 25:19; Josh. 23:1; 2 S. 7:1,11; cf. 1 Ch. 22:9).

4. *Personal Enemies*. Some passages speak of one's relationship to personal enemies. If the ox or ass of a person's enemy goes astray or is weary, he shall help it (Ex. 23:4f.). The instructions concerning killing in Nu. 35:16-34 make a distinction between killing with a hostile intention ("in order to do him *ra'ah* [harm]," parallel to "out of hate" or "in enmity," *sin'ah*, vv. 20f.) and without such an intention, "without enmity" or "though he was not his enemy" (*vehu' lo' 'oyebh lo*, vv. 22f.). Prov. 24:17 says: "Do not rejoice when your enemy falls," but this saying is rather unique in the OT.

5. *God As Enemy*. The enemies of Israel are also the enemies of Israel's God (1 S. 30:26; 2 S. 12:14); Yahweh intervenes to fight them. Accordingly, God promise Israel in Ex. 23:22 that if they hearken to him he will be an enemy to their enemies and an adversary to their adversaries.

It is unprecedented when in Lam. 2:4f. God is accused of appearing as an enemy against his people: "he has bent his bow like an enemy ... and put to death like a foe ... Yahweh has become like an enemy, he has destroyed Israel." Similarly, Trito-Isaiah says that God has become Israel's enemy because of the disobedience of the people (Isa. 63:10).

III. The Problem of Enemies in the Psalms. A somewhat different picture, or at least a much more complex picture, appears in the Psalms. Here, especially in the Songs of Lamentation and of Thanksgiving, there are references to enemies in which a psalmist laments the work of the enemies or gives thanks to God for their defeat. In psalms where the nation is the subject, it is natural to think that the enemies are external, national enemies, while in Individual Psalms the identification of the enemies is very difficult to determine. It is advisable to deal with the National Psalms and the Individual Psalms separately.

1. *National Psalms and Royal Psalms.* As far as the national enemies are concerned, [18] there is no basic difference between psalms in which the subject is "we" and psalms in which the king speaks in the name of the people. The relevant passages for a discussion of *'oyebh* in this sense are Ps. 18:4,18,38,41,49 (3,17,37,40,48); 21:9(8); 61:4(3); 89:23,43(22,42); 110:2; 132:18 (Royal Psalms), or 44:17(16); 74:3,10,18; 80:7(6) (National Psalms of Lamentation); add to this 1 S. 2:10 in Hannah's Song of Praise. The synonyms of *'oyebh* which occur in these passages [19] are *sone'* or *mesanne'*, "one who hates," Ps. 21:9(8); 44:8,11 (7,10); 89:24 (23); *tsar*, "oppressor," 44:6,8,11(5,7,10); *qam*, "assailant," 18:40, 49(39,48); *mithnaqqem*, "avenger," 44:17(16). In several instances the enemies are explicitly designated as foreigners: *goyim*, "nations," 18:44(43); 79:1,6,10; *'ammim*, "peoples," 18:48(47); *bene nekhar*, "foreigners," 18:45f.(44f.); 144:7,11.

It is often said in these passages that the national enemies do not seek or worship Yahweh (14:1f.,4; 28:5; 44:17[16]; 58:4[3]; 74:10,18; 79:6,10,12), therefore they are Yahweh's enemies (74:4,18,22f.; 83:3,6[2,5]; 89:52[51]; 1 S. 2:10). They are characterized by their pride, which expresses itself especially in arrogant words (Ps. 12:4f.[3f.]; 18:28[27]; 1 S. 2:3) and scoffings (44:17[16]; 74:10,18; 79:10,12; 89:52[51]). Their corruption is depicted with designations like *resha'im*, "wicked" (28:3; 58:4[3]; 125:3; 1 S. 2:9), *po'ale 'aven*, "evildoers" (14:4; 28:3; 125:5), *'anshe chamas*, "men of violence" (18:49[48]), *ben 'avlah*, literally "son of injustice," so "wicked" (89:23[22]), and *dobhere khazabh*, "speakers of lies" (58:4[3]). Thus, theologically the "enemies of the people" are regarded as "enemies of God." For this reason, one prays for help against them, and the king receives the promise that he will triumph over them.

2. *Individual Psalms.* In the Individual Psalms, *'oyebh* occurs in the following passages: 3:8(7); 6:11(10); 7:6(5); 9:4,7(3,6); 13:3,5(2,4); 17:9; 25:2,19; 27:2, 6; 30:2(1); 31:9,16(8,15); 35:19; 38:20(19); 41:3,6,12(2,5,11); 42:10(9); 43:2;

---

18 Birkeland, *Feinde,* 23-66.
19 *Ibid.,* 60-62.

54:9(7); 55:4,13(3,12); 56:10(9); 59:2(1); 64:2(1); 69:5,19(4,18); 71:10; 102:9 (8); 119:98; 138:7; 143:3,9,12. The most frequently used synonyms of *'oyebh* in these psalms are *tsar* (*tsorer*), "oppressor, adversary" (3:2[1]; 6:8[7]; 7:7[6]; 13:5[4]; 27:2,12; 31:12[11]; 42:11[10]; 69:20[19]; 119:139,157) and *sone'* or *mesanne'*, "one who hates" (9:14[13]; 35:19; 38:20[19]; 41:8[7]; 69:5,15[4, 14]); in addition, *qam*, "to rise up against" (3:2[1]); *mithqomem*, "to rise up against" (59:2[1]); *shorer*, "slanderer" (?) (5:9[8]; 27:11; 54:7[5]; 56:3[2]; 59:11[10]); as well as forms of the root *radhaph*, "to pursue, persecute" (7:2,6 [1,5]; 31:16[15]; 35:3; 69:27[26]; 71:11; 119:84,86,157,161; 143:3); also occur. This last word describes the work of enemies as that of "pursuing" or "hunting." They are characterized especially by their boastful words and their hostile plans; [20] they are also called *resha'im*, "wicked" (3:8[7]; 7:10[9]; 9:6[5]; 17:9, 13; 55:4[3]; 71:4; 119:53,61,95,110,155), i.e., they arrogantly rebel against God. They are also called *po'ale 'aven*, "evildoers" (6:9[8]; 59:3[2]; 64:3[2]), *mere'im*, "evildoers" (22:17[16]; 27:2; 64:3[2]), *'ish damim*, "men of blood" (55:24[23]; 59:3[2]), *'ish mirmah*, "deceitful men" (43:1; 55:24[23]), and *boghedh*, "treacherous" (25:3; 59:6[5]; 119:158). Occasionally they are compared with lions (3:8 [7]; 7:3[2]; 10:9; 17:12; 22:14[13]; 35:17) or other strong or wild beasts (22:13, 17,21[12,16,20]; 59:7,15[6,14]). Their pride is evident above all in their scornful and boasting words. [21] Particular emphasis is placed on their being hostile to the worshipper without cause (*chinnam*, 69:5[4]; *sheqer*, 35:19).

Nevertheless, the description of suffering in these psalms is either given in very general terms or occasionally refers to illness. Under such conditions, it is hardly justifiable to conclude that the enemies are the same throughout the Individual Psalms. In some psalms, the enemies are identified as *goyim*, "nations" (59:6,9[5,8]; 9:6,16,18,20f.[5,15,17,19f.]; 10:16; perhaps also *goy lo' chasidh*, "an ungodly people," 43:1), *'ammim*, "peoples" (7:8f.[7f.]; 56:8[7]), *le'ummim*, "peoples" (7:8f.[7f.]), *zarim*, "strangers" (54:5[3]), [22] or reference is made to war, strife, etc.; [23] thus, these texts could be speaking of distresses in war or the like. Other psalms very clearly seem to be speaking of illness: Pss. 6, 30, 38, 41, 102, which, among other things, follows from the use of the verb *rapha'*, "to heal" (Ps. 6:3[2]; 30:3[2]; 41:5[4]); but it is not always clear whether the enemies have brought on the illness of the worshipper or only rejoice over his misfortune. In other instances, reference is made to a lawsuit: false witnesses (Ps. 27:12; 35:11), *ribh*, "contend" (35:1,23), "vindicate" (35:23f.), and perhaps *sha'al*, "ask" (35:11).

Perhaps the simplest solution to this problem is to assume that the description of enemies in Individual Psalms has become "stereotyped" to a certain extent, because enemies of the nation are described as beasts and demons and thus are subject to a theological interpretation as people who work against God, while on the other hand personal adversaries or even sorcerers and demons can be

---

[20] *Ibid.*, 78.
[21] *Ibid.*, 66ff.
[22] *Ibid.*, 144ff.
[23] *Ibid.*, 173ff.

described in the same categories. The important thing is not the precise description of the enemies, but the theological classification of their work as contrary to God and chaotic. Beyond this, it is possible in some passages that the worshipper is a king on whom the fate of the land rests.

3. *Present Status of the Debate.* The enemies in the Individual Psalms of Lament have been interpreted quite variously. Duhm [24] and to some extent Kittel [25] thought they were political and religious adversaries of the godly in the Maccabean Period; Puukko still thinks so. [26] Balla expresses himself only briefly on the problem of the identity of the enemies in the psalms; [27] but since he defends the thesis that the "I" in the psalms is an individual, he also identifies the enemies as the personal adversaries of the worshipper, perhaps the ungodly, who are also enemies of God and enemies of the godly who still believe in God. [28] Gunkel-Begrich favor an interpretation that allows for a wider diversity of meaning. [29] Mowinckel thinks that the enemies were primarily sorcerers (*po'ale* → אָוֶן *'āven*), who persecuted the worshipper and sought to harm him by their magical arts. On the contrary, Birkeland maintains that since the enemies in the Individual Psalms of Lament are described with the same words as in the "National" Psalms, they must be external national enemies everywhere in the psalms: in the Individual Psalms, the king may be the worshipper, or the situation may be that of an individual in distress because of war. On the basis of his comparisons of the OT psalms with the Akkadian Psalms of Lament, Widengren emphasizes that the same expressions can be used differently in different contexts, and that stereotyped phrases by no means justify a uniform explanation of the enemies; rather, in each individual case one must make his investigation on the basis of other criteria in order to determine those to whom the expressions refer.

Ringgren

---

[24] Duhm, *KHC*, XIV (²1922).
[25] Kittel, *KAT*, XIII (³⁻⁴1922).
[26] Puukko, *OTS*, 8 (1950), 47-65.
[27] Balla, 19ff., 125f.
[28] *Ibid.*, 26.
[29] Gunkel-Begrich, 196-211.

אֵימָה 'êmāh; אָים 'āyōm; *אֵימְתָן 'êmᵉthān

Contents: I. Occurrences, Etymology. II. Analysis of Use in the OT: 1. Secular Use; 2. Religious Significance. III. Theological Considerations.

I. Occurrences, Etymology. Outside of Biblical Hebrew (including the Qumran literature), the noun 'emah occurs in Jewish Aramaic and Middle Hebrew. Up to the present time no occurrences of this word are known in the ancient Near East outside the OT. It is evident from this that the noun seems to be an exclusively Hebrew word formation.

The same thing applies to the words that are cognate to 'emah: the adjective 'ayom (OT; 1QH 15:23?) and *'emethan (Dnl. 7:7), as well as the denominative root 'ym in Middle Hebrew. Whether the proper noun 'emim, "the Emim," is to be included among these derivatives [1] cannot be determined with certainty. [2]

All this leads to the conclusion that the original meaning of 'emah, which, thanks to the ancient translations, many scholars assume to be "terror," cannot be determined with certainty etymologically. Gaster's attempt to make our word a cognate of Arab. 'ym, at least in Dt. 32:25, and to translate it "widowhood," has found no acceptance among scholars.

II. Analysis of Use in the OT.

1. Secular Use. One can be struck with terror by animals (Job 39:20; 41:6 [Eng. v. 14]: horse, crocodile; Dnl. 7:7: beast) and by man (Prov. 20:2: the king). In Cant. 6:4,10, the beauty of the girl friend is described using this comparison, 'ayummah kannidhgaloth, "terrible as an army with banners." According to Rudolph [3] and Goitein, the latter term here means "stars," and Goitein interprets the adjective to mean "excellent, magnificent," in keeping with the popular understanding. Then this expression would mean, "magnificent as the stars." In Isa. 33:18, 'emah means a "time (or period) of terror" under enemy oppression. In Jer. 50:38, 'emim appears in parallelism with pesilim, "images," and means the idols which for a devout Israelite are nothing but "apparitions" or "phantoms." [4] These examples all come from late literary strata of the OT, and give a faint untypical impression of the basic meaning of 'emah.

'êmāh. T. H. Gaster, "Dtn 32,25," ExpT, 49 (1937/38), 525; S. D. Goitein, "Ajummā Kannidgālōt," JSS, 10 (1965), 218f.; G. von Rad, Der Heilige Krieg im alten Israel (⁴1965), 10f.; F. Schwally, "Über einige palästinische Völkernamen," ZAW, 18 (1898), 126-148, 135-37: II. Die Emim.

[1] Schwally.
[2] KBL.
[3] Rudolph, KAT, XVII, 162.
[4] Rudolph, HAT, 12 (³1968), 304.

2. *Religious Significance.* The basic meaning of *'emah* may be seen in Hab. 1:7. To be sure, it is the Chaldeans who spread abroad terror here. But if according to v. 6 Yahweh is the one who rouses the Chaldeans, and in v. 5 the Israelites are summoned to "wonder and be astounded" (→ תמה *tāmah,* hithpael, qal), then it is clear that Yahweh produces this terror by means of a military invasion, a terror which is expressed by wonder and astonishment. Dt. 32:25 contains a similar idea. Because he is angry with his people, Yahweh smites them with afflictions of war (vv. 19-24), which are summed up in v. 25: "in the open the sword shall bereave, and in the chambers shall be terror." Again, Yahweh is the actor who is responsible for this situation through military invasion, and the *'emah* is equivalent to a deadly weapon. The personification of terror to be observed here also appears in Ps. 88:16(15); Job 9:34; 13:21; 33:7; and most clearly in Ex. 23:27 (J). Yahweh dismisses the people with the promise: "I will send my terror before you." Like the "angel" (v. 20) and "fear" (v. 28), so here terror appears as an independent entity. It acts at Yahweh's instruction, brings about the confusion and flight of Israel's enemies (v. 27), and thus mediates the delivering immanence and protecting presence of Yahweh to his people.

The content of the statements found in Ex. 15:16; Josh. 2:9 (J); and Gen. 15:12 (J) is similar to that which occurs in these passages, but they have a different form. According to Ex. 15, "terror and dread" (*'emethah vaphachadh,* → פחד *pachadh;* so also 1QpHab 3:4; 4:7; 1QS 1:17; 10:15) fall upon the Edomites, Moabites, and Canaanites (v. 15), and cause them not merely to "tremble" (v. 14), "be dismayed" and "melt away" (v. 15), but "to be still as a stone" (v. 16). In this context, there is no explicit reference to Yahweh, and *'emah* is construed with *naphal 'al,* "to fall upon." In Josh. 2, the Canaanites also melt away before Israel because of the terror. Terror falls upon Abraham (Gen. 15) to prepare him for the theophany and the promise which follow (vv. 17f.). The fact that Yahweh acts here also, and that the *'emah* is "in terror and bewilderment," [5] or in fear, confusion, and numbness, connects Gen. 15:12 with the other two passages. But Gen. 15 differs from them in that the setting is not warlike, and the terror does not fall on Israel's adversaries, but on the Israelite Abraham.

This use of the word is very near that found in Ps. 55:5(4); 88:16(15); Job 9:34; 13:21; 20:25; 33:7, all of which are concerned with an individual Israelite. The worshipper in the two Individual Songs of Lament describes his distress in this way: "the terrors of death have fallen upon me," "fear" (→ יראה *yir'āh*) and "trembling" come upon me (Ps. 55:5f.[4f.]), and he says that he had suffered Yahweh's terrors (Ps. 88:16[15]). Job wishes that God would take away his physical suffering, that "his terror" would not "fall upon" (*ba'ath,* piel) him (Job 9:34; 13:21). Zophar expresses his belief in the threatening judgment on evildoers with the statement, "terrors come upon him" (20:25), and Elihu replies to Job in these words: "behold, the fear of me shall not dismay you" (33:7).

In Ezk. 42:16, it is preferable to read *me'oth,* "hundreds," with the *qere* than the MT *'emoth,* "terrors"; and in Ezr. 3:3 it is better to read *be'ebhah,* "in enmity," than the MT *be'emah,* "in fear." Some scholars have suggested

---

[5] Von Rad, *Genesis. OTL* (trans. 1961), 182.

that we should read "thy terror" ('emathekha) instead of "thy faithfulness" ('emunathekha) in Ps. 89:9(8), and "sea monsters" ('emoth) instead of "ships" ('aniyyoth) in Ps. 104:26, but the commentaries should be consulted on these passages.

III. Theological Considerations. The earliest passages in which 'emah is used are Ex. 15, Josh. 2, and Ex. 23. At first in very reserved manner and wholly by implications, but then *expressis verbis,* these passages relate how Yahweh, with the help of a mysterious terror, discouraged Israel's enemics, crippled their power, and put them to flight so that his people could take possession of the land which had been promised to them by their God. Yahweh is the one who acts here. His activity is decisive. The close connection between this idea and the promised possession of the cultivated land along with the occurrence of this idea in Yahweh's speech when Israel was dismissed from Sinai make it probable that the experience of Yahweh's protecting nearness during the exodus event gave rise to the idea of the terror of Yahweh.

On the whole, this agrees with von Rad's suggestion that the terror was rooted in the range of ideas connected with the war of Yahweh. This explains why it is not the secular use, but the religious use of 'emah that stands at the beginning of the history of this idea, and why there are no examples of its use in the ancient Near Eastern world surrounding Israel: the concept of the terror of Yahweh is uniquely Israelite.

The group of ideas connected with the war of Yahweh[6] and the concept of the terror of Yahweh have been reinterpreted, clearly under prophetic influence. Angered by Israel's sins, Yahweh raises up foreign nations to go to war against them; thus, his terror falls upon his own people (Dt. 32; Hab. 1). At the same time, it seems that another concept was also experiencing change, viz., that of individualization. If the object of Yahweh's terror in the beginning was always a nation, now it is the individual. Thus, the approaching theophany is announced to Abraham through the terror of Yahweh (Gen. 15), and the ultimately severe physical punishment and emotional distress in which Yahweh's terror is reflected fall upon the individual worshippers responsible for Pss. 55 and 88, and upon Job.

Zobel

---

6 Von Rad, *OT Theol.,* II (trans. 1965), 119-125.

> אִישׁ 'îsh; אִשָּׁה 'ishshāh

Contents: I. 1. Etymology, Occurrences; 2. Use. II. Secular Use: 1. 'ish; 2. 'ishshah. III. Theological Considerations: 1. Anthropological Concepts; 2. Specifically Theological Concepts; 3. As a Medium of Revelation.

I. 1. *Etymology, Occurrences.*

a. The etymology of *'ish* is uncertain: one root which has been suggested, *'yš, 'wš,* "to be strong," [1] cannot be verified, and the meaning of another root which has been proposed, *'nš,* [2] is not settled (Arab. *atta,* "to sprout up abundantly"?). [3] Elliger thinks the noun *'ish* comes "from the root *'šš* which has come to light in the Habakkuk Commentary from the Dead Sea literature (VI, 11)" [4] (if so, *hith'oshash* means "to take courage," "to act like men" [Isa. 46:8; cf. 1 S. 4:9], and is a denominative from *'ish*). In connection with this, we should mention the Old South Arabic words *'ys, 's,* "man, one, each," [5] and especially Ugar. *'š.* [6] It is possible that *'ish* is a primary noun which is not based on a verbal root. In the OT this word is found in the singular and the plural, and occurs here 2160 times according to *KBL*.

b. The etymology of *'ishshah* is also uncertain. It is usually derived from the root *'nš,* "to be sick, weak"; we are probably dealing with a primary noun here also. The connection between *'ishshah* and *'ish* which is made in Gen. 2:23 is probably to be interpreted as a popular etymology, because *'ishshah* is certainly

---

'îsh. P. J. Bratsiotis, Ἡ γυνή ἐν τῇ βίβλῳ (Athens, ²1940), 13-25; N. P. Bratsiotis, Ἀνθρωπολογία τῆς Παλαιᾶς Διαθήκης, I (Athens, 1967), 24-39, 49-52, 140-151; A. Gonzáles, "Hombre de Dios," *CultBibl,* 120/21 (1954), 143-48; A. Haldar, *Associations of Cult Prophets among the Ancient Semites* (Uppsala, 1945), 126-28; R. Hallevy, "Man of God," *JNES,* 17 (1958), 237-244; J. Hempel, "Gott, Mensch und Tier im AT," *BZAW,* 81 (1961), 198-229; G. Hölscher, *Die Profeten* (1914), 127; H. Junker, *Prophet und Seher in Israel* (1927), 77f.; *idem, Genesis. EB,* I (²1955), 28f.; W. C. Klein, "The Model of a Hebrew Man. The Standards of Manhood in Hebrew Culture," *BiblRes,* 4 (1960), 1-7; E. König, *Genesis* (²,³1925), 217-220; J. Lindblom, *Prophecy in Ancient Israel* (Oxford, 1962), 60ff.; N. W. Porteous, "Man, Nature of, in the OT," *IDB,* III, 242-46; O. Procksch, *KAT²⁻³,* I, 28f.; R. Rendtorff, "Προφήτης, B. נביא in the OT," *TDNT,* VI, 796-812; J. Scharbert, *Heilsmittler im AT und im Alten Orient. QuaestDisp,* 23/24 (1964), 138f., 280ff.; H. V. Schwarz, "Das Gottesbild des Propheten Oseas," *BiLi,* 35 (1961/62), 274-79; A. van Selms, "De uitdrukking 'Man van God' in de Bybel," *Hervormde Teologiese Studies,* 15 (1959), 133-149; de Vaux, *AncIsr;* C. Westermann, "Propheten," *BHHW,* III, 1496-1512; H. W. Wolff, *Hosea* (trans. 1974).

1 *KBL¹.*
2 *KBL².*
3 Baumgartner.
4 K. Elliger, *Festschrift Alt* (1953), 100f.
5 W. W. Müller, *ZAW,* 75 (1963), 306.
6 Cf. *OLZ,* 62 (1967), 537; Gröndahl, *PNU,* 102.

related to Arab. *'untā* (cf. Ugar. *'tt,* "woman," and *t3ntt.).* [7] *'ishshah* is found in the singular and the plural (*nashim*) in the OT, and occurs here 775 times according to *KBL.*

2. *Use.* The word *'ish,* which in a characteristic way is used not only with reference to man, but also to God and even to animals, appears in all aspects of human life, where it usually has a secular sense, and only rarely a theological one. In comparison with other terms that have a similar meaning, *'ish* manifests a rich variety of nuances. The principal meanings are "man," "husband," and "mankind."

The variety of meanings also appears where *'ish* occurs as a parallel to or possibly even as a synonym of other terms, [8] especially of → אדם *'ādhām,* → אנוש *'enôsh,* and → גבר *gebher,* and also → זכר *zākhār* and → בעל *ba'al.* Since *'ish* is found almost uniformly both in OT literature (including Sir.) and in the ancient Hebrew inscriptions, it is impossible to speak of an earlier or later use of this word, as can be done with some combinations of words. [9] The same also applies to *'ishshah.* [10]

II. Secular Use.

1. *'ish.* The various examples of *'ish* come mainly from the secular sphere. We can get a clear picture of the various meanings by the following analysis.

a. *'ish* means "man": first, as a term denoting sex, used in contrast to *'ishshah,* "woman," to designate the one who begets (Eccl. 6:3), or a newborn male child (Gen. 4:1); second, as a term denoting that a person is an adult man in contrast to *yeledh,* "young man" (4:23), or to *na'ar,* "youth" (1 S. 17:33), but also in contrast to → זקן *zākhēn,* "old man" (2:32f.); third, as a term used to emphasize masculine qualities such as manliness in contrast to *'ishshah,* in fact used in parallelism with *gebher,* "man" (Jer. 22:30; 23:9), or such as bravery (1 S. 4:9; 1 K. 2:2; cf. 1 S. 26:15). Physical or spiritual qualities are often expressed by the use of *'ish* in the construct, e.g., *'ish sa'ir,* "a hairy man," in contrast to *'ish chalaq,* "a smooth man" (Gen. 27:11); *'anshe middoth,* "men of great stature" (Nu. 13:32); *'ish to'ar,* "a man of good presence" (1 S. 16:18); *'ish chesedh,* "a man who is kind" (Prov. 11:17); *'ish shalom,* "a man of peace" (Ps. 37:37); *'ish tebhunah,* "a man of understanding" (Prov. 17:27); *'anshe 'emeth,* "men who are trustworthy" (Ex. 18:21; Neh. 7:2); fourth, as a term to designate an office, a profession, and a rank held by men: *'ish kohen,* "priest" (Lev. 21:9); *'ish sar,* "prince" (Ex. 2:14); *'ish saris,* "eunuch" (Jer. 38:7); *'ish sadheh,* "a man of the field" (Gen. 25:27); *'anshe miqneh,* "keepers of the cattle" (46:32); *'ish milchamah,* "a man of war" (Josh. 17:1; cf. Nu. 31:49; Dt. 2:14; Josh. 5:6; Joel

---

[7] *BiOr,* 23 (1966), 132.
[8] See below.
[9] See below.
[10] For further discussion of this, see below.

2:7); *’ish chayil,* "valiant men" (Jgs. 3:29; 1 S. 31:12; 2 S. 24:9; 1 K. 1:42); fifth, as a term used to indicate that one was of a certain nationality: *’ish mitsri,* "an Egyptian" (Gen. 39:1); *’ish ’ibhri,* "a Hebrew" (Ex. 2:11); or of a certain tribe: *’ish levi,* "a certain Levite" (Jgs. 19:1); *’ish ’ephrayim,* "men of Ephraim" (8:1); or to indicate inhabitants of a land: *’anshe ha’arets,* "the men of the land" (Lev. 18:27); of a city: *’anshe ha’ir,* "the men of the city" (Jgs. 19:22); of a house: *’anshe bethah,* "the men of her household" (Gen.39:14); sixth, with the meaning "someone, one" (13:16); "each" (40:5).

b. *’ish* means "husband" (Gen. 29:32; Nu. 30:7ff. [Eng. vv. 6ff.]; 1 S. 1:8; 25:19; Jer. 29:6; Ezk. 16:45; Prov. 7:19): in contrast to *’ishshah,* "wife" (Gen. 16:3; Lev. 21:7; Nu. 30:7ff.[6ff.]; Jgs. 13:6), and as a parallel to → בעל *ba‘al,* "husband" (2 S. 11:26; cf. Dt. 24:3f.).

c. *’ish* means "mankind" (esp. in Jgs. 9:49b, where *’ish,* "mankind" [pl.] is used alongside *’ish,* "man," and *’ishshah,* "woman"): as a designation for the species "man," which includes "man" and "woman," and appears in both the secular and the religious sphere; thus *’anshe qodhesh,* "men consecrated" (Ex. 22:30[31]); *’erets lo’ ’ish,* "a land where no man is" (as parallel to *midhbar,* "desert," Job 38:26). *’ish* is also used as a parallel to *’enosh* and as a synonym of *’adham* (Isa. 2:9,11,17; 31:8; Jer. 2:6; Prov. 6:12; cf. Ps. 22:7[6]; Prov. 30:2) or of *ben ’adham,* "son of man" (Nu. 23:19; Isa. 52:14; cf. 2 S. 7:14), and *ben ’ish* is used synonymously with *ben ’adham* (Jer. 49:18,33; 50:40; Ps. 62:10[9]). It is still uncertain, however, whether *bene ’ish* is used in Ps. 4:3(2); 49:3(2); and Lam. 3:33 as a parallel to or in contrast to *bene ’adham.* Finally, *’ish* sometimes has the meaning "human" (*’ammath ’ish,* "cubit of a man" = "human cubit," Dt. 3:11) or "usual" or "common" (*shebhet ’anashim,* "rod of men" = "common rod," 2 S. 7:14).

2. *’ishshah.* The different uses of *’ishshah* are divided between the two basic meanings "woman" and "wife." [11]

a. *’ishshah* means "woman" in contrast to *’ish,* "man," [12] i.e., first, *’ishshah* in the absolute, Eccl. 7:26 (the feminine sex); *’orach kannashim,* "the manner of women" (Gen. 18:11); *derekh nashim,* "the way of women" (Gen. 31:35); *’ahabhath nashim,* "the love of women" (2 S. 1:26); second, with an adjective or in the construct as a term used to designate rank and characteristics: *’ishshah gedholah,* "a wealthy woman" (2 K. 4:8); *’ishshah zonah,* "a harlot" (Josh. 2:1; 6:22; Jer. 3:3); *’esheth zenunim,* "a wife of harlotry" (Hos. 1:2); *’ishshah zarah,* "a loose (strange) woman" (Prov. 2:16; 5:3,20; 7:5); *’esheth chayil,* "a woman of worth" (Ruth 3:11; Prov. 12:4; 31:10); third, in the sense of "each" (Ruth 1:8,9).

---

[11] Cf. above, II.1.a,b.
[12] See above, II.1.a.

b. *'ishshah* means "wife" in contrast to *'ish,* "husband." Here belong the following expressions which have to do with the man-woman relationship, mostly with regard to sex: *'ishshah,* "fiancée" (Dt. 22:24) or "bride" (Gen. 29:21); *nathan lo le'ishshah,* "(she) gave him (her maid) as a wife" (30:4,9); *laqach lo 'ishshah,* "he took to himself a wife" (4:19; 6:2; cf. Ex. 21:10); *vattehi lo le'ishshah,* "and she became his wife" (1 S. 25:43); *'ishshah bheʿulath baʿal,* "the wife of another man" (Dt. 22:22); *'esheth 'ish,* "a man's wife" (Prov. 6:26); *'esheth neʿurim,* "a wife of youth" (Isa. 54:6; Prov. 5:18); and *'esheth ʿazubhah,* "a wife forsaken" (Isa. 54:6).

c. It is worthy of note that fainthearted or cowardly men are characterized as "women" (Jer. 51:30; 50:37; Isa. 19:16; Nah. 3:13). Moreover, the death of a man was considered to be dishonorable if it was at the hand of a woman. Therefore, the severely wounded Abimelech urged his armorbearer to kill him lest it be said, "a woman killed him" (Jgs. 9:54; cf. also 4:9).

III. Theological Considerations.

1. *Anthropological Concepts.* Some passages in the OT may be interpreted anthropologically. These are passages where *'ish* appears as a synonym of *'adham* and *'enosh,* and where there is an indication of a differentiation of human nature.

a. First of all, man is distinguished from God. This appears in the use of *'ish* in contrast to → אלהים *'elōhîm,* "God" (Gen. 32:29[28]); but also in contrast to → יהוה *yhvh,* "Yahweh, the Lord" (Isa 2:11,17; cf. Sir. 10:7). The relationship between man and God, and the differentiation of human nature from God, are determined by God's creation of man on the one hand, and by the OT belief that all human nature is "in his hand" on the other (*beyadho . . . veruach kol besar 'ish,* "in his hand . . . is the breath of all mankind," Job 12:10).[13] Man is conscious of God's vast superiority. The pride of man is humbled before the exalted magnificence of God (Isa. 2:11,17). Thus, the question is asked, "Who has directed the Spirit of the Lord, or as his counselor has instructed him?" (*'ish ʿatsatho,* Isa. 40:13).

b. But man is also distinguished from animals. This is especially emphasized when *'ish* is contrasted with → בהמה *beⁿhēmāh* (as in Ex. 11:7; 19:13; Lev. 20:15; cf. Ps. 22:7[6]). Such passages express the OT belief that in spite of the many affinities between man and beasts (cf. Gen. 2:19a with 2:7a), there is still a clear distinction between human and animal nature. This is even clearer in passages that impose the death penalty for the transgression of sexual intercourse (Ex. 22:18[19]) between an *'ish* (Lev. 20:15) or an *'ishshah* (18:22; 20:16) and a *behemah,* "beast." A theological reason for this is found in the ancient narrative of the creation of man (Gen. 2:7), both male and female (2:18,20bff.), and of the

---

[13] For certain passages that make a strong distinction between man and God, see below, III.2.a.

animals (2:19f.). It appears as if the creation of the beasts interrupts the whole process of the creation of man. But actually the writer is trying to emphasize the difference between man and beast, and man's position of dominion over the beasts (2:20; cf. v. 19). The beasts do not fulfil the God-given need of man for a partner (2:18,20), and cannot take away his loneliness. Therefore God "builds" (→ בנה *bānāh*) the woman. Thus the nature of man is different from that of animals, which cannot stand by man's side (2:21f.), but are "put under his feet" (Ps. 8:7ff.[6ff.]; cf. Gen. 2:18f.; 1:26,28). Everything that perverts such a relationship between man and beast is rejected. This explains why fornication with animals is considered to be unnatural (Lev. 18:23): it opposes the arrangement ordained by God in the creation of man, and is offensive to the significance of the existence of one's fellow man and especially of the woman (cf. Gen. 2:18,20b).

c. In addition to the external differentiation of man from God and beasts, the OT also speaks of an internal distinction within mankind, but only with regard to the sexual difference between an *'ish,* "a male," and an *'ishshah,* "a female." Gen. 2:18,20bff. develop this distinction. The well-thought-out choice of words (cf. in 2:7a, *min ha'adhamah–'adham,* "from the ground–man"; v. 23b, *me'ish–'ishshah,* "from the man–woman") in the entire narrative (2:4bff.) must be interpreted by theological exegesis. Thus, 2:23 is of fundamental importance, because on the one hand here *'ish* is used for the first time in this narrative, and on the other hand *'ishshah* is explained, indeed one may even say, is defined here. In 2:23, *'ish* and *'ishshah* appear only once apiece (in all likelihood this is deliberate), and both words are spoken by *'adham,* "man," himself. After the "deep sleep" (*tardemah*) which God brought on the *'adham,* for the first time he meets the woman whom God brought to him (2:22), and for the first time he becomes aware of standing in the presence of a fellow creature not merely with the same nature but also of a different sex (2:23a). Previously he had inspected the animals and recognized that he had a different nature and thus came to realize that he was a human being, but now he also realizes that he is of a different sex from the *'ishshah,* "woman," and thus recognizes the peculiarity of his being a "man" (*me'ish*). Therefore, he is *'ish,* and she is *'ishshah.* To express it more precisely, according to 2:23a *'adham,* "the man," characterizes the creature who stands before him as *zo'th,* "this (one, feminine)," apparently in order to establish a blood relationship and thus to emphasize that they are of the same nature, i.e., by using *zo'th* he recognizes that she is a fellow creature. Now for him *zo'th* is an *'ishshah.* But at the same time he also recognizes their mutual relationship (*'ishshah me'ish,* "woman from man"), as well as the position of both in creation. Therefore, it is worthy of note that *zakhar,* "male," and *neqebhah,* "female," which serve only to denote a person's sex, are not used here, as they are in 1:27, but rather *'ish* and *'ishshah.* While these words also mean "husband" and "wife" respectively, they also indicate their position in creation as well as their relationship to and with each other. Thus, by using the expression *'ishshah me'ish,* which calls attention to the striking similarity between the Hebrew words for "man" and "woman," the narrator seems to want to emphasize the identity of the nature of, and the "equality" of, man and woman. [14]

d. Taken strictly, neither *'ishshah* nor *'ish* appears in Gen. 2 as a proper name. For a while, *'ishshah* serves only as a designation for the sole female human being, because not until after the Fall does the woman receive a proper name–Eve (Gen. 3:20). After establishing that there is a fellow creature for man, the narrator uses *'adham,* "Adam," as the man's proper name (so in 2:25, *ha'adham ve'ishto,* "Adam and his wife," cf. 3:8,12; on this cf. 16:3, *'abhram 'ishah,* "Abram her husband"). Because of the appearance of the woman, he is no longer the only *'adham,* but he is still the only male and husband and bears the proper name *'adham,* i.e., he is *'ish,* "man," with reference to the female fellow creature and wife. Only after the appearance of the *'ishshah* did he function as an *'ish.* Thus, both the creation of man in 2:7 and his differentiation into two sexes in 2:21f. are traced back to God. Consequently, God determines not only the position of man in creation in general and his relationship to God and to the other created beings (2:7; cf. 2:19f.), but also the equivalent position of man and woman and their close relationship to each other (2:21ff.), which is an I-Thou relationship. Therefore, this sexual differentiation also has a distinct social character about it (cf. 2:18, where *'ezer,* "helper," is contrasted with *lebhadh,* "alone"; cf. also 2:20b), which is apparent in the use of → ידע *yādha',* "to know," to denote the sexual relationship. But this is not to say that the crucial point is to be found in the sexual relationship, because *'ish* and *'ishshah* extend beyond sex and emphasize that they are partners whose nature is the same, fellow creatures, Gk. *sýzygoi.* If the *'ishshah* is *min ha'adham* and *me'ish,* "from the man," the *'ish* is also *min ha'adhamah,* "from the ground" (2:7). The primacy of the *'ish* over the *'ishshah* is not the same as the primacy of man over the beasts which are subordinate to him, but is only a primacy of age (the man was created before the woman). However, this cannot mean that the man has a natural or ethical superiority over the *'ishshah,* because God himself put the *'ishshah* at his elbow, indeed by his side (2:21f., *tsela',* "rib," which also means "side"). God brought the *'ishshah* to the man as a father gives away his daughter to her husband (→ בוא *bô'* is also used elsewhere of bringing a girl to her husband; cf. Jgs. 12:9), which is apparently intended to indicate that God himself is responsible for establishing marriage. Before God and in the presence of the woman, the man acknowledges (this is the sense of → אמר *'āmar,* "to say," and → קרא *qārā',* "to call," in Gen. 2:23) the equality of the partnership between *'ish* and *'ishshah* which God had established, and before God he makes a covenant with the woman (cf. 2:22b; 3:12, and the use of → נתן *nāthan,* "to give"), which, consequently, is a "covenant of God" (it is explicitly called *berith 'elohim* in Prov. 2:17). In a type of "marriage formula," [15] he acknowledges the woman as "his wife," i.e., *'ishto* (cf. Gen. 2:24; cf. also Ezk. 16:8b), which "indicates

---

[14] Junker, *EB,* I, 28f.
[15] Cf. on this de Vaux, 33ff.

that monogamy is the foundation of the whole human race." [16] Consequently, he sets her beside him in her proper place, which God had appointed for her (cf. Gen. 2:18). Thus, she is now for him *'esheth cheqo,* "the wife of his bosom" (Dt. 28:54; cf. 13:7[6]), just as he is for her *'ish cheqah,* "the husband of her bosom" (28:56). That which is spoken before God in Gen. 2:24 clearly has to do with sexual intercourse, which is also connected with the blessing of God in 1:28 (cf. 4:1), and is regarded as one of the purposes of marriage (cf. 2:24; also 2:18,20b). Thus, the creature (child) produced as a result of this act combines within himself once again *'ish* and *'ishshah.* Here one may seek a theological reason for the prohibition of the homosexual relationship (Lev. 20:13; cf. 18:22), which is considered to be an "abomination" (*to'ebhah*) and a transgression worthy of death, since it perverts sexual differentiation and marriage, which is based on this. [17] For the same reason, transvestism is forbidden (Dt. 22:5), since distinctive clothing for the two sexes also serves as a conspicuous sign of sexual differentiation.

God himself is witness of the marriage mentioned in Gen. 2:22f. This is also explicitly stated in Mal. 2:14f., a passage that probably refers to Gen. 2:22f. Mal. 2:14f. states that God appears as a witness (→ עוּד *'ûdh*) between *'ish* and *'ishshah.* Here, the *'ishshah* is also designated as the *koinōnós* (so the LXX for *chabhereth,* "companion," in Mal. 2:14), and as the *'esheth berith,* "wife of the covenant." This originally intimate relationship between man and woman changes after the Fall, in which the *'ishshah* plays a major role. She appears as it were unfaithful, since she departs from her *'ish,* "husband," or at least acts without him (thus Gen. 3:1-6b). Here the separation of the *'ishshah* from her *'ish* (cf. by way of contrast 2:23b) provides the type of situation in which the Fall can take place. The subsequent jeopardizing of the existing *'ish-'ishshah* relationship [18] may be reflected when the man speaks of his wife merely as *ha'ishshah,* "the woman" (3:12, in contrast to *'ishto,* "his wife," in 2:24). This expression calls to mind the formula that the husband utters when he dissolves a marriage (*hi' lo' 'ishti ve'anokhi lo' 'ishah,* "she is not my wife, and I am not her husband," in Hos. 2:4b[2b]). [19] Before God, to some extent the man retracts what he had felt for his wife at first, when he received her from God (thus Gen. 3:12; see by way of contrast the so-called love song in 2:23f.). Thus a different kind of relationship is formed between man and woman, which as it were is given legal status by that which God says to the woman in prophetic speech form (3:16, in contrast to what is said in prophetic speech form in 2:24). Here woman is placed under man's authority (in 2:24, *'ish... vedhabhaq be'ishto,* "a man... cleaves to his wife"; by way of contrast, 3:6 states "the woman... saw... took... ate" and 3:16 says, *ve'el 'ishekh teshuqathekh,* "yet your desire shall be for your husband"; with 3:16c, *vehu' yimshol bakh,* "and he shall rule

---

[16] Procksch, 29.
[17] But see Elliger, *Leviticus. HAT,* 4 (1966), 241, 275.
[18] See above.
[19] See below, III.2.c.

over you," cf. 3:6b, "*she* gave"; cf. v. 6a). This new state of affairs perhaps begins with the man giving the woman a proper name which she had not had previously (*vayiqra' ha'adham shem,* "the man called the name...," in 3:20 in contrast to 2:23b). In this way the *'ish* becomes → בַּעַל *ba'al,* "lord" (but cf. Hos. 2:18[16]), [20] in relation to the *'ishshah,* and → אדון *'ādhôn,* "lord," a designation of rank which is not even mentioned in Gen. 2:18,20b,23f.

As far as the position of man and woman in the OT is concerned, we can only mention here that both are indeed equal before God, but not socially. [21]

2. *Specifically Theological Concepts.* The passages that use *'ish* in a specifically theological sense may be divided into three groups.

a. In the first group, *'ish* is used in the sense of "mankind," [22] i.e., as a synonym of *'adham* and *'enosh,* and the intention is to make a sharp distinction between man and God. But God and man can be distinguished in different ways. In some cases man may be the point of reference, and in others, God. In the former, the fundamental idea is *'ish lo' 'el,* "man is not God," but in the latter it is *'el lo' 'ish,* "God is not man." In the one case, God bears witness concerning himself; in the other, man turns it around. Hos. 11:9 contains a very typical statement of God's witness concerning himself: *ki 'el 'anokhi velo' 'ish,* "for I am God and not man." God is not man, he is the holy God, who is explicitly far removed from every human emotion and activity. God is omnipresent and all-seeing. God himself asks, "Can a man hide himself in secret places so that I cannot see him?" (Jer. 23:24). Since he sees through everything, he recognizes as false what men express to him as true worship, but which ultimately is only *mitsvath 'anashim melummadhah,* "a commandment of men learned by rote," and thus his people are far from him (Isa. 29:13). The second discourse of Balaam also contains the same sort of distinction: *lo' 'ish 'el vikhazzebh,* "God is not man, that he should lie" (Nu. 23:19), which, like Hos. 11:9, separates the true God from all weakness and fallibility. Thus man understands why he cannot go to law with God: *ki lo' 'ish kamoni,* "for he is not a man, as I am" (Job 9:32). Man should know that nothing is hidden before God: *ki nokhach 'ene yhvh darkhe 'ish,* "for a man's ways are before the eyes of the Lord" (Prov. 5:21), and that no man can resist God's omnipotence, *yisgor 'al 'ish velo' yippatheach,* "if he shuts a man in, none can open" (Job 12:14); God is able to do that which lies beyond human power: *'el yiddephennu lo' 'ish,* "God may vanquish him, not man" (32:13). He helps his people, and therefore they do not need to fear any man (Isa. 41:11-13). But God also punishes *beshebhet 'anashim,* "with the rod of men" (2 S. 7:14), or *becherebh lo' 'ish,* "by a sword, not of man" (Isa. 31:8), and thus he acts without human help: *lebhaddi ume'ammim 'en 'ish 'itti,* "alone, and from the peoples no one was with me" (Isa. 63:3).

---

[20] See below, III.3.c.
[21] Cf. on this P. J. Bratsiotis; de Vaux.
[22] See above, II.1.c.

b. In the second group, Yahweh (at first glance in contradiction to Dt. 4:12, 15ff., etc., and to the passages just mentioned) is described as an *'ish,* e.g., *'ish milchamoth,* "a man of war" (Isa. 42:13; cf. *keghibbor,* "a warrior," in Jer. 20:11). But this does not mean that God is thought to be identical with man; for God continues to be God, *yhvh 'ish milchamah yhvh shemo,* "Yahweh is a man of war; Yahweh is his name" (Ex. 15:3). Rather, this phrase is used to emphasize a particular attribute of God. According to the understanding which always appears elsewhere in Israel (cf. Ex. 14:14,25; Dt. 3:22; 32:30a; Josh. 23:10), when Yahweh fights against any enemy of his people as an *'ish milchamah,* "a man of war," the intention is to emphasize his omnipotence. He is also described as a war lord and a war god, who is recognized as the lord of world history through his dynamic intervention into history in behalf of his people. This metaphor seems to contradict Jer. 14:9 in particular: "why shouldst thou be like a man confused (*nidhham,* hapax legomenon)?" but the interrogative form used here indirectly expresses belief in the omnipotence of God.

c. In the third group, *'ish* and *'ishshah* with the meanings "husband" and "wife" respectively are used figuratively for the relationship between God and his people (or Zion). This is done either by using both substantives together (Hos. 2:4[2]), or by using only one of them with a synonymous word in place of the other (2:9[7]; Isa. 54:6f.; Jer. 3:3; Ezk. 23:2), or finally even by using synonyms of both of these words (Hos. 2:10[8]; Isa. 50:1; Jer. 2:2; 3:1,4,7f.; Ezk. 16:8ff.; 23:4ff.). Hosea especially uses this metaphor (2:4ff.[2ff.]); but it also appears in Deutero-Isaiah (Isa. 50:1; 54:5f.), Jeremiah (2:2; 3:1ff.), and Ezekiel (chaps. 16, 23). It is worthy of note that in Hosea alone *'ish* is used of God, even as a self-designation (Hos. 2:18[16]), [23] and the word *'ishshah* of the people of God (2:4b[2b]), while the other prophets use *'ishshah* in the figurative sense (Isa. 54:5f.; Jer. 3:3; cf. 3:1,20; Ezk. 23:2; cf. 16:32). This marital relationship (making of a covenant) is disrupted by adultery and desertion on the part of the *'ishshah,* so that the *'ish* (God) now no longer recognizes the *'ishshah* (the people) as his wife, and divorces her. When she returns to her longsuffering *'ish,* he declares that he wishes to restore the disrupted marital relationship by making a new covenant. These three stages, marriage–divorce–new covenant, appear in particular in Hosea (2:4ff.,9ff.,18ff.[2ff.,7ff.,16ff.]). In 2:4(2), as *'ish,* "husband," God addresses the children of the *'ishshah,* which are not, however, his own children, but are illegitimate (*bene zenunim,* 2:6[4]). Ezekiel alone, who elsewhere also gives a daring picture of the marital relationship between Yahweh and his people (Ezk. 23:2-4: Yahweh marries two sisters, and they are both prostitutes), mentions legitimate children, and even has Yahweh speak of *benehen 'asher yaledhu li,* "their sons whom they had borne to me" (Ezk. 23:37; cf. 23:4). In Hos. 2:4ff.(2ff.), the *'ish* (God) speaks of the *'ishshah* (people) in the 3rd person until he promises her that their relationship will be restored (2:21f.[19f.]). This indirect form of address, which expresses the husband's feeling of coolness toward his wife, is strengthened by his avoiding use of the

---

[23] On Isa. 54:4, see below.

word '*ishshah*. [24] Another address of the husband to the children of the wife alone is found in Isa. 50:1, but here the word '*ishshah* is not used; instead the husband speaks of a "bill of divorce" (Isa. 50:1; cf. Jer. 3:8). On the other hand, in Hos. 2:4(2), in the presence of the illegitimate children, the husband uses the divorce formula: *ki hi' lo' 'ishti ve'anokhi lo' 'ishah*, "for she is not my wife, and I am not her husband" (with the *lo'*, "not," which appears twice here, cf. the two names of children which have *lo'* as one component in 1:6,9). The word '*ishshah* is used only in the divorce formula; in the form '*ishti*, "my wife," [25] it calls to mind the earlier period of fidelity and love (cf. 2:17b[15b], and also Jer. 2:2; 3:4, where '*abh*, "father," must be understood in a similar way). Thus, the time of the marital relationship is disrupted; according to Ezk. 16:8, as the husband, God himself had "sworn" (→ שׁבע *shābha'*) to the wife and had entered into a "covenant" (*berith*) with her. The "wife" alone is to blame for breaking this covenant because of her continuous adultery (cf. Hos. 2:7[5]) with different "lovers" (2:4ff.[2ff.]), for according to Ezk. 16:59 she "has despised the oath and broken the covenant" (cf. also Isa. 50:1; Jer. 3:20; cf. 3:1; Ezk. 16:32; perhaps also Isa. 54:6f.). Thus, the husband puts into operation the legal consequences of his wife's repeated adultery and dissolves the marriage when he pronounces the divorce formula. In Hos. 2:7ff.(5ff.), the husband speaks of the unchaste behavior of the wife which is reflected in her outward appearance (cf. 2:4b[2b]; cf. Jer. 3:3; Ezk. 23:40b,42b), and on the strength of this he announces measures which will be taken against her. However, he does not seem to have understood his decision as an irrevocable dissolution of the marriage, but uses these measures to try to get her to return (→ שׁוב *shûbh*, which assumes that the wife has run away) (Hos. 2:9[7]), thus demonstrating that he still loves her genuinely. He allows her return on the basis that she understands and admits that it was better with her when she was faithful to her first husband (2:9[7], where he has her say characteristically not '*ish*, "husband," but '*ishi*, "my husband"). This return is not unlawful (cf. Dt. 24:1-4), as Jer. 3:1 explicitly states (in spite of the unqualified divorce formula in Hos. 2:4[2], and in spite of the assumption of a second marriage in the use of *ri'shon*, "first," in 2:9b[7b]), because the woman speaks only of lovers (*me'ahebh* in 2:9a[7a]; cf. vv. 7,12,15[5,10,13]). [26] In order to bring about the return of the wife, he resorts to the use of enticements (→ פתה *pāthāh*, 2:16[14]), for he is convinced that this will cause her to follow him voluntarily (cf. 2:17bf.[15bf.]). However, the return of the wife is viewed as a future event, which is clear from the formula *vehayah bhayyom hahu'*, "and in that day" (2:18a[16a]). But when she returns, as a verification of the genuineness of her decision she will use the address '*ishi*, "my husband" (in antithesis to the divorce formula in 2:4b[2b]), and no longer *ba'ali*, "my Baal (lord, master)" (2:18b[16b]). Here, moreover, a clear distinction is made between '*ish* and the ambiguous word *ba'al*, which can mean the Canaanite god Baal (and thus symbolize idolatry) or marital lord. One cannot fail to see that this

[24] See below.
[25] See above, III.1.d.
[26] But cf. H. W. Wolff, *Hosea*, 36.

passage proclaims a new social relationship between man and woman in which the man is no longer the woman's *baʿal*, "marital lord," but the man with whom God made her an equal, as before the Fall. This distinction seems to mean even more, however, because on the one hand *'ish* repeatedly relates *baʿal* to the lovers (2:10,15[8,13]), while on the other hand *baʿal* also denotes the idols in 2:10(8). Furthermore, the *'ish*, "husband," declares in 2:19(17) that he will intervene dynamically, and as a result the wife will no longer mention the *beʿalim* or even think of them. One is justified in assuming that in 2:18b(16b), *'ishi* is used as a designation for the husband (God), and *baʿali* for his rivals, the "lovers," i.e., the idols. Therefore, the wife of the *'ish* is strongly admonished (*velo' thiqre'i*, v. 18[16]) not only to sever all relationships with the *baʿal*, but also to avoid completely anything that might imperil her marital fidelity. Merely the mention of the ambiguous *baʿali* would remind the wife of her infidelity; in the ambiguity it can be seen that Baalistic syncretism is in the background of this picture.

In light of this, at first glance Isa. 54:5 seems strange. Here Yahweh says to Jerusalem, which is designated as his wife: *ki bhoʿalayikh ʿosayikh yhvh tsebha'oth shemo*, "for your Maker is your Husband, Yahweh of hosts is his name." In order to understand this metaphor, it is necessary to take into consideration what is said in Hos. 2:20ff.(18ff.) concerning the future restoration of the relationship between God and his people. In this passage the *'ish* (God) is repeated, and now he addresses the *'ishshah* (people) in the 2nd person. Three times he promises her, "I will betroth you" (*'aras*, Hos. 2:21f.[19f.]); cf. the thrice repeated expression, "I will establish my covenant with you (i.e., Jerusalem)" in Ezk. 16:60,62. On the other hand, the husband promises to adopt the illegitimate children of the wife (Hos. 2:24f.[22f.]). Thus, the marital relationship between God and his people passes over into an adoption relationship.

d. The last two groups of passages show that God is represented in the OT not only anthropomorphically, but also andromorphically, i.e., as a male. The same thing is also true of his angel. [27] Furthermore, his servants are predominantly men; it is true that in the Yahweh religion there are some prophetesses, but there are no priestesses. But this andromorphic idea of God should not be understood to apply merely to sex, because there are no proofs for such an application. However, this idea of God is made clear by the general view of man in the OT, i.e., his physical and psychic characteristics which distinguish him from the woman and her characteristics. [28] In this regard, the general OT idea of God is different from that of other ancient Near Eastern cultures. Moreover, the deeper theological meaning of this OT idea and its religio-historical interpretation continue on as a fundamental theological belief.

3. *As a Medium of Revelation.* *'ish* also appears in a group of passages which deal with the messenger of God or the medium of revelation.

---

[27] See below, II.3.a.
[28] Cf. II.2.c.

a. Thus, the angel of Yahweh (→ מלאך *mal'ākh*) often appears in the form of an *'ish*, "a man." Either both terms are used interchangeably for an angel (cf. Gen. 18:2,16,22; 19:5,8,10,12,16: *'anashim,* "men," with Gen. 19:1,15: *mal'akhim,* "angels"; also cf. Jgs. 13:3,9,13,15,16,17ff.: *mal'akh,* with Jgs. 13:11: *'ish*), or angels who appear at first only as men afterwards speak with divine authority (Gen. 19:12ff.; Jgs. 13:3ff.; Josh. 5:15) or even as God himself (Gen. 18:9ff.), or they act in the place of God (19:10f.; Jgs. 13:20). In pertinent narratives, the uncertainty of men concerning an angel is clearly expressed (cf. Jgs. 13:16b), although at the first encounter they consider angels to be real men (cf. Gen. 18:2ff.; 19:1ff.; Josh. 5:13). This uncertainty is seen in that *'ish* (Jgs. 13:10,11) and *'ish ha'elohim,* "man of God" (13:6,8), or even *'elohim* (13:22), are used interchangeably to designate an andromorphic angel. But frequently a man asks an angel a direct (Josh. 5:13f.) or an indirect question (Jgs. 13:17f.), or the angel reveals who he is after a while (Gen. 19:12f.). Also in the prophets, the angel of God appears in the form of an *'ish.* Thus, Zechariah speaks of an *'ish* riding (Zec. 1:8ff.), but he realizes later that he is an angel of Yahweh (1:11). Daniel also speaks of the appearance of an *'ish* (Dnl. 10:5ff.; 12:5f.), but without explicitly stating that he is an angel. Thus, he speaks of *'ish gabhri'el,* "the man Gabriel" (9:21), whom he sees flying. Since the word *mal'akh,* "angel," does not occur in the Hebrew portion of Daniel, perhaps this may be rendered "the angel Gabriel."

b. *'ish* and *'ishshah* are used in connection with → נביא *nābhî',* "prophet," and *nebhi'ah,* "prophetess": *'ish nabhi',* lit. "a man, a prophet," or *'ishshah nebhi'ah,* "a woman, a prophetess" (Jgs. 6:8; 4:4). These expressions are used only once apiece, and that in the book of Judges, where the words *nabhi'* and *nebhi'ah* appear only in this combination.

c. It is significant that *'ish* also appears in connection with → רוח *rûach,* "spirit," or *ruach 'elohim,* "spirit of God." This means the divine power which differentiates the *'ish* who possesses it from other men, and emphasizes the special charisma which he has temporarily (Joseph, Gen. 41:38; Joshua, Nu. 27:18; the seventy elders, Nu. 11:25). Thus, the true prophet is also called *'ish haruach,* "the man of the spirit" (Hos. 9:7). It is quite characteristic, therefore, that (as is explicitly stated in 1 S. 10:6) the man on whom the spirit of God falls "is completely changed" (→ הפך *hāphakh*), so that because of it he emerges as "another man" (*le'ish 'acher*), who is called a "madman" (*'ish meshugga',* Jer. 29:26; cf. 2 K. 9:11; Hos. 9:7).

The expression *'ish (ha)'elohim,* "(the) man of God," occurs in all about 75 times in the OT. It is distributed in the OT books as follows: Dt. (33:1), Josh. (14:6), Jgs. (13:6,8), 1 S. (5 times), 1 K. (19 times), 2 K. (37 times), Jer. (35:4), Pss. (90:1), Ezr. (3:2), Neh. (12:24,36), 1 Ch. (23:14), and 2 Ch. (5 times), thus predominantly in the Deuteronomistic literature.

The only persons whose names are given as *'ish (ha)'elohim* are Moses (Dt. 33:1; Josh. 14:6; Ps. 90:1; Ezr. 3:2; 1 Ch. 23:14; 2 Ch. 30:16), Samuel (1S. 9:6ff., 10), David (Neh. 12:24,36; 2 Ch. 8:14), Elijah (1 K. 17:18,24; 2 K. 1:9-13), Elisha

(2 K. 4:7-13,16), Shemaiah (1 K. 12:22; 2 Ch. 11:2), and Igdaliah (Jer. 35:4). In several passages this term refers to men who remain anonymous (1 S. 2:27; 1 K. 13:1-31; 2 K. 23:16f.; 1 K. 20:28; 2 Ch. 25:7,9). All these persons are charismatics who are closely connected with God, but whose offices and duties are different. Sometimes the Bible reports nothing about such a "man of God" other than this name (Jer. 35:4). Also, every attempt to determine with certainty the geographical home of this idea is doomed to failure (the stories of Elijah and Elisha may favor the northern kingdom; but cf. 1 K. 12:22; 13:1ff., esp. v. 18; 2 K. 23:16f.; Jer. 35:4). In addition, there are other questions for which there are no conclusive answers. Thus, e.g., no satisfactory explanation has yet been given as to why Moses and David, as well as Shemaiah or even Igdaliah, are characterized as "men of God." And further: Is it accidental that this expression not only does not occur in the prophetic books, but also is not used to refer to the literary prophets or to other well-known charismatics (only the LXX of 1 K. 12:15 speaks of Ahijah as a "man of God," cf. 14:3), although the book of Jeremiah is familiar with this idea (35:4)? Why is it that the OT never uses the expression 'ish yhvh, "man of Yahweh," as e.g., it uses mal'akh yhvh, "angel of Yahweh," in addition to mal'akh 'elohim, "angel of God?" Although Elijah fought zealously for the success of the Yahweh faith, he is designated only as 'ish ha'elohim. The comparative material from ancient Near Eastern literature which is available to us at the present time is neither adequate nor certain, [29] and thus is unable to help us solve these problems. Also, there is no basis for connecting 'ish ha'elohim with demons. [30]

Hölscher compares the expression 'ish 'elohim with Arab. dū 'ilāhin, "possessor of an 'ilah, i.e., of a divine being or demon," who can also be a kāhin, "soothsayer." Then 'elohim here would not mean Yahweh, but "the demon," and the expression would be comparable with ba'alath 'obh, "a medium" (1 S. 28:7), and 'ish haruach, "man of the spirit" (Hos. 9:7), and originally would have designated one possessed by God. Haldar refers to Sum. lu-dingir-ra, Akk. amēl ili, "man of God," and interprets this expression as "man who is consecrated to the (cultic) service of a God." [31] Lindblom [32] understands 'ish 'elohim as a man who has a close relationship to God and participates in divine characteristics and powers and therefore is peculiarly well suited to be a messenger of God (→ מלאך mal'ākh) (cf. Hag. 1:13; Mal. 2:7). [33]

In view of all these facts, it is necessary to proceed very cautiously in interpreting this concept, and to begin only with data that are certain. It is significant that in the OT there is no 'esheth ha'elohim, "woman of God," corresponding to 'ish ha'elohim, although there is an 'ishshah nebhi'ah, "a woman, a prophetess" (Jgs. 4:4), and also elsewhere there is a nebhi'ah, "prophetess,"

---

29 Cf. Dhorme, RB, 40 (1931), 36.
30 So Hölscher, 127, n., against whom Junker, Prophet, 77f., has already given a reply.
→ אלהים 'elōhîm.
31 Haldar, 29f., 126f.
32 Lindblom, 60f.
33 Haldar, 128.

corresponding to *nabhi'*. Further, it is to be observed that the concept "man of God" is used in many passages as a particularly reverential designation (1 K. 17:24; 2 K. 4:9); thus, it is understandable that in a later period this expression was applied to Moses and David. So also, Manoah and his wife call the angel (whose identity was not yet known to them, but in whose countenance they sensed something supernatural) a man of God (Jgs. 13:6,8). It is characteristic that the angel comes with a specific message from God. Also, at other times the expression *'ish ha'elohim* is prevalent in the popular vernacular (1 S. 9:6ff.; 1 K. 17:18,24; 2 K. 1:9,11,13; 4:9,16,25,40; 23:17). But also the narrator (1 S. 2:27; 1 K. 12:22; 13:1,4ff.; 20:28; 2 K. 4:21; 5:8,14; 23:16) or a prophet (1 K. 13:14,26) uses it. Frequently, the "man of God" comes with a prophetic word to an individual (1 S. 2:27ff.; 1 K. 17:14; 2 K. 4:3; etc.), to the king as well as to the people (1 K. 12:22ff.; 13:1ff.; 17:1f.; 20:28; 2 K. 1:16). He is the one commissioned by God (as is explicitly stated in 1 K. 12:22ff.; 17:2ff.,8f.; 2 K. 1:15; cf. also 1 S. 2:27; 1 K. 13:1f.; 20:28; 2 K. 3:17f.), who, like an angel (Jgs. 13:3ff.), appears and vanishes suddenly (1 S. 2:27; 1 K. 20:28), but also can remain (1 S. 9:6ff.; 1 K. 12:22; 13:1ff.; 17:17ff.; 2 K. 4:9ff.). Quite often the expression "man of God" appears together with *nabhi'*, "prophet" (cf. 1 S. 9:6ff. with v. 9, where *ro'eh*, "seer," and *nabhi'* appear; 1 K. 17:18,24 with 19:16, where *nabhi'* appears). "Man of God" is even equated with "prophet" (1 K. 13:18; but cf. 1 K. 20:28, where a "man of God" appears alongside a *nabhi'* in 20:13,22, and alongside the *nebhi'im*, "prophets," in 20:35). 1 K. 19:16f.,19ff. speaks of the call of a man who serves for a long time as a disciple of a "man of God," only later to become a "man of God" himself (1 K. 19:20f.; 2 K. 2:2ff.). Yet, quite often "men of God" are "prophets" (they are equated in 1 K. 19:16; 18:22). In addition, "man of God" appears in connection with *ruach*, "spirit" (2 K. 2:9f.), and is acknowledged as a "holy man" (→ קָדוֹשׁ *qādhôsh*, 2 K. 4:9). Further, the OT indicates that "men of God" strongly refused to accept any gift for healing people, etc. (1 K. 13:7ff.; 2 K. 5:15ff.; cf. Jgs. 13:7ff.; contra 1 S. 9:7f.,10). Sometimes it seems to be widely known that a certain man is an *'ish ha'elohim* (a self-designation in 2 K. 1:10,12; cf. 1 K. 13:14); this helps us understand why such a man had the courage to appear before the king. The "man of God" often appears as a miracle-worker, either by the express commission of God (1 K. 17:14ff.; 2 K. 2:21f.; 4:43; cf. 1 K. 13:4) or apparently on his own authority (2 K. 2:8,14; 4:16f.). In the latter case, he performs his miracles through the power of God (1 K. 13:6; 17:20ff.; 2 K. 4:33ff.), or simply by prophesying (2 K. 1:10,12; 2:10; 4:4ff.; 5:10ff.). The curse of a "man of God" causes incurable illness (5:27) and even death (2:24f.).

N. P. Bratsiotis

אָכַל 'ākhal; אֹכֶל 'ōkhel; אָכְלָה 'okhlāh;
אֲכִילָה '^akhîlāh; מַאֲכָל ma'^akhāl;
מַאֲכֶלֶת ma'^akheleth; מַאֲכֹלֶת ma'^akhōleth

Contents: I. In the Ancient Near East. II. In the OT: 1. Meaning and Occurrences;
2. Noun Forms; 3. Figurative Use. III. Theological Uses: 1. God Gives Food; 2. Food Laws.

I. In the Ancient Near East. The Egyptian verb *wnm*, "to eat," is used of
men and animals alike, usually has a literal meaning, and often occurs in connection with *swr/swy*, "to drink." Figuratively, it means "to have the right of use
(of a possession)," or "to be absorbed in something" (e.g., sorcery, spiritual
power, hunger). It is also used of demons,[1] flames, diseases, etc., which "consume" something.

The Sumerian word meaning "to eat" is *kú*, which originally meant "to consume, use up." It also occurs with the meaning "to sacrifice."[2] In Akkadian,
akālu is used quite often in a figurative sense: "to spend" money, "to use" things,
"to take" portions, "to get profit from" a field, "to use up" something, and
further in describing "consumption" or "destruction" by enemies, sword, fire,
pestilence, etc.[3] Of particular interest is the use of *akālu* with *ikkibu* or *asakku*
with the meaning 'to break a taboo" (thus originally "to eat that which is forbidden").[4]

II. In the OT.

1. *Meaning and Occurrences.* The root *'kl* is found in all Semitic languages
with the same original meaning, and is used of both men and animals. In Hebrew, the qal, niphal, pual (possibly in reality qal passive),[5] and hiphil forms
occur. *'akhal* is often used with *shathah*, "to drink," in referring to functions

---

'ākhal. J. Gnilka, "Das Gemeinschaftsmahl der Essener," *BZ*, N.F. 5 (1961), 39-55; W.
Herrmann, "Götterspeise und Göttertrank in Ugarit und Israel," *ZAW*, 72 (1960), 205-216;
L. Köhler, "Problems in the Study of the Language of the OT," *JSS*, 1 (1956), 20-22;
F. Nötscher, "Sakrale Mahlzeiten von Qumran," *Festschrift H. Junker* (Trier, 1961), 145-174;
M. Ottosson, *Gilead, Tradition and History* (Lund, 1969); Pedersen, *ILC*, I-IV; J. van der
Ploeg, "The Meals of the Essenes," *JSS*, 2 (1957), 163-175; R. Rendtorff, *Studien zur Ge-
schichte des Opfers im alten Israel. WMANT*, 24 (1967); Y. Rosengarten, *Le concept su-
mérien de consommation dans la vie économique et religieuse* (Paris, 1960); R. Schmid, *Das
Bundesopfer in Israel. Wesen, Ursprung und Bedeutung der alttestamentlichen Schelamim*
(1964); de Vaux, *AncIsr*; J. Zandee, *Death as an Enemy, SNumen*, 5 (1960).

[1] Zandee, 158-160.
[2] Rosengarten.
[3] *CAD*, I/1, 245-259; *AHw*, I, 26f.
[4] See *ZA*, 41 (1933), 218f.; *RA*, 38 (1941), 41ff.
[5] *BLe*, § 42q.

necessary to life or as a sign of well-being and happiness (Gen. 25:34; 26:30; Ex. 24:11; Jgs. 9:27; 19:4,21; 1 S. 30:16; 2 S. 11:11,13; 1 K. 1:25; 4:20; 13:18; 19:6,8; 2 K. 6:22f.; 9:34; Isa. 21:5; 22:13; Jer. 15:16; 22:15; Job 1:4; Prov. 23:7; Ruth 3:3; Eccl. 3:13; 5:17 [Eng. v. 18]; 8:15; 9:7; Est. 4:16; Dnl. 1:12; 1 Ch. 12:40[39]; 29:22).

Frequently the expression *'akhal lechem,* "to eat bread," occurs, but it means nothing more than simply "to eat, to feed on" (e.g., Gen. 3:19; 37:25; 43:32; Jer. 41:1; 52:33; Ps. 14:4; Am. 7:12). The normal result of eating is to become full (*sabha',* which occurs quite often in Dt.: 6:11; 8:10,12; 11:15; 14:29; 26:12; 31:20; elsewhere it is found in Jer. 46:10; Joel 2:26; Ps. 22:27[26]; 78:29; Ruth 2:14; Neh. 9:25; 2 Ch. 31:10.

2. *Noun Forms.* Hebrew has six noun forms built on the root *'kl.*[6] (a) *'okhel,* usually "food, nourishment," but also "prey" when speaking of animals (Job 9:26; 38:41; 39:29; Ps. 104:21); in certain cases it can also mean grain (Gen. 14:11; 41:35; etc.; Joel 1:16; Hab. 3:17; perhaps also Dt. 2:6,28). Cf. Ugar. *'kl,* "grain, flour,"[7] or "harvest."[8] (b) *'okhlah* in general means "food, nourishment" (Gen. 1:29,30; 9:3; Ex. 16:15; Lev. 11:39; 25:6, all in P), but usually it has a figurative meaning; e.g., Ezk. 15:4,6 (the grapevine is given to the fire for "food"); 21:37(32) (Judah will be "fodder" for the fire); further Jer. 12:9; Ezk. 23:37; 29:5; 34:5,8,10; 35:12; 39:4. (c) *'akhilah,* which occurs only in 1 K. 19:8, includes bread and water. (d) *ma'akhal* is used for food of all kinds, e.g., in 1 Ch. 12:41(40), where it encompasses meal, cakes of figs, wine, oil, oxen, and sheep. It is also used figuratively (Ps. 44:12[11]; 74:14; 79:2; Jer. 7:33; 16:4; 19:7; 34:20; Hab. 1:16). (e) *ma'akholeth* occurs only in Isa. 9:4,18(5,19) ("fodder, fuel for the fire"). A cognate form, *makkoleth,* is found in 1 K. 5:25 (11). (f) *ma'akheleth* means "knife" (Gen. 22:6,10; Jgs. 19:29; fig. in Prov. 30:14).

3. *Figurative Use.* *'kl* is often used figuratively in expressions in which the meanings "to destroy, to consume," can be traced. At this point, the Hebrew is closer to the Akkadian (Sumerian) linguistic usage than to the Egyptian. Thus *'akhal* is used to express destructive or other hostile activities (so also in Akkadian).[9]

Consequently, when Israel suppresses her enemies, it can be said that she "devours" them (Dt. 7:16; Ezk. 19:3,6; 36:13; Zec. 12:6). The Balaam discourses use the figure of a lion or a wild beast, which "devours" the enemy (Nu. 23:24; 24:8). In a similar way, other nations "devour" or "consume" Israel and its land (Isa. 1:7; Jer. 8:16; 10:25; 50:7; Ps. 79:7), or "the strength of Ephraim" (Hos. 7:9). "To devour the poor (*dal*)" may indicate a hostile intention (Hab. 3:14) or a social injustice (Prov. 30:14). The king of Assyria "de-

---

[6] Cf. Köhler, *JSS,* 20-22.
[7] Hillers, *BASOR,* 173 (1964), 49.
[8] Dahood, *Greg,* 43 (1962), 72, who finds the same meaning for *'okhel* in Isa. 55:10.
[9] Cf. above, and *CAD,* I, 256.

voured" Israel (in the figure of a sheep that had gone astray, Jer. 50:17), as did Nebuchadrezzar (51:34). However, when Israel is restored, the enemies will be "devoured" by Israel because of Yahweh's intervention on Israel's behalf (30:16), or they will "eat their own flesh" (Isa. 49:26, an expression of complete helplessness, cf. the Kilamuwa Inscription, *KAI*, No. 24,6f., where the king eats his own beard and hand). [10] This is because Israel is holy, and those who "devour" her bring guilt upon themselves (Jer. 2:3). In Biblical Aramaic (as in Akkadian), [11] the root *'kl* means "to eat the pieces of someone" (*'akhal qartsohi*), and consequently to maliciously accuse him (Dnl. 3:8; 6:25[24]).

In the pessimistic report of the spies in Nu. 13:32, they say that Canaan is a land "that devours its inhabitants." [12] The same figure is also used in the description of the apostasy: "the land of your enemies shall eat you up" (Lev. 26:38; cf. v. 16; Dt. 28:51). Naturally, those who do the consuming are usually enemy armies, but one passage states that the "horses of Yahweh" will devour the land (Jer. 8:16), and another pictures Yahweh himself as the devouring foe (Hos. 13:8, which is toned down by the LXX!).

The result of apostasy from Yahweh is internal disorder, which is often described as an *'akhal*, "a devouring, consuming." Thus Micah reproves the princes because they eat the flesh of the people (Mic. 3:3), and Ezk. 22:25 says that the prophets "devour" human lives; by way of contrast, Hos. 7:7 states that the people of the northern kingdom "devour" their judges. This motif also appears in the Psalms: the evildoers "eat up my people as they eat bread" (Ps. 14:4; 53:5[4]; with a singular object in 27:2). One of the consequences of breaking the covenant which is mentioned in the OT is severe famine, as a result of which a person is driven to eat the flesh of his sons and daughters (Lev. 26:29; Dt. 28:53ff.), a theme that becomes historical reality in 2 K. 6:28f., and is used by the prophets as a sign of destruction (Jer. 19:9; Ezk. 5:10; 36:13f.; cf. Lam. 4:10). This feature has parallels in Akkadian. [13]

As in Akkadian, in analogous OT contexts the sword can be the subject of the verb *'akhal*. The sword of Yahweh devours enemies (Dt. 32:42; Jer. 46:10, 14), but it can also be directed against his own people (Isa. 1:20; Jer. 12:12; Hos. 11:6; Nah. 2:14[13]). The expression "the sword devours" belongs to war terminology (2 S. 2:26; 11:25; as well as 2 S. 18:8, where the expression "the forest devoured more people than the sword" illustrates the meaning of the verb in this connection and also contains an interesting tactical reference). The Israelites also used the sword against one another, cf. Jer. 2:30: "your own sword devoured your prophets."

Furthermore, *'esh*, "fire," is often used as the subject of *'akhal*. Yahweh is compared with a "devouring fire" (*'esh 'okheleth*, Ex. 24:17; Dt. 4:24; 9:3). "Devouring fire" goes out of his nose (Dt. 32:22) or out of his mouth (Ps. 50:3). All these expressions are well-known elements of the theophany. The word

---

[10] Dahood, *CBQ*, 22 (1960), 404ff.
[11] *CAD*, I, 255f.
[12] Cf. *CAD*, I, 249, "The country will eat wood and stones."
[13] *CAD*, I, 250, *akālu* 1.b.

of Yahweh is a fire, which burns up the people like wood (Jer. 5:14). The fire of Yahweh consumes the sacrifice (Lev. 9:24; 1 K. 18:38; 2 Ch. 7:1). Prophetic oracles against foreign nations often announce that Yahweh will kindle or send a devouring fire (Am. 1:4,7,10,12,14; 2:2,5; Isa. 10:17; 30:30; Jer. 49:27; 50:32; Ezk. 28:18). But fire can also be used as a means of punishment against his own people: Ezk. 15:7; Zeph. 1:18; against Jacob, Am. 7:4; [14] Lam. 2:3; against Judah, Jer. 21:14; Ezk. 21:3(20:47); Hos. 8:14; or against Jerusalem, Isa 29:6; Jer. 17:27; Lam. 4:11. The fire of God directly devoured the sons of Aaron (Lev. 10:2), the people at Taberah (Nu. 11:3), the rebels with Korah (16:35; 26:10), the embassy of Ahaziah (2 K. 1:10,12,14), and part of Job's possessions (Job 1:16). As in Akkadian, [15] the devouring fire also appears in war contexts. According to Nu. 21:28, fire devours the cities (?) of Moab and the heights of the Arnon, [16] and in Joel 2:3 in a description of the Day of Yahweh it has an almost mythological ring (a feature of the description of the theophany). According to Ob. 18, the house of Jacob will be a fire which will consume the mountains of Esau.

Abstract substantives can also serve as subjects of 'akhal. The heat consumes (Gen. 31:40); the shameful thing has devoured all for which our fathers labored (Jer. 3:24); zeal for the house of God consumes the psalmist (Ps. 69:10[9]); a curse devours the land (Isa. 24:6), as do hunger and pestilence (Ezk. 7:15); disease consumes the limbs of the ungodly (Job 18:13, Bildad).

In some OT passages (as in Akkadian), 'akhal has the meaning "to enjoy." One is said to enjoy the fruit of his lies (Hos. 10:13), or the fruit of his way, i.e., his behavior (Prov. 1:31). The OT speaks of enjoying riches (Eccl. 5:10 [11]), the wealth of the nations (chel goyim, Isa. 61:6), and the spoil of enemies (Dt. 20:14) (on the other hand, 'akhal keseph means "to use up money"; cf. in the Nuzi tablets akālu kaspa). [17] The statement "in toil you shall enjoy it (the earth)" in Gen. 3:17 is parallel to Akk. eqlam ikalu. [18] Job 31:39 says: "have I enjoyed its (the soil's) strength (koach, "yield") without payment?"

The only time Yahweh appears as the subject of the verb "to eat" is in Hos. 13:8. [19] Other gods consume sacrifices (Dt. 32:38), but the OT rejects any such concept of Yahweh, cf. Ps. 50:13. [20]

III. Theological Use.

1. *God Gives Food.* Man's food is a gift of God. In the creation man is given every herb and every fruit tree for nourishment (Gen. 1:29, P). Because of the Fall (which, incidentally, takes place through eating!), the way in which

---

[14] See Hillers, *CBQ*, 26 (1964), 229ff.
[15] *CAD*, I/1, 254, *akālu* 5.b.
[16] Ottosson, 64.
[17] Gordon, *RB*, 44 (1935), 36.
[18] Von Soden, *AHw*, 27.
[19] See above.
[20] Herrmann, 213ff.

man procures his nourishment becomes more difficult; now he must do it with great toil (3:17-19, J). The covenant with Noah introduces something new, viz., that now man may also eat the meat of animals (9:3, P); but he is forbidden to eat meat with its blood (9:4, → נפש nephesh, dam). It is part of Yahweh's divine care to give to his creatures "food ('okhel) in due season" (Ps. 104:27), so that they are filled (v. 28). It is emphasized again and again that God gives man food (Dt. 12:15f.; 32:13; Hos. 11:4; Eccl. 2:24; 3:13). As covenant God, Yahweh takes it upon himself to provide for his people in the wilderness (Ex. 16:4ff.); but here it is emphasized that he gives each person the right amount. Manna is a very special expression of divine care (Dt. 8:16; Ps. 78:25,29). According to Dt. 12:15, the people ought to eat "according to the blessing of Yahweh." At the border of Canaan the manna ceased, and afterwards the people ate the produce of the land (Josh. 5:12). Deuteronomy emphasizes the responsibility of enjoying the yield of the land with thanksgiving to God (6:11f.; 8:10ff.). As long as Israel is faithful to the covenant, the land gives sufficient harvest so that the Israelites "have enough to eat" (Lev. 25:19; 26:3-5) and also can take care of the poor (19:9f.; 23:22; 25:2-22; Dt. 24:19f.). Complete harmony reigns, which also involves the provision of food. But the goodness of God must not be used for revelry (Isa. 22:13; Am. 6:4,6); one must feed and clothe the poor (Isa. 58:7,10). In the coming age of salvation, each man will be able to eat the fruit from his own fig tree (Mic. 4:4; Zec. 3:10). The Rabshakeh promises the Jews the same thing in behalf of Sennacherib to convince them that he would be a good ruler to them (2 K. 18:31; Isa. 36:16), but the deceit of his words is proved in 2 K. 19:29; Isa. 37:30. According to the positive interpretation of the Immanuel oracle, everyone who remains in the land will eat curds and honey (Isa. 7:22– according to v. 15, Immanuel enjoys the equivalent of the food of the gods). [21] Also, Isa. 55:1f. describes the time of salvation under the figure of abundant provision (cf. also 25:6, which describes the feast on Mt. Zion).

Just as abundance of food indicates a right relationship to Yahweh, so also his judgment is manifested by a lack of nutriment (Dt. 28:17f.,23,31,33, etc.), or by one eating without being satisfied (Lev. 26:26; Isa. 9:19[20]; Hos. 4:10; Mic. 6:14; Hag. 1:6; cf. Prov. 13:25). Eating and joy go together, especially when one eats the tithe "before Yahweh's face" (Dt. 12:17f.; 14:23). Dt. 12:11f. and 27:7 mention the joy that accompanied sacrificial meals. [22] Sacrificial meals are mentioned in connection with special occasions, e.g., at the making of a covenant (Gen. 31:46,54; Ex. 18:12) and at the choosing of a king (I K. 1:25). Participation in sacrificial meals in the service of other gods was forbidden (Ex. 34:15), as was "eating upon the mountains" (Ezk. 18:6,11; 22:9), which clearly has in mind a Canaanite cultic practice. While a person was in mourning, he did not eat (Dt. 26:14; 1 S. 1:8), a custom which David broke when his little child died (2 S. 12:21). In a similar situation, Ezekiel obeys Yahweh's command

---

[21] Cf. Herrmann; but see Stamm, "Die Immanuel-Weissagung und die Eschatologie des Jesaja," *ThZ*, 16 (1960), 439-455, esp. 447; R. Kilian, *Die Verheissung Immanuels Jes 7,14. SBS*, 35 (1968), 64; H. Wildberger, *Jesaja. BK*, X/4 (1969), 262-64 (literature), 259f., 306f.

[22] See on this Pedersen, *ILC*, III-IV, 334ff.

not to eat "the bread of men" (lechem ʾanashim, Ezk. 24:17,22). Hosea speaks of lechem ʾonim, "the bread of grief (or mourning)," which defiles those who eat of it (Hos. 9:4). Eating gives life and strengthens the "soul." When eating involves some form of fellowship—with one's family, relatives, or covenant partners—it produces divine power which strengthens the unity. Meals establish harmony, which is the prerequisite for all communal life. It was a serious crime to disrupt such a fellowship (Ps. 41:10[9]). It was unthinkable for someone to eat with his enemies. [23]

2. *Food Laws.* Eating was strictly regulated by numerous food laws in the OT. The broad statement in Gen. 9:3 is restricted by the distinction it makes between clean and unclean (→ טמא ṭāmēʾ) animals (Lev. 11:1ff.; Dt. 14:3ff.). Eating the flesh of an animal that died of itself made one unclean (Lev. 11:40), and it was an abomination to eat animals that had been torn apart by beasts (Ex. 22:30[31]; Ezk. 4:14). No flesh that "had its blood (→ דם dām) in it" was to be eaten (Gen. 9:4; Ex. 12:7; Lev. 3:17; 7:23,26; 17:14; Dt. 12:16,23f.); in general, blood was forbidden food (Lev. 7:26f.; 17:10ff.; 1 S. 14:32ff.; Ezk. 33:25).

There were special regulations for Nazirites, soldiers, Levites, and priests, because their professions placed them in holy isolation. The Nazirite had to abstain from wine; in fact, he could not eat grapes at all (Nu. 6:3f.). It goes without saying that he could eat no unclean food (Jgs. 13:4). The expectant mother of a Nazirite also observed the Nazirite regulations (13:7,14). According to Uriah's words to David in 2 S. 11:11, soldiers in the levies gave up all claim to the pleasures of civilian life ("to eat and to drink, and to lie with my wife"); however, David and his men could eat the bread of the Presence when they were in the situation of the holy war (1 S. 21:1-6). [24] The Levitical priests, who had received no inheritance of their own, were to "eat the offerings by fire to Yahweh, and their rightful dues (nachalah)" (Dt. 18:1; cf. Gen. 47:22, which speaks of the priests of Egypt who "eat their choq," i.e., live on the income allotted to them); thus, they were to live on their portion of the sacrifices and other dues. Dt. 14:27ff. speaks of tithes of produce for priests, sojourners, widows, and orphans. Moreover, the priests were to eat the cereal-offering that remained of the offering by fire to Yahweh (Lev. 10:12f.), the breast that is waved and the thigh that is heaved (10:14). Likewise, the sin-offering was eaten by the priests, but only at holy places (10:17f.; Hos. 4:8). The Levites ate the festival sacrifice (moʿedh, 2 Ch. 30:22). The priest and his house ate of the holy votive offerings (qodhashim), but not when they were in an unclean state (Lev. 22:1ff.). However, neither a foreigner (an outsider) nor a woman married to a foreigner was allowed to eat the holy things (Ex. 29:33; Lev. 22:10,12).

Ottosson

---

[23] *Ibid.,* I-II, 305f.
[24] Cf. *ibid.,* III-IV, 10ff.; de Vaux, 258ff.

אֵל 'ēl

Contents: I. 'ēl in the Semitic Languages: 1. 'ilu > 'ēl As an Appellative of Deity; 2. 'Ilu, El As a Proper Name among the Semites; 3. The Etymology of 'ēl. II. The Character and Function of the God El in Canaanite and Related Texts: 1. El in the Pantheon Lists; 2. The Epithets of El; 3. El in Canaanite Myth; 4. El the Divine Patriarch: Summary. III. El in the OT: 1. El As a Divine Proper Name; 2. El As a Generic Appellative of Deity; 3. A Special Idiom with the Putative Use of El.

I. 'el in the Semitic Languages.

1. *'ilu>'ēl As an Appellative of Deity*. The term '*il* appears to have had the general appellative meaning "god," "deity," in the early stages of all the major branches of the Semitic family of languages. This meaning is well documented in East Semitic, Old Akkadian (*ilu*[*m*], fem. *iltu*, pl. *ilū*), and its daughter dialects beginning in pre-Sargonid times (before 2360 B.C.), and continuing into Late Babylonian. The appellative usage appears also in Northwest Semitic, in Amorite ('*ilu*[*m*]; on '*ila*, see below), in Ugaritic (*ʾl*, fem. *ʾlt*, pl. *ʾlm*, fem. pl. *ʾlht* with the rare byforms *ʾlh*, pl. *ʾlhm*), in Hebrew,[1] and in Phoenician ('*l*[2] usually replaced by the masc. pl. '*lm* [referring to a single god, a "plural of cult manifestations"]). In South Semitic the appellative '*l* (pl. '*l*'*lt*!) is not uncommon in the Old South Arabic dialects, rare in North Arabic where it is replaced by '*ilāh*.

2. *'Ilu, El As a Proper Name among the Semites*. The discovery of the Ugaritic texts beginning in 1929 has removed any doubt that in the Canaanite pantheon 'Il was the proper name of the god *par excellence,* the head of the pantheon. While '*il* may be used as an appellative also, e.g., in such an expression as '*il Haddu,* "the god Haddu," such usage is excessively rare. In mythic texts, in epic texts, in pantheon lists and temple records 'Il is normally a proper

---

'*ēl*. W. F. Albright, *Yahweh and the Gods of Canaan* (London, 1968); C. Clemen, *Die phönikische Religion nach Philo von Byblos* (1939); F. M. Cross, "Yahweh and the God of the Patriarchs," *HThR*, 55 (1962), 225-259; *idem*, "The Origin and Early Evolution of the Alphabet," *Eretz Israel*, 8 (1967), 12; O. Eissfeldt, *Ras Schamra und Sanchunjaton* (1939); *idem*, *El im ugaritischen Pantheon* (1951); *idem*, *Sanchunjaton von Berut und Ilumilku von Ugarit* (1952); *idem*, "El and Yahweh," *JSS*, 1 (1956), 25-37; I. J. Gelb, *Old Akkadian Writing and Grammar* (Chicago, ²1961); P. Miller, "El the Warrior," *HThR*, 60 (1967), 411-431; A. Murtonen, *A Philological and Literary Treatise on the Divine Names* אל, אלוה, אלהים *and* יהוה (Helsinki, 1952); U. Oldenburg, *The Conflict Between 'El and Ba'al in Canaanite Religion* (Leiden, 1969); M. Pope, *El in the Ugaritic Texts. SVT,* 2 (Leiden, 1955). We may mention the following works which are not used in this article: R. de Vaux, "El et Baal, le dieu des pères et Yahweh," *Ugaritica,* VI (1969), 501-518; J. C. de Moor, "The Semitic Pantheon of Ugarit," *UF,* 2 (1970).

1 See below, III.2.
2 On the sing. '*l*, cf. F. M. Cross and R. J. Saley, *BASOR,* 197 (1970), 42-49. The frequent, suffixed form '*ly* is to be taken as pl. with 3rd masc. sing. suffix.

name.[3] That El was the name of a particular deity should have been clear from the beginning from Sakkunyaton's "Phoenician theology" preserved in fragments in Eusebius' *Praeparatio evangelica.*[4]

Moving to East Semitic we find again very ancient evidence that 'Il was the proper name of a deity. 'Il appears often in Old Akkadian in the earliest sources[5] without the case ending (exclusive of the predicate state), unambiguously the divine name and not an appellative. The forms *Ilu* and *Ilum* are ambiguous as are forms written logographically with DINGIR, but many are no doubt the divine name. For example, the pattern *DN-is lum* does not occur, but kinship names (Abu-ilum, Aḫu-ilum, etc.) and like patterns (Ilum-bānī, "God/El is my creator," Ilum-qurād, "God/El is a warrior") are frequent and give the same picture of the god as patron, creator, "god of the father,"[6] and warrior that we find in unambiguous names. One finds also names like I-lī-DINGIR-lum/ Ilī-ilum, "my god is Il(um)." I. J. Gelb has gone so far as to say, "we may note the very common use of the element *Il* in Akkadian theophorous names, which seems to indicate that the god *Il* (later Semitic *El*) was the chief divinity of the Mesopotamian Semites in the Pre-Sargonic Period."[7]

In the Amorite onomasticon of the 18th century B.C. the god 'Il plays a large role.[8] Occasionally the divine name is spelled *ila*, which many scholars have normalized *'ilāh.*[9] It is perhaps best to take the -*a* of *ila* as a morpheme denoting the predicate state both in Amorite and Old Akkadian.[10]

Among the more interesting Amorite names are those compounded with *sumu*, "the name," *sumuhu*, "his name," *sumuna*, "our name," plus a divine name or epithet. The element *sum-* refers to the name of the god of the family or clan (that is, the personal god) on whom he can call or by whom he swears. Frequently we find this element compounded with *Il* or *Ila*: *su-mu-la-AN/ sumu(hu)-la-'il*, "his personal god is indeed 'Il," *sa-mu-ú-i-la/Samuhu-Ila, su-mu-AN/sumu-il*, etc. The same name formation is found in Heb. *shemu'el*, "Samuel" (⟨*šimuhu-'El*⟩*šimû'El*), and in Old South Arab. *śm'l*. Such a hypostatization of the name stands in the background of the Deuteronomistic name theology.[11]

---

3 Eissfeldt, *El im Ugaritischen Pantheon.*
4 The best critical text is that of K. Mras, *Eusebius Werke*, VIII/1 (1954), i.10.1-44. Cf. Clemen; Eissfeldt, *Ras Schamra und Sanchunjaton; idem, Sanchunjaton von Berut.* The most thoroughgoing recent study of Sakkunyaton is the unpublished Harvard dissertation of Lynn R. Clapham, *Sanchuniathon: The First Two Cycles* (1969).
5 The most recent study is J. J. M. Roberts, *The Early Akkadian Pantheon: A Study of the Semitic Deities Attested in Mesopotamia before Ur III* (diss., Harvard, 1969; now published). Cf. also I. J. Gelb, *Glossary of Old Akkadian* (Chicago, 1957), 26-36, esp. 28; *idem, Old Akk. Writing*, 139-142, 145, 148.
6 Cross, "Yahweh and the God of the Patriarchs."
7 *Old Akk. Writing*, 6.
8 Huffmon, *APNM*, 162f.
9 *APNM*, 165.
10 Cf. Gelb, *Old Akkadian Writing*, 146f., and *La lingua degli Amoriti.* AANLR, 13 (1958), 55f., 154.
11 Cf. S. D. McBride, *The Deuteronomic Name Theology* (diss., Harvard, 1969), 136-141.

Another frequent onomastic pattern in Amorite is the compounding of a kinship word with '*Il*: *Abum-’ilu*, "Il is the (divine) father"; '*Adi-ilu*, "Il is my (divine) father" (→ אב ’*ābh*); '*Aḥum-ma-’Il*, "Il is the (divine) brother (→ אח ’*āch*); *Ḥali-ma-Ilu*, '*Ammu-Ilu*, and *Ḥatni-Ilu*, all "Il is my (divine) kinsman."

The divine proper name '*Il* is frequently found in Old South Arabic.[12] As we have noted, some of the patterns of Amorite '*El* names are found in South Arabic.

In view of the appearance of '*Il* as a proper name in the earliest strata of languages belonging to East Semitic, Northwest Semitic, and South Semitic, we may conclude that this denotation belongs perhaps to Proto-Semitic, alongside its use as a generic appellative. To argue that one of the two denotations takes priority is to speculate in the shadowy realm of a pre-Semitic language, and is without point.

3. *The Etymology of ’ēl*. Of the several etymologies of '*Il* that have been offered by scholars,[13] two seem most likely to survive. One proposal is to derive '*il* from a root '*wl* meaning "to be strong" or "to be preeminent." '*il* conforms to the pattern of the stative participle of the weak root, i.e., the pattern of *mith* > *mēth*, '*idh* > '*ēdh*, and Ugar. *ỉb*. Such an etymology would explain the variety of derivatives, especially in Hebrew and Arabic. One must give a caveat here, however, for none of the derivatives of the putative roots coincide in form or meaning in the several branches of Semitic.

An alternate interpretation is to take the verbal root as denominative from a primitive noun: '*il*, like '*im*, "mother" or *shim*, "name." This would provide a better explanation for the fem. pl. *ỉlht*, fem. dual *ỉlhtm*, the sole forms of the fem. pl. and fem. dual in Ugaritic. Such an explanation would require a development like that of Aram. *sheᵉmāhîn*, *sheᵉmāhāt*, "names," or of Aram. '*emāhê*, "the mothers." In such case, the masc. sing. '*ilāh* (> '*lwh*) would be a secondary formation based on the plurals, an innovation of Western Semitic (Ugar., Heb., Aram., Arab.).

One notes also the derivatives *ỉlnym*, "deities," members of El's entourage, in Ugaritic, '*lnm* in Phoenician, vocalized *alonim* by Plautus.

II. The Character and Function of the God El in Canaanite and Related Texts.

1. *El in the Pantheon Lists*. In the three pantheon lists[14] found at Ugarit, first in order came *ỉlỉb* (Akk. *DINGIR-a-bi*) and *ỉl* (Akk. *ilum*). Dagnu (later Dagan) follows with (Haddu) Ba'al-Ṣapān in third position.[15] The designation *ỉlỉb*, Hurrian *en atn*, pl. *enna-šta attanna(šta)* apparently applies to a generic

---

[12] G. Ryckmans, *Les noms propres sud-sémitiques* (Louvain, 1934), I, 1; II, 2ff.

[13] Pope, 16-21.

[14] *CTA*, 29; *Ugaritica*, V, No. 18, 42-64; the third text, as yet unpublished, is described on 63f.

[15] Cf. the Hurrian god lists, *Ugaritica*, V, 518-527.

type of deity, perhaps the divine (dead) ancestors. [16] In any case, the executive gods, those of the cult, begin with El.

2. *The Epithets of El.* (a) A number of epithets reveal El as father and creator. He is called *tr ʾl 'bh ʾl mlk d yknnh,* [17] "Bull El his father, King El who created him." Though Ba'al is called son of Dagan regularly in these texts, here 'Il is called his father and progenitor. However, we are dealing with a fixed oral formula here which could be used of any of the sons of El, that is, any god (in *Praep. evang.* i.10.26, we find the plain statement that Ba'al was born to El). The epithet "Bull" is noteworthy. Names of the males of a number of species of animals were given to nobles and warriors in both Canaanite and Hebrew tradition. One may compare, for example, the epithet of the patriarchal god, the *'abhir Ya'aqob,* "Bull of Jacob" (→ אביר *'ābhîr*).

A like epithet is *bny bnwt,* [18] "Creator of Creatures," and *'b 'dm,* [19] "Father of Man." In *CTA,* 10 [IV AB], we find yet another El epithet: *k qnyn 'lm/ kdrd⟨r⟩ d yknnn,* "indeed our creator is eternal/indeed ageless he who formed us." [20] Yet another formula used of El is *ḥtkk,* "thy patriarch." [21] In later texts we find the liturgical name *'El qone 'arts* (Hitt. *Ilkunirsa*), "El, creator of earth." [22]

(b) Another series of epithets describe El as the "ancient one" or the "eternal one" with gray beard and concomitant wisdom. For example, Asherah speaks of a decree of El as follows: *tḥmk ʾl ḥkm/ḥkm 'm 'lm/ḥyt ḥzt tḥmk,* [23] "Thy decree O El is wise, Thy wisdom is eternal, A life of fortune thy decree."

In *Ugaritica,* V a new text has been published which applies to El the familiar biblical epithet *melekh 'olam,* "Eternal King." [24] A similar epithet of El is *mlk ʾb šnm,* "King father of Years," [25] reminiscent of biblical *'abhi 'adh,* "Eternal father," and *'attiq yomin,* "Ancient of days" (Isa. 9:5 [Eng. v. 6]; Dnl. 7:9; cf. Isa. 40:28).

In the Proto-Sinaitic texts we find the title *'Ēl ḏū 'ōlam,* [26] and *'ōlam simpliciter,* "the Eternal One," in the Arslan Tash Plaque. [27]

---

[16] Gese, *RdM,* 10/2, 104f.; differently → אוב *'ôbh.*

[17] *CTA,* 3 [V AB], V, 43; 4 [II AB], I, 5; IV, 47, etc.

[18] *CTA,* 6 [I AB], III, 5, 10; 4 [II AB], III, 31, etc.

[19] *CTA,* 14 [I K], I, 36; III, 150; VI, 296, etc.

[20] *CTA,* 10, III, 6. The reading is based on the reconstruction of Ginsberg, *Or,* 7 (1938), 1-11. Compare also *qnyt ʾlm,* "Creatress of the gods," a formula applied to El's consort Asherah-'Elath, *CTA,* 4, III, 30; IV, 32; I, 23; etc.

[21] *CTA,* 1 [VI AB], II, 18; III, 6; on *ḥtk,* cf. Cross, *BASOR,* 190 (1968), 45, n. 24.

[22] *KAI,* 26 A III.18; 129.1; see Cross, "Yahweh and the God of the Patriarchs," 241-44.

[23] *CTA,* 4 [II AB], IV, 41; 3 [V AB], V, 38.

[24] Text 2, 1, Verso 4, 5(?), 6; cf. Jer. 10:10. See already Cross, "Yahweh and the God of the Patriarchs," 236.

[25] *CTA,* 6 [I AB], I, 36; 17 [II D], VI, 49, etc.

[26] Cross, "Yahweh and the God of the Patriarchs," 238.

[27] Cross, *BASOR,* 197 (1970), 45; differently *KAI.*

(c) A third group of epithets reveal El as merciful and benign: *ltpn ʾl dpʾd,* "the kindly One, El the Compassionate." [28] From Serābîṭ el-Khādem comes the title *d-ṭb,* "merciful one." [29]

3. *El in Canaanite Myth.* (a) In a recently published text [30] we find El, called *rpʾ mlk ʿlm,* "the Hale One, the eternal king," presiding at a feast.

> El is enthroned with ʿAṭṭart ⟨of the Field⟩;
> El sits as judge with Haddu the Shepherd,
> Who sings and plays on the lyre.

The scene is a lovely one, the old king sitting in state with the shepherd Haddu singing in court as David sang to old Saul. Evidently Baʿal sits at the right hand of the father-god, ʿAṭṭart on his left. The scene fits strikingly with lore to be found in Sakkunyaton: "Astartē the greatest goddess and ... Adōdos, king of the gods, ruled the country with the consent of Kronos (El)" (*Praep. evang.* i.10.31).

The text ends in a broken but intriguing way:

> Let Rapiʾ the eternal king [judge (?)] in might,
> Let [Rapiʾ] the eternal king [judge (?)] in strength,
> Verily let him rule his offspring in his grace:
> To exalt (?) thy might in the earth,
> Thy strength before us (?) thy offspring,
> Thy grace in the midst of Ugarit
> As long as the years of Sun and Moon
> And the pleasance of the years of El.

One notes that the "ancient king" role stands in remarkable contrast to earlier pictures drawn by scholars of El as a receding *deus otiosus.*

(b) Remarkably, the chief text from Ugarit that can be labeled a *hieros gamos* tells of El (not Baʿal) and his two wives, and of the birth of his sons Dawn and Dusk (Shahar and Shalim). [31] The text is the libretto for a cultic drama. It has been badly misunderstood by reason of its impressionistic and repetitious series of scenes. Glimpses of action, El's hunting and feasting, the squeals of his wives being seduced, their love-making and the birth of the gods follow one another, but not in sequence, sometimes anticipating, sometimes repeating actions described earlier. We are given a description of the love-making and the birth, for example, followed by a repetition of the description of love-making and birth. The repetition is a literary or mimetic device, not an account of two different episodes.

----

[28] *CTA,* 6 [I AB], III, 4, 10; I, 49; 4 [II AB], 3, 31; etc.
[29] W. F. Albright, *The Proto-Sinaitic Inscriptions* (Cambridge, 1966), 44, and Nos. 360f.
[30] *Ugaritica,* V, No. 2.
[31] *CTA,* 23 [SS], 31-53.

After some broken text, the drama opens with El at his abode near the sea.

> [31] *El takes two ladlesful,*
>   *Two ladlesful filling a flagon.*
> [32] *Behold one: she bends low*
>   *Behold the other: she rises up*
>   *Behold one cries Sire! Sire!*
> [33] *Behold the other cries Mother! Mother!*
>   *El's power is great like Sea's*
> [34] *El's power is like that of Flood*
>   *Long is El's member like Sea's*
> [35] *El's member like that of Flood*
>   *El takes two ladlesful,*
> [36] *Two ladlesful filling a flagon,*
>   *He takes (it), he drinks in his house.*
> [37] *El stretches his bowstave*
>   *He drew his mighty shaft*
>   *He lifts (it),* [38] *he shoots skyward.*
>   *He shoots a bird in the sky,*
>   *He plucks (it), he sets* [39] *on coals.*
>   *El indeed seduced his wives*
> [40] *Lo the two women cried:*
>   *O husband! husband! stretched your bowstave,*
>   *Drawn is your mighty shaft.*
> [41] *Behold the bird is roasted*
>   *Broiled on the coals.*
> [42] *The women are (now) the wives of El*
>   *The wives of El for ever.*

After repetitions with subtle variations we read:

> [49] *He reclines, he kisses their lips,*
> [50] *Lo their lips are sweet,*
>   *Sweet as grapes.*
> [51] *As they kiss they conceive*
>   *As they embrace, they are made pregnant*
> [52] *The two travail and give birth*
>   *To the gods Dawn and Dusk.*

El in this text lives up to his reputation found in Sakkunyaton's lore that he was a vigorous and prodigiously lusty old man as is fitting for the primordial procreator and patriarch.

We have translated in the historical present since the movement back and forth in time is more easily expressed in this fashion. Line 32: The two wives, no doubt mentioned in the break, bob up and down in embarrassment and excitement. Lines 33ff.: We have expressed the *double entendre* by translating the identical cola differently. For the idiom "long of hand," meaning "great in power," compare Heb. *qitsre yadh,* "short of hand" (2 K. 19:26), or *hayadh yhvh tiqtsar,* "Is the Lord's hand shortened?" (Nu. 11:23). Of course, *'rk yd ʾl* can also mean "El's penis was long." Line 37: *ḥṭ* here means bowstave; cf. *CTA*, 19 [I D], I, 14, where *ḥṭ* seems to be in parallelism with *qšt,* "bow," and *qṣʿt,* "darts, arrows." The idiom *nichath qesheth,* "to string or stretch a bow," is found in 2 S. 22:35 = Ps. 18:35(34). Line 37: *mymmn* is denominative from *yamin,* "right hand." "To draw (with the right hand)" is precisely the meaning of *mayeminim ... bhachitstsim baqqesheth,* "with the right hand ... they could shoot arrows," 1 Ch. 12:2. *mṭ:* Heb. *matteh* means "shaft," "dart," in Hab. 3:9, 14; also in *CTA,* 3 [V AB], II, 15f., *mṭm* and *qšth* are a parallel pair.

(c) In 1948 B. Landsberger observed, "a certain probability for equating Baʿal-ḥammān with El emerges ... from comparing the triad of chief gods (Baʿal-ṣemed, Baʿal-ḥammān, Rakkab-El) [*KAI,* 24.15f.] with the group Hadad, El, Rakkab-El [*KAI,* 214.2,11,18; 215.22]. The variant El-ḥammān appears in late Phoenician inscriptions." [32] W. F. Albright carried the discussion further, noting the identification of Carthage's chief god, "Baʿal-ḥammōn," with Saturn and Kronos, his consort Tannit (the epithet *Tannit* means the "Dragon Lady," and must be identified with Elat-Asherah) [33] with Juno. Moreover he recognized that the popularity of child sacrifice in Carthage depended on an El cultus. It is El among the gods who sacrifices his own children, Yadid and Mot (*Praep. evang.* i.10.21,34,44), a theme repeated thrice by Sakkunyaton. Albright understood his epithet to mean "Lord of the Brazier," vocalizing the second element *ḥammān* or *ḥammōn.* [34]

There are now new data. From Ugarit come a number of names using the theophorous element, *ḫa-ma-nu* in syllabic writing, *ḥmn* in alphabetic (the names include *abdi-ḫa-ma-nu* and *ʿbdḥmn*). [35] In *CTA,* 172, we find the Hurrian reading in alphabetic script: *ʾn ḥmnd,* "god of the (mountain) Haman." These readings render impossible any connection with the brazier or incense altar, *ḥammān.* The laryngeal is wrong, as is the doubling.

There is every reason now to equate *ḥaman* with Mt. Amanus, [36] a form that rests on Gk. *Amanos.* In Old Akkadian the name was written *Am-a-num KUR.ERIN;* in later cuneiform we find *KUR Ḫa-ma-nu KUR. e-ri-ni,* "Amanus, the cedar mountain." The equation solves all the linguistic problems. There is yet more evidence. In *Ugaritica,* V, 510-16, Laroche publishes a hymn to El (RS 24, 278), in which we read the following: *ʾl pbnḫwn/ḥmn,* "El, the one of the mountain Haman" (lines 9f.). Recognizing that El's abode is in the very distant north, we can solve a number of problems. In Isa. 14:13, "I shall be enthroned in the mount of the council (of El), in the distant north," has been taken to be a reference to Mt. Ṣaphon (*Ḫazzi*) immediately south of the Orontes, the traditional abode of Baʿal Ṣaphon. In fact, the expression *yarkethe tsaphon,*

---

[32] *Samʾal* (Ankara, 1948), 47.
[33] Cross, *Eretz Israel,* 12.
[34] *Yahweh and the Gods of Canaan,* 203.
[35] *PRU,* III, 240, or II, 223; Gröndahl, *PNU,* 104f.
[36] Cross, *loc. cit.;* but according to Gröndahl, *PNU,* 135, the reference here is to the Hurrian god of weather.

"the uttermost parts of the north," elsewhere refers to the territory in the Amanus and farther north (Ezk. 38:6,15; 39:2; cf. Ps. 48:3[2], where Zion is identified with the northern mountain!).

(d) The descriptions of the abode of El and his council in the Ugaritic texts have been the subject of much discussion and little agreement. One of the most frequent themes, stereotyped and repetitious, is as follows: [37]

> Then she (Elat) set her face
> Toward El at sources of the two rivers
> In the midst of the fountains of the double deep.
> She came to the domed tent of El and entered
> The tabernacle of King, Father of Years.
> Before El she bowed down and fell
> She did obeisance and honored him.

The passage continues with a charming view of El receiving 'Asherah.

> As soon as El spied her
> He unfastened his scabbard and laughed
> He put his feet on his footstool
> And wiggled his toes.

He offered her food and drink and his conjugal bed before hearing her petition on Ba'al's behalf for a temple.

A second passage relates the arrival of Yamm's two messengers at the council of El:

> Then the two set their faces
> Toward the mountain of El,
> Toward the gathered council.
> Indeed the gods were sitting at table
> The sons of Qudshu(-Elat) at banquet
> Ba'al stands by (enthroned) El (qm 'l, cf. Heb. qum 'al).

The picture of El's abode given in these two passages places it at the cosmic mount of assembly in the north at whose base the cosmic waters well up, where the council of El meets in his Tabernacle of assembly (biblical 'ohel mo'edh), on the shore of the sea (cf. Ezk. 28:2). The description fits the Amanus, which towers over even Mt. Cassius. It also fits with the biblical description of "Eden, the garden of God at the mount of God, guarded by the cherub(im)" (Ezk. 28:2, 13f.,16). The mythic pattern which couples the cosmic river with the mount of God (the place where the gates of heaven and hell are found) is transferred to Zion in the Bible. This is patent in such passages as Ezk. 47:1-12; Joel 4:18 (3:18); Zec. 14:8; Isa. 33:20-22. The theme transformed also is reflected in Gen.

---

[37] *CTA*, 4 [II AB], IV, 20-26; cf. 2 [III AB], III, 4-6; 1 [VI AB], III, 23; 17 [II D], VI, 46-51; 5 [I* AB], VI, 1; 3 [V AB], V, 15.

2:10, where the waters springing from Eden are divided, one identified as Gihon. Perhaps the most extraordinary identification of Zion with the cosmic mount of assembly is Ps. 48:3(2) where Zion, Yahweh's holy mountain, is given the name *yarkethe tsaphon,* "the Far North."

A third form of the theme occurs only in broken contexts: [38]

> *Then he set his face*
> *Toward Luṭpān El, the Compassionate*
> *Toward the mountain* [...
> *Toward] Mount Ks* [...
> *He came to the domed tent of El*
> *He entered the tabernacle of King, Father of Years.*

It serves only to confirm the mountainous character of El's abode; it is interesting that the loanword *huršan* is used parallel to Canaanite *ġr.* One wonders what connotations it carried besides the usual meaning "mountain." Can it refer to the place of the river ordeal (cf. Akk. *ḫuršānu*)?

(e) In another recently published text, we find El feasting in his *mrzḥ,* the thiasos or cultic revel. [39] The gods invited to the banquet prepare food and drink for El, and his lackeys warn the gods to care well for the patriarch, who in consequence becomes drunk as a lord, and finally passes out, meanwhile having been confronted or assisted by a certain Ḫubbay, "he of the horns and tail," about whom we should like to know more.

(f) The exercise of authority by El over his council suggests that his role is more that of the patriarch, or that of a judge in the council of a league of tribes, than that of a divine king. It is extraordinary in this regard to discover two epithets of El, not discussed above, in the Hurrian hymn to El, [40] namely *ʾl brt* and *ʾl dn.* Laroche suggests that we read, "El of the sources (fountains), El of judgment." We should expect, however, "sources" to be written *bʾrt.* Rather, we should read *'Ēl bᵉrīt* and *'El dān,* "God of the Covenant," whose cult at Shechem is well known, and "El the judge" (compare the personal name at Mari, *Šapaṭa-Il,* "El has judged").

If one examines the major decrees of El, he is seen to be a strong but not absolute ruler. In *CTA,* 2 [III AB], e.g., El appears to give in to the desires of Prince Sea, giving Baʿal over to Yamm. Baʿal is the only member of the divine council who is not cowed. He stands by El's throne and rants at the court. Nevertheless Baʿal is given to Mot as his perpetual slave, and apparently he had not enough power to contest El's decision. In *CTA,* 6 [I AB], Mot, "the beloved of El," as he is called here and in Sakkunyaton, is doing battle with Baʿal. Shapshu warns Mot that if El learns of his fighting against Baʿal, "he [El] will overthrow your royal throne / he will smash the scepter of your judgeship."

---

[38] *CTA,* 1 [VI AB], III, 21-25, cf. III, 11f., II, 23.
[39] *Ugaritica,* V, No. 1.
[40] *Ugaritica,* V, 510ff.

Mot is sufficiently afraid of El to break up the battle and seek reconciliation. A final example we shall cite is *CTA*, 4 [II AB]. Ba'al desires a temple of his own. Asherah-Elat goes to El to lobby in Ba'al's behalf, and through flattery and cajolery gains El's reluctant agreement.

(g) Having examined El's role as patriarch and judge, we need to look finally on El's behavior as the divine warrior: El Gibbōr. P. Miller, in a paper entitled "El the Warrior,"[41] describes El's role as patron god of Kirta "the son of El." He instructs Kirta in an incubation to prepare and conduct a campaign of "holy war" in order to secure a bride. While in the mythic texts of Ugarit the great cosmogonic battles were waged by Ba'al and 'Anat, El like an aging David remained at home seducing goddesses; in Sakkunyaton he is a mighty man of war. His battles fit, however, not so much in the context of cosmogonic myth, but in myths of theogony, the story of the old gods, the natural pairs like Heaven and Earth, which "stand behind the pantheon." In the sophisticated, or in any case, typologically more developed cosmogonic myths, the theogony of the old divine pairs often functions as an introduction, giving the complex myth placement in "time." This is the case in Enuma Elish and also in the conflate series of cosmogonies in Sakkunyaton.

Theogonic series are also linked with the great gods in another function: the listing of witnesses to treaty or covenant. An intriguing case is found in the Sefire Treaty Inscription.[42] After listing the major patron deities of each party to the treaty, the text goes on to list primordial pairs: El and 'Elyōn, Heaven and Earth, Abyss and Sources, Day and Night. Similar references are familiar in Hittite treaties. It will be noted that in the list of witnesses the theogonic sequence is reversed, moving between the "executive" deities to more fundamental structures that bind even the gods. This special use of the old gods survives in the OT in the covenant lawsuit oracle; witnesses are called, Heaven and Earth or Heaven and Mountains, to hear the case of the divine suzerain against his rebellious vassal. As a matter of fact, El like Enlil stands at the "transition point" between the old gods and the deities of the cultus. Put another way, El reflects the patriarchal structures of society in many of the myths, the organized institutions of kingship in his titles and functions. He may be a state god or a "god of the father."

The particular wars of El are to establish his headship in the family of the gods. His wars are against his father Shamēm, Heaven, in behalf of his wronged mother 'Arts, Earth; the two, Heaven and Earth, are the last of the theogonic pairs. El takes his sisters to wife, and emasculates his father. The parallels with the Theogony of Hesiod are close: Earth by her firstborn Heaven gave birth to the great gods, among them Rhea and Kronos. It is Kronos who in defense of his mother Earth emasculates Heaven. Zeus, the son of Rhea and Kronos, went to war against Kronos and defeated them, casting them into the nether

---

41 Miller, 411ff.
42 *KAI*, 222.8-12.

world.[43] Similarly in the Kumarbi myth, Kumarbi emasculates his father Anu (Heaven), who in his own time had cast his father Alalu into the nether world. The most extraordinary tradition of what we may call the patricide-incest motif is found in a newly published theogony.[44]

Through some six generations of theogonic pairs, power is transferred by the device of patricide and incest. In the second generation the young god Sumuqan kills his father (whose identity is uncertain), weds his mother Earth and his sister Sea for good measure. Sea also kills her mother and rival wife Earth. In the third through the sixth generations the young god murders the patriarch (twice his mother as well), and regularly weds his sister (only in the third generation his mother also). In the seventh generation the young god holds his father captive. In the broken lines that follow we meet the great gods of the pantheon, Enlil and his twin sons Nushku and Ninurta, who apparently share rule amicably.

The existence of this "baroque" form of the patricidal and incestual pattern of the theogonic myth should make clear once and for all that the succession of the gods: Shamēm to El, and El to Baʿal-Haddu, etc., does not root in the history of a sequence of cults one following the other in the history of the Canaanite (Mesopotamian, Hurrian, etc.) religion. The pattern of violence in the generations of the old gods (one or more) comes to an end at the point of transition to the great gods of the cult, those who finally establish an uneasy, but tolerable peace. In Greece the transition goes over two generations, Zeus "the Father of the gods and man" successfully banishing his old father to Tartarus. In the Canaanite shift from the old gods to the established cosmic state, El like Enlil established himself father of the gods, associating with his son (or nephew) in his rule over the cosmos.

The myths of El present static or eternal structures which establish cosmos in nature and the uneasy order of a patriarchal society. They do not seek to explain the historical course of the rising or falling popularity of a god's cult. In the cosmic family of the gods, the patriarch always stands between the old (or dead) god and his lusty and ambitious son. It is this structure the myth describes, a primordial structure. The older theogonic pairs, at least in the first beginnings, inevitably must be incestuous. Moreover, patriarchal society creates settings in which the temptation to incest on the one side and revolt against the father on the other side constantly threaten peace. In the court history of David these forces are dramatically revealed. The rape of Absalom's sister Tamar by Amnon, another son of David, began a conflict which included fratricide, and ultimately the revolt of Absalom against David. The transfer of power was signaled by the violation by Absalom of his father's harem, and the episode ended only in a test of arms in which Absalom fell. The succession to David's throne by Solomon whom David appointed king in his last days also was marked by fratricidal conflict and harem intrigue. This is the pattern of life of men and gods who live in families, or extended families.

---

[43] Hesiod *Theog.*, 165-180, 455, 490, 650-730.
[44] CT 46, 39; see Lambert and Wolcot, *Kadmos,* 4 (1965), 64-72; Albright, 81ff.

4. *El the Divine Patriarch: Summary.* One cannot describe El as a sky-god like Anu, a storm-god like Enlil or Zeus, a chthonic-god like Nergal, or a grain-god like Dagon. The one image of El that seems to tie all his myths together is that of the patriarch. He is the primordial father of gods and men, sometimes stern, often compassionate, always wise in judgment.

While he has taken on royal prerogatives and epithets, he stands closer to the patriarchal judge ruling over the council of the gods. He is at once father of the family of gods and ruler, functions brought together in the human sphere only in those societies which are organized in tribal leagues or in kingdoms where kinship survives as an organizing power in the society. He is a tent dweller in most of his myths. His tent on the mount of assembly in the far north is the place of cosmic decisions. There are myths of monumental carousals where he appears to live in a palace (*hekhal*) and live like a king. Such uneven layers of tradition in oral poetry should not be surprising.

El is creator, the ancient one, whose extraordinary procreative powers have populated heaven and earth, and there is little evidence that his vigor flagged. To be sure, he rests now from the ancient wars in which he won his patriarchal authority; feats of arms "now" are fought by the younger gods, Baʿal in particular, and he shares El's rule. His old wife, the mother of the gods, is occupied with intrigues in the family. El appears affectionate toward her, but the *hieros gamos* texts we have reveal that he often turns to younger wives. His three major consorts are his sisters, ʿAnat, Asherah (the chief wife), and Astarte. Baʿal also takes ʿAnat as consort, and El shows particular favor to Astarte, the divine courtesan.

In Akkadian and Amorite religion, as also in Canaanite, he frequently plays the role of "god of the father," the "social" deity who governs the tribe or league, leading it in its migrations, directing its wars, establishing its justice, often bound to league or king with kinship or covenant bonds.

His characteristic mode of manifestation appears to be the vision or audition, often in dreams in contrast to the theophany of the storm-god, whose voice is the thunder and who goes out to battle riding the clouds, shaking the mountains with the blasts of his nostrils and his fiery bolts.

III. El in the OT.

1. *El As a Divine Proper Name.* (a) El is rarely if ever used in the Bible as the proper name of a non-Israelite, Canaanite deity in the full consciousness of a distinction between El and Yahweh, god of Israel. In Ezk. 28:2, the prophet's famous oracle on Tyre, he describes Canaanite El in excessively mythological terms, suggesting his awareness that he is singing of the Canaanite deity: "Because your heart was proud you (Tyre) said, I am El (*ʾel ʾani*) / in the seat of Elohim I am enthroned in the midst of the seas." The abode of El is here precisely described in Canaanite language. Yet there are problems. Ezekiel uses *ʾelohim* in parallel to *ʾel* here, and later in vv. 14 and 16 speaks of El's mountain as *har ʾelohim,* "the mountain of God"; and in v. 2 he uses *ʾel* in its fairly frequent generic sense. I am inclined to believe that the prophet was aware of the back-

ground of the language he used. In the phrase, "you are human and not divine/ El," it appears that he plays on the double possibilities of the meaning of 'el: "a divinity" / "the divinity El." Similarly in using the expressions gan 'elohim, "the garden of God," and har 'elohim, "the mountain of God" (cf. hr ʾl in CTA, 4 [II AB], II, 36), he may have been aware that 'elohim could be used with double meaning: the "plural of manifestations" of a proper name (like Ba'alim = Ba'al), as well as a simple plural: "gods." Still there remain problems and the evidence is not wholly clear.

In Jgs. 9:46 there is reference to the temple in Shechem of El-berith. As we have noted above, this appears to be a specific epithet of Canaanite El. Here again, however, one must ask how the epithet was understood in biblical tradition. In view of the parallel titles, "Ba'al-berith," the god was evidently understood to be a pagan deity.

Some have suggested that the expression 'adhath 'el in Ps. 82:1 be taken as "the council of El," and the poem read to mean that Yahweh (revised to 'elohim in the Elohistic Psalter) stood in El's council. I doubt that this is so, and would place this passage among those in early poetry where El is clearly regarded as a proper name of Yahweh. [45] However, there can be no doubt that the origin of the designation 'adhath 'el is in Canaanite myth. It appears at Ugarit in the form 'dt ʾlm, "Council of El." [46]

A similar frozen, archaic phrase having its origin in Canaanite mythic language is kokhebhe 'el, "the stars of El." The expression has turned up in the Pyrgi Inscription in the form hkkbm 'l. [47]

In the same category, I think, are the expressions 'arze 'el, lit. "the cedars of El" (Ps. 80:11[10]), and harere 'el, "the mountains of El" (36:7[6]; cf. 50:10). The ordinary explanation, that 'el here means "preeminent," or "grand," appears weaker, especially in view of El's abode in "the cedar mountains of the Amanus," to use the Babylonian designation. In the case of all these archaisms, it is unlikely that their original connotations survived in Israelite usage after the era when Yahweh ceased to be an epithet of El. [48]

The use of the apparent plural 'ēlîm requires special treatment. (We need not treat here the use of 'ēlîm and 'ēlê in such passages as 'ēlê gibbôrîm, lit. "gods of the mighty ones," in Ezk. 32:21, or 'ēlîm, lit. "gods," in Job 41:17[25]. These are simply orthographic variants of 'êlê and 'êlîm, "rams" in passages where the animal name is used as a military or noble appellation. Such usage [with various animal names] is frequent in Canaanite literature and in the Bible.) It occurs in the Bible only four times, three times in early Hebrew poetry: Ps. 29:1; 89:7(6); and Ex. 15:11. [49] The original referent was, of course, the family of El, or the members of the Council of El. In late apocalyptic (Dnl. 11:36; 1QM 1:10; 14:16) it comes back into use in reference to angelic members of

---

[45] See below.
[46] CTA, 15 [III K], II, 7, 11.
[47] Cf. M. Dahood, Or, 34 (1965), 170-77; J. A. Fitzmyer, JAOS, 86 (1966), 285-297.
[48] See below.
[49] See further Cross, JThC, 5 (1968), 1-25.

Yahweh's court, and is appellative in use. The two sole uses of *bene 'elim*, "sons of the gods," both in archaic texts, one evidently a borrowed Baʻal hymn,[50] require special consideration in view of the Canaanite evidence. In the Ugaritic texts the council of gods is designated by *dr bn ʾl*, *mpḫrt bn ʾl*, or *pḫr bn ʾlm*. El is called *'b bn ʾl*. Epithets of a single member of the family include *bn ʾl* and *bn ʾlm*. These data strongly suggest that *ʾlm* in the first two of the three phrases is a singular with the enclitic. In later Phoenician *bn 'lm* appears, e.g., *kl bn 'lm* in the Arslan Tash Plaque[51] of the 7th century B.C. Like the biblical occurrences, it is in archaizing poetry, and hence ambiguous. *'lm* may be taken as a singular with enclitic, a plural applied to a single god, or as a plural of the appellative. The *m*-enclitic survives as late as the 5th century B.C. in Phoenician. The balance of evidence suggests that *'elim* of the two Hebrew passages was the proper name *'el* plus the enclitic, a usage long dead in Hebrew when the apocalyptists revived the use of *'el* and *'elim*, taking the latter as an appellative plural. In Ex. 15:11 we have our only biblical example of the living use of the pl. *'elim* as an ordinary generic appellative before the time of late apocalyptic (Dnl. 11:36).

(b) In the patriarchal narratives of Genesis, there is a series of names or appellations of deity beginning with the element *'el* combined with a substantive or adjective, among them *'el 'olam*, "the Everlasting God" (Gen. 21:33; *yhvh* is secondary here), *'el 'elyon*, "God Most High" (14:18ff.; in v. 22, omit *yhvh* with LXX and Syr., as well as for traditio-historical reasons; → עֶלְיוֹן *'elyôn*), *'el shaddai*, "God Almighty" (this is in Priestly contexts: 17:1; 28:3; 35:11; 43:14; 48:3; and Ex. 6:3; the epithet also appears once in an archaic poetic context, Gen. 49:25 [with the tradition of the Old Greek] in parallel to *'el 'abhikha*, "the God of your father," which is sufficient evidence that P draws on an old tradition; → שַׁדַּי *shaddai*), *'el 'elohe yisra'el*, "God, the God of Israel" (33:20), and *'el ro'i*, "a God of seeing" (16:13). These epithets are tied to specific patriarchal sanctuaries or altars, El 'Olam to Beer-sheba, El 'Elyon to Jerusalem, El Elohe Israel to Shechem, El Ro'i to Beer-lahai-roi. El Shaddai, unlike the other epithets, is not firmly rooted in tradition, though P attaches it to Bethel in 48:3.

The epithets El 'Olam, El 'Elyon, El Shaddai, and El Ro'i are capable philologically of more than one interpretation. We may read the element *'ēl* as the generic appellative "god" with a divine name following in apposition, or with a substantive in a genitival relationship, or with an attributive adjective or participle. Alternately, we may take the first element as the proper name El, the second element as an adjective or a substantive in apposition, arising out of a liturgical formula or mythic epithet. Thus El 'Olam, for example, is capable of being interpreted as "the god 'Olam," or as the "god of eternity," which may or may not be an El epithet; or again, we may interpret El 'Elyon as "the

---

50 Cross, *BASOR*, 117 (1950), 19ff.
51 *KAI*, 27.11.

god 'Elyon" or as "El, the highest one." We have noted examples above of Ugaritic epithets which follow some of these patterns.

Evidence is available, however, that as in the case of Ugaritic epithets of deity, most fit the pattern proper name plus attribute (in one of the syntactical relationships listed above). The pattern *ʾl hd,* "the god Haddu," appellative plus divine name, is rare.

We must emphasize that these epithets, however, were interpreted in the tradition that preserved them as names by which Yahweh was called. At the same time, the Elohistic tradition of Ex. 3:13-15, and Priestly tradition in 6:2f. retained the memory that the name Yahweh was not revealed until the Mosaic age. These texts claim continuity between the religion of the Fathers and the Yahwistic faith of later Israel. At the same time, the texts, precisely in the insistence that Yahweh is to be identified with the god of the Fathers, disclose to the historian that the old religion and the Mosaic religion were historically distinct, or in any case belonged to two stages in a historical development.

There can be little doubt that El 'Olam must be read "the eternal (or ancient) god," and taken as a standard epithet of the divine patriarch El. The evidence from Ugarit, the use of *'olam* in poetic parallelism to "Asherah" in the incantation from Arslan Tash, and above all in the archaic epithet from Sinai, *'El dū 'ōlami,* "El, the ancient one," [52] all seem to point in this direction.

In the case of *'el 'elyon qoneh shamayim va'arets,* the translation "El most high, creator of heaven and earth" appears to be best. The widespread epithet of El, *'El qone 'arts,* "El, creator of the earth," including its borrowing into Hittite versions of Canaanite texts, is quite striking. A question remains about the epithet 'Elyon. It appears as an old god in Sakkunyaton, father of Heaven and Earth. In the Sefireh text the pair *'l v'lyn* is placed at the transition between the patron gods and the old natural pairs. It is possible to interpret the pair as a hendiadys or better as a double name of a single god as often at Ugarit. These develop from fixed formulaic pairs used in parallelistic poetry. The case is not clear.

I am inclined to believe the 'Elyon serves as an epithet of El and is not an intrusive element in the formula (the epithet also occurs in an early biblical context in Ps. 78:35). Such epithets expand and contract in a variety of lengths suitable to metrical form in orally composed poetry. [53] In any case, 'Elyon and El (to be read, e.g., in 2 S. 23:1 where MT reads *'al,* early orthography for *'eli,* 4QSamᵃ *'el,* presumably the *lectio facilior*) become epithets of Yahweh.[54]

The epithet *'El shaddai,* while the most frequent of these epithets, is the most enigmatic. The element *shaddai* is a familiar pattern of divine name formation: a natural element plus an adjectival suffix. One thinks of *'Arṣay, Ṭallay,* and *Pidray,* wives of Baʿal whose names mean "One of the Earth," "the Dewy One," and "the Misty One" or "the Lady of the Mist." Of the many etymologies suggested for the name, we have argued in the past that the best derivation of

---

[52] Cross, "Yahweh and the God of the Patriarchs," 236-241.
[53] A. Lord, *The Singer of Tales* (Cambridge, 1966), 30-67.
[54] Albright, 50, 164.

the name was from *ṭdw/y*, "breast," "mountain." [55] From Ugaritic have come new data confirming the existence of *ṭdy* in Canaanite with the meaning "mountains," and distinguishing it from *šd*, "field." [56] Thus, the personal name *šdyn* is related to ᵐA.ŠÁ-ia-nu with the ideogram for "field," while *ṭdy ṭdyn* belongs with ᵐša-du-ia and ᵐKURᵈᵘ-ia and contains the element "mountain." [57] Shaddai is thus the "one of the Mountain." We cannot yet determine whether El Shaddai was (1) Ba'al-Haddu of Mt. Ṣaphon, (2) an epithet of El like the other discussed above, or (3) an old Amorite god of the mountains who was identified early by the Fathers with Canaanite El. The importance of El's mountain is such that we are inclined to accept (2) or (3), or a combination in which Amorite El is identified with Canaanite El.

In summary we have found that the epithets *'El 'Olam, 'El qoneh 'arts*, and *'El 'elohe yisra'el* are epithets of El taken over from patriarchal tradition: *'El 'elyon* probably is to be added, and there is a possibility, at least, that *'El shaddai* is an El epithet. To these we should add *'El berith* and *Ba'al berith*, or what was probably the unshortened epithet, *'El ba'al berith*.

(c) The term *'el* is also used in the formation of epithets of Yahweh in the early cultus of Israel. Some of these persist in usage until late times. Late in Israel's history, for example in the sectarian literature of Qumran, there is a revival of the formation of epithets after the ancient pattern of El plus a substantive, adjective or verbal adjective.

In the archaic liturgical material preserved by the epic source in Ex. 34:6, the God of Israel recites his names *yhvh yhvh 'el rachum vechannun*, etc. Are we to read "El the compassionate and merciful" or "the merciful and compassionate god"? It must be said that the epithets here are reminiscent of El's, expressing the same benign attributes, and I am inclined to think that at least this portion of the long liturgical name is pre-Yahwistic. In any case, this archaic epithet is found in later tradition in slightly variant forms: Dt. 4:31; Jonah 4:2; Ps. 86:15 (probably *'el nose'*, "a forgiving God," in Ps. 99:8 is a reminiscence of the long formula with *nś' 'wn*). A formula somewhat similar is *'el qanna'*, "a jealous God," found in Yahwistic tradition (Ex. 34:14), Elohistic tradition (20:5; Josh. 24:19) as well as later tradition (Dt. 4:24; 5:9; 6:15; Nah. 1:2). There appear to be no parallels in Canaanite polytheism to the exclusive loyalty demanded by Yahweh in his covenant forms. We judge this epithet to have arisen in the very early cultus of Israel, patterned upon living liturgical epithets of the day.

In Ps. 29:3 is the epithet *'el kabhodh* (the article is secondary here). Probably it meant originally not "the god of glory," or "El the Glorious," but "god of the thunder cloud," the *'anan kabhedh* (cf. Ex. 19:16), an epithet of Ba'al originally. Much of the language of the storm theophany used of Yahweh is taken from

---

[55] Albright; Cross, "Yahweh and the God of the Patriarchs," 244-250.
[56] So A. F. Rainey.
[57] Cf. Gröndahl, *PNU*, 191f., 417.

Ba'al epithets. An obvious example is *rokhebh ba'arabhoth*, the Cloud-Rider (Ugar. *rkb 'rpt.*).

Another group of epithets combines *'el* with an abstract feminine plural: *'el de'oth*, "God of knowledge" (1 S. 2:3 in the Song of Hannah), *'el neqamoth*, "God of vengeance" (Ps. 94:1; cf. 2 S. 22:48), *'el gemuloth*, "God of recompense" (Jer. 51:56). Behind the variants *'el yeshu'athi*, "God is my salvation" (Isa. 12:2), and *ha'el yeshu'athenu*, "God is our salvation" (Ps. 68:20[19]), we should like to see an earlier formula: *'el yeshu'oth*, "God of salvation." But this is speculative.

Another epithet, likely to have stemmed from Israel's pre-Yahwistic past, is *'el gibbor;* probably it should be reconstructed as the original text of Ex. 15. It appears also in Isa. 9:5(6); 10:21, and in degraded form in Ps. 77:15(14).

In Ps. 68 another old epithet turns up, *'el yisra'el*, "the God of Israel," which is to be related to *'el 'elohe yisra'el* discussed above (Gen. 33:20) and probably was the inspiration for an imitation in Ps. 146:5: *'el ya'aqobh*, "the God of Jacob."

A popular epithet was *'el gadhol venora'*, "the great and terrible god." It appears in its most pristine form in Dt. 7:21 (cf. Jer. 32:18; Dnl. 9:4; Neh. 1:5; 9:32; Dt. 10:17; Ps. 96:4). None of the contexts in which it appears is early, however, and it has little claim to be an old liturgical cliché.

Next we should like to single out the epithet *'el chai*, "the living god," in Josh. 3:10, where it is placed in the context of holy war. It appears also in Hos. 2:1(1:10); Ps. 84:3(2); and 42:3,9(2,8). In late usage the expression seems to be used over against pagan gods, especially the dead idols. We doubt if this is its origin, however, and find it probable that it was the epithet of a god who dies and rises, in short a Ba'al epithet. Compare, e.g., the Ugaritic myth of Ba'al's return from death. The climactic cry is: *whm ḥy 'l3yn b'l/whm 3t zbl b'l 'rṣ*, "And behold, mighty Ba'al lives, and behold, the Prince, lord of earth exists." [58]

A number of other epithets of similar pattern exist (Isa. 45:21; Ps. 57:3[2]). It will be sufficient, however, to examine one more, an epithet used in Priestly tradition: *'el 'elohe haruchoth lekhol basar*, "El, god of the spirits of all flesh" (Nu. 16:22; cf. 27:16). Is the epithet merely a latish creation of the Priestly school using an archaic pattern? Or is the epithet a filling out of a more primitive and shorter epithet, *'el 'elohe ruchoth*, "El, god of spirits"? *ruchoth* is a proper early designation of members of the divine council (compare the description of the members of the Council of Yahweh by the term *haruach* and the council here called the "army of heaven," *tsebha' hashshamayim*, 1 K. 22:19-23). In this case, *'el 'elohe ruchoth* would be semantically nearly equivalent to *yhvh tsebha'oth*, "Yahweh of hosts."

(d) El in biblical tradition is often used simply as an alternate name of Yahweh. The distribution of the use of El as a proper name equivalent to Yahweh is highly irregular and hence significant. In Israel's earliest poetry this usage is

---

58 *CTA*, 6 [I AB], III, 3f.; cf. already G. Widengren, *Sakrales Königtum* (1955), 73.

frequent. In the Oracles of Balaam ’el as the name of the God of Israel appears six times, once parallel to Yahweh (Nu. 23:8), once parallel to ‘elyon (24:16), once parallel to shaddai (24:4), once in contrast to ’adham, "man" (23:19; the other two places where ’el occurs are 23:22 and 24:8). It is used also in 2 S. 23:5 (the "Last Words of David"), and Ps. 89:8(7) in a similar way.

In the book of Job, El is used some 50 times as the proper name of the God of Israel, parallel to Shaddai 12 times. The pattern of use of divine names in Job actually warrants a separate study. Yahweh is never used in the dialogues (Job 12:9 would appear to be an exception; however, the textual evidence is divided between ’eloah and yhvh). On the other hand Yahweh is regular in the Prologue and Epilogue, and in the rubrics of the Yahweh speeches; i.e., Yahweh only appears in the prose parts of the book. One must argue, I believe, that the poet of the dialogues belongs either to a different tradition, or is engaged in a heroic attempt to archaize, or both (Job is unusual also in using the rare ’eloah some 40 times versus some 16 occurrences in all other books).

The closest parallels to Job's use of El, other than the usage in the Balaam Oracles, are found in a few passages of the Elohist (Gen. 35:1,3; 46:3; Nu. 12:13) and in the so-called Elohistic Psalter. Some 15 times in Pss. 43–83, El is used as the proper name of God, more often in its 42 psalms than in all the remaining 108 psalms belonging to other collections.

These data suggest strongly the northern or non-Judean Israelite origin of the book of Job.

In describing the use of El as the proper name of deity in the Psalter, we must note also that El tends to be used in early poetry, especially the early psalms of the Elohistic Psalter (e.g., Ps. 78 has six instances of the use of El as a proper name of Yahweh), and in quite late psalms throughout the Psalter. This late usage of El presumably signalizes the revival of the use of El which we find highly developed in the Qumran and contemporary Jewish literature.

We have not dealt with the onomasticon of Israel in this study. [59] One or two generalizations should be made. The use of El both as a proper name of the god of Israel and as an appellative in personal names is most frequent in the earliest period of Israel's existence, and in the postexilic period. Thus we find the curve of distribution of El-names paralleling the general usage of the divine names in the literature of Israel. In the intervening period of the first temple, "Yahweh" displaced El as a proper name, ’elohim replaced ’el as the generic appellative. Presumably the increasing sense of the sacredness of Yahweh and the fully conscious universalism of the postexilic age converged to stimulate the revival of El as the name of Israel's god and as a proper element in proper names.

In the late literature of Israel only Second Isaiah other than Job makes extensive use of El as a proper name of the god of Israel (see, e.g., Isa. 40:18; 43:10,12; 45:14). We judge the phenomenon to be explained by his reutilization of old liturgical forms [60] and his general impulse to archaize much in the same way as does the author of the dialogues of Job.

---

[59] See Noth, IPN, 82-101.
[60] Cross, JThC, 6 (1969), 161-65.

(e) The phenomenon of the use of El as a proper name for Israel's God has some implications for the history of religion. Eissfeldt has argued strenuously that the free use of El epithets by Israel for their God on the one side, and the rejection and indeed hostility of Yahwists to the use of Ba'al-Haddu names and epithets on the other side, require explanation if the reconstruction of the origins of Yahweh is to be successful. [61]

The wide overlap in attributes, epithets, and names of Yahweh with El suggests that Yahweh originated as an El figure, splitting apart from the old god as the cult of Israel separated and diverged from its polytheistic context. The failure of polemic against El, and the free use of his image as the patriarch of the divine assembly, all tend to support such a thesis. We have argued elsewhere [62] that the name Yahweh itself originated as a hypocoristicon of a liturgical title of El, of the type beginning with a verbal element, a familiar phenomenon in Amorite and Canaanite divine names and appellatives. [63] Such a liturgical formula would be *'El dū Yahwê tsᵉbhā'ôth* or the like, "El who creates the (heavenly) armies" (cf. *ʾl mlk d yknn* above), an appropriate epithet of El.

2. *El As a Generic Appellative of Deity.* The use of *'el* is rather infrequent in Hebrew except as a designation for a pagan deity, and then its distribution tends either to be quite early or quite late. In the Yahwistic tradition of the Decalog in Ex. 34:14 we find *'el 'acher*, "an alien god." This usage is displaced in Ex. 20, as well as generally in Deuteronomistic rhetoric, by *'elohim 'acherim*, "other gods" (→ אחר *'achēr*).

Among the early contexts are the following: *'el nekhar*, "foreign god" (Dt. 32:12; cf. 3:24; Mic. 7:18; Lam. 3:41; cf. *'el nekhar* in Mal. 2:11, *'el zar*, "foreign god," in Ps. 81:10[9]; in Ex. 15:11 we have the single example of the appellative use of the pl.); *lo' 'el*, "no god" (Dt. 32:21); *mi 'el mibbal'adhe yhvh*, "who is God, but Yahweh?" (2 S. 22:32 par.); and *'el yeshurun*, "the god of Jeshurun" (Dt. 33:26). The form *'eli*, "my god," is rather frequent early: *zeh 'eli*, "this is my God" (Ex. 15:2); *'eli tsuri*, "my God, my rock" (Ps. 18:3[2]–note the replacement by *'elohe* in the parallel 2 S. 22:3–Ps. 89:27[26]); *'eli malki*, "my God, my King" (Ps. 68:25[24]; cf. 22:2[1]; 102:25[24]). Another phrase is widely distributed: *'eli 'attah*, "thou art my God" (Isa. 44:17; Ps. 22:11[10]; 63:2[1]; 118:28; 140:7[6]). Another widely found use is in the contrast between the human and the divine: *'adham velo' 'el*, "a man, and no God" (Hos. 11:9; Ezk. 28:9; Isa. 31:3).

Second Isaiah makes a considerable use of *'el* to denote pagan gods or idols which are no gods: Isa. 44:10,15; 46:6; 44:17; 45:20; cf. 45:15,22; 46:9.

3. *A Special Idiom with the Putative Use of El.* There is a series of passages (Gen. 31:29; Dt. 28:32; Mic. 2:1; Prov. 3:27; Neh. 5:5) that utilize a frozen

---

61 *JSS*, 1 (1956), 25-37.
62 *HThR*, 55 (1962), 250-59.
63 *Ibid.*

idiom: *'en/yesh le'el yadhi* and variants, meaning "It is/is not within my power." No suitable explanation has ever been made of the use of *'el* in this idiom even though the meaning of the phrase is clear enough from context.

The idiom is to be explained, I believe, by redivision of the words: *'en lo' leyadhi*, "my hand has no power." The root *l'y* is extremely common in Canaanite as well as other Semitic languages in the meaning "be powerful"; it has indeed been identified in a number of biblical passages, [64] and clearly is to be read here.

Cross

---

[64] Cf. Dahood, *Psalms,* I. *AB,* XVI (1965), 46.

אָלָה ʾ*ālāh;* אֵלָה ʾ*ālāh;*
תַּאֲלָה *ta'ᵃlāh*

Contents: I. 1. Etymology, Meaning; 2. Related Ideas in the Ancient Near East. II. Use in Legal Situations: 1. Protection of Property; 2. Proof of Guilt; 3. Execution of Authoritative Commands; 4. Ratification of Treaties. III. Use in the Religious Sphere, Covenant Ratification. IV. Metonymic Use. V. Theological Evaluation. VI. Qumran, LXX.

I. 1. *Etymology, Meaning.* Outside the OT, the root *'lh* is authenticated in Arab. *'lw* IV and V, "to swear, curse," *'alwe,* "oath, curse," and the Phoenician stative construct *'lt,* only in *KAI,* 27.9,13-15 with the meaning "curse" and "promise" (*krt 'lt 'lm*). In the OT, the verb occurs in the qal (Jgs. 17:2; Hos. 4:2; 10:4) and in the hiphil (1 S. 14:24: *vayyo'el;* 1 K. 8:31 = 2 Ch. 6:22: *leha'alotho*), and the noun *'alah* appears 36 times. The noun *ta'alah* in Lam. 3:65 is probably also to be derived from this root. In translating the different forms, one should always begin with the meaning, "to pronounce a conditional curse."

'ālāh. S. H. Blank, "The Curse, Blasphemy, the Spell and the Oath," *HUCA,* 23 (1950/51), 73-95; H. C. Brichto, *The Problem of "Curse" in the Hebrew Bible. JBL Monograph Series,* 13 (Philadelphia, 1963), 22-76; T. Canaan, "The Curse in Palestinian Folklore," *JPOS,* 15 (1935), 235-279; *idem,* "Flüche unter den Arabern Jordaniens," *Studii Bibl. Franciscani,* L.A. 13 (1962/63), 110-135; J. Hempel, "Die israelitischen Anschauungen von Segen und Fluch im Lichte altorientalischer Parallelen," *ZDMG,* 79 (1925), 20-110; F. Horst, "Der Diebstahl im AT," *Festschrift P. Kahle* (1935), 19-28; *idem,* "Der Eid im AT," *EvTh,* 17 (1957), 366-384; both of these articles now appear in *Gottes Recht=ThB,* 12 (1961), 167-175, 292-314; S. Mowinckel, *Segen und Fluch in Israels Kult und Psalmendichtung. Psalmenstudien,* V (1923), 61-135; J. Pedersen, *Der Eid bei den Semiten* (1914), 64-118; J. Scharbert, "'Fluchen' und 'Segnen' im AT," *Bibl,* 39 (1958), 1-26, esp. 2-5; further literature may be found under → ארר *'ārar.*

2. *Related Ideas in the Ancient Near East.* The use of *'lh* in Hebrew corresponds almost exactly with Phoen. *'lt* in *KAI*, 27 (see above, 1), which, according to the context, also signifies a conditional curse, i.e., in the ratification of a promise, but then by metonymy can mean the binding promise, the "covenant" (of the deity with a man), and thus can be the object of *krt*.[1] Akk. *māmītu* has almost the same meaning. Sometimes it appears with the meaning "ban" (esp. in the series of exorcisms), and sometimes with the meaning "oath" (in court, as the ratification of a treaty, in promises to be faithful).[2] One should also compare *arratu/erretu* (→ ארר *'ārar*).

II. **Use in Legal Situations.** *'alah* does not denote curses and imprecations absolutely, but only conditional curses which a person pronounces upon others or upon himself to protect legal rights or religio-ethical orders.

1. *Protection of Property.* It is clear from Jgs. 17:2 that one function of such curses is to protect a person's property: Micah returns the pieces of silver which he had stolen from his mother, because she had pronounced a curse upon the thief, and he must have been afraid that calamity would strike him because of it. When his mother learned that her son was the thief, she made the curse ineffective by pronouncing a blessing on Micah. Unfortunately, only the wording of the blessing is preserved in the text, and not the wording of the curse. But it must have had a form similar to that of the blessing, as is customary even today among the Bedouins in such cases. If a Bedouin loses something, he declares among his own tribe and among neighboring tribes: "I hold the person who finds this thing responsible for it. If he keeps it, may Allah cut off his property and his family from him." Then no one dares keep this article which he has found; he returns it immediately in order to escape the curse.[3] It is on this basis that one can best understand Lev. 5:1: "If any one sins in that he hears an audible curse (*qol 'alah*) to testify and, though he is a witness, having either seen or come to know about the matter, yet does not speak, he shall bear his iniquity." The "audible curse" is the conditional imprecation which the person who has been wronged pronounces on the thief, the thief's partner, or the dishonest person who finds what he has lost. According to Prov. 29:24, the thief's partner "hates his own life" because he has heard the curse and yet shares the spoil with the thief. In these cases, a private person legally pronounces the imprecation as soon as his property loss has been discovered, in order to make the thief or the person who finds it return it. Thus, the curse is in effect only under certain conditions, viz., when the thief or the one who finds the lost article does not return it. Furthermore, for the curse to be in effect, it is necessary for it to be pronounced publicly or made known openly.[4]

---

1 Cf. F. M. Cross-R. J. Saley, *BASOR*, 197 (1970), 42-49.
2 Cf. *AHw*, 599f.; Pedersen, 2f.; Brichto, 71-76.
3 Canaan, *JPOS*, 240; for further examples see Hempel, 38f.
4 Cf. Horst, "Diebstahl," 169f.

2. *Proof of Guilt.* In a legal proceeding, an *'alah,* "curse," serves to prove whether a person is guilty after the manner of an ordeal. Thus, the judge or the plaintiff puts the defendant under a curse which will take effect if the defendant is guilty. The procedure is described clearly in Nu. 5:21-28. The priest, functioning as a judge, "adjures" (*vehishbia'*) a woman accused by her husband for adultery "with the oath of the curse" (*bishebhu'ath ha'alah*): "Yahweh make you an execration (*le'alah*) and an oath among your people, when Yahweh makes your thigh fall away and your body swell. . . . " At the same time, he gives her the water of the curse to drink, into which the formula of the curse which had been written on a leaflet was rubbed off. The woman must acknowledge this curse by repeating *'amen* twice. Vv. 27f. state that the curse will take effect only if the woman is actually guilty. 1 K. 8:31 = 2 Ch. 6:22 is to be understood in a similar way: "If a man sins against his neighbor and is made to take an oath (curse) in order to put him under the oath (curse) (*venasa' bho 'alah leha'alotho*), [5] and comes and swears his oath (curse) (read *ubha' be'alah*) before thine altar in this temple. . . . " Here, *'alah* is the curse which a plaintiff pronounces against his neighbor who is accused of wrong, in order to force a divine judgment. In both cases the procedure takes place in holy places. Job affirms that he has never asked for the death of an enemy by pronouncing this kind of curse (31:30). Ps. 10:7; 59:13 (Eng. v. 12) (both passages use the noun); and Hos. 4:2 (which uses the qal inf.) have to do with this kind of curse in unrighteous or unscrupulous accusations against another person. As Nu. 5:21 shows, such curses are always prayers to Yahweh to prove that the accused is guilty. The prohibition in Ex. 20:7 is directed primarily against such unscrupulous ordeal curses connected with unrighteous accusations. [6]

3. *Execution of Authoritative Commands.* Furthermore, *'alah* is the conditional curse with which an authority forces his subjects to observe a command. According to 1 S. 14:24, "Saul laid an oath on the people" (or, Saul put the people under a curse) (hiphil *vayyo'el*), and in this way emphasized his command that no one was to be hindered from pursuing the enemy by eating a meal before evening. The wording of this curse is given: "Cursed (*'arur*) be the man who eats food before it is evening!" Also in Gen. 24:41, "my oath (curse)" (*'alathi*), from which Abraham will set his servant free if he finds no wife for Isaac in Mesopotamia, cannot be the oath which the servant took before him, but is the adjuration with which Abraham bound the servant to his task, though to be sure, nothing is said about this at the beginning of the narrative.

4. *Ratification of Treaties.* An *'alah* guarantees fidelity to a treaty. Both partners, or only the weaker who is forced into the treaty, take an oath in which they pronounce a curse on the partner who breaks the treaty. Then "a curse stands between them," as in the case of the treaty between Abraham and the

---

[5] On the emendation of the MT *venasha',* "and lends," to *venasa',* see M. Noth, *BK,* IX; and Brichto, 52-55.

[6] Brichto, 40-67; differently Scharbert, 4.

king of Gerar (Gen. 26:28). According to Ezk. 17:13, the king of Babylon "put him (the king of Judah) under the curse" (*vayyabhe’ ’otho be’alah*); but according to 16:59; 17:16,18, the king of Judah "despised" the "oath (curse)" (*’alatho*) and the treaty which he made with his overlord. Of course, it is not entirely clear whether the vassal pronounced the curse on himself or the overlord pronounced it over his vassal in case of infidelity to the treaty. But when Yahweh calls the curse "my curse" (*’alathi*), i.e., clearly "curse made by calling on my name," it is little likely that the heathen overlord called on the name of Yahweh; only the king of Judah would have mentioned him in his oath (curse). [7] In Hos. 10:4, the expression *’aloth* (probably inf.) *shav’*, "with empty oaths," can also refer to confirming a treaty with an oath by pronouncing a conditional curse on oneself, but in this case with the malicious intention of breaking the treaty again soon. [8]

III. Use in the Religious Sphere, Covenant Ratification. Since the covenant between Yahweh and Israel in the OT is understood according to the analogy of a treaty, this covenant is also said to be ratified by an *’alah*, "curse, oath." As a rule, this means the ratification of the curse with which Yahweh threatened the partner who broke the covenant (Dt. 29:18,20[19,21]; 30:7; Isa. 24:6; Jer. 23:10; Ezk. 16:59; Dnl. 9:11; 2 Ch. 34:24). According to Deuteronomy, Daniel, and 2 Chronicles, stipulated curses are written down in the document recording a given covenant. Zec. 5:3 reflects the same idea: the prophet sees a flying scroll. The angel explains to him that this is the *’alah* that goes out over the whole land. Here *’alah* is the curse written by God which threatens all evildoers, and also the destructive power which has already been released by their evil deeds. Similarly, written curse formulas and released destructive power are not clearly distinguished in Dt. 29:19f.(20f.); 30:7; and Dnl. 9:11 either. But in Neh. 10:30(29), "the people enter into a curse and an oath" (*ubha’im be’alah ubhishebhu‘ah*), which probably means that they pronounced a curse on themselves in case they should fail to keep the law. Since such curses are basic constituents of the ritual of transacting a covenant, *’alah* can almost be used as a synonym of *berith*, "covenant," or together with it as a hendiadys, in the expressions "to enter into a covenant and a curse" (*’abhar bibhrith ubhe’alah*, Dt. 29:11[12]), and "to make a covenant and a curse" (*karath ’eth habberith ve’eth ha’alah*, Dt. 29:13 [14]). [9] The noun *ta’alah* in Lam. 3:65 is the total calamity that, on the basis of the *’alah* which threatens all evildoers and protects the covenant law, overtakes the wicked.

IV. Metonymic Use. *’alah* can be used metonymically as a noun for persons on whom the curses pronounced in the contexts mentioned above come as devastating calamities. The expressions "to make someone a curse" (*nathan le’alah*,

---

[7] On Ezk. 17, cf. M. Tsevat, "The Neo-Assyrian and Neo-Babylonian Vassal Oaths and the Prophet Ezekiel," *JBL,* 78 (1959), 199-204.

[8] Scharbert, 4; Brichto, 39f., has a different view.

[9] Cf. further *KAI,* 27.8f.; see I, above.

Nu. 5:21; Jer. 29:18) and "to become a curse" (*hayah le'alah*, Nu. 5:27; Jer. 42:18; 44:12) are to be understood in this way. They mean that the person under consideration would be placed in such a dreadful situation that if someone wanted to curse his fellow, he would refer to the fate of that person. Jer. 29:22 and Ps. 83:12(11) show one way such imprecations were stated: "Yahweh make you like So-and so!" The words → שְׁבוּעָה *sh*e*bhû'āh* and → קְלָלָה *q*e*lālāh* are used in a similar way. [10]

V. Theological Evaluation. The meaning of *'alah* overlaps with that of *'arar* and *qalal*, but also with that of *shebhu'ah*, "oath." Therefore, many theological questions which are raised by *'alah* must be treated first under these key words. Reference must also be made to *barakh* and *dabhar*, inasmuch as *'alah* is related to word-magic, which attributes to the spoken and written word the power to actually bring about that which is stated in the word, whether it be good or evil. Such magical ideas are still in the background of many passages in the OT that use *'alah*. This is true perhaps of 1 S. 14:24. Here the narrator is convinced that the curse is effective only when it is publicly pronounced, even on those who transgress the command ratified by the curse without knowing anything about it. He thinks the first indication of the power of this curse is that there is no reply to Saul's inquiry from the oracle (v. 37). However, the magical element here is arrested and largely neutralized by faith in Yahweh. According to v. 45, a contrasting affirmation, in which one called on the name of Yahweh (whereby the people placed the person threatened by the curse under his protection), is sufficient to make even the curse of the king ineffective. In the curse of Saul, the name of Yahweh was not mentioned; this also indicates that it was close to magic. Usually the curses designated as *'alah* in the OT were already prayers to Yahweh that he would bring calamity on the evildoer and thus call him to account. This would also apply to Jgs. 17:2, even though we do not know the wording of the curse here. Like the blessing with which the mother neutralized the curse, the curse must also have contained the name of Yahweh.

In Ezk. 17:19, Yahweh explicitly acknowledges that it is his duty to guarantee a treaty which was transacted under a sworn oath in his name, even though the overlord to whom the king of Judah made the oath is a heathen. If a person put a defendant under a curse in a holy place, it was obvious that he was calling on Yahweh. In Nu. 5:21, the curse which the priest pronounced on the woman accused of adultery is explicitly put in the form of a prayer to Yahweh that he may bring calamity on the woman if she is guilty. Indeed, the Israelites were convinced that Yahweh would comply with this prayer and because of this the curse would not fail to take effect. Its efficacy was made even stronger by requiring the woman to hold the offering in her hand during the curse ritual. But the words of the priest leave no doubt that the Israelites knew they could not force Yahweh to act by word and ritual. This understanding is made even clearer in 1 K. 8:31 = 2 Ch. 6:22.

The Deuteronomist, to whom Solomon's prayer of dedication of the temple

---

[10] Cf. Scharbert, 11f.

is probably to be ascribed, knows that the curse does not necessarily come upon the guilty. One must ask God to put the curse into operation and to prove whether the person is guilty. It is obviously realized from the very first that a curse pronounced on an accused person may not be effective in every case and immediately, and thus his guilt may not be satisfactorily proved. Therefore, such a curse could also be abused in making unjustified accusations. Once the accusation was made and the ordeal curse pronounced, the matter was put in suspense because the curse might begin to take effect on the accused only after a long time, in the form of illness or some other misfortune. In any case, the person accused carried a public blemish if his innocence was not evident. Therefore, there is much in favor of Brichto's conjecture that the prohibition in Ex. 20:7 and the Liturgy of Entrance into the Temple in Ps. 24:4 represent attempts to put an end to this kind of abuse of an 'alah in which one called on the name of Yahweh. [11] Hosea denounces this sort of abuse (4:2), and the godly man expects such an 'alah to fall upon the unrighteous accuser when Yahweh calls him into account (Ps. 10:7; 59:13[12]).

It was only because 'alah was no longer understood as real magic that it could be connected with the covenant idea. Indeed, the curse with which Yahweh himself ratified his covenant with Israel constantly threatened the covenant-breaking people; but at the same time, the written curse formulas which were attached to the covenant law did not operate on the principle of magic, but only because Yahweh himself put the curse into effect from time to time. If Yahweh is in control of the curse, he is also free to stop it or to revoke it. But since the 'alah is a very effective instrument in God's acts of punishment, the godly can also see a meaning behind a dreadful event that comes upon the people in their history, and can recognize God's power in it.

VI. Qumran, LXX. In connection with accepting a new member into the Qumran community, the Qumran literature declares a blessing to the faithful, but curses to those who become unfaithful to the rule of the community, which is called a covenant (berith). In 1QS 2:16 and 5:12, these curses are called "curses of the covenant" ('aloth [hab]berith). But in the Damascus Document, the "curses of the covenant" are obviously the curses that ratify the Mosaic Law (CD 1:17; 15:2f.). In 9:12, a "sworn curse" (oath of malediction) is required to prove whether the accused has committed a theft, as in Lev. 5:1. The LXX renders 'alah in Gen. 24:41 (only the second occurrence, evidently for stylistic variation) and Lev. 5:1 by horkismós, in Prov. 29:24 by hórkos, and in Ezk. 17:18f. by horkōmosía, all of which mean "oath," corresponding completely to the meaning of the MT. Several times there is no word in the LXX corresponding to 'alah in the MT (Jer. 23:10; 29:18; Ezk. 16:59; 2 Ch. 34:24). In all other passages, the noun is rendered by ará and katára, "curse," and the verb by arásthai, "to curse." No striking variation in meaning is to be found in the LXX.

Scharbert

---

[11] Brichto, 59-67, 70f.

אֱלֹהִים   ʾelōhîm

Contents: I. Concepts of God in the Ancient Near East: 1. Egypt; 2. a. Sumer; b. Babylon and Assyria; 3. The Western Semites. II. 1. The Three Words for God; 2. Etymology. III. Definition: 1. Negation; 2. Adjectives and Verbs. IV. ʾelohim As an Appellative: 1. The Gods of Other Nations; 2. The God of Israel; 3. The God of an Individual; 4. "My God," "Your God"; 5. Simple ʾelohim; 6. Images of God; 7. Irregular Use. V. Assertions of Incomparability. VI. ʾelohim As a Designation of Yahweh.

I. Concepts of God in the Ancient Near East.

1. *Egypt.* The derivation of the common Egyptian word for "god," *ntr* (Copt. *noute*), is uncertain. The connection of this word with *ntr*, "soda" (used as a purifying agent, thus "pure"), which was advocated most recently by von Bissing,[1] cannot be proved.[2] The hieroglyphic sign for *ntr* was understood as an axe for a long time, and was interpreted as a symbol for power; but it has now been shown that it represents a pole with a flag or something similar on it, and probably symbolizes the sacred precincts.[3] When we look for other words for "god" with the help of synonyms, above all we find words like *šḫm*, "power, might"; *ȝḫ*, "spirit, glorified"; and *bȝ*, "soul," or according to the most recent investigation "ability to take shape."[4] A statement in a text in the Book of the Dead is instructive: "I was pure (holy, *wʿb*), I was *ȝḫ*, I was strong (*wsr*), I was *bȝ*."[5] Most of these ideas could refer also to men (at any rate, to the dead), who were thus transferred to the divine sphere. But even if the boundary between them is fluid, the repeated antithesis between "gods and men" shows that the Egyptians recognized that they were distinct. In any case, the idea of strength or power is common to the different synonyms for "god" and "divine." The

---

ʾelōhîm. F. Baumgärtel, *Elohim ausserhalb des Pentateuch. BWANT,* 19 (1914); U. Cassuto, "Il nome divino ʾEl nell'antico Israele," *SMSR,* 8 (1932), 125-145; *idem,* "Gottesnamen in der Bibel," *EJ,* VII (1931), 551-59; *idem, The Documentary Hypothesis and the Composition of the Pentateuch* (Jerusalem, 1961); O. Eissfeldt, "'My God' in the OT," *EvQ,* 19 (1947), 7-20 (cf. *KlSchr,* III, 35-47); J. Hehn, *Die biblische und die babylonische Gottesidee* (1913); C. Steuernagel, "Jahwe, der Gott Israels," *BZAW,* 27 (1914), 329-349.

On I: J. Černý, *Ancient Egyptian Religion* (London, 1952); J. van Dijk-W. G. Lambert, "Gott," *RLA,* III, 532-546; H. Frankfort, *Ancient Egyptian Religion* (New York, 1948); E. Hornung, *Der Eine und die Vielen* (1971), 20-55; S. N. Kramer, *The Sumerians* (Chicago, 1963); A. L. Oppenheim, *Ancient Mesopotamia* (Chicago, 1964); E. Otto, *Gott und Mensch. AHAW,* 1 (1964).

[1] Von Bissing, *SBAW* (1951), 2.
[2] S. Morenz, *Egyptian Religion* (trans. 1973), 19.
[3] Goldammer, *Tribus,* 4/5 (1956), 13ff.
[4] E. M. Wolf-Brinkmann, *Versuch einer Deutung des Begriffes bȝ* (1968).
[5] E. A. W. Budge, *Chapter of Coming Forth by Day,* 174, 15.

special power of a god is often called ḥkȝ, which is often translated "magic." [6]

From the proper names of the Old Kingdom, Černý derives the following characteristics of a god: he "abides" and "appears" (like the sun), he "lives," is "great," "powerful," and "strong," he is also "good" (nfr, "beautiful"), "merciful," "exalted," and "just." Like men, the gods have one or several ka, which are also mighty, good, pure, great, exalted, and abiding. Their ba (external manifestations) "appear" and are great and good, they give a child, protect it, sustain its life, help it, etc. [7] In the Middle Kingdom, other attributes are added, e.g., "sweet" and "pleasant," and here people are called "sons" or "daughters" of the deity. [8]

In the texts of the Late Period, Otto, among others, finds the following characteristics of a god: he is unique ("he has no equal"), omnipotent ("that which he says comes to pass"), omniscient ("he knows what is in the heart"), inscrutable ("no one knows his nature or his form," "his nature is hidden"), and righteous, connected with the maʿat; he also helps and answers prayers. [9] Otto also emphasizes "the ability of the deity to give light," [10] and the intimate connection between light and life (→ אוֹר ʾôr). Here the prominent position of the religion of the sun is clearly evident. By way of summary, Otto emphasizes "how strong an anthropomorphic concept of God exists here," i.e., human characteristics are ascribed to the gods, but of greater power. However, this fact in no way stands in opposition to the animal forms of most gods. Furthermore, nṯr is used not only of gods in the literal sense, but also of the deified dead (Pyr. 25; 394; 754; 2097; 2108; Tell er-Rīma XI, 55; Book of the Dead 101:10) and of the king, who is called among other things nṯr pn, "this god," nṯr ʿȝ, "the great god," and nṯr nfr, "the good (beautiful) god."

The Egyptian religion is essentially polytheistic. For various reasons, certain gods maintain a leading position, and then other gods are identified with them. Perhaps we are to understand by this that the great god takes on their form and manifests himself in them. [11] Among these relationships, it is worthy of note that the Wisdom Books often speak of "God" or of "the God" (nṯr, pȝ nṯr). This has been interpreted in different ways. Drioton found here a monotheistic tendency, [12] a faith in a single god, omnipotent, lord of events, providential ruler of man, judge and rewarder of good and evil acts. [13] Most other scholars reject this interpretation; e.g., Frankfort translates simply "the god in question." [14] A concept of the divine in general, which manifests itself in different deities, would be conceivable here.

---

[6] Černý, 56f.; cf. Ringgren, Word and Wisdom (Lund, 1947), 27f.

[7] Cf. also H. Junker, Pyramidenzeit (1949), 26-49; J. Sainte-Fare Garnot, L'hommage aux dieux (Paris, 1954), 171-184.

[8] Černý, 54f.

[9] Otto, 11-31.

[10] Ibid., 47.

[11] Cf. Frankfort, 20.

[12] E. Drioton, Cahiers d'histoire égyptienne, 1, 149-168.

[13] Ibid., 161.

[14] Frankfort, 67.

The relationship between the god and his image is considered in the Memphitic theology: "the gods entered into their bodies made of all kinds of wood, stone, clay, etc." Stated more precisely, the *ba* of the gods manifest themselves in their images.

The relationship of the gods to men is expressed by the genitive, as "the god of the city" or "the god of his city." Suffix forms are particularly frequent in the phrase "the man and his god," but there are also other examples (*Urk.*, IV, 114, "chief of the sculptors, who praised his god"; *p3y.k ntr*, "this your God"; [15] *ntr.y imn*, "my god Amun," "Upuaut, your favorite god"). On the whole, however, the examples are rather scanty.

2. a. *Sumer*. The Sum. *dingir*, "god," is written with the sign of a star, which can also be read *an*, "heaven."

"God is the object of religious awe." [16] This awe is called forth by the numinous power *me*, which the god possesses and which shines forth in *me-lám*, "divine, awe-inspiring splendor." On the other hand, *me* is a comprehensive term for a great number of forces and powers (orderly principles) which govern the various phenomena in the world, which are at the god's disposal and which he distributes. [17] When Ḫuwawa loses his seven *ní-te* ("terrors") or *me-lem*, he is a helpless man. [18] When the godly Gilgamesh ascends the wall of Uruk, his enemies fall upon the ground before his *me-lám*. [19]

The gods are understood as persons, and the same is true of natural phenomena: *en-ki*, Lord Earth. This personification implies anthropomorphism; but according to van Dijk it is doubtful whether we are to assume an older view with Jacobsen that the natural phenomenon is itself a god, and then anthropomorphism would represent a later stage. [20]

The creative power of the divine word is characteristic; everything the god says comes to pass, just as the word of a king is carried out. [21] Closely connected with this is the idea that the god "determines destiny," which is not to be understood in the sense of some sort of predestination, but rather as "the distribution of vital energy." [22] As a rule, the gods are considered to be immortal; only rarely does one find the idea of a dying god (in particular Dumu-zi). [23] The pantheon is understood as an assembly of people with the king at the head. [24] Generally speaking, demons are not called gods, but sometimes they appear in the lists of gods. Besides the great gods, "the personal god of the individual" also plays an important role. Usually the references are to gods of

---

15 Sethe, *Ägyptische Lesestücke* (²1928), 76, 20.
16 Van Dijk, 532.
17 Kramer, 115ff.
18 *CahTD*, I, 70, 52ff.
19 "Gilgameš und Agga," *AJA*, 52 (1949), 8f., 84ff.; cf. EnEl I, 138.
20 Jacobsen, *Proceedings of the American Philosophical Society*, 107 (1963), 473ff.
21 Kramer, 115.
22 Van Dijk, 541.
23 Kramer, 117.
24 *Ibid.*, 114f.

the family and of the dynasty, or personal tutelary gods. A man who is in distress turns first to "his god," who can in turn intercede for him to the great god if it is necessary. Another connection between god and man is expressed by the term "god of the land" or "the god of his land." The address "my god" appears occasionally. [25]

b. *Babylon and Assyria*. In Akkadian, the word for "God" is *ilu*, usually written with *AN* as in Sumerian. Occasionally the plural is used when referring to one god. The plural is often used in speaking of "gods and goddesses" (*ilāni u ištarāti*). [26]

According to Lambert, [27] *ilu* includes all superhuman beings and powers: (1) gods in the city and state pantheon; (2) the personal god of the individual, of which little is known, unfortunately; (3) demons, which are sometimes designated as gods. Deified men are rare; outside Gilgamesh and Tammuz (which is questionable), there are only a couple of examples of little significance.

One might derive a type of definition from EnEl I, 138; II, 24: *melammē uštaššâ iliš umtaššil,* "she (Tiamat) endowed them with splendor and made them like gods." Thus a god has *melammū* (cf. the Sumerian). Another characteristic is indicated in Gilg. XI, 194: "up to this time Utnapishtim was human, now he and his wife are (immortal) as we gods are" (*lū emû kī ilāni nāši*). Thus, the gods are immortal. In the so-called Theodicy it says: "The heart of the gods is far away like the interior of heaven," i.e., they are inscrutable and hidden. [28] The biblical idea that man cannot "see God and live" should be compared with Gilg. V, 4, 12 ("if a god did not pass by, why did my members shudder?"). The gods are also merciful and good, as is clear from *VAS,* 1, 37, III, 41: "The king has regarded him mercifully with shining face like a god." But when it is said to Engidu, "You are beautiful, you are like a god" (Gilg. I, 4, 34), it is doubtful whether beauty can be considered a characteristic of the gods; instead, it may mean general excellence.

The statement in Ludlul bēl nēmēqi II [29] is also significant: "when (men) are full, they feel like a god," i.e., they cross over the boundary placed between god and man, and live on their own responsibility (*ina ramānišu*). [30] The relationship between god and man is expressed in this way in CT XVI, 12, I, 44f.: "The god is the shepherd of man, and he seeks pasture for mankind." [31]

The character of a god can be determined more precisely when he is connected with a place or a function; thus, there are "gods of heaven" (*ilāni ša šamê*), "gods and goddesses of the land," [32] "gods of the Amurru," "god or gods of the

---

[25] *ANET³*, 590.

[26] *CAD,* VII, 97.

[27] *RLA.*

[28] *BWL,* 86, 256.

[29] *BWL,* 40-45.

[30] G. Widengren, *The Accadian and Hebrew Psalms of Lamentation* (1937), 141f., 162.

[31] *CAD,* VII, 95.

[32] *CAD,* VII, 92f.

city," gods of certain temples, etc. Here it is noteworthy that the gods of a land or of a city can leave their dwelling place and return to it. [33] There is also a "god of dreams," "gods of the battle," and "gods of the night," i.e., stars. [34] Furthermore, there are expressions which indicate different relationships between the gods and men, e.g., "gods of the king," "the god of the man" (il amēli), [35] and "the god of my father" (→ אב ʾābh). Suffix forms ("my, your, his, our, their god") occur rather frequently to express the special relationship between man and god; cf. especially "a man speaks to his god in behalf of his friend in tears," "his god is not helping him," "I want to sacrifice to my god," "my (his) god is angry with me (him)," "I strove to praise my god and my goddess." [36] The address "my god" is found in certain psalms of lament. [37] Success and happiness are ascribed to supernatural powers which fill the body of man or preserve it. These may be called lamassu or šēdu (tutelary gods), but they may also be called simply ilu. Thus, "a man who has a god" is a successful and happy man. In such cases, ilu is a kind of spiritual gift which brings about a man's good destiny. [38]

The Sumerian gods were more numerous than the Semitic, which so to speak "claimed more power." [39] Therefore, the Babylonian theologians created a theology of identification quite early, which "sublimated the majority of Sumerian gods to mere names and hypostases of a smaller number of gods." Thus, e.g., Marduk received his 50 names. Later (after ca. 1200 B.C.), the "great gods" were identified with each other, or they were interpreted as personified attributes or parts of one god. [40]

3. The Western Semites. In Ugaritic, ʾl with its plural ʾlm is the usual word for "god"; the singular is also a proper name, El (→ אל ʾēl). There is also a feminine form ʾlt, pl. ʾlht. Perhaps a cognate form ʾlh, which would correspond to Heb. ʾelohim, is to be inferred in some damaged passages; [41] the corresponding pl. ʾlhm is rare, and its exact meaning is debated (gdlt ʾlhm, "godlike cow," i.e., splendid cow, or "a cow belonging to the gods"?). [42] In Phoenician, ʾl with the pl. ʾlm or ʾlnm (transliterated into Latin as allonim; also appearing sometimes in Ugaritic) and the fem. ʾlt is the usual word for "god"; the Aramaic inscriptions use ʾlh, fem. ʾlht. [43]

Neither the Ugaritic texts nor the inscriptions are especially productive with regard to the attributes of deity. In Ugaritic and Phoenician, qdš, "holy,"

---

[33] Examples in CAD, VII, 92f.
[34] CAD, VII, 94f.
[35] Cf. above.
[36] CAD, VII, 95f.
[37] SAHG, No. 79; IV R, 10; ANET, 391f.
[38] Oppenheim, 199f., 206.
[39] Von Soden.
[40] E.g., SAHG, 301f., 258f.; cf. W. von Soden, MDOG, 96 (1965), 45f.
[41] Pope, 7.
[42] Ibid., 7f.
[43] DISO, 13f.

appears as a divine epithet; perhaps it may be assumed that the meaning of this word is not far from that of the Hebrew. Theophorous proper names characterize the deity as "mighty," "exalted," and "just," but also as one who "gives," "helps," "liberates," "protects," "sustains," "blesses," and "is gracious." Here we get a general picture of the concept of god. [44]

The Aqhat Epic adds another feature. When the goddess Anat offers Aqhat immortality in exchange for his bow, she sends him away, pointing out that as a man he must still die. [45] It is clear from this that immortality is a divine prerogative. The same thought lies behind the question addressed to Keret: "Should you die, then, like men?" [46]

II. 1. *The Three Words for God.* The OT uses three different words for "God," viz., *'el, 'eloah,* and *'elohim.* In general these words are interchangeable, as is clear from the following examples: in Ps. 29:1 and 89:7 (Eng. v. 6), we find *bene 'elim,* lit. "sons of the gods" (RSV–"heavenly beings"), while in Gen. 6:2; Job 1:6; 2:1; 38:7 we find *bene 'elohim,* with the same meaning. The OT has *'el chai, 'elohim chayyim,* and *'elohim chai,* all meaning "the living God," as well as *'el nekhar* and *'elohe nekhar,* meaning "foreign god." [47] In Ex. 34:14 we find *'el 'acher,* "other god," while elsewhere we find *'elohim 'acherim* (→ אַחֵר *'achēr*). Ps. 18:32(31), "Who is *'eloah* (God) but Yahweh?" is parallel to 2 S. 22:32, "Who is *'el* but Yahweh?" Ex. 15:11 has, "Who is like thee *ba'elim* (among the gods)?", while Ps. 86:8 expresses the same thought in this way: "There is none like thee *ba'elohim.*" In Dt. 32:17 we find the expression *lo' 'eloah,* "no god," and in v. 21 *lo' 'el.* No clear rule for the use of these words can be recognized in the OT, but *'el* occurs mainly in poetic and archaic or archaizing texts (→ אל *'ēl*).

Of the 57 occurrences of *'eloah,* 41 are found in Job, viz., in the Dialogue, where Job and his friends, who are not Israelites and thus do not know the God of Israel, use designations for God other than Yahweh exclusively (besides *'eloah, 'el* occurs in Job 55 times, *'elohim* 4 times, and *shaddai* 31 times). *'eloah* is used rarely as an appellative (only in Dt. 32:17; Isa. 44:8; Ps. 18:32[31]; Dnl. 11:38; 2 Ch. 32:15), only once with a suffix (Hab. 1:11), once in the expression "God of Jacob" (Ps. 114:7), and once in the expression "God of forgiveness" (*'eloah selichoth,* Neh. 9:17).

The form *'elohim* occurs 2570 times in all, with both the plural ("gods") and the singular ("a god," "God") meaning. As a rule, verbs and adjectives used with *'elohim* are either singular or plural in conformity with the meaning; there are only rare exceptions. Why the plural form for "God" is used has not yet been explained satisfactorily. Perhaps the plural also or even originally desig-

---

[44] F. Jeremias, "Chantepie de la Saussaye," *Lehrbuch der Religionsgeschichte,* I (²1925), 635.

[45] *CTA,* 17 [II D], VI, 25-35.

[46] *CTA,* 16 [II K], I, 17f.

[47] See below.

nated not a plurality, but an intensification; then *'elohim* would mean the "great," "highest," and finally "only" God, i.e., God in general. [48]

2. *Etymology.* *'elohim* also presents a difficult etymological problem. An exact cognate appears only in Aramaic (*'elah[ah]*) and in Arabic (*'ilāh*). There are only late derivatives from Aram. *'elah* (as *'elahotha'*); the same is true of Arab. *'ilāh* (verb *ta'ullaha*, "to devote oneself to godly practices," etc.). Thus, we cannot assume a verbal root. On the other hand, *'el* is a common Semitic word (lacking only in Ethiopic and perhaps classical Arabic), and appears sometimes as a proper name and sometimes as an appellative (→ אל *'ēl*). It could be derived from the root *'wl,* and then it would denote either might or first in rank (cf. Arab. *'awwal,* "first"). These two meanings may have belonged together originally. [49] It is usually assumed that *'el* and *'elohim* are related, viz., *'elohim* would be a plural form of *'el* expanded with the *he.* This sort of expansion also occurs elsewhere in Hebrew and Aramaic. [50] Then *'eloah* would be a late singular form derived from *'elohim.* However, this hypothesis is not completely without difficulties. First, plural forms expanded with *he* are usually derived from originally biconsonantal roots, which would not agree with the derivation of *'el* from *'wl.* Second, the Arab. *'ilāh* opposes the assumption of a special Hebrew-Aramaic development. Perhaps originally two different roots existed, which were later combined (because of the similarity of their sounds?). At the same time, nothing in the linguistic use of these words opposes the assumption of an original meaning "might, power."

Zimmermann's suggestion that these words are to be derived from the root *'ll* [51] is particularly improbable, because no form with the double *lamedh* occurs in any Semitic language.

III. Definition.

1. *Negation.* However, in order to attain a more exact definition of the idea of "God," it is necessary to begin with the passages in which *'elohim* (or *'el*) stands in antithesis to something else, or where it is denied that a creature is a god.

"Man" especially appears in antithesis to "God." "God (*'el*) is not man (→ אישׁ *'îsh*), that he should lie, nor a son of man (*ben* → אדם *'ādhām*), that he should repent (→ יתנחם *yithnechām*)" (Nu. 23:19, the Oracles of Balaam, E), i.e., what God has said stands firm for ever, while human words are deceptive and changeable (cf. v. 20). "The Egyptians are men (*'adham*), and not God (*'el*); and their horses are flesh, and not spirit" (Isa. 31:3); thus the same contrast which stands between God and man also stands between spirit and flesh (→ בשׂר *bāśār*). The context shows that what the writer has in mind is the power

---

[48] Cf. *GK,* § 124e, g.
[49] Cf. Ringgren, *RdM,* 26, 59.
[50] Cf. *BLe,* § 78f.: vocative?
[51] Zimmermann, *VT,* 12 (1962), 190-95.

and strength of God and the defenselessness of human enemies. In Ezk. 28:2, the king of Tyre says: "I am a god (*'el 'ani*), I sit in the seat of the gods" (*moshabh 'elohim yashabhti*). But when the enemies come, saying he is a god will not help him, "since you are but a man, and no god" (*ve'attah 'adham velo' 'el*, v. 9). Thus the hubris of the king stands in contrast to his actual helplessness as a man. Further, Yahweh says in Hos. 11:9: "I am *'el* and not man (*'ish*), the Holy One in your midst." It follows that the holiness of God here is not manifested in punitive wrath, but in compassion and forgiveness–a typical Hoseanic idea.

It is worthy of note that all these passages use *'el*, not *'elohim*. On the other hand, the passages which deny that someone is a god exhibit a greater variety of expression.

In Dt. 32:15-21, the idolatry of the Israelites is reproved. This passage says that they sacrificed to *shedhim*, "demons" (→ שֵׁד *shēdh*), which were no gods (*lo' 'eloah*) (v. 17), and stirred up the jealousy of Yahweh "with what is no god" (*lo' 'el*). The context says that they had forsaken the God (*'eloah* or *'el*) who had made them (*'asah*) (v. 15) and had begotten them (*cholel*). They had served strange (gods) (→ זרים *zārîm*) or "new gods," whom their fathers had not known (v. 17); finally these gods are designated as → הבלים *haᵇbhālîm*, "good-for-nothing" (v. 21). It is significant that the foreign gods are designated not only as worthless, but also as those which had had no earlier relationship to Israel. In contrast, Yahweh is really God, and initiated the relationship with Israel.

In Jeremiah this aspect of the question is discussed repeatedly. The Israelites had forsaken Yahweh and had sworn by "those who are no gods" (*belo' 'elohim*), in spite of Yahweh's having fed them to the full (5:7). They had exchanged their God for that which is of no avail (*belo' yo'il*), while no other nation had exchanged its gods, "even though they are no gods" (*vehemmah lo' 'elohim*, 2:11). The idols they had made could not save them (*yoshia'*, 2:27f.). It follows from this that a god who is worthy of being called *'elohim* can also help and save (cf. also v. 13, "broken cisterns," in contrast to Yahweh as the fountain of living waters, and 16:20, where the same theme is taken up).

Hos. 8:6 states that the calf images of Samaria are no gods (*lo' 'elohim*), but only the works of men's hands. Perhaps the same idea is reflected in 2 Ch. 13:9, where it says that the priests of the northern kingdom had consecrated themselves to no gods (*lo' 'elohim*), whereas "Yahweh is *our* (the southern kingdom's) God, and we have not forsaken him." We see from Gen. 3:5 that a god possesses a special kind of knowledge which man cannot attain (→ ידע *yādha'*, טוב *tôbh*),[52] whether we connect *yodhe'e tobh vara'*, "knowing good and evil," directly with *'elohim* or with man who had become "like God." Similarly, Job 32:13 says that only God can surpass Job in wisdom, and not a man. Three times the book of Job emphasizes that no man can be righteous before God (*ha'enosh yitsdaq 'im 'el*, 4:17; 9:2; 25:4). According to 1 K. 8:27, normally *'elohim* does not dwell on the earth ("with man," 2 Ch. 6:18); nevertheless,

---

[52] Cf. the comms.

he will be present in the temple (cf. Ps. 115:3, "Our God is in the heavens; he does whatever he pleases," which also refers to his omnipotence).

2 K. 5:7 points out that a god has power over life and death ("Am I God, to kill and to make alive?"; Gen. 50:19 shows in a similar expression that it is God's prerogative to judge man). Finally, it is considered to be obvious that no one can "see God and live" (Ex. 33:20; Jgs. 13:22; cf. Gen. 16:13), i.e., that he is so completely different that a man cannot endure the sight of him.[53] The same thing is said in Ex. 20:19 and Dt. 5:24 of those who hear his voice.

2. *Adjectives and Verbs.* It is also possible to define the words for "God" more exactly by investigating the expressions in which *ʾelohim* occurs, e.g., the adjectives that are used with it, the verbs of which it is the subject, etc.

Relatively speaking, adjectives are used with *ʾelohim* in the attributive sense in a surprisingly small number of instances. Also, it is worthy of note that the expressions using *ʾel* are much more numerous than those using *ʾelohim*. Perhaps *ʾelohim* was avoided because it would require either a plural form of the adjective or a grammatical incongruity (like *ʾelohim chai*).[54]

Here only a simple list of the expressions using adjectives with words for "God" can be given; for a more detailed explanation, one should consult the articles of these different adjectives at the proper places in this Dictionary.

The following expressions occur using *ʾelohim: ʾelohim qedhoshim,* "holy God" (Josh. 24:19), *ʾelohim tsaddiq,* "righteous God" (Ps. 7:10[9]), *ʾelohim chai (chayyim),* "living God" (Dt. 5:26; 1 S. 17:26,36; Jer. 23:36; 10:10; 2 K. 19:4,16 = Isa. 37:4,17), and *ʾelohim qerobhim,* "a God who is near" (Dt. 4:7). The following adjectives are used with *ʾel* in the attributive position: *qadhosh,* "holy" (Isa. 5:16), *tsaddiq umoshiaʿ,* "a righteous God and a savior" (45:21), *chai,* "living" (Josh. 3:10; Hos. 2:1[1:10]; Ps. 42:3[2]; 84:3[2]), *qannaʾ,* "jealous" (Ex. 20:5; 34:14; Dt. 4:24; 5:9; 6:15; Josh. 24:19; Nah. 1:2–in the last passage also *noqem,* "avenging"), *zoʿem,* "angry, having indignation" (Ps. 7:12 [11]), *rachum,* "merciful" (Dt. 4:31), *rachum vechannun,* "merciful and gracious" (Ex. 34:6; Ps. 86:15; Jonah 4:2; Neh. 9:31), *gadhol,* "great" (Ps. 77:14 [13]; 95:3; Jer. 32:18), *gadhol venoraʾ,* "great and terrible" (Dt. 7:21; 10:17; Neh. 1:5; 9:32; Dnl. 9:4; also with *gibbor,* "mighty," in Dt. 10:17; Jer. 32:18; Neh. 9:32), *gibbor,* "mighty" (Isa. 9:5[?] [6]; 10:21), *neʾeman,* "faithful" (Dt. 7:9), *noseʾ,* "forgiving" (Ps. 99:8), and *mistatter,* "hiding, who hidest" (Isa. 45:15).

We may add to this a group of expressions in construct, which express the functions or attributes of God. But these also are rather rare. Here again, both *ʾel* and *ʾelohim* are used. The connection of "God" with *yeshuʿah,* "salvation," or a variant from this word (*yeshuʿathi, yeshuʿathenu, yishʿi*) is common to both groups: *ʾel yeshuʿathi,* "God of my salvation" (Isa. 12:2) (cf. *haʾel yeshuʿathenu,* "God is our salvation," (Ps. 68:20[19]); *ʾelohe yeshuʿah* (or *yeshuʿathi, yeshuʿathenu, yishʿi*) 13 times. The following construct expressions

53 Cf. above, I.2.a.
54 Cassuto, *SMSR,* 132.

appear only with *'el: 'el hakkabhodh,* "the God of glory" (Ps. 29:3), *'el 'emunah,* "a God of faithfulness" (Dt. 32:4), *'el 'emeth,* "God of truth, faithful God" (Ps. 31:6[5]; cf. also 2 Ch. 15:3), *'el de'oth,* "a God of knowledge" (1 S. 2:3), *'el gemuloth,* "a God of recompense" (Jer. 51:56), *'el neqamoth,* "God of vengeance" (Ps. 94:1), and *'el simchath gili,* "God my exceeding joy" (43:4). And the following construct expressions occur only with *'elohim: 'elohe tsidhqi,* "God of my right" (Ps. 4:2[1]), *'elohe ma'uzzi,* "the God in whom I take refuge" (43:2), *'elohe mishpat,* "a God of justice" (Isa. 30:18; Mal. 2:17), *'elohe thehillathi,* "God of my praise" (Ps. 109:1), *'elohe 'amen,* "the God of truth" (Isa. 65:16); cf. also *'elohe miqqarobh,* "a God at hand," and *lo' 'elohe merachoq,* "not a God afar off" (Jer. 23:23).

Other construct expressions indicate the area in which God lives or exercises his authority, e.g., "God of heaven" (Gen. 24:7; Jonah 1:9; 2 Ch. 36:23; Ezr. 1:2; Neh. 1:4,5; 2:4,20–mostly late passages!), "God on high" (*marom,* Mic. 6:6), "God of heaven and of the earth" (Gen. 24:3), "God of the earth" (Isa. 54:5) or "of the land" (2 K. 17:26f.; Zeph. 2:11), "God of all flesh" (Jer. 32:27), "God of the spirits of all flesh" (Nu. 16:22; 27:16), and finally "God of gods," i.e., the highest God (Dt. 10:17; Ps. 136:2). If one attempts to analyze the verbs used in connection with *'elohim,* such a complex picture appears that an entire theology emerges. But it is noteworthy that the verbs all denote personal activities; in other words, the activity of God is presented entirely in personal categories. Observe in addition that it has a certain connection with "light" (cf., e.g., Ps. 118:27, *'el yhvh vayya'er lanu*). [55]

IV. 'elohim As an Appellative.

1. *The Gods of Other Nations. 'elohim* is above all an appellative, and is frequently used as a plural with reference to the gods of different nations. Thus e.g., the OT speaks of the gods of Egypt (Ex. 12:12), the gods of the Amorites (Josh. 24:15; Jgs. 6:10), and the gods of Syria, Sidon, Moab, the Ammonites, and the Philistines (Jgs. 10:6). In other instances, this word has a singular meaning, e.g., Baal-zebub the god of Ekron (2 K. 1:2f.,6,16), Ashtoreth the deity (goddess–here also *'elohim!*) of the Sidonians, Chemosh god of Moab, and Milcom god of the Ammonites (1 K. 11:33).

Such expressions are natural and a matter of course in the mouth of non-Israelites. Thus the king of Assyria speaks contemptuously of "the gods of the nations," which he has conquered (2 K. 18:33f.); the Philistines speak of the "God of Israel" as if it were a matter of course (1 S. 5:7f.,10f.); etc. But the earlier Israelite tradition also simply assumes that each nation has its god (or gods) (Mic. 4:5; Jonah 1:5; cf. 2 K. 17:29, which, however, is discussing images).

This same view also lies behind the wording of the first commandment in the Decalog: "You shall have no other gods besides (etc.) [56] me" (Ex. 20:3). This thought was then further developed in Deuteronomic/Deuteronomistic statements concerning the service of other gods (→ אחר *'acher*). The Israelites were

---

[55] See further under → אור *'ôr.*
[56] See the comms.

not to serve the gods of the peoples living round about them (Dt. 6:14; 13:7f. [6f.]; 29:17[18]; 31:16; Jgs. 2:12; cf. also Ex. 23:32f.). The heathen peoples in the land must be destroyed, and Israel must not serve their gods (Dt. 7:16), but must destroy the places at which they were worshipped (12:2f.). The transgression of this prohibition is related as a fact, e.g., in Jgs. 3:5f.: "they dwelt among the Canaanites ... and served their gods." The warnings against strange (foreign) gods (*elohe → נכר *nēkhār, Dt. 31:16; Josh. 24:20,23; Jgs. 10:16; 1 S. 7:3; Jer. 5:19; 2 Ch. 33:15) have the same goal. No question is raised as to whether these gods existed; their existence was simply accepted as a fact.

2. *The God of Israel*. On the other hand, Yahweh is the God in Israel, which is expressed linguistically by the phrase *'elohe yisra'el*, "the God of Israel," and by forms of *'elohim* with suffixes, as "thy God," "your God," and "our God."

The place to begin is Dt. 32:8f.: "When Elyon gave to the nations their inheritance ..., he fixed the bounds of the peoples according to the number of the *bene 'el*, "sons of God" (to be read with the LXX instead of the MT *bene yisra'el*, "children of Israel"); but Yahweh's portion is his people." Each one of the "sons of God" received his people; Yahweh's portion is Israel. Here an ancient tradition shines through that is rather unique in the OT. Usually the OT says that Yahweh himself chose Israel and became her God. According to Dt. 4, [57] Yahweh "your God" allots to the peoples of the earth the service of the sun and the moon and the stars, while he chooses Israel to be a people of his own possession (4:19f.). No other god has ever attempted to lead a nation out in this way, as Yahweh did in Egypt (4:34); and no other god has spoken to a people and made known his will like Yahweh (4:33).

The result is the covenant, which can be described in the statement, "I will be your God, and you will be my people." This statement occurs in different variations in about 25 passages. It means that Yahweh appeared to Israel in the special relationship that should exist between a people and its God, and between a God and his people. This statement is worded in different ways: simply in Ex. 6:7 and Lev. 26:12; in expanded form in Dt. 26:17f.; in modified form in 29:12 (13); as well as in 2 S. 7:24; Jer. 11:4b; 30:22; 31:33; 32:38; Ezk. 11:20; 14:11; 36:28; 37:23,27.

Lev. 11:45; 22:33; 25:38; and Nu. 15:41 state merely that Yahweh brought Israel out of Egypt to be their God—they do not specifically say that Israel is his people. Ex. 29:45; Lev. 26:12; and Ezk. 37:27 emphasize that Yahweh dwells among his people, and thus he is their God. In Gen. 17:7f., the promise to be the God of Abraham's descendants is connected with the promise of the land. Jeremiah and Ezekiel have in mind the renewal of the covenant. The expression "to be with the people" (→ את *'ēth*) must also be considered in this connection. It suggests a rather clear picture of God's role: he actively intervenes in behalf of his people, he is continually present in the midst of his people, and thus he has a rather intimate and active relationship with them.

---

[57] Which N. Lohfink, *Höre Israel* (1965), 72ff., sees as the latest form of the homiletic interpretation of the First Commandment.

The consequences of this relationship can at least partly be determined in passages that use the expressions "our, your, thy God." A large number of these expressions are found in Deuteronomy ("our God" 23 times; "thy God" 218 times; "your God" 44 times). "Yahweh thy (your, our) God" is more or less a stereotyped formula, and an analysis of these passages amounts to almost the same thing as an analysis of the Deuteronomic idea of God/Yahweh in general. He is a God who is "one" (Dt. 6:4), who makes a covenant (5:2), who gives statutes and commandments (11:1; etc.), and who gives Israel the land (4:21,40; 5:16; 7:16; 13:13[12]; 15:4). Further, he is a God whom one must fear (6:2, 13; 10:20) and love (6:5; 11:1), and to whom Israel is a holy people (7:6; 14:2, 21). We also encounter similar expressions outside the Deuteronomistic literature, e.g., in Ex. 20:2, "I am Yahweh your God, who brought you out of the land of Egypt"; 20:12, "the land which Yahweh your God gives you"; Hos. 12:10 (9); 13:4, "I am Yahweh your God from the land of Egypt"; Ps. 50:7, "I am God, your God" (a Covenant Festival Psalm); 95:7, "he is our God, and we are the people of his pasture"; Isa. 26:13, "Yahweh our God, other lords besides thee have ruled over us, but thy name alone we acknowledge"; Jer. 14:22, "Are there any among the false gods of the nations that can bring rain? Art thou not he, Yahweh our God, and must we not hope in thee?" Other motifs, which are connected to 'elohenu, "our God," are trust (2 K. 18:22; Isa. 36:7), help, salvation (Isa. 37:20; 52:10; Ps. 106:47), forgiveness (Isa. 55:7), "is with us" (1 K. 8:57), and "fights for us" (Neh. 4:14[20]).

Although all these could be general statements concerning Yahweh, in context it is significant that the relationship is expressed by the suffix, and consciously appears as something traditional and natural.

The expression 'elohe yisra'el, "God of Israel," is also explained by the covenant. Thus, its use is not limited to texts in which heathen speak of the God of Israel (1 S. 5:7f.,10f.; 6:3,5), or in which the national character of Yahweh is portrayed to a heathen (Ex. 5:1; cf. Josh. 24:2). Steuernagel saw in this divine name an ancient cultic epithet used at Shechem, which denoted the God of the tribal group called Israel, as may be deduced from Gen. 33:20 and Josh. 8:30. [58] This theory can hardly be proved; in any case, it does not explain all the passages in which this epithet occurs. Of particular interest is that some of the most important examples appear in traditions of the Holy War (Josh. 7:13; 10:40,42; 14:14; Jgs. 4:6; 5:3,5; 6:8; 11:21,23; etc.), or in connection with the ark of the covenant (1 S. 5:7f.,10f.; 6:3,5). The variant 'el yisra'el also appears in Ps. 68:36 (35), "Terrible is God in his sanctuary, the God of Israel, he gives power and strength to his people." Here, the national connection as well as (through the context of the psalm) the connection with war and the ark are clear. The majority of the other examples are found, as Steuernagel has shown, [59] in the framework of the prophetic literature ("Thus says Yahweh, the God of Israel"), especially in Jeremiah and Ezekiel. He thinks that Ezekiel adopted this expression from priestly circles, and that in Jeremiah it is to be assigned to a redactor (Deuter-

---

[58] Steuernagel, 345f.
[59] Ibid., 333f.

onomistic?). Examples in the Historical Books indicate that this phrase was used
to refer to the Jerusalemite Yahweh, "meaning the genuine Israelite Yahweh
as distinguished from the ethnicized Yahweh worshipped on the high places." [60]
It is noteworthy that 'el yisra'el is used frequently in the War Scroll from
Qumran. [61]

3. *The God of an Individual.* Other construct expressions designate a god
as the god of an individual. To this group belong the phrases "the God of
Abraham" (Gen. 24:12,27,42,48; 26:24; 31:42), "the God of Abraham and
Isaac" (28:13; 32:10[9]), "the God of Abraham, Isaac, and Jacob" (Ex. 3:6,15;
4:5; 1 K. 18:36), "the God of your father" (Gen. 46:3; 50:17; cf. 31:42; Ex.
3:6), etc. These epithets, which appear in particular in the patriarchal narratives,
could contain the reminiscence of a belief in God comparable with the Sumerian
idea of the "God of man." [62] Here also is the point of departure for Alt's reflections on "the God of the fathers," in connection with which he has made use
of the material concerning the family gods of the Nabateans from the Hellenistic
period. The conclusion that a "God of the individual" or "God of the family"
was known is obvious.

In the Historical Books especially, "the God of the fathers" is an expression
of the (often broken) continuity in the Israelite belief in God (→ אב 'ābh).

In other passages, "the God of Jacob" especially is synonymous with "the
God of Israel" (2 S. 23:1; Isa. 2:3; Mic. 4:2; Ps. 20:2[1]; 75:10[9]; 76:7[6];
81:2,5[1,4]; 84:9[8]; 94:7). Other references to the God of an individual are
rare, cf. however "the God of Shem" (Gen. 9:26), "the God of Elijah" (2 K.
2:14), and "the God of David" (20:5).

4. *"My God," "Your God."* As Eissfeldt emphasizes, the expression "my
God" ('elohai or 'eli–this is the only suffix form of 'el) is used with different
nuances of meaning. "My God" can appear in contrast to other gods, e.g.,
in Nu. 22:18, where Balaam says "Yahweh, my God"; 2 S. 24:24, where
David uses the phrase "Yahweh, my God" in speaking to Araunah; and 1 K.
5:18f.(4f.), where Solomon uses the same expression in a message to Hiram
(here the relationship between Solomon and his God is to be observed: Yahweh
has given him peace, and Solomon wants to build him a house). Ruth 1:16 is
of particular interest. Here Ruth says to Naomi: "your people shall be my
people, and your God my God," i.e., she renounces her ethnic and religious
associations, and accepts the nationality and religion of her mother-in-law.

Often the phrase "my God" has no special significance. But in certain psalms
it is the expression of a personal relationship between the worshipper and God,
whom he regards as "his God." In these prayers (as also in certain other examples), the phrase "my God" emphasizes that the worshipper is convinced
that his God is ready to hear his prayer favorably. Thus, e.g., we read in Ps.

---

[60] *Ibid.,* 339.
[61] P. von der Osten-Sacken, *Gott und Belial* (1969), 38.
[62] Ringgren, *RdM,* 26, 17f.

38:22f.(21f.): "O my God, be not far from me, make haste to help me, O Lord, my salvation (*'adhonai teshu'athi*)." Ps. 22 also affords an impressive example with the introduction, "My God, my God, why hast thou forsaken me?" in comparison with v. 12(11), "be not far from me, for trouble is near and there is none to help"–the previous verse contains the confession, "since my mother bore me thou hast been my God." 31:15(14) should also be mentioned: "But I trust thee, O Yahweh, I say, 'Thou art my God'"; cf. v. 6(5), "Into thy hand I commit my spirit; thou hast redeemed me, O Lord, faithful God."

The expressions with the suffix *-kha,* "your," are a little different when they do not refer to the people. Above all, those who are addressed are men that one would normally expect to be in a particularly close relationship to God, like kings and prophets. [63] Thus, e.g., the people say to Samuel: "Pray for your servants to Yahweh your God, that we may not die" (1 S. 12:19). Saul speaks to Samuel of "Yahweh your God," to whom sacrifice is to be made (15:21). The woman of Tekoa says to David: "Pray let the king invoke Yahweh your God" (2 S. 14:11), and in v. 17: "Yahweh your God be with you." King Jeroboam I says to a man of God: "Entreat now the favor of Yahweh your God, and pray for me" (1 K. 13:6). Similarly, Hezekiah says to Isaiah: "It may be that Yahweh your God heard" (2 K. 19:4 = Isa. 37:4). Cf. also Ps. 45:8(7): "God, your God, has anointed you." Thus, this phrase emphasizes the special relationship of the person named to God, and it is assumed that the results of this relationship extend out to those who come in contact with them. Here the question, "Where is your God?" (*'ayyeh 'elohekha*) should also be mentioned. It is put in the mouth of the enemies of the psalmist, who ask triumphantly: Where is the God with whom you have a relationship and from whom you expect help? (Ps. 42:4,11[3,10]; cf. Mic. 7:10; in the third person, Ps. 79:10; 115:2; Dt. 32:37; Joel 2:17). This question hints scornfully that God is not fulfilling his function as God of the person addressed: "What a useless God you have!" (cf. also the words of the Rabshakeh: "Where are the gods of Hamath and Arpad? ... Who among all the gods of the countries have delivered their countries out of my hand?" [2 K. 18:34f.]).

5. *Simple 'elohim.* Simple *'elohim* often has an appellative meaning: "a god," "a deity." In his investigation of Elohim outside the Pentateuch, Baumgärtel has studied these examples, and thinks he is able to prove that all or almost all occurrences outside the Pentateuchal sources E and P and the Elohim Psalter have this meaning. Although many of the passages which he cites can be interpreted in a different way, the following deserve special consideration.

When the person who denies God says *'en 'elohim,* "There is no God" (Ps. 14:1), "he is not referring to Yahweh, but to the concept of God in general." [64] Similarly, the skeptics say that it is not worthwhile to serve *'elohim* (Mal. 3:14f., 18). The reference here is not to Yahweh, but to God in general. But it is doubt-

---

[63] Cf. above, IV.3, the God of David and of Elijah.
[64] Baumgärtel, 24.

ful whether Yahweh is to be completely excluded in the expression *da'ath 'elohim*, "knowledge of God" (Hos. 4:1; 6:6; Prov. 2:5). [65] The antithetical passages discussed under II above also refer to God in general.

Baumgärtel also includes in this category passages which speak of seeking (*darash*) or inquiring of (*sha'al*) God. When 2 S. 12:16 says: *vayebhaqqesh davidh 'eth ha'elohim*, "David therefore besought God," Baumgärtel thinks this means: David went to the sanctuary. But it is hardly to be assumed that a God other than Yahweh or that "God in general" is intended here. Likewise, in the case of Jgs. 18:5, *she'al na' be'lohim*, "Inquire of God, we pray thee," the following verse shows that Yahweh is meant. But Baumgärtel could be right insofar as this expression as such was a technical term for seeking and inquiring of God in general.

The phrase → מלאך *mal'akh 'elohim*, "angel of God" (7 times), is used alternately with *mal'akh yhvh*, "angel of Yahweh." [66] But *'ish 'elohim*, "man of God," is unequivocal, because *'ish yhvh* never occurs. A "man of God" is a man who has an intimate relationship with a God or with the deity. Likewise, *mar'oth 'elohim* (Ezk. 1:1; 8:3; 40:2) are visions of God in general; *debhar 'elohim* (Jgs. 3:20; 1 S. 9:27; 2 S. 16:23; 1 K. 12:22) is the word of God in general, an "oracle"; and *ma'aneh 'elohim* (Mic. 3:7) is an answer of God without reference to a particular God.

An ancient stereotyped expression lies behind the statement, *mahpekhath 'elohim 'eth sedhom ve'eth 'amorah*, "God overthrew Sodom and Gomorrah" (Isa. 13:19; Jer. 50:40; Am. 4:11). That *yhvh* occurs in the same passage in Amos does not show that the prophet made a distinction between *yhvh* and *'elohim*, but only that he used this traditional expression.

'elohim is also found in phrases expressing the great and enormous. Thus *'ir gedholah le'lohim* in Jonah 3:3 certainly means "a vastly great city." But also *cherdath 'elohim* could be a "dread of God" in the sense of "great dread," as e.g., in 1 S. 14:15. But *pachadh yhvh*, "dread of Yahweh," also occurs. [67] Likewise, the most natural meaning of *chokhmath 'elohim* is "exceedingly great wisdom" (1 K. 3:28). The interpretation of *ruach 'elohim* in Gen. 1:2 as "great wind" is in line with this observation. [68] *'el* also occurs with this meaning, e.g., *'arze 'el*, "great cedars." [69]

6. *Images of God.* In some instances, *'elohim* is used with reference to images of God. Thus, Ex. 20:23 prohibits the making of "silver and gold gods." The golden calf is called a "god (made) out of gold" (*'elohe zahabh*, Ex. 32:31) (cf. also Lev. 19:4; Dt. 4:28; Josh. 24:14; 2 K. 17:29; 19:18,37). In Isa. 42:17, the idol worshippers say concerning their idol: "This is our God." Jer. 16:20 says: "Can man make for himself gods? Such are no gods!"

[65] Contra *ibid.*, 27.
[66] *Ibid.*, 52f.
[67] *Ibid.*, 29ff.
[68] Westermann, *BK*, I, with Bibliography.
[69] Cf. Smith.

7. *Irregular Use.* Finally, we may mention certain passages in which *'elohim* has a somewhat irregular meaning. In 1 S. 28:13, the medium at Endor calls the spirit of Samuel which had come up an *'elohim,* i.e., a nonhuman or "supernatural" being. The same idea appears in Isa. 8:19: "Should not a people consult their *'elohim,* the dead on behalf of the living?" In Ps. 8:6(5) ("Thou hast made him [man] little less than *'elohim*"), the most natural meaning of *'elohim* is "divine being" (cf. the LXX *par' angélous,* "than angels"); the crucial thing here is the similarity with the divine in general. Ps. 45:7(6), where the king apparently is addressed as *'elohim,* is an entirely different matter. If one is unwilling to conclude from this that the king, at least in some circles, was considered to be "divine" (and thus somehow elevated into the superhuman sphere), then one must either connect *'elohim* with *kis'akha* ("thy divine throne"), which is grammatically strained, or consider *'elohim* as an Elohistic substitution for *yhvh* and explain it as a faulty writing of *yihyeh: kis'akha yihyeh 'olam va'edh,* "thy throne will endure (exist) for ever and ever." The first explanation seems to be the simplest.

V. Assertions of Incomparability. But the claims about a being who may justifiably be called "God" can also be increased. In fact, one of the fundamental questions of the Hebrew religion is, Who is really God?

An ancient formula, which, indeed, has parallels in the Akkadian (and to some extent Egyptian) hymnic literature, appears in Ex. 15:11: "Who is like thee among the gods (*mi khamokhah ba'elim*)? Who is like thee, majestic (*ne'dar*) in holiness, terrible in glorious deeds, doing wonders (*pele'*)?" Such questions have a logical meaning in a polytheistic context like in the Babylonian-Assyrian religion, where even several gods are represented as incomparable. In Israel, Yahweh can be compared with the gods of other nations (and this is perhaps the case in Ex. 15); but as time passed by, the conviction became stronger that in reality Yahweh is the only one who rightly wears the attributes "glorious," "holy," "terrible," etc., i.e., who is really God.

A similar statement appears in Ps. 89:7(6): "Who in the skies can be compared (*'arakh*) to Yahweh? Who among the *bene 'elim* (sons of God) is like Yahweh?" The comparison here clearly refers to the other divine or heavenly beings, the Israelite vestige of the Canaanite assembly of the gods. Cf. also Ps. 113:5f.: "Who is like Yahweh our God ... in heaven and on earth?"

These passages indicate that the origin of the assertion of Yahweh's incomparability is to be sought in the hymnic literature. The idea is then further elaborated in Deuteronomy and in the Deuteronomistic history, as is clear from the following quotations: Dt. 3:24: "What God is there in heaven or on earth who can do such works and mighty acts as thine?"; 4:7: "What great nation is there that has a god so near to it as Yahweh our God is to us?" 4:34f.: "Has any god ever attempted to go and take a nation for himself ... ? Yahweh is God; there is no other besides him" (*yhvh hu' ha'elohim 'en 'odh milebhaddo*); 4:39: "Yahweh is God in heaven above and on the earth beneath; there is no other." The main emphasis here is on God's working in history, the choice of Israel and their deliverance from Egypt; but one observes the tendency to deny that there is really any God other than Yahweh. But in their context, these passages have in mind the only God of Israel, whose commandments Israel must keep.

2 S. 7:22 dispenses with the use of comparison in asserting the uniqueness of Yahweh: "There is none like thee, and there is no God besides thee" (*ʾen kamokha veʾen ʾelohim zulathekha*). That which follows is interesting because it shows that the main point is neither the superiority of Yahweh nor that of Israel, but the unique relationship between Yahweh and Israel. A similar statement appears in Solomon's prayer at the consecration of the temple, 1 K. 8:23, "There is no God like thee, in heaven above or on earth beneath" (*ʾen kamokha ʾelohim bashshamayim mimmaʿal veʿal haʾarets mittachath*). Here also what follows shows that the incomparability of Yahweh has to do with his relationship to Israel: "keeping covenant and showing *chesedh* (steadfast love) to thy servants who walk before thee with all their heart." But evidently the Deuteronomistic tradition has developed a type of monotheistic formula (or perhaps better, a formula of incomparability), which is based on the hymnic formula *mi kamokha,* "Who is like thee?"

Of course, there are other expressions that convey this idea, e.g., in Dt. 10:17: "Yahweh your God is God of gods and Lord of lords," i.e., the highest God and the most powerful Lord. But again the context emphasizes that the God who is lord of the whole world (v. 14) has loved and chosen Israel (v. 15), so that Israel must keep his commandments (v. 13).

Very much in harmony with this theoretically formulated principle, the Deuteronomistic history relates two conflicts between Yahweh and Baal in which the question is, Who is really God? In the first example, the question is merely mentioned in passing, viz., in Jgs. 6:31, where we read: "Is Baal a god?" i.e., does he really have divine power so that he can contend for himself? The problem is stated much more clearly in the encounter of Elijah with the prophets of Baal on Carmel (1 K. 18). Here the question, "Who is really God?" is explicitly raised, but again this means, "Which of these two gods (Yahweh and Baal) has the right to receive Israel's worship?" When Yahweh has shown his power by setting the sacrifice on fire, the people cry out: "Yahweh is God; Yahweh is God."

The assertions of Yahweh's incomparability reach their high point in Deutero-Isaiah. Although the prophet quite clearly is dependent on the hymnic tradition, he develops this motif independently. The interrogative form of the hymn is still found in Isa. 44:7: "Who is like me?" (*mi khamoni*). The context speaks of declaring beforehand what is going to happen (no one has done this like Yahweh), but then this conclusion is drawn: "Is there a God besides me?" (*hayesh ʾeloah mibbalʿadhai*) (v. 8). The interrogative form is also retained elsewhere, but the wording is different: 40:18: "To whom will you liken God (*ʾel*), or what likeness compare with him?"; 40:25: "To whom will you compare me, that I should be like him?"; 46:5: "To whom will you liken me and make me equal, and compare me?" Only in the last passage is an answer given: "For I am God, and there is no other; I am God, and there is none like me" (*ki ʾanokhi ʾel veʾen ʿodh ʾelohim veʾephes kamoni*, 46:9). 43:10-13 is even more detailed:

"Before me no god was formed, nor shall there be any after me. I, I am Yahweh, and besides me there is no savior. I declared and saved and proclaimed, when there was no strange god among you . . . I am God, and also henceforth I am He; there is none who can deliver from my hand." The wording of v. 11 seems to indicate that "savior" (*moshiaʿ*) and "God" are more or less synonymous, which is confirmed by 45:21f. Thus, "to be God" is not intended statically or abstractly, but is also and especially "to be a savior," to intervene in behalf of those with whom God stands in intimate relationship. As would be expected, Deutero-Isaiah contains several phrases referring to God with suffix forms: "thy God" (41:10,13; 43:3; 48:17; 51:15); "your God" (40:1,9); "our God" (40:3,8; 52:10; 55:7).

VI. ʾelohim As a Designation of Yahweh. Finally *ʾelohim* was simply a designation of Yahweh, and characterized him as God absolutely. But it is worthy of note that this use of *ʾelohim* is restricted to certain portions of the OT, especially the Pentateuchal sources E and P and the Elohistic portions of Psalms. Baumgärtel even thinks that all the occurrences of simple *ʾelohim* outside the Pentateuch and the E Psalter are to be understood appellatively.

Opponents of the literary-critical source division of the Pentateuch like Cassuto and Engnell deny the validity of using the names of God as a criterion for dividing the material into different written sources. Cassuto thinks that the use of different names for God has a theological significance. According to him, the OT uses *yhvh* when it is speaking of the Israelite concept of God and of God's working in the history of Israel, while it uses *ʾelohim* when it intends to refer to the abstract idea of the deity, of the universal God, and of the creator of the world. It uses *yhvh* when the characteristics of the deity are clear and concrete, and *ʾelohim* when they are more abstract and obscure. *yhvh* suggests that God is personal and that he stands in direct relationship with people and nature, while *ʾelohim* indicates the transcendent nature of God. [70]

Undoubtedly, these distinctions fit quite well in a number of OT passages. But they cannot be applied consistently to all passages. It is possible, however, that certain circles preferred to use the divine designation *ʾelohim* for theological reasons that at least to some extent correspond to Cassuto's explanations. The preference for the use of *ntr* rather than names of individual gods in the Egyptian Wisdom Literature would be analogous to the OT use of *ʾelohim*, although these two words are not necessarily identical in meaning.

On the one hand, *ʾelohim* is used abstractly as a substitute for the name of God: the concrete personal Yahweh, understood anthropomorphically, is identified with the deity in general, which suggests a more abstract understanding of God. On the other hand, this identification is on a plane with the monotheistic concept: only when there is but one God and he is acknowledged to be the only God is it fully meaningful to characterize that specific God as God absolutely (*ʾelohim*).

Ringgren

---

[70] *Documentary Hypothesis*, 31; *SMSR*, 125-145.

אֱלִיל ’elîl

Contents: I. Occurrences. II. Etymology. III. Use in the OT.

I. Occurrences. The substantive *’elil*, which appears in the singular only in Isa. 10:10 (should *ha’elleh*, "these," be read here? This verse is probably a late insertion) and Zec. 11:17 (should we read *ha’evili*, "my foolish [shepherd]," here?), and everywhere else in the plural (Lev. 19:4; 26:1; Isa. 2:8,18,20; 10:11; 19:1,3; 31:7; Ezk. 30:13 [read here *’elim*, "gods," cf. the LXX]; Hab. 2:18; Ps. 96:5; 97:7; 1 Ch. 16:26; cf. also Sir. 30:19), is one of the words in the OT used to ridicule idols. The LXX renders it by *bdelýgmata*, "detestable things," *eídōla*, "idols," *daimónia*, "demons," *cheiropoíēta*, "made by human hands," and even by *theoús*, "gods," in Isa. 19:3. The Qumran texts also know the idea (1QM 14:1; cf. Isa. 19:1). [1]

II. Etymology. Since *’elil* is used with debilitating intention and with scornful undertones in all OT passages where it occurs, it seems to have been created expressly for this purpose. By true analogy with → גלולים *gillûlîm*, "dungy things, balls of dung," → שקוצים *shiqqûtsîm*, "horrible things, monsters," and perhaps also → תרפים *terāphîm*, "the rotting things"? "old rags, scraps"? (cf. Ugar. *’ll*, "garment"?), words which are used to ridicule idols, and which also were consciously created to strike a discordant note with the sound of *’elohim*, *’elil* (an Aramaizing form? Cf. *kesil* and *lamedh* as a diminutive ending) [2] was created as a disparaging pun on and as a diminutive of *’el* or *’elohim* (Ps. 97:7) ("little god, godling"). This helped to bring about a conscious antithesis between *’elil* and *’el*, "the Strong One." Furthermore, it is likely that the noun *’elil* is intentionally reminiscent of the adj. *’elil*, "weak, insignificant, worthless," which we also encounter in contexts where the speaker uses scornful words (Job 13:4; Jer. 14:14; cf. Zec. 11:17; also Sir. 11:3). We may also compare the Akk. *ulālu*, "powerless," Ugar. *ʒll*, "destruction," [3] Syr. *’allîl*, "weak" and Arab. *’alāl*, "useless." It is unlikely that *’elil* was derived from the South Arab. *’l’lwt* or the Babylonian god Ellil. [4] But all attempts to derive *’elil* linguistically from the nations surrounding Israel run into difficulties, because in these nations we do

---

’elil. W. W. Graf Baudissin, "Die Anschauung des AT von den Göttern des Heidentums," *Studien zur semitischen Religionsgeschichte,* I (1876), 102f.; R. H. Pfeiffer, "The Polemic against Idolatry in the OT," *JBL,* 43 (1924), 229-240; H. D. Preuss, *Verspottung fremder Religionen im AT. BWANT,* 92 (1971), 58, 136f., 139, 173, 240, 248-250, 281; H. Wildberger, *BK,* X, 102f., with additional literature on the etymology; see also the comms., esp. on Isa. 2:8 and Ps. 96:5.

1 On the adj., see below, II.
2 In addition, cf. R. Meyer, *Hebräische Grammatik,* II (³1969), 28, 40.
3 So Driver, *CML,* but this is doubtful.
4 See Wildberger, 102.

not find scornful polemics against foreign gods to the extent of completely opposing the idea that they are really gods. On the contrary, the negative *'al* may have come into being through the influence of the form *'elil*.

According to another explanation, *'elil* is to be interpreted as a qutail form with a diminutive, pejorative meaning. If this is the case, it is conceivable that either *'el* or *'al* is a basis for it.

III. Use in the OT. The earliest examples of the use of *'elil* occur in Isa. 2:8,(18?); 10:11; 19:1,3, while 2:(18?),20, as additions in 2:6-22; 10:10; and 31:7, can hardly have come from Isaiah, although they do make it clear that *'elil* came to be used more extensively in ridiculing idols. Occasionally, scholars have even supposed that *'elil* is a word created by Isaiah himself. And the later texts that use this word depend on Isaiah and indicate that it was used predominantly in the Jerusalem tradition. [5]

In the oracles on the coming of the Day of Yahweh (Isa. 2:6-22), one of the reasons given for punishing God's people is that they have gone away after vain idols (v. 8). Therefore, the idea that idols are only the work of men's hands is a theme that was present in the OT ridicule of idols before Isaiah. The existence of idols is scornfully denied; they are only inferior human works. Isaiah, who does not speak of idols very often, calls them little gods, weaklings, nothings. According to Isa. 10:11, the Assyrians (cf. 2 K. 19:10-13) attempt to identify idols and Yahweh, against which Isaiah cites Yahweh's punishment as counter-evidence. According to Isa. 19:1-15, in which only vv. 5-10 are an addition, Yahweh's coming for judgment also brings the destruction of idols (19:1,3; cf. 2:8,18). They cannot help in distress, which the addition in 2:20f. vividly emphasizes. As always in texts of the OT which ridicule idols, here the idols are identified with their images. The final redactor of Isa. 2:6-22 saw the exposure of the powerlessness of the idols and their downfall as the real intention of this section.

This is analogous to Hab. 2:18f. These verses are clearly a later addition to the series of Woe Oracles in 2:6b-20. They are different from the surrounding material in form, function, and content; they do not have the expected threat of punishment; and they presuppose Jeremiah, Deutero-Isaiah, and Isa. 57:12f. In their present position, these verses stand in conscious contrast with the statement concerning Yahweh in v. 20, and serve the redactor's purpose to make explicit the wickedness of those who were addressed. Moreover, the *'elilim* are still characterized as dumb (*'illemim*, so here only), which hardly goes back to an original *'elim*, "gods," [6] but is a (frequently later) theme in the ridicule of idols.

Ps. 96:5 and 97:7 (as well as the text of 1 Ch. 16:26, which is taken from Ps. 96) presupposes Deutero-Isaiah here as elsewhere. The ridicule of idols is complementary to the Yahweh hymn. The proof that idols are nothing, which is also founded on the creation faith, is a component of eschatology, i.e., the

---

[5] *Ibid.*
[6] Thus A. Geiger, *Urschrift und Übersetzungen der Bibel* (²1928), 293.

final accomplishment of Yahweh. These verses are well integrated into their contexts. On the intentionally sharp contrast between ’elilim and ’elohim in Ps. 96:5, which is supposed to produce or strengthen the intended ridicule, cf. 97:7, and similarly Lev. 19:4; 26:1. In Ps. 97:7 this contrast, which intended to speak of Yahweh in the highest possible way, has in fact helped those "nothings" to new life.

Thus, ’elil is used to contrast the power and greatness of Yahweh with the weakness and vanity of idols. It appears as part of a contrast motif in hymns exalting Yahweh as king (Ps. 96:5; 97:7; cf. 1 Ch. 16:26), and in the oracle of the coming day of Yahweh (Isa. 2:6-22), since Yahweh's coming will also bring the end of idols (19:1,3), as well as the recognition of their weakness by their worshippers. Since the OT polemical ridicule of idols is predominantly a polemic ridiculing images of idols, ’elil is also used in speaking of these images (Lev. 19:4; 26:1; cf. Ps. 97:7), for the prohibition of the worship of idols and the prohibition of making images to idols are necessarily related. The texts in the Holiness Code (Lev. 19:4; 26:1) again use ’elil in contrast to the totally different I of Yahweh in apodictic prohibitions, which are intimately connected with the Decalog, even though Leviticus contains the plural address and uses different negatives.

Hosea's classification of idols as "not (no) God" (8:6) reflects an assumption on his part concerning the origin and use of ’elil. And when Jeremiah calls foreign gods → הבל hebhel, "worthlessness" (2:5; 8:19; 14:22; 16:19f., and also texts which depend on these), he is following this same line of thought even further.   Preuss

---

אַלְמָנָה ’almānāh; אַלְמָנוּת ’almānûth

Contents: I. 1. Etymology and Related Terms; 2. Sumerian-Akkadian; 3. Egyptian; 4. Hittite; 5. Ugaritic and Phoenician. II. Position of the Widow: 1. Existence or Non-existence of Children; 2. Remarriage; 3. Property Rights; 4. Vows; 5. As an Example of Pious Devotion. III. Protection and Care of the Widow. IV. Figurative Use of the Word.

I. 1. *Etymology and Related Terms.* In most ancient Semitic languages, the word for "widowed" (originally an adj., not a subst. as is clear from constructions like ’ishshah ’almanah, lit. "a widowed woman") contains the basic

---

’almānāh. H. Donner, "Die soziale Botschaft der Propheten," *OrAnt*, 2 (1963), 229-245; G. R. Driver-J. C. Miles, *Assyrian Laws* (Oxford, 1935), 212-250; A. Erman-H. Ranke, *Ägypten und ägyptisches Leben* (²1923), 129; F. C. Fensham, "Widow, Orphan and the Poor . . . ," *JNES*, 21 (1962), 129-139; H. Grapow, *Die bildlichen Ausdrücke des Ägyptischen* (1924), 134f.; T. Mayer-Maly, "vidua," *PW*, II, 8; 2, 2098-2107; B. Meissner, *BuA*, I, 172, 423; A. F. Rainey, *A Social Structure of Ugarit* (Heb.) (1967), 28f., 42, 98f., 101, 106f.; R. de Vaux, *AncIsr*, 39f., 54f., 149.

consonants *ʾlmn:* Heb. *ʾalmanah,* Akk. *almattum* (<*ʾalmantum*), Ugar. *ʾlmnt* (*ʾalmanatu*), Phoen. *ʾlmt* (<*ʾalmant*), and possibly Arab. *ʾarmalatun* (<*ʾalmanatun?*). It is certain that *-(a)t* is the feminine ending, and it is possible (although not certain) that the *ʾa-* is also the preformative of an adjectival *ʾaqtal* form. Then the root would be *lmn* (cf. Akk. *lemnu,* "poor," though possibly *lemnu* derives from *lā imnu*). Other ancient Near Eastern terms for "widow" are Sum. *nu-mu-(un)-su* (cognate form *na-ma-su*) and *nu-kúš-ù* ("one who does not have any peace"), Egyp. *ḫꜣr.t,* Hitt. *wannumiyaš SAL-za,* Gk. *chḗra.* In all these instances, with the possible exception of the Sumerian, the crucial term is an adjective, and often the substantive "woman" appears with it.

In Biblical Hebrew, the word *ʾalmanah* has a completely negative nuance. It means a woman who has been divested of her male protector (husband, sons, often also brothers). As a person without a living relative, money, or influence, the widow is often mentioned together with the orphan (→ יתום *yāthôm,* Job 22:9; 24:3; Isa. 10:2; Job 31:16f.; Ps. 94:6; Mal. 3:5), the sojourner (→ גר *gēr,* Ps. 94:6; Mal. 3:5; Zec. 7:10), the hireling (*sakhir,* Mal. 3:5), the poor (→ דל *dal,* Isa. 10:2; Job 31:16; → עני *ʿānî,* Isa. 10:2; Job 24:4,9; Zec. 7:10; → אביון *ʾebhyôn,* Job 24:4; 31:19), and the Levites (Dt. 14:29).

2. *Sumerian-Akkadian.* As in the OT, widows, orphans, and other persons who are deprived of normal protection and care are a special concern in the laws of ancient Mesopotamia. But this concern, about which the lawgiver publicly boasts, [1] often is not given corresponding expression in the actual wording of the law. Nevertheless, it is the expressed intention of the lawgiver to defend the powerless classes (the weak [*enšu*], young girls without a family [*ekūtu*], and widows [*almattu*]). In this endeavor, the human official merely takes as his model the divine protectors of such helpless persons: Marduk[2] and Nanshe.[3] "Although *almattu* usually corresponds to the modern word 'widow,' it does not mean simply a woman whose husband is dead, but a married woman who enjoys no financial support from a male member of her family (husband, grown son, or father-in-law), and thus on the one hand needs legal protection, and on the other is able to exercise freedom either by entering into a second marriage or by starting a profession."[4]

3. *Egyptian.* Of course, there are no formal legal documents from Pharaonic Egypt in existence, but the administration of justice was ordinarily in the hands of the monarchs, and these (esp. in the Middle Kingdom) boast in the tomb inscriptions that they had been concerned about the protection of the helpless. Thus, e.g., Ameni, provincial prince of the sixteenth province under Sesostris I, says: "There was no daughter of a citizen whom I mistreated, no widow to whom

---

[1] F. Thureau-Dangin, *SAK,* 52, XII, 23-25; Gudea Statue B, VII, 42f.; Gudea Cylinder B, XVIII, 6f.; CH § 40, 61.

[2] L. W. King, *Babylonian Magic and Sorcery,* (1896), 12f.

[3] E. I. Gordon, *Sumerian Proverbs* (1960), 197.

[4] *CAD,* I/1, 364.

I did violence.... There was no poor... or hungry in my time.... I gave to the widow just as I gave to the woman who had a husband, and never showed partiality in giving to the great more than to the small" (Ameni, 20; Document VII, 16). [5] The Eloquent Peasant compliments his judge Rensi as follows: "You are a father to the orphan, a husband to the widow, a brother to the divorced" (B 1, 63). [6] The same word ḫ3r.t, "widowed," is used figuratively of countries (Israel Stela, 27).

4. *Hittite.* In the Hittite texts, widows are seldom mentioned. Once the wife of the Egyptian king, Nebhururiya (Tutankhamen), who is mentioned in the Hittite text only with her Egyptian title *taḫamunzu,* "wife of the king," is called "widow" (*wannumiyaš*). Another text, which tells of the administration of a great (royal?) estate, contains an instruction to the major-domo to provide the widows with work so that they can earn their living (1966/c, line 7). [7] A collection of orders of the Hittite lord for the commandants of the provincial garrison contains the following instruction: When the commandant comes to a city on his circuit, he shall summon all who have legal claims and assemble them at the city gate; then he shall deal with the case of each to the satisfaction of the plaintiff. He must be particularly careful to give satisfaction to three groups, viz., the male slaves, the female slaves, and the widows. [8]

5. *Ugaritic and Phoenician.* In the Ugaritic epics, we encounter as an essential function of the king setting right (i.e., defending) the cause of the widow. In the Aqhat Epic, king Danel sits at the city gate and *ydn dn ’lmnt yṭpṭ ṭpṭ ytm,* "he sets right the claim of the widow, he decides in favor of the orphan." [9] We see how important this royal function is in the accusation of the young prince Yaṣib, who reproves his royal father and says: "You do not set right the claim of the widow, or decide in favor of the oppressed (?)..., therefore step down from your kingdom that I may become king." [10] Phoenician texts from later centuries do not explicitly refer to this royal function. King Esmun‘azar of Sidon is called on his coffin inscription "orphan, son of a widow" (*ytm bn ’lmt ’nk*), [11] i.e., he was born after the death of his father.

II. Position of the Widow.

1. *Existence or Nonexistence of Children.* As has been said above, the term "widow" was used for the woman who had no financial support from an adult male member of her family (husband or grown son). When the husband of a married woman died, she became an *’almanah,* "widow," and her children

---

[5] Erman-Ranke, 105.
[6] *ANET*, 408.
[7] *ArOr*, 33 (1965), 337f.
[8] *KUB*, XIII, 2, III, 29f.
[9] *CTA*, 17 [II D], V, 7-9.
[10] *CTA*, 16 [II K], VI, 33f., 37.
[11] *KAI*, 14.3, 13.

yethomim, "orphans" (Ex. 22:23 [Eng. v. 24]). As long as a woman had her sons, she was not entirely without means as a widow. Therefore, the prospect of losing her sons was especially bitter for a widow (2 S. 14:5-7; 1 K. 17:20). The widow who brought her sons to manhood by remarrying or by supporting herself was often honored by her name instead of the father's being mentioned with the name of her son. Zeruah was the widowed mother of Jeroboam I, the first king of Israel (1 K. 11:26). Hiram, the foreman of the men of Tyre who helped build Solomon's temple, was the son of a widow from the tribe of Naphtali who had married a man of Tyre (7:14). Examples of widows without living children are Naomi, Ruth, and Tamar (Judah's daughter-in-law, Gen. 38:11). Cf. in the NT 1 Tim. 5:5.

2. *Remarriage.* When a woman's husband died, three ways stood open to her. She could marry again if she was young or had a rich dowry. She could remain unmarried and support herself by following a profession. Or she could return to her father's house. A widow to whom no son had been born would often marry a brother of her husband in a so-called Levirate marriage (→ יבמה *yibbᵉmāh*). The Levirate marriage was also practiced in priestly families (Ezk. 44:22), although a priest was openly forbidden to marry a widow, a divorcee, or a prostitute (Lev. 21:7,14).

3. *Property Rights.* Widows who had no grown sons were entrusted with the property of their deceased husbands. If a widow had a young son, as soon as he was of age he took over his father's property and the responsibility of caring for his mother. If she had no son, the brother of her husband (→ גאל *gōʾēl*) bought the property of the deceased and simultaneously took her as his wife. The son who was born first into this union was regarded as son of the deceased husband and thus inherited his property (Ruth 4). When the OT warns against coveting the land of a widow or defrauding her in civil cases (Dt. 10:18; 27:19; Isa. 1:17,23; Jer. 7:6; 22:3; etc.), it is implied that a widow who had not remarried could (and she in fact did) possess property. God took it upon himself to protect the widow's boundaries (Prov. 15:25). Widows who had no possessions could either return to their father's house or consecrate themselves as prophetesses (Anna, Lk. 2:36ff.).

4. *Vows.* As long as a woman's husband was alive, and if she preferred after his death to return to her father's house, she had no right to dispose of the family possessions, and thus could not consecrate them to fulfil a vow made to God without the consent of her father or husband. But if she lived as a widow on her husband's land without being subject to the veto of her husband or father, she could consecrate part of her property to the temple to fulfil a vow (Nu. 30:10).

5. *As an Example of Pious Devotion.* In the OT and NT alike, widows, since they are usually poor, are often praised because of their liberality and piety (1 K. 17:9f.; Mk. 12:42ff.; Lk. 21:1ff.).

III. **Protection and Care of the Widow.** A widow's needs were of two kinds: protection against exploitation, and help in time of distress. These responsibilities to a woman, which under normal circumstances were the duty of her husband or father, were taken over by society in general when these two means of support were missing. But expressed religiously, it was said that God assumed this responsibility and put society under obligation to her. He was the protector of the widow and the father of her children (Ps. 68:6[5]). She was protected from her creditors and from the creditors of her deceased husband; they could take no pledge from her (Dt. 24:17; Job 24:3), nor could they regard her or her property as spoil (*shalal*) (Isa. 10:2). She received the benefit of the doubt in any civil suit (Ex. 22:21[22]; Dt. 10:18; 27:19; Isa. 1:17,23; 10:2; Jer. 7:6; 22:3; Zec. 7:10; Mal. 3:5). In addition to protection from exploitation, the widow enjoyed certain privileges, which represented a kind of social security. Every third year, the tithes of the agricultural products were supposed to be given to the widows, orphans, Levites, and sojourners (*ger*) (Dt. 14:28f.; 26:12f.). At the Feast of Weeks (16:11) and the Feast of Booths (16:14), widows and other poverty-stricken and dependent people received portions of food and wine with the families who were celebrating. Every year when the wheat and barley were harvested, and the grapes, olives, and other fruits were gathered, the gleanings of the fields, vineyards, and fruit trees were left for the poor, including widows (Lev. 19:9; Dt. 24:19-21; Ruth 2).

IV. **Figurative Use of the Word.** The word "widow" is frequently used in a figurative sense in all ancient Near Eastern literature. On the Israel Stele (line 27), the word *ḫ₃r.t* is used to describe the plundered enemy lands. In Stymphalos, the goddess Hera, in harmony with her ancient character as a nature deity, was called *país*, "child, girl" (or *parthénos*, "virgin") in the spring, *teleía*, "full-grown," in the summer, and *chéra*, "widow," in the winter (Pausanias viii.22.2). When God forsakes his people Israel and their land, they can be characterized as an *’almanah*, "widow" (Isa. 47:8), and their situation as *’almanuth*, "widowhood" (54:4).

Hoffner

אָמַן 'āman; אֱמוּנָה 'emûnāh;
אָמֵן 'āmēn; אֱמֶת 'emeth

Contents: I. Etymology. II. Derivatives. III. Qal. IV. Niphal: 1. Forms; 2. Secular Use of the Participle and Perfect; 3. Theological Use of the Participle; 4. Imperfect; 5. Meaning. V. Hiphil: 1. Problem; 2. Discussion; 3. Distribution in the OT; 4. Strictly Human Use; 5. Theological Use; 6. Summary; 7. History. VI. 'emeth: 1. Form; 2. Distribution in the OT; 3. Problem; 4. Strictly Human Use; 5. God's 'emeth. VII. 'emunah: 1. With Reference to Man; 2. With Reference to God. VIII. 'amen. IX. Summary.

I. **Etymology.** It is hardly possible to get a good understanding of the Hebrew root 'mn from related Semitic languages. Up to the present time, it has not been authenticated with certainty in Akkadian or in Ugaritic or Canaanite-Phoenician; thus, at present the Hebrew examples are the earliest. Then the hiphil form of the Hebrew was taken over by Syriac and Arabic, and possibly by Ethiopic. However, Aramaic-Syriac also has this root independent of Hebrew, but, as it seems, especially to denote duration of time. [1] Accordingly, the earliest Aramaic example [2] can best be translated: "(May the Pharaoh or his throne be) as *permanent* as the days of heaven." Wehr gives as the meaning of the Arabic verb: "to be faithful, reliable, or to be secure"; corresponding to this, the cognate nouns mean: "security, rest, peace, or reliability, faithfulness."

In light of this, it is difficult to draw conclusions about an "original meaning" of the root from the Aramaic and Arabic languages, which are much later from

---

'āman. J. Alfaro, "Fides in terminologia biblica," *Greg*, 42 (1961), 463-505; P. Antoine, "Foi," *DBS*, 3 (1938), 276-291; J. Barr, *The Semantics of Biblical Language* (1961); F. Baumgärtel, "Glaube. II, Im AT," *RGG³*, II, 1588-1590; M. Buber, *Two Types of Faith* (trans. 1951); J. C. C. van Drossen, *De derivate van den stam* אמן *in het Hebreeuwsch van het OT* (Amsterdam, 1951); G. Ebeling, *Word and Faith* (trans. 1963); A. Gelin, "La foi dans l'AT," *Lumière et Vie*, 22 (1955), 431-442; A. G. Hebert, "'Faithfulness' and 'Faith,'" *Theology*, 58 (1955), 373-79; M.-L. Henry, *Glaubenskrise and Glaubensbewährung in den Dichtungen der Jesaja-apokalypse. BWANT*, 5/6 (1967); P. Michalon, "La foi, rencontre de Dieu et engagement envers Dieu, selon l'AT," *NRTh*, 85 (1963), 587-600; A. Schlatter, *Der Glaube im NT* (⁴1927), 557ff.; G. Segalla, "La fede come opzione fondamentale in Isaia e Giov," *Studia Patavina*, 15 (1968), 355-381; T. F. Torrance, "One Aspect of the Biblical Conception of Faith," *ExpT*, 68 (1956/57), 111-14=*Conflict and Agreement*, II, 74-82; S. Virgulin, *La 'Fede' nella profezia d'Isaia. BeO*, 2 (1961); *idem*, "Isaian and Postisaian Faith," *Euntes Docete*, 16 (1963), 522-535; 17 (1964), 109-122; Th. C. Vriezen, *Geloven en Vertrouwen* (Nijkerk, 1957); A. Weiser, *Glaube und Geschichte im AT. BWANT*, 4/4 (1931).

On V: L. Bach, "Der Glaube nach der Anschauung des ATs," *BFChTh*, 4/6 (1900), 1-96; J. Boehmer, "Der Glaube und Jesaja," *ZAW*, 41 (1923), 84-93; H. W. Heidland, *Die Anrechnung des Glaubens zur Gerechtigkeit. BWANT*, 4/18 (1936); C. A. Keller, "Das quietistische Element in der Botschaft des Jesaja," *ThZ*, 11 (1955), 81-97; Pedersen, *ILC*, I-II, 336ff.; E. Pfeiffer, "Glaube im AT," *ZAW*, 71 (1959), 151-164; R. Smend, "Zur Geschichte

(continued on p. 293)

[1] Cf. the translations in Brockelmann, *LexSyr²*, 25: for 't 'mn, *perseveravit;* for 'myn', *constans, semper, continuo.*
[2] *KAI*, 266.3.

a literary standpoint; if an original meaning is still possible at all, it must be deduced from the Hebrew rather than from the Syriac or Arabic. Of course, it is possible that old meanings were preserved in later languages. But in this case, it is difficult to determine whether the original meaning is closer to the Arabic and thus meant "faithful" or "secure," or to the Syriac and thus meant "enduring." Furthermore, we cannot confidently deduce the meaning of a word in the later development of a language even if we clearly establish the original meaning of that word. Thus, the meaning of the words derived from the root 'mn can hardly be explained by determining its original meaning. And when we do not know the original meaning, the development of a word can lead us far from that meaning to something entirely different. The meaning of a word cannot be inferred from the (more or less certain) etymology, but only by a careful study of the way it is used in the language. [3]

II. **Derivatives.** The root 'mn appears in the following forms:

1. As a verb in the qal, niphal, and hiphil. To be sure, it is a matter of debate whether the qal forms really belong to the root being treated here. Thus, in opposition to GesB and KBL², Baumgartner assumes two different roots in KBL³.

2. As a noun: (a) in the form 'emeth, probably from 'amint; [4] (b) in qaṭul or qᵉṭul forms: 'emûnâh, 'ēmûn, 'emûnîm, 'emûnê; [5] (c) in a segholate form following quṭl: 'ômen, fem. 'omnâh; with adverbial ending, 'omnām, 'umnām; (d) in the form 'ᵃmānâh.

---

von האמין," Hebräische Wortforschung. Festschrift W. Baumgartner. SVT, 16 (1967), 284-290; A. Weiser, "Glauben im AT," Festschrift G. Beer (1935), 88-99; idem, "The Stem אמן and Related Expressions," TDNT, VI, 183-196; H. Wildberger, "Erwägungen zu האמין," Hebräische Wortforschung. Festschrift W. Baumgartner. SVT, 16, 372-386; idem, " 'Glauben' im AT," ZThK, 65 (1968), 129-159; E. Würthwein, "Jesaja 7,1-9," Theologie als Glaubenswagnis. Festschrift K. Heim (1954), 47-63.

On VI: R. Bultmann, "Der Begriff der Wahrheit im AT und unter alttestamentlichem Einfluss," ZNW, 27 (1928), 113-134; W. A. Irwin, "Truth in Ancient Israel," JR, 9 (1929), 357-388; L. J. Kuyper, "Grace and Truth," Reformed Review, 16/1 (1962), 1-16; D. Michel, "'Ämät. Untersuchung über 'Wahrheit' im Hebr.," Archiv für Begriffsgeschichte, 12 (1968), 30-57; E. T. Ramsdell, "The OT Understanding of Truth," JR, 31 (1951), 264-273.

On VII: M. A. Klopfenstein, Die Lüge nach dem AT (1964); E. Perry, "The Meaning of emuna in the OT," JBR, 21 (1953), 252-56; S. Virgulin, "La אמונה in Abacuc 2,4b," Divus Thomas, 99 (1969), 92-97.

On VIII: G. Dalman, The Words of Jesus (trans. 1909), 226-29; H. W. Hogg, "Amen," JQR, 9 (1897), 1ff.; A. R. Hulst, "Het woord 'Amen' in het OT," Kerk en Eredienst, 8 (1953), 50-68; I. Lande, Formelhafte Wendungen der Umgangssprache im AT (1954); E. Pfeiffer, "Der alttestamentliche Hintergrund der liturgischen Formel 'Amen,'" KuD, 4/2 (1958), 129-141.

3 This is also emphasized by Pfeiffer, KuD, 131, in harmony with Albright and Delitzsch, even if it is not practiced in the ZAW.
4 For particulars, see below, VI.
5 See below, VII.

3. As an original adjectival form following qaṭil: ’āmēn. [6]

Again, the extent to which these different derivatives have a similar meaning, or whether from time to time they have acquired a special meaning, can be determined only by studying the way they are used in the language.

III. Qal. The qal of the verb occurs clearly only in the active participle, in the masculine in Nu. 11:12; 2 K. 10:1,5; Est. 2:7; Isa. 49:23; and in the feminine in 2 S. 4:4; Ruth 4:16. It is used of men and women who are entrusted with the care of, or who take it upon themselves to care for, dependent children. 2 K. 10 must have to do with an official commission; the ’omenim could hardly be guardians, but are probably those entrusted with the responsibility of leadership and education. Also, according to Est. 2:7 (cf. v. 20), Mordecai appears in the role of Esther's father and mother. Now, whether we wish to characterize him as a guardian or not, to Esther he is more than a provider and a guardian. The same is true of the women. In all likelihood, the ’omeneth of the five-year-old Meribbaal did not nurse him, nor did Naomi nurse Obed. Rather, in the former (and perhaps also in the latter) case, it is to be assumed that this woman had the responsibility of taking care of the child. The child has been entrusted "to faithful hands," or like Naomi, she assumed the responsibility of caring for him.

Moses denies that he has the kind of responsibility toward Israel that an ’omen has toward a child (Nu. 11:12). But kings must accept the responsibility of "caring for" Israel when they return home from Babylonian captivity (Isa. 49:23).

’omnah, "care" (Est. 2:20), fits the meaning "a man who cares for, a woman who cares for." But if this is indeed the meaning of the qal participle, it is not necessary to separate these forms from the other forms of the root ’mn. Perhaps the qal participle has taken on a special meaning, that of responsible care, but still its connection with the other forms of ’mn is quite discernible.

The suggestion of Albright [7] that ’omenim is to be derived from Akk. ummānu, with which Baumgartner seems to agree, cannot be justified by the form or the meaning of the word; and so the reason for assuming that the qal forms of ’mn are from a special root, which is so crucial to Baumgartner's position, is gone also.

IV. Niphal.

1. *Forms.* The niphal of the root ’mn appears predominantly in the participle–32 times, while it is found in the perfect only 5 times and in the imperfect 8 times. We must omit Hos. 5:9 and 12:1 (Eng. 11:12) from these passages as unintelligible or corrupt. [8] We should probably also omit 1 Ch. 17:24 for the same reason, but one should read Rudolph's comments on this passage. [9] Thus,

---

[6] See below, VIII.
[7] Albright, *BASOR,* 94 (1944), 18, n. 28.
[8] Cf. comms. *in loc.*
[9] Rudolph, *HAT,* 21 (1955), *in loc.*

it would seem best to try to determine the meaning of the participle first; but since it is evident that the perfect had the same meaning, the perfect forms will be treated with the participle.

The ptcp. *ne'eman* is always used in a nominal, i.e., adjectival sense. Therefore, it is not appropriate to begin with the verbal derivative, for this seems hardly to have been known any more.

2. *Secular Use of the Participle and Perfect.* a. In the relatively few passages in which *ne'eman* is used in connection with "things," it means "lasting, continual, firm." Thus, Dt. 28:59 speaks of afflictions and sicknesses which do not cease; Isa. 33:16 and Jer. 15:18, of water which will flow continually, and of water which will flow no more, respectively; and Isa. 22:23,25, of a firm (RSV–sure) place into which a peg may be driven so that it will hold.

b. Prov. 25:13; Isa. 8:2; Jer. 42:5; Neh. 13:13; and 1 S. 22:14 indicate what *ne'eman* means when it is used in connection with people. In all these passages it means men who are reliable. Thus Prov. 25:13 speaks of the messenger on whom his master can rely; Isa. 8:2, of the witness whose statement is reliable (in Jer. 42:5, God himself is called the "faithful witness"); Neh. 13:13, of the priests who faithfully carry out the task to which they are appointed; and finally, 1 S. 22:14, of David, for on whom among the servants of Saul could one rely, if not on him? Still, in these passages the emphasis seems to be that such reliability is not obvious; it must be pointed out in particular.

c. This also calls to mind the small number of passages, especially in the Wisdom Literature, that speak of the *ne'emanim* in general. Thus, Prov. 11:13 says: "He who is trustworthy in spirit (*ne'eman ruach*) keeps a thing hidden"; and 27:6 states: "Faithful are the wounds of a friend; profuse are the kisses of an enemy." Therefore, faithful people such as these are particularly favored by the king (Ps. 101:6). But it is an indication of divine omnipotence that God himself takes away the speech of those who are faithful (Job 12:20).

3. *Theological Use of the Participle.* In strictly theological use, this word appears in different connections. a. It is rarely applied to God himself. [10] Yahweh is called *ne'eman*, "faithful," only in Isa. 49:7. And in Dt. 7:9, he is called *ha'el hanne'eman*, "the faithful God," i.e., the God on whom one can rely, who keeps his promise. In Jer. 42:5, Yahweh is invoked as the true and faithful witness, as if he were the only one who could be considered as such. Sometimes God's precepts and commandments are called *ne'eman*, "sure," as precepts on whose validity one can rely because they partake of God's reliability. Here it is hardly possible to translate *ne'eman* as "lasting, enduring," its usual meaning when applied to things.

---

[10] But cf. below on *'emeth*.

b. *ne'eman* is used only a few times to refer to the relationship of individuals to God, again probably indicating that these are being emphasized in a particular way. It is applied to Abraham in Neh. 9:8, where it says in the prayer of the community: "Thou didst find his heart *ne'eman*, 'faithful,' before thee," i.e. probably, completely devoted to thee. It is uncertain whether this alludes to Abraham's faith in Gen. 15:6 or to his behavior in Gen. 22. Sir. 44:20 would seem to favor the latter view, for it says: *benisuy nimtsa' ne'eman*, "when he was tested he was found *ne'eman*," i.e., faithful, loyal, reliable. (This wording is also presupposed in 1 Macc. 2:52, where *pistós* occurs.) Since there is no priest whose behavior can be said to be *ne'eman*, "faithful," God must raise up a priest on whom he can rely (1 S. 2:35). The refining of God makes it necessary for a citizenship (*qiryah*, "city") which was at one time steadfast, loyal, and reliable to God to become so again (Isa. 1:21,26). It is clear that a personal relationship is intended here too.

The precise translation of two other statements that belong here is debated, viz., the words concerning Moses in Nu. 12:7, and the words concerning Samuel in 1 S. 3:20. One possibility is that *ne'eman* is to be understood as "reliable," as above. In this case, it is said of Moses: in contrast to Aaron and Miriam, he is faithful and loyal in my whole house; and of Samuel: all Israel knew that Samuel was faithful as a prophet of Yahweh. However, both statements fit into the context very poorly. Therefore, some scholars have suggested that the participial forms here should be understood more like verbs: "he is entrusted, he is authorized." In this case, Nu. 12:7 would mean: "He (alone) is entrusted with all my house"; and 1 S. 3:20: " ... that Samuel was appointed as a prophet of Yahweh." [11] No objection can be made to such a verbal meaning in itself; however, the derivation from '*mn* causes difficulties. But in both cases it is clear that a statement was made about Moses and Samuel which expressed a unique relationship to the deity, indeed, a special divine evaluation of these two men. [12]

c. *ne'eman* appears more often with regard to the promise made concerning the dynasty of David. This is stated in different ways. 2 S. 7:16 and 1 S. 25:28 state that his house shall be *ne'eman*, "sure"; Ps. 89:38(37) says his descendants shall be *ne'eman;* 89:29(28) says God's *berith*, "covenant" = "promise," shall be *ne'eman*; and Isa. 55:3 states that the tokens of God's love for David are *ne'eman*. Only translations like "continuous, enduring, lasting," are suitable here, as is confirmed by the parallel '*olam*, "ever," in the last three passages. The promise made to the house of the priest whom God raised up (1 S. 2:35), and the one made to the house of Jeroboam I (1 K. 11:38), are probably both derived from this promise made to the house of David. In all three cases, it is assumed that the durability of a house is not a natural thing, but is guaranteed

---

[11] So according to the older commentators; cf. Calmet *in loc.*, Klostermann, Hertzberg, *GesB, KBL*[3], etc.

[12] On the difficulties of the textual continuity of 1 S. 3:19-21, cf. the comms., esp. Klostermann, Budde, and Caspari.

by a promise of God. Such promises of God also have durability and permanency. [13]

d. Israel's conduct, as it is described in Ps. 78:8,37, stands in contrast to the conduct of God. Here also, as in the other three passages that use the perfect, the most obvious meaning is "to be ne'eman." In both verses ne'eman stands in parallelism to: "Their (his) heart was not steadfast (nakhon)"; therefore a translation like "they were not faithful" is the most natural. V. 37 would then read: "Their heart was not steadfast toward him and they were not faithful to his promise." V. 8 could also fit in with this understanding with its statement about the stubborn and rebellious generation: "a generation whose heart was not steadfast and whose spirit was not faithful to God."

4. *Imperfect.* The seven forms of the niphal imperfect may be divided into two groups. In five passages, the imperfect is connected with *dabhar*, "word." First of all, we may mention Gen. 42:20; here Joseph has his brothers prove that their word to him was "true, reliable," thus that a person could rely on their word. The other passages speak of the word of God. First we may note 1 K. 8:26, where Solomon prays that God's promise to David might prove to be a reliable word. The Chronicler takes over this passage (2 Ch. 6:17), and inserts the same formula in his reproduction of 1 K. 3:6 in 2 Ch. 1:9, and of 2 S. 7:25 in 1 Ch. 17:23. The Chronicler seems to have attached particular importance to the fact that God's word, his promise, should be fulfilled, and thus prove to be reliable. Thus, "to prove to be reliable" would probably be the best rendering of this formula. But we still need to discuss Isa. 7:9 and its reproduction in 2 Ch. 20:20, which can be interpreted best in connection with the hiphil forms.

5. *Meaning.* This analysis of the linguistic use of the niphal has shown that the niphal forms of 'mn are used very predominantly of God and man, or of what they say, while they are used of things very rarely. Therefore, Weiser is probably using a *petitio principii* (a fallacious approach) when he begins with the passages in which the niphal forms are used of things, develops a formal idea from these, and then applies this idea to the uses of these forms with regard to persons. Following Weiser, Ebeling reaches the conclusion that ne'eman means "that a thing corresponds to what it promises to be." [14] On the contrary, virtually all that can be determined from the use of the word is that when ne'eman is used of things, a meaning like "lasting, continual," is to be assumed, but when it is used of persons, it means "reliable." In neither case is a specific quality in view, namely, what the thing or person promises to be. Neither sicknesses and afflictions, nor water, nor even a dynasty promises to endure. Rather, one could say that that which is not specific, indeed that which is unexpected, is declared in promise ("house") and threat ("afflictions"), viz., that a dynasty will continue, or

---

[13] See below on Isa. 7:9.
[14] Ebeling, 208.

that a disease will not cease. The personal use conveys even less the idea of something specific: that the priests of Nehemiah are faithful is not an evaluation of their priesthood, but of their persons, and the same applies to other persons and groups of persons mentioned. When *ne'eman* is used, it always indicates something special, not something obviously to be expected.

If one were to try to find a translation in English that would embrace the different meanings of this word, the closest would probably be "constant," which can include both the permanency of things and the stability and reliability of persons. The result is that one may build or rely upon the thing or person giving proof of constancy.

V. Hiphil.

1. *Problem.* The problem of the hiphil form can be seen clearly by examining the various translations and explanations that have been suggested for this word. A selection of some of the views that have been proposed should make the issues clear.

Pedersen writes: "To make a man true, *he'emin,* means the same as to rely on him. It implies confidence in his having the will and power to maintain the claims of the covenant.... The weaker members of the covenant help to uphold the stronger by their confidence. They *make* him 'true,' i.e., firm, sure, and strong"; "to consider a soul firm and thus to contribute to its firmness, that is to 'make true,' to believe in it." [15]

Eichrodt says: "In several passages the word *he'emin,* 'to consider firm, trustworthy, to find to be reliable,' is used to describe this (positive) relationship; and it does indeed very happily strike the exact note of the adventurous attitude toward God." And in a footnote he adds: "Since the basic meaning of the root *'mn* in Arabic is 'to be secure, out of danger,' one could choose as the preferable translation of the Heb. *he'emin,* 'to regard as assured,' 'to find security in.'"[16]

Weiser paraphrases: "To say Amen to something with all the consequences that this involves for object and subject," and then comments: "The concept *'mn* relates the totality of the manifestations of human life to the relationship with God." [17] Ebeling concludes from this: "The Hiph. form האמין has, in the causative or declarative sense, the meaning: to let something be נאמן or declare it to be נאמן, that is, to let it be valid or adjudge that it corresponds to what it promises." [18]

On the other hand, von Rad says: "In Hebrew 'to have faith' is literally 'to make oneself secure in Yahweh' (hence the prep. *be* after *he'emin*). But the object to which, according to Gen. 15:6, Abraham directed his faith is—as is usual in the OT—something in the future." [19]

---

[15] *ILC,* 347; cf. also 348.
[16] Eichrodt, *TheolOT,* II (trans. 1967), 276.
[17] Weiser, *TDNT.*
[18] Ebeling, 209.
[19] Von Rad, *OT Theol,* I (trans. 1962), 171.

Procksch translates *he'emin* "to become trustworthy, to become faithful." [20] Schlatter says: "The antithesis to this unfortified condition of the soul, the manifestation of its inner stability through trust and confidence, which is also essential to the preservation of the community, is called *he'emin*." [21] Similarly, Wildberger writes: "The original and wholly concrete meaning of the root *'mn* is 'firm, reliable,' and therefore the meaning of the hiphil is 'to be (or become) firm, to have or gain stability.'" [22]

These examples must suffice to indicate the varied breadth of possible interpretations of *he'emin*, ranging from the idea of making one sure to that of having stability oneself. Scholars have arrived at these different meanings in the following ways: (1) by means of etymology, in which one tries to derive the meaning of the verb from the original meaning of the root *'mn*; cf., e.g., Eichrodt and Wildberger; (2) by considering the meaning of the hiphil–but the hiphil can be understood in different ways, and this gives rise to different interpretations; cf., e.g., Pedersen and Ebeling; and (3) by a varied assessment of the concept of faith in the OT and in the NT. While Schlatter deals with the root *'mn* from the NT viewpoint alone, Weiser and (following him) Ebeling think that the OT idea of faith is the immediate precursor to the NT concept.

2. *Discussion*. First of all, it is necessary to examine the tenability of these three criteria. As far as deriving the meaning from the root *'mn* is concerned, no more need be added to what has already been said above. It might seem more to the point to begin with the meaning of the hiphil. But when we consider what the grammars say about the meaning of the hiphil, [23] this approach immediately becomes very questionable, because they indicate a great diversity in its use. Not only is its relationship to the meaning of the root causative ("to cause something to happen" or "to make someone do something"), but it must be translated in the greatest variety of ways if the shades of meaning in the various OT contexts are to be understood correctly. When Brockelmann gives six other possibilities besides the causative meaning (*to declare* to be right; *to become* fat; *to act* foolish; *to obtain* horns; *to break out* in rejoicing; = qal), this shows that the classification of the hiphil in a specific category of meaning comes from the linguistic usage of the hiphil in the first place, and thus that we cannot begin with this sort of classification. The whole discussion about the meaning of the hiphil of *'mn*, the purpose of which is to clarify first of all whether the hiphil here is to be understood as a causative, a declarative, or an internal transitive, [24] cannot be resolved. First, we must learn how the word was used; then perhaps we will be in a position to determine the category in which the hiphil form *he'emin* belongs. Theoretically, it would even be conceivable that

---

[20] O. Procksch, *ThAT* (1950), 604.
[21] A. Schlatter, *Glaube*³, 560.
[22] Wildberger, 385.
[23] E.g., *GK*²⁸, § 53c-g, or Brockelmann, *Synt.*, § 36.
[24] Cf., e.g., Pfeiffer and Wildberger.

the hiphil of this word represents a special category different from what is usually observed. Thus, the question about the grammatical classification of the hiphil of this word can be asked only at the end.

With regard to the third point, the difference in the outlooks of Schlatter and Ebeling is clear. Both wish to investigate the meaning of *he'emin*. But Schlatter deals with the OT word in an Appendix; he is able to define the meaning of faith in the NT without first dealing with the OT word. Indeed, he seems to have intentionally ignored the connection between faith in the OT and in the NT in order to emphasize what is distinctive in the NT idea. Ebeling intentionally refers to the OT concept in order to discover a root of the NT idea of faith. But what he goes on to present is not merely an interpretation of *he'emin*, but the development of the OT view of God in its entirety. In view of his purpose, this is quite correct; what OT faith in God means as a prerequisite for NT faith can be determined only from a study of the entire OT (cf., e.g., his statements: "God and faith belong together"; the concept of faith is connected with the idea "that the God of Israel is the God of history," and also his conclusion from Dt. 6). But all this goes far beyond what is to be inferred from the linguistic use of *he'emin*. Our task is to determine the meaning this form has in the OT. Only after we have done this will we be in a position to determine whether this meaning is related to the NT concept of faith, and if so, how it is related.

3. *Distribution in the OT*. *he'emin* appears in the following constructions: with *be*, "in, on": Gen. 15:6; Ex. 14:31; 19:9; Nu. 14:11; 20:12; Dt. 1:32; 28:66; 1 S. 27:12; 2 K. 17:14; Jer. 12:6; Jonah 3:5; Mic. 7:5; Ps. 78:22,32; 106:12; 119:66; Prov. 26:25; Job 4:18; 15:15,31; 24:22; 39:12; 2 Ch. 20:20; with *le*, "in": Gen. 45:26; Ex. 4:1,8 (twice), 9; Dt. 9:23; 1 K. 10:7; 2 Ch. 9:6; Isa. 43:10; 53:1; Jer. 40:14; Ps. 106:24; Prov. 14:15; 2 Ch. 32:15; with an inf.: Ps. 27:13; Job 15:22; with a *ki* clause: Ex. 4:5; Job 9:16; 39:12; Lam. 4:12; absolutely: Ex. 4:31; Isa. 7:9; 28:16; Hab. 1:5; Ps. 116:10; Job 29:24; 39:24.

It is very likely that the text of Jgs. 11:20 and Isa. 30:21 should be emended; it is at least so uncertain that no conclusions can be drawn from the occurrence of *he'emin* in these passages. [25]

Equally important is the analysis of the literary types in which *he'emin* appears: it is found 24 times in narrative contexts, as well as in four Psalms passages; 7 times in prophetic oracles; 4 times in other psalms; and 11 times in the Wisdom Literature. This (very rough) distribution shows that *he'emin* is not used very often in the Prophets and the Psalms, but does appear frequently in the narratives of Israel's early history and in the Wisdom Literature. Since the historical narratives have a predominantly theological concern, and the Wisdom Literature has a secular concern, it seems advisable to begin with the latter.

4. *Strictly Human Use*. In both Prov. 14:15 and 26:25, *he'emin* has a clearly negative ring. It is characteristic of a fool to trust in every word, to believe

---

[25] On Jgs. 11:20, however, cf. Fohrer on Job 24:22.

everything. Caution is all the more necessary when a flatterer speaks, especially when he speaks graciously: Do not believe him. When it is a question of depending on someone or something and relying on something, to do so is always dangerous. On whom can one really rely?

The same negative ring also seems to determine the use of this word in the book of Job; at any rate in all nine passages this word is connected with a negation (in 39:12, the negative sense is in the question).

God can put no trust in his servants, his holy ones (4:18; 15:15), to say nothing of man. No one is so pure and reliable that God can depend on him. These statements speak of God, but their intention is to evaluate man as untrustworthy. Man is no more reliable than a wild ox, and thus what can be said of one can be said of the other: "Can you have faith in him that he will return?" (39:12). His strength is too unruly to tame or to rely on.

The same expression used in Dt. 28:66 also appears in Job 24:22, which speaks of the ruler whose life is prolonged by God's help when he himself "can no longer rely on his life," i.e., despairs of life. The meaning of this expression is certain, even if the connection in the book of Job is doubtful, for the only thing it can mean in Dt. 28:66 is: "you will despair of life."

Uncertainty as to another is also clearly the meaning of 9:16. Here it is God whom Job doubts: "If I called and he answered me, I could still not rely on it that he really heard my voice." The usual translation, "I would not believe that...," weakens the statement. [26]

The same meaning is also to be recognized in 15:22. The evildoer "cannot rely on it, cannot count on it that he might return out of darkness, that he might escape from it"; rather, he is destined for the sword.

In all these passages he'emin is used when the writer wishes to state that one cannot rely on someone or something else. In these cases it would be a frivolous, foolish undertaking against which a warning is given.

The text and context of the last three passages in the book of Job are difficult, and thus these passages can hardly aid in determining the meaning of he'emin. 15:31 certainly agrees with the conclusions that have been reached so far: "Let him (the evildoer) not rely on emptiness"; but this demand does not correspond with the description of the evildoer and his fate. Therefore, it is usually regarded as a gloss. [27] 29:24a is syntactically difficult, and thus is interpreted in many different ways; often the lo', "not, no," is deleted, but on this see above. With van Doorsen, Pfeiffer, and Wildberger, it is possible to interpret lo' ya'aminu as an abbreviated relative clause: "I smiled on them when they despaired," i.e., when they had nothing on which they could rely. 39:24 has been interpreted in many different ways. If one is not willing to conjecture an original yemin, "to turn to the right," with Duhm, etc. (which could be suggested by Isa. 30:21), the only possible subject of he'emin would be an animal, which to be sure is probably not to be excluded in this context.

The syntactical structure is more difficult: ki qol shophar hardly makes sense.

---

[26] Cf. Budde, in loc.
[27] Cf. Beer, Duhm, Budde, Fohrer, et al., in loc.

The meaning "it (he) does not stand still" is assumed for *lo' ya'amin,* without really making this statement clear. It may be that this is a technical term of equestrians, whose precise meaning is not known. In any case, this obscure passage can hardly be a proper starting point for determining the meaning of the root *'mn* or of the hiphil form.

On the whole, the use of *he'emin* in the Wisdom Literature seems to be associated with a certain skepticism. However, the warnings in the book of Proverbs and the negations in Job surely make it clear that "not to rely on" is usually more desirable than too hasty confidence.

This impression is reinforced by the other passages in which *he'emin* is used in the secular sense. This is the case in Jer. 12:6, where Yahweh warns Jeremiah about his brothers: "Do not rely on them when they speak fair words to you," and in Mic. 7:5 in the description of the coming time of terror: "Do not rely on a neighbor, have no confidence in a friend!" The word *he'emin* is used in a positive statement only once, viz., in 1 S. 27:12: "And Achish relied on David, thinking, 'He has made himself utterly abhorred by his people Israel; therefore he shall be my servant always.'" But the narrator indicates to the reader that Achish should not have been so gullible, though of course he did not know what David was doing behind his back.

When *he'emin* is construed with *le,* the text has something to do with a messenger or a message, and the meaning is: "to have confidence in a messenger, to believe a message." In these passages also, the word is always connected with *lo',* "not." One simply cannot be careful enough when it comes to an incredible message. How could Jacob believe that Joseph was still alive and was ruler over all the land of Egypt (Gen. 45:26)? And how could anyone believe the reports of the fabulous wisdom and prosperity of Solomon? (1 K. 10:7: "I did not believe it"). Thus, Gedaliah also was not willing to believe that a Davidide could be solicited to murder him (Jer. 40:14). What Hezekiah says to the Jews about the coming help of Yahweh is to be viewed in the same way: Unbelievable! Therefore, the servants of Sennacherib urge the Jews: "Do not believe him!" (2 Ch. 32:15). The question in Isa. 53:1 is to be understood similarly: "Who has believed what we have heard?" This message of the servant of God, who is suffering here, is incredible; it is not surprising that no one believes it. And yet in all these cases the messages were correct; people should have believed them, but they did not. After all, on whom can one rely?

Thus, *he'emin* here means the same thing as "to consider a statement trustworthy or reliable, true or possible."

The two passages in which *he'emin* is followed by a *ki* are not quite so clear. In Lam. 4:12, the final clause refers to the fact that Jerusalem has been conquered. But the whole world had considered this fact to be incredible, indeed impossible, and yet it is a fearful reality. Thus, this passage agrees with those we have just discussed. The construction in Hab. 1:5 is different in that the *ki* clause does not indicate the contents of the *he'emin,* but speaks of a message. Two translations have been proposed. Some read: "You would not believe it if it were told." In this case, this sentence would have to do with considering a message to be true, which would agree well with the examples that have just been discussed. However, Wildberger has objected to this interpretation because it demands that an "it" be added as an accusative object, which is not found anywhere else in the OT. Therefore, he suggests that *he'emin* is to be taken absolutely and that the last line of Hab. 1:5 is to be translated: "You would not be able to stand fast" or "You would lose all confidence, if it were told." Since Isa. 7:9 yields a similar translation, [28] Wildberger's rendering is probably to be preferred.

Thus, in all secular usages *he'emin* occurs in a negative context; there are too many men and relationships on which one cannot rely, and too many messages one cannot consider to be true. It is probably no accident that frequently → בטח *bāṭach*, "to trust," stands in parallelism to *he'emin* (Mic. 7:5; Job 39:11); *batach* is also often used of a false security. It is easy to understand why a person would have reservations about men or messages, and thus would not "believe" something until he was convinced of its reliability or truth. One can be ruined all too easily by his good "faith," as was the case with Achish.

5. *Theological Use.* On this basis, perhaps we can understand how Moses, as a messenger of God, could be afraid that the people would be skeptical of his message: "But behold, they will not believe me or listen to my voice, for they will say, 'The Lord did not appear to you'" (Ex. 4:1). Could not anyone come and assert that God had appeared to him? Basically, the people's doubt is considered to be logical, because now Yahweh gives Moses power to do two signs that will attest to his genuineness, "that they may believe that the Lord... has appeared to you" (v. 5). If they do not believe the first sign, they will believe the second (v. 8). As a matter of fact, Yahweh even gives Moses a third sign (v. 9). And indeed, when the signs are performed, the people "believe" (vv. 30f.). As far as this point is concerned, the composition of this section is not important; it is clear that even God recognizes that it is quite likely that the people will not believe; therefore, he gives signs as a ground on which the people can accept the message of Moses as originating from God. [29] A person can and should rely on the messenger of God who is verified by signs. To this extent, this narrative has a somewhat different ring: God's signs and deeds should motivate people to hear his words and to take his promises seriously. "The people gained confidence," i.e., in what Moses said. Ex. 19:9 has in mind a similar verification of Moses to overcome the people's doubt; when the people hear Yahweh speaking with Moses, they will gain confidence in Moses from then on. Such confidence in a man requires a special basis.

The only other passage in which this positive statement is made about Israel is in Ex. 14:31 (it is repeated in Ps. 106:12). After they passed through the sea and the Egyptians were destroyed, Israel gained confidence in Yahweh and in his servant Moses, for Yahweh's promises through Moses had been fulfilled. God's deeds, his signs and wonders, led the people to "believe," and left no more room for doubt.

---

[28] See below.
[29] → אות *'ôth*, III.1.

However, the Israel of the wilderness period and even Moses and Aaron themselves are often accused of unbelief and doubt. When the people refuse to go into Canaan after the spies return, Yahweh says to Moses: "How long will this people despise me? And how long will they not believe in me, in spite of all the signs which I have wrought among them?" (Nu. 14:11). Israel's doubt may have been understandable at first, but now it is sin for the people not to believe that God was able to lead them into the promised land. The OT refers to this event several times as a sign of "unbelief." Thus, we find in the speech of Moses: "In spite of this word you did not believe Yahweh your God" (Dt. 1:32; cf. also 9:23; Ps. 78:32; 106:24). It is clear what the OT wished to emphasize in connection with this event: the people of Israel were expected to rely completely on their God and his promises; if they did not manifest this kind of trust, they would be punished, their existence would be threatened. Ps. 78:22 refers to a situation that is different, though analogous. The statement in 2 K. 17:14 is a general reference to the fathers who did not rely on the Lord their God.

The temptation to unbelief is so great that even Moses and Aaron succumbed to it. They did not believe that God was able to supply water for the people without their help, without smiting the rock. But that which seems possible and even necessary to men is sin for Moses and Aaron, since it has to do with their attitude toward God; sin, the consequence of which can only be punishment—premature death. Like the generation that did not trust in God, so also Moses and Aaron were not allowed to enter into the promised land. Anyone who is not prepared to take God's promises seriously perishes.

Where confidence in man is often dubious and trust in God's almost incredible promises is so difficult, it is easy to understand why positive statements are so rare. When the poet of Ps. 119:66 says: "Teach me good judgment and knowledge, for I believe in thy commandments," it is significant that although he likes to repeat words elsewhere in this psalm, he ventures to use *he'emin* only once. Did this word still have the ring of uncertainty for him? Or (as is more likely) is the assurance of trust so unusual that he cannot say it but once? In either case, this positive statement is connected with something absolute.

The meaning of two other passages in the book of Psalms in which *he'emanti* is used in a positive sense is so uncertain that no conclusions can be drawn from them: Ps. 27:13; 116:10. Perhaps 116:10 can be translated this way: "I have kept my confidence, even if I had to say: I am utterly bowed down." [30] 27:13 is hardly more intelligible: "If I had not relied on seeing. . . ." In both of these passages, if anything we must examine the use of *he'emin* elsewhere in the OT in order to draw conclusions about its meaning here.

The more astonishing, then, is that which the author of the book of Jonah says about the Ninevites. When Jonah preaches, "Yet three days, [31] and Nineveh will be destroyed" (3:4), the men of Nineveh did that which Israel, and even Moses and Aaron, were not able to do: They relied on God, and they did so without

---

[30] Cf. Wildberger, 376; but cf. the careful formulations of Kittel, *in loc.*
[31] This is to be read with the LXX; cf. Duhm, *in loc.*

seeing wonders and signs (in contrast to the Israelites, who believed when they saw signs and wonders, Ex. 4:31; 14:31); they believed wholly on the basis of the word of Jonah. The translation, "they believed in God," weakens the idea somewhat. It would be better to paraphrase the idea this way: They took Jonah's message seriously as a message which actually came from God, although nothing is said about God in Jonah's message. As a result of this, they fasted, put on garments symbolizing their penitent attitude, and (v. 10) turned from their evil way. Thus, it is the intention of this narrator to show that a metropolis (3:3) whose wickedness was so great that God felt compelled to destroy it (1:2) accepted the word of God which was preached to it, considered it to be true, and was willing to do all that it required. It is almost as if the narrator wanted to say: I have not found such faith in Israel. It is not without reason that Mt. 12:41 referred to this behavior of the Ninevites. A third positive statement appears in Gen. 15:6: *vehe'emin bayhvh vayyachshebheha lo tsedhaqah*. This statement is fundamental to the evaluation of Abraham in Judaism and Christianity.[32] It forms the conclusion of a brief promise of Yahweh to Abraham that his descendants would be as numerous as the stars of heaven. It would be necessary to divide this section into sources in order to put this statement about Abraham's faith in a historical setting. However, such a source analysis is almost impossible here. There is no real justification for assigning this statement to E, as has often been proposed. It is more likely that this section is a late insertion with a strong theological character.[33] All we can do, then, is to investigate the meaning of this statement apart from its historical setting.

This much is clear: Abraham reacts to the promise of Yahweh and its allusion to the stars by taking this promise of God seriously, by relying on it, or to be more specific, by relying on God and by believing that he is able to fulfil his promise. Although it is often very difficult to trust in man, it is still possible to trust in God. This is the only possible right conduct toward God, and therefore it is recognized by God as such. Thus, it is clear from this passage what the right conduct toward God is in the view of this narrative (*tsedhaqah*, "righteousness"): trusting in him, relying on his promise without doubting, indeed contrary to all appearance. The real meaning of Abraham's "belief" in this passage has been the subject of much discussion among Jews and Christians (cf. in the NT, Rom. 4:3; Jas. 2:23).

The special importance of such rare statements about faith is also clear in that among the prophets Isaiah alone dares to use the word *he'emin* in his preaching, and then only twice (7:9; 28:16). Of course, the precise interpretation of both passages is greatly debated. This is largely because in both cases the word *he'emin* is used absolutely, which makes it necessary to ask whether something like "in God" must be supplied in the text, or whether the absolute use is intelligible as it stands. Since *he'emin* is used absolutely elsewhere in the OT (although admittedly very rarely), it is necessary to begin by studying these passages. Ex. 4:31 says: The people gained confidence; and in Job 29:24 we

32 Cf. *TDNT*, s.v. Ἀβραάμ.
33 Cf. Kaiser, *ZAW*, 70 (1958), 101ff.

find: I smiled on them when they despaired. Thus in Isa. 7:9 it is also possible to translate: "If you do not gain confidence," or: "If you should doubt or despair"; in this case, no augmentation of the text is really necessary.

Würthwein has suggested a more exact interpretation, especially since the house of David is addressed here, and the statement refers back to the promise that the house of David would endure. [34] The situation is clear: The allied armies of Syria and Israel draw near to fight against Judah and Jerusalem. For reasons that may not be clear, they intend to dethrone the house of David and to make someone else king over Jerusalem. The real concern, then, is the existence of the house of David, and what is more the stability of God's promise. Thus, the final clause must be translated in connection with the promise to the house of David: You will not be *ne'eman*. Taken all together, the idea would be: "If you do not gain stability, you will have no stability." The existence of the house of David, like the stability of the promise, depends on your (the house of David) gaining confidence, on your not doubting the promise of God. This is Würthwein's view. Here *he'emin* means to take seriously a very concrete word of God; the existence of the house of David depends on taking it seriously.

What is involved here? For the Ninevites faith meant to fast, to repent, and to turn from their evil way. What does Isaiah expect of Ahaz? The answers to these questions are various: Isaiah wants the king to discontinue any plans for making a league with Assyria, or for taking up arms against the invaders, or even for carrying out defense measures such as the inspection of the water supply. Each of these answers indicates that Isaiah is interfering with the responsible political affairs of the king, and thus the problem is the relationship of the prophet to politics. This raises a further question of whether the intervention of Isaiah in this situation, perhaps opposing the league with Assyria, was purely utopian, or whether his advice did not indicate political insight. But is it correct to state all these questions in this way? The text says nothing about concrete instructions of Isaiah in one direction or another. All that he does is to warn against any fear and unrest. There is no reason for this because God's promise is steadfast. The house of David has stability as long as it clings to this promise and acts on the basis of this assurance. Isaiah does not tell the king what is the reasonable thing to do at this moment. He wants to give him more than this: security in the promise of his God. Only out of this "faith" could Ahaz decide what was the right thing for him to do politically at that moment.

An early interpretation of this passage is found in 2 Ch. 20:20, where the Chronicler puts a speech to the army of Judah in the mouth of King Jehoshaphat: "Believe in Yahweh your God, and you will have stability; believe his prophets, and you will succeed." That which follows in the narrative shows what is meant by "believe" here. Israel does nothing at all. At Yahweh's inducement, the enemies destroy one another, and Israel merely brings home the spoil. Here, however, Isaiah's admonition seems to have been interpreted in a very unilateral

---

[34] Cf. above on the niphal.

manner,[35] in the sense of doing nothing, and leaving everything to God alone. It is also significant that here faith in the prophetic word appears side by side with faith in God, as though the word of the prophet had power within itself. Is an age speaking here which sees itself divested of all means of power and views its existence as rooted in blind trust in Yahweh alone?

The second passage in which Isaiah uses the word he'emin (28:16) is so difficult in itself that it can hardly contribute to the clarification of the concept. For first of all, the way in which this little sentence fits into the context dealing with the "cornerstone" (→ אֶבֶן 'ebhen) can hardly be determined with certainty. Second, the meaning of the statement in which he'emin appears is debated. Does lo' yachish mean "he does not need to hasten,"[36] or "he does not need to be anxious,"[37] or should we emend the text, possibly to yebhosh, "to be ashamed," with the LXX,[38] or to something else? But all conjectures are based on the assumption that it is known already what is meant by ma'amin, "he who believes." Thus the question is that of the traditional wording, and this is what is difficult. Nevertheless, the Akkadian parallels discussed by Ellermeyer may indicate the direction in which the meaning must be sought: "The ma'amin should not be anxious." But this does not say anything about the ma'amin himself. However, it would be possible to assume from Isa. 7:9 that the ma'amin is the one who urges the people of Judah to trust in the divine promise of the foundation which is yet to be built. God's word points to the future, and he who takes it seriously does not need to be anxious.

Deutero-Isaiah uses the form he'emin only once. Thus this verb does not belong among those words which are significant for his theology. In 43:10, it is used in connection with the aim of God's choice of Israel: "'You are my witnesses,' says Yahweh,/ 'and my servant whom I have chosen,// that you may know and believe me/ and understand that I am He.// Before me no god was formed,/ nor shall there be any after me.'//'" The two middle half-verses stand in parallelism to one another: What Israel is to understand is that Yahweh alone is God, and what she is to know is that this God alone deserves to be trusted. Israel was to bear witness to this among the nations. If there is only one God for Israel (and therefore, for the world), then there is also only one God in whom she can completely trust.

6. *Summary.* On the basis of this survey, we can make some summary statements. he'emin contains primarily a statement about the subject which gains confidence, mostly with reference to a person or a message. Even though it does not occur very often, the absolute use shows that he'emin can occur without any reference to something or someone else, and thus actually something is being said about the subject. Of course, in most cases the text indicates in whom or in what confidence is placed. Thus he'emin contains a judgment about what de-

---

[35] Cf. Wildberger, *BK,* X, 285, who speaks of a "far-reaching reinterpretation of the concept of faith."

[36] So Lindblom.

[37] Ellermeier, *ZAW,* 75 (1963), 213f., following Driver, *JTS,* 32 (1931), 253f.

[38] So Procksch, *in loc.*

serves or does not deserve confidence. Perhaps the best paraphrases that have been suggested to convey the meaning of *he'emin* are: "to gain stability, to rely on someone, to give credence to a message or to consider it to be true, to trust in someone."

7. *History.* As far as the history of the word *he'emin* is concerned, its occurrences in the OT are much too scanty for anyone to be able to venture a reconstruction. Only detached observations can be made.

a.   As far as man and his words are concerned, *he'emin* seems to be something that it is best for a person not to do. Thus the OT contains warnings against a rash confidence, or statements one should not believe. Men and their words are not always trustworthy.

b.   With this may be connected the fact that, comparatively speaking, *he'emin* is rarely used in the OT in speaking of man's attitude toward God. At the same time, the statement that the people did not believe appears frequently. Caution may be recommended toward men, but it is sin when directed toward God. Only rarely does the positive statement of faith appear: Gen. 15:6; Ex. 4:31; 14:31; Ps. 106:12; Jonah 3:5; Ps. 119:66 (cf. 116:10; 27:13). We may add to this the promises which are made to *he'emin*: Isa. 7:9 (repeated in 2 Ch. 20:20); 28:16; and *he'emin* as a goal of divine action: Ex. 19:9; Isa. 43:10.

c.   Accordingly, it can hardly be maintained that *he'emin* is a fundamental word in OT theology. Perhaps the negative emphasis which was connected with the human *he'emin* prevented this word from being used for man's attitude toward God in a positive sense. Nevertheless, surely this much can be said: Whenever the OT speaks of *he'emin* as man's attitude toward God, it is based on God's signs (Ex. 4:31), miracles (14:31; Ps. 106:12), and word (Gen. 15:6; Jonah 3:5). This reaction of man is alone *tsedhaqah,* right conduct. "Unbelief," doubting God's promise, leads the wilderness generation, and even Moses and Aaron, to death; relying on God's word leads to existence. This explains the promise to the house of David: Your existence depends on your maintaining your trust.

d.   We do not know whether Isaiah was the first who dared introduce this somewhat loaded word into the religious vocabulary, because we cannot date passages like Gen. 15:6; Ex. 4:31; 14:31; and Nu. 14:11 precisely. But the following development would be possible:
First of all, the general idea of "not believing" in men was transferred to the wilderness generation: They did not have any confidence in God at all; they treated him as if he were a man, and thus perished.
Isaiah took over this formula, but used it positively: "If you do not have confidence in the promise of which you have become a partaker, then you (also) will not have stability." Positively, then, this means: "Your stability depends on your taking God's promise seriously." Then certain narrators and singers who succeeded Isaiah adopted this formula, and used *he'emin* in positive statements.

e. It is hardly possible to determine a *Sitz im Leben* for this use of *he'emin*. We certainly cannot consider the "holy war" as such a setting. First, the occurrences of this word are much too late and too scanty. Second, they almost never stand in relationship to war; one exception would be Isa. 7, but this passage is hardly adequate to establish such a thesis. Third, the predominantly negative use opposes the conjecture that Israel learned *he'emin* in the holy war.

f. But in spite of the relatively rare use of *he'emin* with reference to man's attitude toward God, it brings a significant concept into the group of words that are used to describe this attitude, namely, that of an absolute trust in God and his word, the like of which one cannot manifest toward another man, a trust on which the existence of man somehow depends.

g. In light of this analysis, it is not very easy to evaluate correctly the immediate significance of the OT statements for the development of "faith" in the NT. It would hardly be possible to develop the entire scope of the OT experience of God from an exegesis of *he'emin*. But in connection with other OT words, *he'emin* was of considerable importance to the Rabbis. "Belief" must have acquired its distinctively Christian character in its discussion with them, especially in Paul and John.

h. As an appendix, the question of the meaning of the hiphil may be taken up once again. In light of the linguistic usage which has been examined above, it is most likely that *he'emin* is to be understood to mean: "to become steadfast (stable)," and is thus analogous to *hishmin*, "to become fat." The different nuances would best be explained from this fundamental idea, even if each peculiar shift in meaning does not find here its logical explanation. One hardly does justice to the meaning of *he'emin* by taking the hiphil causatively or declaratively.

VI. 'emeth.

1. *Form.* Of the nominal derivatives of the root *'mn, 'emeth* occurs the most frequently. It is found 126 times in the OT, or 121 if we take the doublets into consideration.

The derivation of *'emeth* from *'mn* would seem to be assured by suffix forms like *'amitto,* since this pronunciation is understandable only if there was an original form *'aminto.* The explanation for the Massoretic pointing of *'emeth* is debated. *BLe* must assume that in place of the normal phonetic development which would have to progress from *'amintu > 'amittu > 'amatt > 'āmath,* first the construct form *'amath* appeared in place of the absolute form (for which there are hardly any examples elsewhere), secondly this construct form was intentionally changed to *'emeth* because it was identical with *'amath,* "maid," and then thirdly the *seghol* is changed to *pathach* when the accent shifts with the addition of the suffix. On the whole, this is probably an admission that a normal phonetic derivation is impossible. Even Brønno's suggestion that we assume that '*imitt* was the original form instead of '*amitt* [39] is only a little more helpful. Certainly, this would provide a better explanation for the Hexaplaric forms (Gk.) *ēmeth: emeththach;* but at the same time, the Massoretic pointing is still unintelligible. Thus, until strong evidence is produced to the contrary, it still seems best to maintain that '*emeth* is to be derived from '*mn,* which is also suggested by the meaning of these two words, without being able to say anything conclusive about the form '*emeth.*

2. *Distribution in the OT.* The distribution of '*emeth* in the OT is peculiar. It occurs 37 times in the Pss., 12 times in Isa., 11 times in Jer., 11 times in Prov., and 6 times each in Zec. and Dnl. In the other books, it appears from 1 to 6 times each. But it does not occur at all in Lev. and Nu., or in the P sections of Gen. Since Ezk. also uses this word only twice in one context (18:8,9), it seems to have been used very rarely in distinctively priestly language. But it is even more remarkable that the Joban poet does not use it at all. Was there nothing on which he could rely? Or had God's '*emeth* become so uncertain to him that he preferred to say nothing about it? Also, in early prophecy before Jeremiah, '*emeth* appears assuredly only in Hos. 4:1 (Isa. 10:20 and 16:5 are probably not from Isaiah, and Mic. 7:20 is probably not from Micah). Among the prophets, it is used frequently only from Jeremiah on. On the other hand, statements about human '*emeth* appear in Proverbs and in certain narratives, while statements about divine '*emeth* appear especially in the Psalms. In any case, the statements about '*emeth* do not seem to have been understood in the same way everywhere.

3. *Problem.* As far as the meaning of '*emeth* is concerned, the LXX (which translates this word by *alḗtheia, alēthinós* most of the time) and the Aramaic (*qushta'*) have largely been responsible for the translation "truth." *KBL*[3] gives these different meanings for '*emeth:* 1. stability, reliability; 2. durability, permanence; 3. faithfulness; 4. truth. Torrance understands by '*emeth* "the faithfulness of God as the foundation of all truth." [40] But Quell argues: "The translation 'faithfulness' nowhere commends itself. . . ." [41]

As von Soden has observed, [42] the Akk. root *kūn* (→ כון /*kûn*) has undergone the same development in meaning as '*mn.* The meaning "to be true" has arisen from the original meaning "to be constant, permanent, faithful." Truth is that which is constant and unchangeable.

4. *Strictly Human Use.* a. In some passages, '*emeth* is used to characterize an object. In Josh. 2:12, Rahab asks for a sign on which she can rely. In Jer. 2:21, *zera' 'emeth* is seed which promised to produce good fruit. Prov. 11:18 refers to a reward of which a person can be certain. Each passage refers to something on which someone can rely, which will prove to be true in the future.

---

[39] E. Brønno, *Studien über hebräische Morphologie und Vokalismus* (1943), 157.

[40] According to Barr, 190.

[41] *TDNT,* I, 233, n. 2; cf. 236, n. 12. On the method of investigation, cf. Barr, 190ff., who also thinks "truth" is the correct translation.

[42] Von Soden, *WO,* 4 (1967), 44.

The same idea would seem to be intended when *'emeth* appears in connection with → חסד *chesedh*, "steadfast love," and → שׁלוֹם *shālôm*, "peace," in a hendiadys relationship. The OT speaks of a "kindness," a good deed, on which one can rely, which is requested (Gen. 24:49; 47:29), promised (Josh. 2:14), wished for another (2 S. 15:20), and contemplated (Prov. 14:22), and which can even cover and atone for sins (16:6). It also speaks of a sure peace which is announced for the future (Est. 9:30), and desired (Isa. 39:8). (Cf. also as a divine promise Jer. 33:6; and as a word of the lying prophets 14:13.) To the extent that such a "reliable" kindness or peace continues, the translation in *KBL³*, "lasting, abiding kindness," is essentially correct, even if it does not express a positive personal relationship of "being able to rely on."

Thus, frequently something that is characterized as *'emeth* is not simply present at that time, but must prove to be really *'emeth* some time in the future.

b. *'emeth* is often connected with *dabhar*, "word." The word is characterized as "true." But here also *'emeth* seems to have a special ring. There are so many words on which a person cannot rely, that he is almost astonished if a report is "really true." Thus, the queen of Sheba is astonished at Solomon's kingdom, 1 K. 10:6: "It is true; it is real"; it was not exaggerated.

'emeth is probably to be understood in a similar way in the ordinances of Deuteronomy. Here it has been reported that some Israelites had apostatized and now belonged to other gods; but this cannot be. However, if after careful examination it is proved that the rumor is "really true," then one must intervene (Dt. 13:15[14]; 17:4; the double apposition to *haddabhar*, "thing": *'emeth nakhon*, is probably intended to emphasize the astonishment that would be aroused if the examination showed that an Israelite really did serve other gods: really true!). The same thing applies to the incredible proposition that a young woman has lost her virginity before marriage; but if it is "really true," then ... (22:20).

c. A similar astonishment is probably intended in Jotham's fable (Jgs. 9:15), where we should paraphrase: "If it is really true, incredible as it may seem, that you want to anoint me king." And Jotham uses *'emeth* in the same sense (vv. 16,19): If you really acted uprightly.... But one cannot really believe it.

d. *'emeth* is not obvious. This probably explains why it is not applied to man very often. The direct statement, *hu' ke'ish 'emeth*, "he had the manner of a reliable man," occurs only one time (Neh. 7:2). [43] In Ex. 18:21, Jethro gives Moses good advice: "Moreover choose able men from all the people, such as fear God, men who are trustworthy and who hate a bribe." One must be able to "look into the heart" (perhaps this is the meaning of *chazah*) of men in order to find men of *'emeth*. Perhaps it is significant that in relating this scene in Dt. 1:13, the Deuteronomist avoids these expressions and speaks of "wise, understanding, and experienced men" whom the tribes should choose. "Reliable" men

---

[43] On this construction cf. Brockelmann, *Synt.,* § 109c.

are not so easy to find. Therefore also, it is not surprising that Joseph declares that he would first have to test the words of his brothers before he could know whether there was really *'emeth* in them (Gen. 42:16).

e. In the last passage, *'emeth* is a value which can and should be in a man. Therefore, it is understandable that admonitions to *'emeth* and laments over its absence occur about the same number of times in the OT. Once the OT admonishes people to speak *'emeth*, i.e., probably, to speak that on which people can rely: "Speak *'emeth* to one another" (Zec. 8:16). The OT promises that the reliable tongue will endure (Prov. 12:19). Instruction should consist of words of *'emeth* (22:21). It is the highest praise when words of *'emeth* are attributed to the Preacher (Eccl. 12:10).

Second, justice should be carried out in *'emeth:* "Render in your gates judgments that are *'emeth* . . . " (Zec. 8:16); and "Render a *mishpat 'emeth*" (7:9), i.e., judgments that are in accordance with *'emeth*, with the actual facts, so that they prove to be right and just. Cf. also Ezk. 18:8f., where one characteristic of the *tsaddiq*, "righteous," is that of executing a judgment of *'emeth*. A witness is also essential in a legal judgment: An *'edh 'emeth*, i.e., a witness on whose testimony one can depend, who speaks the truth, saves lives (Prov. 14:25). Witnesses should appear and say: *'emeth*, this is the truth! (Isa. 43:9). In Jer. 42:5, Yahweh himself is called upon as "a true and faithful witness."

The king in particular is advised to practice *'emeth*. If a king judges the poor in *'emeth*, his throne will be established for ever (Prov. 29:14). Thus, *chesedh*, "loyalty," and *'emeth* will preserve him (20:28; cf. also Ps. 61:8[7]), i.e., uphold his throne. [44]

But in spite of all admonitions, Jeremiah is compelled to lament: "No one speaks the truth; they have taught their tongue to speak lies" (9:4[5]). And (Deutero-)Isa. 48:1 speaks of those "who swear by the name of Yahweh, and confess the God of Israel, but not in *'emeth*," i.e., one cannot rely on their oath.

f. In addition to these concrete admonitions to speak and perform reliable words, judgments, and oaths, *'emeth* is also used in a general sense as something of the highest value, which man should seek. Thus Prov. 23:23 admonishes: "Buy *'emeth*, and do not sell it." Here *'emeth* is mentioned in parallelism with wisdom, instruction, and understanding, and thus it is considered to be one of the elements essential to human life. Similarly, 3:3 urges: "Let not *chesedh* (loyalty) and *'emeth* forsake you; bind them about your neck, write them on the tablet of your heart." *'emeth* belongs to the heart, i.e., to the innermost nature of man. Thus, this admonition appears in Zec. 8:19: "Love *'emeth* and peace." Also, one thing that is mentioned in the OT picture of the future is that *'emeth* will spring up from the ground, and *chesedh*, "steadfast love," and *'emeth* will meet (Ps. 85:11f.[10f.]).

---

[44] On the same idea transferred to God in Ps. 89:15(14), see below. The extent to which Isa. 16:5 belongs in the same category is uncertain in light of the very controversial exegesis of Isa. 15f.; cf. on this Rudolph in *Hebrew and Semitic Studies Presented to G. R. Driver* (1963), 130ff.

But the more important *'emeth* is considered to be, the more sobering is a lament such as that found in Hos. 4:1: "There is no *'emeth* or *chesedh,* and no knowledge of God in the land!" Or when justice and righteousness disappear because "*'emeth* has fallen in the public squares," and "*'emeth* is lacking" (Isa. 59:14f.), it is clear that *'emeth* is the prerequisite for justice and righteousness.

g. It can be said by way of summary: *'emeth* was used of things that had to be proved to be reliable; of the word that is really true, on which a person can rely; of a man who is really trustworthy, and thus to whom an office can be entrusted; of judgment that is righteous; and in general, of the innermost nature of man, that which determines his character and his actions. But OT admonitions to *'emeth* and laments over its absence show that such *'emeth* is not something that is obvious in man. Indeed, only rarely does the OT dare to say that some man (or men) is a man of *'emeth,* and it is almost astonishing when a word is really true. And yet *'emeth* is the prerequisite for justice and order. Actually, therefore, it is very difficult to translate accurately the meaning of *'emeth.* It denotes the nature of the man who is said to be faithful to his neighbor, true in his speech, and reliable and constant in his actions. Apart from the form of the word, "reliability" would be the best comprehensive word in English to convey the idea suggested by Heb. *'emeth.* It always involves one's relationship to his fellow men, and pertains to his speech and actions: *'emeth* is that on which others can rely. To this extent, *'emeth* involves a personal relationship, it is not merely an objective fact.

5. *God's 'emeth.* But Yahweh is an *'el 'emeth,* "faithful God": "Thou hast redeemed me, O Yahweh, thou God whose nature is determined by *'emeth*" (Ps. 31:6[5]). That which is only all too often absent in man is present in God; it belongs to him. Therefore, the OT often speaks of "thy" and "his" *'emeth.* Here again the translation is difficult, because God's *'emeth* operates in different directions. The meaning of the OT assertion that God is *'emeth,* however, is that Yahweh is the God in whose word and work one can place complete confidence. This God is not *'emeth* in himself, but in his conduct toward man, and particularly toward his community and its members. This helps to explain the frequent allusions to God's *'emeth* in prayers in the OT.

As creator, God "keeps *'emeth,*" and man can rely on him "for ever" (Ps. 146:6). *chesedh* and *'emeth* go before him (89:15[14]). He is great in *chesedh* and *'emeth* (Ex. 34:6; Ps. 86:15). Thus, *'emeth* belongs to God.

This applies to the word of God in particular. The word of man may often be deceitful, but God's speech is *'emeth!* Thus in his confession David says: "O Yahweh, thou art God and thy words are 'reliable'!" (2 S. 7:28). It is characteristic of Yahweh's deity that a person can rely on his words. Thus we read in Ps. 132:11: "Yahweh swore to David in trustworthiness, from which he will not turn back." Frequently the poet of Ps. 119 emphasizes the reliability of the divine word (vv. 43,160), divine instruction (v. 142), and divine commandments (v. 151; cf. Ps. 19:10[9]; Neh. 9:13). Thus also, the divine Wisdom can only speak *'emeth* (Prov. 8:7).

Of course, the reliability of the divine word in the mouth of a prophet is a problem. In Jer. 23:28 we read: "Let the nabi who has a dream tell the dream, but let him who has my word speak my word faithfully." But how can it be known which prophets are really speaking 'emeth? To be sure, Jeremiah maintains that Yahweh "really" sent him to speak what he spoke (26:15). But did not Hananiah make the same claim (Jer. 28)? And Jeremiah knows of no other criterion for deciding this other than the fulfilment of promises which a given prophet had made; on this basis alone could one know the prophet whom Yahweh had really sent. Also, that which Micaiah ben Imlah declares to be true in the name of Yahweh cannot be proved to be true until it is fulfilled (1 K. 22:16). And it is not until her son is revived that the mother knows that Elijah is a man of God, and that the word of Yahweh in his mouth is 'emeth, "reliable." The truth and reliability of the prophetic word remain a problem. The Maccabean redactor of the Daniel tradition naturally claims that the revelations which he inserts are reliable (Dnl. 8:26; 10:1,21; 11:2).

Unhampered by such doubts, faith in God's 'emeth in his works remains: "The works of his hands are faithful and just" (Ps. 111:7; in this verse, the subject that is characterized as 'emeth umishpat, "faithful and just," is ma'ase yadhav, the "works of his hands"; the meaning is not that "truth and justice" are works of God). His precepts are "executed, faithful and just" (111:8). [45]

That which God promises in deeds is "most certain." "Most certainly" God gives the promised recompense (Isa. 61:8); he plants the people in their land (Jer. 32:41); indeed, he will be their God (Zec. 8:8). That which applies to the future, the worshipper of Neh. 9:33 confesses of the past: "Thou hast been just in all that has come upon us, for thou hast dealt faithfully and we have acted wickedly."

In one passage, 'emeth seems to be the goal of the activity of God through his servant (Isa. 42:3). The solitary le'emeth can only be translated: "that (reliable) truth will be (known), he (my servant) will make known the sentence of judgment." This means that it will be recognized and known as reliable that Yahweh alone is God (it is hardly possible to translate le'emeth here as "in faithfulness" or "faithfully").

Frequently God's 'emeth is connected with his chesedh. It might be asked whether 'emeth is only a characteristic of chesedh, or whether it stands independent of it. However, the parallelism of these two words in adjoining half-verses and the plural form of verbs used with these two words as subject favor the idea that chesedh and 'emeth were understood as two separate attitudes of God, who manifests himself in active kindness and protective faithfulness respectively. David expressed the desire that such kindness and faithfulness might come on the inhabitants of Jabesh (2 S. 2:6). And Jacob thanked God for the kindness and faithfulness he had done to him (Gen. 32:11[10]).

Since Yahweh is an 'el 'emeth, a faithful God, the worshipper can rely on him, his words and deeds, at all times. This reliability of God is clearly intended for man's protection: "His 'emeth is a shield and buckler" (Ps. 91:4). "Let thy

---

[45] So Baethgen, Kittel, and Gunkel; contra Kraus.

steadfast love and thy faithfulness ever preserve me" (40:12[11]). Thus, we find the prayer: "Let me walk in thy faithfulness" (25:5; similarly 26:3; 86:11); for: "All the paths of Yahweh are steadfast love and faithfulness, for those who keep his covenant and his testimonies" (25:10), i.e., he leads them in active kindness and faithfulness. Abraham's servant learns this (Gen. 24:27,48), and he thanks God because he did not withhold his kindness and faithfulness from his master, but led him (the servant) in the "right" way, directing him reliably to his goal. The psalmist prays for this kind of escort: "O send out thy light and thy 'emeth, let them lead me" (Ps. 43:3). As light illuminates the way, God's 'emeth (i.e., God in his reliability) leads in the right way. In expectation of reliable deliverance, the worshipper in 69:14(13) prays that God will give him an answer. But the community of Mic. 7:20 expects God's "faithfulness" and "kindness," which in time past he had sworn to the fathers.

Since Yahweh is a God on whom one can rely completely (both on his words and on his deeds), this 'emeth of God is the object of praise in the OT: "I will also praise thee with the harp for thy faithfulness, O my God" (Ps. 71:22); "the father makes known to the children thy faithfulness" (Isa. 38:19). The extent to which this praise is a vital element of prayer in the OT is shown in that different Israelites remind God that the dead can no longer praise him for his 'emeth (Ps. 30:10[9]; Isa. 38:18). Thus it is in the hymn that God's chesedh and 'emeth stand side by side as the objects of man's confession of praise to God: Ps. 40:11(10); 117:2; 57:11(10); 108:5(4); 115:1; 138:2.

But such a God is not one God among many, but he is the "true" God, besides whom none other has any claim to deity, as is made clear in the late passage, Jer. 10:10. And the preacher-prophet of 2 Ch. 15:3 describes the time without the "true" God as the "godless," terrible time. The God on whom one can rely, and he alone, is the one true God (the text of Ps. 54:7[5] and 57:4[3] is uncertain).

Since God is an 'el 'emeth, man's relationship to this God is possible only through 'emeth. Whether it is a matter of walking before God (1 K. 2:4), calling upon him (Ps. 145:18), or swearing by his name (Jer. 4:2), it must always be done be'emeth, honestly, genuinely, reliably. Only the person who, among other things, "speaks 'emeth in his heart," who means it honestly and genuinely from the bottom of his heart, has access to God's holy hill (Ps. 15:2). This explains the admonitions of Joshua (Josh. 24:14) and Samuel (1 S. 12:24): "Fear the Lord and serve him be'emeth, reliably."

But in view of man's situation treated under 4 above, it is not surprising that such an attitude of man toward God is expressed only rarely. Thus, the prayer is put in the mouth of Hezekiah: "Remember now, O Yahweh, I beseech thee, how I have walked before thee with a genuine and sincere heart" (Isa. 38:3; 2 K. 20:3). Similarly, Solomon speaks of his father, "who walked before thee in faithfulness" (1 K. 3:6); and the Chronicler says of Hezekiah: "He did what was good and right and faithful before Yahweh his God" (2 Ch. 31:20). Only once does a prophet put in the mouth of God the judgment: "Sincere instruction was in his (the priest's) mouth" (Mal. 2:6); but what once was has long ago passed away. Thus, looking retrospectively, OT writers dared attribute sincerity, genuineness, and reliability before God to none but David and Hezekiah.

Thus, all that remains is the prospect for the future. E.g., Zec. 8:3 says that one day Jerusalem will be called *'ir ha'emeth,* a city of faithfulness and genuineness, on which God can rely in every respect. In a similar way, Isa. 10:20 speaks of a day in which the remnant of Israel will lean upon Yahweh, the Holy One of Israel, in reliability, stability, and faithfulness. Only then will that be reality which now is often absent.

Two passages in the book of Psalms are difficult to classify correctly, viz., 51:8(6) and 45:5(4). 51:8(6) states: "Behold, thou (God) desirest *'emeth* in the inward being; therefore teach me wisdom in my secret heart." If *'emeth* stands in parallelism to "wisdom," it probably means something like "truth," which is pleasing to God, and which the worshipper can share "in the inward being" as he can "wisdom." [46]

Ps. 45:5(4) can hardly be made intelligible without emending the text. By themselves the words *rekhabh 'al debhar 'emeth* could mean: "Ride on for the sake of *'emeth,*" but we could not conclude exactly what *'emeth* means in context. The first thing that comes to mind is truth and reliability for which the king is established among the nations. *'emeth* should be omitted in 2 Ch. 32:1. [47]

Thus, *'emeth* is something which determines God's nature, which belongs to his deity, and which makes it possible for man to trust in him. *'emeth* is God's reliability, which is given to man so that he might seek its protection. Certainly, *'emeth* should also determine the nature of man, his deeds and actions, especially in his conduct toward God. But continually there is uncertainty as to whether *'emeth* is in man, and lament that this is not the case. "Truth," "faithfulness," and "reliability" are God's; but they are required of man, though he often rejects them.

VII. 'emunah.

1. *With Reference to Man.* a. Related to *'emeth,* but clearly distinct from it, are the qāṭūl or qᵉṭūl forms *'emunah, 'emun* and *'emunim.* The historical relationship of these forms to one another is obscure. According to *BLe,* § 61 dβ, *'emun* perhaps represents an involution from *'emunim.* In any case, these words are closely connected in meaning. Their peculiar meaning can hardly be derived from the form, as Perry seems to assume. It is true that the form qāṭūl, fem. qᵉṭūlāh, is the form of the passive participle. But this does not prove that all words having this form must be understood as originally passive. Rather, *'emunah* belongs to the class of abstract forms like *gebhurah,* "strength," *gedhullah,* "greatness," and *melukhah,* "kingship," and as such is derived from the root *'mn.*

b. *'emunah* is used only once in speaking of "hands" in the OT, viz., in Ex. 17:12. When Aaron and Hur held up the hands of Moses, "his hands were *'emunah* until the going down of the sun," i.e., they were raised continually and firmly.

---

[46] Cf. the comms.
[47] Cf. Rudolph, *in loc.*

c. In all other passages where 'emunah appears, it refers to the conduct of persons, about the same number of times of God and of man.

Ps. 119:30, which speaks of derekh 'emunah (RSV-"the way of faithfulness"), is no exception; for this passage is not dealing with a way, but with the man who chooses 'emunah in opposition to → שֶׁקֶר sheqer, "falsehood" (v. 29). Besides, derekh was used here only to preserve the alphabetic arrangement of the acrostic; in the context, the important thing is the contrast between 'emunah and sheqer.

d. In spite of coming from the same root, 'emunah and 'emeth must be differentiated. This is clear, first of all, in that outside the book of Psalms 'emunah is translated by Gk. pístis, not by alḗtheia. Second, 'emunah does not appear in many constructions where 'emeth is quite common. Thus, the OT says that the "word" is 'emeth, but it never says that it is 'emunah. Similarly, the OT does not say that an object is 'emunah, and yet it speaks of an 'oth 'emeth, a "reliable sign," or a zera' 'emeth, "genuine seed" (descendant). [48] On the other hand, it could be said that workmen worked be'emunah; be'emeth would hardly be suitable in this case. Thus 'emunah is not so much an abstract quality, "reliability," but a way of acting which grows out of inner stability, "conscientiousness." Whereas 'emeth is always used in relationship to something (or someone) on which (or whom) one can rely, 'emunah seems more to emphasize one's own inner attitude and the conduct it produces. The frequently suggested translation, "conscientiousness," would seem to come closest to the meaning intended in many passages.

e. Thus 2 K. 12:16(15) (repeated in 2 K. 22:7 = 2 Ch. 34:12) says that no accounting was asked of the men into whose hand they delivered the money to pay to the workmen, because they worked be'emunah, "conscientiously." Most passages in Chronicles that use this word are also to be understood in this way. 1 Ch. 9:22 speaks of the gatekeepers whom David and Samuel had established in their office "because of their conscientiousness." In 2 Ch. 19:9 Jehoshaphat charges the judges whom he appointed to work "in the fear of Yahweh, with a conscientious and honest heart." 31:12,15 speak of the conscientious work of the priests and Levites. Also, the term "conscientious" fits the context of 1 Ch. 9:31 at least as well as "continual"; the preparation of "flat cakes" would certainly require special care. Since the text of 2 Ch. 31:18 should probably be emended, [49] the only other passage in Chronicles that uses 'emunah is 1 Ch. 9:26. But it is so difficult to establish the context [50] that the meaning of be'emunah can hardly be known. The instances in which the meaning is certain, however, would suggest that 'emunah conveys the idea of inner stability, integrity, conscientiousness, soberness, which is essential for any responsible service. But a special meaning "official duty" cannot be derived from this. [51]

---

[48] See above.
[49] Cf. Rudolph, in loc.
[50] Cf. the comms.
[51] So correctly Rudolph in his comments on 1 Ch. 9:22.

f. Second, 'emunah is characterized by being contrasted relatively often with sheqer, "falsehood": Prov.12:17,22; 14:5; Jer. 5:1,2; 9:2(3); Isa.59:4; Ps.119:29, 30 (also 89:34[33]; 119:86). But Klopfenstein says correctly concerning sheqer: "Therefore, the character of falseness or sincerity always affects the whole person." [52] Thus, this terminology has to do with more than merely false or true words. Unlike 'emeth, 'emunah never refers to speech only, but to the conduct of the whole person, who, determined by 'emeth, acts in 'emunah. Accordingly, 'emunah is a type of behavior that may be defined as "genuineness, reliability, conscientiousness."

g. A witness who acts conscientiously does not lie (Prov. 14:5), and a messenger who acts conscientiously brings healing (13:17). He who speaks 'emunah, i.e., sincerely, proclaims order (12:17). Thus 'emunah is an element in that kind of conduct which maintains order among men.

How terrible it is if 'emunah is absent! This is the lament of Jeremiah (5:1,3; 7:28; 9:2[3]); where there is no 'emunah in the land, justice and order perish. Isa. 59:1ff. describes the same condition and points out that in legal cases tsedheq, "righteousness," and 'emunah are lacking. The 'emunim have vanished (Ps. 12:2[1]). Who can find an 'ish 'emunim (Prov. 20:6)? Thus, God's lament is also intelligible: "They are sons lo' 'emun" (Dt. 32:20).

h. This explains the OT admonition to such 'emunah, that inner attitude which is prerequisite to a genuine life (Ps. 37:3). It also explains the psalmist's statement that he had chosen a life of 'emunah in preference to a life of "falsehood" (119:30). This sort of connection between life and conduct characterized by 'emunah is stated in different passages. Prov. 28:20 makes this general affirmation: 'ish 'emunoth rabh berakhoth, i.e., many blessings are attached to 'emunah. 12:22 shows that God is favorably disposed toward those who practice 'emunah: "Lying lips are an abomination to Yahweh, but those who practice 'emunah are his delight." Similarly Ps. 31:24(23) states: "Yahweh preserves the 'emunim," and 1 S. 26:23 says: "Yahweh rewards every man for his tsedhaqah and his 'emunah," i.e., for his conduct that is in accordance with order and truth. Hab. 2:4 also belongs to this group of passages, at least as it stands in the MT: "The righteous (tsaddiq) shall live be'emunatho." Here 'emunah hardly means merely "godly honesty" [53] or even "faithfulness," [54] but it is that conduct which is in accordance with 'emeth, which includes sincerity, faithfulness, reliability, and stability. Such 'emunah is peculiar to the tsaddiq and brings him to life. Of course, this sentence should not be isolated from its context. 2:4 is the antecedent to v. 5, [55] and does not refer to the faith of the prophet.

At a later time, of course, this passage must have been interpreted according to the LXX, which reads: ek písteōs mou, thus making the statement refer to

---

[52] Klopfenstein, 25 (cf. 26).
[53] Sellin, KAT², in loc.
[54] So recently Klopfenstein, 204.
[55] So Sellin and Horst, in loc.

God's faithfulness: "Out of my faithfulness the righteous will live." It may be asked whether the LXX here assumes a different Hebrew text *(vav* and *yodh* are difficult to distinguish in the Qumran MSS), or whether it contains a well-known interpretation which makes the life of the righteous dependent, not on its own quality, but on God. When Paul omits the pronoun in Rom. 1:17 and Gal. 3:11 (perhaps, but not certainly, in connection with the LXX reading), it is possible to interpret this statement in two different ways. [56] He. 10:38 connects the *mou* with *díkaios,* "my righteous one," and thus produces a different meaning, perhaps in connection with LXX[A], etc.

2. *With Reference to God.* There are certain problems with the OT use of *'emunah* with reference to God. First, *'emunah* is used of God only in poetic speech. Second, the evidence seems to indicate that most of the passages in which *'emunah* is used of God are of exilic or postexilic origin (only in Ps. 89 is an earlier origin possible). Finally, in approximately one-third of the passages, *'emunah* appears in parallelism with *chesedh,* which elsewhere is found in parallelism with *'emeth.* Is one to conclude from this that *'emunah* was not used with reference to God until a late period, when it came to be used in place of *'emeth,* and therefore that *'emunah* and *'emeth* have approximately the same meaning? This explanation is especially attractive in passages that praise the divine *'emunah,* which seems to be parallel to the divine *'emeth* (Ps. 40:11[10]; 92:3[2]; 88:12[11]; 89:2,6[1,5]). Then it would have to be assumed that *'emunah* had taken over some of the functions of *'emeth.*

But it may be asked whether the use of *'emunah* with reference to God does not indicate more the conduct growing out of *'emeth.* Ps. 89, which is clearly characterized by the term, might suggest such an explanation. Five times the psalmist calls attention to God's *'emunah* (vv. 2,3,6,9,50[1,2,5,8,49]), and twice God himself acknowledges it (vv. 25,34[24,33]). In this case, *'emunah* would be conduct in which God acts in a way true to his character, as it were. Indeed, the concern of this psalm is that God be reminded of his deity, of his word, which he cannot break without forsaking his deity, himself, his very *'emunah,* i.e., his conduct that is inseparably connected with faithfulness and reliability, which, therefore, also includes steadfast endurance.

Thus it is proper to ask whether this peculiar meaning cannot be detected in the other passages. It could be present in Dt. 32:4. The poet desires to praise the greatness of Yahweh, and calls him *'el 'emunah,* i.e., a God who is faithful, and thus in whom there is no fault. In Lam. 3:23, *'emunah* seems to be connected with *chesedh* (v. 22); the confession on which the worshipper relies says: "Great is thy *'emunah.*" Kraus's explanation of *'emunah* here is good: "The constant, irrevocable stability in which Yahweh remains who he is." [57] It is this *'emunah* also with which Yahweh betroths Israel to himself (Hos. 2:22[20]). Isa. 25:1 has this same meaning when it praises God because he has done wonderful things in faithfulness, in keeping with his nature (the additional *'omen* here

---

[56] Cf. K. Barth, comm. on Rom. 1:17.
[57] Comm. *in loc.*

should probably be interpreted as a strengthening of this idea, and not as an additional thought, like "truth"). Also in the passages in the book of Psalms, 'emunah has been chosen with great care. Ps. 33:4 says that all God's work is done in 'emunah, i.e., in constant faithfulness characteristic of his nature. 96:13 makes a similar statement concerning God's judgment (the same combination of tsedheq and 'emunah is also found in Isa. 11:5 in the description of the coming messianic king). This 'emunah of God extends to the clouds (Ps. 36:6[5]), and endures to all generations (100:5; 119:90). God remembers his chesedh and 'emunah, i.e., that faithfulness characteristic of his nature (98:3), and answers the worshipper in his 'emunah (143:1). In it he afflicts the psalmist (119:75). Indeed, it is claimed that God's commandments ultimately are 'emunah (119:86, 138). Certainly it must be considered whether in many of these passages, perhaps in Ps. 119, the distinction between 'emeth and 'emunah has not been removed. But on the whole, the distinction will have to be maintained fundamentally: while 'emeth describes the character of a person on whose words and deeds one can rely, 'emunah denotes the conduct of a person corresponding to his own inner being. 'emeth is used of God's words and deeds on which man can rely; 'emunah is used of God's conduct, which corresponds to the nature of his deity. It has already been pointed out that 'emunah appears infrequently in the OT, and that it is found in late texts primarily. Does this indicate that Israel's poets now attempted to see the nature of Israel's God in his 'emunah? It is God's stability, which is a true reflection of his deity, that is the motivation for calling on him in time of distress and for praising him.

VIII. 'amen. The best-known word built from the root 'mn is 'amen, which was transliterated into the Greek of the NT as amēn, and from there became a part of the language of the Christian Church. It does not occur very often in the OT–only 24 times; and of this number it appears 12 times in Dt. 27:15ff. alone. Thus it is difficult to trace its function in the course of history.

The form of this word is qatil, which could suggest an adjectival meaning. However, the use of this word in certain passages suggests that it is to be interpreted as a particle, so that no certain conclusion can be drawn about the meaning of 'amen from its form.

a. In 1 K. 1:36, Benaiah gives this reply to David's instruction to anoint Solomon king: "Amen! May Yahweh, the God of my lord the king, say so. As Yahweh has been with my lord the king, even so...." In a similar way, 'amen appears in Jeremiah's reply to Hananiah's prophecy in Jer. 28:6: "Amen! May Yahweh do so; may Yahweh make the words you have prophesied come true...." In both cases "Amen" introduces the wish that God would give his blessing to that which had already been planned and said. In both passages reference is made to the speakers only because they acknowledged what had been said previously and wished that it might be fulfilled. Their statements might be paraphrased this way in English: "Precisely! I feel the same way about it, may God do it!" Jer. 11:5 conveys the same idea in the briefest form. Here Jeremiah makes the oracle God had delivered his own: "Amen, Yahweh."

b. The use of 'amen in Dt. 27:15ff.; Nu. 5:22; and Neh. 5:13 is different. All three passages have to do with curses that are uttered and then accepted by saying "Amen." Dt. 27:15ff. contains curses uttered against those who commit secret sins and thus are not brought before human judges. By this curse ceremony, they are handed over to the divine court of justice. But when the people say "Amen," they acknowledge that this curse is to become effective against anyone who transgresses secretly or otherwise. In the same way, the priest in Nu. 5:21f. hands over the accused woman to God's court of justice: "The Lord make you...." But the woman places herself under this divine judgment by saying "Amen." In Neh. 5:13, Nehemiah utters a curse formula: "So may God shake out every man who...." But the assembly takes this curse upon itself by saying "Amen."

Thus in both groups of passages "Amen" is an acknowledgment that the divine word is an active force: May it happen in just this way. The extent to which this use can be said to be cultic or liturgical is yet to be decided, because (with the exception of Nu. 5) these passages have to do with specific incidents. But it is clear that the "Amen" has reference to words and deeds of God, to which the speaker submits himself.

c. In the third place, 'amen is used in passages that praise God. So we find in Neh. 8:6: "And Ezra blessed Yahweh, the great God; and all the people answered, 'Amen, Amen,' lifting up their hands." Here for the first time "Amen" is attested as a response of the community to a prayer. It seems that by using "Amen" the community makes the prayer (in this text in particular the prayer of praise) its own. It is not clear whether the community is following an already existing custom here, or whether this incident is related because it presents something new. In any case, the custom of responding to a prayer of praise by saying "Amen" came into vogue, as is indicated by 1 Ch. 16:36, where it is put back into the time of David. This is further confirmed by the fact that it was used in the Synagogue (Ber. v.4; viii.8), and that it was taken over by Primitive Christianity (1 Cor. 14:16).

d. From this use in public worship has probably arisen the practice of ending individual books of the Bible with an ascription of praise to God and its accompanying "Amen." This may be shown especially in the books into which the psalms have been collected. That the doxologies at the end of Pss. 41, 72, 89, and 106 are different allows one to reach only one conclusion, viz., that the complete book of Psalms was not divided into five books at a later time, but that at least the first three books were provided with concluding doxologies before they were brought together. That the psalms that were inserted later (perhaps at first only 90–119) were then subdivided at Ps. 106 may have its basis in the present account in 1 Ch. 16. [58] In any case these concluding verses, in which

---

[58] Cf. further Gunkel-Begrich, *Einl. in die Psalmen* (1933), 438ff.; Rudolph, comm. on 1 Ch. 16 (*HAT,* 21).

"Amen" occurs once or twice, form a unit, and thus "Amen" is not a later addition, as Kraus seems to assume in his comments on Ps. 41.

For the scribes, the confirmatory "Amen" was an essential element in prayers of praise to God, and they added "Amen" themselves. The later scribes (if not the authors) of Tobit, 3 and 4 Maccabees, and many manuscripts of the Gospels took over this use of "Amen" from the ancient books of psalms.

Thus, what was said later about "Amen" among the Amoreans can also be said about it in the OT: "Amen is affirmation, Amen is curse, Amen is making something one's own." [59] When he utters the word "Amen," the hearer affirms the wish that God may act, places himself under divine judgment, and joins in praise to God.

e. The text of Isa. 65:16 and 25:1 is difficult. *be'lohe 'amen* is often emended to *be'lohe 'emun* or *be'lohe 'omen* both times this expression appears in 65:16, because it hardly seems that the MT can be translated "the God of the Amen." However, it should be observed that *'amen* was in the Hebrew text used by Aquila, for he translates by *pepistōménos* here, which is how he always renders *'amen* (cf. Nu. 5:22; Dt. 27:15; Ps. 41:13; 72:19; 89:53[52]; Jer. 11:5). The reading *'amen* in Isa. 65:16 is also attested by Symmachus, who transliterates it in this passage. Therefore, it has been assumed (probably correctly) that Rev. 3:14 presupposes the same tradition when it reads *ho amēn*. Thus the Massoretic pointing of Isa. 65:16 goes back to an ancient tradition, and should not be rejected so quickly. It is uncertain whether the LXX translation *tón theón tón alēthinón*, "the true God," assumes a different Hebrew text or represents an attempt to paraphrase *'elohe 'amen*. On the other hand, in Isa. 25:1 the LXX translation *génoito* presupposes an *'amen* after *'emunah*. Aquila assumes that this is the case with his reading *pepistōménos*. However, by reading *pístei* Symmachus seems to be translating a form like *'emun* or *'omen*. Thus, at a very early period both passages were read in different ways. But in Isa. 25:1 *'amen* can hardly be translated intelligibly, while the Massoretic reading *'omen* can probably be understood as a strengthening of *'emunah*. On the other hand, *'amen* is probably to be preferred in Isa. 65:16; that *'amen* is connected with *barekh*, "to bless," in Neh. 8:6, and with *nishba'*, "to curse," in Nu. 5:22, certainly favors the view that here also blessing and cursing are meant to be connected with the God of "Amen." This would mean that blessing and curse should be uttered by the God who confirms blessing and cursing, because he also says "Amen" to his own word and stands by it. [60] This expression may have been taken up in Rev. 3:14, where Christ is called *ho amēn*. [61]

IX. Summary. When a Hebrew heard the various words derived from the root *'mn*, the basic idea that came to his mind was apparently "constancy." When they were used of things, they meant "continual"; and when they were

---

[59] Dalman, *The Words of Jesus*, 226.

[60] Cf. Delitzsch, *comm. in loc.;* and Pfeiffer, *KuD.*

[61] On the question of whether Jesus, when he used "Amen," understood it as a word of divine omnipotence, cf. J. Jeremias, *Abba* (1966), 148ff.

connected with persons, "reliability." However, derivatives could have special meanings in any given context.

Thus, the qal participle acquires the meaning "one who cares for." The niphal means "to endure," and thus the participle means "enduring, lasting," and when applied to persons "stable, reliable." Then the hiphil means "to become stable (steadfast)," "to acquire stability," and is used especially of a person or his word: to build steadfastly on someone, or to rely on his word. From "stability" through "reliability," 'emeth acquires the meaning of "truth," while 'emunah conveys more the idea of "conduct that grows out of reliability," i.e., "faithfulness." Finally, 'amen has gotten its meaning through a specific function. [62] Thus, in spite of the different ways in which the words derived from 'mn developed, generally speaking the meaning of the root was retained throughout.

In keeping with this, all forms are quite predominantly personal, i.e., they are used in connection with man and God. While they have a negative ring when used of man, they are used of God absolutely: God is and has 'emeth, he acts in 'emunah, his word is ne'eman, and therefore demands he'emin. Thus, the root 'mn is especially important in OT anthropology and theology.

Jepsen

---

[62] See above.

> אָמֵץ 'āmats; אֹמֶץ 'ōmets; אַמְצָה 'amtsāh; אַמִּיץ 'ammîts; מַאֲמָץ ma'ᵃmāts

Contents: I. Occurrences; Meaning. II. Secular Use. III. Figurative, Religious Meaning: 1. In the Royal Ideology; 2. The Formula of Encouragement; 3. With *lebh;* 4. Other Uses.

I. Occurrences; Meaning. The root '*ms* occurs at Ugarit, [1] where it is used in a sense which the OT attests as its original meaning. It is doubtful whether '*ms* is related etymologically to '*sm* [2] or even to the Copt. *oumot* (Egyp. *wmt*) [3]; these etymological relationships are not decisive for understanding the words built on the root '*ms* in the OT anyway, since this must be determined by the context, especially in connection with the root → חזק *chāzaq*, "to be strong." The original meaning is "to be strong" [4]: this meaning suits the different kinds of activity with which this root is connected in the OT. The root '*ms* occurs in verb forms in the qal 16 times, the piel 19 times, the hiphil twice, and the hithpael 4 times; in the adjectival forms '*ammits* 4 times, and '*amots* twice; in

---

[1] *UT*, 361, No. 228: '*ms yd*, "strong of hand."
[2] So Levy, *WTM*, I, 99.
[3] So *GesB*[17].
[4] *KBL*[3].

the substantival forms *'omets, 'amtsah,* "strength," and *ma'amats,* "effort," once each; and in the name Amaziah (*'amatsyah*) with the shortened forms Amzi (*'amtsi*) and Amoz (*'amots*).

The various forms of the root *'ms* are translated in the LXX as follows: the qal by *ischýein, stereoún,* and *hyperéchein;* the qal and piel by *andrízesthai* and *katischýein;* the qal, piel, and hiphil by *krataioún;* the piel by *apostérgein, apostréphein, enischýein, ereídein, thársos peritithénai, ischyrón poiein, ischýs esti, kratein,* and *parakalein;* the hithpael by *anthistánai, anistán, anistánai, speúdein,* and *phthánein;* and *'ammits* by *ischyrós, krataiós, kratein, krátos,* and *sklērós.*

II. Secular Use. "To have or give strength and power" is the basic meaning of the root *'ms* and its derivatives as they appear in the secular realm. This root is used primarily in connection with war and conflict. Successful defense and deliverance depend on whether man has strength and can preserve it (Am. 2:14). But even in the daily activities of life, as Wisdom says, strength is necessary if one is to be successful. Thus the proficient housewife "girds her loins with strength and makes her arms strong" (Prov. 31:17). Words that instruct and strengthen help and encourage the weary, the discouraged, and the weak (Job 4:4; 16:5). The wise man who speaks is, in an argument, superior to the strong; for a victory can be won only by clever, well-planned strategy (Prov. 24:5f.). However, when Israel revolted against the house of David, Rehoboam "showed himself strong" (*hith'ammets la'aloth*) only in fleeing (1 K. 12:18; 2 Ch. 10:18), and not against the empty-headed, worthless scoundrels who had gained the upper hand over him (hithpael with *'al*) because he was young and his courage weak (2 Ch. 13:7). By way of contrast, Ruth was strong (hithpael with *le*), and firmly resolved to go with Naomi to Israel (Ruth 1:18). Strength, when it is designated by the root *'ms,* is almost always viewed as a quality of a person. It is also used, however, to refer to the strength of a great tree among the trees of the forest (Isa. 44:14), and to Absalom's conspiracy (*vayehi haqqesher 'ammits,* "and the conspiracy grew strong," 2 S. 15:12). Finally, 2 Ch. 24:13 refers to the repair of the temple as a strengthening of the house of God. It is possible that the royal ideology grew out of this interpretation:[5] the temple, and not the kingship, would be the supporting pillar of the theocracy; it had to be strengthened.

III. Figurative, Religious Meaning.

1. *In the Royal Ideology.* In order to understand the essential content and aspect of the figurative and theological use of *'ms,* it is probably best to begin with the royal ideology. In the ancient Royal Hymn of Thanksgiving, Ps. 18, we find the confession: "He delivered me from my strong enemy, and from those who hated me; for they were too mighty for me" (v. 18 [Eng. v. 17]). Here was fulfilled in a victorious battle that for which Yahweh's people had waited

---

[5] See below.

since the Davidic period, viz., that their God would strengthen the king whom he had chosen, his anointed one, and thereby save his people. Thus, according to 89:21f.(20f.), Yahweh had promised: "I have found David, my servant; with my holy oil I have anointed him; so that my hand shall ever abide with him, my arm also shall strengthen him." In a lament to Yahweh, probably from the time of Josiah, Israel prayed that Yahweh might hold his hand over the "son" to protect him (Jerusalemite theology used this terminology to convey the idea of the special relationship the king had to Yahweh), a man whom he had reared and made strong for himself (80:16,18[15,17]). Thus, the people pray that Yahweh may give the king the power to be the mediator of salvation so that Israel may be restored. In the two expressions "son" and "man of thy right hand," the Psalms refer to the anointing oracle (2:7) and the enthronement decree (110:1). In these fundamental acts, Yahweh "made" the king "strong" to accomplish his task. The present hour demands demonstration and actualization, for apparently the northern kingdom (80:2f.[1f.]) will be restored, and all Israel will be reestablished. The claim and the confidence that Yahweh would strengthen his chosen one, representative, and servant lived on after Josiah's failure and even after the downfall of the kingdom, at least in a reinterpreted sense. Yet, during the exile, the prophet can proclaim this divine promise to his servant, Israel: "I will strengthen you, I will help you, I will uphold you with my victorious right hand" (Isa. 41:10). And as a belated echo, the plaintiff in Ps. 142 calls to mind (to that extent correctly the author of the heading over this psalm refers to David's affliction during his flight from Saul) the Royal Hymn in Ps. 18 and says: "Deliver me from my persecutors; for they are too strong for me" (142:7[6]). One of the people now makes the same request that had once been uttered by the king.

2. *The Formula of Encouragement.* Although a direct connection cannot be demonstrated, the formula of encouragement, "Be strong and of good courage," has to be explained from the royal ideology. The basic passage is Dt. 31:23, a text that is usually thought to belong to JE (31:14,15,23).[6] Here Yahweh commissions Joshua and says: "Be strong and of good courage; for you shall bring the children of Israel into the land I swore to give them: I will be with you." In the course of the military conquest, Joshua was to lead the people, win the victory, and help the people establish "justice" (the realization of their claim to the land). He assumes tasks that constitute the essential functions of the royal office (1 S. 8:20). The promise that Yahweh would be with him points in this direction.[7] This promise appears in the same words when Yahweh speaks to David (2 S. 7:9), in a context that has to do with ensuring (cf. also Jgs. 6:16) and completing the conquest. According to E, Moses was commissioned by God (who promised to be with him, Ex. 3:12) to bring forth the Israelites out of

---

[6] So Eissfeldt, *Hexateuchsynopse* (1922); Noth, *Überlieferungsgeschichtliche Studien*, I (1943), 40, 191, 214f.; but in *A History of Pentateuchal Traditions* (trans. 1971), 32f., n. 126f., Noth says it is "secondary Deuteronomistic."

[7] Cf. H. D. Preuss, "... ich will mit dir sein!" *ZAW*, 80 (1968), 139-173; W. Richter, *Die sog. vorprophetischen Berufungsberichte. FRLANT*, 101 (1970), 146ff.; etc.

Egypt. In the view of the Yahwist, it was Joshua who was commissioned by Yah-weh (who promised to be with him) to bring the people of Israel into the promised land. In addition, and as a demand for the inevitable personal reaction of Joshua to Yahweh's promise of help, Yahweh commands Joshua to be strong and of good courage. His strength comes from Yahweh; he must rely on him in attitude and action. Then the strong God will be with him. The theologian interprets the formula of encouragement chiefly in this way: Yahweh will not fail (→ רפה *rāphāh*) or forsake (→ עזב *'āzabh*) him (Dt. 31:6,8; Josh. 1:5; cf. 1 Ch. 28:20). He goes before him (Dt. 31:8); therefore no man will be able to stand before him (Josh. 1:5). But the Deuteronomistic interpretation also makes clear from the context what is meant by being "strong and of good courage": since the success and prosperity of the conquest depend on fidelity to the law, it means for Joshua, "Be careful to do according to all the law which Moses my servant commanded you," do not deviate from it, yea, keep the book of the law of Yahweh in mind in all activities (Josh. 1:7f.). Therefore, the formula which originally pertained to the execution of the conquest is reinterpreted in harmony with the viewpoint of the Deuteronomistic history. The new element of a person demonstrating that he is strong and of good courage by conscientiously observing the divine statutes and ordinances remains the formula in all Deuteronomistic passages, and is also preserved in the Chronicler's final instruction of David (1 Ch. 22:13; 28:20), where Solomon is entrusted with building the temple. As a word of commission, "be strong and of good courage" fits most appropriately in the mouth of Yahweh. However, this Deuteronomistic meaning makes it possible for Moses, the Deuteronomistic proclaimer of the law, to admonish and encourage his "successor" Joshua (Dt. 31:7f.), as Yahweh had commanded him (3:28), and even the people (31:6), with the formula of encouragement. In a similar manner also, Joshua, the leader of the army (Josh. 10:25), and Hezekiah (2 Ch. 32:7) inspire and admonish the people with their courage. Even the people use this formula in order to encourage Joshua in his obedience to this commis-sion by Yahweh (Josh. 1:18). [8]

3. *With lebh.* The formula of encouragement also makes its way into the lament (Ps. 27:14; 31:25[24]), where it is expanded by the addition of → לב *lēbh*, "heart." In this form it is an encouragement to the oppressed: "Hope in Yahweh; be strong, and let your heart take courage" (27:14); and to the godly (31:25[24]). However, in Deuteronomistic terminology, the expression "to make the heart strong" has a negative connotation. In the laws having to do with caring for the poor, we find the warning against hardening the heart (*lebhabh*), i.e., against making it unsympathetic, and against shutting the hand against a poor tribal brother (Dt. 15:7). And when Yahweh hardens the spirit of King Sihon and makes his heart strong, he is making him obstinate in order to give him over to destruction (2:30). The Chronicler also knows this expression (2 Ch. 36:13), but here it is Hezekiah himself who is obstinate.

---

[8] Cf. N. Lohfink, "Die dtr Darstellung des Übergangs der Führung Israels von Moses auf Josua," *Scholastik,* 37 (1962), 32-44.

4. *Other Uses.* Only God and the man to whom he gives strength are strong. Wisdom Theology locates the statement about the strong God in the framework of the concept of creation: he makes the sources of the deep strong (Prov. 8:28); he brings out the host of stars, which he has created, by number, "calling them all by name; by the greatness of his might, and because he is strong in power not one is missing" (Isa. 40:26). The prophetic word speaks of God's strength in the context of judgment. God can put strength and might into his service (28:2). The most courageous among heroes is not stronger than the Lord (Am. 2:16), and the mighty Nineveh is not able to withstand the strong enemy whom Yahweh had raised up (Nah. 2:2[1]). Human strength which is able to preserve and succeed is from God. To the Judeans, he is a strong help against enemy nations (Zec. 12:5). Therefore, when he comes to deliver Israel, God's people are to "strengthen the weak hands, and make firm the feeble knees"–another echo of the formula of encouragement (Isa. 35:3). But the Levites are able to strengthen Rehoboam only as long as they walk in the way of David, which as viewed by the Chronicler (2 Ch. 11:17) is wholly faithful to Yahweh. Similarly, in the reign of Abijah the Judeans prevail over the Israelites because they rely upon Yahweh (13:18). Also, in the Yahwistic word of salvation in the oracle to Rebekah, Yahweh says that Jacob's descendants will be stronger than those of Esau, and he brings this to pass (Gen. 25:23). Here, "to be stronger" is an early proclamation of the consciousness and affirmation of the choice of Israel. On the other hand, it could be that at times man wished to compete with God, and it is quite possible that he attempted to do so. In this regard Job affirms that God alone has power and strength; man is wholly inferior to him, even if he believes himself to be in the right (Job 9:19): "He (God) is wise in heart, and mighty in strength–who has hardened himself against him, and succeeded?" (9:4). Elihu adds that no human effort can avail against God (36:19). Thus Job's advice is: "The righteous should hold to his way, and he that has clean hands should grow stronger and stronger" (17:9). On the whole, the theological content of 'ms is viewed as an explicit or veiled praise of God, who alone is strong.

Schreiner

אָמַר 'āmar; אֹמֶר 'ōmer; אֵמֶר 'ēmer;

אִמְרָה 'imrāh; אֶמְרָה 'emrāh;

מַאֲמָר ma'ᵃmār; מֵאמָר mē'mar

Contents: I. The Root: 1. Etymology and Occurrences; 2. Meaning and Radius of Function. II. General Use: 1. A Communication Term; 2. A Term That Signifies; 3. A Term for Imputation; 4. Thinking and Reflecting; 5. lē'mōr. III. Theological Use: 1. Term for Revelation: a. 'amar in Connection with God Identifying Himself; b. The Creative Word; c. Demand; d. Encouragement; 2. Messenger Formula and Messenger Oracle; 3. Man Speaking to God. IV. Derivatives: 1. 'omer; 2. 'emer, ma'amar, Aram. me'mar; 3. 'imrah, 'emrah.

I. The Root.

1. *Etymology and Occurrences.* '*mr* is a common Semitic root, which can mean "to be bright," "to be visible," "to make visible," "to see," or "to inform." [1] The etymological connection between Ugar. '*mr* I, "to be visible," "to see," [2] and Heb. '*mr* is no longer disputed. [3] However, there is still discussion as to whether Akk. *amāru*, "to see," and Ethiop. '*ammara*, "to show," belong to the linguistic history of Heb. '*mr*. In Hebrew and Biblical Aramaic (as well as in the Mesha Stela) the original meaning recedes entirely, giving way to the concept "to say" in the sense of imparting information. We encounter '*mr* in the verb form throughout the OT, in both early and late texts, and in all conceivable literary connections. Its use is not limited to specific types and forms. In both the Hebrew and Aramaic sections of the OT the verb form of '*mr* appears about 5300 times. [4] '*mr* is found almost exclusively in the qal (or Aram. peal). In the few instances in which it appears in the niphal, it is to be understood passively or impersonally (in the sense of "one says, it is said"). There are only two examples of its use in the hiphil, and both of them occur in the same context

---

'āmar. P. R. Ackroyd, "The Vitality of the Word of God in the OT," *ASTI*, 1 (1962), 7-23; J. Barth, *Wurzeluntersuchungen zum hebr. und aram. Lexicon* (1902); M. Dahood, "Hebrew-Ugaritic Lexicography I," *Bibl*, 44 (1963), 289-303; F. Delitzsch, *Prolegomena eines neuen hebr.-aram. Wörterbuchs zum AT* (1886); L. Dürr, *Die Wertung des göttlichen Wortes im AT und im Antiken Orient. MVÄG*, 42/1 (1938); A. Ehrman, "A Note on the Verb אמר," *JQR*, 55 (1964/65), 166f.; O. Grether, *Name und Wort Gottes im AT. BZAW*, 64 (1934); V. Hamp, *Der Begriff "Wort" in den aramäischen Bibelübersetzungen* (Munich, 1938); O. Procksch, *TDNT*, IV, 91-100; F. Rundgren, "Hebräisch *bäṣär* 'Golderz' und '*āmar* 'sagen.' Zwei Etymologien," *Or*, 32 (1963), 178-183; C. Westermann, *Basic Forms of Prophetic Speech* (trans. 1967).

[1] *KBL*; Rundgren; Delitzsch, 28, n. 1.
[2] Cf. *WUS*³, 25, No. 283; cf. with No. 284.
[3] Cf. Dahood, 295f.
[4] According to *KBL*³.

(Dt. 26:17,18). Here '*mr* is to be interpreted primarily in the causative sense, but from this meaning comes the use of this form in the sense of an official, binding statement. [5] In Mishnaic Hebrew, the causative form means "to betroth." [6] '*amar* is frequently used with → דבר *dibbēr*. Often these two words are used synonymously, but they are also used synthetically: *dibber* is used first to announce or declare to the reader that someone is going to speak, then '*amar* is used to indicate that the speaker's words follow immediately, and this may be done in the style of direct or indirect discourse, e.g., we find in Gen. 19:14(J), "...Lot spoke... and said..." (*vayedhabber... vayyo'mer;* but quite often this idea is expressed by Heb. *vayedhabber... le'mor;* cf. also Isa. 7:10; 8:5, *vayyoseph dabber le'mor*). '*amar* is also used in other passages to indicate that the speaker's words follow immediately, where '*amar* follows verbs like → קרא *qārā'*, "to call," → ענה '*ānāh*, "to answer," → נגד *nāghadh*, "to announce," → שאל *shā'al*, "to ask," → צוה *tsivvāh*, "to command," etc., and appears after expressions like *hayah dabhar 'el*, "the word came unto," e.g., in Jer. 1:4. The nouns built from the root '*mr*, viz., '*omer, 'emer, 'imrah, 'emrah, ma'amar*, and Aram. *me'mar*, correspond in meaning to the ordinary sense of the verb in the OT, and thus are to be translated "saying," "speech," "announcement," and "word," and less frequently like *dabhar*, "matter," "thing," "affair" (Job 22:28). The noun forms from the root '*mr* occur approximately 100 times in the OT, and are found primarily, although not exclusively, in late and poetic (wisdom) texts. [7]

2. *Meaning and Radius of Function.* '*amar* has a very diverse breadth of meaning, and the variety of its nuances of meaning is exceptionally rich. In the German language, compound words built from the same root often provide a striking clue to the variety of meanings in Hebrew words and their uses in different contexts; and indeed, if we look at the various German compounds with *sagen*, "to say," we find that these correspond with the various meanings of '*amar*, e.g.: *ansagen* (to announce), *aussagen* (to state, declare), *zusagen* (to promise), *absagen* (to refuse), *vorhersagen* (to predict), *nachsagen* (to repeat), etc. But in order to convey correctly the wide variety of meanings connected with '*amar*, it is necessary to use many other German words which are not built from *sagen*, e.g., *mitteilen* (to inform), *nennen* (to name, call), *benennen* (to name, call), *erwähnen* (to mention), *zusichern* (to assure, promise), *widersprechen* (to contradict, oppose), *antworten* (to answer), *rühmen* (to praise), *lästern* (to slander), *befehlen* (to command), *zu sich selber* (or *zu seinem Herzen*) *sagen* (to speak to oneself [or to one's own heart]), *denken* (to think), *überlegen* (to reflect, consider), *erwägen* (to consider), *erörtern* (to discuss), *deuten* (to explain), *bedeuten* (to mean), etc.

'*amar* always indicates reasonable statements by a subject which may be heard and understood by others.

---

[5] Cf. R. Smend, *Bundesformel* (1963), 7f., in agreement with Ben Yehuda, *Thesaurus,* I (1960), 297: "to proclaim."

[6] See *KBL;* cf. *GesB*.

[7] See below, IV.1-3.

Its purpose is never to describe the technique of speaking, but to call attention to what is being said. Therefore, 'amar always appears in a subject-object relationship (even the nouns built from the root 'mr require a logical subject), and quite often takes two objects, viz., an accusative object designating the direct object of the verb, and the person or persons addressed. And in passages where direct or indirect discourse is introduced by 'amar to indicate that the speaker's words follow immediately, the direct or indirect discourse that follows forms the object. The object of 'amar is designated not only by the simple accusative, but also by the use of the prepositions 'el, le, "to," and 'al, "over." [8]

'amar always expresses a personal relationship, no matter what it may be. 'amar functions in all phases of social life (culture, custom, law, religion), in all human relationships (with regard to classes, personal feelings, teaching and learning, wisdom and foolishness, communication and isolation), in man's relationships to nature, the world, and creation, and by no means least in the relationships between God and man and man and God. It follows from all this that the varieties of relationships with which 'amar is connected are many and diversified. This is equally true of both object and subject relationships. The personal relationship indicated by 'amar can be applied to matters, things, abstracts, lands, cities, animals, plants, parts of the body (as pars pro toto, e.g., lebh, "heart," in Ps. 27:8, and 'atsamoth, "bones," in Ps. 35:10), elements in nature such as water and fire, weather phenomena, and mythical monsters, tehom (the Deep), maveth (Death), yam (the Sea), and 'abhaddon (Abaddon) (Job 28:14,22). All these can be the subject of the verb 'amar, not only as graphic descriptions in figurative speech or in figurative reality depicted by man in his various functions, but also as actual subjects, e.g., the seraph in Isa. 6:3, and Egypt (Ex. 12:33), Edom (Ezk. 35:10-12; Ob. 3), Jerusalem (Jer. 10:19; 51:35; Isa. 57:10), Babylon (Isa. 47:10), Tyre (Ezk. 27:3), and Nineveh (Zeph. 2:15) as corporate entities in which actions and conditions are concentrated in an intelligible statement, an 'amar-deed. Here 'amar is the result of a process which probably extended over a long period of time. The words of the trees and the bramble in Jotham's Fable (Jgs. 9:8-15) and of the objects and articles in OT parables (e.g., the thing made speaks against its maker, the clay against the potter, Isa. 29:16; 45:9) are easy to understand. But it is more difficult to interpret the 'amar-activity of the serpent in Gen. 3. If through his creative power God is able to make lightning and weather his messengers (Ps. 104:4), this means they are able to speak (Job 38:35). Personified Wisdom and Folly (Prov. 1:21; 9:4,16) and the mashal, "proverb," in themselves are potential speakers, which occasionally make concrete statements in which experiences are evaluated, representing the sum total of events and their interpretation. Hence chokhmah, "wisdom," or kesiluth, "folly," is the subject of the 'amar-event in such cases. In a similar way, 'amar appears in a bold figure in Job 3:3, where (poetically, of course) the author has the Night, cursed by Job, say that a male child (viz., Job) has been conceived, i.e., the Night speaks by means of the deed that took place in it. Thus 'amar can also be understood as the deed that is

---

[8] See KBL.

indicated by what is said. Until the 'amar, that which is said, takes place, a wide variety of activities occur in the realm of personal relationships from the most sublime reflection on one's own attitude to the active deed. Sometimes these activities speak an intelligible language of their own, and thus are regarded as a function of 'amar or are themselves the execution of 'amar.

The relationships between 'amar and its objects are also diverse and have many dimensions. They cover a wide range of things which are defined by 'amar. One can talk about anything, and can make anything the object of "speaking": love and hate, turning to and turning from, claim and promise, judgment and pardon, law and order, action and conduct, cursing and blessing, war and peace, wounding and healing, sin and confession, demanding and offering, joy and grief, revealing and hiding, information and communication, etc.

This should help us understand why it is difficult to make 'amar fit into a neatly worked out pattern, for the meaning and radius of function of 'amar are best characterized as extensive, transparent, many dimensional, and complex.

II. General Use. The general and theological uses of 'amar in the OT cannot be distinguished from each other as far as function is concerned. The distinction lies in the subject-object relationships. Here, of course, subject and object function in their own unique way, and yet not every subject or every object functions in the same way. However, OT Hebrew does not use one term for God speaking to man, another for man speaking to God, and still a third for man speaking to his fellow man. The general and theological uses both share in the broad radius of function outlined under I above, and in the widely divergent meaning of 'amar. What is about to be said about the general use also applies *mutatis mutandis* to the theological use.

1. *A Communication Term.* 'amar is used to denote communication between two personal entities (or entities regarded as personal). The goal of 'amar is that another person (or persons) might hear and understand, and might reply, in the broadest sense of the word (reaction). 'amar is used in dialogues (Gen. 3). In these instances, 'amar is construed with prepositions ('el, le, 'al) to indicate the object of the verb. The refusal to accept that which is proposed, in contexts using 'amar, only confirms the communicative intention of the 'amar-event (Nu. 20:14-21). The communicative aspect of 'amar in covenant-making (e.g., Josh. 9:6ff.), marriage contracts (Gen. 24), explanatory statements (2:22,23), invitations (45:17), bearing a message (45:9), etc., is instructive. The subject of 'amar is stated and in this way offered to the community. In OT legends, there are passages in which 'amar is used in connection with a person's intentions, ideas, desires, and sentiments (e.g., in Jgs. 9:1-6, where it appears in connection with dibber). Communication occurs and becomes reality in the "response" (again, often expressed by 'amar) (9:3). This aspect of the use of 'amar is particularly clear in passages in which a person is identifying himself (Gen. 45:3f.; this use of 'amar prevails throughout chap. 45). [9] On the other hand, to refrain from speak-

---

[9] Cf. also the formal expressions in passages in which God identifies himself; see below.

ing (to be silent) signifies a conscious abrogation of the personal relationship (Am. 6:10; Job 32:1).

2. *A Term That Signifies.* '*amar* is used in the OT in connection with giving the meaning of something. It can mean "to show," either in a purely local sense as, e.g., in Gen. 22:2f., or as part of the explanation of the meaning of a quotation, as in Nu. 21:14. '*amar* is used in different ways to designate an object, a phenomenon, or a personal entity. It is connected with giving names, by means of which it is possible to understand the nature of a thing or of a person and the relationship of that which is named to the one giving the name and his frame of reference (cf. Gen. 2:23 and the preceding verse, which explains the *vayyo'mer* of v. 23). Moreover, in this kind of '*amar*-event there is a subtle assumption that the one giving the name seizes and overpowers that which is named (2:23; 4:1; cf. in this connection the OT etymologies [involving proper names] and etiologies). The characteristic '*amar*-deed qualifies or disqualifies (Isa. 5:20) and determines the nature of its object, which acts in keeping with this nature (8:12; Hos. 2:1 [Eng. 1:10]) until someone gives it a new name (Hos. 2:1 [1:10]; Isa. 32:5). Praising (Neh. 6:19) and dishonoring (Ps. 41:6 [5]) are forms of expressing significance. The niphal of '*amar* in particular (of course, not alone) is used in connection with signifying (Gen. 32:29 [28]; Isa. 4:3; 32:5; 61:6). Occasionally, '*amar* in the niphal (with and without → שֵׁם *shēm*) is also used in connection with giving names, a special form of signifying (Gen. 32:29 [28]; Isa. 4:3; 19:18); however, → קרא *qārā'* (with and without *shem*) is the more common term used in connection with giving names in the OT (cf. Gen. 2:18-23).

3. *A Term for Imputation.* '*amar* is used extensively in the sense of imputation. By pledges, assurances, promises, wishes, blessings, curses, punishments, and judgments, importance, goodness, strength, wisdom, and power are imputed to people or things, and from that moment on, they are affected, burdened, blessed, and endowed by what is imputed to them. The validity of this imputative aspect of '*amar* can be confirmed by covenant, treaty, or oath (cf. Gen. 21:22-33; 26:15-33). A pledge can be recalled (1 K. 1:28-30, and context), a promise can be considered reliable (Gen. 33:1-18). Gen. 27 is typical of the imputation of a blessing by using '*amar*. The stories of Elijah and Elisha, especially 2 K. 2:8-10, impressively illustrate the imputative '*amar*-event in succession in office (transfer of office, succession). The efficacy of the curse (2 S. 16:5-13, esp. v. 7, where '*amar* is connected with *qalal*) has to be neutralized by counteractions (19:16-24[15-23]; in v. 24[23], there is a sworn assurance). Imputative speaking functions in judicial language (1 K. 3:16-28; Jer. 26:7-19). Declaration, proclamation, and acclamation have an imputative '*amar* character (2 S. 15:10; 1 K. 1:24,25,34,39). Imputation is intended both for the one(s) addressed and for those who hear what is declared. The imputative event also takes place in wishes irrespective of whether its content is good or evil (Ps. 41:6 [5]; 2 S. 15:9; 18:28).

Finally, the command should be mentioned in this connection (1 K. 1:33).

Even though the usual word for "command" is *tsivvāh,* sometimes *'amar* has this meaning. "Commanding" means that a person forces his own will on someone else with the expectation that that person will do what he wills. It is easy to see that the imputative aspect of *'amar* plays an important role in the theological use of this root.

4. *Thinking and Reflecting.* It is clear from the expression *'amar 'el libbo,* "speak to his heart," or the like, that *'amar* is used in the sense of "thinking" in the OT. This cognitive function can be rendered in English by using other verbs also: "to consider," "to discuss," "to reflect," thus the activity preceding a decision. This use is immediately understandable if we keep in mind that in the ancient Near East "thinking processes" and "intellectual processes" often transpire as phonetically perceptible "expressions." According to Ps. 1:2, observation of the law is accomplished by unceasing "muttering" (→ הגה *hāghāh*). *'amar* is used in a similar way in the OT. Not only does it have this meaning when it occurs with *lebh,* "heart" (1 S. 1:13; 27:1; Gen. 17:17; 27:41; Jer. 5:24; Hos. 7:2 with *lebh + le*), but also without *lebh* (Gen. 26:9; 44:28, see esp. the passages that use *'amarti!*). Here *'amar* means to accept something as a fact after careful reflection, so that in Ps. 10:6 and 14:1 *'amar* expresses the conviction at which the respective persons arrive after grappling with a phenomenon intellectually for a long time. Even God can "speak to his heart" (Gen. 8:21). Secret reflection (1 K. 12:26) acquires the character of understanding, planning, and intending. The construction *'amar* followed by the infinitive construct + *le* states the intention of the thinking subject to do this or that, e.g., in 2 S. 21:16; 1 K. 5:19(5).

5. *lē'mōr.* The uses of *le'mor* (qal inf. const. + *le =* "to say") in the OT are more diverse than the most widely used Hebrew lexicons would seem to indicate. [10] First of all, we encounter the proper use of *le'mor* as an infinitive in sentences like these: "he proceeded to say" (2 S. 2:22), "he feared to say" (Gen. 26:7), and "he came to say" (47:15; Jer. 32:7). But this use of *le'mor* is more frequent than, e.g., Lisowsky-Rost, *Konkordanz,* might lead one to believe when it lists only nine occurrences of this word in the OT. Probably all the passages in which *le'mor* comes after *shalach,* "to send" (Nu. 21:21; Dt. 9:23; Josh. 2:1,3; 10:3,6; 2 K. 3:7; Am. 7:10), should be included in this group: This man or that man sent (a messenger) to say (followed by the message that was supposed to be related). Sometimes the qal here has a causative meaning. Conceivably there are other verbs after which *le'mor* should be interpreted in the simple sense as an infinitive, e.g., after *shama'* ("he heard said," "he heard that it was said," etc.), Gen. 41:15; Dt. 13:13(12); 1 S. 13:4; 1 K. 16:16; Isa. 37:9. To a large extent, this also applies to cases in which *le'mor* indicates an intention to speak or give information, e.g., after verbs of motion like *'amadh,* "to stand" (Nu. 27:2); *'alah,* "to go up" (1 S. 23:19); *qarabh,* "to come before" (Josh. 17:4); and *ngš,* "to approach" (Ezr. 9:1). In the majority of cases,

---

[10] Including even *KBL.*

le'mor introduces direct or indirect discourse (on the latter, cf. 1 Ch. 21:18), and therefore has often crystallized into a formula, conjunction, or introductory particle (Gen. 34:4). In English, then, it is best to render *le'mor* by a subordinate clause: "as he (or some other subject) said (spoke, talked, etc.)." Since it is usually found after verbs of saying (*'amar, dibber, naghadh, za'aq, 'anah, tsivvah, tsa'aq, sha'al,* etc.) or nouns that are cognate with them (*dabhar, mitsvah, tse'aqah,* etc.), it can also be translated more simply by "in the following manner," "as follows," "thus," or "so." Like the Gk. *hóti*, it sometimes represents a colon (Josh. 1:10-13).

Of course, *le'mor* also appears after verbs which primarily have nothing to do with "speaking." Here the word-event indicated by *le'mor* is integrated into the entire event designated by the main verb. The word-event can be a motivation for the main verb, or one of its consequences, or it can further the course of the main event; in each of these constructions, *le'mor* has to be translated in a different way. The *'amar*-deed expressed by *le'mor* has the function of interpreting or defining, and conversely sometimes it is clarified by the main verb on which it depends. The man of God from Judah gives a sign in Bethel followed by its interpretation (*nathan mopheth le'mor,* "he gave a sign, saying," 1 K. 13:3). Sarah laughs about the wondrous words of the three men after concrete reflection (Gen. 18:12f.). Potiphar's wife takes hold of Joseph's garment with specific intention (39:12; cf. Neh. 6:9). The brothers of Joseph are frightened, perplexed (Gen. 42:28). In Egypt, the overseers of the Israelites are beaten by the taskmasters, who justify this treatment by asking the overseers why the Israelites had not made their normal quota of bricks (Ex. 5:13f., *vayyukku ... le'mor,* "and they were beaten ..., saying"). In the Sinai account, Yahweh tells Moses to set bounds around the place where he would appear, and to explain to the people what he was doing (19:12). According to Lev. 10:16, Moses was angry, "as he said ... " ("he was angry *le'mor*"). The spies dishearten the people with their report (Dt. 1:28), and according to the Assyrians Hezekiah misleads his people when he advises them to resist the Assyrians (2 K. 18:32; cf. Isa. 36:15,18; 37:10). The meaning of the trumpet blast is explained after *le'mor* (1 S. 13:3). The men of Anathoth make an attempt on Jeremiah's life, and in connection with this use specific words (Jer. 11:21); and Jeremiah's persecutors lay hold of him and sentence him to death (26:8, *taphas ... le'mor*).

In a number of cases, the main event follows as a consequence or result of that which is designated by *le'mor*. Although the *le'mor* sentence is placed after the main verb, its contents logically precede the action depicted in the main sentence, e.g., in 1 S. 27:12; 2 K. 7:12; Jer. 36:29. Sarah reflects on her being too old to bear children, and laughs about the announcement of the visitors (Gen. 18:12f.). When the *le'mor* sentence occurs after the event to which it refers, it is always to be translated in the past or the pluperfect. In all the examples mentioned above, *le'mor* could still be rendered by "and (he) said" or "and (he) had said," or "with the words," thus preserving the meaning of *'amar*. This concept experiences a certain abstraction and spiritualization when *le'mor* introduces the content of something that is written after the act of writing (2 S. 11:15; 1 K. 21:9; 2 K. 10:6; Jer. 36:29). Here, what is written speaks, as it were. A similar idea occurs in Ps. 119:82 ("my eyes fail with watching for thy promise, *le'mor* [saying], when wilt thou comfort me?"). That *le'mor*, when it is not a simple formula, can also represent a finite verb form, is understandable from what has already been said. But beyond this, there are passages in the OT in which *le'mor* occurs as a finite verb form completely independent from any other verb, e.g., Jgs. 16:2; Isa. 44:28; 49:9.

III. Theological Use. What was said at the beginning of II above must be emphasized here once again. Many functions of *'amar*, in spite of their use in the theological realm, function *mutatis mutandis* in the "secular" realm. This is the case in particular with the communication delivered by messengers and its individual formal elements, e.g., the formula used by messengers. Even though this genre is also used in the prophetic literature, one should not therefore fail to see that the communication delivered by messengers is a "secular" speech form. We shall have to discuss this more fully under the appropriate section below.

1. *Term for Revelation.* Frequently in the OT God is made the subject of an *'amar*-event. The expressions "God has spoken (said)," "God speaks (says)," and "God will speak (say)," imply that God can be heard in the realm of nature and history, the arena of human experience and understanding. This is also true of passages where God does not speak to man, but when he addresses, e.g., the heavenly council (1 K. 22:20-22; Isa. 6:8), animals (Gen. 1:22; 3:14; Jonah 2:11[10]), and the elements of nature (Isa. 5:6, here, admittedly, using *tsivvah*, "to command"), or even when heaven and earth are summoned to be witnesses (Isa. 1:2, a summons to hear; but here using *dibber*). In these instances, what God says does not concern man directly, but at least he can perceive and record it. In addition, we encounter words of God in the "I style" (Gen. 22:2; Ex. 3:17; 1 S. 2:30; 9:17; Hos. 2:25[23]; Jer. 3:19; Ps. 95:10, using *'amarti* or *'omar*), and statements in the "thou style" which refer to something God has said: "Thou, O God, hast said..." (*'amarta, vatto'mer;* Ex. 33:12; Ps. 90:3). The use of *'amar* briefly outlined here shows that theologically this root is a term for revelation. God has the power to speak so that he can be understood. God expresses himself; God manifests himself and his will and his acts. When he speaks, he discloses himself to those addressed. The communicative aspect of God's words is particularly clear in Gen. 3:9ff., and their significatory function in 22:2; 26:2. More will be said about their imputative role under 1.d below. There are even examples of the use of *'amar* in the sense of "thinking," "reflecting," etc. in the theological realm, 8:21 (with *'el libbo*, "to his heart"); 2:18; Ps. 95:10 (without *lebh*, "heart").

a. *'amar in Connection with God Identifying Himself.* The theological function of *'amar* as a term for revelation appears most clearly in the formulas in which God identifies himself. The content of these formulas is to be understood as the object of an *'amar*-deed performed by God.[11] In Ex. 3:6, the statement

---

[11] Cf. W. Zimmerli, "Ich bin Jahwe, Gottes Offenbarung," *ThB*, 19 (1963), 11-40.

in which God identifies himself, *'anokhi 'elohe 'abhikha*, "I am the God of your father," immediately follows *vayyo'mer*, "and he said" (so similarly 3:14; 6:2–*'ani yhvh*, "I am Yahweh"–; Gen. 15:7). In Ex. 20:1f., the statement in which God identifies himself is introduced by *le'mor* after *vayedhabber*. Also in Ezk. 20:5 it is introduced by the infinitive, but after a different verb: "I swore to them, *le'mor* (saying), I am Yahweh your God." In Dt. 5:5f., *le'mor* is used as a finite verb, and means "he spoke." According to Lev. 18:1f., the statement in which God identifies himself is represented as mediated by human speech, although the mediator is expressly commissioned by God to do this. In all instances (the examples mentioned here could be multiplied many times), [12] the content of the speaking event is the declaration in the "I style." The enunciation of the formula in which God identifies himself (the *'amar*-deed) signifies God's self-proclamation to the one (or ones) addressed, who is usually mentioned by name (with the prep. *'el*). Yahweh is present in the word as the one who acts, as is clear from all the passages or from the context. The execution of the *'amar*-deed of God in the statement in which God identifies himself is not merely an announcement, but also an actualization of God, who is present in his acts. The speaking act of God (in the past, present, and future), which is inseparably connected with the statement in which God identifies himself, defines God as the God who is thus present. God is able to speak in his nature and acts, and this means that he can be heard.

b. *The Creative Word.* The theological use of *'amar* also manifests itself in the creative word of God. In the account of creation in P (Gen. 1), creation is depicted as a word (or speech) event. Each individual creative act begins with *vayyo'mer 'elohim*, "and God said," after which stands a jussive. As far as form is concerned, the *'amar*-event here is a command, and it is followed by a statement to the effect that what God had commanded came to pass. [13] The creative will of God is capable of being spoken; the creative word does what it says. That references are made, in the course of the larger account of the creative act, to differentiated creative acts of God (word account and deed account), is worthy of note and often discussed. In P's opinion, the statement that the creative act was accomplished (the deed account) can be understood only as an explication of the divine word which had been uttered (the word account). Each individual divine act is identical with the creative word that precedes it. The word is the deed, that which is said is that which is done. Theological references to creation in the Psalm literature, especially in Ps. 33:4,6 (cf. Isa. 44:26f.; Lam. 3:37), are closely related to the ideas of P. Examples like Ps. 105:31,34 or 107:25 (conjec.) show that the creative power of God in speaking was also considered to be effective in other contexts. Although the idea that God created by speaking a word may be relatively late, [14] the relationship between word and event was

---

[12] Cf. Zimmerli.

[13] Cf. W. H. Schmidt, *Die Schöpfungsgeschichte der Priesterschrift. WMANT*, 17 (²1967), 49ff., 163ff., esp. 169ff.

[14] Cf. W. H. Schmidt and C. Westermann, *Genesis. BK*, I (1967), 116ff.

present at an early time in the pledge, in the promise of God (here perhaps proleptically), in the oracle in which the psalmist expresses his belief that God will hear his prayer, and in the divine blessing or curse. [15]

c. *Demand*. In the proclamation of the will of God, in the divine address to man, in the demand of God on man, *'amar* is the bearer of the revelation of the law: Ex. 20:1 (Decalog, after *dibber le'mor*); 20:22 (Book of the Covenant); 34:1,10 (the so-called Yahwistic Decalog); Lev. 17:1 (the Holiness Code, *vayedhabber* with *le'mor*); Dt. 1:5,6; 5:1 (Deuteronomic Law). *'amar* is also bearer of the revelation of the law when the proclamation of the will of God is mediated through human speech, e.g., in Ex. 20:22. Indeed, Deuteronomy is considered to be entirely the speech of Moses. In the course of prophetic speech, too, we encounter the revelation of the will of God (2 S. 7:4f.; Isa. 7:3,4,10). The creative word of God is a command, but *'amar* can retain the meaning "to command" in other contexts also, e.g., at the beginning of the Abraham stories (Gen. 12:1), in the flood traditions (6:13; 7:1; 8:15), etc. It can be asked whether the revelation of the law might not also be included in the category of command. To be sure, "to command" often translates the Heb. → צוה *tsivvāh*; especially in Deuteronomy and the Deuteronomistic literature, the word for law and precept is *mitsvah* (= command). However, *'amar*, at least in the form *le'mor*, is often used along with *tsivvah* in such cases, and several times *'amar* by itself means "to command." The functional aspect, uttering a command and making it binding, is carried out in deed by *'amar*. The judgment of God, which transcends God's decision to judge (Gen. 6:7, *vayyo'mer yhvh*, "So the Lord said") in becoming reality through *'amar*, "speaking" (2 S. 12:1, mediated through Nathan; cf. Isa. 3:16–4:1; Am. 3:11; etc.), is no different. In this connection, one should not forget that the curse belongs to the category of speaking (Gen. 3:14, 17; 4:10f.; Dt. 27:14). Thus in the OT the "demands of God" (which are made known and carried out) are also and often expressed by *'amar*.

d. *Encouragement*. The imputative aspect of the *'amar*-event in the theological use of this root is expressed in the strongest way in the encouragement (pledge, promise) of God. The promise to Abraham in Gen. 12:2f. is dependent on *vayyo'mer yhvh 'el 'abhram*, "Now the Lord said to Abram" (12:1; cf. 18:10). The divine decree, which is evoked by a question (→ דרש *dārash*, "inquire of"), is also an *'amar*-event and has an imputative character (25:22f.). The same thing is true of the divine blessing in 9:1-7 (*vayyo'mer lahem*, "and he said to them," comes after *vayebharekh*, "and he [God] blessed"; cf. 1:28; this combination appears with *le'mor* in 1:22), and of the covenant God gives in 9:8-17. By special divine commission, men impart the divine blessing (Nu. 6:22-26). By pronouncing the benediction, they place (→ שים *śîm*) the divine name on those who are (or are to be) blessed. The contents of the blessing or the covenant or the promise are given in the text after *vayyo'mer* or *le'mor* in direct discourse, and

---

[15] On the question of ancient Near Eastern parallels and influences, as well as the problem of the word of God, cf. → דבר *dābhār*.

thus are considered to be imputed, according to the view of the narrator, through the act of 'amar. This is also true of making the covenant, which is explicitly described as mediated, e.g., in Ex. 24:8. The same may be said of 24:3-8 as a whole, where the imputative act of speaking is given vivid emphasis by being connected with the account of Moses' sprinkling blood on the people. Moreover, the way in which the covenant with its contents, its covenant statutes, is accepted, is that those to whom it is offered say audibly that they will abide by it (24:3,7). The promise of victory before the beginning of the battle plays a decisive role in the Holy War (Josh. 6:2; Jgs. 7:9). The promise of victory is stated in the perfect. It is either given by God directly (a divine decree, a divine judgment) or declared to the army by their leader who was made sure and confident by God (Josh. 6:16; Jgs. 7:15). [16]

That the call event [17] in the OT is a word event (of course, not alone) can be demonstrated from the well-known call accounts, Jer. 1:4 (with dabhar and le'mor); Ex. 3:4ff.; 6:2-8. These accounts show that the call event is also a dialogue (introduced with 'amar). The "charge to accept the office" takes place by means of speaking (vayyo'mer 'elai, Am. 7:15). We also encounter declaratory action and imputative speaking connected with it in the enthronement ceremony (esp. of the Davidic king, Ps. 2:7; cf. Ps. 110).

Not only are the covenant, the promise, the pledge, and the blessing in the OT understood as the direct utterance of God, but they are often represented as the mediated word of God. This is expressed quite clearly in the prophetic oracle and in the priestly oracle of salvation; see Isa. 7 and Jer. 45 for the prophetic oracle, and Isa. 41:8-13; Lam. 3:57; and Ps. 35:3 for the priestly oracle of salvation. [18] The communication of a → תורה tôrāh, "law," which is given in answer to a question by an 'amar-deed (Hag. 2:11-13), also belongs to this group. [19] Declaratory formulas should be included here in the broader sense. [20] Finally, we should not fail to mention here the seeking and giving of oracles (Jgs. 20:23,27f.; 1 S. 23:2,4,9-12–with the ephod), the encouragement of God through an (oracle) technique whatever its constitution may be, and for the second time the ordeal (Nu. 5, esp. vv. 19-28), where the word of adjuration is represented as an act, and the person undergoing the ordeal accepts this divine judgment by saying 'amen (ve'amerah, "and [she] shall say," Nu. 5:22).

2. *Messenger Formula and Messenger Oracle.* The saying of God mediated by man appears most clearly in the prophetic oracle. Here we encounter pas-

---

[16] Cf. G. von Rad, *Der Heilige Krieg im alten Israel* (⁴1965), esp. 7-9; W. Richter, *Traditionsgeschichtliche Untersuchungen zum Richterbuch. BBB*, 18 (²1966), 177-186.

[17] Cf. W. Richter, *Die sogenannten vorprophetischen Berufungsberichte. FRLANT*, 101 (1970), esp. 136-169.

[18] Cf. on this J. Begrich, "Das priesterliche Heilsorakel," *ZAW*, 52 (1934), 81-92 = *ThB*, 21 (1964), 217-231.

[19] Cf. J. Begrich, "Die priesterliche Tora," *BZAW*, 66 (1936), 63-88 = *ThB*, 21 (1964), 232-260.

[20] Cf. G. von Rad, "Die Anrechnung des Glaubens zur Gerechtigkeit," *ThLZ*, 76 (1951), 129-132 = *ThB*, 8 (²1961), 130-35; R. Rendtorff, *Die Gesetze in der Priesterschrift. FRLANT*, 62 (²1963), 74-76.

sages with a fixed structure in which *’amar* is used, viz., the commission of the messenger, the messenger formula, and the messenger oracle. These individual pieces belong to the general context of conveying a message, which was clearly used throughout the ancient Near East in a uniform way. Attention has repeatedly been called to this with reference to extrabiblical texts.[21] Originally, a message was no doubt conveyed orally. Because of the stereotyped pattern for doing this, probably it made its way into the ancient Near Eastern style of letter writing also (see, e.g., the Amarna correspondence and the letters in the Mari literature). A message can be conveyed in the most diverse spheres of social life, but it seems to have been rather firmly entrenched in international (diplomatic) correspondence. Outside the prophetic literature, the OT also contains numerous "secular" examples of conveying a message. The best-known examples are to be found in Gen. 32:4-6(3-5); Jgs. 11:12-16; Gen. 45:9-11; Nu. 22:15-17; 2 K. 18:19,28-31; 19:1-4,5-7,9-14,20. Thus, the genre of conveying a message, with all its individual formal elements, does not function only in the theological realm in the OT. Rather God's revelation event proceeds in a generally widespread, and therefore quite intelligible, form.

Baumgärtel's attempt to show that the prophetic message formula is to be derived from priestly speech forms is unsuccessful.[22] However, we must not overlook the fact that individual elements of the typical genre of conveying a message also function in priestly circles.[23]

Using Gen. 32:4-6(3-5) as a model, it is possible to outline the event of conveying a message as follows: sending of the messenger (B) by the sender (A) to the designated recipient of the message (C) at a certain place (D), commission of the messenger ("Thus shall you say to C," *koh tho’mar ’el*), messenger formula ("Thus has A spoken," *koh ’amar*),[24] and messenger oracle (the message is conveyed in direct discourse).[25] Not all elements are present in the account of the delivery of the message. Occasionally the messenger formula can be anticipated by the commission of the messenger. The messenger formula represents a self-confirmation of the messenger and his legitimation before the person(s) addressed (2 K. 9:1-3,4-10,11-13). The messenger comes to deliver not his own word, but the word of someone else. He is mediator of a word. OT prophetism is to be understood exclusively as the conveying of a message. This consists of

---

[21] L. Köhler, *Deuterojesaja. BZAW*, 37 (1923), 102-109; *idem, Kleine Lichter* (1945), 11-17.

[22] *ZAW*, 73; see below.

[23] So, e.g., the messenger's commission; see below. On the whole problem, see H. W. Wolff, *Dodekapropheton. Amos, BK*, XIV/2(1969), 164-67; on the discussion with Baumgärtel, p. 167; on the formula *ne’um yhvh*, p. 174; Westermann, *Basic Forms*, 98ff.; A. H. van Zyl, "The Message Formula in the Book of Judges," *OT Werkgemeenskap in Suid-Afrika* (1959), 61-64; F. Baumgärtel, "Die Formel ne’um jahwe," *ZAW*, 73 (1961), 277-290; *idem,* "Zu den Gottesnamen in den Büchern Jeremia und Ezechiel," *Verbannung und Heimkehr. Festschrift W. Rudolph* (1961), 1-29; R. Rendtorff, "Botenformel und Botenspruch," *ZAW*, 74 (1962), 165-177; W. Richter, *BBB*, 21 (1964), 100f.; *idem, FRLANT*, 101 (1970), 93, 155f.

[24] Differently Rendtorff, 167, who translates by the present tense.

[25] Cf. Westermann, 101.

sending the prophet, which is connected with his commission, and of his conveying the message, in which he announces the one who has sent him by means of the messenger formula, e.g., Jer. 7:1-3 (and in general quite often in Jer. and Ezk., frequently in brief accounts, but always with the messenger formula); 2 K. 1:2-8. In Amos, the sending of the prophet is assumed to be once for all (Am. 7:15); it is not expressly mentioned any more in the record of the delivery of the message (3:11f.; 5:3f.). Deutero-Isaiah often uses the messenger formula before the message when it is given in direct discourse, and here the messenger formula adds more detailed information about the one who sent the messenger. These (often in participial style, in this resembling the hymns of praise) make affirmations concerning God's actions and being in history (Isa. 42:5-9; 43:1; 44:1f.). Also, the address to a person can be followed by appositional statements describing that person (45:1). In Deutero-Isaiah, the individual elements in the conveying of the message appear in modified form. However, the words in 40:1f. are hardly to be understood as a messenger formula.[26] The repetition of the messenger formula after the message delivered in direct discourse (45:11-13) is worthy of note also.

A formal sending and commission to deliver a message is connected with the call of Moses (Ex. 3:10). The commission of the messenger is worded in the traditional way (3:14f. with the jussive; 3:16 with the perfect of ʾamar plus the vav-consecutive). The messenger formula is replaced the first time by the statement (found in the conveying of the message to the hearers) that the messenger was sent by God (perf., Ex. 3:12-15), and the second time by the affirmation (expressed in the delivery of the message to the hearers) that God had appeared to the messenger (perf.) and had spoken (leʾmor) to him. Then the direct discourse follows.

Elements of conveying a message also appear in the traditions of the appearance of Moses and Aaron before Pharaoh (Ex. 4:19-23: sending of the messenger, commission to deliver the message, veʾamarta ʾel, "and you shall say to," messenger formula, koh ʾamar yhvh, "thus says Yahweh," message in direct discourse; cf. 5:1). If the prophetic element in the picture of Moses is more prominent in the traditions rooted in the Elohistic tradition, the individual elements of conveying a message in the context of reporting the revelation of the law and the covenant are harder to understand from prophetic phenomena, Ex. 19:3; 20:22 (koh thoʾmar ʾel, or le, "thus you shall say to"). The same is also true of the formal introductions to the priestly legal material in the book of Leviticus presented as the words of Moses (Lev. 1:1f. with dibber, leʾmor, and veʾamarta ʾel; similarly 4:1f.; 11:1).

Individual elements of conveying a message can be recognized clearly in the introduction to the Holiness Code (Lev. 17:1f.), where the commission to the messenger is worded in the traditional way, and the messenger formula is represented by the expression zeh haddabhar ʾasher tsivvah yhvh leʾmor, "This is the thing which the Lord has commanded" (cf. further 18:1f.; 19:1f.; etc.). The

---

[26] Cf. Köhler, Deuterojesaja, 102-109.

same thing is also to be observed in Numbers (Nu. 5:11f.; 6:1f.,22f.; etc.). Occasionally, individual elements of conveying a message appear in Deuteronomy, e.g., the commission to the messenger (Dt. 1:3,5,6). Other elements of this genre occur in Deuteronomy in greatly modified form. It may well be asked, on the basis of these facts, whether (modified) forms of the commonly used conveying of a message were not also preserved in the process of priestly conveying of law.

3. *Man Speaking to God.* In sketching the theological use of *'amar* it is necessary to include not only the idea of God speaking to man, but also the idea of man speaking to God. In the OT, men speak so that God is the one addressed and the object of what they say. This can take place in a variety of ways, such as through prayer, song or hymn, praise and thanksgiving, but also through lament, and even accusation, discussion, objection, assent, etc.[27] As surely as all these speech types have their own unique terminology (→ פלל *pālal*, "to pray"; → הלל *hālal*, "to praise"; → זעק *zāʿaq* "to cry out"; → שיר *shîr*, "to sing"; → ברך *bārakh*, "to bless"; → ידה *yādhāh*, "to thank"; etc.), they are all connected with an *'amar*-event. Thus, e.g., the ancient confessions are speaking events (Dt. 26:3,5, *vaʿanitha veʾamarta*, "and you shall answer and say"). Moses' Song of Victory is introduced by *vayyoʾmeru leʾmor*, "and they (Moses and the people of Israel) said, saying" (Ex. 15:1), and the introduction to the Song of Deborah is worded in a similar way, *vattashar ... leʾmor*, "then she (Deborah) sang ... and said" (Jgs. 5:1). In the final literary form of the text of 2 S. 7 as we now have it, David utters *(vayyoʾmer)* a prayer after Nathan has promised him the dynasty (7:18). The *'amar*-deed appears in the account of Solomon's dedication of the temple (1 K. 8:12,15,22f.). The entire book of Job is composed of discussions conducted before God and with God, of lament and accusation (e.g., Job 7; 9; 10). Mention should be made of objections expressed to God by those whom he has called (Ex. 3:11,13; 4:1,10, *vayyoʾmer mosheh*, "But Moses said"; Jer. 1:6). These establish a type of dialogue relationship between God and man through the *'amar*-event. Of course, this is delineated more clearly in Ex. 33:11, but *dibber* is used in this verse instead of *'amar*. However, *'amar* appears in the following passage, which can be understood as a discussion between God and man (33:12-23). The remarks anointed kings make after the prophetic promise (designation) (Saul, 1 S. 9:21; David, 2 S. 7:18; cf. 1 S. 18:18 for a similar kind of remark in the secular sphere) are interesting, and almost stereotyped. Isaiah asks God how long the calamity will last (Isa. 6:11, *vaʾomar*, "then I said"), and he receives an answer from God *(vayyoʾmer*, "and he said"). Human assent to God's deeds is expressed in audible speech (Ex. 24:3,7). The refusal to heed the warning of God through Samuel not to set up a king in Israel is introduced by the words, *vayyoʾmeru loʾ ki ʾim*, "and they said, No! but ... " (1 S. 8:19). These various human means of speaking to God express the urgent desire to communicate with God. Here also, *'amar* is a communication term.

---

[27] Cf. I.1.

IV. Derivatives. In Hebrew, nouns are formed from the root *'mr,* which should also be rendered in English as nouns. According to Aistleitner, it is possible that this sort of noun existed in Ugaritic with the meaning "wish," "speech." [28] It is worthy of note that in the OT (apart from a few exceptions) the nominal derivatives of *'mr* are to be found predominantly in late literary contexts.

1. *'omer. 'omer* occurs only six times in the OT. It is noteworthy that it is used in the very ancient (originally perhaps non-Israelite) hymn, Ps. 19:3f.(2f.), which deals with the theology of creation. This hymn states that the heavens are telling (*sipper*) the *kebhodh 'el,* "glory of God," and the *raqia',* "firmament," proclaims *ma'aseh yadhav,* "his handiwork." Day choirs and night choirs (so to speak) are also included among those who praise God here. In ecstasy, the day choirs pour forth *'omer,* "speech," and the night choirs declare *da'ath,* "knowledge." The first works of creation, which then were witnesses to all the other creative acts of God, have secret knowledge concerning them, and a living tradition which they hand down daily and nightly in their praise of God, even though their language is unintelligible (i.e., by men). Man is prevented from hearing what is spoken by these creative works, and yet he is aware that these creatures praise God because they function so smoothly (in a sort of natural revelation). Thus, *'omer* here has to do with praising God's glory and creatorhood which is borne by secret knowledge. It is (put in terms of a natural theology) at the same time *'omer* and not *'omer.* It is audible speech, but not in the usual intelligible sense. The *'omer* is fact, but it is not necessarily evident and clear. [29] In Ps. 68:12(11), *'omer* is the word of God given before the victorious battle (in the Holy War). In 77:9(8), also, *'omer* is the word of God. By being used here in parallelism with → חסד *chesedh,* "steadfast love," it is defined by the context as "promise, pledge." The meaning of *'omer* in Hab. 3:9 is not clear. Finally, *'omer* occurs in Job 22:28, where it must be understood as a stated intention, a professed program of action, to which God grants or denies success. Here *'omer* acquires the meaning of *dabhar,* "matter, business."

2. *'emer, ma'amar, Aram. me'mar. 'emer* appears nearly 50 times in the OT. Its frequent occurrence in Psalms, Job, and Proverbs is striking. It is used to designate God's words and man's words. We encounter this word in a lament in the Individual Laments (Ps. 5:2[1]; 54:4[2]), and in a confession at the end of Ps. 19. It takes on a wisdom character in 78:1. Here *'emer* is connected with *torah,* "teaching," *mashal,* "parable," and *chidhah,* "dark saying." In this context, "wisdom" should be interpreted as "instruction," "teaching," which, e.g., explains the meaning of history to those who are taught. *'emer* has the broad general meaning "word of God" in 138:4, and the meaning "word of God" in the sense of "commandment" in 107:11. In the book of Job, *'emer* is connected with parallel terms like *dabhar* and *millah* (Aram.) in the description of the

---

28 Aistleitner, *WUS,* No. 284.
29 Cf. the comms. *in loc.*

dialogue between God and man, in which man contends with God and defends him. Here *'emer* can take on several meanings, as "words spoken by man publicly" (Job 6:25; 33:3), "words of a despairing man" (6:26), "violent, harsh, angry words" (8:2), and "man's words against God" (34:37); but it can also have the general meaning of words spoken in the debate (32:12,14). *'emer* can also mean the words of God, especially with reference to instruction and reproof (22:22; 23:12), and to the proclamation of the divine will understood and received by man (6:10). (In 20:29, *'imro* is probably an incorrect reading; [30] furthermore, it is the only example of the singular use of this noun in the OT.)

In the book of Proverbs, *'emer* appears in the following collections: Prov. 1–9; 10:1–22:16; 22:17–24:22. In the second collection, it is found only from chap. 15 on. Here *'emer* is entirely a wisdom category (again, in agreement with other terms like *mitsvah*, "command," and *torah*, "instruction"), whether it be instruction of the "son" given by the wisdom teacher (to teach him how to live a successful and rewarding life, 2:1; 4:5,10,20; 5:7; 7:1,5), or the words of personified Wisdom (→ חכמה *chokhmāh*), which knows how to speak just and righteous words (8:8; 1:21; cf. 1:2 [*binah*, "insight"]), or the words of wisdom which the "student" has accepted for himself in the school of the "Wise," so that he can pass it on as a reliable and true word (22:21), as a word of knowledge (23:12, *da'ath*). School, instruction, and the words of wisdom belong together (19:27; 23:12, *musar*, "instruction"). *'amarim*, "words," are elevated to the position of a wisdom category when they are *'imri no'am*, "words of pleasantness" (15:26; 16:24), delightful, pleasant words, which are the antithesis of the thoughts of the wicked and thus are not oriented to evil, but cause one's fellow man to rejoice. To be sure, the words of the strange seductive woman seem to be "smooth," they seem to be wise (2:16; 7:5), but a warning is given against them. The wisdom teacher utters the summons: "My son, keep my words and treasure up my commandments with you" (7:1). In this connection, reference should be made to Isa. 32:7, where the knave is contrasted with one who is noble in the style of wisdom maxims. By his "lying words," the knave is able to ruin the poor. The danger of indiscreet words is seen throughout. Not every example of *'emer* is to be interpreted as belonging to wisdom thought, even if it seems to be expressed in the sense of wisdom (cf. Isa. 32:7 with Prov. 6:2); thus, e.g., the reference to one being snared and caught in the words of his own mouth when he becomes surety for his neighbor (Prov. 6:2). In one statement, he who restrains his words can be regarded as truly prudent (17:27). 19:7 is no longer intelligible, and possibly is defective.

The other occurrences of *'emer* in the OT can be made to conform to uniform categories only with difficulty. In Hos. 6:5, *'emer* is the word of judgment proclaimed through the prophets, by means of which God encountered his people in the past. In Isa. 41:26 *'emer* means prophetic proclamation, but the use of the term in Deutero-Isaiah is singular. When Balaam speaks, he declares the revealed word of God, i.e., the word of God which he received in vision and audition (Nu. 24:4,16). The parallel members in these two verses have the form

---

[30] See the comms. *in loc.*

of a *figura etymologica* (etymological figure): Balaam is described as one who has the knowledge of the Most High and sees the vision of the Almighty, and he is also the one who *shomea' 'imre 'el,* "hears the words of God." From the analogy of the parallel members, it would be best to interpret *'emer* as audible, perceptible, understandable. *kol 'imre yhvh,* "all the words of Yahweh," in Josh. 24:27 signifies all the words which Joshua spoke to the Israelites at Shechem, and which establish and guarantee the covenant between God and his people and set forth the contents of the covenant together with its duties. Scholars are still debating whether *'emer* in Gen. 49:21 is original, but Zobel favors the interpretation "words of the triumphant message."[31] The introduction to the so-called Song of Moses (Dt. 32:1) calls upon heaven and earth to hear that which is expressed in what follows. Here *'imre phi,* "the words of my mouth," stands in parallelism with *va'adhabberah,* "and I will speak." In any case, both of these expressions have reference to an official announcement. In v. 2, the same phenomenon occurs again with *liqchi,* "my teaching," and *'imrathi,* "my speech." It may well be that this passage is fundamental to an understanding of *'emer* in the OT outside the Wisdom and Poetic Literature: *'emer* means the official announcement. It might also be possible to interpret Jgs. 5:29 in this way.

As an appendix, we may also discuss *ma'amar* here. This noun appears only in the book of Esther, where it always means human "directive," the "expression of the will" to which the person(s) addressed must accommodate himself (1:15; 2:20; 9:32). The two examples from Biblical Aramaic are to be understood basically in the same way (*me'mar,* Dnl. 4:14[17]; Ezr. 6:9). Here also, one would be correct in translating "rule" or "regulation."

3. *'imrah, 'emrah.* The overwhelming majority of the occurrences of *'imrah* in the OT appear in the Psalms. Ps. 119 has a special affinity for this word. *'imrah* means purely and simply the word of God in its comprehensive theological sense, as this is developed in Ps. 119. Here *'imrah* is not the only term used to describe the word of God, but it stands in parallelism with other words, which help to define it, e.g., with → חֹק *chōq,* "statute," *mitsvah,* "commandment," *mishpat,* "judgment," *piqqudhim,* "precepts," *'edhoth,* "testimonies," *dabhar,* "word," etc. But the definition of *'imrah* can also be determined by studying all sorts of activities which God does or intends to do for the worshipper "according to his word." It is in keeping with the whole tenor of Ps. 119 when the legal, the directive function of the "word of God" is emphasized (119:11,67). But the word can also be used in the sense of pledge, promise, protection, support, and comfort (119:38,58,41,76,82,116,170). It gives life (vv. 50,154), and enables a man to walk acceptably with God (vv. 133,158). It is worthwhile to meditate on it and to study it (v. 148); it is a righteous word (*'imrath tsidhqekha*) and a word creating justice (vv. 123,172). He who accepts it rejoices in it (v. 162), it is sweet to him (v. 103), he longs for it (v. 82), he can only extol it. But this *'imrah* is also pure and tried (v. 140), reliable and true (cf. also Ps. 12:7[6];

---

31 H.-J. Zobel, *Stammesspruch und Geschichte. BZAW,* 95 (1965), 5, 20, 21.

18:31[30]; 2 S. 22:31; Prov. 30:5). In the other passages in the Psalms (except for Ps. 17:6, where *'imrah* is the human word of prayer directed to God), this noun again means the "word of God," e.g., the word preceding deliverance (105:19), or the word authenticating the steadfast love and faithfulness of God in his promise (138:2), or finally the word sent forth to earth and now running swiftly (with *dabhar* in the parallel line, 147:15).

In the context of priestly concerns with covenant and law, instruction and precept, sacrifice and altar, *'imrah* appears in the Levi Oracle of the so-called Blessing of Moses (Dt. 33:9), so that its meaning here must be based on the firmly established word of God known to the priests. God's *torah* and *'imrah* also appear together in Isa. 5:24, where it is indicated that they are to be respected and kept. In 28:23 and 32:9, *'imrah* means the prophetic word, in particular the announcement of calamity. According to Lam. 2:17 (in the statement concerning *'emratho*), those who lie under the catastrophe of the punishment that had come upon Israel remember God's word of calamity which had been announced long before. God has carried out his "threat."

There are two other passages that use *'imrah* to refer to man's words. Isa. 29:4 states that those who were smitten by God's punishment could speak only in muffled and humiliated tones. And Gen. 4:23 refers to Lamech's so-called Song of the Sword as *'imrah,* as an official announcement.

It is difficult to try to determine when *'imrah* came into use in Biblical Hebrew. Ps. 119 is a late postexilic psalm, but we encounter *'imrah* here and there in very early texts. One can only conjecture as to when *'imrah* came into use, and the same is true of all the derivatives mentioned here. They occur predominantly in later literary traditions, especially in Poetic and Wisdom Literature, and in this context they mean "law," "wisdom," "instruction," and "teaching." In this sense, then, they also mean the "word of God." Outside this context, they can mean "oracle," "prophetic oracle," "announcement," "official announcement," and finally "oracle of God."

Wagner

אֱנוֹשׁ *'enôsh*

Contents: I. Distribution, Etymology. II. Meaning in the OT.

I. Distribution, Etymology. *'enosh* is widely attested along with *'adham* in the earliest representatives of the Semitic language group. Akk. *enēšu* means "to be weak, feeble" (like the Biblical Heb. *'anash* I, 2 S. 12:15; cf. *'anush,* "incurable," which occurs 8 times in the OT), and in the 'iphtael it means "to

---

'enôsh. For literature, see under → אדם *'ādhām* and → אִישׁ *'ish.*

be sociable." *tenēštu,* "man, mankind," and *nīšu,* "people, persons," belong to this root, [1] but not *iššu, aššatu,* "woman." [2] This word is common already in the earliest Aramaic. [3] In Biblical Aramaic, where *'adham* does not occur, we encounter *'enash* 25 times. [4] In the Ras Shamra material, *'nš* means "to be manly, brave": *CTA,* 2 [III AB], I, 38, "Then Prince Baal took courage," etc.; [5] and *nšm* (pl.) and *bnšm* (written syllabically *bu-nu-šu* and rendered by Akk. *awîlu*; perhaps < *bn nš*) mean "men." [6] Arab. *'insān* (pl. *'ins,* coll. *nās*) means "man"; the verb *'ns* means "to be sociable." [7] According to the usual view, *'ish* (but not *'ishshah,* "woman"; cf. Ugar. *'nt,* and Aram. *'antah*) and the plurals *'anashim,* "men," and *nashim,* "women," as well as *'enosh,* are to be traced back to the same stem. Scholars assume that the original meaning was "to be weak" or "to be sociable." Since there is a problem with deriving the sing. *'ish* from *'nš,* it has been suggested that *'ish* comes from another root meaning "to be strong." [8]

II. Meaning in the OT. *'enosh,* "man, men, mankind" (masc.; never with the article), occurs 42 times in the OT, and Aram. *'enash* 25 times. *'enosh* is found only once in the Pentateuch (Dt. 32:26), and it does not appear at all in Joshua, Judges, Samuel, or Kings. It occurs most frequently in Job (18 times), Psalms (13 times), and Isaiah (8 times, in late verses except for 8:1); it also appears in Jer. 20:10 and 2 Ch. 14:10 (Eng. v. 11) (in the prayer of Asa). Thus, *'enosh* is found almost exclusively in poetic texts. Isa. 8:1 is in prose, and is the only passage using this word that can be dated with some degree of certainty from the preexilic period. Thus, this ancient Semitic word is missing in the early writings of the OT, but it occurs quite often in the late literature. Several scholars question *'enosh* in Isa. 8:1 (*becheret 'enosh,* which is usually translated "with human stylus" or "in popular writing"), and emend the text to *'anush,* "hard, uneffaceable" (?). [9] Wildberger begins with *'anush* and translates "stylus of calamity," which he justifies by referring to the expression "stylus of life" in 1QM 12:3. [10]

'enosh is often translated "mortal" or something similar, which would agree with the original meaning "to be weak." But there are only a few passages in which this meaning is clearly intended, and which would permit a corresponding distinction between *'enosh* and *'adham.* Of course, the creatureliness, frailty, and danger of man is often emphasized in the OT, especially in Ps. 103:15 (as for *'enosh,* "his days are like grass; he flourishes like a flower of the field"); Job 7:1 ("Has not *'enosh* a hard service upon earth...?"); 15:14; and 25:4 (where *'enosh*

---

[1] F. Delitzsch, *Assyrisches Handwörterbuch* (1896 [1968]), 105f.

[2] *BLe,* § 78d,g, where the root is *'nt.*

[3] *DISO,* 19.

[4] Bauer-Leander, *Grammatik des Biblisch-Aramäischen* (1927), § 87d.

[5] *WUS,* 28.

[6] *WUS,* 28, 54; *UT,* No. 486.

[7] H. Wehr, *A Dictionary of Modern Written Arabic* (1961), 30f.

[8] *GK,* § 96.

[9] O. Kaiser, *Isaiah 1-12. OTL* (trans. 1972), 110, following Gressmann, *Der Messias* (1929), 239; cf. Galling, *ZDPV,* 56 (1933), 215-18.

[10] Wildberger, *BK,* X, 312.

appears in parallelism with *yeludh ʾishshah*, "born of woman"). In addition, we should mention the statements that emphasize the distance between God and man: Ps. 9:20f.(19f.) ("...Let not *ʾenosh* prevail; let the *goyim*, 'nations,' know that they are but *ʾenosh!*"); 10:18 ("...so that *ʾenosh* who is of the earth [!] may strike terror no more"); Job 5:17 ("happy is the man [*ʾashre ʾenosh*] whom God reproves"); 33:12,26 (God is greater than *ʾenosh* and heals him); 9:2; 10:4; 13:9; 14:19; and 32:8. But all this can be said of *ʾadham* or *ben ʾadham*, "son of man," in the OT (→ אדם *ʾādhām*), for several times *ʾenosh* stands in parallelism with (*ben-, bene-*) *ʾadham*, and is usually synonymous with it, as in two of the three parallel passages where we find "What is man...?" (Ps. 8:5[4], *ʾenosh–ben ʾadham;* 144:3, *ʾadham–ben ʾenosh;* Job 7:17, *ʾenosh* without a parallel word); [11] and also Isa. 13:12 (*ʾenosh–ʾadham*); 51:12 ("...Who are you that you are afraid of *ʾenosh*, who dies, of *ben ʾadham*, who is made like grass?"); 56:2 (*ʾenosh–ben ʾadham*); Ps. 73:5 (*ʾenosh–ʾadham*); 90:3 ("Thou turnest *ʾenosh* back to the dust, and sayest, 'Turn back, O *bene ʾadham!*'"); Job 25:5f. ("Behold, even the moon is not bright and the stars are not clean in his sight; how much less *ʾenosh*, who is a maggot, and the *ben ʾadham*, who is a worm!"); and 36:25 (*ʾadham–ʾenosh*). Also, *ʾenosh* appears in parallelism with "inhabitants of the earth" (Isa. 24:6), and with → גבר *gebher*, "man" (Job 4:17; 10:5). Four times *ʾenosh* is used of violent or hostile men (Isa. 51:7; Ps. 56:2[1]; 66:12; 2 Ch. 14:10[11]), twice of unfaithful friends (Jer. 20:10; Ps. 55:14[13]), and twice of those suffering in punishment (Isa. 13:7; 33:8). The four other passages in the OT that use *ʾenosh* are quite general. They deal with remembrance among men (Dt. 32:26), miners who are far from men (Job 28:4), wine and bread, which gladden and strengthen man's heart (Ps. 104:15), and the price (or way) of wisdom, which no man knows (Job 28:13).

In Biblical Hebrew, *ʾenosh* nowhere functions as an indefinite pronoun, as *ʾadham* does. However, in Biblical Aramaic it serves as an indefinite pronoun four times (Dnl. 3:10; 5:7; 6:13[12]; Ezr. 6:11, in every case *kol ʾenash*, "every man"="everyone").

The Aram. *ʾenash* usually occurs in stereotyped expressions (the Most High rules the kingdom of men, Dnl. 4:22,29[25,32]; 5:21; the king will be driven from human society, 4:22,29,30[25,32,33]; 5:21; loses his human heart and obtains the heart of an animal, 4:13[16]; cf. 7:4b; no one is allowed to make a petition to any god or man except the king, 6:8,13[7,12]). Dnl. 4:14(17) says that God can also set over the kingdom the lowliest man (read with the *qere: shephal ʾanasha*), and 2:38 states that the king has dominion over men and beasts. The Chaldean astrologers defend themselves by saying, "There is not a man on earth who can meet the king's demand" (2:10). The expression "mix by the seed of men" refers to marriage (2:43). The mysterious writing on the wall was written by the fingers of a man's hand (5:5). In Ezr. 4:11, the Transjordanian vassals are called *ʾenash ʿabhar naharah*, "the men of the province Beyond the River."

---

11 On these three passages, see W. Zimmerli, *Was ist der Mensch?* (1964).

The three remaining occurrences of *'enash* are found in Dnl. 7. The lion was made to stand upon two feet like a man (7:4); the little horn had eyes "like the eyes of a man" (7:8); and after the four beasts rose up out of the sea, the fourth beast was destroyed, and the power of the others was taken away, one "like a man" (*kebhar 'enash*) came with the clouds of heaven and came to the Ancient of Days (7:13). In this vision, the *bar 'enash*, lit. "son of man," is purely figurative; just as the four beasts represent the four preceding empires, so he represents the coming kingdom of the saints of the Most High (7:17f.). Nevertheless, the predominant interpretation at the present time is that the *bar 'enash* of Dnl. 7:13 is a product of the King-Messiah or Primal Man tradition. [12] About fifty years after Daniel, in the symbolic words of Enoch, the Son of Man is an independent individual, a Messianic figure (1En. 46:2; 48:2; 69:26-29; etc.). A symbolic figure is made independent in other literary contexts as well (e.g., *'anani*, "man of the clouds," also according to Dnl. 7:13; Midr. *Tanchuma, Toledhoth* 14, etc.).

Maass

---

[12] See esp. A. Bentzen, *HAT*, 19 (²1952), 62-67, and the literature cited there; R. Marlow, "The Son of Man in Recent Journal Literature," *CBQ*, 28 (1966), 20-30; cf. further *ben* → אדם *'ādhām*.

אֲנִי *'anî* → הוּא *hû'*.

אָנַף *'ānaph;* אַף *'aph* (*za'am, za'aph, chemah, charah, 'abhar, qatsaph, raghaz*)

Contents: I. The Concept of "Anger" in the Ancient Near East: 1. Egypt; 2. Mesopotamia; 3. In West Semitic Languages. II. Words for "Anger" in the OT: 1. Etymology; 2. Distribution, Meaning. III. Human Anger. IV. Divine Anger: 1. Linguistic Analysis; 2. Reason for Divine Anger; 3. Manifestations of Divine Anger; 4. Positive Value of Divine Anger.

I. The Concept of "Anger" in the Ancient Near East.

1. *Egypt*. The most common Egyptian words for "anger," "to be angry," are *knd*, "rage, fury," *dndn, dnd,* "anger," and *nšn(y)*, "to rave, rage." The translations of these words do not always capture the exact nuance of meaning. The hieroglyphic signs which are used for these words well illustrate their char-

---

'ānaph. J. Fichtner-O. Grether, "ὀργή," *TDNT*, V, 392-412; H. M. Haney, *The Wrath of God in the Former Prophets* (New York, 1960); J. L. Palache, *Semantic Notes on the Hebrew Lexicon* (Leiden, 1959); H. Ringgren, "Vredens kalk," *SEÅ*, 17 (1953), 19-30; *idem*, "Einige Schilderungen des göttlichen Zorns," *Tradition und Situation. Festschrift A. Weiser* (1963), 107-113; R. V. G. Tasker, *The Biblical Doctrine of the Wrath of God* (London, 1951).

acter. In addition to the sign of "smiting a poor person (or a man)," which indicates the violence of the situation or of the action, *ḳnd* is often represented by the "raging baboon" or the "raging panther." An angry ox head or antelope head usually means "anger," while "rage, fury," is usually denoted by the beast of Seth, and from the New Kingdom on by the "raging baboon."

Other words are also worthy of note in this connection. *dšr*, "red," which occurs, e.g., in the Metternich Stela (line 12) in an appeal to the sun god ("Come in your might, in your anger, in your redness!"), can refer to the redness of the battle fury as well as to the blood poured out in battle. *fnd*, which can mean "nose," "snorting," and "anger," and thus forms a parallel to Heb. ʾaph, is a rather rare word. A much more important word is *bȝw*, which appears, especially from the New Kingdom on, in several royal texts and prescription formulas, with the meaning "anger" expressed concretely in vengeance and punishment. [1]

The hieroglyphic signs for anger, which have to do with the animal world and the disorganized world of Seth, testify to the fact that anger has no place in the ideal Egyptian conception of man. The humanity proclaimed by the wisdom teaching aims at "righteous self-control" (*gr mȝʿ*). A quick temper is stigmatized from the earliest teaching (e.g., Ptahhotep 18:12) to the latest. "Silence," which is understood to rule the heart as well as the mouth, characterizes the ideal man: he is "the cool one" (*ḳbb*), over against whom "the hot one" (*šmm*) stands out as a warning example. [2] Quick temper is censured because of *šd ḥrw* or *kȝ ḥrw*, which does not mean "to make a noise, uproar," but in general "to behave oneself in an unbecoming manner, to bring about unrest, tumult." [3] Now since this is characteristic of the god Seth, one who becomes angry is represented as a man of Seth, which is emphasized especially by *nšny*.

Seth stands out as "the raging one" among the gods. [4] However, the rage (fury) of Seth is directed in particular against the Apophis serpent, and thus is justified. His rage against order in the framework of the Myth of Horus and Osiris characterizes the chaotic aspect of the world. The enumeration of primordial conditions (Pyr. 1463) begins in a typical way: "Before anger originated," and after this there are references to the struggle between Horus and Seth. The Pyramid Texts (e.g., 1501) also speak of the anger of other gods, something to which frequent later reference is also made.

An important elaboration of the divine anger, which is directed against disobedient mankind, appears in the Myth of the Destruction of Mankind. The anger of the creator-god takes on a personalized form in his daughter Hathor-Sekhmet, who comes forth as a fierce lioness. All mankind would have fallen victim to the raging goddess if the creator had not planned to save man. The goddess is intoxicated and appeased by blood-red beer. Several temple texts

---

[1] L. V. Žabkar, *A Study of the Ba Concept in Ancient Egyptian Texts* (Chicago, 1968), 62ff., 85ff.

[2] H. O. Lange, *Das Weisheitsbuch des Amenemope* (Copenhagen, 1925), 20ff.; E. Otto, *Die biographischen Inschriften der äg. Spätzeit* (Leiden, 1954), 67ff.

[3] Otto.

[4] H. Te Velde, *Seth, God of Confusion* (Leiden, 1967), 23ff., 101.

mention the ritual *śḥtp śḥm.t*,[5] which means not only "to appease Sekhmet," but also "to break down the anger of Sekhmet."[6] However, here other myths like "the goddess in the strange land" and the Onuris Legend must also be taken into consideration. The appeasement of the raging goddess, who is often localized in Philae, is expressed in the pregnant phrase, "She is angry as Sekhmet, she is gracious as Bastet."[7] Along with the libation, the sistrum played an important role in the appeasement. In a temple scene from Thebes (*Urk.*, VIII, 7c), the king, offering the sistra to the goddess Mut, says: "I take away your anger, I remove your fury, when I appease the rage of your Ka."

The Myth of the Eye of the Sun also presents a special elaboration of the anger motif. The anger of the eye or of the uraeus is directed against the possessor himself.[8] This calls attention to the tension in the character of the Egyptian deity, who is both merciful and raging.

The same ambivalence can be observed in the character of the Pharaoh.[9] According to the teaching of Sehetepibre, the king is "a Bastet who protects the two lands. He who worships him will be one whom his hand defends. He is a Sekhmet against him who transgresses his commandment." The anger or rage of the king falls especially on his enemies in battle. He is "raging like a lion"[10] or "raging like a panther."[11]

Finally, man is threatened by the anger of certain powers in the realm of the dead.[12]

Bergman

2. *Mesopotamia*. The anger of the gods appears occasionally in the Sumerian Hymns as one of several characteristics causing fear ("Who can appease your angry heart?" *SAHG*, 78; "As An had looked angrily at all lands," *ibid.*, 190). It is obvious that no thought was given to the reason for their anger.

In Akkadian, the linguistic expression for "anger" is strikingly quite different from the Hebrew. The two most frequently used words, *agāgu* and *ezēzu* (root ʿzz, "to be strong"!), differ from each other in that *agāgu* denotes the momentary excitement, while *ezēzu* indicates an abiding characteristic, but also means "wild, furious," and can be used of natural phenomena.[13] The references to human anger are rather few, and offer little that is of theological interest. The statements concerning the anger of the gods, however, have some significance. First of all, the gods could be angry with each other (Gilg. XI, 171: "Enlil saw the ship and became angry, he was filled with anger against the Igigi gods"; EnEl I, 42: "She was angry and screamed at her husband"; Atraḫasīs III, i, 42f.: "Enki and Enlil

---

[5] J. Bergman, *Isis-Seele und Osiris-Ei* (Uppsala, 1970), 16, n. 13.

[6] For the antithesis *nšny-ḥtp*, see the examples in *WbÄS*, II, 340.

[7] H. Junker, *Der Auszug der Hathor-Tefnut aus Nubien* (Vienna, 1911), 32; *idem, Die Onurislegende* (Vienna, 1917), *passim*.

[8] Junker, *Onurislegende*, 132.

[9] H. Brunner, *ZÄS*, 79 (1954), 81ff.; 80 (1955), 5ff.

[10] *WbÄS*, V, 57, 3 and 8.

[11] *WbÄS*, III, 244, 3.

[12] J. Zandee, *Death as an Enemy* (Leiden, 1960), 191.

[13] *CAD*, IV, 428.

were angry with each other"). Second, the gods became angry with men, which led them to forsake their cities or lands, or to plan the destruction of the land. [14] Furthermore, it is said in the psalms of lament and the prayers of adjuration that the god or the goddess is angry, and it is asked that he (or she) might be appeased (e.g., *SAHG*, 332, 352f.). Occasionally the sin of man is mentioned as a reason for the anger of the gods.

3. *In West Semitic Languages.* Examples of anger in the West Semitic inscriptions are rare. The statement in the Mesha Inscription, therefore, that the god Chemosh was angry at his land and thus Omri had afflicted Moab for some time, [15] is particularly interesting. Further, a day of anger (*ywm ḥrn*) is mentioned in one of the Sefire treaties, [16] but the context is not clear. In an inscription from Zinjerli it also is said: "Hadad will pour out anger... and shall give him nothing to eat in anger" (*vhdd ḥr' lytkh...'l ytn lh l'kl brgz*), [17] and "you shall kill him... in anger" (*bḥm'*). [18]

II. Words for "Anger" in the OT.

1. *Etymology.* "Anger" is represented in Hebrew by several words of different origin. a. One root is *'np* with the subst. *'aph,* which sometimes means "nose" and sometimes "anger." The verb stem occurs in Arab. *'anifa,* "to despise, refuse," the noun in Akk. *appu,* Ugar. *'p,* and Arab. *'anfun,* all meaning "nose"; it is doubtful that Ugar. *'p* means "anger." [19] Scholarly opinions differ on the original meaning of the root. Fichtner [20] and *KBL* think the original meaning was "to snort," because both "nose" and "anger" could be derived from this meaning. But Palache argues that there was a development in meaning from "nose" to "anger." Blachère-Chouémi [21] starts with the Arab. root with the original meaning "to be at the head," and derives from this the words for "nose" and "to be haughty"; then from the latter, under the influence of *'anafa,* would come the meaning "to despise."

Thus the double meaning of *'aph* as "nose" and "anger" appears evidently only in Hebrew. It is interesting that in the OT the nose plays a certain role in the description of anger: Ezk. 38:18, "my anger will rise up in my nose" (text uncertain); and Ps. 18:8f. (Eng. v. 7f.), "for he was angry; smoke rose up in his nose" (*charah lo 'alah 'ashan be'appo*). Moreover, there is a clear connection between anger and snorting, e.g., in Ex. 15:8; Ps. 18:16(15); Job 4:9.

The verb *'anaph* appears in the qal and hithpael. The nouns built from this root are *'aph* and *'appayim.*

---

[14] For examples, cf. *CAD,* I/1, 139f.; IV, 427f.; cf. Albrektson, *History and the Gods* (Lund, 1967), 91.

[15] *KAI,* 181.5.

[16] *KAI,* 223 B.12.

[17] *KAI,* 214.23.

[18] *Ibid.,* 33; speaking of a man.

[19] Aistleitner, *WUS.*

[20] Fichtner, 392.

[21] Blachère-Chouémi, 257ff.

b. *za'am* means "to be angry" and "to curse" in the OT. Neither of these meanings can be shown to be the older. In the Qumran literature this root means only "to curse," and in modern Hebrew only "to be angry," "to be dissatisfied." [22] Gray [23] and *GesB* connect *za'am* with the rare Syr. *za'em*, "to reproach," but this also could not be derived from the Hebrew. Arab. *za'ama* means simply "to maintain," while *tazaġġama* can denote angry speaking. [24] Gray finds the key to understanding this word in Nu. 23:7 and Prov. 24:24, where it appears as a synonym of "to curse" (→ ארר *'ārar* or *qalal*). In this case, originally *za'am* was a part of the curse formula, and later it came to denote the emotional condition that lay behind the curse. This helps explain why it is said of Yahweh, "his lips are full of *za'am*" (Isa. 30:27). According to Wolff, *za'am* means "curse" in Hos. 7:16. [25] Further, it is possible to connect the expressions "day of *za'am*" (Ezk. 22:24) and "weapons of *za'am*" (Isa. 13:5; Jer. 50:25) with the realization of the curse. *za'am* appears in the qal and niphal, and the noun form is *za'am*.

c. *za'aph* is cognate with Syr. *za'eph*, "to address angrily, to be angry," and Arab. *za'afa*, "to kill on the spot." Modern Hebrew and Aramaic words derived from this root are used to describe the violence of the rain or of the storm. [26] If we suppose that the original meaning was "to be excited," this would explain the use of *za'aph* with reference to natural phenomena (Jonah 1:15, the raging of the sea; Ps. 11:6, *ruach zil'aphoth*, "whirlwind") and to man (of emotional excitement). *za'aph* has this latter sense in Gen. 40:6 and Dnl. 1:10, where it is not necessary to assume another root. [27] The idea in 1 K. 20:43 and 21:4 is "out of humor" (parallel with *sar*). In Prov. 19:3, the LXX translates *za'aph* by *aitiátai* ("to accuse"), but it is better to read, "because of Yahweh his heart is excited." In 2 Ch. 26:19 also, "excitement" is the correct translation. *za'aph* means "anger" in the other passages where it occurs in the OT (Prov. 19:12; Mic. 7:9; Isa. 30:30; 2 Ch. 16:10; 28:9). It is a natural step from "excitement" to "anger"; perhaps *za'am* influenced this development. *za'aph* occurs in the qal, and the nouns built from this root are *za'aph*, *za'eph*, and *za/il'aphah*.

d. *chemah* is derived from *yacham*, "to be hot" (cf. Arab. *waḥim*, "hot," *waḥima*, "to lust after"); cf. Aram. *chema'*. [28] According to *GesB*, in five cases it means "venom" (Dt. 32:24; Ps. 58:5[4]–twice; 140:4[3], the venom of a serpent; Job 6:4, poison of arrows). Driver thinks that in some passages it also denotes "fiery wine" (Isa. 27:2-4; Hab. 2:15; Job 36:16-18). [29] It is easy to understand how bodily "heat" is brought about by anger as well as by poison or wine.

---

[22] Levy, *WTM;* Jastrow.
[23] Gray, *ICC* on Nu. 23:7.
[24] *GesB*.
[25] H. W. Wolff, *BK in loc.*
[26] *GesB*.
[27] Against Kopf, *VT,* 9 (1959), 254.
[28] *KAI,* 214.33.
[29] Driver, *ThZ,* 14 (1958), 131ff.

e. *charah* still appears in modern Hebrew and Jewish Aramaic, and its original meaning was probably "to glow, to burn." Syr. *'eth⁽e⁾rī*, "to struggle," the Talmudic *ḥry* in the pael, "to cause to burn," and Aram. *chera'*, "anger,"[30] and *charan*[31] are cognates of this Hebrew root. In Hebrew, the verb appears either with *'aph* as subject ("anger is kindled") or impersonally (*charah lo*, "he became angry"); and the cognate noun *charon*, "burning anger," also occurs.

f. *ka'as* (in Job this root is spelled also with a *sin* instead of a *samekh*) denotes an inner action, which as a rule does not take an object. It usually means the feeling that comes from being treated unjustly, and thus should be translated "grief" or "sorrow" rather than "anger" (Eccl. 7:3; Ps. 6:8[7]; 31:10f.[9f.]; Job 17:7). This root also appears in modern Hebrew and Jewish Aramaic. In exceptional cases, *ka'as* in the sense of "anger" is directed against other men (Job 10:17; 2 Ch. 16:10; Ps. 85:5[4]). The verb *ka'as* appears in the qal, piel, and hiphil, and the noun form built from this root is *ka'as*.

g. In the hithpael of the verb and in the noun *'ebhrah*, the root *'br* means "to be angry." It is debated as to whether these forms are derived from *'br*, "to pass over," or whether they presuppose a different root. Driver's explanation, "to pass over prescribed boundaries,"[32] renders the assumption of two roots unnecessary, and explains the entire scope of this root's meaning from "pride" and "exaltation" to "destructive anger."

h. *qatsaph* appears as a Canaanite gloss in the Amarna Letters; it is also found in Aram. *qetsaph*, "to be angry." Whether there is a connection between this root and Arab. *qaṣafa*, "to break," is uncertain; cf., however, Heb. *qetseph*, "bent twig, splinter."

i. The original meaning of *raghaz* (cf. Aram. *reghaz*, "to tremble," "to be angry," Phoen. *rgz*, "to be angry," and Arab. *raḡaz*, "trembling," "anger") is "to be excited, shaken," "to tremble"; the word is used in Biblical Hebrew only in isolated cases with regard to anger (hiphil–Job 12:6; 37:2; 2 K. 19:27f.; Hab. 3:2). One can also tremble for joy (Jer. 33:9) or fear (Ex. 15:14).

j. *ruach*, "wind," is translated "anger" six times by *GesB* (Jgs. 8:3; Isa. 25:4; 30:28; Zec. 6:8; Prov. 16:32; 29:11). According to *GesB*, this meaning is to be derived from "breath" by way of "snorting" (Job 4:9). But it seems more likely that it was derived from heavy breathing brought about by great excitement.

2. *Distribution, Meaning.* a. *'anaph* is the word most frequently used for "anger" in the OT. The verb occurs 14 times, always with God as the subject (with the exception of Ps. 2:12, where the subject is the king as the son of God).

---

[30] *KAI*, 214.23.
[31] *KAI*, 223 B.12.
[32] Driver, *ICC* on Dt. 3:20.

But the nouns (*'aph, 'appayim*) denote both human (40 times) and divine (170 times) anger. *'np* is found in a relatively equal proportion in the various text types of the OT. Although it was clearly connected originally with angry snorting, it often expresses the idea of anger as "fire." Of the 78 times *'aph* is used as a subject in the OT, it appears as the subject of *charah*, "to glow," "to burn," 54 times (in fact, the verb *charah* is used only with *'aph* as subject). The expression *charon 'aph*, "burning anger," occurs 35 times, and *chari 'aph* is found 6 times. *'aph* is used as the subject of *ba'ar*, "to burn," and *'ashan*, "to smoke," twice each. *chemah*, which is derived from *yacham*, "to be hot," is the word used most frequently in parallelism with *'aph* (33 times, of which *'aph* appears in the first line 25 times). Other words used synonymously with *'aph* are *'ebhrah*, "fury" (10 times), *za'am*, "indignation" (8 times), and *qetseph*, "wrath" (4 times). Words meaning "compassion," "grace," and "mercy" (*rechem*, Dt. 13:18[17]; Ps. 77:10[9]; 78:38; *chesedh*, Mic. 7:18; *ratson*, Ps. 30:6[5]; *nicham*, Isa. 12:1), are used as antonyms of "anger."

b. The root *z'm* occurs 12 times as a verb, and 22 times as a noun. With the exception of Nu. 23:7f., this root is found only in the Later Prophets and the Writings, always in poetic texts. *z'm* means both "anger" and "curse." In five of the six occurrences of the verb with God as the subject, the idea is clearly that of "anger," and even in the sixth passage (Nu. 23:8) this meaning is possible. However, in the five passages in which man is the subject, it is never necessary to translate this root as "to be angry." The noun has reference to the anger (wrath) of God in all 22 passages where it occurs. [33] In apocalyptic texts, *za'am* has the special meaning "time of wrath" (Isa. 26:20; Dnl. 8:19; 11:36). [34] *'aph* (8 times), *'ebhrah* (3 times), *qetseph* (twice), and *chemah* (once) are used as synonyms of *za'am*. Also, the expression "to wish harm (on someone)" appears in parallelism with *za'am*.

c. *za'aph* appears four times as a verb. Of the nouns built on this root, *za'aph* occurs 7 times, *za'eph* twice, and *zil'aphah* 3 times. With the exception of Gen. 40:6, all forms of *z'p* are found in the Later Prophets and the Writings. This root is used in connection with God, man, and natural phenomena. The synonyms of this root mean "grief" and "discontent" more often than "anger": *sar*, "discontented" (1 K. 20:43; 21:4); *ra'*, "troubled" (Gen. 40:6f.); *ka'as*, "anger" (2 Ch. 16:10). A clear word for "anger" from this root occurs only once, viz., in the expression *za'aph 'aph*, "furious anger" (Isa. 30:30). *ratson*, "favor," appears in antithesis to *za'aph* (Prov. 19:12).

d. Next to *'aph*, *chemah* is the second most frequently used word in the OT for "anger." It occurs 118 times, 90 of which have to do with the anger (wrath) of God. Like *'aph*, it is found in all text types. Other than *'aph*, we may note the following as synonyms used with *chemah*: *qetseph* (7 times), *ka'as* (twice),

---

33 *TDNT*, V, 393.
34 *Ibid.*

za'am and *za'aph* (once each). *ge'arah*, "rebuke," is used as a synonym of *chemah* in Isa. 51:20 and 66:15. In Ezk. 5:15 and 25:17, *chemah* is connected with chastisement (*tokhechah*), and Ps. 6:2(1) and 38:2(1) speak of "chastening in anger (wrath)."

Since its derivation from *yacham* is clear, it is not surprising that in *chemah*, several times the idea of anger as fire is found (Jer. 4:4; 21:12; Nah. 1:6; Ps. 89:47[46]; Lam. 2:4). The OT also speaks of anger "being kindled" (*yatsath*, 2 K. 22:13,17). On the other hand, *chemah* can also be poured out like water, [35] and the two figures can be combined: "anger is poured out and burns" (Isa. 42:25; Jer. 7:20; 44:6).

e. *charah* appears 92 times as a verb in the OT, either with *'aph* as a subject (50 times) or impersonally. The cognate noun *charon* is always used with reference to divine anger (wrath); it occurs 41 times, and 35 of these in connection with *'aph*. However, the expression *chari 'aph* (6 times) can refer to both divine and human anger. When *charon* is used without *'aph* (6 times), obviously heat as a psychic phenomenon is attributed to anger in general. In some passages, *charah* means "to be zealous" (Neh. 3:20; Jer. 12:5; 22:15), i.e., one is heated because of zeal.

f. *k's* appears as a verb 54 times (43 times of God and 11 times of man), and as a noun 25 times (8 times of God and 17 times of man). This word is characteristic of the Deuteronomistic theology; most of the passages in which it is found are in Deuteronomy, Kings, and Jeremiah. The verb is found usually in the hiphil (in 42 out of 46 occurrences) of the divine wrath brought about by the apostasy of the people. Yahweh is offended when the people prefer idols. Usually the anger denoted by *ka'as* is not an objective phenomenon; rather, it is an internal feeling. Other words for "anger" are rarely connected with *ka'as;* sometimes *qana'*, "jealous," appears as a parallel word (Dt. 32:16,21; Ps. 78:58). Sometimes *ka'as* means "grief," e.g., in Eccl. 7:3 "*ka'as* is better than laughter"; 1 S. 1:6, "to grieve her"; Ps. 6:8(7); 31:10f.(9f.); Job 17:7.

g. The hithpael of *'br* occurs 8 times with the meaning "to be angry," and in 5 of these cases it refers to God. The noun *'ebhrah* appears 30 times, and 24 of these refer to God. With the exception of two passages in the Pentateuch (Gen. 49:7; Dt. 3:26), this root is found only in the Later Prophets and the Writings. *'aph* (10 times) and *za'am* (3 times) are used as synonyms of words built from *'br*. The expression "fire of anger (wrath)" occurs 4 times (Ezk. 21:36[31]; 22:21, 31; 38:19); elsewhere, fire (→ אֵשׁ *'esh*) is connected only with *'aph* and *chemah*. The "day of wrath" is mentioned 5 times (Ezk. 7:19; Zeph. 1:15,18; Job 21:30; Prov. 11:4).

h. *qsp* as a verb is used 16 times of God and 17 of man. But the noun is used almost exclusively of God (it is used of man only in Eccl. 5:16[17] and

---

[35] See below, IV.3.

Est. 1:18). The verb is almost always used with an object. *'aph* (5 times), *chemah* (7 times), *za'am* (twice), and *ka'as* (once) appear as synonyms of words built from the root *qṣp*.

III. Human Anger. On the whole, the OT uses the same expressions to denote human and divine anger, but all together it does not speak of human anger as much as it does of divine anger. Individual men function as the subject of anger. Only in exceptional cases does the OT mention that groups of men are angry. Human anger is usually directed against other men. The reason for human anger can be that someone has been treated unjustly (e.g., Gen. 27:45; 30:2; 39:19; Nu. 24:10), that one sees how other men are exploited (e.g., Gen. 34:7; 2 S. 12:5; 13:21), or that one's fellow men manifest disobedience or unbelief in God (e.g., Ex. 16:20; 32:19; 2 K. 13:19). Although the examples are scarce, there are also some passages in the OT that speak of men becoming angry with God. In this case, the reason is that one views his actions as inexplicable (e.g., Gen. 4:5; 2 S. 6:8; Jonah 4:1,4,9).

In the large majority of cases, the OT censures human anger. Human anger is never clearly approved. But there are instances (esp. in the narrative books) in which the biblical writer does not make a judgment on this. It is simply stated that someone was angry. It follows from Gen. 4:5-7 that human anger is something negative. Furthermore, anger is criticized because it produces negative results (e.g., 49:6f.).

Value judgments of anger appear most frequently in Job, Proverbs, and Ecclesiastes, and they are clearly negative. In these books we find statements like "anger is cruel" (*'akhzeriyyuth chemah*, Prov. 27:4), and "strife is pressed out of anger" (30:33). "To still anger" is good, as is clear from 15:1; 21:14. The wise stills anger (29:8,11). The ideal of wisdom is the quiet man who does not err in anger, or as 17:27 puts it, is "a calm and understanding man" (*qar ruach 'ish tebhunah*). Thus, here *qar*, "cool," is used in antithesis to the man who is kindled and heated by anger. The OT censures a man who is hot-tempered (15:18; 29:22). Therefore we also find admonitions not to be angry or not to err in anger (Ps. 37:8; Prov. 16:32; Eccl. 7:9; Job 36:18). Anger characterizes the fool, the irrational, and the evildoer (Prov. 14:17,29; 29:11; Eccl. 7:9; Job 5:2). Job 36:13 speaks of those who are disposed to godlessness (*chanephe lebh*, "the godless of heart"), who cherish anger, and Job 19:29 calls anger sin.

IV. Divine Anger.

1. *Linguistic Analysis.* Words for anger are connected with God three times as often as they are connected with man in the OT. Some words are used almost exclusively with God as subject, e.g., *'anaph* and *charon*. The nouns *za'am*, *'ebhrah*, and *qetseph* predominantly have God as their subject, and in the majority of cases *chemah* and *'aph* are used of the divine anger. With few exceptions (*chari 'aph*, 4 times), combinations of several words for "anger" have to do with the divine wrath exclusively: *charon 'aph* (33 times), *za'aph 'aph* (Isa. 30:30), *za'am 'aph* (Lam. 2:6), and *'ebhroth 'aph* (Job 40:11); so also the following

groups of two or three terms: *'aph* and *chemah* (15 times), *charon 'aph* and *'ebhrah* (Isa. 13:9), *za'am* and *qetseph* (Ps. 102:11[10]), *'aph, chemah,* and *qetseph* (Dt. 29:27[28]), and *charon 'aph, 'ebhrah,* and *za'am* (Ps. 78:49). In construct expressions involving a word for "anger" and God, the word used for God is almost always *yhvh,* "Yahweh" (50 times, 40 of which consist of the expression *'aph yhvh*). The expression *'aph 'elohim* appears only twice (Nu. 22:22; Ps. 78:31).

2. *Reason for Divine Anger.* If one asks the motive for God's anger, sometimes there are instances described in the OT in which God's actions seem to be completely inexplicable. In texts like Gen. 32:23-33(22-32) and Ex. 4:24f., he acts without perceptible inducement. However, in most cases the anger of God is brought about by the actions of men. Thus, his anger must be understood within the framework of the covenant relationship. God has made known his desire to save through his promises and through the historical leadership of his people, and therefore he has a claim on their obedience and trust. The making of the covenant presents the people with the possibility of a twofold divine reaction depending on whether the people keep the covenant or not (Ex. 20:5ff.). If God's anger comes upon Israel (as a whole, or on one individual as a member of the people), as a rule the reason is that the people have not performed their covenant responsibilities. Dt. 29:27(28); Jgs. 2:20; Josh. 23:16; and Ezr. 9:14 state clearly that the reason for Yahweh's anger is that his people have broken the covenant. Yahweh's anger is aroused especially when his people turn to other gods (Ex. 32; Nu. 25; Dt. 2:15; 4:25; 9:19; 29:27[28]; 31:29; Jgs. 2:14; 1 K. 11:9; 14:9,15; 2 K. 17:18). In this connection, the word *ka'as* plays a significant role in the Deuteronomistic theology. It has become a technical term for Yahweh becoming vexed over the apostasy of his people to other gods. Sometimes the OT says that Yahweh is angry because the people have sinned, without going on to specify the nature of the sin more precisely (1 K. 8:46; 2 Ch. 6:36). The disobedience of the people (Nu. 32:11-14) and their lack of faith in Yahweh (11:33) arouse Yahweh's anger. Yahweh also becomes angry because of social offenses, e.g., when widows are treated wickedly (Ex. 22:23[24]). Transgression against one's fellow man is a violation of the covenant.

In the preexilic prophets, especially Jeremiah and Ezekiel, we often find threats of Yahweh's anger. Everything Yahweh has done for Israel is emphasized (Am. 2:9-11; 3:2; Hos. 11:3f.; Isa. 1:2). But the people consider themselves to be the chosen people and are deluded with false security (Jer. 6:14; Ezk. 13:10). Thus, they have forgotten their covenant responsibilities and arouse the anger of Yahweh. The prophets point to social injustice (Isa. 1:15-17; Jer. 5:28; Am. 5:7,10-12; Mic. 3:1), the syncretistic cult (Isa. 1:10-17; Jer. 6:20; Hos. 6:6; Am. 5:21-27), and foreign policy (Isa. 30:1-5; 31:1-3; Jer. 2:35-37; Ezk. 16:26; Hos. 5:13; 7:11) as signs that the people had forsaken God and deserved the anger of God. Thus, here also God's anger is due to violating the covenant. [36]

But Yahweh's anger is also directed against other nations. In the postexilic

[36] *TDNT,* V, 404.

period, this anger is clearly connected with the intervention of these nations into the destiny of Israel. Thus, Yahweh becomes angry with Edom because she has dealt violently with Israel (Ob. 1-15), and the prophet asks Yahweh to pour out his anger on the nations who have devastated Israel (Jer. 10:25). Respect for the people is also respect for God (Isa. 48:9-11). This thought also governs the earlier history, where Yahweh's desire to save demands that he act in anger against other nations (Ex. 23:27-30; Josh. 24:12).

3. *Manifestations of Divine Anger.* The manifestations of divine anger are often described with the help of figurative language. The two most frequently used figures are those of fire (→ אֵשׁ 'ēsh) and water. Thus, the OT speaks of the fire of Yahweh's wrath (Ezk. 21:36[31]; 22:21,31; 38:19), or it says that the anger of Yahweh is like fire (Jer. 4:4; 21:12; Nah. 1:6; Ps. 89:47[46]; Lam. 2:4). The anger of Yahweh can also be compared with a blazing oven (Ps. 21:10[9]). Several passages state that Yahweh's anger burns, smokes, or is kindled (Isa. 30:27; Ps. 2:12; Jer. 7:20; Isa. 42:25; Jer. 44:6; Dt. 29:19[20]; Ps. 74:1; 2 K. 22:13,17). The use of *charah* and its cognates also belongs here. [37]

Isa. 30:28 says that Yahweh's anger is like an overflowing stream; thus, here anger is compared with a flood of water. The same motif also lies behind the expression "anger is poured out." Three verbs are used to convey this thought, viz., *shaphakh, puts,* and *nathakh.* When *shaphakh* is used, it is always God who "pours out" anger (Isa. 42:25; Jer. 6:11; Ezk. 7:8; 14:19; 20:8,13,21,33f.; 21:36[31]; 22:22,31; 30:15; 36:18; Hos. 5:10; Zeph. 3:8; Ps. 79:6; Lam. 2:4; 4:11). Hos. 5:10 says that anger is poured out like water. Remarkably, twice this expression is connected with fire (Lam. 2:4; Isa. 42:25), although actually the two figures are logically incompatible. *puts* is used of anger in Job 40:11. The verb *nathakh,* which otherwise can denote rain coming down out of the sky, is used of anger in the following passages: Jer. 7:20; 42:18; 44:6; Ezk. 16:38 (conjec.); Nah. 1:6; 2 Ch. 12:7; 34:21,25. When this verb is used, it is never said that God pours out his anger, but that anger streams forth of its own accord. It is worthy of note that in four of the eight cases where this verb is used, the figure of anger shows similarities with fire (Jer. 7:20; 44:6; Nah. 1:6; 2 Ch. 34:25). Moreover, *nathakh* is used only with 'aph and *chemah,* thus with the two words that are most strongly connected with fire and heat.

In some passages the anger of Yahweh is represented by the figure of a cup filled with wine, which certain peoples must drink (Isa. 51:17,22; Jer. 25:15); the point of comparison is always their helplessness due to drunkenness. [38]

When the OT says that Yahweh is angry, it means that punishment is coming (Isa. 10:4). Therefore, "to be angry" can be synonymous with "to destroy" (Ezr. 9:14). When Yahweh's anger is kindled, this often means extermination or destruction (Ex. 32:10; Dt. 6:15; 7:4; Josh. 23:16).

Frequently, the figure used for anger passes over into a graphic description of the divine activity. In Ezk. 21:36(31), Yahweh says that he will blow the fire

---

[37] See above, II.2.e.
[38] Ringgren, *SEÅ.*

of his wrath upon Israel; however, the text does not maintain this figure, but continues: "I will deliver you into the hands of brutal men, skilful to destroy; you shall be fuel for the fire." In Ezk. 22:21, the figure of fire is extended in a similar way: "and you shall be melted in the midst of it." Similarly, Ps. 21:10(9) combines the figure of the blazing oven with words like "swallow" and "consume." In Isa. 42:25, the statement about pouring out anger is followed by a reference to burning; here anger is also connected with the fury of war. Thus, this text is dealing not only with a "psychic" behavior of the deity, but with a concrete action; the same is true when "fierce anger" (heat of anger) appears as a synonym of destruction (Hos. 11:9) and perishing (Jonah 3:9). Jer. 25:38; 30:24; 49:37; Ps. 69:25(24); and Job 20:23 also use the term "fierce anger." In Ps. 78:49, "fierce anger, wrath, indignation, and distress" are said to be "a company of destroying angels." Here anger is on its way to becoming an independent power separated from the divine subject, and its presence is evident in concrete acts. [39]

Hostile nations are the weapons of Yahweh, the instruments of his anger, who carry out judgment against his people. The expression "weapon of anger" is used first of Assyria (Isa. 10:5), in connection with which cf. Isa. 13:3ff. This is already regular terminology in Jer. 50:25. "The rod of his wrath" in Lam. 3:1 is ambiguous: it could refer to Babylon, or it could be a comprehensive term for all the suffering that results from the anger of God.

In addition to the passages that speak only in a general way of destruction and ruin in connection with Yahweh's anger, there are statements describing the destruction in concrete terms. Ezk. 13:13 says that a deluge of rain will come because of the anger of God. Isa. 30:30 states that the arm of Yahweh will descend with a flame of devouring fire, a cloudburst, a tempest, and hailstones. Ezk. 38:22 describes how Yahweh will rain fire and brimstone in his anger. This passage is probably influenced by descriptions of the theophany. [40] On the other hand, Nu. 11:1 is a sober description of how fire breaks out and consumes the camp.

Another effect of Yahweh's anger is that the earth does not yield its fruit. Dt. 11:17 says that in his anger, God shuts up the heavens so that no rain falls, and the land does not yield its fruit. The same idea lies behind Ezk. 22:24, "You are a land that is not cleansed, or rained upon in the day of indignation."

Yahweh's anger can also be manifested against Israel by his not driving their enemies out of the land (Jgs. 2:20f.), or by his giving them into the hand of their enemies (2 K. 13:3).

4. *Positive Value of Divine Anger.* The OT does not consider divine anger to be merely a negative thing. It can also be an indication of the unlimited greatness and sovereignty of God. According to Job 9:4f., God's might and strength is manifested in that he removes and overturns mountains in his anger. Job 9:13 says that God can act in anger because in creation he was able to overcome the powers of chaos. In Job 37:2,5, and 40:9f., thunder is a manifestation of God's

---

[39] Ringgren, *Word and Wisdom* (Lund, 1947), 153.
[40] Ringgren, *Festschr. Weiser,* 108, 111f.

anger. In 40:9f., the goal of anger is the humiliation of the enemy, which is often the case in descriptions of the theophany. In order to destroy the enemy, God can deal with creation as a sovereign (Isa. 30:27,30).

The OT positively affirms that God is an *'el za'am*, "God of indignation," and a *ba'al chemah*, "lord of wrath" (Ps. 7:12[11]; Nah. 1:2). Nah. 1 has to do with punishing Israel's enemies, and Ps. 7 praises God as the one who helps the righteous maintain his right and who punishes the evildoer.

Naturally, the OT extols the idea of God turning away his anger from his own people. Here there is often a certain duality. Nah. 1:2 leaves the impression that it is good that Yahweh manifests his anger against his enemies, while v. 7 affirms that he is good to those who trust in him. Ps. 78:49f. describes the way in which God's anger is carried out against the Egyptians, but the same psalm praises God because he turns away his anger from his own people (v. 38: "Yet he, being compassionate, forgave their iniquity, and did not destroy them; he restrained his anger often, and did not stir up all his wrath").

Nevertheless, Yahweh's anger often comes upon his own people, sometimes with destructive consequences. God's anger is obviously a reaction to Israel's ingratitude and unfaithfulness. Israel was not faithful to the covenant, and therefore God, who wanted to manifest love to his people (Hos. 11:9), appears as an angry God. There are passages in the OT that indicate that this idea was well known and that the anger of God was expected when people did unrighteousness. E.g., Mic. 7:9 says, "I will bear the indignation of the Lord because I have sinned against him"; and Ezr. 8:22 states, "The power of his (God's) wrath is against all that forsake him."

Yahweh's anger against his people is mixed with a clearly expressed element of compassion. Yahweh is a compassionate and merciful God; therefore he is longsuffering (*'erekh 'appayim*) and does not become angry easily (Ps. 103:8; Ex. 34:6; Mic. 2:7). And when he does become angry, "he does not retain his anger for ever" (Jer. 3:5; Mic. 7:18). Paradoxically, it is even said, "in wrath remember mercy" (Hab. 3:2). The OT emphasizes that his anger ceases, and then he comforts (Isa. 12:1).

But a problem arises when anger seems completely to gain the upper hand. Ps. 77:10(9) raises the question, "Has God forgotten to be gracious? Has he in anger shut up his compassion?" And Ps. 85:6(5) asks, "Wilt thou be angry with us for ever? Wilt thou prolong thy anger to all generations?"

God's anger is also questioned in the OT when it is considered to be unjust, e.g., in Nu. 16:22: "Shall one man sin, and wilt thou be angry with all the congregation?" or Job 19:11: "He has kindled his wrath against me, and counts me as his adversary."

E. Johnson

אֶפֶס 'ps; אֶפֶס 'ephes

Contents: I. Occurrences in Extrabiblical Literature. II. Occurrences and Meaning in the OT. III. Theological Significance.

I. Occurrences in Extrabiblical Literature. The substantive *'ps*=(upper) "end" (of the throne) occurs once in Ugaritic,[1] once in Phoenician,[2] and six times quite late in the Hymns from Qumran (1QH 2:33; 3:30,36; 6:17; 12:10; fragm. 3,10) with the same meaning as this word has in the OT ("end, nothing"). It is not possible to determine the original meaning of the word etymologically, but possibly it is connected with Akk. *apsū* ("fresh water sea").[3] This is the ocean encircling the earth (which to some extent is personified mythically) as well as the uttermost depths of the earth.

II. Occurrences and Meaning in the OT. If there is a relationship between Heb. *'ephes* and Akk. *apsū*, the idea suggested by *apsū* is greatly limited in the OT and is no longer used independently, but only in the stereotyped formula *'aphse 'erets*, "the ends (limits) of the earth." It occurs 16 times (including Sir.) in hymnic-poetic texts, the antiquity of which is to some extent uncertain (Psalms, the Blessing of Joseph, Dt. 33:17!). Often, *qatseh*, *yarekhah*, and *kanaph* are used for "the ends of the earth." 1QH 6:17; 12:10 have the phrase *'en 'ephes*, "without end" (limit). *'ephes* is never used for "end" in the temporal sense, thus in Isa. 52:4 it should not be translated "in the end."[4]

The original meaning of the substantive, "limit, end," is also preserved in the use of *'ephes* as a restrictive particle "only" ("limited"): Nu. 22:35 (=v. 20, *'akh*); 23:13; similarly *'ephes ki*, "only (save) that," "however (howbeit)": Nu. 13:28; Dt. 15:4; Jgs. 4:9; Am. 9:8; 2 S. 12:14; 1 S. 1:5 (conjec.); cf. 1QH 2:33.

It is worthy of note that the root *'ps* appears as a verb in a fairly early text, Gen. 47:15f. If it is correctly pointed at all, it is certainly denominative and means "to be at the end"; the same is true in the spurious passages, Isa. 16:4; 29:20 (where *'aphes* is parallel to *karath*, "to be cut off," *tamam*, "to vanish," and *kalah*, "to cease"), and in Ps. 77:9 (Eng. v. 8) (where *'aphes* is parallel to *gamar*, "to be at an end").

No doubt only secondarily did *'ephes* develop from the meaning "end" to complete nonbeing, which is beautifully expressed in the late oracle, "Whatever

---

'ephes. W. Eichrodt, *Theol OT*, I (trans. 1965), 472-511; H. Gross, *Weltherrschaft als religiöse Idee im AT* (Bonn, 1953); M. H. Pope, *El in the Ugaritic Texts* (Leiden, 1955), 71f.

[1] *CTA*, 6 [I AB], I, 68.
[2] Karatepe, *KAI*, 26 A IV.1; the translation is disputed; cf. *DISO*, 22.
[3] Cf. Pope, 72.
[4] Contra F. Zorell, *Lexicon Hebraicum* (1966), 74; *ZDMG*, 70 (1916), 557.

is from nothing returns to nothing" (*kl m'ps 'l 'ps yšwb,* Sir. 41:10). The privative meaning, "nothing," appears in Isa. 34:12; 40:17; 41:12,29; 52:4, where *'ephes* stands in parallelism with *ruach,* "wind," *'en,* "there is not," and *tohu,* "emptiness." Thus, like *'en, 'ephes* serves as a particle of negation (Isa. 5:8; 54:15; Am. 6:10), or as a finite verb (Dt. 32:36; 2 S. 9:3; 2 K. 14:26). *be'ephes,* "without," occurs in Prov. 14:28; 26:20; Job 7:6; Dnl. 8:25. Deutero-Isaiah loves the formula, "(elsewhere) there is none" (Isa. 45:6,14; 46:9). The *chireq* in *ve'aphsi 'odh* in Isa. 47:8,10 and Zeph. 2:15 probably is not a suffix, but a *chireq compaginis,* [5] parallel to *ve'en 'odh* (Isa. 45:6,14,18,22).

III. Theological Significance. The passages in which *'ephes* means "nothing," where God appears directly or indirectly as the one acting, are of theological significance. God puts all opposing powers to an end. The statement that the princes of Edom shall be nothing (Isa. 34:12) belongs to the genre of the prophetic lawsuit. All nations are as nothing before God (40:17). Already well-established monotheism (which appears elsewhere in Deutero-Isaiah) enunciates the confession that besides Yahweh there is no other god.

Faith in the unlimited omnipotence of God goes back even farther. He rules over Jacob and to the ends of the earth (Ps. 59:14[13]); he judges the ends of the earth (1 S. 2:10), for as creator he has established them (Prov. 30:4). The nations come to Yahweh from the ends of the earth (Jer. 16:19); they shall fear him (Ps. 67:8[7]). Deutero-Isaiah's announcement of universal salvation, that all the ends of the earth will turn to Yahweh in order to be saved (Isa. 45:22; Ps. 22:28 [27]), in particular agrees with this. They see the salvation of our God (Isa. 52:10; Ps. 98:3), and come to know him (Sir. 36:17).

The Davidic king of the present and future participates in this omnipotence of God. He is great to the ends of the earth (Mic. 5:3[4]), and as the "son" of God's grace, he receives the ends of the earth for a possession (Ps. 2:8). He rules from sea to sea, and from the River to the ends of the earth (72:8; Zec. 9:10). This formula (which also occurs in Sir. 44:21) seems to have been used in Babylon. [6] Such a Utopian "court style" has a unique religious meaning in the OT, since the king, as God's representative, has the right and even the duty to bring about the complete dominion of God. The expectation of the Messiah in the End Time was nourished by these promises, until finally in the NT the message of the gospel goes out to the ends of the earth (Acts 1:8; 13:47).

Hamp

---

[5] *GK,* § 90 l.
[6] On the problem of terms used for "limit, boundary, end," cf. Gross, 11-18.

אֲרוֹן ’aron

Contents: I. 1. Etymology; 2. Meaning. II. Secular Use. III. Religio-Cultic Use: 1. External Description; 2. Parallels Outside the OT; 3. Origin and Antiquity; 4. Religious Significance; 5. Function; 6. History.

I. 1. *Etymology.* The noun *'aron* is a West Semitic word. Besides Biblical Hebrew (where it occurs about 200 times), Christian Palestinian, Syriac, and Arabic (which is derived from the Syriac), it appears in a group of West Semitic inscriptions, and in Late Babylonian as a loanword.[1] In spite of this widespread evidence, its etymology is unknown. The attempts of Meinhold and Morgenstern

'aron. W. R. Arnold, *Ephod and Ark* (Cambridge, 1917); A. Bentzen, "The Cultic Use of the Story of the Ark in Samuel," *JBL*, 67 (1948), 37-53; K.-H. Bernhardt, "Lade," *BHHW*, II, 1038-1041; H. A. Brongers, "Einige Aspekte der gegenwärtigen Lage der Lade-Forschung," *NedThT*, 25 (1971), 6-27; C. Brouwer, *De ark* (Baarn, 1955); M. Buber, *Kingship of God* (trans. 1967), 99ff., 186-88; K. Budde, "Die ursprüngliche Bedeutung der Lade Jahwe's," *ZAW*, 21 (1901), 193-97; *idem*, "War die Lade Jahwes ein leerer Thron?" *ThStKr*, 79 (1906), 489-507; *idem*, "Ephod und Lade," *ZAW*, 39 (1921), 1-42; W. Caspari, "Die Bundeslade unter David," *Festschrift Th. Zahn* (1908), 25-46; H. Cazelles, "Israël du nord et arche d'alliance (Jér. III 16)," *VT*, 18 (1968), 147-158; L. Couard, "Die religiös-nationale Bedeutung der Lade Jahves," *ZAW*, 12 (1892), 53-90; G. H. Davies, "The Ark in the Psalms," *Promise and Fulfilment. Essays Presented to S. H. Hooke* (Edinburgh, 1963), 51-61; *idem*, "The Ark of the Covenant," *ASTI*, 5 (1966/67), 30-47; M. Dibelius, *Die Lade Jahves* (1906); L. Dürr, "Ursprung und Bedeutung der Bundeslade," *BZTS*, 1 (1924), 17-32; J. Dus, "Der Brauch der Ladewanderung im alten Israel," *ThZ*, 17 (1961), 1-16; *idem*, "Noch zum Brauch der 'Ladewanderung'," *VT*, 13 (1963), 126-132, 475; *idem*, "Der Beitrag des benjaminitischen Heidentums zur Religion Israels. Zur ältesten Geschichte der heiligen Lade," *ComViat*, 6 (1963), 61-80; *idem*, "Die Länge der Gefangenschaft der Lade im Philisterland," *NedThT*, 18 (1963/64), 440-452; *idem*, "Die Thron- und Bundeslade," *ThZ*, 20 (1964), 241-251; *idem*, "The Dreros Bilingual and the Tabernacle of the Ancient Israelites," *JSS*, 10 (1965), 55-57; *idem*, "Herabfahrung Jahwes auf die Lade und Entziehung der Feuerwolke," *VT*, 19 (1969), 290-311; W. Eichrodt, *Theol OT*, I, 107-115; O. Eissfeldt, "Lade und Stierbild," *ZAW*, 58 (1940/41), 190-215=*KlSchr*, II, 282-305; *idem*, "Jahweh Zebaoth," *Miscellanea Academica Berolinensia*, II, 2 (1950), 128-150, Abb. 1-4=*KlSchr*, III, 103-123, Taf. V 1-4; *idem*, "Silo und Jerusalem," *SVT*, 4 (1957), 138-147=*KlSchr*, III, 417-425; *idem*, "Lade und Gesetzestafeln," *ThZ*, 16 (1960), 281-84=*KlSchr*, III, 526-29; *idem*, "Die Lade Jahwes in Geschichtserzählung, Sage und Lied," *Altertum*, 14 (1968), 131-145; G. Fohrer, *History of Israelite Religion* (trans. 1972), 106-111; T. E. Fretheim, *The Cultic Use of the Ark of the Covenant in the Monarchical Period* (diss., Princeton, 1967), cf. *DissAbs*, 28 (1967/68), 325 A; *idem*, "The Ark in Deuteronomy," *CBQ*, 30 (1968), 1-14; K. Galling, "Kultgerät. 4. Lade," *BRL*, 343f.; M. Görg, *Das Zelt der Begegnung. BBB*, 27 (1967); H. Gressmann, *"Die Lade Jahves und das Allerheiligste des salomonischen Tempels* (1920); H. Gunkel, "Die Lade Jahves ein Thronsitz," *ZMR*, 21 (1906), 33-42; M. Haran, "The Ark and the Cherubim," *Eretz Israel*, 5 (1958), 83-90 (Heb.)=*IEJ*, 9 (1959), 30-38, 89-94 (Eng.); *idem*, "'oṭfe, maḥmal and ḳubbe. Notes on the Study of the Origin of Biblical Cult Forms: The Problem of Arabic Parallels," *D. Neiger Memorial Volume* (1959), 215-221; *idem*, "The Disappearance of the Ark," *IEJ*,

[1] *KBL³*.

(continued on p. 364)

to postulate an original meaning "box (throne)" or "object similar to a tent," on the basis of alleged archeological parallels, are not convincing, because the texts with one accord speak against these explanations.

2. *Meaning*. In its linguistic usage both in and out of the OT, *'aron* denotes objects used in everyday human life, but in the majority of occurrences in the OT it has to do with an Israelite cult object. Thus, it seems best to begin by attempting to determine the meaning of our word in secular use.

13 (1963), 46-58; R. Hartmann, "Zelt und Lade," *ZAW*, 37 (1917/18), 209-244; J. Herrmann, "ἱλαστήριον, 1," *TDNT*, III, 318f.; D. R. Hillers, "Ritual Procession of the Ark and Psalm 132," *CBQ*, 30 (1968), 48-55; W. H. Irwin, "Le sanctuaire central israélite avant l'établissement de la monarchie," *RB*, 72 (1965), 161-184; E. Klamroth, *Lade und Tempel* (n.d. [1932?]); K. Koch, *Die Priesterschrift von Exodus 25 bis Leviticus 16. FRLANT*, 71 (1959); H.-J. Kraus, *Worship in Israel* (trans. 1966), 125-28; W. B. Kristensen, *De ark van Jahwe* (1933); E. Kutsch, "Lade Jahwes," *RGG*³, IV, 197-99; W. Lotz, "Die Bundeslade," *Festschrift der Universität Erlangen*, I (1901), 143-186; H. Lubsczyk, "Die katechetische Verwertung der Überlieferungen von der Bundeslade," *BiLe*, 2 (1961), 206-223; W. McKane, "The Earlier History of the Ark," *TGUOS*, 21 (1965/66), 68-76; J. Maier, *Vom Kultus zur Gnosis. Studien zur Vor- und Frühgeschichte der "jüdischen Gnosis". Bundeslade, Gottesthron und Märkābāh* (Salzburg, 1964); *idem, Das altisraelitische Ladeheiligtum. BZAW*, 93 (1965); H. G. May, "The Ark–a Miniature Temple," *AJSL*, 52 (1935/36), 215-234; J. Meinhold, *Die Lade Jahves* (1900); *idem,* "Die Lade Jahves. Ein Nachtrag," *ThStKr*, 74 (1901), 593-617; J. Morgenstern, "The Ark, the Ephod and the 'Tent of Meeting'," *HUCA*, 17 (1942/43), 153-266; 18 (1943/44), 1-52; E. Nielsen, "Some Reflections on the History of the Ark," *SVT*, 7 (1960), 61-74; M. Noth, *Das System der zwölf Stämme Israels* (1930, ²1966); *idem,* "Jerusalem und die israelitische Tradition," *OTS*, 8 (1950), 28-46 = *ThB*, 6, 172-187; Pedersen, *ILC*, III-IV, 229-234; G. von Rad, "Zelt und Lade," *NKZ*, 42 (1931), 478-498 = *ThB*, 8 (²1961), 109-129; *idem, OT Theol*, I (trans. 1962), 17-21, 237-39; L. Randellini, "La tenda e l'arca nella tradizione del VT," *Studii Bibl. Franciscani*, L.A. 13 (1962/63), 163-189; W. Reichel, *Über die vorhellenischen Götterkulte* (1897); W. Reimpell, "Der Ursprung der Lade Jahwes," *OLZ*, 19 (1916), 326-331; L. Rost, *Die Überlieferung von der Thronnachfolge Davids. BWANT*, 3/6 (1926), 4-47 = *Kleine Credo* (1965), 122-159; *idem,* "Königsherrschaft Jahwes in vorköniglicher Zeit?" *ThLZ*, 85 (1960), 721-24; S. Saba, *L'arca dell'alleanza: Storia, descrizione, significato* (Rome, 1948); H. Schmidt, "Kerubenthron und Lade," *Eucharisterion für H. Gunkel*, I (1923), 120-144; W. H. Schmidt, *Alttestamentlicher Glaube und seine Umwelt* (1968), 105-108; J. Schreiner, *Sion-Jerusalem* (1963), 22-56; Waltraud Seeber, *Der Weg der Tradition von der Lade Jahwes im AT* (diss., Kiel, 1956); cf. *ThLZ*, 83 (1958), 722f.; T. P. Sevensma, *De ark Gods het oud-israëlitische heiligdom* (Amsterdam, 1908); F. Seyring, "Der alttestamentliche Sprachgebrauch inbetreff des Namens der sogen. 'Bundeslade'," *ZAW*, 11 (1891), 114-125; R. Smend, *Yahweh War and Tribal Confederation* (trans. 1970), 76-97; J. A. Soggin, "Zwei umstrittene Stellen aus dem Überlieferungskreis um Schechem," *ZAW*, 73 (1961), 78-87, esp. 78-82; *idem,* "Der offiziell geförderte Synkretismus in Israel während des 10. Jahrhunderts," *ZAW*, 78 (1966), 179-204, esp. 182-88; H. Timm, "Die Ladeerzählung (1. Sam 4-6; 2. Sam 6) und das Kerygma des deuteronomistischen Geschichtswerks," *EvTh*, 26 (1966), 509-526; H. Torczyner, *Bundeslade und Anfänge der Religion Israels* (²1930); *idem* (N. H. Tur-Sinai), "The Ark of God at Beit Shemesh (1 Sam VI) and Pereṣ 'Uzza (2 Sam VI; 1 Chron XIII)," *VT*, 1 (1951), 275-286; de Vaux, *AncIsr*, 297-302; *idem,* "Les chérubins et l'arche d'alliance, les sphinx gardiens et les trônes divins dans l'Ancien Orient," *MUSJ*, 37 (1960/61), 91-124 = *Bible et Orient* (Paris, 1967), 231-259; *idem,* "Arche d'alliance et Tente de réunion," *À la rencontre de Dieu. Mém. A. Gelin* (Le Puy, 1961), 55-70 = *Bible et Orient* (Paris, 1967), 261-276; A. Weiser, "Die Tempelbaukrise unter David," *ZAW*, 77 (1965), 153-168, esp. 163-65; T. Worden, "The Ark of the Covenant," *Scripture*, 5 (1952), 82-90; M. H. Woudstra, *The Ark of the Covenant from Conquest to Kingship* (Philadelphia, 1965).

II. Secular Use. In the OT the coffin of Joseph (Gen. 50:26), and the chest furnished by the priest Jehoiada, set up at the entrance of the Jerusalem temple and appointed as the receptacle for the money that was brought (2 K. 12:10,11 [Eng. vv. 9,10]; 2 Ch. 24:8,10,11), are called 'aron. In texts outside the OT, this word is used for a "box," "ossuary," "sarcophagus." [2] It is clear from this that 'aron means a container, chest, ark, etc.

III. Religio-Cultic Use.

1. *External Description.* This meaning obtained from the secular sphere also holds true for the religio-cultic use of the word. For the only description of the cult object called 'aron preserved for us in the OT (Ex. 25:10-22; 37:1-9; cf. Dt. 10:1,3) speaks of an ark of acacia wood, made at the command of Yahweh at Sinai, $2^1/_2$ cubits long, $1^1/_2$ cubits wide, and $1^1/_2$ cubits high, overlaid inside and out with gold. Attached to this ark were rings for poles, which were not supposed to be removed. The testimony (→ עֵדוּת 'ēdhûth) was placed in this ark; the *kapporeth,* which was $2^1/_2$ cubits long and $1^1/_2$ cubits wide and was made out of gold, and which was adorned with a cherub on each end, but in a technical sense perhaps is to be understood as a "cover plate" rather than a "means or place of atonement," [3] was placed on top of the ark; and the entire structure was put in the "Tent of Meeting" (→ אֹהֶל 'ōhel mo'edh).

a. This description comes from P, who has taken over various ancient traditions and has combined them with his own theological ideas. As far as the external form is concerned, the cover plate of the ark is an invention of P. *kapporeth* appears only in P, and one gets the impression that the plate is an object to be distinguished from the ark itself, which indicates that originally it was not connected with the ark, but was later connected with the essential cultic function of the ark. [4] With regard to the ornamentation of the *kapporeth,* P borrows from the pattern of the Solomonic temple insofar as the two cherubim which are connected with the temple (1 K. 8:6f.) also appear in his description of the ark. Of course, the cherubim in P are greatly reduced in size, are made from pure gold, and are inseparably connected with the *kapporeth.*

b. It is clear that P has a preference for expensive objects in the sanctuary, and therefore he must have been responsible for the idea that the ark was richly ornamented with gold, although this is not to be taken to mean that originally the ark was not adorned at all. For the view of P, that the gold ornamentation of the ark was made out of pieces of jewelry donated by the Israelites (Ex. 25:1-7; 35:21-29), is in harmony with Ex. 33:3-6 (JE). Twice this passage speaks of the Israelites giving jewelry, and it is correct to infer that this was used in making the ark. Since it is clear here again that P is dependent on earlier traditions (in this

---

[2] *DISO,* 25; *KAI,* 1.1; 11.21; 29.1; etc.
[3] Herrmann, 320; von Rad, "Zelt," 110; Weiser, 310.
[4] Herrmann, 319; de Vaux, *AncIsr,* 300f.; Weiser, 310; cf. H. Schmidt, 137-144.

case, J and E), one is certainly justified in generalizing and in thinking that the external form of the ark is from earlier traditions. Several scholars correctly assume that P, both in the general outline of his work and in various individual sections (including the narrative on the making of the ark), followed the pattern of R^JE, but replaced it with his own description, [5] and perhaps even connected rituals from Israel's monarchical period with it. [6] It follows from this that we should consider the description given by P of the main features of the ark, as a transportable wooden box adorned with precious metal, to be authentic. [7]

c. In a similar way, because of the inferior material, one will also have to deal with the very difficult question of the connection between the ark and the tent. As we have seen, in P they are connected with each other and are said to originate at Sinai. But Deuteronomy speaks only of the ark, and says nothing about the tent (9:7–10:5). However, like P the historical reminiscenses of Deuteronomy are dependent on R^JE. Thus, one could reason this way: originally there was a tension between the ark and the tent, which is reflected in the tent's not being mentioned in Deuteronomy; they were connected for the first time by P, who made the tent the dwelling place of the ark in conjunction with the pattern of the Solomonic temple projected back into the wilderness period. [8]

But this is not altogether convincing, because the uniqueness and purpose of Deuteronomy do not sufficiently explain why it does not mention the tent. Von Rad's argument [9] carries more weight. He thinks that the concept of God's dwelling place or throne was attached to the ark, while the idea of mo'edh, "meeting (God)," was connected with the tent. Thus the ark emphasized the immanence, and the tent the transcendence, of God who continually revealed himself in Israel's history. This penetrating emphasis on these two ideas is useful in gaining a deeper understanding of the function of these two cult objects. It is doubtful, however, whether we should place such a logical idea of God or such a self-contradictory reality of God [10] at the beginning of the history of the religion of Israel, i.e., whether we should assume that originally there was a connection between the ark and the tent.

2 S. 7:6, where Yahweh says that he had not dwelt in a permanent house from the exodus to the days of David, but in a tent, suggests that the ark and the tent were originally connected. It also supports the validity of the frequently suspected passage, 1 S. 2:22, which states that the women served at the entrance to the tent, thus indicating that in the Shiloh temple, ark and tent were combined. [11] We cannot really exclude altogether the possibility that at one time the lo of

---

[5] Davies, "Covenant"; Dibelius, 112; Eichrodt, 109f.; Eissfeldt, KlSchr, II, 283f., etc.; Schreiner, 24; for a different view Fohrer, 109; Kutsch, 198.

[6] Koch, 97.

[7] So, among others, Budde, "Ephod," 33f.; Couard, 81; Kraus, 125f.; H. Schmidt, 144; W. H. Schmidt, 108.

[8] Kraus, 125f.; cf. de Vaux, AncIsr, 297.

[9] Von Rad, "Zelt."

[10] Eichrodt, 111.

[11] Eissfeldt, "Lade Jahwes," 134f.; cf. Woudstra.

Ex. 33:7 (E) referred to *'aron,* which is especially construed as a masculine. If so, the E account contained the statement that Moses took the tent and pitched it for the ark (*lo*) outside the camp. [12] Therefore, P follows the earlier Pentateuchal tradition in connecting the ark with the tent. However, due to his high regard for Sinai, he has the tent built there for the first time, whereas in E the tent was already in existence before Sinai. [13] When everything is taken into consideration, it is most likely that from the very first the ark of Yahweh was housed in the → אהל *'ōhel mo'edh,* which therefore is called the tent of meeting or revelation. [14]

2. *Parallels Outside the OT.* In order to shed light on the origin, age, meaning, and function of the Israelite ark of Yahweh, in the past scholars have compared it with a number of cult objects from both nomadic and settled cultural areas.

a. *'utfa, mahmal,* and *qubba* originated among the Bedouins. The *'utfa,* which is also called *markab* because it can be transported from place to place, is a richly ornamented wooden trellis-work which is carried on a camel. It chooses the way and the camp site each night, gives oracles, and leads in battle. The *mahmal* is quite similar to the *'utfa.* It is a tentlike structure also carried on a camel, which is usually empty, but is sometimes furnished with a small wooden box containing a copy of the Koran, and resembles the *'utfa* in meaning and function. To a certain extent, the same thing is also true of the *qubba,* a holy tent tied on the back of a camel, which seeks new pastures, gives oracles, and is present at decisive battles. It contains two holy stones as representations of the clan or tribal deities. [15] As Morgenstern has established, [16] the *'utfa* and *mahmal* are semi-Islamic forms of the ancient *qubba,* so that in the final analysis we are dealing with only one cult object.

The question of the similarity between this object and the Israelite ark has been answered in different ways by outstanding scholars. Hartmann reached the conclusion that possibly the tent corresponds to the *qubba,* but not the ark; therefore, the tent and the ark are two fundamentally different things, because they are objects that originated in two separate milieux, viz., a nomadic society and a settled, civilized society. On the other hand, Morgenstern, like Torczyner before him, [17] sees in the *qubba* a striking religio-historical parallel to the Israelite ark, although he is not able to explain why the ark is called *'aron,* "box," and not perhaps a "tent" or something similar. These views sufficiently illustrate the difficulties that stand in the way of a direct identification of the two objects. There are certainly similarities between the *qubba* and the ark as far as mobility and several functions are concerned. But the ark differs so greatly from the

---

[12] So also de Vaux, *AncIsr,* 302.
[13] Eissfeldt, "Lade Jahwes," 131f. Dus, "Dreros," thinks this is unlikely.
[14] So still Irwin, 164; de Vaux, "Arche"; *AncIsr,* 302; cf. Buber, 102 and n. 8.
[15] Hartmann, Morgenstern.
[16] Morgenstern, *HUCA,* 17, 223.
[17] Torczyner, 47-51; more recently, Irwin, 164.

qubba in form and shape that we cannot regard the two as genuinely comparable. [18]

b. Reimpell conjectures that in the framework of thought that existed in the civilized land of Canaan, the ark is to be explained as the "stage of Yahweh," and is to be compared with the holy stages in Petra and among the Hittites; but this view has rightly found no advocates. Gressmann refers to Egyptian shrines for deities and procession barques, and postulates that in form the ark was a double chest containing the images of two deities, viz., the bull and Astarte; but this view also rightly has been rejected. [19]

Finally, referring to pre-Hellenistic divine thrones, Reichel wanted to understand the Israelite ark as an empty throne, thus originating in the civilized land of Canaan; and this view has had several followers. [20] Certainly we encounter the idea of Yahweh's throne in connection with the ark while it was in Shiloh and Jerusalem, and therefore the ark could be understood as a throne of God, similar to thrones of deities which have been demonstrated in other earlier ancient Near Eastern religions. But again, against this is the fact that the ark is not called a "throne," but an *ʼaron,* a designation which was never abandoned. [21] Thus, this comparison is also useful only to a limited extent. [22]

3. *Origin and Antiquity.* Now as we turn to the question of the origin and antiquity of the ark, which some scholars trace back to Israel's nomadic period and others to the period after Israel's settlement in Canaan, initially we will examine the arguments that seem to oppose the OT tradition and favor the view that the ark did not exist among the Israelites until they came into Canaan. The first argument is based on the evaluation of the tradition of the ark in 2 S. 6. Beginning with Dibelius, [23] the historicity of this chapter came to be suspected, because comparable Pentateuchal narratives are sagas and, like the narratives in Josh. 3–6, are unhistorical. The beginning of the Ark Narrative, to use Rost's terminology, [24] contains "more stories than history." Secondly, 2 S. 6:2 reveals "a sort of renaming" of the ark from an original "ark of God" to "the ark of Yahweh Sebaoth who sits enthroned on the cherubim." [25] The third argument is included in the second, viz., that Israel could not have known of the idea of Yahweh's throne until they settled in Canaan. [26] The conclusion that originally the ark was a Canaanite sanctuary which the Israelites adopted and appropriated to Yahweh seems to be inevitable. [27]

---

18 Recently W. H. Schmidt, 105.
19 Von Rad, *ThB,* 118f.; W. H. Schmidt, 105.
20 Dibelius, Dus, Gunkel, Meinhold, Nielsen, etc.
21 Budde, "Bedeutung der Lade"; Davies, "Covenant"; von Rad, *ThB,* 118.
22 Kutsch, 198.
23 Dibelius, 112ff.
24 Rost, *Kleine Credo,* 122-159.
25 Dibelius, 116; Fohrer, 110f.; von Rad, *ThB,* 120f.
26 Dibelius, 117f.
27 So also Kutsch, 198; Maier, *Ladeheiligtum;* von Rad, *ThB,* 120-29; similarly Fohrer, 110. Gressmann and Arnold incorrectly conclude from the text of 1 S. 14:18, emended according to the LXX, that there were several Canaanite arks.

The view that the supposed narratives of the making of the ark are sagas like the passages corresponding to them in Josh. 3–6 is no longer uncontested today.[28] But even if this were true, by no means does it necessarily follow that they are unhistorical.[29] The so-called Ark Sayings (Nu. 10:35f.), although connected with the ark only by the framework, can hardly be separated from it,[30] for their content assumes the situation of the wilderness wandering found in the context of Nu. 10 as well as the connection of the ark with war indicated in Nu. 14:40-45 (J).[31] And Smend's idea that the name Israel could hardly have been in use during the wilderness period[32] is not convincing, because nothing certain has been deduced about the origin of this name. And as far as the narratives pertaining to the ark in Joshua are concerned, the recollection of the ark's participation in the initial entrance into Canaan is clearly an essential part of the whole.[33] Finally, the argument that the ark was renamed is not convincing. For one thing, the juxtaposition of "the ark of Elohim" (20 times) and "the ark of Yahweh" (26 times) in 1-2 Samuel is to be interpreted just like the juxtaposition of Yahweh and Elohim in the Pentateuch and in the Psalms, i.e., these expressions are to be assigned to different strata of tradition.[34] For another thing, the statement in 2 S. 6:2 can be understood just as well, or perhaps even better, as a legitimation of the new title which Yahweh received as God of the ark and which now reads, "Yahweh Sebaoth who sits enthroned on the cherubim."[35]

We are indebted to Noth for this last decisive argument. "For only a cult object with a tradition which had already been established and was unique could procure for the non-Israelite Jerusalem that cultic role which soon the supporters of the kingship would no longer need." Not only does this "confirm the statements concerning the ark in the pre-monarchical period," but it also confutes conjectures that Israel borrowed the ark from the Canaanites.[36]

The conclusion that the ark originated in the wilderness period and was built by the Israelites at Sinai[37] finds a welcome confirmation in Jgs. 20:27f.[38] That the note about the sojourn of the ark in Bethel and the genealogy of the ark priests from the time of Moses to the middle of the period of the judges are secondary literary pieces proves nothing about their historical value. Jgs. 2:1, with its statement that the messenger of Yahweh went up from Gilgal to Bochim (which is located near Bethel, according to Gen. 35:8), confirms that the ark was

---

[28] Seeber.

[29] Eissfeldt, *KlSchr,* II, 283ff., also on the following.

[30] Noth, *Numbers. OTL* (trans. 1968), 79; Rost, "Königsherrschaft," 724.

[31] Eichrodt, 108f.; Seeber.

[32] Smend, 79.

[33] De Vaux, *AncIsr,* 298.

[34] Budde, "Ephod," 13; Lubsczyk; cf. Couard and Seyring.

[35] Schreiner, 41; de Vaux, "Chérubins," 259.

[36] *ThB,* 6, 184; similarly earlier Caspari.

[37] Couard, 75; Buber, 77f.; Davies, "Covenant"; Dus, "Beitrag"; Irwin, 164; Kraus, 125ff.; W. H. Schmidt, 105; Torczyner, 21f.

[38] Eissfeldt, *KlSchr,* II, 289f.; Lotz, 5; de Vaux, *AncIsr,* 298.

stationed at Bethel. [39] And the internal probability that this was the case is evident in that a later generation would never have connected the ark with Bethel because Bethel was hated for its idolatry. Furthermore, the ark priest at that time was Phinehas, the grandson of Aaron, who was probably the father of Eli, who had a son also called Phinehas. Since this agrees best with the course of history, the Egyptian name Phinehas agrees with the origin of the Elides given in 1 S. 2:27f., [40] and further supports the probability of the pre-Canaanite origin of the ark.

4. *Religious Significance.* These observations have already led us to a certain a priori judgment concerning the religious significance of the ark, viz., that originally it could hardly have been an empty throne seat of Yahweh.

a. In P, it is always called *'aron ha'edhuth,* "the ark of the testimony" (Ex. 25:22; 26:33f.), because it contains the two tablets of the law as it is designated by P. The idea in Deuteronomy is similar. As the box containing a copy of the Decalog, it is called in Deuteronomy and in the traditions influenced by it *'aron berith yhvh,* "the ark of the covenant of Yahweh," or something similar (Nu. 10:33; Dt. 10:8; etc.). As Eissfeldt has shown, [41] Deuteronomy has taken over from RJE "the interpretation of the tablets from Ex. 34 as a substitute for the view in 24:12-14,18b; 31:18b; 32"; but the interpretation of the ark as a container for the tablets is his own work, for in the passages cited from J and E the ark has nothing to do with the tablets, but functions as a symbol of divine leadership to the Israelites departing from Sinai/Horeb. It also has this meaning in other passages. Nu. 10:33 (J) describes its task as that of going out before the army and finding a resting place for it. The Ark Sayings cited in this context (vv. 35f.): "Arise, O Yahweh, and let thy enemies be scattered; and let them that hate thee flee before thee," and "Return, O Yahweh, to the ten thousand thousands of Israel," also assume the situation of breaking camp and resting. In addition, with its use of military terminology the first saying makes it clear that the ark was considered to be a symbol of military leadership. It has the same function in Nu. 14:40-45 (J), where the defeat of the Israelites is attributed to their not taking the ark with them into battle, as well as in the narratives of the crossing of the Jordan (Josh. 3:1–4:1) and of the conquest of Jericho (6:1-27). The ark plays the same role in 1 S. 4 and 2 S. 11:11; but the statement that the Israelites did not take the ark into the battle against the Philistines until they had been severely defeated (1 S. 4:1-4), and the fact that it was not used in every battle, indicates that the ark was not merely and exclusively a war palladium. [42]

b. These traditio-historical considerations raise the question: "What is the historical reality lying behind the biblical traditions?" With its new understanding

---

[39] Most recently Eissfeldt, *KlSchr,* II, 283, n. 2, and 286, with reference to Wellhausen and Smend.

[40] Fohrer, 152.

[41] Eissfeldt, *KlSchr,* III, 526-29.

[42] Couard, 79.

of the role of the ark, Deuteronomy has diminished its significance,[43] which indirectly favors the credibility of the view of the ark reflected in the ancient tradition. The ark was an important symbol of leadership in time of both war and peace. [44]

Beyond this, it seems conceivable that when Deuteronomy speaks of putting the tablets into the ark, it is not inventing something completely new, but is following an earlier tradition, elsewhere unknown to us, that there was something in the ark. This conjecture may be supported by the fact that the name for the ark is ʾaron, which means a box or a container, [45] even if all the attempts to determine the contents of the ark more precisely (a divine image, [46] a covenant treasure, [47] covenant documents, [48] slingstones or meteorites, [49] or [what is most nearly conceivable] holy stones from Sinai [50]) must remain purely hypothetical. [51]

c. Besides this meaning of the ark, the above-mentioned designation of the ark of God as the ark "of Yahweh Sebaoth, who is enthroned on the cherubim" (1 S. 4:4; 2 S. 6:2; similarly 2 K. 19:15 = Isa. 37:16), in connection with passages like Jer. 3:16f. (the ark shall no longer be remembered, but Jerusalem will be called "the throne of Yahweh") and Isa. 66:1; Ps. 99:5; 132:7; Lam. 2:1, which speak of Yahweh's "footstool," perhaps referring to the temple and thus to the ark, and also Nu. 10:35f., have led to the thesis that the ark was understood either exclusively or additionally as the throne of Yahweh. [52] But the Ark Sayings in Nu. 10:35f. cannot be interpreted in this way, [53] and the other passages prove only that there was an idea of a throne of Yahweh in Jerusalem, but not that the ark was such a throne. [54] There are several difficulties with this interpretation. The Hebrew expression does not mean that Yahweh is enthroned "between," [55] but "upon, over" the cherubim, a statement that (as von Rad has correctly ascertained [56]) "can by no means be connected" with the cherubim of the Solomonic temple: they cover the ark, but do not function as figures supporting a throne. It follows that the Jerusalem ark was not a throne of God, but that Yahweh was worshipped there as the one enthroned on the cherubim. In connection with the above-mentioned passages from Samuel and Ps. 24:7-10,

---

43 Fretheim.

44 Smend, 76ff.; cf. McKane; W. H. Schmidt, 105; Seeber; Soggin, "Stellen," 80ff. Symbol of an anti-Philistine league: Maier, Ladeheiligtum; Fohrer, 110.

45 Von Rad, ThB, 118.

46 Gressmann; Sevensma.

47 Maier, Ladeheiligtum.

48 Irwin; Randellini; Torczyner, 31-38; de Vaux, AncIsr, 301; Woudstra.

49 Couard, 75.

50 Most recently Morgenstern, HUCA, 17, 154-57; Eissfeldt, "Lade Jahwes," 132.

51 Fohrer, 110; W. H. Schmidt, 108; Schreiner, 24.

52 Among others Dus; Eichrodt; Nielsen; von Rad, ThB; Randellini; de Vaux, "Chérubins"; AncIsr; Weiser.

53 Among others Buber, 187f.; Rost, "Königsherrschaft," 724.

54 Cf. Haran, "Ark."

55 Gressmann; but contrast Torczyner.

56 Von Rad, ThB, 114.

which was probably composed for the transporting of the ark to Jerusalem, [57] this leads to the conclusion that the cult name "Yahweh Sebaoth" was associated with the ark and had been connected with it before the ark was brought to Jerusalem. This favors the credibility of our tradition tracing this title back to the ark of God in Shiloh. [58] Thus it supports the conjecture that we are dealing here with a divine epithet which Israel took over from the Canaanites, and which could also indicate the military power of the ark of God (1 S. 17:45). [59] Finally, since it may be supposed that there was an object corresponding to the new title, i.e., a Canaanite cherub throne, the connection between the two will perhaps have to be explained in terms of the ark standing under or in front of the throne (as a footstool?). [60]

5. *Function.* The pertinent texts reflect a broken picture of the function of the ark. Side by side with an apparent identification of Yahweh and the ark we encounter a clear-cut distinction between the two. [61] In the so-called Ark Narrative and in 2 S. 7:6, the same direct connection of Yahweh with the ark is assumed that we find in the references to the ark in J and in the narratives in Joshua. Throughout these passages, the ark embodies the valid presence of Yahweh, [62] and thus is able to help someone perform marvelous powerful deeds and to serve as a place of revelation. The picture is different in E. In order to punish the Israelites for their transgression, God refuses to accompany them. As an imperfect substitute for his presence, he has the ark brought; and when God reveals himself, he does so by descending in a pillar of cloud on the tent containing the ark.

This shifting and emptying of the ark's function, which can be discerned by comparing J and E, can also be observed in 1 K. 8, where "one can hardly find any trace of tension between the divine presence and the ark," [63] and it continues through D and on into P. [64]

It cannot be determined with certainty whether the ark made any contribution to the fusion of Israel's election traditions after it was transferred to Jerusalem. [65]

6. *History.* The observations made above concerning the origin, antiquity, meaning, and function of the ark in the early history of Israel make it clear that the ark was the sanctuary of the house of Joseph, [66] and perhaps only of that portion of the house of Joseph which is called Benjamin. [67] This is indicated in

---

[57] Eissfeldt, most recently "Lade Jahwes," 144.

[58] Eissfeldt, *KlSchr*, III, 113-121; most recently "Lade Jahwes," 135ff.; W. H. Schmidt, 107.

[59] Smend, 59-62.

[60] Cf. H. Schmidt, 144; Seeber.

[61] Seeber; Woudstra has a different view.

[62] Eissfeldt, *KlSchr*, III, 526f., also for the following.

[63] Seeber, *ThLZ*, 723.

[64] Fretheim, *CBQ*, 30; von Rad, *ThB*, 110ff., etc.

[65] Lubsczyk.

[66] Dibelius, 119f., with reference to Stade; most recently Eissfeldt, "Lade Jahwes," 134; W. H. Schmidt, 106.

[67] Dus, "Beitrag"; Nielsen.

that after the ark was made at Sinai, and after the period of the wilderness wandering and the crossing of the Jordan, the places where the ark was kept were located in the tribal territory of Benjamin. At first it was taken to Gilgal near Jericho (Josh. 4:19; cf. 9:6; 10:6). Its transfer from there to or near Bethel (Jgs. 2:1; cf. 20:26ff.) may be connected with the further expansion of the Benjaminite territory, but it can also have been a result of pressure applied by the Moabites when they extended their power even beyond Jericho (Jgs. 3:11-30).

As the period of the judges continued, the ark was brought to the Shiloh temple, which was the first real high point in its history (1 S. 1-3). Since Shiloh was in the territory of Ephraim, its transfer there must surely be traced back to a dispute between Ephraim and Benjamin as to which of these two tribes had the preeminence in the house of Joseph, which is reflected in Jgs. 19–21. We may suppose that Benjamin lost the struggle and the ark to Ephraim.

It is unlikely that the ark had formerly been kept at Shechem (Josh. 8:30-35: a Deuteronomistic revision) and since that time had enjoyed the rank of a central sanctuary, [68] or that the Israelites had a custom of carrying the ark in procession following a regular itinerary. [69]

As a result of the defeat of the Israelites, the ark fell into the hands of the Philistines, who had little delight in it because they experienced the manifestations of Yahweh's power which emanated from the ark, [70] and after seven months [71] they sent it back again into the Israelite territory where it had been before, but which was under their control (1 S. 4:1–7:2). [72] David found it there (Ps. 132:1-9) [73] and transferred it to his new capital (2 S. 6) after he decisively defeated the Philistines and circumscribed their territory (5:17-25). This gave Jerusalem not only a political significance, but also the dignity of a cultic-religious metropolis. [74] Here the ark experienced its second period of glory, which reached its high point and climax when it was brought into the temple of Solomon (1 K. 8).

We are no longer able to determine with certainty whether the ark served as a procession sanctuary during this period and the period that followed, and whether it played a conspicuous role in certain festivals, e.g., the Feast of Tabernacles, [75] or in the great Day of Atonement, [76] even if the meaning of the ark for times of peace suggested above seems to favor these possibilities.

Nothing is known about the later fate and end of the ark. It is possible that it fell into the hands of Pharaoh Shishak (1 K. 14:26). [77] But it could also have

---

[68] Noth, *System*, 95f., 116ff.; Kraus, 127; Schreiner, 25f. To the contrary, Smend and most recently Irwin.

[69] Dus, "Ladewanderung."

[70] Schreiner, 45; Timm.

[71] Dus, "Länge," differs.

[72] Caspari, 7-12; Eissfeldt, *KlSchr*, III, 420; Schreiner, 33.

[73] Cf. Davies, "Psalms."

[74] Eissfeldt, *KlSchr*, III, 417-423; Noth, "Jerusalem."

[75] Fretheim, *Cultic Use;* Seeber; cf. Bentzen and Nielsen.

[76] Eissfeldt, "Lade Jahwes," 141.

[77] Couard, 83.

fallen victim to the reform of Hezekiah (2 K. 18:5), or have been removed to give room for the image of the Asherah which Manasseh set up in the temple (21:7). [78] But by no means did it survive the destruction of Jerusalem in 597 or 587 B.C. [79] After that it was never restored.

Zobel

---

[78] Haran, "Disappearance."

[79] Lotz, 2f.; Dibelius, 126; W. H. Schmidt, 106; de Vaux, *AncIsr*, 299. The different possibilities are given in Eissfeldt, "Lade Jahwes," 139.

אֲרִי 'ºrî; אַרְיֵה 'aryēh; גוּר gûr;

כְּפִיר kephîr; לָבִיא lābhî';

לַיִשׁ layish; שַׁחַל shachal

Contents: I. Words for Lion in the OT, Related Expressions, Occurrences: 1. 'ari; 2. 'aryeh; 3. gur; 4. kephir; 5. labhi' and Derivatives; 6. layish; 7. shachal. II. In the Ancient Near East: 1. Egypt; 2. Mesopotamia; 3. Ancient Syria. III. The Lion in the OT: 1. General Survey; 2. Yahweh in Lion Metaphors; 3. Israel and Her Princes; 4. Israel's Enemies; 5. Individual Persons, Situations, and Maxims; 6. Basic Types of Comparisons Using the Lion.

I. Words for Lion in the OT, Related Expressions, Occurrences. Hebrew has seven words for lion with different examples and meanings in the various Semitic dialects.

'*arî.* Y. Aharoni, "On Some Animals Mentioned in the Bible," *Osiris*, 5 (1938), 461-478; *idem,* "Vues nouvelles sur la zoologie biblique et talmudique," *RES* (1938), 32-41; K.-H. Bernhardt, *Gott und Bild* (1956); J. Blau, "Etymologische Untersuchungen auf Grund des palästin. Arabisch," *VT*, 5 (1955), 337-344; F. S. Bodenheimer, *Die Tierwelt Palästinas. Land der Bibel*, III, 3/4 (1920); *idem, The Animals of Palestine* (Jerusalem, 1935); *idem, Animal and Man in Bible Lands* (Leiden, 1960); G. J. Botterweck, *Die Tiere in der Bildersprache des AT unter bes. Berücksichtigung der äg. und akk. Literatur* (inaug. diss., Bonn, 1953); *idem,* "Gott und Mensch in den at.lichen Löwenbildern," *Festschrift J. Ziegler* (1971); E. D. van Buren, *The Fauna of Ancient Mesopotamia as Represented in Art. AnOr,* 18 (Rome, 1939); *idem, Symbols of the Gods in Mesopotamian Art. AnOr,* 23 (Rome, 1945); J. Calvet-M. Cruppi, *Les animaux dans la littérature sacrée* (Paris, 1956); C. M. Clark, "The Animal Series in the Primeval History," *VT,* 18 (1968), 433-449; Dalman, *AuS,* VI; J. Feliks, *The Animal World of the Bible* (Tel Aviv, 1962); H. Gabelmann, *Studien zum frühgriechischen Löwenbild* (diss., Marburg, 1965); K. Galling, "Das Löwenrelief von Bethsean–ein Werk des 8. Jahrhunderts," *ZDPV,* 83 (1967), 125-131; H. Gese, "Die Religionen Altsyriens," *RdM,* 10/2 (1970), 1-232; H. Grapow, *Die bildlichen Ausdrücke des Ägyptischen* (1924); *idem, Vergleiche und andere bildliche Ausdrücke. AO,* 21, 1/2 (1920); W. Hartner-R. Ettinghausen, "The Conquering Lion. The Life Cycle of a Symbol," *Oriens,* 17 (1964), 161-171; W. Heimpel, *Tierbilder in der sumerischen Literatur* (Rome, 1968); J. Hempel, "Jahwegleichnisse der israelitischen Propheten," *ZAW,* 42 (1924), 74-107=*Apoxysmata. BZAW,* 81 (1961), 1-29;

(continued on p. 375)

1. *'ari.* a. *'ari,* "lion," corresponds to the Old South Arab. *'rw,* "ibex," [1] the Harari *ūri,* "wild bull," [2] and Akk. *erū(m), arū,* "eagle." [3]

b. *'ari* occurs 35 times in the OT: twice in the Balaam Oracles; 10 times in Isa., Jer., Ezk., Am., Nah., and Zeph.; 16 times in Jgs., S., K., and Ch.; 3 times in Prov.; once each in Pss. (?), Cant., Lam., and Sir. *'ari* appears twice in connection with *labhi',* 5 times with *kephir,* twice with the bear, and once each with the prairie wolf and the snake. *'ari* is used 7 times for a lion ornament of sculpture. The LXX always translates *'ari* by *léōn,* "lion."

2. *'aryeh.* a. *'aryeh,* "lion," corresponds to Egyp. *rw,* [4] Ethiop. *'arwē,* "wild animal," Tigr. "snake," [5] Berbian *awar,* Cushite *ār,* [6] and Arab. *'arwīyat,* "ibexes, wild sheep." Its connection with Akk. *armū,* "mountain billy goat"(?), which is

---

idem, "Die Grenzen des Anthropomorphismus Jahwes im AT," *ZAW,* 57 (1939), 75-85; *idem,* *Das Bild in Bibel und Gottesdienst. SgV,* 212 (1957); M.-L. Henry, *Das Tier im religiösen Bewusstsein des at.lichen Menschen* (1958); H. Hilger, *Biblischer Tiergarten* (1954); Th. Hopfner, *Der Tierkult der alten Ägypter nach den griechisch-römischen Berichten und den wichtigeren Denkmälern. Denkschrift der Akademie der Wissenschaften, Wien,* 57/2 (1913), 40ff.; E. Hornung, "Die Bedeutung des Tieres im alten Ägypten," *StudGen,* 20 (1967), 69-198; H. Kees, *Der Götterglaube im Alten Ägypten* (²1956); L. Koehler, "Lexikologisch-Geographisches," *ZDPV,* 62 (1939), 115-125; L. Kopf, "Arabische Etymologien und Parallelen zum Bibelwörterbuch," *VT,* 8 (1958), 161-215; B. Landsberger, *Die Fauna des alten Mesopotamien nach der 14. Tafel der Serie ḪARRA=ḪUBULLU* (1934); H. Möbius, "Die Göttin mit dem Löwen," *Festschrift W. Eilers* (1967), 449-468; S. Morenz, *Egyptian Religion* (trans. 1973); S. Mowinckel, "ša̜hal," *Festschrift G. R. Driver* (Oxford, 1963), 95-103; H. W. Müller, "Löwenskulpturen in der Ägyptischen Sammlung des Bayerischen Staates," *Münchener Jahrbuch der bildenden Kunst,* 16 (1965), 7-46; W. Nagel, "Frühe Tierwelt in Südwestasien," *ZA,* 55 (1963), 169-236; H. Otten, "Noch einmal hethitisch 'Löwe,'" *WO,* 5 (1969/70), 94f.; E. Otto, "Die Religion der alten Ägypter," *Religionsgeschichte des Alten Orients* (Leiden, 1964), 1-75; W. Pangritz, *Das Tier in der Bibel* (1963); R. Pinney, *The Animals in the Bible. The Identity and Natural History of All the Animals Mentioned in the Bible* (Philadelphia, 1964); H. Schmökel, "Bemerkungen zur Grossfauna Altmesopotamiens," *Jahrbuch Kleinasiat.-Forschungen,* 2/1 (Istanbul, 1967), 433-443; A. Schott, *Die Vergleiche in den akkadischen Königsinschriften. MVÄG,* 30 (1926); U. Schweitzer, *Löwe und Sphinx im alten Ägypten. ÄF,* 15 (1948); W. von Soden, "aqrabu und našru," *AfO,* 18 (1957/58), 393; K. Tallqvist, "Typen der assyrischen Bildersprache," *Ha-Kedem,* 1 (1907), 1-13, 55-62; *idem,* *Akkadische Götterepitheta. StOr,* 7 (1938); C. H. Wallace, *Several Animals as Symbols in the OT* (diss., Basel, 1961); J. A. Wharton, *The Role of the Beast in the OT. An Investigation of the Impact of the Animal World upon OT Literature* (diss., Basel, 1968); H. Wohlstein, "Zur Tier-Dämonologie der Bibel," *ZDMG,* 113 (1963), 483-492; A. Wünsche, *Die Bildersprache des AT. Ein Beitrag zur ästhetischen Würdigung des poetischen Schrifttums im AT* (1906).

[1] W. W. Müller, *Die Wurzeln Mediae und Tertiae Y/W im Altsüdarabischen* (diss., Tübingen, 1962), 26.

[2] W. Leslau, *Etymological Dictionary of Harari* (Los Angeles, 1963), 31.

[3] *AHw; CAD;* cf. von Soden, *AfO,* 393: "etymologically ... naturally connected with the Heb. *'aryeh/'ari,* 'lion'; the eagle is the 'lion' of the air."

[4] *WbÄS,* II, 403; cf. Egyp. *ir* (?), I, 106.

[5] Littmann-Höfner, *Wörterbuch der Tigrē-Sprache* (1962), 359b.

[6] Cf. *Linguistica* (Rome, 1961), 158.

to be distinguished from the common Semitic *arwaị* because of the etymological *m*, according to Landsberger, [7] is doubtful. Since Koehler, [8] *'ari* and *'aryeh* have been regarded as terms referring to the African lion, in which case the mammals of southern Palestine (as well as of the Sinai Peninsula, Egypt, and Nubia) would belong to the Ethiopian region.

b. *'aryeh* occurs 42 times in the OT (or 43, if one includes an additional *kethibh* reading): once each in Gen. 49 and Dt. 33; 13 times in Jgs., S., K., and 1 Ch.; 22 times in Isa., Jer., Ezk., Hos., Joel, Am., Mic., and Nah.; 5 times in Pss.; and once each in Job and Eccl. With two exceptions in which it translates by *léaina*, "lioness," the LXX always translates *'aryeh* by *léōn*, "lion."

3. *gur*. *gur* (*gor*) means "young animal," especially "young lion," [9] although in Lam. 4:3 it means "jackal"; cf. the Middle Heb.-Jewish Aram. "young dog," Syr. *gūryā*, "young lion," Arab. *ğurw*, "beast of prey, young dog," Akk. *gerru*, "young beast of prey," [10] and Moabite *grn, gr(t)*. *gur* occurs 6 times in the OT, and *gor* twice. The LXX always translates *gur/gor* by *skýmnos*, any young animal, especially "a lion's whelp."

4. *kephir*. a. *kephir* is isolated etymologically. Blau suggests that it may be connected with Arab. *ğafr*, "a four-month-old lamb." [11] Originally *kephir* meant a "young animal," but then especially a "young lion" who goes out on his own in search of prey. [12]

b. *kephir* occurs 31 times in the OT: 17 times in Isa., Jer., Ezk., Hos., Am., Mic., Nah., and Zec.; twice in Job; 3 times in Prov.; and once in Jgs. It appears 6 times in connection with *'ari* or *'arayoth;* twice each with *labhi'* and *gore* (*'arayoth*), and once each with *shachal* and *tannin*, "jackals." The LXX translates *kephir* by *léōn* (19 times), *skýmnos* (8 times), and once each by *drákōn*, "dragon," *kōmē*, "village," and *skýmnos léontos*, "young lion" (and *ploúsios*, "rich, wealthy").

5. *labhi' and Derivatives*. a. *labhi'* (*lebhi, lebhiya'*) corresponds to the Akk. *lābu(m)* or Late Bab. *labbu*, [13] the Old South Arab. *lb'*, Arab. *lab'a*, and Egyp. *rw*. [14] The Ugar. *lb'* appears only in the name of the goddess *'bdlb't*, and perhaps is to be found in the proper name *šmlb'*. [15] Further, Koehler refers to

---

7 Landsberger, *Fauna*, 94f., 100.
8 L. Koehler, *ZDPV*, 115-125, esp. 122ff.
9 Cf. *VG*, I, 251.
10 *AHw*, I, 285; Landsberger, *Fauna*, 76f.
11 J. Blau, *VT*, 342.
12 Cf. Th. Nöldeke, *Beiträge zur semit. Sprachwissenschaft* (1904), 70, n. 10; L. Koehler, *ZDPV*, 121.
13 *AHw*, I, 526; according to Landsberger, *Fauna*, 76 and n. 7, *lābu* originally meant "lioness," while *nēšu* meant "lion."
14 *WbÄS*, II, 403; cf. also the Copt. *labei*, Demotic *labei;* Ward, *JNES*, 20 (1961), 35.
15 *UT*, 1347.

Saho/ʿAfar *lubāk,* Somali *libāh.* [16] *labhiʾ* could mean the Asiatic lion if Nehring is correct in arguing that the fauna of northern Palestine and Syria essentially belong to the Paleartic region.

b. *labhiʾ* occurs 11 times in the OT: once each in Gen. 49 and Dt. 33; twice in Nu. 23f.; 5 times in Isa., Hos., Joel, and Nah.; and twice in Job. The LXX translates *labhiʾ* 6 times by *skýmnos* and 5 times by *léōn,* and *lebhiyaʾ* once by *skýmnos.*

6. *layish.* a. *layish,* "lion," corresponds to the Jewish Aram. *laitāʾ,* Arab. *lait,* and would seem to be related to Akk. *nēšu,* either by the approximation of **nait* to **labʾ,* [17] or by assimilation. [18]

b. *layish* is found only 3 times in the OT: once each in Isa., Prov., and Job. The LXX translates this word twice by *skýmnos léontos,* and once by *myrmēkoléōn,* "ant lion" (Job 4:11).

7. *shachal.* a. Etymologically, the meaning of *shachal* is not clear, but the context suggests that it means "lion," "young lion." [19] Kopf calls attention to the Arab. *sahl,* "lamb." [20] The Ugar. *šḥlmmt: šd šḥlmmt* is variously explained: "shore of death," "lion that kills," [21] or "lion of the Mametu." [22] Because of the connection of *shachal* with *pethen,* "venomous serpent," *tannin,* "serpent," and *bene shachats,* "proud beasts" (lit. "sons of pride") (cf. Job 28:8; Ps. 91:13), S. Mowinckel supposes that *shachal* means not only "lion," but also "serpent," in support of which he appeals to *nachash,* "snake," and the Akk. *nēšu,* "lion," or *ʾaryeh* and Ethiop. *ʾarwē,* "snake"; "šaḥal may have meant the serpent dragon, the mythical wyvern or 'Lindwurm.'" Because of the connection of snake and lion "in mythopoetical and artistic fancy," *shachal* was also adopted as a term for "lion."

b. *shachal* occurs 7 times in the OT: once each in Pss. and Prov.; twice in Hos.; and 3 times in Job. The LXX translates this word by *pánthēr,* "panther," *léōn,* 4 times, and *léaina.*

II. In the Ancient Near East.

1. *Egypt.* In both Upper and Lower Egypt, the lion (*rw, mꜣy*) plays an important role in the cult, the royal symbolism, and art.

---

16 Koehler, *ZDPV,* 122ff.
17 So Landsberger, *loc. cit.*
18 *VG,* I, 231; cf. *lis* in Homer *Iliad* xi.239; xv.275; xviii.318 (Liddell-Scott).
19 Cf. Koehler, 121: "the young lion who no longer sucks."
20 L. Kopf, *VT,* 207.
21 Cf. *UT,* 488, No. 2396.
22 *WUS,* 303.

a. In Upper Egypt, especially at the mouths of the wilderness wadis, we encounter mainly lioness cults: Matit of Der el Gebrawi, Mehit of This, Mentit of Latopolis, Pachet of Speos Artemidos, Sachmet of Memphis, Menet, etc. Frequently the lioness is called "lady of the mouth of the wilderness valley." [23] Lion cults are particularly prominent in the Delta: near Sile, Bubastis, On with the cult of the lion pair (rw.ty), etc. While the lion pair of On was associated with Atum and was identified with the children of Atum, Schu and Tefnut, the lion advanced beyond the local deities almost to the sun-god, and was regarded as a manifestation of the sun-god not only in comparisons and figures, but also in reality. Besides the ancient witnesses, [24] this is confirmed by representations of a lion with a solar disk on its head and is promoted by the increasing animal cults in the New Kingdom. We may compare with this the representation of the sun in the fifth (or sixth) hour of the day as a lion in the Greco-Roman magical papyri. [25] Also, because of his relationship to the sun, Horus can be represented as Harachte with a lion's head. Occasionally, he was worshipped as a frontier-guard in the form of a lion, e.g., in Sile. [26] Others like Nefertem, Shesmu, Aker, and Bach seem to have appeared for the sake of certain characteristic features (e.g., the bloodthirstiness of Shesmu) or to have become secondary to the lion-gods. Many goddesses were represented (possibly secondarily) with a lion head: Uret-Hekau, Uto, Mut, etc. Min is assimilated to the ithyphallic lion-god. [27] In Egyptian metaphors, [28] the sun-god is called "lion of the lower heaven," "mysterious lion of the eastern mountain," and "lion of the night." Amun is "the mysterious lion with a loud roar, which tears apart that which falls into his claws ... a lion for his people." Horus appears as "the great lion who routs his enemies," etc.

b. From very early times, the ruler has been represented as a lion; many figures of lions in temples are attested as symbols of the king, e.g., Amenophis III at the temple of Soleb. [29] Lion metaphors for the king are especially popular: [30] Thutmose III is "the wild-looking lion, the son of Sekhmet," or "the wild-looking lion, who kills his enemies in their valleys." Similarly, Seti I is regarded as a "wild-looking lion, who treads upon the inaccessible ways of every land." In battle, Rameses III is called "the raging lion, whose claws are on the peoples of the new mountain," "the strong lion, who seizes with his claws," or "which seizes game with his teeth."

c. As a decoration or ornament, the "wild-looking lion" has a majestic or apotropaic function, as guard or pillar at the throne or the entrance of the temple

[23] Kees, 7.
[24] Hopfner, 40ff.
[25] Hopfner; Bonnet, RÄR, 427f.
[26] H. Brugsch, ZÄS, 10, 19; F. Mariette, Dendérah (1870-74), IV, 75; E. H. Naville, Textes relatifs au Mythe d'Horus (1870), Plate 18; RÄR, 427.
[27] Cf. RÄR, 428.
[28] Evidence in Grapow, Bildliche Ausdrücke, 71ff.
[29] RÄR.
[30] Evidence in Grapow, 70f.

or the outer walls. Also, like lion-headed demons, they have apotropaic significance, and keep watch over the god.

d. In the cult of the dead, two lions carry the bier and watch over the deceased; amulets in the shape of lions were supposed to protect their owner. On
the other hand, the dead were used in spells against lions. The doors of the Underworld are guarded by lions (cf. The Book of the Dead 146:7).

2. *Mesopotamia.* a. In Mesopotamia, the Sumerians and the Babylonians seem
to have known no theriomorphic gods, but certain animals were associated with
gods. [31] According to Seidel, [32] from the period of Akkad on, the lion is regarded
as an attribute of a goddess, often of the warlike Ishtar. [33] It appears only rarely
as a symbol, e.g., on a cylinder seal from the time of Gudea. Ishtar also stands
on a lion; [34] according to Tallqvist, she appears as *labbu, labbatu,* and *nēšu.* [35]
She has also been identified with the deified *Labatu.* [36] "Seven harnessed lions"
are allotted to Ishtar. [37] According to the Gilgamesh Epic, in Primeval Time
Ishtar offered her love to Dumuzi, to the "many-colored bird," to the lion, etc.
Ningirsu is also connected with the lion and the lion-headed eagle; [38] cf. the
Vulture Stela of Eannatum and the silver vase of Entemena of Lagash. [39] According to van Buren, [40] the standards depicting a lion carrying a discus along
with a deity could perhaps also be connected with Ningirsu. The lion sceptre
appears from the Akkad period on, and is the symbol of Nergal. [41] From the
Ur III period on, the double-lion club is a divine symbol; on the Kudurru and
the Neo-Assyrian Royal Relief, it is the symbol of Ninurta. [42]

In Sumerian and Akkadian literature, the fierce, roaring, fearless lion (*pirig,
ug, pirig-tur, ur-maḫ, ur-gu-la; labbu, nēšu*) is a favorite way of referring to the
gods of the Sumerian and Akkadian pantheon: [43] thus Inanna has "roared like
a lion in heaven and on the earth, and upsets the people." [44] Ishkur appears as
a "fierce" and "raging" lion, [45] as a "lion of heaven," [46] and Ishkur's temple
"as a fullgrown lion which strikes terror." [47] Ishmedagan moves "like a fierce

[31] Cf. J. van Dijk, *RLA,* III, 534, 538.
[32] U. Seidel, *RLA,* III, 487.
[33] E.g., on seal figures, *EGA,* Illustrations 382-84, 387, 389.
[34] *BuA,* II, 28f.
[35] Tallqvist, *Götterepitheta,* 116, 139.
[36] Thureau-Dangin, *RA,* 37 (1940), 105; E. Dhorme, *Les Religions de Babylonie et d'Assyrie*
(1945), 71.
[37] *VAB,* IV, 274: III, 14f.; *BuA,* II, 29.
[38] Cf. Dhorme, *Religions,* 103, 201; D. O. Edzard in *WbMyth,* I (1965), 112.
[39] Moortgat, *Die Kunst des alten Mesopotamien* (1967), Taf. 118, 113.
[40] E. D. van Buren, *Symbols,* 39f.
[41] Dhorme, *Religions,* 44, 52; Seidel, *RLA,* III, 488.
[42] Seidel, *loc. cit.;* on the lion-dragon, cf. 489.
[43] Evidence in Heimpel and Schott.
[44] Heimpel, 36.1; on Inanna cf. further 36.2, 21, 37, 55, 56; 37.4.
[45] *Ibid.,* 36.5, 39.
[46] *Ibid.,* 36.57.
[47] *Ibid.,* 36.33.

lion of the steppe" "in his raging power" . . . "for fighting and battle." [48] Again
and again the "roaring," "destroying," "fierce," "terror-striking," "fighting" lion
is used to characterize the gods Martu, [49] Nanna, [50] Nergal, [51] Ninazu, [52] Ningirsu, [53] Ningizzida, [54] Ninurta, [55] Numushda, [56] Shulgi, [57] Utu, [58] and Zabada. [59]

Lion metaphors, figures, or epithets appear in Akkadian Literature: in a prayer,
Irnini is called a "raging lion"; [60] "Irnini, strong, fierce lion, calm your heart."
In a hymn, Ishtar, "lioness of Igigi," [61] is addressed in this way: "Thou art a lion
that stalks over the meadow." [62] Nergal appears as a "lion, violent with terrifying
splendor." [63]

b. Lion metaphors or figures appear for the following kings, among others:
Ashurnasirpal says concerning himself, "I am a lion." [64] At the beginning of a
battle, Sargon II becomes furious "like a lion," [65] and stalks through the lands
of his enemies "like a raging lion which strikes terror." [66] Similar comparisons
occur in statements made concerning Sennacherib, [67] Esarhaddon, [68] etc. [69]

Because of its majestic demeanor, the lion is a favorite motif as a decoration
on temples and palaces; lions appear on gates as early as the Ur I period; cf. also
the lions on gates at Tell Ḥalaf, Arslan Tash, Till Barsip, Mari, etc. [70] Representations of lions on stone slabs or enameled tiles adorn the walls of temples and
palaces. [71] The lion appears as a pillar for a throne on a stele of Gudea (for the
first time?). [72] Finally, we may mention the battle between the half bull, half
man hero and the aggressive lion.

---

[48] *Ibid.*, 36.3; cf. also 36.51.
[49] *Ibid.*, 36.35, 45, 48.
[50] *Ibid.*, 36.12, 19, 54.
[51] *Ibid.*, 36.16; 37.6, 7; 39.7.
[52] *Ibid.*, 36.18.
[53] *Ibid.*, 36.14.
[54] *Ibid.*, 39.6.
[55] *Ibid.*, 36.4, 26, 50, 53, 60, 61, 63, 64, 65; 39.1; 40.1.
[56] *Ibid.*, 36.13.
[57] *Ibid.*, 36.9, 11, 15.
[58] *Ibid.*, 36.59, 68 (?); 39.9.
[59] *Ibid.*, 37.5.
[60] E. Ebeling, *Die akkadische Gebetsserie 'Handerhebung'* (1953), 132, line 51.
[61] *Ibid.*, line 31.
[62] *KB*, V, 12, 118, 14.
[63] K 9880, 9 = Böllenrücher, *Gebete und Hymnen an Nergal* (1904), 50f.
[64] Schott, III, 14a.
[65] *Ibid.*, I, 123.
[66] *Ibid.*, I, 178.
[67] *Ibid.*, I, 123.
[68] *Ibid.*, III, 14b.
[69] Cf. Seux, 147f.; I. Engnell, *Studies in Divine Kingship* (Uppsala, 1943), 183. On hunting
lions, cf. *BuA*, I, 73ff.
[70] Van Buren, *Fauna,* 7.
[71] *BuA*, 236, 283.
[72] Cf. Moortgat, Taf. 188.

3. *Ancient Syria.* Since the Ugaritic texts make no contribution to the understanding of the lion, [73] we must largely depend on archeological evidence.

a. In the religion of ancient Syria in the second millennium B.C., the fertility
goddess Qadshu is represented on a lion naked and wearing a Hathoric wig, and
in one hand (or both) she is carrying some snakes. According to Pritchard, [74]
the fertility goddess appears many times in Syria from the end of the Middle
Bronze to the end of the Late Bronze periods. At Ugarit there was found a
representation of a golden appendage with the naked goddess standing on a lion,
with two ibexes in her hands. [75] On a three-storied clay house at Beth-Shan
(12th century B.C.), two gods are depicted fighting over the possession of Qadshu,
who watches above in the window with her animals (a lion and a snake) facing
the two fighters. [76] According to Gese, [77] the relationship of Qadshu to the lion
calls to mind the association of the Felidae to the mother or fertility goddess in
the Neolithic Age (cf. the fertility goddess of Çatal Hüyük with the leopard!).
On a Ugaritic cylinder seal dating between 1450 and 1365 B.C., [78] there appears
a goddess (probably ʿAṭtart) on a lion alongside ʿAnat on a cow. In the pantheon
list, ʿAṭtart appears as Ishtar. [79]
The double-lion club appears in the hand of the goddesses Ishtar, ʿAstarte, and
ʿAnat, [80] or as a life-size rod on the "earth," worshipped by two men. [81]

b. From the 5th century B.C. on, there appears among the Carthaginians the
ʿAstarte-like goddess Tinnit, who is represented on a lion, and was especially
widespread in North Africa and in Punic colonization territories. According to
Gese, [82] its absence in Syria is probably due to its Libyan origin.

c. From the North Phoenician town of Marathus comes a stele depicting the
beardless god Shadrapa standing on a lion, holding in his right hand a kind of
club, and holding in his left hand a small lion by the hind legs. [83] Lion reliefs
have been found in the sanctuary of Baʿal Shamem on the island of Arwad at
Apamea, which perhaps point to a triad: [84] the bull (Baʿal Shamem), the cypress
(the local ʿAstarte), and the lion (the young god).

---

[73] Cf. I.5a, 7a.
[74] J. B. Pritchard, *Palestinian Figurines* (1943), 32ff.
[75] C. F. A. Schaeffer, *Ugaritica,* II (1949), 36, Fig. 10.
[76] A. Rowe, *The Four Canaanite Temples of Beth-Shan* (1940), Table 17.2 and 56 Al and
3; also W. F. Albright, *Yahweh and the Gods of Canaan* (1968), 107f.
[77] Gese, 154.
[78] RS 5089 = *AO* 17242.
[79] Cf. also B. Hrouda, *RLA,* III, 393.
[80] H. H. von der Osten, *Ancient Oriental Seals in the Collection of Mrs. Agnes Baldwin
Brett. OIP,* 37 (1936), No. 93; B. Hrouda, *RLA,* III, 493.
[81] *CANES,* 957.
[82] Gese, 207.
[83] *ANEP,* No. 486.
[84] Gese, 201.

d. From Northern Syria, Lucian's description of the sanctuary at Hierapolis (Mabbug)[85] establishes the existence of a triad: Zeus (Hadad), Hera (Atargatis), and Semeion. Hera (Atargatis) was represented on a lion, [86] and characterized as a mother-goddess. [87]

e. In a similar way, the goddess Gad of Palmyra is portrayed on two temple figures at Dura as Atargatis standing on a lion. [88]

III. The Lion in the OT.

1. *General Survey.* According to Prov. 30:30, the lion is mightiest among beasts. He was noted for his courage (2 S. 17:10) and strength (1:23). Roaring and rapacious (Ezk. 22:25), he is eager for prey (Ps. 17:12). The mother lioness who brings up her young also teaches them to catch prey (Ezk. 19:2f.). In the thicket (Jer. 4:7; 25:38; 49:19), the lion lurks after his victim (Ps. 10:9; 17:12) and waits in ambush (Lam. 3:10); with his fierce teeth (Joel 1:6; Ps. 58:7 [Eng. v. 6]; Job 4:10), he tears it in pieces (Ps. 7:3[2]; Mic. 5:7[8]). He carries off prey (Hos. 5:14; Isa. 5:29) into his cave; he fills his dens with it (Nah. 2:13[12]). Then he devours it and his young lions growl over his victims (Am. 3:4). When he rushes down upon a sheepfold (Jer. 49:19; 50:44) to tread it down and tear it in pieces (Mic. 5:7[8]; Jer. 50:17), the shepherd must defend his flock; and when a sheep is killed, the shepherd must present a bone or a piece of hide to avoid having to pay the stipulated compensation for the loss (Am. 3:12). Even man is not safe from the ravening lion (Isa. 15:9; Ezk. 19:6) and trembles when he hears his roar (Hos. 11:10; Am. 3:8). Man uses pits and nets to catch a lion (Ezk. 19:8). 2 S. 23:20 states that Benaiah, one of David's heroes, slew a lion in a pit. The ravening lion even obeys the command of Yahweh: a young prophet is attacked and killed by a lion because he did not obey the disciple of Yahweh (1 K. 20:36). Similarly, a prophet from Judah is killed by a lion because he transgressed Yahweh's command not to stay and eat (13:24). In the lion's den, God sent an angel to Daniel, who closed the mouths of the wild beasts so that they could not tear Daniel in pieces (Dnl. 6:22f.[21f.]). And in the Messianic Age, peace will prevail among the beasts, the cow and the lion shall feed together peacefully, and the lion shall eat straw instead of prey (Isa. 11:7). The meaning of the wedding riddle in the Samson story (Jgs. 14:18) is uncertain. [89]

Lion motifs appear on seals from Megiddo, Tell en-Naṣbeh, Ramath-rachel, Shechem, En-gedi, etc. An impression of a roaring lion was found on a jug in En-gedi. [90]

---

[85] Comm. and trans. in C. Clemen, *AO,* 37 (1938), 3f.; additional literature in Gese, 218, n. 24.

[86] Cf. the Hierapolitanic coin from the 3rd century B.C., *AOB,* No. 364.

[87] Gese, 220.

[88] Eissfeldt, *AO,* 40 (1941), 13.1; 15.1.

[89] Cf. H. Bauer, *ZDMG,* 66 (1912), 473f.; F. M. Th. de Liagre Böhl, *Opera Minora* (Groningen, 1953), 16; J. R. Porter, *JTS,* n.s. 13 (1962), 106ff.

[90] *IEJ,* 14 (1964), 125.

2. *Yahweh in Figures Using the Lion.* Yahweh is found in the following figures using the lion: according to Am. 1:2, "Yahweh roars from Zion, and utters his voice from Jerusalem." Here Amos' message of judgment is introduced with a sort of motto in the style of the earlier theophany tradition.[91] Here *sha'agh,* "to roar," has reference to the powerful and overpowering revelation of Yahweh to the prophet.

The figure of the lion stands in a series of cause-and-effect analogies in order to illustrate the causal connection between the revelatory word and the prophetic proclamation: just as one can conclude from the roaring of the lion (*'aryeh*) and from the growling of the young lion (*kephir*) that he has taken his prey (Am. 3:4), or just as there is a direct connection between the roaring of a lion and the fear that comes from being startled (3:8), so the prophetic proclamation (*yinnabhe'*) must be traced back to the overpowering word of Yahweh addressed to the prophet.[92]

The parallelism between God's voice (thunder), → קוֹל *qôl,* and Yahweh's roaring, → שָׁאַג *shā'agh,* also appears elsewhere, but especially in Job 37:4.

Possibly a Judean redactor (from the time of Josiah?) wanted to emphasize especially the announcement of judgment by using the theophanic voice, *qol* (thunder); cf. Ps. 50:3ff.; 76:9(8). Jer. 25:30[93] and Joel 4:16(3:16) may have been derived from Amos.[94] According to Weiser[95] and Mowinckel,[96] this saying goes back to a common cult tradition.

In the comparable saying on the day of Yahweh in Am. 5:19, the lion (*'ari*), the bear (*dobh*), and the serpent (*nachash*) are used to characterize the fatal danger of the day of Yahweh. The figure of the lion has a greater impact on the book of Hosea, which directly compares Yahweh's individuality and deeds with the lion and other wild beasts: in the chaotic conditions of the Syro-Ephraimitic War and the events that followed it,[97] Yahweh describes himself as a "lion (*shachal*) to Ephraim" and as a "young lion (*kephir*) to the house of Judah," who "rends" (*taraph*) and "carries off" (*nasa'*) prey without any being able to "rescue" (*matstsil*) (Hos. 5:14). The catastrophe which is described here is the result of the punishment of Yahweh, who attacks like an overpowering lion, tears the land and the people asunder like prey, and carries them away. Hos. 13:7f. is even more menacing. Here Yahweh describes himself as a lion (*shachal*),[98] a leopard (*namer*), and a bear (*dobh*), so that the end of Ephraim is inevitable. It is possible that Tiglath-pileser III stands behind the figures of Yahweh as a powerful lion in Hos. 5:14, and Shalmaneser V in Hos. 13:7f., as historical in-

---

91 Cf. A. Weiser, *Die Profetie des Amos. BZAW,* 53 (1929), 82-85; J. Jeremias, *Theophanie. WMANT,* 10 (1965), 12-17, 130-138, 154.

92 Cf. H. Junker, *TrThZ,* 59 (1950), 4-13; H. Graf Reventlow, *FRLANT,* 80 (1962), 24-30.

93 According to Duhm, Rudolph, Nötscher, etc., this passage is post-Jeremian.

94 Budde, Nötscher, Rudolph, Wolff, etc.

95 Weiser, *ATD,* XXIV (⁴1963).

96 S. Mowinckel, *RHR* (1926), 409ff.; *Le Décalogue* (1927), 120.

97 Cf. A. Alt, *KlSchr,* II, 163-187; modified by H. W. Wolff, *Hosea* (trans. 1974), 110ff.

98 Mowinckel, 96, thinks this word may mean "serpent."

struments of the divine wrath and punishment. According to Jer. 49:19, [99] Yahweh comes upon the Edomites suddenly like a lion that attacks a flock of sheep
in the oasis from the thicket of the Jordan by surprise; [100] here Nebuchadnezzar
seems to be the instrument that is intended. Like Hos. 5:14; Ps. 50:22 uses the
figure of a lion to characterize those who forget God as threatened by the judgment of God: "lest I rend (taraph), and there be none to deliver ('en matstsil)."
Occasionally, the individual also feels himself threatened by Yahweh. Thus, the
ailing king Hezekiah laments because Yahweh has broken (yeshabber) his bones
like a lion ('ari) (Isa. 38:13). But the figure in the lament in Lam. 3:10f. is even
more terrifying: like a bear (dobh) lying in wait and a lion ('aryeh) in hiding, he
leads the unfortunate off his way, disables him (the piel of pashach is a hapax
legomenon, but cf. the Akk. pašāḫu, "to calm down"), and causes him to be
paralyzed (cf. Job 10:16). However, it is not only the speaking-revealing and
punishing God who appears under the figure of a lurking and destroying lion.
According to Isa. 31:4, Yahweh fights for and defends Zion against her enemies
like a lion that is not terrified or daunted by a band of shepherds calling forth
against him. Hos. 11:10 is not clear (the text and genuineness of this verse are
debated): [101] Yahweh's lion-like roar (v. 10b) summons Israel to return home,
drives away her enemies, and guarantees her certain return.

3. *Israel and Her Princes.* According to Nu. 23:24, Israel rises up as a lion
(labhi'–'ari) and does not lie down until it "devours the prey, and drinks the
blood of the slain." According to Nu. 24:8f., "he eats up the nations" and "breaks
their bones." These figures of a lion which Balaam uses contain a clear warning
to Balak not to underestimate the power and threat of Israel. As Balak's outburst
of anger shows (v. 10), he understood this warning correctly.

In the Tribal Oracles of Jacob (Gen. 49) and the Blessing of Moses (Dt. 33), [102]
the tribes are characterized and identified by word plays and comparisons with
animals. According to Gen. 49:9, "Judah is a lion's whelp" (gur 'aryeh); "from
the prey you have gone up." As a lion ('aryeh) or a lioness (labhi') Judah has
stooped down, and no one dares raise him up, i.e., Judah has occupied the land
with certainty by courage and heroic power, and need fear no enemy. Similarly,
in Dt. 33:20 Gad is compared with a lion (labhi') that "tears the arm and the
crown of the head," which probably means that Gad sought out the best of the
spoil, the best portion of the conquered territory. Dan is also compared with a
young lion (gur 'aryeh) (cf. 1 Ch. 12:9[8]).

Some scholars have wanted to see in these comparisons and identifications with
animals remnants of totemistic ideas. [103] Others see in the wordplay and the comparison with animals "forms of self-representation" of those who are specifically

---

[99] According to Cornill, Rudolph (*HAT*, 12 [³1968]), Nötscher, etc., this passage is post-
Jeremian.
[100] The text is uncertain. *BHS* reads *'aritsem,* "I will make them run away." But Rudolph
in loc., reads *'argiʿah,* "I will startle them."
[101] Cf. Wolff, *Hosea,* and Rudolph, *in loc.*
[102] Cf., among others, H.-J. Zobel, *Stammesspruch und Geschichte. BZAW,* 95 (1965).
[103] W. R. Smith; G. B. Gray; B. Stade; etc.

mentioned, i.e., the amphictyons, and thus suppose that the amphictyonic cele-bration of the theophany is the *Sitz im Leben*. [104]

According to Jer. 2:30, the sword of Judah devoured the prophets like a lion (*'aryeh*) (perhaps in the time of Manasseh) because of their annoying admoni-tions (cf. 2 K. 21:16). Judah (Yahweh's heritage) aggressively revolts against her God like a roaring lion (*'aryeh*) and therefore hates him (Jer. 12:8). In Mic. 5:7 (8), [105] the enormous and overpowering might of the remnant of Jacob is pro-claimed by using the figure of a lion. The remnant of Jacob "shall be among the nations, in the midst of many peoples, like a lion (*'aryeh*) among the beasts of the forest, like a young lion (*kephir*) among the flocks of sheep, which, when it goes through treads down and tears in pieces, and there is none to deliver" (*'en matstsil*). The courage which the Maccabeans (2 Macc. 11:11) and Judas Maccabeus (1 Macc. 3:4) manifested in battle is compared with a lion. In the political funeral dirge over the downfall of Judah and its kings in Ezk. 19 the prophet uses an allegory concerning lions (vv. 1-9): the mother lioness, which probably represents Judah (or the royal house; it is less likely that the reference is to the queen mother, Hamutal), was a lioness (*lebhiyya'*) among lions (*'arayoth*), i.e., among other royal powers; she couched among lions (*kephirim*) and reared her whelps (*gurim*). She brought up (hiphil of *'alah*) [106] one of her whelps (*gurim,* v. 3), which eventually was captured by Pharaoh Necho and was carried away to Egypt in the deportation (v. 4); this young lion represents Jehoash. Then, when hope was destroyed, she took another of her whelps and made him a young lion (*kephir,* v. 5), but he met a similar fate (vv. 8f.); the context would indicate that this text has Jehoiachin in mind. [107] The detailed description of the second young lion, Jehoiachin, can hardly be applied to the king in its individual features, but the prophet's intention was to characterize King Jehoiachin as very rapacious and violent, and his punishment as just. In commenting on vv. 6f., Zimmerli points out "the nearness of Ezk. to Jehoiachin, who is 'his king' in a particularly fateful way." [108] The way the king's punishment is described is based on the habits of lions and on the customs of hunting and capturing lions in the ancient Near East. The figure of the lion in Ezk. 22:25 characterizes "in a drastic way the unscrupulous selfishness of the Judean officials." [109] The princes (read *nesi'eha*) of the land are like "a roaring lion tearing the prey" (*'ari sho'egh toreph*), which devoured human lives, took treasure and precious things, and made many widows. Zeph. 3:3f. also compares the princes (*sarim*) of Judah with roaring lions.

---

[104] A. H. J. Gunneweg, "Über den Sitz im Leben der sog. Stammessprüche (Gen 49, Dtn 33, Ri 5)," *ZAW*, 76 (1964), 245-255, esp. 254.

[105] On the genuineness and antiquity of this verse, cf. B. Renaud, *Structure et attaches littéraires de Michée IV-V. CahRB*, 2 (Paris, 1964).

[106] G. R. Driver, *Bibl*, 35 (1954), 154.

[107] However, E. Klamroth, "Die jüdischen Exulanten in Babylonien," *BWANT*, 10 (1912), 10f.; M. Noth, "La catastrophe de Jérusalem en l'an 587 avant Jésus-Christ et sa signification pour Israel," *RHPR*, 33 (1953), 81-102, etc., think the reference is to Jehoiakim.

[108] Zimmerli, *BK*, XIII/1, 426.

[109] Nötscher, *EB, in loc.*

4. *Israel's Enemies*. The enemies of Israel, as Egypt, Assyria, and Babylon, are also described in figures of lions. Thus, in the biting irony of Amos, the "rescue" of Israel is "as the shepherd who rescues from the mouth of the lion (*'ari*) two legs, or a piece of an ear" (Am. 3:12). Actually, this "rescue" from the power of the enemy means Israel's downfall, after which only infinitesimally small portions survive. According to Isa. 5:29, the Assyrians (or Tiglath-pileser III) fall on Israel "like a roaring lion (*kephir/labhi'*), which growls, seizes its prey, and carries it off without any being able to rescue (*matstsil*)." According to Jer. 2:14b,15 (v. 16, which alludes to an Egyptian danger, is a later addition), [110] Israel has become the prey of Assyria, and against this prey lions (*kephirim*) roar and roar loudly. Apparently 4:7 means that the Scythians, as a lion (*'aryeh*) and a destroyer of nations, ruin the land and its cities and make them a waste. The *kephir*, "lion," in 25:38 (a later addition?) is an allusion to 4:7. Similarly, in 5:6 the enemy (the Scythians or the Babylonians) [111] is characterized as a lion (*'aryeh*), a wolf, and a leopard, all of which tear in pieces. The figure of the roaring lion (*kephirim*) or the growling lion's whelp (*gore/'arayoth*) also appears in 51:38 (cf. also 50:17).

In an ironic funeral dirge over the downfall of Nineveh (and the Assyrians, Nah. 2:12f.[11f.]; cf. 1:10f.; 2:2-11[1-10]), Nahum (not less drastically than Jeremiah) figuratively characterizes "the political and economic despoiling system of the Assyrian world power, which pitilessly impoverished its subject peoples," as a lion's den (*me'on 'arayoth*) filled with prey. [112] Like lions (*'aryeh, labhi', gur 'aryeh*), the Ninevites plunder and strangle (*taraph*) and fill their dens with prey (*tereph, terephah*). But Yahweh will cut off (by Babylonians and Medes) their prey (*hikhrith tarpekh*), and cause their voice (*qol*) to be heard no more (2:14[13]). Without clearly identifying the enemy concretely, one prophetic lampoon (*mashal*) (Zec. 11:1-3) describes the catastrophes of a world power as like catastrophes that strike cypresses, cedars of Lebanon, oaks of Bashan, and roaring lions (*kephirim*) of the jungle of the Jordan. These figures poetically illustrate the power, pride, and rapacity of the hostile world power.

5. *Individual Persons, Situations, and Maxims*. Finally, the figure of the lion is used of individual persons or situations or maxims. In the book of Proverbs, the king's wrath is compared with the growling of a lion (Prov. 19:12; 20:2); when they become angry, Oriental despots are as dangerous and unpredictable as roaring lions. In a maxim concerning the oppression of the poor in Prov. 28:15, "a wicked ruler (*moshel rasha'*) over a poor people (*'am dal*)" is compared with "a roaring lion (*'ari nohem*) or a charging bear (*dobh shoqeq*)." *rasha'*, "wicked," is apparently illustrated by *shoqeq*, "charging," and *nohem*, "roaring," as especially dangerous and violent.

In the Psalms of Lament, the worshipper characterizes irremedial oppression by his persecutors or enemies by using the figure of lions who lurk in the thicket

[110] Cf. Rudolph, *HAT*, 12 (³1968), 15.
[111] Cf. C. Rietzschel, *Das Problem der Urrolle* (1966).
[112] F. Nötscher, *EB*, III, *in loc.*; cf. K. Elliger, *ATD*, XXV (⁶1967), 14f.

for their prey (Ps. 10:9; 17:12b), or who rend and devour the godly (7:2f.[1f.]; 57:5[4]). The figure in 22:14,22(13,21) is even more drastic. Here, the danger that threatens the worshipper at the hand of his rapacious opponents is compared with vengeful lions who open wide their mouths. Thus another psalmist prays: "Break the teeth in their mouths; tear out the fangs (methalle'oth) of the young lions (kephirim), O Yahweh!" (58:7[6]). Eliphaz describes the evildoer for whom God prepares an end in a similar way: "The roar of the lion ('aryeh), the voice of the fierce lion (shachal), the teeth of the young lions (kephirim), are broken. The strong lion perishes for lack of prey, and the whelps of the lioness (labhi') are scattered" (Job 4:10f.).

Further, the figure of the lion is used in a general way as a figure of danger. Thus, in his admonition against making a covenant with Egypt, Isaiah warns the negotiators and diplomats of a dangerous road "through a land of trouble and anguish, of the lion (labhi') and the roaring lion (layish nohem; MT reads layish mehem, 'from which come the lion'), of the viper ('eph'eh) and the flying serpent (saraph me'opheph)." The sluggard tries to justify his laziness by calling attention to the danger that "there is a lion ('ari) outside!" (Prov. 22:13; 26:13). In Cant. 4:8, the expression "dens of lions" is used to denote a land of danger and terror. When Ps. 91:13 says that the godly man can tread on the lion (shachal), the adder (pethen), the young lion (kephir), and the serpent (tannin), these animals denote dangers which can have no effect on the godly who enjoys the protection of God. In order to depict the destructive power of locusts, Joel 1:6 says figuratively that their teeth are like the teeth or fangs of lions ('aryeh, labhi'). The author of Ben Sira says, "I would rather dwell with a lion and a dragon than dwell with an evil wife" (Sir. 25:16).

Finally, "the lion, which is mightiest among beasts and does not turn back before any" (Prov. 30:30), is a figure of strength, security, and courage. Thus according to Prov. 28:1, the righteous are bold as a lion (kephir). According to 2 S. 1:23, Saul and Jonathan were stronger than lions (me'arayoth). Similarly, in 17:10, the courage of the valiant man is compared with the courage of a lion ('aryeh). 1 Macc. 3:4f. says concerning Judas Maccabeus, "He was like a lion in his deeds, like a lion's cub roaring for prey. He searched out and pursued the lawless...."

6. *Basic Types of Comparisons Using the Lion.* Among the figures using the lion there are some specific basic types of comparisons, metaphors, and images. The particular nuances in various texts may be determined by the respective verbs used, by the adjective or participle occurring in the attributive position, and by analyzing the different situations that are described. The lion always remains "mightiest among beasts" (Prov. 30:30b), the superior, majestic, and terrifying beast. He represents a norm of comparison for strength (2 S. 1:23; Prov. 28:1; 30:30; etc.).

The *roaring lion* is a popular and widely used figure: Am. 3:4; Hos. 11:10; Isa. 5:29; (31:4); Jer. 2:15; 12:8; 25:30; 51:38; Zeph. 3:3; Ezk. 22:25; Zec. 11:3; Prov. 19:12; 20:2; 28:15. It gives the same impression as a fearsome enemy which is eager for plunder. On the other hand, the lion growling (haghah) over his prey

388   'arî אֲרִי

assumes a special role in that he defends his prey and thus is used to symbolize
the protection or care of Yahweh.

The *attacking and hunting lion* is used as a figure for immediate danger: Jer.
4:7; 5:6; 49:19; 50:17; Ps. 7:3(2); cf. 22:22(21); 35:17; 57:5(4); 58:7(6). Closely
connected with the figure of the hunting lion is that of the *tearing lion*, which is
used to symbolize a threatening, fierce, and destructive power: Am. 3:12; 5:19;
Hos. 5:14; (13:7); 13:8; Isa. 38:13; Mic. 5:7(8); Gen. 49:9; Nu. 23:24; 24:9; Dt.
33:22.

Finally, the figure of the *hunted or slain lion* often appears in the OT: Nah.
2:12,14(11,13); Ezk. 19:8f.; Job 4:10f.; 10:16.

Botterweck

 אֶרֶץ *'erets*

Contents: I. In Ancient Near Eastern Literature: 1. Egyptian; 2. Sumerian-Akkadian;
3. West-Semitic. II. In the OT: 1. Cosmological Sense: Earth; 2. Ground; 3. Underworld;
4. Land; 5. Theological Sense.

I. In Ancient Near Eastern Literature.

1. *Egyptian.* a. The most frequently used Egyptian word for "earth" and
"land" is *t3*.[1] The usual hieroglyphic symbol for *t3* has a flat floodland with grains

'erets. Y. Aharoni, *The Land of the Bible* (London, ²1968); M. Delcor, "Les attaches
littéraires, l'origine et la signification de l'expression biblique 'prendre à témoin le ciel et la
terre,'" *VT*, 16 (1966), 8-25; O. Eissfeldt, "Himmel und Erde als Bezeichnungen phönikischer
Landschaften," *Ras Schamra und Sanchunjaton* (1939), 107-127=*KlSchr*, II, 227-240; J.
Geyer, "קצות הארץ–Hellenistic?" *VT*, 20 (1970), 87-90; J. Harvey, *Le plaidoyer prophétique
contre Israël après la rupture de l'alliance* (Bruges, 1967); H. B. Huffmon, "The Covenant
Lawsuit in the Prophets," *JBL*, 78 (1959), 285-295; E. Lipiński, *La royauté de Yahwé dans
la poesie et le culte de l'ancien Israël* (Brussels, 1965); I. Oppelt, *RAC*, V, 1113-1179; M.
Ottosson, *Gilead, Tradition and History* (Lund, 1969); J. G. Plöger, *Literarkritische, formgeschichtliche und stilkritische Untersuchungen zum Deuteronomium. BBB*, 26 (1967); G.
von Rad, "Verheissenes Land und Jahwes Land im Hexateuch," *ZDPV*, 66 (1943), 191-204=
ThB, 8, 87-100; L. Rost, "Bezeichnungen für Land und Volk im AT," *Festschrift O. Procksch*
(1934), 125-148=*Das kleine Credo* (1965), 76-101, cited herein; K. Rupprecht, "עלה מן הארץ
(Ex 1,10; Hos 2,2); 'sich des Landes bemächtigen'?" *ZAW*, 82 (1970), 442-47; L. I. J. Stadelmann, *The Hebrew Conception of the World. AnBibl*, 39 (1970); R. de Vaux, "Le pays de
Canaan," *JAOS*, 88 (1968), 23-30; J. N. M. Wijngaards, *The Dramatization of Salvific History
in the Deuteronomic Schools. OTS*, 16 (1969); H. Wildberger, "Israel und sein Land," *EvTh*,
16 (1956), 404-422; G. E. Wright, "The Lawsuit of God," *Israel's Prophetic Heritage. Essays
in Honor of J. Muilenburg* (New York, 1962), 26-67.

On I.1.: A. de Buck, *De Egyptische Voorstellingen van den Oerheuvel* (Leiden, 1922); J. J.
Clère, "Fragments d'une novelle représentation égyptienne du monde," *Mélanges Maspéro*,
I (1934), 30-46; S. Morenz, *Egyptian Religion* (trans. 1973), esp. 29f., 42ff.; H. Schäfer,
Ägyptische und heutige Kunst und Weltgebäude der alten Ägypter (1928).

1 *WbÄS*, V, 212-228.

of sand underneath it as an explanatory sign. The scope of the meaning of *tȝ* is quite extensive, ranging from "earth" as an antithesis of heaven to "dust," and even "dirt." Another Egyptian word for "earth" is *sȝtw,* which is partly synonymous with *tȝ,* but not as widely used. [2] Further, *gb(b)* sometimes is the name of the earth-god Geb, but sometimes it means "earth, ground," e.g., as a place where vegetation grows. [3] We cannot determine which of these meanings is original, as Morenz has shown. [4] Foreign lands, which are mountainous by contrast to the flat land of Egypt, are usually called *ḫȝś.t.*

b. *tȝ* is used most extensively in the stereotyped antithesis between *p.t* and *tȝ,* "heaven" and "earth," which means the entire cosmos. In this antithetical pair, which expresses a totality, *tȝ* denotes the lower half of the universe, or perhaps better the way it spreads out horizontally. This is illustrated in a Hymn of Amun, where this expression is used: "to the height of heaven and to the breadth of earth." The same idea appears in the familiar description of the all-embracing cosmic jubilation over the appearance of God. The Book of the Dead 16:5f. says, "Heaven is engaged in a festival, and earth in joy," or again we read, "The praise of God reaches to the height of heaven, the bowing down before God to the breadth of the earth" (this refers to the gesture of worship, *sn-tȝ,* "the touching of the earth").

There are other typical examples of this antithetical pair. As creator of everything, Khnum is "the potter who made heaven and earth." As one who rules over everything, a goddess is "mistress of heaven, princess of earth." Amun is "the greatest of heaven, the oldest of earth," which is summed up in the expression *nb-r-dr,* "lord of all." In a Hymn to the Sun, we read: "Heaven rejoices on your account, because your Ba is so great; Earth is afraid of you, because your form is so magnificent." Schäfer and Clère provide a good orientation to the different representations of heaven and earth in Egyptian literature. But the twofold division of the universe suggested above is often replaced by a threefold division, in which the underworld or water is added as the third part. Thus, the praise of God also reaches "into the depth of the sea," and "heaven, earth, and underworld are under his command." "From heaven to earth and the underworld" is a stereotyped formula (e.g., in the Esna Text 17, 21; 18, 13). The gift of nature includes "what the earth creates, what the heaven gives, and what the Nile brings." "Those in heaven, on earth, and in the underworld" are to fear Khnum (Esna Text 277, 19ff.). Gradually, the number of divisions in the universe increases. In the Hymn of Amun at the Hibis Temple (col. 31), we read: "You are the heaven, the earth, the underworld, the water, and the air which is in between." Similar pantheistic formulas appear in the Late Period in connection with other gods. Since *tȝ* also means "land" in antithesis to "water," other two-stage formulas also occur, e.g., "on water and on land."

---

2 *WbÄS,* III, 423.
3 *WbÄS,* V, 164.
4 Morenz, 29f.

c. Common to all Egyptian cosmogonies is the prominent role played by the Primal Hill, the peculiar form of the Primal Land (Primal Earth) caused by the amphibious nature of the land. [5] Almost every cult place claimed to have within its sphere of control the first land which came forth out of the Primal Sea. In the great Leiden Hymn of Amun, it says concerning the city of Thebes (II, 10): "The water and the earth existed at first. The sand became arable land (?), causing its ground (s3tw) to form a hill, and thus the land (or, the earth) was formed." In certain local traditions, the name of the hill contains the word t3, especially in Memphis: t3 tnn, "the elevated land."

The extremely close connection between Primal Land and Primal God is characteristic of Egyptian literature. Frequently they are even identified: Atum is "the hill," Tatenen "the elevated land," etc. Geb is both God and earth. It is worthy of note that in contrast to the neighboring peoples, earth is masculine and heaven is feminine.

Certain eschatological events which have to do with heaven and earth are indicated in the Egyptian texts. PSalt 825, XVII, 8ff. speaks of the rotation of the earth as something from which man should want to be saved, and chapter 175 of the Book of the Dead indicates that in the End Time, the earth will sink back into the Primal Sea.

d. t3 also means "land, nation," especially Egypt. [6] But since t3 can also be used for foreign lands, one preferred to speak of t3 pn, "this land," when referring to Egypt. An even more frequent name for the land of Egypt is t3.wy, "the two lands," i.e., Upper and Lower Egypt, a name which really goes back to the prehistoric twofold division of the Nile Valley. As a royal ceremony, "the union of the two lands" (sm3 t3.wy) plays an important role.

e. Finally, t3 also means "earth as matter" and "ground," e.g., in the name of an agricultural festival ḥbs t3, "the chopping up of the ground."

Bergman

2. *Sumerian-Akkadian.* In Sumerian and Akkadian, a distinction is made between earth (ki or erṣetu) and land (kur, kalam, or mātu). The Sumerian and Akkadian ideas of the world are not very uniform, and it can hardly be assumed that all the ideas found in the different texts represent a coherent world view. [7] In Sumerian texts two cosmogonic-cosmological views in particular appear. One is the "chthonic motif," according to which the water of the abzu and mother earth constitute the life principle, and man is formed from clay. The other is "the cosmic motif," according to which heaven and earth are united in a holy marriage and men sprout up out of the earth. [8]

Akk. erṣetu first has the cosmic meaning "earth" in contrast to "heaven." As in Egyptian, "heaven and earth" (šamû u erṣetu) means the universe. The

---

[5] *Ibid.*, 45.

[6] On the Egyptocentric concept of the world, see Morenz, 46ff.

[7] Cf. Meissner, *BuA*, II, 107.

[8] J. van Dijk, *AcOr*, 28 (1964/65), 1-59.

earth, which is divided into four regions (*kibrāt arbaim*), rests on the *apsû* (sweet-water ocean, underground water), which surrounds it on all sides. *Kippat šamê u erṣeti* means the circumference or the edge of the earth; but Akkadian literature also speaks of four *kippāti*. [9]

The earth, in order to be secured, is connected with heaven by a rope. This rope is the Milky Way. [10] One chamber in the temple of Enlil is called *Dur-an-ki* or *markas šamê u erṣeti*, "bond of heaven and earth," and thus is understood symbolically as the bond making the earth secure. [11] Similarly, the palace in Babylon is called *markas māti*, "bond of the land," and thus is (so to speak) the center of the land, the means by which the land is held together.

The earth can be divided into an upper earth where men live, a middle earth– the kingdom of the water-god Ea, and a lower earth–the dwelling place of the gods of the Underworld. [12] There is also the idea of seven earth-days (*tubuqāti*). [13] Several gods wear the title, "Lord of heaven and earth" (*bēl šamê u erṣeti*), [14] or "king (*šarru*) of heaven and earth." [15] Shamash is caretaker (*pāqidu*) and ruler (*muštēširu*) of heaven and earth. [16]

Heaven and earth are symbols of permanence ("firmly established like heaven and earth," "may his descendants continue as long as heaven and earth"). [17] "You shall swear by the name of heaven, you shall swear by the name of earth," is a stereotyped formula in exorcisms. [18]

Further, *erṣetu* denotes the Underworld, which is *erṣet lā târi*, a land without return. Thus it is said, "Ishtar has descended *ana erṣeti*, into the earth, i.e., into the Underworld," [19] and the spirit of Enkidu rises *ultu erṣetim*, out of the earth or out of the Underworld (Gilg. XII, 83f.).

Less often, *erṣetu* denotes a defined territory: "land" (e.g., of a king; [20] usually *mātu* is used to convey this idea), "territory," "district," [21] or even "ward." [22] Finally, *erṣetu* means "ground" in phrases like "he soaks the earth with his blood," "the earth shakes," "to plow the earth," "to paw the ground" (cf. Job 39:24), "to bury in the earth," etc. [23] In addition to *šamû u erṣetu*, the expression *šamû u qaqqaru* also occurs; *qaqqaru* is also used in the sense of "territory," and it is the most frequently used word for "ground." [24]

---

[9] Examples in *AHw*, 471, 482f.
[10] *BuA*, II, 111.
[11] E. Burrows, in *The Labyrinth*, ed. S. H. Hooke (London, 1935), 46f.
[12] *BuA*, II, 110.
[13] *BuA*, II, 375.
[14] Tallqvist, *Akk. Götterepitheta* (1938), 54.
[15] *Ibid.*, 239.
[16] *Ibid.*, 153 or 106.
[17] *CAD*, IV, 309.
[18] See the examples in *BuA*, II, 215-17, 222, 230, 233, 236.
[19] Ishtar's Descent Into Hell, verso 5, *AOT*, 208.
[20] *CAD*, IV, 311.
[21] *CAD*, IV, 311f.
[22] *CAD*, IV, 312.
[23] Examples in *CAD*, IV, 312f.
[24] *CAD*, IV, 313; *AHw*, 900f.

On the other hand, *mātu* means "land, territory" as a political entity, but also "the country" in contrast to city or mountains. Both *bēl māti* or *mātāti* and *šar māti* or *mātāti*, "lord" and "king" of the land or of the lands, occur as divine epithets. [25] The king is *šarri mātāti* "the king of (all) lands," [26] which makes clear his claim to world dominion (cf. Shamash as *nūr mātāti*, light of [all] lands). [27]

3. *West Semitic.* Ugar. *ʼrṣ* means "earth, ground, Underworld." Here also earth stands in antithesis to "heaven" and clouds: Baal raises his voice in the clouds and hurls lightning on the earth. [28] The earth is the sphere of living men: "Hadad will come among the peoples (*lʾmm*), Baal will return to the earth." [29] The substitute king ʻAthtar ʻAriz *ymlk bʼrṣ*, "rules over the earth," in connection with which *ʾl klh*, "as god of its entirety," indicates the extent of his rule. *zbl bʼl ʼrṣ*, "the prince, lord of the earth" as a divine title should also be mentioned here.

There are several cases in which *ʼrṣ* means "ground," among which the following may be mentioned: *CTA*, 5 [I* AB], VI, 8f., "Baal has fallen to the ground" (*npl lʼrṣ*); VI, 27, "Anat searches to the interior of the earth" (*lkbd ʼrṣ*); *CTA*, 10 [IV AB], II, 24, "we wish to knock my enemy to the ground"; *CTA*, 16 [II K], III, 5, "rain for the earth" (par. "field"); *CTA*, 5, II, 5, *ybl ʼrṣ*, "produce of the earth." There are several instances in which this word means "Underworld," which speak of descending "into the earth," e.g., *CTA*, 5 [I* AB], VI, 25; V, 14f., *wrd bt ḫptt ʼrṣ/tspr byrdm ʼrṣ*, "Go into the depths (cf. *chophshi*, Ps. 88:6 [Eng v. 5]) of the earth below, be numbered among those who descend into the earth."

For our purposes, the West Semitic inscriptions are not very fruitful. In the Mesha Inscription, [30] *ʼrṣ* occurs three times with the meaning "land" (in line 5, Chemosh is angry with his land, line 29 speaks of "cities which I had annexed to the land," and line 31 refers to the sheep of the land), and once with the more limited meaning "territory" (*ʼrṣ ʻtrt*, "the territory of Ataroth," line 10).

The following examples from the Phoenician inscriptions should be mentioned: (a) earth: Baal of heaven and El, creator of the earth (*ʼl qn ʼrṣ*); [31] (b) land: "I enlarged the land of the plain of Adana (*ʼrṣ ʻmq ʼdn*); [32] "I subjugated strong lands in the west." [33] The meaning of the expression *ṣdn ʼrṣ ym*, "Sidon of the sea land," in *KAI*, 14.16, 18, is debated, but it is probably to be understood as a part of Sidon. [34]

---

[25] Tallqvist, *Akk. Götterepitheta*, 48, 245.
[26] Seux, 315f.
[27] Tallqvist, 133; see further *AHw*, 633f.
[28] *CTA*, 4 [II AB], IV-V, 70f.
[29] *CTA*, 10 [IV AB], I, 8f.
[30] *KAI*, 181.
[31] Karatepe, *KAI*, 26 III.18.
[32] *KAI*, 26.14f.
[33] *KAI*, 26 I.18.
[34] Cf. *DISO*, 26 and the literature cited there.

The following examples may be cited from the Aramaic inscriptions: *KAI*, 216.4, *rb'y 'rq'*, "the four regions of the world"; 266.2, "(Astarte the mistress) of heaven and earth (i.e., of all)"; 214.7, "they cultivate the land and the vineyards" (*y'bdw 'rq vkrm*); Driver, *Aramaic Documents*, 6, 2, *'bwr 'rqt'*, "produce of the earth"; *KAI*, 215.5, 7, *'rq y'dy*, "the land Ya'udi."

II. In the OT. The Heb. *'erets* combines the same nuances of meaning as the related words discussed above: "earth" in the cosmic sense as an antithesis to "heaven," "land" in antithesis to "sea," "ground" and "land" = sovereign territory, the extent of which can be defined more precisely by a genitive, a possessive suffix, or a relative clause; we may add to this other examples where *'erets* means "Underworld," "Hades."

It is not always easy to determine whether *'erets* means "earth" or "land" in a given instance. As an example of this, some passages where the expression *kol ha'arets*, "the whole earth (land)," appears may be discussed here. It would seem to be evident that man was intended to have dominion over the whole *earth* (Gen. 1:26,28). Also, Gen. 7:3 has reference to the animals of the earth, and 8:9 means that the water covered the whole earth. 11:1 means that the whole earth had one language. However, in 13:9,15 *kol ha'arets* means "the whole *land*," and in 41:56 it means Egypt. There is none like Yahweh in all the earth (Ex. 9:14,16); similarly, Ex. 19:5 says, "all the earth is mine"; 9:29 may convey the same idea, but some scholars think the expression here has reference to Egypt. In Dt. 11:25; 19:8; 34:1; Josh. 6:27; 10:40; 11:16,23; 21:43; 1 S. 13:3; and 2 S. 24:8, it means "the whole land," but its meaning is doubtful in Josh. 4:24 ("the peoples of the whole earth," or "of the land"), and in 7:9, "they will cut off our name from the earth (or, out of the land)." Ex. 23:31; Nu. 33:52,55; Josh. 2:24; and 9:24 refer to "the inhabitants of the whole land." In 2 S. 18:8, *kol ha'arets* means the territory east of the Jordan. 1 S. 17:46 is often translated, "that the whole land may know that there is a God in Israel"; but "all the earth" would be a conceivable reading, just as when Naaman says: "Behold, I know that there is no God in all the *earth* but in Israel" (2 K. 5:15). *derekh kol ha'arets*, "(I go) the way of all the earth" (Josh. 23:14; 1 K. 2:2; cf. Gen. 19:31) is an interesting expression.

In Isa. 7:24, clearly the meaning is that "all the *land* will be briers and thorns," and 10:23; 28:22 have reference to "the whole land" (of Israel). In 13:5, it is not clear whether the enemies will destroy the whole earth or the whole land; vv. 9 and 11 seem to favor the view that the reference is to the earth. The meaning "earth" is to be preferred in 6:3; 10:14; 12:5; 14:7,26; 25:8; and 54:5. In Jeremiah *kol ha'arets* usually means "the whole land" (of Israel) (Jer. 4:20,23,27; 8:16; 12:11; 15:10; 23:15; 25:11; 40:4), but it means "earth" in the secondary passages, 50:23 and 51:7. In 45:4, "all flesh" (v. 5) favors the translation "earth."

Joel 1:2,14; 2:1; and Zec. 11:6 speak of "all the inhabitants of the land," while Zeph. 1:18 means "all the inhabitants of the earth." Again, Am. 8:8f. is difficult: does it mean that the land (North Israel) or the whole earth will tremble? The expression *kol ha'arets* has a cosmic dimension in Hab. 2:20; Zeph. 1:18; 3:8,19. According to Zec. 1:10f., the riders patrol the earth and declare that the whole *earth* is at rest; the translation "land" is less likely because of v. 15. But in Zec. 5:3,6, the meaning "the whole land" appears, while 14:9 has a cosmic dimension (cf. v. 8). [35]

1. *Cosmological Sense: Earth.* a. We encounter the bipartite division of the universe especially in texts describing creation or the greatness of the creator God. Yahweh is called "the God of heaven and of the earth" (Gen. 24:3), for he has created heaven and earth (1:1). In the ancient formula of Gen. 14:19,22, El Elyon is called "creator of heaven and earth" (*qoneh shamayim va'arets*). [36] Yahweh has established the ordinances (→ חק *chōq*) of heaven and earth; heaven and earth are his (Ps. 89:12[11]). Heaven is his throne and earth is his footstool (Isa. 66:1; cf. Lam. 2:1), and so he fills the entire creation. From heaven he looks down on the earth (Ps. 102:20[19]).

According to P, heaven was created on the second day (Gen. 1:6-8), and earth on the third (1:9-13). But J says (2:4ff.) nothing about the creation of heaven, but speaks only of the earth, which at first is dry and unfruitful, and is brought to life by water ('*edh*) going up from the earth. The creation of the earth is denoted by different verbs: → ברא *bārā'*, "to create" (Gen. 1:1; 2:4; Isa. 40:28); → עשה *'āśāh*, "to make" (Gen. 2:4; Ex. 20:11; 31:17; 2 K. 19:15; Isa. 37:16; 45:12,18; Jer. 10:12; 27:5; 32:17; 51:15; Ps. 115:15; 121:2; 124:8; 2 Ch. 2:11 [12]; etc.); → יסד *yāsadh*, "to lay the foundations of, found" (Isa. 48:13; 51:13, 16; Zec. 12:1; Ps. 24:2; 78:69; 102:26[25]; 104:5; Job 38:4); *talah*, "to hang" (Job 26:7); *qanah*, "to obtain, create" (Gen. 14:19,22; cf. Ps. 104:24); *raqa'*, "to stretch out, spread out" (Isa. 42:5; 44:24; Ps. 136:6); → יצר *yātsar*, "to form, fashion" (Isa. 45:18); *hekhin* (→ כון *kûn*), "to set up, establish" (Ps. 24:2; 119:90; cf. also *takhan*, "its pillars are established," 75:4[3]). None of these verbs is connected with the Primal War motif, but rather with the idea of the creative word of God (33:9). In the strange variant on the creation narrative in Prov. 8:22-31, personified wisdom is the first work of God and rejoices "in his inhabited world" (*bethebhel 'artso*). As Yahweh's creation, the earth is "his earth" (Job 37:13; Prov. 8:31; cf. Ps. 24:1; 89:12[11]; Ex. 9:29; 19:5). He fills heaven and earth (Jer. 23:24), he is the Lord (→ אדון *'adhôn*) of the whole earth (Mic. 4:13; Zec. 6:5; Ps. 97:5), its king (Ps. 47:3,8[2,7]) and God (Isa. 54:5; [37] or is *'erets* here "land"?); he is "the Most High" (→ עליון *'elyôn*) over all the earth (Ps. 83:19[18]; 97:9; 98:4; 100:1). His honor and glory (→ כבוד *kābhôdh*) extend over all the earth (57:6,12[5,11]; Isa. 6:3). In these statements, which for the most part belong to the tradition of God's royal sovereignty, Yahweh appears as the guarantor of world order. This is based on his having set a bound for the waters of chaos (Gen. 1:9; Ps. 104:9; 148:6); thus the earth is established on its pillars in the sea or "upon the rivers" (Ps. 24:2; 104:5; 136:6).

---

[35] On the Psalms, see below, II.1.
[36] Cf. above, I.3.
[37] Cf. the parallels in a tomb inscription, J. Naveh, *IEJ*, 13 (1963), 4-92.

The passages in the Psalms mentioned above and similar passages in the Psalms again show now and then the difficulty of determining whether *'erets* means "land" or "earth." Lipiński thinks that Ps. 47 reflects the time of the holy war, and according to him Yahweh here is "a great king over all the land (of Canaan)" (vv. 3,8[2,7]), [38] and "giver of the land" (*maghinne 'erets,* v. 10[9]). [39] But expressions like *'ammim,* "peoples" (vv. 2,4,10[1,3,9]), *le 'ummim,* "nations" (v. 4[3]), and especially "God reigns over the nations" (v. 9[8]) favor the meaning "earth." However, it is true that in the Psalms *'erets* often means "land." This is particularly the case in the historical psalms (44:4[3]; 80:10[9]; 106:38; 105:16; 135:12), but also when the fulfilment of the law is emphasized. [40] He who fears God will possess the land (25:13; cf. 37:3,9,11,22,29,34), and vice versa (140:12[11], "let not the slanderer be established in the land"). But in the hymns, "all the earth" is a familiar expression: Yahweh's name is majestic in all the earth (8:2,10[1,9]), his glory fills all the earth (57:6,12[5,11]; 108:6 [5]–par. "heaven"–72:19). The peoples of the earth shall sing praises to him (66:1,4; 96:1,9; 98:4; 100:1). 82:1,8 pictures God as judge of all the world; and the same cosmic aspect is dominant in the judgment motif (94:2; 98:9; 76:9[8]). When the God of Israel is called "the Most High over *kol ha'arets,* all the earth" (83:19[18]; cf. 89:28[27]; 97:9), "the Lord (*'adhon*) of all the *'erets,* earth" (97:5; cf. 114:7; Josh. 3:11,13; Mic. 4:13; Zec. 4:14; 6:5), or "king of the *'erets,* earth" (Ps. 97:1; 47:3,8[2,7]), these are indeed similar to ancient Near Eastern titles, which denote the god as lord of the land; [41] but in Israel the context seems to show that the OT writers have in mind the sovereignty of the world.

Because of man's unrighteousness, Yahweh determines to "destroy" the earth (Gen. 9:11). The flood signifies the temporary return of chaos over the earth. But Yahweh repents; he causes a wind to blow over the earth (8:1) so that the water subsides, and the rainbow is the sign that he will never again destroy the earth (9:11).

As part of creation established by God, heaven and earth are used as examples of durability (Ps. 78:69; cf. Eccl. 1:4; the same is true of the sun and moon, Ps. 89:37f.[36f.]). By way of contrast, there are passages that say the earth will wear out (→ בלה *bālāh*) like a garment (Isa. 51:6; cf. Ps. 102:27[26]), and a new heaven and a new earth will arise as a new creation of Yahweh (Isa. 65:17; 66:22; → ברא *bārā',* → חדש *ḥdš*.

The Israelite world view is the same as that generally held throughout the ancient Near East, according to which the earth is a disk resting in the ocean on foundations or pillars. This world view is expressed, e.g., in the verbs used to describe creation, *yasadh* and *raqa'.* [42] The earth has four corners (*kanephoth ha'arets,* Isa. 11:12; Ezk. 7:2; Job 37:3; 38:13; cf. Akk. *kippāt irbitti*), [43] or an edge or hem (*kanaph,* Isa. 24:16), an end (*qatseh,* Dt. 28:49; Isa. 5:26; 42:10;

---

[38] Lipiński, 427f.
[39] On *maghen,* see *ibid.,* 400f.
[40] Cf. Plöger, 91.
[41] Lipiński.
[42] See above.
[43] See above, I.2.

43:6; 48:20; 49:6; Ps. 61:3[2]; 46:10[9]; Prov. 17:24) or ends (*qetsoth*, Isa. 40:28; 41:5,9; Job 28:24; *qatsve*, Ps. 48:11[10]; 65:6[5]; Isa. 26:15; cf. "from the one end of the earth to the other," Dt. 13:8[7]; 28:64; Jer. 12:12; 25:33; → אפס *'ephes*, Dt. 33:17; 1 S. 2:10; Isa. 45:22; 52:10; Jer. 16:19; Mic. 5:3[4]; Zec. 9:10; Ps. 2:8; 22:28[27]; 72:8; 98:3; Prov. 30:4), sides or remote parts (*yarkethe 'arets*, Jer. 6:22; 25:32; 31:8; 50:41). The earth also has a center or "navel" (*tabbur*, Ezk. 38:12; cf. Jgs. 9:37), which clearly means Jerusalem. [44]

The expanse of the earth is defined very vaguely in the OT: it is called "the great earth" (*'erets rabbah*, Ps. 110:6; cf. Akk. *erṣetu rapaštu*). According to Zec. 14:8f., "all of the earth" over which Yahweh will become king will be bounded by "the eastern sea" (the Persian Gulf) and "the western sea" (the Mediterranean Sea). In Ps. 72:8, the dominion of the king is described as being "from sea to sea, and from the Euphrates to the ends of the earth."

The surface of the earth has been given to man as a dwelling place (Gen. 1:28; Ps. 115:16; Ezk. 41:16; 43:14); the wild beasts (*chayyath ha'arets*, Gen. 1:24) live on it (Isa. 18:6; Jer. 15:3; Ps. 79:2; Prov. 30:24); locusts can cover its face (Ex. 10:5,12,15); plants, herbs, and trees grow out of it (Gen. 1:11f.,29; 7:3; Am. 7:2). The creator gave man the commission to fill the earth and to have dominion over everything that lives on the earth (Gen. 1:28ff.). It is the creator's intention to make the earth a place of blessing. Thus, he causes snow (Job 37:6) and rain (2 S. 14:14; Hos. 6:3; Ps. 72:6; 147:8; Job 5:10; 12:15; 38:26; Eccl. 11:3) to fall on it, and that which grows upon it serves man and beast as food (Gen. 1:29f.; Am. 7:2; Job 28:5; etc.).

In an entirely general sense, men are called "inhabitants of the earth" (*yoshebhe ha'arets*, Isa. 24:5f.,17; Jer. 25:29f.; Zeph. 1:18; Ps. 33:14; 75:4[3]). Other expressions also occur: *goye ha'arets*, "nations of the earth" (Gen. 18:18; 22:18; 26:4; Dt. 28:1; Jer. 26:6; 33:9; 44:8; Zec. 12:3) or *'amme ha'arets*, "peoples of the earth" (Dt. 28:10; Josh. 4:24; 1 K. 8:43,53,60; Ezk. 31:12; Zeph. 3:20; 2 Ch. 6:33; cf. 1 Ch. 5:25; Est. 8:17; Ezr. 10:2,11; Neh. 10:31f. [30f.], "peoples of the land," → גוי *gôy*, → עם *'am*), and *mishpechoth ha'arets*, "families of the earth" (Zec. 14:17). Additional comparable expressions are *mamlekhoth ha'arets*, "the kingdoms of the earth" (Dt. 28:25; 2 K. 19:15; Isa. 37:20; Jer. 25:26), cf. *malkhe ha'arets*, "the kings of the earth" (Ps. 2:2; 89:28 [27]; 102:16[15]; 138:4; 148:11), *kol 'attudhe 'arets*, "all who were leaders of the earth" (Isa. 14:9), and *nikhbadde 'arets*, "the honored of the earth" (23:8f.). The assumption lying behind these expressions is an overall view of the (then known) world as a unity under Yahweh.

In theophany scenes and elsewhere, when Yahweh manifests his power, the earth reacts in submissiveness and fear. It trembles and quakes (1 S. 14:15; Isa. 13:13; 41:5; Jer. 10:10; 49:21; 50:46; 51:29; Joel 2:10; Ps. 18:8[7]; 68:9[8]; 99:1), it staggers and sways like a drunken man (Isa. 24:19f.), it mourns (24:4; 33:9; Jer. 4:28; 12:4; 23:10; Hos. 4:3). When Yahweh comes down upon the earth, the mountains melt and are cleft (Mic. 1:3f.), he speaks to the earth and summons it from the east to the west (Ps. 50:1). "He looks on the earth and it

---

44 Stadelmann, 147-154.

trembles" (104:32); when he utters his judgment from the heavens, the earth fears and is still (76:9[8]); the earth wears out like a garment (Isa. 51:6; Ps. 102:27[26]). [45] In contexts such as these, 'erets often is used in the sense of "inhabitants of the earth": all the earth is to fear its creator (Ps. 33:8), worship him (66:4), and praise him (148:13).

In the prophetic lawsuit (*rîbh* motif), again and again heaven and earth are summoned as witnesses: "Hear, O heavens, and give ear, O earth; for Yahweh has spoken" (Isa. 1:2); cf. "Hear, you mountains, the controversy (*ribh*) of Yahweh, and listen (read *ha'azinu*), you foundations of the earth" (Mic. 6:2). In Dt. 31:28 we find the formula, "that I may speak these words in their ears and call heaven and earth to witness against them." This also appears in a cultic context in Ps. 50:4, "He calls to the heavens above and to the earth, that he may judge his people." Further, the Song of Moses in Dt. 32 is introduced with similar words (v. 1). According to some scholars, [46] the origin of this prophetic speech form is to be sought in a judgment scene in the covenant cult, which could be indicated by Dt. 31:28 and Ps. 50 in particular. Extrabiblical parallels are found in Sumerian-Akkadian incantations ("swear by heaven, swear by earth"), [47] in Hittite and Aramaic treaties where heaven and earth are summoned as witnesses, [48] in Ugaritic treaties where heaven and earth appear as avengers of the treaty, and in the Akkadian Epic of Tukulti-Ninurta, where heaven and earth are mentioned as "watchmen of our oath." [49]

b. Along with the bipartite division, there is also a tripartite division of the universe into heaven, earth, and sea (water) in the OT. In Gen. 1:10, 'erets is defined as "the dry land," and forms the antithesis to the gathering together of the water, i.e., to the sea. The complete tripartite division occurs, e.g., in the prohibition against making graven images in Ex. 20:4 ("you shall not make any likeness of anything that is in heaven above, or that is in the earth beneath, or that is in the water under the earth"). However, Hag. 2:6 divides the universe into two antithetical pairs: "I will shake the heavens and the earth, the sea and the dry land (*charabhah*)." Ps. 135:6 says, "Whatever Yahweh pleases he does, in heaven and on earth, in the seas and all deeps (*tehomoth*)." [50] The OT also distinguishes between heaven, earth, and the Underworld, in which heaven is the dwelling place of God, earth is the dwelling place of the living, and Sheol is the home of the dead. [51]

2. *Ground.* 'erets often means "ground" when a given passage is speaking of the constitution of the earth or of its produce. It gives fatness (Gen. 27:28), increase (*yebhul,* Lev. 26:4,20; Dt. 32:22; Jgs. 6:4; Ezk. 34:27; Hag. 1:10; Zec. 8:12; Ps. 67:7[6]; 85:13[12]), fruit (*peri,* Nu. 13:20,26; Dt. 1:25; Isa. 4:2; Jer.

---

[45] Cf. Rost, 82.
[46] Huffmon, Wright.
[47] See above, I.2.
[48] Huffmon, 294.
[49] Harvey, 86-90; Delcor.
[50] Cf. Stadelmann, 9f., 126-28.
[51] See below, II.3.

2:7), growth, shoots (*tsemach,* Isa. 61:11), produce (*tebhu'ah,* Lev. 23:39; Josh. 5:12), bread (Ps. 104:14; Job 28:5), [52] in connection with which several passages mean the land of Canaan primarily. The fundamental idea is given in the story of creation, Gen. 1:11f.: let the earth put forth (hiphil of *yatsa'*) vegetation, i.e., herbs and trees bearing fruit.

On the other hand, the OT also speaks of the unfruitful land, [53] the desert (*'erets midhbar,* Dt. 32:10; Prov. 21:19). It is a "dry and weary land" (*'erets tsiyyah ve'ayeph,* Ps. 63:2[1]; only *'ayephah,* Isa. 32:2; Ps. 143:6), a parched land (*'erets tsiyyah,* Hos. 2:5[3]; Joel 2:20; Ps. 107:35; Isa. 41:18; 53:2) or "a dry and thirsty land" (*'erets tsiyyah vetsama',* Ezk. 19:13). Yahweh led Israel "in a land of deserts and pits, in a land of drought and deep darkness, in a land that none passes through, where no man dwells" (Jer. 2:6; cf. 51:43). The wilderness is "a land not sown" (*'erets lo' zeru'ah,* Jer. 2:2; cf. Dt. 29:22[23]), "a salt land" (*'erets melechah,* Jer. 17:6; Job 39:6), "a terrible land" (*'erets nora'ah,* Isa. 21:1), "a land of darkness" (*'erets choshekh,* Isa. 45:19, *ma'pelyah,* Jer. 2:31).

Moreover, the barrenness of the land was considered to be a divine punishment. Yahweh turns a fruitful land (*'erets peri*) into a salty waste because of the wickedness of its inhabitants (Ps. 107:34). Babylon is a land of drought and a desert, through which no one passes (Jer. 51:43). Egypt will become a desolate land (Ezk. 32:15). But the same is also true of Israel: the whole land is made desolate (Jer. 12:11; Ezk. 12:19), the land mourns because of the drought (Jer. 12:4), Jerusalem will become an uninhabited land (6:8, cf. the antithesis of this in Ex. 15:12).

The Deuteronomistic view in particular is that the transformation of the earth is a consequence of the curse that comes on the land because of disobedience, e.g., in Dt. 28:23: "the heavens shall be like brass, and the earth shall be like iron"; cf. also Lev. 26:19f. (H): "your land shall not yield its increase, and the trees of the land shall not yield their fruit." According to 26:32f., Yahweh will devastate the land, so that it will be a desolation (*'erets shemamah*).

'erets means "ground" in several expressions in the OT. From the earth one measures the high place (Ezk. 41:16; 43:14; cf. 42:6), the horse paws the earth (Job 39:24), the earth is plowed and distributed (Ps. 141:7). References are made to the ground in connection with different acts. Abishai wants to pin Saul to the ground (1 S. 26:8); Abner smites to the ground Asahel, who is following him (2 S. 2:22); Amasa's bowels are shed to the ground (2 S. 20:10); Jehoash of Israel smites the ground three times with arrows (2 K. 13:18). [54] David says: "Let not my blood fall to the ground," i.e., go unnoticed (1 S. 26:20); "not one hair of your son shall fall to the ground" (2 S. 14:11; cf. 1 K. 1:52); "no word of Yahweh will fall to the ground," i.e., remain unfulfilled (2 K. 10:10); "my liver was poured out on the earth," i.e., I was wholly in despair (Lam. 2:11).

To be struck or thrown to the ground is an expression meaning defeat. This

---

52 On the whole idea, see Rost, 80.
53 *Ibid.*
54 *Ibid.,* 81.

expression appears in several variants: Babylon is cut down to the ground (Isa. 14:12; 21:9), and so is Egypt (Ezk. 32:4). "The enemy has crushed my life to the ground" (Ps. 143:3); Yahweh casts the wicked or the proud to the ground (147:6; Ezk. 28:17); the lofty city will be laid low to the ground (Isa. 26:5; par. with 'aphar, "dust"; cf. Dnl. 8:7,10,12). Edom says proudly: "Who will bring me down to the ground?" (Ob. 3). Amos says: "you cast down righteousness to the ground" (Am. 5:7). Similar expressions are used of the sanctuary (Ps. 74:7), the king's crown (89:40[39]), and the king's throne (89:45[44]).

The mourner sits on the ground (Job 2:13; Lam. 2:21; Ezk. 26:16), as does one who has been deprived of his political power (Isa. 3:26; 47:1; Ob. 3). The OT speaks of persons casting themselves to the ground in reverence (hishtachavah, Ex. 34:8; Isa. 49:23; etc.)–before Yahweh (Gen. 24:52; Neh. 8:6), before the king (1 S. 25:23; 1 K. 1:31), or before a prophet (2 K. 2:15; 4:37). [55]

According to Gen. 2:7, man was created of dust ('aphar) from the earth (→ אדמה 'adhāmāh). Thus, man, who was formed out of dust, returns to the earth (Eccl. 12:7; cf. Job 10:9; Gen. 3:19 has 'aphar). 'aphar and 'erets stand in parallelism in Ps. 22:30(29); Isa. 25:12; 26:5; and perhaps 34:7. "Dust of the earth" is also a figure for a multitude and innumerability ("like the dust of the earth," Gen. 28:14; Ex. 8:12f.[16f.]; 2 S. 22:43; cf. "who can measure the dust of the earth?" Isa. 40:12).

3. *Underworld.* The earth is 'erets chayyim, "the land of the living" (or "of life"), i.e., the earth as the place of human life is contrasted with the Underworld (Isa. 38:11; 53:8; Jer. 11:19; Ezk. 26:20; 32:23-27,32; Ps. 27:13; 52:7[5]; 116:9; 142:6[5]; Job 28:13). In Ecclesiastes, sometimes 'erets is used pessimistically in the sense of earthly existence: 5:1(2); 7:20; 8:14,16; 11:2f.

Since the Underworld is located in the earth or under the earth, it can be denoted as 'erets tachtith, "the nether world" (Ezk. 31:14,16,18; 32:18,24), or tachtiyyoth 'arets, "the depths of the earth" (Isa. 44:23; Ezk. 26:20; Ps. 63:10 [9]). (Ps. 139:15, "I was woven in the depths of the earth" [tachtiyyoth 'erets], betrays a half-forgotten mythological idea of the origin of man in the bosom of Mother Earth.) Expressions like tehomoth ha'arets (Ps. 71:20) and mechqere 'arets, "the depths of the earth" (Ps. 95:4), also occur.

Occasionally, 'erets alone (like Akk. erṣetu) can mean the Underworld or in any case point to a connection with Sheol, [56] e.g., in Isa. 26:19, "the earth will again bring forth the shadows." At any rate, those who go down into the earth" are the dead (Jonah 2:7[6]; Ps. 22:30[29]; Job 17:16); this expression has a direct parallel in Ugar. yrdm 'rṣ. [57]

As the Underworld of the Sumerians and Akkadians is a land from which there is no return, so the Heb. she'ol, "Sheol," is a land of gloom and deep darkness, from which one does not return (Job 10:21). It is "a land of forgetfulness" ('erets neshiyyah, Ps. 88:13[12]). Since Yahweh is the God of the living,

---

55 *Ibid.*
56 Stadelmann, 128, 167.
57 Dahood, *Mélanges E. Tisserant* (1964), I, 85; Lipiński, 325ff.

the Underworld is not part of his sphere of influence. However, some texts maintain that he is present there too (Ps. 139:8; cf. Jonah 2:3 [2]).

4. *Land.* When *'erets* denotes a circumscribed territory, i.e., when it means "land," it can be defined more concretely in various ways.

a. It can be defined by a genitive indicating the direction: *'erets tsaphon,* "land of the north" (Jer. 3:18; 16:15; 23:8; Zec. 6:6,8), *'erets hanneghebh,* "land of the south" (Gen. 24:62; Nu. 13:29; Jgs. 1:15), *'erets mebho' hashshamesh,* "land of the sunset" (Zec. 8:7), *'erets mizrach,* "land of the sunrise" (8:7), and *'erets qedhem,* "land of the east" (Gen. 25:6).

b. It can be defined by topographical statements, e.g., *'erets hakkikkar,* "land of the circle," i.e., the plain of the Jordan (Gen. 19:28), *'erets ha'emeq,* "the valley region" (Josh. 17:16), *'erets hammishor,* "land of the plain" (Jer. 48:21), and *'erets hakkarmel,* "garden land" (2:7). Perhaps we should also mention here *'erets (hag)gil'adh,* the land east of the Jordan (Transjordan), if *gil'adh* is originally a designation for a natural phenomenon: "rough country." [58]

c. It can be defined by a genitive that puts the land in relationship to a person or a group: *'erets moledheth,* native land (Gen. 11:28; 24:7; 31:13; Jer. 22:10; 46:16; Ezk. 23:15; Ruth 2:11), *'erets 'abhoth,* "land of the fathers" (Gen. 31:3; 48:21), *'erets meghurekha,* "land of your sojournings" (28:4; Ex. 6:4; Ezk. 20:38), *'erets 'achuzzatham,* "land of their possession" (Gen. 36:43; Lev. 14:34; 25:24; Nu. 35:28; Josh. 22:4,9), *'erets yerushshatho,* "land of his possession" (Dt. 2:12; 1 K. 9:19; Jer. 51:28; 2 Ch. 8:6), *'erets shobhehem,* "land of their captivity" (1 K. 8:47; Jer. 30:10; 46:27; Neh. 3:36[4:4]; 2 Ch. 6:37f.), and *'erets 'oyebhehem,* "land of their enemies" (Lev. 26:41,44; cf. 26:34,38; 1 K. 8:48; Jer. 31:16).

d. It can be defined by a genitive of the name of the land or of the people that lives in it, e.g., *'erets mitsrayim,* Egypt, the name for a land used most often in the OT; [59] *'erets kena'an,* Canaan, which was never a kingdom in the political sense, but rather a colonial territory of varying size; [60] *'erets mo'abh,* Moab, *'erets 'edhom,* Edom, both of which were political territories of high rank; [61] *'erets hakkena'ani,* "land of the Canaanites" (Ex. 13:5,11; Dt. 1:7; Josh. 13:4; etc.); *'erets ha'emori,* "land of the Amorite" (always sing.), cf. Akk. *māt amurri* (Am. 2:10; Ex. 3:17; 13:5; Nu. 21:31; Josh. 24:8; Jgs. 10:8; 11:21); *'erets pelishtim,* "land of the Philistines" (Gen. 21:32,34; Ex. 13:17; 1 S. 27:1; 29:11; etc.); *'erets kasdim,* "land of the Chaldeans" (Isa. 23:13; Jer. 24:5; 25:12; etc.); and *'erets bene 'ammon,* "land of the Ammonites" (Dt. 2:19). It is worthy of note

---

[58] Ottosson, 15f.
[59] Plöger, 100ff.
[60] De Vaux; Aharoni, 61ff.
[61] Plöger, 115ff.

that the expression *'erets yisra'el*, "land of Israel," seldom occurs in the OT (it appears as a designation of the entire land only in 1 S. 13:19; Ezk. 40:2; 47:18; 1 Ch. 22:2; 2 Ch. 2:16[17]; 34:7; it is also found in 2 K. 5:2,4; 6:23; Ezk. 27:17; 2 Ch. 30:25, where it refers to North Israel). Perhaps the reason for this is that *'erets* denoted the territory of each tribe, e.g., *'erets gadh*, "the territory of Gad," *'erets naphtali*, "the territory of Naphtali," [62] and *'erets binyamin*, "the territory of Benjamin" (Jer. 1:1). In Ezk. 35:10, Judah and Israel are called "the two countries (lands)," and in 1 Ch. 13:2 we find the expression *bekhol 'artsoth yisra'el*, "in all the tribal territories (lands) of Israel." Further, in Jer. 12:15, "to return to his land" stands in parallelism with "to his heritage," and thus means: to return to his tribal territory. However, *'adhamath yisra'el*, "land of Israel," occurs 16 times in Ezekiel.

e. It can be defined by the name of a city or a prince, e.g., *'erets tappuach*, "land of Tappuah" (Josh. 17:8), *'erets ra'amses*, "land of Rameses" (Gen. 47:11), *'erets hammitspah*, "land of Mizpah" (Josh. 11:3), *'erets chamath*, "land of Hamath" (2 K. 23:33; 25:21; Jer. 39:5; 52:9,27; cf. the Moabite expression *'rṣ 'trt*; [63] Phoen. *'rṣ* is a "city-state," a meaning Dahood also finds in Prov. 29:4; 31:23; Eccl. 10:16; 2 Ch. 32:4; [64] Akk. *erṣetu* is also used for a city and its administrative territory [65]), *'erets sichon*, "land of Sihon" (Dt. 4:46), and *'erets 'ogh*, "land of Og" (4:47). Names of mountains also occur in connection with *'erets*, e.g., *'erets 'ararat*, "land of Ararat" (2 K. 19:37; Isa. 37:38), and *'erets hammoriyah*, "land of Moriah" (Gen. 22:2).

5. *Theological Sense.* In particular, the statements using *'erets* that refer to the land of Canaan are of special theological significance. The defining of the land is not always exact in this case. In Gen. 15:18, its greatest extent is indicated by the expression "from the river of Egypt to the Euphrates," but in other passages it is called quite generally "the land of the Canaanites" (Ex. 3:17; Nu. 34:2) or "of the Amorites" (Dt. 1:7); it also includes the territory east of the Jordan (Nu. 32:1ff.; Dt. 2:24ff.; Josh. 13:8-33; 22; Ps. 135:11f.; 136:19-22). [66]

In reality, this land belongs to Yahweh. It is called "his heritage" (→ נחלה *naḥⁿlāh*) (1 S. 26:19; 2 S. 14:16; Jer. 2:7; 16:18; 50:11; Ps. 68:10[9]; 79:1), and once *'adhamath yhvh*, "land of Yahweh" (Isa. 14:2); cf. also *'adhmathi*, "my land" (2 Ch. 7:20), and *'achuzzath yhvh*, "land of Yahweh," of the land west of the Jordan (Josh. 22:19). Also, the OT says concerning the land east of the Jordan, "Gilead, you belong to me" (*'attah li*) (Jer. 22:6; Ps. 60:9[7]; 108:9[8]).

In Lev. 25:23, this divine claim of possession is emphasized so strongly that the Israelites are regarded as strangers and foreigners: "The land (*ha'arets*) shall

---

62 Cf. von Rad, 88f.
63 *KAI*, 181.10.
64 Dahood, *Bibl*, 47 (1966), 280.
65 See Watson, *VT*, 20 (1970), 501f.
66 Cf. Ottosson, 74ff., 119f.

not be sold in perpetuity, for the land is mine (*ki li ha'arets*), for you are strangers (→ גר *gēr*) and sojourners with me." [67] The regulations for the sabbath year and the year of jubilee in Lev. 25 can be understood only on the assumption that the land is actually the possession of Yahweh. One must obey the possessor of the land if one wishes to live there in peace. Disobedience to Yahweh violates the sacral character of the land: Jer. 2:7, "when you came in you defiled *my* land, and made my heritage an abomination"; 16:18, "I will doubly recompense their iniquity..., because they have polluted *my* land with the carcasses of their detestable idols, and have filled my inheritance with their abominations." Indeed, it can be said of Israel: "These are the people of Yahweh, and yet they had to go out of *his* land" (Ezk. 36:20). Nor can Yahweh tolerate the encroachments of other nations against his land. He speaks jealously against Edom and other nations "who gave *my* land to themselves as a possession" (Ezk. 36:5). Joel 1:6 speaks of "a nation that has come up against *my* land." Enemies will attack the land in vain. Thus we read concerning Assyria in Isa. 14:25: "I will break the Assyrian in *my* land, and upon my mountains trample him under foot." Joel 2:18 says: "Yahweh became jealous for *his* land, and had pity on his people." And Joel 4:2(3:2) predicts that the nations will be judged in the valley of Jehoshaphat "because they have divided up *my* land." It is said of Gog, "I will bring you against *my* land, that the nations may know me" (Ezk. 38:16).

Only Hos. 9:3 has the expression *'erets yhvh,* "land of Yahweh," in a context that speaks of the apostasy of the nation: "they shall not remain in the land of Yahweh"–they will have to return to Egypt and Assyria. In these examples, nation and land usually stand in parallelism (cf. Dt. 32:9). Deuteronomy in particular enlarges on this idea, because it regards the land as the inheritance of all Israel (4:21,38; 12:9; 19:10; 20:16; 21:23; 24:4; 25:19; also Ps. 135:12). However, in the texts that relate the distribution of the land, the idea of *nachalah* (inheritance) is connected with the sovereign territory of the tribe. [68]

The concept of Canaan as the land of Yahweh makes Yahweh a God of the land. Just as Chemosh rules over the land of Moab, Yahweh rules over his territory. [69] This idea is often put into the mouth of a foreigner (2 K. 5:17; 18:33ff.; Isa. 36:18ff.). Yahweh lives in the land, in the midst of the people (Nu. 35:34)– thus land, people, and God belong together. Other gods rule in foreign lands among foreign peoples (1 S. 26:19; Hos. 9:3f.; Am. 7:17). The land is defiled by heathen cults, and "vomits out its inhabitants" (Lev. 18:25). This is what happened to the Canaanites; but if Israel keeps away from foreign cults, she will not be vomited out of the land (18:28; 20:22).

The OT emphasizes that Israel did not obtain the land because of her own merit, but received it as a gift from God (Dt. 1:36; etc.). Because of their wickedness Yahweh drove out the former inhabitants, and gave the land to the Israelites (1:8; etc.).

As Yahweh's inheritance, the land is given exuberant epithets. It is "the good

---

[67] See Wildberger, 404ff.
[68] Von Rad, 88; Lipiński, 411.
[69] *KAI,* 181.5ff.

(→ טוב *tôbh*) land" (Ex. 3:8; Nu. 14:7; Dt. 1:25; etc.), an expression that combines "fruitfulness, wealth, beauty–in short, the fulness of blessing"; "it is the abundantly blessed, glorious land." [70] Dt. 8:7-10 speaks hymnically of abundance of water, fruitfulness, plenty of food, and the presence of ore; an aesthetic element appears also in 11:10-12. [71] Further, it is a land flowing with milk and honey (Nu. 13:27; Dt. 6:3; 11:9; 26:9,15; 27:3; Jer. 11:5; 32:22), which could be regarded as gifts from God; and the expression may have a paradisiacal-mythological background. Sometimes the OT speaks also of a "broad land" ('*erets rechabhah*) (Ex. 3:8; Neh. 9:35; cf. *rachabhath yadhayim*, "broad," Jgs. 18:10; Isa. 22:18; 1 Ch. 4:40), which does not denote so much national boundaries, but refers to freedom and prosperity in connection with the "nomadic perspective on life." Expressions like '*erets chemdah*, "land of pleasantness," "precious land" (Jer. 3:19; Ps. 106:24), and '*erets tsebhi*, "the glorious land" (Dnl. 8:9; 11:16,41), also occur.

The promise of the land runs through the patriarchal narratives like a red thread (Gen. 12:7; 13:15,17; 15:18; 17:8; 24:7; 26:3f. [pl. "lands"]; 28:13f.; 35:12; 48:4; 50:24). According to Hoftijzer, the two central passages are 17:1-8, where Abraham is promised numerous descendants who shall receive "all the land of Canaan for an everlasting possession," and chap. 15, where Abraham is promised numerous descendants (v. 5) and the land (v. 7), but not until the fourth generation (v. 16). According to Hoftijzer, the other allusions to these promises are secondary from a traditio-historical point of view. In 12:1, J formulates his own version of the promise: "Go from your country . . . to the land that I will show you, and I will make of you a great nation, and I will bless you . . . , and by you all the families of the earth shall be blessed (or, shall bless themselves, → ברך *bārakh*)." The break with the family of Abraham and with his fatherland, as well as Abraham's acceptance of the promise, are presented very beautifully. The exact meaning of the concluding words is not clear, but they obviously predict that Abraham's obedience will have positive consequences for the whole earth.

According to Alt, the original promise, corresponding to the vital interests of nomads, had to do with descendants, while the land promise was added after the settlement in Canaan. [72] Von Rad thinks that the idea of the conquest did not belong to the ancient cult saga, but went back to the pre-Yahwistic patriarchal religion. The land promise originally had reference to the patriarchal groups and was later transferred to the twelve-tribe league. [73] According to Noth, both the land promise and the promise of descendants were a part of the patriarchal religion. When the patriarchal history was combined with the traditions of the exodus and the conquest, the element of fulfilment in the patriarchal narratives lost its significance and was transferred to the conquest tradition. [74]

---

[70] Plöger, 90.
[71] *Ibid.*, 89.
[72] Alt, *GF*.
[73] G. von Rad, *Formgesch. des Pentateuchs* = *ThB*, 8, 9, 86; "Verheissenes Land," *ThB*, 8, 87-100.
[74] See also Plöger, 63ff.

Deuteronomy understands the patriarchal narrative exclusively in the sense of land promise. "Possession of the land is a prerequisite for the existence of, and a condition for the continuation of, the people. Loss of the land means the end of the national existence."[75] "The land that Yahweh swore to give to the fathers" is a favorite expression in Deuteronomy (Dt. 1:8,35; 6:10,18,23; 8:1; 10:11; 11:9; 19:8; 26:3; 30:20; 31:7,23; also with 'adhamah).[76] It emphasizes that Israel possesses the land not because of her own righteousness, but because of the wickedness of its earlier inhabitants and "that he (Yahweh) may confirm the word" (Dt. 9:4ff.). In 4:37f., Yahweh's love to Abraham is specified as the ultimate reason for the possession of the land.

But it is established that the land "is the proper milieu for the fulfilment of the law."[77] Again and again it is emphasized that the people are to learn the law "that they should do it in the land Yahweh is giving them" (Dt. 4:5,14; 5:31; 6:1; 11:31f.). Thus 12:1 says: "These are the statutes and ordinances which you shall be careful to do in the land ... all the days that you live in the land." Frequently, this formal introduction is used: "When you come into the land Yahweh your God is giving you." The commandment to honor one's parents promises long life in the land[78] for those who keep it–however, 'adhamah is used here. But in other passages also, obedience and disobedience have consequences for the land. The series of blessings and curses in Dt. 28 pronounce a blessing upon the land (v. 8) and its fruit (v. 11), and a curse upon the fruit of the land (v. 18). Finally, expulsion from the land is mentioned among the results of the curse (v. 63). Similarly, chap. 4 (late?)[79] speaks of utter destruction from the land as a consequence of disobedience (v. 26): "you will not live long upon it, but will be utterly destroyed."[80] But similar ideas also occur in the final chapter of H (Lev. 26). If the people walk in God's statutes, he will "give peace in the land" (v. 6); but if not, the land will not yield its fruit (v. 20), Yahweh will devastate the land (v. 32), the people will go into the lands of their enemies (v. 36), and "the land of your enemies shall eat you up" (v. 38).

Ordinarily, the earlier prophets do not question the possession of the land. But occasionally, we find references to enemy devastation of the land (Isa. 1:7, "your land lies desolate [shemamah]"; 6:12, "the forsaken places are many in the midst of the land"; 9:18[19], "through the wrath of Yahweh the land is burned"; Mic. 7:13, "the land will be desolate"). The land is mentioned more often in Jeremiah and Ezekiel. Here a new element is added, viz., the exile from the land "into the lands." Thus, we find statements like these in Jeremiah: Yahweh wanted to give Israel a pleasant land (Jer. 3:19), and if she would improve her conduct, he would allow her to remain in the land (7:7). The people had defiled the land by their sins (2:7), and so, just as they had served foreign gods in their own land, now they would serve strangers in a foreign land (5:19).

---

75 Ibid., 81.
76 Ibid., 63f.; Wijngaards, 77ff.
77 Plöger, 91f.
78 Cf. Wijngaards, 41.
79 Cf. Lohfink, Höre Israel (1965), 87ff.
80 Cf. Wijngaards, 41.

Yahweh will hurl them out of the land into a land they had not known (16:13; cf. the statement concerning Jehoiachin in 22:26). But finally, Yahweh will bring them back into the land which he had given to the fathers (3:18; 24:6; 30:3).

Ezekiel knows that the land is full of bloodguilt, and that people say, "Yahweh has forsaken the land" (Ezk. 9:9). In chap. 20, he narrates the entire story of the choice and apostasy of the people in traditional terminology: Yahweh swore to bring Israel out of the land of Egypt "into a land that I had searched out for them, a land flowing with milk and honey, the most glorious of all lands" (v. 6). Yet he did not bring the rebellious into the land (v. 15). And when the Israelites came into the promised land, they sacrificed to idols (v. 28), and therefore they must go into exile (vv. 23,35). But now Yahweh will gather them out of the countries (v. 34), and "on my holy mountain ..., all the house of Israel shall serve me in the land" (v. 40). The idea of gathering those who were scattered among the nations (12:15; 20:23; 22:15) and those who were dispersed through the countries is a favorite theme in Ezekiel's oracles of salvation (20:41; 34:13; 36:24); "then you shall dwell in the land which I gave to your fathers" (36:28).

Ottosson

אָרַר 'rr; מְאֵרָה *me'ērāh*

Contents: I. 1. Etymology, Forms; 2. *arāru* I in Akkadian. II. *'rr* in Hebrew: 1. The *'ārûr*-Formula in the OT; 2. Other Forms of the Root *'rr* in the OT; 3. *'rr* in Hebrew Inscriptions, the Qumran Literature, and the LXX. III. Words for "Curse": 1. In the Ancient Near East; 2. In the OT. IV. The Religious Significance of the Curse: 1. In the Ancient Near East; 2. In Israel.

I. 1. *Etymology, Forms.* The Semitic root *'rr* is found in South Arabic (Soqotri), Ethiopic (Tigriña), Akkadian, and Hebrew. In Akkadian, it seems necessary to divide *arāru* into two[1] or three[2] roots: (a) *arāru* I, "to curse,"

'rr. In addition to the Bibliography under → אלה *'ālāh*, cf. P. Buis, "Deutéronome XXVII 15-26: Malédictions ou exigences de l'Alliance," *VT*, 17 (1967), 478; L. Dürr, *Die Wertung des göttlichen Wortes im AT und im Antiken Orient. MVÄG*, 42/1 (1938); F. C. Fensham, "Malediction and Benediction in Ancient Near Eastern Vassal-Treaties and the OT," *ZAW*, 74 (1962), 1-9; *idem*, "Common Trends in Curses of the Near Eastern Treaties and *kudurru*-Inscriptions compared with the Maledictions of Amos and Isaiah," *ZAW*, 75 (1963), 155-175; S. Gevirtz, "West-Semitic Curses and the Problem of the Origins of Hebrew Law," *VT*, 11 (1961), 137-158; P. Heinisch, *Das "Wort" im AT und im Alten Orient. BZfr*, 10/7-8 (1922); D. R. Hillers, *Treaty Curses and the OT Prophets* (Rome, 1964); B. Landsberger, *Das "gute Wort." MAOG*, 4 (1928/29); I. Lewy, "The Puzzle of Dt 27," *VT*, 12 (1962), 207-210; H.-P. Müller, *Ursprünge und Strukturen at.licher Eschatologie. BZAW*, 109 (1969), 129-171;

(continued on p. 406)

[1] *AHw.*
[2] *CAD.*

with the derivatives *arru* (a verbal adj.), "accursed," *āriru*, "a priest who pronounces a curse" (?), *arratu* and *erretu*, "curse"; (b) *arāru* II, "to tremble, to flicker, to burn, to be excited, stimulated"; (c) *arāru* III,[3] "to rot." The Arab. *'arra*, "to stimulate (sexually), to drive away," may be cognate with Akk. *arāru* II. But Soq. *'erer*, "to curse,"[4] and Tigr. *'arar*, "shame," are certainly related to Akk. *arāru* I and Heb. *'rr*. The Heb *'rr* appears only in the sense of "curse." In the OT, the form that occurs most frequently is the qal passive participle in the so-called *'ārûr*-formula (39 times). Other forms of the qal are found 14 times, scattered throughout the entire OT. The niphal (Mal. 3:9) and the hophal (Nu. 22:6) appear only once each, and the piel occurs 7 times (in Gen. 5:29 in the perf. 3rd masc. sing., and in Nu. 5:18-27 in the pl. ptcp. in the expression *hammayim hame'ararim*, "the water that brings a curse"). The only derivative of this root that we encounter in the OT is the noun *me'erah*, "curse" (5 times).

2. *arāru I in Akkadian.* Perhaps the occurrences of Akk. *arāru* I may be analyzed along the following lines.[5] (a) Formal statements such as "May the god A (and the god B) curse (*li-ru-ur*) so-and-so (with an evil curse, *erretam maruštam*)," etc. are found on documents, building inscriptions, and boundary stones as ratifications of treaties, authoritative commands, and private contracts between citizens having equal rights. They were intended to deter those entering into agreements from breaking the treaty or the contract, or subjects from

---

M. Noth, "Die mit des Gesetzes Werken umgehen, die sind unter dem Fluch," *In piam memoriam A. von Bulmerincq = Abh. d. Herder-Ges. u. d. Herder-Inst. zu Riga*, VI/3 (Riga, 1938), 127-145; now in: *GSAT = ThB*, 6 (³1966), 155-171; G. Offner, "A propos de la sauvegarde des tablettes en Assyro-Babylonie," *RA*, 44 (1950), 135-143; A. Parrot, *Malédictions et violations de tombes* (Paris, 1939); Pedersen, *ILC*, 411-452; J. G. Plöger, *Literarkritische, formgeschichtliche und stilkritische Untersuchungen zum Deuteronomium. BBB*, 26 (1967), 130-217; A. Schächter, "Bundesformular und prophetischer Unheilsspruch," *Bibl*, 48 (1967), 128-131; J. Scharbert, *Solidarität in Segen und Fluch im AT und in seiner Umwelt. BBB*, 14 (1958); W. Schottroff, *Der altisraelitische Fluchspruch. WMANT*, 30 (1969); H. Schulz, *Das Todesrecht im AT. BZAW*, 114 (1969), esp. 61-70; M. de Tuya, "El problema bíblico de las imprecaciones," *Ciencia Tomista*, 78 (1951), 171-192; 79 (1952), 3-29; K. R. Veenhof, "An Aramaic Curse with a Sumero-Akkadian Prototype," *BiOr*, 20 (1963), 142-44.

On the Psalms of Imprecation: F. Baumgärtel, "Der 109.Psalm in der Verkündigung," *Monatsschrift für Pastoraltheologie*, 42 (1953), 244-253; H. A. Brongers, "Die Rache- und Fluchpsalmen im AT," *OTS*, 13 (1963), 21-42; E. Charpentier, "Comment prier les 'Psaumes de malédiction'?" *BVC*, 41 (1961), 52-57; P. van Imschoot in *BL²*, 488f.; O. Keel, *Feinde und Gottesleugner. SBM*, 7 (1969), 226-231; A. Miller, "Fluchpsalmen und israelitisches Recht," *Angelicum*, 20 (1943), 92-101; G. Sauer, *Die strafende Vergeltung Gottes in den Psalmen* (diss., Basel, 1957), cf. *ThLZ*, 83 (1958), 721f.; *idem*, in *BHHW*, I, 488f.; R. Schmid, "Die Fluchpsalmen im christlichen Gebet," *Theologie im Wandel = Festschrift d. Kath.-theol. Fakultät Tübingen 1817-1967* (1967), 377-393; F. Steinmetzer, "Babylonische Parallelen zu den Fluchpsalmen," *BZ*, 10 (1912), 133-142, 363-69.

[3] See *AHw, s.v. erēru.*

[4] W. Leslau, *Lexique soqotri* (Paris, 1938), 11.

[5] For the evidence, see *AHw, CAD*, Brichto (→ אלה *'ālāh*, Bibliography); Schottroff, 31-35, 69f.

transgressing the command, or evildoers from falsifying the document, or from damaging the building, the grave, etc. The object that is cursed can be a person, but it can also be the "kingdom," "destiny" (*šimtu*), or "land" of the king of another country or of a succeeding king. This kind of statement was considered to be an indirect petition to the deities, who were implored to bring calamity upon a particular lawbreaker. In light of the importance the Akkadians attributed to the word of the gods, which was powerful and determined fate,[6] we must assume that "to curse" was understood in the sense of pronouncing a curse formula which would bring about or set in motion the desired evil.

(b) In omina, we find statements such as, "The god so-and-so curses/has cursed the land" (*māta irrar/ītarar*), etc. Actually, such statements have to do with the result of an event interpreted as a sign of misfortune. We cannot be absolutely sure whether the verb *arāru* here was understood to mean that people believed that the gods pronounced a curse formula before the announced misfortune began, or whether it was understood in the sense of "determining or causing misfortune."

(c) When human beings are the subject of this verb, it is used less frequently in the formal sense. One person believes that his enemies can "curse" their opponent or his father, and thus bring calamity upon him. The king "curses" an unruly subject, and the father a spoiled son. Those who enter into a contract or covenant "curse" themselves or one another in case the contract or covenant is broken. It is obvious that in these instances curse formulas were pronounced. This is further established by the internal object *arratum īrur*, "he curses with a curse," which appears in this kind of context, and by passages like Gilg. VII, 5-20, where the announcement that Enkidu "became so angry that he cursed (*arāra*) the prostitute" is followed by the text of a long curse formula.

(d) When subordinate people (subjects of a king, slaves, court personnel) are the subject, however, and persons in position of authority (a king, the master of a slave, the women of a harem) are the object, of *arāru*, the meaning "to curse" seems to be inappropriate, while "to speak disrespectfully of so-and-so" or "to act disrespectfully toward so-and-so" seems to convey the intention more accurately. This is close to the meaning of the Heb. *qillēl*.[7] The concept of a formal curse is hardly present here.[8] To be sure, this kind of behavior potentially may be threatened with punishment, but it is not considered to be perilous, evidently because such a "curse" has no real power. Consequently, it seems that *arāru* is to be understood in the sense of "curse" only when persons in positions of authority (gods, kings, parents), or with the responsibility of defending someone's rights in legal matters (in the case of treaties or contracts and legal transactions, against a malicious enemy), pronounce a curse formula.

(e) Ordinarily the noun *arratu* or *erretu* denotes formal curses, curse formulas which are pronounced and therefore "are on the lips," or which "are written down" on a document. People are afraid of such curses, especially when they

---

[6] Cf. the investigations of Dürr, Heinisch, and Landsberger.

[7] → קלל *qālal*, and cf. below, III.2.

[8] Cf. *CAD*, I/2 s.v. *arāru* A 2.

are formuated by their own parents or when they believe that the gods have pronounced them. In view of this, the nouns *arratu* and *māmītu,* "oath, ban," seem to be almost synonymous in the specific ways in which they are used (cf. Šurpu IV, 58 [*arratu*] and V, 42ff. [*mamitu*]). Once they are pronounced and set in force in a given situation, both are efficacious, because they bring about the calamity invoked in the curse. But in spite of the occasional appearance of the attribute *arrat/māmīt lā napšuri,* "an indissoluble curse," both can be counteracted by efficacious incantations which are just as strong or stronger, or by the opposite decision of a deity whom the accursed person petitions. The very abundant incantation literature and the Psalms of Lament have this purpose, among others, in mind.

   (f) Sometimes, of course, the noun also denotes the misfortune caused by the curse. In this case, it is said that the *arratu* "lays hold of" someone, "falls upon" him, and "plunges him into terror and fear." Finally, like the Heb. → אָלָה *'ālāh* [9] and *qᵉlālāh* (→ קלל *qālal*), the noun can be used metonymically for a person who is smitten with misfortune because of a curse; he is a "curse of the gods" (*arrat ilāni*). In spite of numerous curse formulas in which the root *arāru* is used, as far as is known there is no formula in Akkadian that would correspond to the Heb. *'ārûr*-formula.

II. 'rr in Hebrew.

1. *The 'ārûr-Formula in the OT.* Among the various uses of the Heb. root *'rr,* the *'ārûr*-formula, formed with the qal passive participle, occupies a very special position. It is a substantival expression beginning with the predicate *'ārûr* followed by the subject, which can be a pronoun of the 2nd or 3rd person singular or plural, or a person, or a thing. This formula can be expanded by a reason for the curse, or by a more precise explanation of the nature of the curse. The question of whether the mood of the substantival expression was understood as the indicative statement of a curse, or as a wish, must be determined by the context. However, the only passage in which the mood can be assumed with certainty to be a wish is Jer. 20:14f., since the parallel expression in v. 14b says, "let it not be blessed" (*'al yehi bharukh*). In 1 S. 26:19, which Schottroff interprets in this way, [10] in reality we do not find a wish, but a conditional sentence. In all other passages where the *'ārûr*-formula occurs, it is most natural to understand it in the indicative sense.

   We must assume that the original *Sitz im Leben* of the expression *'arur 'attah* or *'arurim 'attem,* "Cursed art thou/are they," was the immediate reaction of a person to a suspicious misbehavior on the part of someone else, and that the intention of the one pronouncing this expression was to vigorously keep himself aloof from that person and his action. But the relevant passages in the OT show that the person who was smitten by a curse was in a subordinate relationship to the one who had uttered the curse, and had been expelled from a community

---

   [9] Cf. below, IV.
   [10] Schottroff, 48.

relationship where he had enjoyed security, justice, and success. Thus, according to Gen. 4:11, after Cain had murdered his brother, he was denied close fellowship with God and was driven away from the fruitful land; and according to 3:14, God deprived the serpent of his former place in the animal community. According to Josh. 9:23, after Joshua discovered the deception of the Gibeonites, he lowered them from the status of vassals to the status of slaves. The adverbial phrase, "from (*min*) the ground/away from all cattle," was not part of the formula originally, but probably was inserted in the course of the development of the narrative. However, we must assume that from the time the formula first became stereotyped, reasons could have been added, as perhaps "because (*ki*) you have done this...," which always precede the curse formula in the OT (Gen. 3:14,17). The question, "Why have you done this?" or something similar, which also precedes the curse and is connected to the curse formula by "and now" (*ve'attah*, 4:11; Josh. 9:23), may be part of the original *Sitz im Leben*. One can also see why a curse formula might be directed against the territory in which a person lived or against things necessary to his sustenance as well as against the person himself. This explains the use of the curse formula with reference to the ground in Gen. 3:17. In Dt. 28:16-19, the curse pronounced on "thou" involves a curse upon the necessities of life ("harvest basket," "kneading-trough," "the fruit of your body and the fruit of your ground"). Here it is clear that in reality the *'arur* has in mind the exclusion of a person from the community, the tribe, or the people who stand under the blessing. The present formulation of 28:16-19 assumes that either the whole people ("thou") or some individual whom the community has not punished properly and thus has protected, has transgressed the covenant law. In this case also, the curse is intended to affect the whole realm of life, but the writer still feels it necessary to define this realm explicitly ("in the city"–"in the field"–"when you come in"–"when you go out"). Schottroff may be correct in suggesting that this passage is speaking of rural farm life ("coming in" from working in the field, and "going out" to work in the field). [11]

The curse formula was changed to the 3rd person when the person being cursed was not present, or when the person pronouncing the curse had determined that he would never see the one he was cursing again because the behavior of the latter had destroyed their relationship, a situation that may be assumed in Gen. 9:25. The 3rd person is also used especially in a curse pronounced by a person who is suspicious that an undefined circle of persons is responsible for a calamity that has come upon him, but cannot verify this as a fact, as in 1 S. 26:19. Yet, in this case the curse formula can be expressed only conditionally (*'im*).

The *'arur*-formula was also used when the intention was to discourage someone from transgressing a commandment, a commonly accepted responsibility, or a far-reaching legal or ethical demand. In this case, the curse formula is the most severe means of separating the community from the evildoer. It is significant that the only ones who pronounce such a curse in the OT are God, the

---

[11] *Ibid.*, 61f.

king, those in positions of authority, or the whole assembly of the people. This sort of curse is always conditional, and thus takes effect only when the situation it is intended to prevent exists. This situation that makes a curse effective can be expressed in two different ways: (a) by a participial construction, or (b) by a relative clause, "the man who does (or does not do) this or that" (ha'ish 'asher, and sometimes without ha'ish). In narrative contexts, both forms occur side by side when the passage has to do with a concrete reason for preventing something that is undesirable. In Jgs. 21:18, the participial curse formula threatens anyone who transgresses the resolution of the tribal league not to let their daughters marry men of the tribe of Benjamin. The relative clause is used in 1 S. 14:24, where a curse is placed on anyone who does not observe the king's order to abstain from food until evening, and in Josh. 6:26, where a curse is placed on the man who rebuilds the city of Jericho. But the OT shows preference for the participial construction when the purpose of the curse is to prevent legal situations that would threaten an intimate relationship in the family, in the clan or tribal league, and in the local community, or that would threaten the fundamental rights of socially weak members of the tribe.

Dt. 27:16-25 is composed of a "decalog" of ten curse formulas pertaining to situations such as dishonoring one's parents, removing a neighbor's landmark, endangering the blind, perverting justice due to the sojourner, the fatherless, and the widow, sexual abuses (incest and bestiality), murder, and bribing judges or witnesses. This series of ten curses is hardly original, but probably was put together from earlier smaller series and individual formulas for the first time when Dt. 27 was compiled. In particular, the four curses against sexual offenders formulated by the expression, "Cursed be he who lies with...," must have belonged to an earlier series. A traditionist has placed the curse against the maker of cult images in the form of a relative clause before the series in 27:16-25, and has added at the end (vv. 15 and 26) a curse against anyone who transgresses the entire Torah corpus of Dt. 6–26. In this way, he has made this series a striking conclusion to Dt. 6–26, and in its present position it is analogous to the decalog in Dt. 5, which introduces the entire corpus. [12] We can assign the series in 27:16-25 to a cultic Sitz im Leben for the first time in this stage of the tradition process, because now for the first time the 'arur-formula is used as a ratification of the Yahweh-covenant regulations governing the whole life of Israel, which were proclaimed in the cult. The formula in Jer. 11:3, where the person who does not heed "the words of this covenant" is placed under a curse (in the form of a relative clause), is influenced by this Deuteronomic use. Gen. 27:29 and Nu. 24:9—where, to be sure, the syntactical order of predicate-subject is reversed: 'orerekha 'arur, "Cursed be every one who curses you," which is parallel to the barukh-formula mebharakhekha, bharukh, "Blessed be every one who blesses you" (→ ברך bārakh)—are older than Dt. 27:15-26. Here the Yahwist has taken over a tradition which the entire twelve-tribe league understood as a sacral regulation and as something established by Yahweh, which was itself guaranteed by a formula of curse and blessing. In Gen. 27:29, the author-

---

[12] Cf. H. Schulz, 67-71.

itative guarantee was considered to be the formula Isaac spoke to the patriarch Jacob, and in Nu. 24:9 it was thought to be the formula that a foreign seer spoke at the direction of Yahweh. According to this formula, those nations who seek friendly relationships with ("bless") Israel are placed under a blessing, but those who are hostile to Israel by means of curse formulas are placed under a curse. In Gen. 12:1-3, J has apparently freely transferred the earlier *barukh-* and *'arur-* formulas to the promise given to Abraham.

If the curse formula was used at one time in order to discourage disrespect for the will of Yahweh found in the Deuteronomic law, then this formula could also be used by the prophets in order to threaten men who doubted Yahweh's power and help (Jer. 17:5; here *ha'ish 'asher* is replaced by *haggebher 'asher*, "the man who"), or who did the work of Yahweh with slackness (48:10, participial form). Mal. 1:4 uses the participial *'arur-*formula to threaten those who offer an inferior sacrifice, and Ps. 119:21 uses it to distinguish between those who are wise in the Torah and insolent rebels. It is clear that this curse formula was intended to defend sacral, social, and national regulations, and therefore could be expressed legitimately only by persons in positions of authority, because it is never in the OT used in private situations against personal enemies. This is the case in spite of the numerous private curses and imprecations in the OT, for these always appear in different, or at least less stereotyped, formulations, and use some form of the root *qll*. The only exception to this is Jer. 20:14f. To be sure, this text has to do with the private life of the prophet; but it makes reference not to a personal enemy or to a concrete event in the prophet's career, but to his birthday and to the anonymous person who brought the news of Jeremiah's birth to his father. Here the curse formula has become an emotional indirect self-imprecation, expressing the prophet's despair.

The use of the curse formula in Gen. 49:7 also falls outside the common usage elsewhere in the OT. Here the curse is directed not against Simeon and Levi, the sons of Jacob, but against their uncontrolled anger. We can see from the way the curse is delineated, however, that actually Simeon and Levi are the ones placed under the curse. Thus, what we have here is an indirect curse in which the author attempts to avoid naming those who are cursed.

Sometimes the delineation of the curse following the curse formula describes more precisely the misfortune that the catastrophe brought about by the curse produces: lack of success in agricultural pursuits and restlessness (Gen. 4:12), dispersion and destruction of the tribe (49:7), loss of children (Josh. 6:26), reduction to slavery (9:23; Gen. 9:25), frustration and unhappiness in every respect (Jer. 17:5). Dt. 28:15-19 contains the most detailed delineation of the curse in the following verses down to v. 68. Here the misfortune (brought about by the curse) that will fall on the whole people if they break the covenant is depicted in the most gruesome colors.

Thus the *'arur-*formula is the most powerful "decree" expressed by an authority, and by means of it a man or a group that has committed a serious transgression against the community or against a legitimate authority (God, parents) is delivered over to misfortune. Moreover, originally it was probably thought that the word became effective in and of itself the moment the conditions for the activation of the curse were present. And yet, the expansion of the *'arur*-formula to *'arur liphne yhvh,* "Cursed before Yahweh" (Josh. 6:26; 1 S. 26:19), which already occurs in ancient texts, justifies the conjecture that the activation of misfortune was closely connected with an intervention of Yahweh. This conjecture is strengthened by the delineation of the curse in Dt. 28, [13] by the many amorphous curses in the OT in which Yahweh is invoked explicitly or is named as the one working misfortune, and by the antithetical formula *"barukh* so-and-so *leyhvh,"* "Blessed is so-and-so for Yahweh," or "May so-and-so be blessed for Yahweh" (→ ברך *bārakh*). [14] Therefore, one must be careful about adopting a purely magical understanding of the curse formula. [15]

2. *Other Forms of the Root 'rr in the OT.* The qal passive participle is used elsewhere in the OT only with reference to Jezebel, whom Jehu calls "this cursed woman" (2 K. 9:34). One subject of the other forms of *'rr* in the qal is God, who in the 1st person (*'a'or,* "I will curse," Gen. 12:3; *'arothi,* "I will curse," Mal. 2:2) "curses" those who refuse the blessing of Abraham, or changes the blessings of priests who perform their service unconscientiously into a curse. Another subject is the seer Balaam (Nu. 22:6,12; 23:7); and a third, the army of the tribes which was called up to "curse" (*'oru*) those who had not participated in the war of Yahweh (Jgs. 5:23). Apparently, a fourth subject is specific persons who allegedly have the power to pronounce powerful curses, and whom, therefore, different people ask to curse their enemies, as Balak king of Moab asked Balaam. Thus Job calls on "those who curse the day" (*'orere yom,* Job 3:8), and we are compelled to understand the "ones who curse" (*'orerekha*) Jacob-Israel in Gen. 27:29 and Nu. 24:9 as professional "cursers" of the same sort as Balaam, whom enemy nations call upon to render Israel harmless before them. But Yahweh rescinds their curse, and puts them under a curse. In Gen. 12:3, the Yahwist has undoubtedly enlarged the circle of people who wanted to "curse" Israel or its patriarch Abraham, and thus refers to all persons or nations who despise and curse Israel; therefore, here he has used the piel active participle of *qll* [16] (→ קלל *qālal*) instead of the qal active participle of *'rr*. It may also be that Ex. 22:27(28) is not to be interpreted as a prohibition of all "private" imprecations or amorphous "curses" against a tribal prince or a king, but of a formal curse pronounced by this sort of professional "curser," especially since *'rr* is never used in other passages to denote imprecations or curses pronounced by subjects against persons in positions of authority or against God; *qillel* is always used to convey this idea.

No significant difference between the niphal (Mal. 3:9, pl. ptcp.) and the hophal (Num. 22:6, 3rd person sing.) can be ascertained; both mean something like "to be smitten by a curse." At the same time, Nu. 22:6 testifies to the belief that one who has been cursed by a man like Balaam is certain to fall under the misfortune

---

[13] Cf. Plöger.
[14] Cf. Schottroff, 167-69.
[15] Cf. Brichto, 205-215.
[16] Cf. below, III.2.

brought about by the curse. Nor can any appreciable difference be ascertained between the qal and the piel in Gen. 5:29: the subject is God and the object, the ground; the expression, "the ground that Yahweh has cursed," refers back to the 'arur-statement in Gen. 3:17. The expression hammayim hamme'arerim, "the water that brings the curse," in Nu. 5:18-27 is used of the ritual of the ordeal, as a technical term for the water which (by virtue of the curse formula spoken over the woman suspected of adultery, then written down and washed off into the water) was supposed to have the power to bring about misfortune if the woman had really committed adultery. It is quite clear that the origin of the curse here is to be traced to magic; but the magical character of this rite has, of course, been weakened in that the ritual is attributed to a commandment of Yahweh. Therefore, Yahweh himself is to be regarded as the real judge of the woman under suspicion: it is he who causes the misfortune announced in the curse to become effective if the woman is guilty. The noun me'erah in Dt. 28:20; Mal. 2:2; 3:9; Prov. 3:33; and 28:27 means a "curse" in the sense of a misfortune which has already struck, and not in the sense of a curse formula or a word of curse. "Yahweh sends" it, and it can be seen "in the house of the wicked" as a calamity that has already occurred. This noun is not used metonymically for a man smitten with a curse, like → אלה 'ālāh and qelalah.

3. 'rr in Hebrew Inscriptions, the Qumran Literature, and the LXX. The 'arur-formula occurs, once with certainty [17] and once after appropriate restoration and correction, [18] on a tomb inscription, which pronounces a curse on anyone who desecrates the tomb. Thus here also it serves to protect an important legal commodity and a sacral and ethical ordinance, the repose of the dead. In the Qumran literature, the curse formula occurs several times, and it is used in a way similar to that found in Dt. 28, viz., as a ratification of the rule of the community. It was pronounced in particular against apostates when a new member was taken into the community and when the community celebrated the renewal of the covenant (1QS 2:5,7), but also against Belial and his followers in the ritual which introduces the eschatological holy war against the "sons of darkness" (1QM 13:4). According to CD B, 2:8(20:8), "all the holy ones of the Most High" "curse" ('ereruhu) the apostate, and therefore no member of the community is allowed to associate with him. Such apostates are "eternally cursed" ('arure 'olamim, 1QS 2:17). "An accursed man" ('arur, 4QTest 23) is "a fowler's net" to others, because they also fall under the curse through association with him. The descendants of Israel should walk according to the divine rule, so that they "do not fall under the curse" (hophal: yu'aru, CD A, 12:22; similarly the niphal in 1Q26 1:6). The 'arur-formula occurs often as well in the Rabbinic literature when someone wishes to separate himself from transgressors of the Torah. [19]

In the LXX, 'rr is almost always translated by (epi)katarásthai, "to curse";

---

[17] KAI, 191 B.2.
[18] Schottroff, 26.
[19] Cf. St.-B., III, 446.

but since this verb also ordinarily translates *qillel,* it is hardly possible to tell from the deuterocanonical books whether *'rr* or *qll* stood in the primitive Hebrew text, if indeed such existed. However, no form of *'rr* in the Hebrew text of Sirach has been translated by this verb in the Greek text. It is only in the Greek text of Tob. 13:12 and Wisd. 3:12; 14:8 that the curse formula "*epikatáratos* so-and-so," "Cursed is (be) so-and-so," bears a close similarity to the Hebrew *'arur*-formula. In Wisdom, the curse is directed against the ungodly in general or against graven images and those who make them, while in Tobit, it is directed against the heathen who refuse to acknowledge the God of Israel. Thus, the different forms of the root *'rr* in this literature essentially have retained those nuances of meaning that are attested in the OT.

III. Words for "Curse."

1. *In the Ancient Near East.* Other than *arāru,* one of the most important words for "curse" in Akkadian is *māmītu,* which corresponds to the Sum. *namerim* in the Sumerian-Akkadian word list, and means "oath" (when it applies to a conditional curse), "curse" in the sense of the destructive power that is produced by violating an oath or by committing some other evil, and "ban," and therefore approximates the meaning of the Heb. → אלה *'ālāh.* [20] Another important word for "curse" is Akk. *nazāru* (*ezēru*), which corresponds to Sum. *áš-bal-e,* and is translated in the lexicons by "curse" and "revile." Since this verb has as its object gods, one's parents, and personal enemies, and is used in connection with private arguments between personal enemies, it corresponds to the Heb. *qillel* and its derivatives. [21] In Phoenician-Punic we find *'lt,* "treaty-curse," "oath-curse," [22] and the root *qbb* with the meaning "curse" in a curse formula to protect a votive offering from being profaned, [23] with a deity as subject. In the Aramaic Targumim, the root *lvt* corresponds to the Heb. roots *'rr* and *qll.* However, in Ahikar 151 the context (to humble–to exalt) hardly allows the meaning "to curse," but indicates that the idea is "to disparage (with words), to speak about contemptuously," which would correspond to the meaning of the Heb. *qillel.* In Nabatean tomb inscriptions there are curse formulas against grave robbers which use the root *l'n* and have a god as subject; this usage clearly corresponds to Heb. *'rr* and should be translated "to curse." [24] In Egyptian [25] it is possible to distinguish between two formulations of the curse, corresponding closely to the distinction between *'rr* and *qll.* Possessions and graves are protected, [26] and enemies are threatened, in conjunction with symbolic acts (as smashing images, or vessels and potsherds on which the name of the enemy has

---

[20] Cf. above, I.2.

[21] On the Akk. *qullulu,* → קלל *qālal,* cf. *AHw,* 893.

[22] Cf. → אלה *'ālāh* I.1.

[23] Schottroff, 70.

[24] Cf. *ibid.,* 70f.

[25] On this see *RÄR,* 195f.

[26] Cf. H. Sottas, *La préservation de la propriété funéraire dans l'ancienne Egypte* (Paris, 1913).

been written), by the use of the formula *ḥwy šdb(r)*, "(The god A.) will bring evil (against so-and-so)," which means the same thing as "will curse him" (this expression occurs in literature all the way from the period of the Old Kingdom to the period of the New Kingdom [27]), or by the use of the Demotic expression "*ḫyṯ A ḥwy r* so-and-so," "May the wrath/curse of the (god) A fall upon so-and-so." However, amorphous curses, whose object can also be the king, are often formed with the root *wꜣ*, which *WbÄS* also translates "curse," [28] but which means rather "to blaspheme" or something similar. [29] In the ancient Near East, one was not limited to the expressions we have cited here if he wished to curse someone or to depict the curse and its effects. Numerous figurative phrases and expressions had been developed to convey this idea (including curses that do not belong to the special category of *terminus technicus*), which cannot be described more precisely in a lexicon. [30]

2. *In the OT*. In Hebrew, apart from *'rr*, the words for "curse" are the verbal and substantival derivatives of the roots → אלה 'ālāh and → קלל qālal. Brichto and Scharbert [31] have shown the mutual relationship of these various terms. *'alah* denotes conditional curses, which are spoken or written down in an oath or as a deterrent to transgressors against the law. But even when it is used in similar contexts, *'arar* predominantly designates curses which an authority pronounces to aid in carrying out his ordinances, public interests, or religio-ethical commands. The passive participle is the typical form used by such an authority in typical Hebrew-OT curse sayings. The terms for "curse" built from the root *qll* are basically more comprehensive. Unlike terms from the other two roots, they are used in amorphous imprecations in private situations against personal enemies, and in blasphemies against God, the king, or one's parents (→ קלל qālal). Apart from the word of curse itself, the nouns *'alah* and *qelalah* could also mean the destructive power produced by the curse, or concretely the affliction resulting from this power, or metonymically even the person smitten by the curse as a warning.

Among the other terms occasionally used in the sense of "curse" are *qabhabh* or *naqabh* (Nu. 22:11,17; 23:8,11,13,25,27; 24:10; Job 3:8; 5:3; Prov. 11:26; 24:24), which really means "to revile," "to express contempt for," and *za'am* (Nu. 23:7f.; Mal. 1:4; Prov. 24:24), which elsewhere in the OT means "to threaten." All these expressions appear in contrast with the only commonly used expression meaning "to bless" in the OT, viz., → ברך bārakh (*berakhah*, "blessing"), whose meaning extends from "greet" to "speak of with appreciation, praise" to the formal "bless." But in addition to stereotyped terms, Hebrew

---

27 Cf. *WbÄS*, IV, 382f.

28 *WbÄS*, I, 246.

29 Cf. Schottroff, 72f.

30 Cf. the studies of Dürr, Fensham, Gevirtz, Heinisch, Hillers, Offner, Parrot, Scharbert (esp. 37-71), Steinmetzer, and Veenhof, as well as the statements concerning curses among the modern Arabs in Scharbert, 100-109, and among the Canaanites (cf. the literature under → אלה *'ālāh*).

31 *Bibl*, 39 (1958), 1-26. Cf. the literature under → אלה *'ālāh*.

also developed a rich store of forms, and numerous figures and expressions, from which curses could be formulated for all situations.

IV. The Religious Significance of the Curse.

1. *In the Ancient Near East.* That the curse, as a forceful word producing destructive powers, is connected with the magical view of life of ancient cultures, is undisputed. But it is clear that in the high cultures of the ancient Near East the magical element is covered over by religious ideas, although it is not completely suppressed. A curse is considered to be unlawful as a magical spell for producing destruction, i.e., as a private means of revenge to smite a personal enemy, or as a means of gaining personal advantage by getting rid of other people, and therefore is prohibited by law. [32] By way of contrast, a lawful curse is connected very closely with the deity, whether it take the form of a wish that the deity would "curse" the evildoer himself, or of a curse formula in which the deity somehow is mentioned by name, or curse formulas connected with religious rites or deposited at a sanctuary on written records ratified by a curse. [33] To be sure, the plentiful ancient Near Eastern "incantation literature" also shows us that it was difficult to draw the line between religion and magic. The very fervent prayers to the gods to annul a curse or to curse unrighteous enemies, which sometimes appear in the incantation texts, are so intimately connected with abstruse symbolic acts which sometimes are reflected in ritual instructions, that it is impossible to avoid the impression that people in the ancient Near East actually believed that the gods could be forced by such formulas and acts to intervene in the manner desired. In contrast to this magical interpretation is the equally well-attested belief that the gods could render an unrighteous curse ineffective or prevent it from becoming effective, that a person could even render a legal curse inoperative by confessing his sins and praying to the deity for forgiveness, and that in the final analysis the deity was free to work good or evil.

The *Sitz im Leben* of the legal curse may be the sacral, the public-legal, or the private sphere. In private everyday life, its main purpose is to prevent unjust harm; thus, a person curses his enemy whom he cannot prosecute, or discourages would-be thieves, dishonest people who discover lost possessions, violators of the family tomb, etc., by proclaiming or writing down a curse formula. Both the civil law and the public and sacral law use the curse in order to guarantee the truth of an oath or of a testimony, the observance of a contract or treaty, and the safety of records and public or sacral monuments and buildings, as well as entire legal corpora and religious institutions. Indeed, both for the individual and for the community, the curse is often the only or last legal method of effectively discouraging violators of the law and evildoers, or of finding out what is true. The curse was able to accomplish this task because people were convinced of its effectiveness. [34] Together with blessing formulas, curses played a signif-

---

[32] Cf. the examples in Schottroff, 17, n. 2.

[33] Egyptian examples of both kinds are given in *RÄR*, 195.

[34] See the examples given in the works of the scholars mentioned above under III.1, and also in V. Korošec, *Keilschriftrecht, HO* I, suppl. vol. III (Leiden, 1964), 49-219.

icant role in the ratification of treaties. In this setting, more or less extensive series of curses, formulated in a wide variety of ways, were placed after the enumeration of the conditions of the treaty. They pronounced misfortune upon would-be violators of the treaty. When the ritual of making the treaty took place, and, among the Hittites, when high governmental officials and military officers were sworn into office, such curses were accompanied by symbolic acts which effectively emphasized the curses (cutting off the head of an animal, pouring out blood or water, or sprinkling salt). [35]

2. *In Israel.* From this background, we get an insight into the variety of ideas concerning the curse reflected in the OT. We detect a *Sitz im Leben* in the private sphere in texts like Jgs. 17:1-3; [36] Jer. 17:12-18; 18:18-23; Ps. 58; 59:13f. (12f.); 69:21-29(20-28); and 109. Here a woman endangered by a thief, one who is unjustly persecuted, and a person threatened by a malicious sorcerer, see no other way to protect themselves than to pronounce a curse, but all of these appear in the form of prayers that Yahweh would intervene. The Israelite law also prohibits the use of malicious sorcery upon penalty of death (Ex. 22:17 [18]). As the study of *'alah* and of the *'arur*-formula has shown, the curse found its way into Israelite law very early as a part of the oath, and as a guarantee of treaty agreements, authoritative ordinances and statutes, and public and sacral institutions. Moreover, Jer. 34:18 shows that the curse also could be replaced by or accompanied by symbolic acts, pointing to the death of violators of the treaty. When Israel adopted the idea of a treaty or of a unilateral legal union of God with his people, which is without analogy elsewhere in the ancient Near East, she went so far as to transfer the form of the symbolically expressed conditional oath-curse to Yahweh (Gen. 15:17f.; [37] so also, in the sprinkling of the blood not only on the people but also on the altar, in Ex. 24:6, the altar is probably intended as a representation of Yahweh). In the cult tradition found in D and H, the whole ethico-religious system, which now was considered to be the Yahweh covenant, was also secured by long ratifications of curses and blessings (Dt. 27f.; Lev. 26), analogous to the ancient Near Eastern treaty texts. It was probably under the influence of this cult tradition that the people also adopted many forms of the curse saying in their proclamation of calamity. [38]

Even though rituals like that found in Nu. 5:11-30 strongly suggest magical practices, the curse has a stronger religious emphasis in the OT than it does in the ancient Near Eastern literature. This is the case because in the OT the curse is a means of seeing to it that the will of God, divine judgment, and divine acts of vengeance proclaimed in the judicial system, in ethics, and in religion are executed. Viewed in this light, the so-called Imprecatory Psalms and other

---

[35] See the examples in Scharbert, 37-44; D. J. McCarthy, *Treaty and Covenant* (Rome, 1963); V. Korošec, *Hethit. Staatsverträge* (1931); the most detailed ratifications by curse are found in the text published by D. J. Wiseman, *The Vassal-Treaties of Esarhaddon* (London, 1958), lines 397-668.

[36] Cf. → אָלָה *'ālāh* II.1.

[37] Cf. N. Lohfink, *Die Landverheissung als Eid. SBS,* 28 (1967).

[38] Cf. Hillers, Fensham, Müller, and Schächter.

imprecatory texts, which seem strange to the modern reader, are expressions of faith in the just rule of Yahweh in situations in which the godly person or the people sees no other source of help or possible means of securing just treatment. If a person knows that an unwarranted curse will recoil on its author (Ps. 10:7-15; 109:16-19), that God will turn such a curse into a blessing for the person who is cursed unjustly (2 S. 16:12; Ps. 109:28; cf. the Oracles of Balaam in Nu. 22–24), that "like a sparrow in its flitting, like a swallow in its flying, a curse that is causeless does not alight" (Prov. 26:2), then the curse has lost its dread as a terrifying and effective decree. [39]

Scharbert

---

[39] On the historical problem, and on the various views concerning the OT concepts of the curse, cf. now esp. Schottroff, 11-24.

אֵשׁ 'ēsh; אִשֶּׁה 'ishsheh

Contents: I. In the Ancient Near East: 1. Egypt; 2. Mesopotamia. II. Philological Considerations. III. Earthly Fire: 1. In Everyday Life and in Comparisons; 2. In the Cult. IV. Fire in Connection with God: 1. As a Means of Punishment; 2. The Fire of God's Wrath; 3. In the Theophany. V. In Apocalyptic Literature: 1. Ezekiel and Daniel; 2. Eschatological Fire.

I. In the Ancient Near East.

1. *Egypt*. a. Besides *ḫ.t*, the most common Egyptian word for fire, and *śḏ.t*, which also in general means "fire," there is a whole series of special terms[1] which are translated "flame, blaze, heat," etc.; but the precise meaning of any of these words is not clear. Usually, all these words have a brazier with a flame

---

'ēsh. C.-M. Edsman, "Feuer," *RGG*[3], II, 927f.; W. Eichrodt, *TheolOT*, II, 15ff.; J. Fichtner, "The Wrath of Men and the Wrath of God in the OT," *TDNT*, V, 392-409; H. Fuchs, "Feuer," *Jüd. Lexikon*, II, 637-39; H. W. Haussig, ed., *Götter und Mythen im Vorderen Orient. WbMyth*, I (1965); D. R. Hillers, "Amos 7,4 and Ancient Parallels," *CBQ*, 26 (1964), 221-25; J. Hoftijzer, "Das sogenannte Feueropfer," *Festschrift W. Baumgartner. SVT*, 16 (1967), 114-134; J. Jeremias, *Theophanie. WMANT*, 10 (1965); F. Lang, *Das Feuer im Sprachgebrauch der Bibel, dargestellt auf dem Hintergrund der Feuervorstellungen in der Umwelt* (diss., Tübingen, 1950); idem, "πῦρ," *TDNT*, VI, 928-948; R. Mayer, *Die biblische Vorstellung vom Weltenbrand. BoSt*, N.S. 4 (1956); P. D. Miller, "Fire in the Mythology of Canaan and Israel," *CBQ*, 27 (1965), 256-261; E. Pax, ΕΠΙΦΑΝΕΙΑ (1955); G. von Rad, "כָּבוֹד" in the OT," *TDNT*, II, 238-242; A. Vögtle, *Das NT und die Zukunft des Kosmos* (1970); P. Volz, *Die Eschatologie der jüdischen Gemeinde* (1934).

[1] See *WbÄS*, VI, *s.v.* "Feuer" and "Flamme."

in it as a determinative. Several of the words for "flame," etc. (esp. *nśr.t* and *nby.t*), are also designations for goddesses like Sachmet, who is depicted in the form of a lion, perhaps suggesting the idea of her fiery nature. Apparently, this is also related to their connection with the Royal Serpent/Royal Crown, which was often called "The Fiery One."

The ambivalent nature of fire is clearly evident especially in the cult and in all sorts of magical customs. On the one hand, fire has a purifying effect and represents an effective protection against evil powers; on the other hand it is the element of destruction and thus a dangerous power.

b. We hear little about fire as a part of the cosmos. Series of elements like "wind, light, water, and fire" (by the effect of which everything lives) are rare and late (perhaps under Greek influence).

In the cosmogonic views, fire is connected especially with the sun. In the Hermopolitan Cosmogony, "the Flaming Island" [2] is the birthplace of Re. Apparently, the "Fiery Lake," which is mentioned in chap. 17 of the Book of the Dead, is a Herakleopolitan parallel to this. This text often speaks of the "fiery sunny eye," which destroys the enemy of Re with its flame. As the sun and Re could simply be said to be a "flame," so we hear that Amun was "the torch of life which came forth out of the Primal Sea and gives light to mankind" (*Urk.*, IV, 111, 11). Similarly, Khnum in Esna is "the one who comes forth out of the Primal Sea and looks like a flame" (Text 378, 10).

c. The chaotic powers could also be described as flames. Pyr. 237 speaks of a hostile flame which comes forth out of the Primal Sea. In a coffin text, [3] Apophis is called "flame." According to the little developed eschatological views, one day the world will be threatened by a flame. [4]

d. In the Egyptian temple cult, fire performed several important functions. Thus, on the day of its consecration, a temple was supposed to be purified with torches. [5] In the daily cult, a flame was kindled at the entrance into the Most Holy Place. [6] In the burnt offering, the ambivalence of the burning is particularly clear. For one thing, the sacrificial animals represent the enemies of the god which had to be burned and destroyed; yet the burnt offering is considered to be a roast offering whose smell pleased the god.

Fire also plays a role in the tomb cult, which naturally was connected with the ceremonies of the Osiris tombs. After the ritual of the hourly watch, [7] lamps were lighted on the bier of Osiris at the breaking of dusk. Frequently, the protective function of these lamps or torches is emphasized (e.g., in the Book of the Dead 137). In this connection, reference is made alternately to the "torch in the

---

[2] See *RÄR*, 194.
[3] De Buck, *CT*, V, 244d.
[4] PSalt 825.17, 19ff.; Schott, *AnBibl*, 12 (1959), 327.
[5] R. Lepsius, *Denkmäler aus Ägypten und Äthiopien* (1849ff.), III, 84.
[6] A. Moret, *Rituel du culte divin journalier* (1902), 9ff.
[7] H. Junker, *Die Stundenwachen in den Osirismysterien* (1910), 65.

night" and to the Eye of Horus (cf. *Urk.*, IV, 117, 2; 148, 13). This combination is of greatest importance, for it made it possible for goddesses who were regarded as the Eye of Horus to assume the role of flame goddesses. Thus, among the transformations that the dead person wishes to experience are "the change into a flame," [8] and "the change into the glowing Eye of Horus": [9] as Eye of Horus and flame, he is able to defeat his enemies.

e. On the other hand, fiery streams, fiery lakes, and all sorts of fire-breathing demons appear among the perils of the Underworld. It is clear from the imposing collection of material made by Zandee [10] that punishment and destruction played a great role in that terror-filled world.

f. As far as the figurative use of "fire," "flame," etc., is concerned, [11] the Egyptians liked to speak of flames and fire, e.g., in connection with poisons and diseases. And the same is true of expressions for wrath and violence ("the fire of speech," etc.). In the royal ideology, "the fire in its time" is a term that denotes the fighting Pharaoh; he is comparable to a "fire which can reduce its aggressor to ashes."

Bergman

2. *Mesopotamia*. In daily life, fire (Sum. *izi*, Akk. *išātu* or *girru*) played the role it had had from of old: fragments discovered by archeologists, in written sources dating from a half to a whole millennium later, indicate that from the third millennium B.C. artificial fire was used to produce light and heat (and heat was used to prepare food, to manufacture glass, etc., and to bake clay tablets and sun-dried bricks). Thorns and cane especially, and rarely charcoal, were used as fuel to produce heat. [12]

Mention should be made in particular of fire as it was used in cultic acts, although we are not able to specify more precisely the "purposes" of fire in such acts: cf. the Sumerian name for a month, *gu₄-rá-izi-mú-a-ᵈnanše*, "(Festival) of the goddess Nanshe, in which a (torch-)fire is kindled for the bull (to be sacrificed?)," which appears from approximately 2500 B.C. on. [13] In a ritual instruction concerning an exorcism from the 7th century B.C., we read, "with a sulphur fire you (= the priest) set fire to a torch, and then you set the wood-pile on fire (with it)." [14] In another ritual instruction from the same period we read, "You make a pile of poplar shavings, set it on fire, and sprinkle... (= aromatic substances for a smoke offering) into it." [15]

---

[8] De Buck, *CT*, I, 250c-d.
[9] *Ibid.*, VI, 98ff.
[10] J. Zandee, *Death as an Enemy* (1960), 133-146.
[11] See H. Grapow, *Die bildlichen Ausdrücke des Ägyptischen* (1924), 47, 166.
[12] Cf. A. Salonen, *Die Hausgeräte der Alten Mesopotamier*, I (1965), 130ff. ("Beleuchtungsgeräte"); *idem*, "Die Öfen der Alten Mesopotamier," *Baghdader Mitteilungen*, 3 (1964), 100ff.
[13] Cf. the examples in B. Landsberger, "Der kultische Kalender," *LSS*, 6, 1-2,46.
[14] E. Ebeling, *ArOr*, 17/1 (1949), 187-89.17.
[15] Ebeling, *Die akkadische Gebetsserie 'Handerhebung'* (1953), 136, lines 108f.

We find this statement in a commentary on cultic procedures presumably of the New Year Festival: "the fire which is kindled before the goddess Ninhil, the sheep which they lay 'on the oven,' which the fire burns: this is Kingu, as he is burned in the fire." [16] According to the Babylonian song of creation, Enuma Elish, after the defeat of Marduk the god Kingu is slain and men are created from his flesh.

Apart from the realm of the destructive power of fire, fire signals (Akk. *išātum*, lit. simply "fire") in particular should be mentioned. They were used to convey messages, as we know especially from the Mari texts (early second millennium B.C., in the region around the central Euphrates). [17]

It is probably only accidental that there few references are made to signs of ownership on animals in the form of brands; cf. the statement from the Middle Babylonian period (*ca.* 1310 B.C.), "one ... cow which has no brand (lit. fire sign, Akk. *šimat išātim*)." [18]

With regard to the destructive power of fire, we hear of its use in this way in the earliest group of historical Sumerian texts; cf. the frequent repetition of the statement, "the man of Umma (= the hostile king) has set the ... sanctuary on fire (Sum. *izi ba-SUM*)," in an inscription of the city prince Urukagina of Lagash (*ca.* 2355 B.C.). [19] From a later period, we may compare the statement by the Assyrian king Shalmaneser I (1274-1245 B.C.), "the remainder of his (= the enemy's) cities I burned down with fire" (Akk. *ina išāti lûqelli*). [20] Quite similar expressions are numerous in the accounts of the wars of Assyrian kings down to Ashurbanipal (669-631 [?] B.C.) (Akk. *ina išāti ašrup* or *ina girri aqmu*). For reflections of such expressions in literary texts, we may compare this epithet of the god Nusku from a Sumerian hymn, "he who casts fire on the enemy" (*erím-e izi sum-mu*). [21] In a collection of omina, on the basis of observing animal intestines (hepatoscopy) this proclamation is given: "(under such and such conditions) you shall set fire to the hut of (your) enemy (*išātu tanaddi*)." [22]

Finally, § 25 in the penal code of the Code of Hammurabi should be mentioned here. It declares: "(he who comes to extinguish a fire in someone else's house, but then steals something from that house:) this man shall be cast into that fire (*ana išātim šuāti innaddi*)." [23]

Destruction by fire also plays a role in magic. Thus, according to the incantation ritual called Maqlû ("burning"), often images of the sorceress or sorceresses by whom someone thinks he is being persecuted are made out of wood or wax, and then during the recitation of the incantations are burned with fire. These incantations are directed to the image of the sorceresses or of the sorceress,

---

[16] CT 15, 44, 8ff.=H. Zimmern, "Zum babylonischen Neujahrsfest," *BSGW*, 58, 131, 8ff.
[17] See G. Dossin, *RA*, 35 (1938), 174ff.
[18] *PBS*, 2/2, No. 27, 1.
[19] F. Thureau-Dangin, *SAK*.
[20] E. Ebeling, *et al., Die Inschriften der altassyrischen Könige*, 118f., 3, 7.
[21] J. van Dijk, *Sumerische Götterlieder*, II (1960), 109 and 112, 1. IV 5.
[22] F. Thureau-Dangin, *TCL*, 6, Nos. 4, 13; copy from the Seleucid Period.
[23] For further literature, cf. M. San Nicolò, *RLA*, III, 59.

whose death is supposed to be caused by burning, or to the fire god.[24] The Assyrian king Esarhaddon (681-669 B.C.) observed a similar ritual when he made international treaties with different ones of his vassals. He puts wax figures into the fire, and, according to the wording of the treaties, just as they burn in the fire, so shall his vassals burn if they violate the treaty.[25] A related idea stands behind the rituals in which wool is plucked, or an onion is peeled, or a mat is torn in pieces, and then is cast into the fire. In these incantations it is stated, "As... is cast into the fire (and) the consuming fire consumes it..., so today the fire... shall burn the ban,... the sin... (etc.), the ban shall go out from (me)..." (*kīma... ana išāti innaddû girru qāmû iqammû... girru qāmû liqmi...).*[26]

Here the destructive power of fire stood in the service of magic, but contrariwise magic (primarily the incantation from the mouth of the incantation priest) was invoked against fire.[27] "Fire" here also means the fever of a sick person.

The myth of the fire-god Gibil (Sum.) or Girra, Girru (Akk.) is known from the Fara Period on (*ca.* 2550 B.C.). Nusku (Nuska), the son and vizier of the chief Babylonian god Enlil (Ellil), is also considered to be the god of light and of fire. However, as far as we know there is no myth explaining the creation or dedication of fire somewhat comparable with the tale of Prometheus. According to the "Lament over the Destruction of the City of Ur," Enlil secures the help of the fire-god Gibil for his work of destruction.[28] In the incantations of the Maqlû series mentioned above, Nusku and Gibil are invoked to burn the sorceresses or the sorceress.[29] In the Erra Myth, Marduk has Gibil clean his imperial insignia that had become dirty.[30]

But Gibil/Girra and Nusku are not the only lords of fire among the gods: Inanna of Uruk, the goddess of love and war, "rains (Sum. *šèg*)" fire (in the war) on men.[31] The fire she kindles "does not go out" (Sum. song in which Inanna praises herself).[32] Among the (Sum.) *me,* "divine powers" or "cultural values," which Inanna procured from Eridu through the cunning of Enki, are the abilities "to kindle a fire" and "to extinguish a fire."[33]

Other gods (Marduk, Nergal, Ninurta, Papullegarra) are also given the epithet "wild fire," etc., especially in a later period.[34] And the Babylonian song of

---

[24] See below. Cf. G. Meier, *Die assyrische Beschwörungssammlung Maqlû* (1937); E. Reiner, *Šurpu* (1958), 2f.

[25] D. J. Wiseman, *Iraq,* 20 (1958), 75f., 608-610.

[26] E. Reiner, *Šurpu. BAfO,* 11 (1958), tables V-VI, 60-122.

[27] See W. G. Lambert, "Fire Incantations," *AfO,* 23 (1970), 39-45.

[28] A. Falkenstein, *SAHG,* 200, line 180.

[29] Meier, pp. 11f., lines 122-134; pp. 13ff., lines 1f.; etc.; see also W. von Soden, *SAHG,* 347-352.

[30] L. Cagni, "L'epopea di Erra," *StSem,* 34 (1969), 72f., line 141. On the fire god, see D. O. Edzard in *WbMyth,* I, 68f. and 116f.; J. van Dijk in *Heidelberger Studien zum Alten Orient* (1967), 249[60]; 250[63].

[31] W. Hallo-J. van Dijk, *The Exaltation of Inanna* (1968), 16f., line 13; copy *ca.* 1800 B.C.

[32] CT 42, No. 48,5 ‖ *ASKT,* 126, 27f.

[33] *PBS,* 5, 25 V 8f.; see Å. Sjöberg in *Heidelberger Studien zum Alten Orient,* p. 203; see further *CAD* under *išātu* 1 b 1'.

[34] See K. Tallqvist, *Akkadische Götterepitheta* (1938), 77 *s.v.* II. *girru.*

creation [35] says of Marduk, after he was created, "when he moved his lips, a fire was kindled" (I, 96). Furthermore, in the Gilgamesh Epic, the friend and servant of the hero describes the giant Ḫumbaba in this way: "his roar is a flood; yea, his mouth is fire; his breath, death." [36] And the Assyrian king Ashurbanipal says in a song of praise to the goddesses of Nineveh and Arbela: "the word of their lips is a kindled fire *(girru napḫu)*." [37]

The incantations frequently speak of the raging of demons "with fire" or "as (with) fire": "the Asakku-demon (a disease) ... lights a fire in the depth (of the Primal Ocean) and cooks the fish there"; [38] "the evil Namtar-demon that burns the land as (with) fire." [39]

By the fire not kindled by men or gods, the Babylonians clearly had in mind the fire (perhaps ignited by a flash of lightning) in the dry reeds and in the grassy steppe. In any case, the comparison with the reed and grass fire that blazes high but soon goes out frequently occurs; cf. the statement from a Sumerian incantation *(ca.* 1800 B.C.), "then his (=the man's) Asakku-illness will terminate of its own accord as a reed-grass fire that (swiftly) goes out." [40] For lightning (Sum. *nim-gír;* Akk. *birqu,* also *miqit išāti* [fire falling]) as a natural cause of fire, cf. *CAD* under *išātu* 1 a 1', and from the Sumerian Lugalbanda Epic, the prayer of Lugalbanda that the Anzu-bird might make it his lot to be able "to rise up like a flame" and "to flash (down) like lightning." [41]

Krecher

II. Philological Considerations.
According to *KBL*[3], 89, *'esh* occurs 380 times in the OT. It is found in all Semitic languages except Arabic. We are to understand that in Hebrew the second radical was reduplicated (probably at a later time). [42] The gender is feminine. [43] The pl. *'eshoth* appears only in Sir. 48:3. The substantive lacks a verbal cognate in the OT.

III. Earthly Fire.

1. *In Everyday Life and in Similes.* The importance of fire as dispenser of heat and light in daily life is obvious; see the enumeration in Sir. 39:26. The practice of starting a fire by striking flint, which was well known throughout the world, is mentioned in 2 Macc. 10:3. Because of the exertion of energy connected with this practice, starting a fire on the Sabbath day was forbidden (Ex. 35:3). Of course, the devastating power of insatiable fire was familiar (Prov. 30:16). Those guilty of starting fires that caused damage were punished (Ex.

---

[35] See above.

[36] A. Schott-W. von Soden, *Das Gilgamesch-Epos* (1958), pp. 34, 110.

[37] S. Langdon, *Babylonian Penitential Psalms. OECT,* 6 (1927), 68, 6.

[38] R. Borger, *JCS,* 21 (1967), 7 and 14, line 66.

[39] CT 17, 29, 1f.

[40] A. Falkenstein, *Die Haupttypen der sumerischen Beschwörung. LSS,* N.F. 1 (1931), 63 with n. 2; further W. Römer, *lišān mitḫurti, AOT,* 1, 285f., 42.

[41] C. Wilcke, *Das Lugalbandaepos* (diss., Heidelberg, 1969), 108f., 173.

[42] *BLe,* 454.

[43] *ZAW,* 16 (1896), 63.

22:4f. [Eng. vv. 5f.]). Particularly in war, cities were plundered and "consumed (→ אכל 'ākhal) by fire." Thus distress in war is characterized poetically as fire (Nu. 21:28; Isa. 10:16; Ps. 78:63). We encounter the figure "tongue of fire" in Isa. 5:24 (cf. Acts 2:3). The heat of the sun is also compared with consuming fire (Joel 1:19; Am. 7:4). The expression "melt like wax before the fire" (Mic. 1:4; Ps. 68:3[2]; cf. 97:5) was proverbial for devastation wrought in judgment. Since dry thorns burned very quickly, they could be used as a figure for swift destruction (Ps. 118:12 and perhaps also 58:10[9]; Eccl. 7:6; Isa. 10:17; 64:1[2]). Burning as a death penalty for serious ethical crimes was probably an unusual kind of punishment in Israel (but cf. CH 25, 110, 157) (Gen. 38:24; Lev. 20:14; 21:9; Josh. 7:15). Fire is used in a furnace to refine metals, a process employed to symbolize afflictions and cleansing judgments (Isa. 1:22,25; Jer. 6:27-30; Ezk. 22:17-22; Mal. 3:2; Zec. 13:9; Ps. 66:10; Prov. 17:3; Sir. 2:5). The Wisdom Literature compares different passions with the heat of fire (Job 31:12; Prov. 6:27f.; 26:20f.; Sir. 9:8; 23:16; 28:10f.). In the prophetic literature, the word of Yahweh is designated as fire (Jer. 5:14; 20:9; 23:29). Without explicit comparison, the flame of fire is used directly in figurative language for prosperity, in parallelism with light (Job 18:5f.; a burning lamp, Prov. 13:9; 20:20), for the passion of love (Cant. 8:6), and for danger, in parallelism with "water" (Ps. 66:12; Isa. 43:2; Sir. 51:4).

2. *In the Cult.* In the OT cult, the sacrifices were burned, completely or partly. The fire on the altar of burnt-offering was not allowed to be extinguished (Lev. 6:2,5f.[9,12f.]). The paschal lamb had to be roasted with fire (Ex. 12:8). Among the sacrificial terms, we encounter the word *'ishsheh* over 60 times, mainly in priestly texts. From the LXX on, this term has been connected with *'esh*, "fire," and is usually translated "offering made by fire." But this meaning is uncertain and more recent exegetes find other etymological explanations. [44] Incense was burned on coals of fire (Lev. 16:12f.; unlawful, and therefore called *'esh zarah*, "strange fire," 10:1, → זר *zār*), and the cleansing power produced by this was used ritually (in connection with pieces of spoil taken in war, Nu. 31:23; or in connection with the ordination of a prophet, Isa. 6:6). The remains of animals used in the cult had to be protected from profanation by burning (Ex. 12:10; 29:34; Lev. 4:12; etc.). Under Canaanite influence child sacrifice was practiced in Israel, especially in the late monarchical period. The term used to describe this was "make one pass through the fire" (*he'ebhir ba'esh,* 2 K. 16:3; etc.). 2 Macc. 1:18 (-36) mentions a particular feast of fire. The historicity of this narrative is admittedly very doubtful, but still the author knows of "naphtha," unrefined oil from the earth.

IV. Fire in Connection with God.

1. *As a Means of Punishment.* Fire plays a very important role in statements concerning God, his appearances and actions. In harmony with theocentric faith,

---

[44] Hoftijzer, 114-134.

lightning (as fire from heaven) is sent out as an arrow by God himself (Ps. 18:15 [14]; 29:7; 144:6; etc.). These poetic passages in the Psalms have in mind a kind of theophany, in which Yahweh rides on the storm-clouds. [45] "He makes fire and flame his ministers" in Ps. 104:4 means "He makes lightning flashes his ministers" (cf. 148:8: fire and hail). God sends thunder, lightning, and hail as plagues (Ex. 9:23). "Fire of God" falls from heaven: Job 1:16; 1 K. 18:38; 2 K. 1:10,12; 2 Ch. 7:1; Sir. 48:3. Related to, but not quite identical with the lightning is the idea that God expressly (usually to punish, but in Jgs. 6:21; Lev. 9:24; 1 K. 18:38; 2 Ch. 7:1 to consume the sacrifice) sends fire (Nu. 11:1-3; 16:35; Lev. 10:2; Lam. 1:13). The concept of the Holy War probably lies behind this idea, particularly in the formal transitional verse, "I will send a fire upon . . . , and it shall devour his palaces" (Am. 1:4,7,10,12,14; 2:2,5; Jer. 17:27; 49:27; Hos. 8:14). According to Gen. 19:24, Yahweh rains brimstone and fire on Sodom and Gomorrah (so similarly Ezk. 38:22; 39:6; and with a slight textual emendation Am. 7:4 [Hillers reads "rain of fire"]). Isa. 34:9 mentions burning pitch and brimstone.

2. *The Fire of God's Wrath.* In the passages that have been mentioned, lightning and fire are instruments of divine judgment. The connection between fire and the fierce anger (*charon 'aph*) of Yahweh is even more intimate. We encounter this expression using a verb, *charah 'appo*, "his nose was hot = his anger was kindled." [46] Since *'aph* (→ אָנַף *'ānaph*) means both "nose" and "anger," it is difficult to decide the extent to which the concrete original meaning "nose" is still present or at least is still felt. The original meaning is clear only in the description of the theophany in 2 S. 22:9 = Ps. 18:9(8): "Smoke went up from his nostrils, and devouring fire from his mouth"; cf. Isa. 30:33: "the breath of Yahweh is like a stream of brimstone"; 33:11: "my breath is like a fire that will consume you"; 65:5: "These (people) are a smoke in my nostrils, a fire that burns all the day." This bold figure of anger originated in the world of legends which tell of fire-breathing creatures (see Job 41:10-13[18-21], and the fire-breathing Primal Serpent in Egyptian art). But usually it is more in keeping with the evolution of ideas and with an advanced theology to translate *'aph* by "anger" when it is connected with fire, which is also suggested by the free alternation of the parallel expressions using *'aph* (Isa. 66:15; Jer. 15:14 = 17:4; Dt. 29:19[20]; 32:22), *qin'ah*, "anger" (Dt. 29:19[20]; Ezk. 36:5; Zeph. 1:18; Ps. 79:5), *'ebhrah*, "wrath" (Ezk. 21:36[31]; 22:21,31; 38:19), *chemah*, "wrath" (Jer. 4:4 = 21:12; Nah. 1:6), and *ge'arah*, "rebuke" (Isa. 66:15). As a rule, fire is used only in comparisons, and therefore we do not encounter the concept of real judgment by fire. Also the idea of "partial judgment" remains in the preexilic period in a rather narrow sphere. The (hardly genuine) statement that "in the fire of his jealous wrath (*be'esh qin'atho*), all the earth shall be consumed" is found for the first time in Zeph. 1:18 (= 3:8); cf. also the late passages, Isa. 33:11f.; Joel 2:3; Zec. 12:6. [47]

[45] See below, 3.
[46] *KBL³*, 74.
[47] *TDNT*, VI, 936, n. 46.

3. *In the Theophany*. a. In God's angry judgment the lightning flashes, his anger burns like fire, and he even breathes out fire. Here already it is clear more or less that what we are dealing with is God's powerful manifestation, which is made known, among other ways, through fire. The best-known example is the theophany at Sinai. According to the Elohistic tradition (Ex. 19:16,19; 20:18,21), the accompanying natural phenomena are claps of thunder and flashes of lightning, dark clouds and trumpet blasts (a cultic motif), thus predominantly aspects of a storm. According to the Yahwistic tradition (19:18), Yahweh descends on the mountain in fire, accompanied by smoke like the smoke of a kiln; the smoking mountain in 20:18 also is probably an element of the Yahwistic narrative. The picture reflected in this source [48] may be based on that of a volcano, if indeed it is true that fire and smoke (see Isa. 4:5; 6:4; etc.) are not usually included in the description of a theophany. In Ex. 34:5, J also speaks of the "cloud." Similarly, P says (Ex. 24:16f.) that the cloud covered the mountain, and the *kabhodh*, "glory," of Yahweh looked like a devouring fire. Frequently Deuteronomy mentions that Yahweh spoke "out of the midst of the fire" (Dt. 4:12,15,33,36; 5:4, 22-26; 10:4; stated in more detail in 4:11). Jeremias emphasizes that in the Sinai theophany "fire is the phenomenon that accompanies or mediates the manifestation of Yahweh." [49] But in the true genre of theophany descriptions, it is "either Yahweh's irresistible weapon, ... or a symbol and actualization of his burning anger."

b. This essentially different form-critical category appears in the hymnic theophanies of judgment, which exhibit a strong mythological hue (esp. Ps. 18:8-16[7-15]; 77:17-20[16-19]; 97:2-5; Isa. 29:6; 30:27-31; Hab. 3:2-15). In these passages, we encounter the following motifs having to do with fire: smoke going out from Yahweh's nostrils and devouring fire from his mouth, glowing coals, lightnings (Ps. 18:9,13,15[8,12,14]); lightnings (77:18f.[17f.]); fire and lightnings (97:3f.); furious anger and devouring fire (Isa. 29:6; 30:27,30); brightness like light, rays, fiery anger, light of thine arrows, flash of thy glittering spear (Hab. 3:4,8,9,11). "Before him is a devouring fire, round about him a mighty tempest" (Ps. 50:3).

c. In addition to the storm theophanies, there is a series of other manifestations involving fire through which God's presence is made known. In the story of God's covenant with Abraham, God's presence is made known mysteriously by the expressions "smoking fire pot" and "flaming torch" (Gen. 15:17). Yahweh appears to Moses in a flame of fire in the bush (Ex. 3:2). In the wilderness wandering, the pillar of cloud by day and the pillar of fire by night are signs of the divine presence and leadership, Ex. 13:21; 14:24(J); Nu. 9:15(P); 14:14(J); Dt. 1:33; Ps. 78:14. Of course, the ancient narrators would have understood this literally. But in Dt. 9:3, the motif of the pillar of fire is transferred figuratively to the conquest of Canaan: "he who goes over before you as a devouring fire is

---

[48] According to J. Jeremias, 104, also P and D.
[49] Jeremias, 108.

Yahweh your God." Similarly (without the comparative particle), in Dt. 4:24 Yahweh is "a devouring fire, a jealous God." The second explanatory expression shows that the first is understood only in a figurative sense. The motif of the pillar of fire also has its effect on the symbolic language of the prophets in Isa. 4:5; 58:8; Zec. 2:9(5): Yahweh will be a wall of fire round about Jerusalem and the glory within her. In contrast to the judgment theophany, here the positive, protective, and bright side of fire is always emphasized. Isa. 10:17 characterizes Yahweh as the "light of Israel" (cf. 9:1[2]), which will become a fire and a flame against his enemies. The original and certainly early connection of Yahweh's revelation of himself with the storm and with the devouring fire in general is replaced more and more by its connection with the manifestation of light (→ אור 'ôr) in the later period, thus also in Hab. 3 [50] and Dt. 33:2; Job 37:3,15.

d. Fire is not limited to any form; it blazes up to an intensity pure and inaccessible, it disseminates light and heat like the stars and lightning flashes, and it can be either beneficial or destructive. All this gave it the nimbus of the mysterious, the terrifying, the immaterial. Thus, like other religions, according to the OT view fire has a close connection with the spiritual world, but of course this does not mean at all that the OT reflects the view that the heavenly beings by their nature were composed of fire. [51] Even the seraphim, "the burning ones," are described in corporeal terms in Isa. 6:2. According to Jgs. 13:20, the messenger of Yahweh ascended in the flame of the altar toward heaven. Fire was always at God's disposal as a means of punishment. The chariot of fire ("sun chariot"?) in the Elijah narrative came down out of heaven (2 K. 2:11), and so did the horses and chariots of fire in 2 K. 6:17.

From a traditio-historical point of view, the terrifying appearance of Yahweh in the storm seems to be very old. From a religio-historical perspective, terminology applied to the storm gods of the ancient Near Eastern mythologies concerning Ba'alshamēm, Ba'al/Hadad, Teshub, etc., [52] stand behind OT statements concerning Yahweh which use expressions derived from the storm. However, it must be observed that (as also very frequently elsewhere) mythological themes in the OT should not be isolated and overemphasized, even when they have been borrowed above all in their actual concreteness. [53] It is typical of mythological speech not to make a distinction between figurative symbolism and sober reality. Moreover, alongside the natural mythological elements, we encounter the more historical motifs of the holy war in the OT. [54] In the divine revelation to Elijah on Horeb (1 K. 19:11f.), the traditional phenomena are even deliberately rejected: Yahweh is not in the storm, the earthquake, or the fire, but in the whisper (silence) (→ דממה d^emāmāh). Thus, when we look at the OT picture of God as

---

[50] See above.
[51] However, cf. Rabbinic views: Jüd. Lex., II, 639.
[52] See WbMyth, I; Miller, 256-59.
[53] Cf. Eichrodt, 17-20; Jeremias, 38.
[54] Miller; see above, IV.1.

a whole, Yahweh is by no means regarded as a storm-god or a fire demon. Usually the personality of Yahweh (his name and, in the prophets, his word), which is revealed especially in historical acts, is depicted to man in such a way as to make the storm phenomena (which are also mentioned later) symbols of the mighty acts of God. This is always the case in a poetic-hymnic literary genre, and in the prophets only in a visionary revelation. But fire is also a form of the external manifestation of God, since it is a gracious sign of his presence, e.g., in the bush, on Sinai, or in the pillar of fire, and yet his nature is more hidden behind it than revealed. The priestly theology in particular has substituted the idea of → כבוד kābhôdh, "glory," for that of fire, i.e., his "glory" is veiled, usually in the cloud (Ex. 16:10; 24:15-17; 40:34-38; etc.). [55] In this way an attempt is made to reconcile the tension between the visible manifestation and the invisible nature of God. To be sure, there is a connection between kabhodh, "glory," and fire, but it is not close and inseparable.

V. In Apocalyptic Literature.

1. *Ezekiel and Daniel.* In the growing apocalypticism with its heavenly visions, again light and fire frequently are features of the transcendental world. "The appearance of the likeness of the kabhodh, 'glory,' of Yahweh" was a brightness like that of the rainbow (Ezk. 1:28). God himself has a human form, whose outlines are enveloped in brightness (vv. 26f.). The "Ancient of Days" in Dnl. 7:9 is described more clearly. His raiment is white as snow, his throne is fiery flames whose wheels are burning fire. An angelic being is described in this way in 10:6: "his face was like the appearance of lightning, his eyes like flaming torches." 1 En. 14:9-22; Rev. 1:13-16; 4:3-5 contain similar figures from the late period.

2. *Eschatological Fire.* The concept of the eschatological destruction of the enemies of God either on earth or in the fire of Hell is late and not typical for the OT. Mal. 3:19(4:1), "the day that comes will burn them up," was the point of departure for this idea. Moreover, using the murderous fire of Topheth in the Valley of Hinnom as the basis of comparison, the late postexilic passage Isa. 66:24 (quoted in Mk. 9:48) says, still quite obscurely, "their worm shall not die, their fire shall not be quenched." Jth. 16:17, "fire and worms he will give to their flesh," is dependent on this. [56]

The Apocalyptic Literature connects the end of the world with the belief in a conflagration of the world, [57] which is also found in the NT (2 Pet. 3:7). The view that the idea of the conflagration of the world probably already existed in Zephaniah [58] is not tenable. [59]

Hamp

---

55 See Eichrodt, 29-35; von Rad, 243.
56 On the important role of fire in the Apocrypha and in Revelation, cf. Volz, 318f., who also discusses hell fire, 323f.; *TDNT*, VI, 937ff.
57 Volz, 353f.; Mayer, 120ff.
58 Bousset-Gressmann, *Die Religion des Judentums* (³1926), 503.
59 Mayer, 95-99.

אִשָּׁה 'ishshāh → אִישׁ 'îsh

אָשָׁם 'āshām; אָשֵׁם 'āsham;

אָשֵׁם 'āshēm; אַשְׁמָה 'ashmāh

Contents: I. Etymology. II. The noun 'āshām: 1. In Preexilic Passages; 2. In the Priestly Code and in Postexilic Texts; 3. Isa. 53:10. III. The Verb. IV. The Adjective. V. 'ashmāh.

I. Etymology. 1. The oft discussed question of whether the Ugar. 'ṯm or ṯtm is cognate with Heb. 'šm[1] must be answered negatively,[2] because in CTA, 169 and 180 (UT, 34, 45, 27), 'ṯm is Hurrian, and ṯt, "existence," with enclitic mem lies behind ṯtm in CTA, 5 [I* AB], III, 24. Also m'šmn cannot be connected with Heb. 'šm because of the š.[3] Recently in UT, 2104 (PRU, V, No. 104), a verb 'ṯm seems to be indicated by the forms yṯttm (1. 5) and tṯttmn (11. 2f.). It is impossible to conclude from the connection of the signs preserved elsewhere on this tablet, which has been handed down only in fragmentary form, that 'ṯm is a sacrificial term, as C. H. Gordon has suggested. When this text speaks of oxen (line 1) and horses (line 4), this does not mean a priori that it is a sacrificial text. On the contrary, it is much more likely that we are dealing with an administrative text here.[4] The precise meaning of the verb cannot be determined from its occurrences in UT, 2104.

2. In Arabic the root appears in the form 'aṯima, which means "to sin, to go astray, to transgress, to be guilty." The subst. 'iṯm, "sin, transgression, outrage, guilt," is cognate with this. This root occurs frequently in Old Arabic poetry in a wide variety of contexts, as well as in the Koran.[5]

'āshām. H. Cazelles, VT, 8 (1958), 314f. (review of L. Moraldi, Espiazione [1956]); K. Elliger, Leviticus. HAT, 4 (1966); P. Joüon, "Notes de Lexicographie Hébraïque XV. Racine אשׁם," Bibl, 19 (1938), 454-59; D. Kellermann, "'āšām in Ugarit?" ZAW, 76 (1964), 319-322; S. Łach, "Różnica czy tożsamość ofiary haṭṭā't i 'āšām," Collectanea Theologica, 37 (1967), 41-53; A. Médebielle, L'Expiation dans l'Ancien et le Nouveau Testament, I. L'AT (1924); idem, "Expiation," DBS, 3 (1938), 1-262; L. Moraldi, "Espiazione nell'Antico e nel Nuovo Testamento," RivBibl, 9 (1961), 289-304; 10 (1962), 3-17; idem, Espiazione sacrificale e riti espiatori nell'ambiente biblico et nell'Antico Testamento. AnBibl, 5 (1956); L. Morris, "'Asham," EvQ, 30 (1958), 196-210; R. Rendtorff, Studien zur Geschichte des Opfers im alten Israel. WMANT, 24 (1967); P. P. Saydon, "Sin-Offering and Trespass-Offering," CBQ, 8 (1946), 393-98; D. Schötz, Schuld- und Sündopfer im AT (1930); N. H. Snaith, "The Sin-offering and the Guilt-offering," VT, 15 (1965), 73-80; H. C. Thomson, "The Significance of the Term 'Asham in the OT," TGUOS, 14 (1953), 20-26; R. de Vaux, Studies in OT Sacrifice (1964), esp. 98-112.

[1] Cf. recently J. Gray, "Social Aspects of Canaanite Religion," SVT, 15 (1966), 171; C. H. Gordon, UT, Glossary, No. 422; J. Heuschen, "Sündopfer," BL[2] (1968), 1686.

[2] Cf. D. Kellermann, ZAW, 319-322.

[3] Cf. GGA, 216 (1964), 192f.; W. von Soden, SVT, 16 (1967), 294 on mišmunnu.

[4] But cf. J. C. de Moor, UF, 1 (1969), 178.

[5] See Ringgren, Temenos, 2 (1966), 101-103.

3. The root *'šm* is not found in South Semitic. Neither the Ethiop. *hašämä*, "to be wicked, offensive," nor the Tigr. *ḥasämä*, "to be wicked" (which is to be compared with Tigré *ḥasama*, "pig") have anything to do with Heb. *'šm*. This connection goes back to Dillmann, [6] was considered possible by Leslau, [7] and thus found its way into *KBL²*, where, however, it is followed by a question mark. [8] According to the principles of phonetics, a "primitive Semitic" root *'tm* must have produced in Geʿez *'sm*, but not *ḥšm*. Furthermore, the root *ḥšm* is by no means limited to Abyssinia (Ethiopia), but appears as well in Syriac, where it has the meaning "to envy," and is found in Arabic with the meaning "to shame." [9]

4. It is impossible to demonstrate an etymological connection between the Heb. root *'šm* and the divine names *'šmvn* or *'šmbyt'l*, or between *'šm* and *'ashimah*. [10] And it is equally difficult to accept the recent conjecture of Zimmerli that etymologically the root *'šm* can hardly be detached from *šmm*, "to be desolated," which was apparently motivated by the translation of various forms of the root *'šm* in the sense of *šmm* in the ancient versions (e.g., the LXX in Hos. 5:15; 10:2; 14:1[13:16]). [11]

Thus outside Hebrew, the root *'šm* occurs only in Arabic and perhaps in Ugaritic. In postbiblical Hebrew, it does not exhibit any special characteristics worthy of note.

II. The noun *'ashām*. The greatest diversity of meaning appears in the noun *'ashām*, while the verb reveals very few nuances in meaning.

1. *In Preexilic Passages*. a. In the Pentateuch, *'ashām* occurs in the ancient source J in Gen. 26:10 (cf. the adj. in E, Gen. 42:21). In the oldest form of the tradition of the betrayal of the tribal mother, Isaac, who had said that Rebekah was his sister, is reproved by Abimelech of Gerar, because by his deception Isaac risked occasioning for Abimelech the guilt of open adultery. *'ashām* also appears in the later period with this meaning of guilt, which brings punishment in the time of Yahweh's vengeance, e.g., in Jer. 51:5. Ps. 68:22(21) states that he who walks arrogantly before Yahweh in his guilty ways (pl. here only) will certainly perish.

b. 1 S. 6 presents a different meaning. When the Philistines send the ark back into Israelite territory in order to be delivered from the catastrophes they had suffered, at the advice of the Philistine clergy they put five golden tumors and

---

[6] A. Dillmann, *Lexicon Linguae Aethiopicae* (1865), 80b; cf. also the reference in *BDB*, 79b.

[7] Leslau, *Contributions*, 12.

[8] *KBL²*, 92b.

[9] Cf. C. Brockelmann, *LexSyr²*, 274a. I am indebted to W. W. Müller of Tübingen for information concerning the South Semitic.

[10] Cf. below on Am. 8:14.

[11] W. Zimmerli, *Ezechiel. BK*, XIII, 508.

five golden mice beside it on the cart as an *'āshām* for Yahweh. We are unable
to go into details here (as into the question of whether the combination of tumors
and mice is original), but it is clear that *'āshām* in 1 S. 6:3,4,8,17 (LXX *básanos*,
"torture, torment") means "propitiatory sacrifice, compensation, indemnifica-
tion." The verb *shubh* in the hiphil, "to return," which is also connected with
'āshām, e.g., in Nu. 5:7, and the number five, which calls to mind the law that
20 percent was to be added to the *'āshām* (Lev. 5:16,24[6:5]; 22:14; Nu. 5:7),
allow us to conjecture that in 1 S. 6 *'āshām* is to be seen in close connection with
the earlier idea that *'āshām* is a technical term used in the law of retribution, a
usage that can still be detected in P.

2. *In the Priestly Code and in Postexilic Texts.* Out of all the occurrences of
'āshām in the OT (48), the overwhelming majority (32) appear in P. Of course,
scholars have long recognized that *'āshām* does not always have the same meaning within P. Furthermore, it is hardly possible to distinguish between *'āshām*
and *chatta'th* in the texts as they exist in their present form.

a. The uncertain distinction between the roots *ht'* and *'šm* can already be
seen in the ancient versions. Thus, e.g., in Lev. 5:5 the Samaritan Pentateuch
has *yecheta'* for *ye'sham* of the MT (cf. also Nu. 18:9, where the Samaritan
Pentateuch has *ye'shamu* for *yashibhu*, "to render," of the MT). The LXX omits
Lev. 5:2b where the MT reads *'ashem*, has nothing corresponding to *ye'sham*
in Lev. 5:5a, and seems to want to read *'al chatta'tho*, "for his sin," instead of
'eth 'ashamo in Lev. 5:7. The rendering of *'āshām* by the root *plēmmel-*, "sin-,"[12]
in the LXX makes it quite clear that an interpretation has replaced a sacrificial
term in this translation. The Syriac Peshitta also, by its very general translation
of *'āshām* by *qwrbn'*, e.g., in Lev. 5 and 7, indicates that it has a sacrificial idea
in mind. But at the same time, the rendering of *'āshām* by *hth'* in Lev. 7:5;
chap. 14; and 19:21f., and of Heb. *chatta'th* in the same way, shows that the
translators of the Peshitta were unable to find an appropriate term in Syriac to
correspond to Heb. *'āshām*.

Furthermore, ancient authors no longer knew the meaning of *'āshām*. Thus,
Philo of Alexandria tries to explain the difference between *'asham* and *chatta'th*
on the basis of the use of these words in the LXX. He argues that *chatta'th* refers
to all unintentional transgressions against man, while *'asham* is used for unintentional sins against the Holy One and for intentional sins against man.[13]
Flavius Josephus, who is a little later than Philo, has no more precise information about the meaning of *'āshām* than Philo did, in spite of having come from
a priestly family. The distinction he makes (*Ant.* iii.9.3) is that a *chatta'th*
was to be sacrificed for sins of ignorance, while an *'āshām* was to be sacrificed
for all deliberate sins which no one witnessed. Origen thinks that the *chatta'th*
was the sacrifice offered to atone for mortal sins, and that the *'āshām* was the

12 Cf. S. Daniel, *Recherches sur le vocabulaire du culte dans le Septante* (1966), 299-326
and 341-361.
13 *De specialibus legibus, I, de victimis*, ed. L. Cohn, V (1906), 226-238.

sacrifice offered to atone for venial sins. [14] Augustine adopts the translation of
the Vulgate and thinks that *chatta'th* referred to sinful deeds (*peccatum*), thus
to intentional transgressions, and that *'āshām* referred to unintentional transgressions. [15] Jerome, whose translation Augustine adopts, agrees with this interpretation when he defines *'āshām* as a sacrifice *pro delicto sive pro ignorantia*,
"for sin or for ignorance." [16]

The views of modern authors are just as different as those of ancient writers.
Herrmann sees no fundamental difference between the meaning of *chatta'th*
and *'āshām*. [17] Médebielle believes that the unique feature of the *'āshām* is that
it is a restitution for trespasses, which presupposes a more severe sin than is
assumed in the fundamental idea of propitiation, which is denoted by *chatta'th*. [18]
Schötz concludes that ultimately the purpose of the *'āshām*-sacrifice was to atone
for a sacrilege, [19] viz., "a transgression against the deity himself as pertains to
holy things or holy persons, either against a specifically required holiness or by
unauthorized use of the divine name." [20] Again, the distinction Saydon makes [21]
amounts to differentiating between deliberate transgressions ("which are due to
human frailty" [22]), which are to be expiated by a *chatta'th*, and unintentional,
inadvertent transgressions which are to be expiated by an *'āshām*. Conversely,
Thomson thinks that *'āshām* was considered to be atonement for intentional
sins. [23] Moraldi concludes that both the *chatta'th* and the *'āshām* serve as atonement for sins and transgressions, but that in the *'āshām* the aspect of restitution
is added. [24] Gaster emphasizes the reparational aspect of *'āshām* even more. [25]
He argues that the *'āshām* is a "fine." Snaith argues that the *'āshām* serves as a
restitution, especially for wrongs that have actually been committed. [26] Rendtorff
conjectures that the *'āshām* was the "older form of the expiatory sacrifice for the
individual," which was largely replaced by the *chatta'th*. [27]

b. Questions concerning the difference between *'āshām* and *chatta'th*, and
concerning a possible development of the meaning of *'āshām* within P, can be
answered only by a thorough analysis of the texts. Elliger has already done this
in Leviticus, [28] and his conclusions will be discussed here. *'āshām* is used several
times in the sacrificial laws of Lev. 1–7. In the first supplement to the law of

---

14 *MPG*, 12, 453.
15 *MPL*, 34, 681f.
16 Cf. Jerome's comm. on Ezk. 40:39; 42:13; 44:29; *CChr*, LXXV, 582, 703.
17 J. Herrmann, *Die Idee der Sühne im AT* (1905), 78f.
18 A. Médebielle, 57, 61, and *DBS*, 3, 56-59.
19 D. Schötz, 32ff.
20 *Ibid.*, 45.
21 P. P. Saydon, 397f.
22 *Ibid.*, 398.
23 H. C. Thomson, 24.
24 L. Moraldi, 180ff.; *RivBibl*, 294f.
25 T. H. Gaster, "Sacrifices and Offerings, OT," *IDB*, IV, 147-159, esp. 152.
26 N. H. Snaith, 79f.
27 R. Rendtorff, 207-211.
28 K. Elliger, *HAT*, 4.

the sin-offering in 5:1-5, which gives regulations concerning specific cases, such as neglecting the responsibility of testifying in court or becoming contaminated by touching an unclean thing or the carcass of unclean animals, 'āshām is not yet understood as a sacrifice, but means "compensatory payment" (5:6). It means the same thing in 5:7 in the later section 5:7-10, concerning the sin-offering of a poor person. The first time 'āshām is introduced as a new designation for a sacrifice is in 5:14-16. When someone sins in the matter of paying his holy dues, he must bring a ram as an offering. In v. 15, 'āshām is used twice and in different senses: in v. 15bα it means compensatory payment as in 5:6,7, but in v. 15bβ it assumes the special meaning of penitential offering. But this kind of transition is nothing unusual in the Hebrew language as, e.g., the twofold meaning of chatta'th, "sin" and "sin-offering," in 4:3 shows. In all likelihood 'āshām in 5:15 is simply an alternate word for chatta'th, "sin-offering." The section concerning the ram offered as a guilt-offering, 5:17-19, the meaning of which is not immediately clear, seems to understand 'āshām as a sacrifice with its own ritual. The latest section, 5:20-26 (6:1-6), which is separate from that which precedes it, as its new introduction shows, delineates the guilt-offering for perjury in cases of theft. It is no longer the transgression, but the guilt that is emphasized. Presumably a development took place: "along with the restitution which originated in the civil law, . . . the sacrificial demand forced its way into the law of restitution, and thus a cultic law was produced out of a piece of civil law." [29] The restitution consists in restoring the complete value of that which was acquired unlawfully plus an additional tax of a fifth (cf. 5:16), and also a ram without blemish for a guilt-offering as atonement.

As a supplementary law to Lev. 5:20ff.(6:1ff.), Nu. 5:5-8 assumes a knowledge of the institution of the guilt-offering, and gives regulations concerning the restitution of embezzled goods in cases where the person wronged is dead and has not left a kinsman behind to inherit his estate. Such goods are to be used as payment to the priests. [30]

One should consult the Mishnah Kerithoth iii.1; iv.1f. for the peculiar form of the 'šm tlwy, which represents a special later development, and which was offered in cases of doubt.

In addition to the situations for which regulations are given in Lev. 4f. and Nu. 5:5-8, the 'āshām-sacrifice is also mentioned in Lev. 6:10(17); in the laws of cleansing in Lev. 14:12,13,14,17,21,24,25(twice),28; in the Holiness Code in Lev. 19:21(twice),22; in the Nazirite law in Nu. 6:12; and in 18:9; Ezk. 40:39; 42:13; 44:29; 46:20; 2 K. 12:17(16); Ezr. 10:19 (conjec.); and Sir. 7:31.

In the sacrifice for cleansing a person who is healed from leprosy (Lev. 14:12ff.), one male lamb is required as a guilt-offering (another as a burnt-offering, and a ewe lamb as a sin-offering). The importance of the guilt-offering is shown in that, in the supplement concerning the poor person's sacrifice for cleansing in Lev. 14:21-32, the burnt-offering and sin-offering are reduced to two pigeons while the guilt-offering remains unchanged as one lamb. It seems

[29] Ibid., 78.
[30] Cf. BZAW, 120 (1970), 66ff.

that the separation between God and the sick was considered to be so serious that only an *'āshām* could make restitution for the sin as a compensation.

An *'āshām*-sacrifice is also necessary when a man lies carnally with a woman who is a slave, betrothed to another man, Lev. 19:21f. Since in this case the wrongdoer cannot be punished according to civil law, although he is guilty, in dependence on 5:25(6:6) a ram is required as a compensatory sacrifice for the trespass.

The *'āshām*-sacrifice, which the Nazirite must offer in addition to cleansing ceremonies when his Nazirite vow is violated as a result of his having touched a dead body (Nu. 6:12), is usually understood as a later addition. However, since *'āshām* should probably be understood as a "restitution" here, and since the violation of the vow is an offense against Yahweh's possession, viz., the time pledged to him, the *'āshām* a priori will have belonged to the sin-offering and the burnt-offering of the Nazirite. [31]

The *'āshām*-sacrifice is not an ancient type of sacrifice, but developed from the *chatta'th* as an atonement sacrifice for all cases of gross negligence, and ultimately as a guilt-offering in difficult cases.

c. Some conclusions can be drawn from the ritual handed down in Lev. 7:1ff.: killing the animal in the holy place, the blood rite, offering the fat, burning the fat, and the regulations about eating the sacrifice. It is worthy of note that the rite of laying hands on the *'āshām* is not mentioned. The blood rite differs from that of the sin-offering: the blood is not sprinkled on the horns of the altar with the finger, nor is the remaining blood poured out at the base of the altar, but it is sprinkled on the altar round about, as in the burnt-offering and the sacrifice of peace-offering. The rite of burning the fat resembles that of the sin-offering of a sheep. The clear dependence of the ritual in Lev. 7 on various other sacrifices indicates that in its present form it is a relatively late development, the purpose of which was to distinguish between the rite of the *'āshām* and that of the sin-offering, and to provide a form of sacrifice which would stand between the sin-offering and the burnt-offering. Perhaps this is one reason why the *'āshām* is not a part of the ritual of one of the great festivals in Israel, in contrast to the *chatta'th* and even more naturally to the *'olah* (cf. Nu. 28f.).

d. A verse some scholars like to cite as a proof of the great antiquity of the *'āshām*-offering is 2 K. 12:17(16), which speaks of the *keseph 'asham*, "money from the guilt-offerings," and the *keseph chatta'oth*, "money from the sin-offerings," in connection with the account of the beginning of the collection to pay the men who worked on repairing the temple. But this argument cannot stand up under scrutiny because v. 17 is a later addition, [32] reflecting conditions in the postexilic period.

---

[31] Cf. *ibid.*, 88ff.
[32] Cf. also Rendtorff, 54.

e. The experiences that are intensified in times of great catastrophe, when sins and guilt severely strain the relationship between God and man, explain why the Jews in the postexilic period had such a lively interest in thinking about and reflecting on means of expiating sin. The literary remains from this period in the Priestly Code reveal the fervor with which the movement to guilt-offerings and sin-offerings was carried out.

a. *Isa. 53:10.* A particularly prominent passage in the last Ebhedh-Yahweh Song, Isa. 52:13–53:12, also speaks of *āshām.* Not only does this song compare the servant with a lamb that is led to the slaughter (53:7), but it also says that he makes his soul an *'āshām* "offering for sin." [33] The vicarious suffering of the righteous is the guilt-offering for the many. Like a guilt-offering, the death of the Servant results in atonement, the salvation of sinners from death.

It is not clear how *'āshām* is to be understood in Prov. 14:9. The parallel *ratson* could indicate that it means a guilt-offering, but the text is probably corrupt. [34]

III. The Verb. 1. The verb *'āsham* appears in the OT 33 times in the qal and once in the hiphil (Ps. 5:11[10]). The formal example of the niphal in Joel 1:18 should be read *nāshammu,* "are dismayed," with the LXX and derived from *shamem.* [35] With regard to the 33 occurrences of this verb in the qal, we should omit it in Hab. 1:11 as a textual error (and read *veyasim,* "and he set," with 1QpHab), but add it in Ezk. 35:6 (reading *'ashamta,* "you are guilty," with the LXX instead of *sane'tha,* "you have hated"). [36] A concrete sense of *'asham* probably preceded the abstract range of its meaning in the qal, "to act wrongly, to become guilty, to become culpable, to atone for guilt," perhaps in a way similar to the verb *chatta',* "to miss a target" > "to sin." But this concrete sense can no longer be determined from the existing occurrences of *'asham.* *'asham* can be connected with a preposition, and then it means to become guilty of something mentioned previously in the context (Lev. 5:4f.), or of a crime against other people (Nu. 5:7), or in particular of a crime against Yahweh (Lev. 5:19; 2 Ch. 19:10).

2. No change in the meaning of *'asham* can be ascertained between the pre-exilic and postexilic periods. In connection with the abduction of the Benjaminite women, Jgs. 21:22 emphasizes that the relatives of these women were not held guilty because the abduction occurred without their knowledge.

a. In Hosea, the verb occurs five times (4:15; 5:15; 10:2; 13:1; 14:1[13:16]). The contention that in Hosea *'asham* means "to make a sin-offering, to atone

---

33 Cf. recently E. Kutsch, *Sein Leiden und Tod–unser Heil. BSt,* 52 (1967); K. Elliger, "Jes 53,10: alte crux–neuer Vorschlag," *Festschrift R. Meyer. MIO,* 15 (1969), 228-233; W. Zimmerli, *SVT,* 17 (1969), 238ff.

34 Cf. the comms. *in loc.*

35 Cf. H. W. Wolff, *BK,* XIV/2, 22, n. 18c.

36 W. Zimmerli, *BK,* XIII/2, 852, n. 6c.

for sin," as Nyberg tries to show, [37] is not correct, in spite of *KBL²*, 92b, "to plead guilty by making atonement." [38] In all these passages, *'asham* means "to act wrongly, to become guilty," and thus "to make oneself culpable." For Hosea, one becomes guilty by practicing and following the Baal cult, and thus he uses *'asham* to denote a final culpability before God.

b. *'asham* occurs four times in Ezekiel (6:6; [39] 22:4; 25:12; and 35:6 [conjec.]). In the accusation against Jerusalem, one who sheds blood is considered to be guilty (so similarly 2 Ch. 19:10), and therefore he will be punished (Ezk. 22:4). Edom's vengeance against Judah is the grievous guilt (*vayya'shemu 'ashom*) which now causes Yahweh to take vengeance on them.

3. The occurrences of the verb *'asham* in the Priestly Code (Lev. 4:13,22,27; 5:2,3,4,5,17,19[twice],23[6:4]; Nu. 5:6,7) are nowhere influenced by the technical term *'āshām,* "guilt-offering." In these passages also *'asham* means "to become guilty," and except for Lev. 5:19, as a consequence of *chata',* "to sin."

4. Those who hurt Israel become guilty before Yahweh and will be punished (Jer. 2:3; 50:7). Those who transgress Yahweh's commandments must suffer for it; the consequences they must endure are a curse and devastation (Isa. 24:6).
Ps. 34:22(21) says, "those who hate the righteous will suffer for it," and it follows from the parallel lines that the death of the wicked is their punishment, while those who trust in Yahweh are protected from guilt and punishment (v. 23[22]).
Like Sir. 9:12, the wise counsel in Prov. 30:10, "do not slander a servant to his master, lest he curse you, and you be held guilty," shows how strictly the verb *'asham* was understood to have the meaning "to be guilty," even in the realm of human relationships, and to lead to automatic punishment, which means destruction and even death.

5. The hiphil is found only once in the OT (Ps. 5:11[10]) as the causative of the qal. In his request for divine judgment, the psalmist prays that Yahweh will make his enemies suffer and cast them out because of their transgressions (*pish'ehem*).

IV. The Adjective. The adj. *'ashem* occurs in Gen. 42:21 (pl.); 2 S. 14:13 (sing.); and Ezr. 10:19. However, we should read *va'ashamam,* "and their guilt-offering," in Ezr. 10:19 with the LXX and 3(1) Esd. 9:10, following Lev. 5:15, instead of *va'ashemim,* "and the guilty ones," of the MT. [40] The example in Gen. 42:21 belongs to the Old Pentateuchal source E. On their first trip to

---

[37] H. S. Nyberg, *Studien zum Hoseabuche* (Uppsala, 1935), 30f., 101.
[38] Cf. C. van Gelderen, *Het Boek Hosea* (1953), 124; W. Rudolph, *KAT,* XIII, 113; and H. W. Wolff, *Hosea* (trans. 1974), 89.
[39] Cf. on this W. Zimmerli, *BK,* XIII/1, 140, n. 6b.
[40] Cf. W. Rudolph, *HAT,* 20 (1949), 96.

Egypt, the brothers of Joseph understand by his order, to leave one brother in prison until their youngest brother be brought as verification of their word, that they were guilty and were having to suffer [41] for what they had done to Joseph. In this passage also *'ashem* means "guilty" or "suffering," unless one wishes to adopt the interpretation of Jerome in the Vulgate, *merito haec patimur, quia peccavimus,* "we deserve to suffer this, because we have sinned." In 2 S. 14:13, in the explanation of her parable, the woman of Tekoa compares David with a guilty person when he refuses to bring Absalom back home again because of his transgression in killing his brother Amnon. Here *'ashem* does not mean "guilty" in a forensic sense (for it is a law and a duty to avenge a murder), but in a purely moral sense, with a view to perpetuating the family.

V. 'ashmāh. *'ashmah,* the formal feminine derivative from the root *'shm,* means as a *nomen actionis* (noun of action), "guiltiness, becoming guilty," and thus is a qal infinitive construct, as it was undoubtedly understood in Lev. 4:3; 5:24,26(6:5,7); and 2 Ch. 28:13aδ. In other passages, [42] *'ashmah* hardly has the character and function of an infinitive construct, but means "sin, guilt." The plural occurs in Ps. 69:6(5); 2 Ch. 28:10; and perhaps also 2 Ch. 28:13aγ. The reading, "oath by the guilt of Samaria," in Am. 8:14 is a later attempt to improve the original text, which in all probability referred to the goddess *'ashimah* (cf. 2 K. 17:30). [43] All the other occurrences of *'ashmah* are found in P (Lev. 4:3; 5:24,26[6:5,7]; 22:16), the Chronicler's historical work (Ezr. 9:6,7,13,15; 10:10, 19; 1 Ch. 21:3; 2 Ch. 24:18; 28:13 [3 times]; 33:23), and Ps. 69:6(5) (postexilic). Thus, *'ashmah* is a relatively recent word which was popular in a later time. It does not reveal any more precise meaning of the root *'šm.*

In the prayer of repentance which he uttered in connection with the act of dissolving mixed marriages involving Jews, Ezra spoke of the great guilt that has mounted up to the heavens (Ezr. 9:6). Marrying foreign women increased the guilt of Israel (10:10). Sin against Yahweh (2 Ch. 19:10) evokes his wrath as punishment (24:18). Guilt is incurred through folly (Ps. 69:6[5]) and evil deeds (Ezr. 9:13). *'ashmah* appears in parallelism with *'avonoth,* "iniquities" (9:6,7), which calls to mind the phrase *'avon 'ashmah,* "iniquity of guilt" (RSV, "iniquity and guilt"), found only in Lev. 22:16 in the OT. When a priest profaned the holy things, the guilt was considered to be particularly serious, not only to the priest himself but also to the whole community.

D. Kellermann

---

[41] Thus H. Gunkel *in loc.*
[42] Including Lev. 22:16, notwithstanding R. Meyer, *Hebräische Grammatik,* II ([3]1969), § 65.10.
[43] Cf. the comms. *in loc.* and A. Alt, *KlSchr,* III, 295; *LidzEph,* III, 260ff.; A. Vincent, *La religion des Judéo-Araméens d'Éléphantine* (1937), 654ff.

אֲשֵׁרָה 'ašhērāh

Contents: I. 1. Etymology; 2. Occurrences. II. In the Ancient Near East. III. 1. Goddess; 2. Cult Object; 3. Religious Significance.

I. 1. *Etymology*. The name of the goddess Asherah is found in the following forms: Akk. DN *Ašratu(m)*, Ugar. DN *'trt*, Ugar. PN *'abdi-a-šar* (or *šir₉?*)*-ti*, El Amarna PN *'abdi-aš-ra-tum*, *'abdi-a-ši-ir-ta/ti*, Tell Taanach DN *a-ši-rat*, Hitt. DN *Ašertu, Ašerduš*, Qatabanic DN *'trt*, Thamudic PN *b'trt*, Aram. (Tema) DN *'šyr'*, and Heb. *'ašhērāh*. The Ugaritic list of gods in *Ugaritica*, V, chap. I, Nos. 18,19, mentions *ᵈAš-ra-tum* instead of *'trt* in the corresponding alphabetic version. But it should not be concluded from this that the Ugaritic pronunciation was *'aṯratu* because the scribe chose as his standard the ordinary Babylonian name. The widely divergent traditions of pronunciation can be explained by two equivalent original forms, both of which are feminine forms from *'aṯr*: 1. *'aṯr-t* → *'aṯirt*, perhaps also *'aṯart;* 2. *'aṯr-at* → *'aṯrat*. The form *'aṯirat* is to be understood as a mixed form of these two.

The root *'ṯr* can have different meanings. On the basis of the Ugar. *'trt ym*, the name Asherah is sometimes interpreted to mean "she who walks on (in) the sea." But for this to be correct, it must be assumed that *ym* was an original part of the name. Furthermore, it is very difficult to explain the different traditions of pronunciation from an original form *'āṯirat*. And finally, Ugar. *'ṯr* does not mean "to stride, to walk," but "to follow."

If the second name of the Ugaritic goddess really is to be vocalized *Qudšu*,[1] this means "holiness" or "sanctuary." This latter meaning may also be assumed for *'ṯrt*[2] if it is a feminine next to the Ugar. *'ṯr*, "holy place";[3] in fact, feminine forms of this word are used next to the masculine in Akkadian (*aširtu*) and Phoenician (*'šrt*). The deification of holy places often occurs among the Semites and is also well attested at Ugarit. If the original meaning is still reflected in *'ṯrt ym*, as is often the case also in other divine names, then this phrase can be translated, "sanctuary near the sea."[4]

'ašhērāh. W. F. Albright, *Archaeology and the Religion of Israel* (²1946), 74ff.; idem, *Yahweh and the Gods of Canaan* (1968), 105ff.; H. Bauer, *ZAW*, 51 (1933), 89f.; K.-H. Bernhardt, *MIO*, 13 (1967), 163ff.; R. Dussaud, *RHR*, 105 (1932), 275ff.; H. Gese, "Die Religionen Altsyriens," *RdM*, 10/2 (1970), 3-232, esp. 149ff.; A. S. Kapelrud, *Baal in the Ras Shamra Texts* (1952), 75ff.; A. Kuenen, *The Religion of Israel* (1882), 88ff.; Du Mesnil du Buisson, *RHR*, 164 (1963), 134ff.; idem, *Études sur les dieux phéniciens* (1970), 58, 98ff., 121ff.; M. J. Mulder, *Kanaänitische Goden in het OT* (1965), 39ff.; F. Nötscher, *RAC*, I, 730f.; U. Oldenburg, *The Conflict Between 'El and Ba'al* (1969), 28ff.; R. Patai, "The Goddess Ashera," *JNES*, 24 (1965), 37-52; M. H. Pope, *WbMyth*, I (1965), 246ff.; W. L. Reed, *The Asherah in the OT* (1949); P. Torge, *Aschera und Astarte* (1902).

[1] See below, II.
[2] Albright, *AJSL*, 41 (1925), 100; Oldenburg, 28, n. 4; Gese, 150.
[3] *CTA*, 17 [II D], I, 29 par.; 33, 24; possibly 5 [I* AB], VI, 24; cf. Akk. *ašru* and Phoen. *'šr*.
[4] Cf. Cowley, *AP*, No. 71,20 *b'tr ym*['], "at a place near the sea."

There is possibly some connection between '*trt* and the god '*tr*,[5] but this can hardly be proved.[6]

2. *Occurrences.* The word '*asherah* occurs 40 times in the OT, but only 4 times in the Pentateuch (Ex. 34:13; Dt. 7:5; 12:3; 16:21). It appears 18 times in the singular, and of these 6 times without the definite article, and 3 times in the plural form '*asheroth*, and of these once without the definite article. The pl. '*asherim* occurs 3 times without the definite article, 10 times with the definite article, and 6 times with suffixes. The plene form (the fully written *tsere*) appears in Dt. 7:5; 2 K. 17:16; and Mic. 5:13 (Eng. v. 14). Neither the definite article nor the plural necessarily excludes an interpretation of '*asherah* as a divine name.

II. In the Ancient Near East. The goddess *dAs̆-ra-tum* is first mentioned in lists of gods from the third dynasty of Ur, and later in Early Babylonian and Late Babylonian texts. She was the consort of the Amoritic god Amurru,[7] and as a West Semitic goddess should probably be identified with Atirat[u]/Asherah.

At Ugarit, Atirat is the consort of El (→ אל '*ēl*), the head of the pantheon. She is to be identified with the Babylonian mother-goddess dNIN.MAH.[8] Just as El is called "father of the gods" and "procreator of the generations of the gods," so Atirat is the *ʾm ʾlm*, "mother of the gods," and the *qnyt ʾlm*, "one giving birth to the gods." Consequently, the gods collectively can be called *dr (bn) ʾl*, "the family of (the sons of) El," or *bn 'trt*, "sons of Atirat."

In keeping with her role, Atirat sometimes performs functions typical of a mother. In *CTA*, 4 [II AB], II, 1-9, we find her on the beach, where she devotes herself to the duties of housekeeping: spinning, washing, and boiling her clothes. According to *CTA*, 4, II, 10f., she does this to please El. But when she goes to see El on a business matter, this does not mean she is reacting to his amorous advances.[9] She is able to exert influence on El.[10] It is uncertain, however, whether she had enough independence from him to live alone. Some scholars have suggested this was so, but *CTA*, 6, I argues against their view.

With her daughter 'Anat, Atirat appears as the nurse of gods and princes.[11] This indicates that at Ugarit Atirat was also given a fertility status. Thus she begins to resemble 'Anat and 'Attart, whose functions appear in the late period of Ugarit as different aspects of a single goddess. This development may be documented in the curious scribal error '*ttrt* in *CTA*, 4 [II AB], II, 13.

Another name for Atirat at Ugarit is *Qds̆* (presumably pronounced *Qudshu*).[12]

---

[5] Cf. *KBL*[3], 94.

[6] For additional etymologies of '*asherah*, see Reed, 91; Kopf, *VT*, 8 (1958), 165; Pope, 246; Gese, 150.

[7] J. R. Kupper, *L'iconographie du dieu Amurru* (1961), 61ff.

[8] *Ugaritica*, V, chap. I, No. 170,16.

[9] *CTA*, 4, IV, 38ff.

[10] *CTA*, 4, IV-V; 6 [I AB], I, 43ff.

[11] *CTA*, 15 [III K], II, 26f.; 23 [SS], 24, 59, 61; cf. *Syr*, 31 (1954), Table VIII; Ward, *Syr*, 46 (1969), 225ff.

[12] Albright.

From Egyptian texts we know *Qdš* as the name of a fertility goddess,[13] who forms a triad with 'Aṯtart and 'Anat.[14] A Canaanite myth in Hittite tradition tells us that Aṯirat tried to take over the role of 'Anat, the consort of Ba'al.[15] Finally, we may cite lists of sacrifices at Ugarit, in which the name Aṯirat often stands immediately after the name Ba'al, whereas in other lists this position is held by 'Anat.

There is no trace of such development in the older Ugaritic literature. As a matter of fact, it reflects a certain hostility between Aṯirat and her children on the one hand, and Ba'al and 'Anat on the other. Only lavish gifts can persuade Aṯirat to plead with El to grant Ba'al's request that he be allowed to build a palace. In the so-called canonical list of gods from Ugarit, *'ṯrt* occurs in fourteenth place (which is astonishingly low in the list) after goddesses like *ktrt* (in 7th place) and *pdry* (in 11th place), but before *'nt, špš, 'rṣy, ʒšḫry,* and *'ṯtrt* (in 15th through 19th places respectively). Also her name rarely appears in proper names. Apparently, at this time her popularity was in the process of declining. However, Aṯirat must have been important in the seaport towns (at Ugarit a Tyrian-Sidonian form of the goddess was also known),[16] because she was the one who opened the shipping season.[17] A small bronze figurine, which very probably represents Aṯirat, has been published by Schaeffer.[18]

In spite of an occasional interpretation to the contrary, trees and stones were certainly worshipped at Ugarit, as might have been expected on the basis of parallels in the Semitic world. Trees and stones seem to have played a role particularly in the giving of oracles: they "whisper" or "murmer" messages.[19] To be sure, they are never used in connection with Aṯirat, but rather with Ba'al and 'Anat. And yet, the Taanach Letter No. 1, 20f. mentions a mantic of Asherah.[20]

The goddess Asherah is no longer prominent in the first millennium B.C. It is impossible to decide whether the Aramaic incantation from Arslan Tash actually mentions her.[21] Apart from statements in the OT, the only allusions to the goddess Asherah which we know come from the Arabian peninsula. These include references in an Aramaic inscription from the 5th-4th centuries B.C. from Tema,[22] a Thamudic PN *b'ṯrt,* and finally the Qatabanic goddess *'ṯrt,* who appears several times in connection with the moon-god.[23] Gradually, Asherah probably came to be identified with Astarte and Anat, who in turn had already been united in one goddess as the Syrian Atargatis. The triad Rhea (Asherah), Diōnē/Baaltis (Anat), and Astartē in Philo of Byblos also points in this direction.[24]

---

[13] R. Stadelmann, *Syr.-pal. Gottheiten in Ägypten* (1967), 110ff.
[14] Edwards, *JNES,* 14 (1955), 49ff.
[15] Otten, *MIO,* 1 (1953), 125ff.
[16] *CTA,* 14 [I K], IV, 198f.
[17] *CTA,* 4 [II AB], II, 28ff.; see *AOT,* 16, 143ff.
[18] Schaeffer, *Syr,* 43 (1966), 5f.
[19] *CTA,* 3 [V AB], C, 20; *PRU,* II 1, verso 13.
[20] Albright, *BASOR,* 94 (1944), 18.
[21] Donner-Röllig, *KAI,* II, 45.
[22] *KAI,* 228.3, 16.
[23] Höfner, *WbMyth,* I, 497.
[24] Clemen, *MVÄG,* 42/3 (1938), 27.

III. 1. *Goddess.* While Aṭirat was still the wife of El at Ugarit, in the OT Asherah appears as the companion of Baal (Jgs. 3:7; 1 K. 18:19; 2 K. 23:4; cf. Jgs. 6:26; 1 K. 16:32f.; 2 K. 17:16; 2 Ch. 33:3, where the symbol of the goddess is connected with the worship of Baal). This OT picture probably represents a later development, which begins to appear toward the end of the second millennium B.C., and can be attributed to the gradual fusion of the Canaanite fertility goddesses Anat and Astarte with the mother-goddess Asherah.[25] This fusion is also evident from the occurrence in the OT of the expression *habbeʿalim veha'asheroth*, "the Baals and the Asheroth" (Jgs. 3:7; cf. 2 Ch. 33:3), in addition to the proverbial phrase *habbaʿal vehaʿashtaroth*, "the Baal and the Ashtaroth" (Jgs. 2:13), or *habbeʿalim vehaʿashtaroth*, "the Baals and the Ashtaroth" (10-6; 1 S. 7:4; 12:10), while the LXX translates *'asherah* by *Astartē* in 2 Ch. 15:16, and *'asherim* by *Astartai* in 2 Ch. 24:18. When one compares 2 K. 23:4-6 with 23:13f., the cult object *'asherah* seems to be connected with both the Asherah cult (in v. 4 probably a proper name; cf. 21:7) and the Astarte cult.

The genuine character of the mother-goddess is forced entirely into the background in this fusion process, and now Asherah appears primarily as a fertility goddess. Women in particular were attracted to her cult (1 K. 15:13; 2 K. 23:7; also 1 K. 11:1-8 with regard to 2 K. 23:13f.). They would weave *battim* for Asherah, viz., in the temple area where the hierodules lived (2 K. 23:7). This weaving of *battim* may be a euphemism for sexual intercourse.[26] According to another explanation, *bath* here is an article of clothing[27] with which the image of the goddess was clothed. On this, one should compare not only Egyptian, Babylonian, and Greek parallels, but also Ugaritic texts in which articles of clothing are mentioned for the images of ʿAṭṭart and other goddesses. In any case, erotic ideas were often connected with spinning and weaving in the ancient Near East.[28] Now it is interesting that at Ugarit neither ʿAnat nor ʿAṭṭart is represented as patroness of this typical female activity, but Aṭirat,[29] so that here possibly an element of the original Asherah concept has been preserved.

If the conjecture made by Wellhausen that we should read *'anatho ve'ashratho,* "his Anat and his Asherah," in Hos. 14:9(8) instead of the MT,[30] were correct, this would mean that Asherah and Anat were explicitly put side by side. This would also provide a good contact with v. 9b(8b), viz., that her symbol was an evergreen tree. However, this conjecture is probably "more ingenious than correct."[31]

2. *Cult Object.* The goddess and her cult object of the same name were not sharply differentiated, as a comparison of 2 K. 21:3 with 21:7 and of 23:4 with 23:6 shows. This is nothing unusual in the history of religion; Canaanite examples

---

[25] See above, II.
[26] Murmelstein, *ZAW,* 81 (1969), 223f.
[27] *KBL*³, 159.
[28] Murmelstein, *ZAW,* 81, 215ff.; Hoffner, *JBL,* 85 (1966), 326ff.
[29] See above, II.
[30] J. Wellhausen, *Skizzen and Vorarbeiten,* V (²1893), 131.
[31] Sellin.

also make this clear (cf. Dagon). There is no precise description of the ʾasherah as a cult object in the OT, which is certainly related to its being offensive to the OT writers. As a result, there is uncertainty as to the true nature of the ʾasherah in the ancient versions: frequently this word has been understood as grove, sometimes as a single tree, as a pole, cult image, or goddess. [32] Modern research has not been able to remove this uncertainty. Due to the inadequacy of the written sources, various archeological identifications can be nothing more than very hypothetical.

The Mishnah considered the ʾasherah to be a living tree (Orla i.7f.; ʿAbodah Zarah iii.7,9f.; Sukkah iii.1-3). As a matter of fact, with reference to Dt. 16:21 one could think of ʾasherah as a living tree which is "planted" (nataʿ). But kol ʿets, "any tree," is ambiguous and can refer just as well to dead wood. The verb nataʿ may have been used in a figurative sense with the meaning "to drive in (a pole)" (cf. Eccl. 12:11; Dnl. 11:45), because in other passages the Asherim were "set up" (hiphil of natsabh, 2 K. 17:10; hiphil of ʿamadh, 2 Ch. 33:19; sim, 2 K. 21:7), and according to Isa. 27:9 they "stood" (qum). These verbs probably indicate an oblong object which was driven vertically into the ground. This is confirmed by Jgs. 6:25,28,30, according to which the ʾasherah jutted up beside the altar (for this use of ʿal, cf. Gen. 16:7; 18:8; etc.; of course an object of wood did not stand on the altar).

"Asherim" in Mic. 5:13(14) could also refer to a tree, as could be indicated by the verb nathash, "root out" (cf. Jer. 12:14,15; 24:6; etc.), and by the parallel to "Asherim" in the next line, ʿarekha, which since J. D. Michaelis has often been understood as a species of tree. However, nathash can very well have the more general meaning "pluck up"; and even if *ʿr indicates a species of tree, it is not necessarily in synonymous parallelism with "Asherim."

If Albright is correct in conjecturing that we should read vekhaʾallon ʾasher(ah) in Isa. 6:13, [33] this could be used as evidence that the oak was consecrated to Asherah. But this suggestion is probably too daring. [34] The same is true of Wellhausen's conjecture on Hos. 14:9(8). [35]

Although living trees and bushes are still worshipped in Syria and Palestine, and holy trees (→ עץ ʿēts) played a role in the OT, it is not to be assumed that the name ʾasherah was used in this connection. Undoubtedly the ʾasherah was an object made of wood (Dt. 16:21; Jgs. 6:26), which was driven into the ground. [36] Thus, it could also be hewed down (Dt. 7:5; 2 Ch. 14:2[3]; 31:1), cut down (Ex. 34:13; Jgs. 6:25f.,30; 2 K. 18:4; 23:14), rooted out (Mic. 5:13[14]), pulled down (2 Ch. 34:7), and burned (Dt. 12:3; Jgs. 6:26; 2 K. 23:6,15). But a living tree cannot be intended, because the Asherim were "made" (1 K. 14:15; 16:33; 2 K. 17:16; 21:3,7; Isa. 17:8), and they stood under green trees (1 K. 14:23; 2 K. 17:10).

---

[32] Reed, 6ff.; Barr, JSS, 13 (1968), 14ff.
[33] Albright, SVT, 4 (1957), 254.
[34] Wildberger, BK, X, 324.
[35] See above.
[36] See above.

Once the OT mentions the making of a graven image (*pesel*) of Asherah (2 K. 21:7); it is called *pesel hassemel,* "the image of the idol," in 2 Ch. 33:7, and simply *hassemel,* "the idol," in 2 Ch. 33:15 (which is not to be identified with *semel haqqin'ah,* "image of jealousy," in Ezk. 8:5). Another passage says that a *miphletseth,* "an abominable image," was made for Asherah (1 K. 15:13). These passages also indicate that the cult object actually represented the goddess Asherah, as the name itself would lead us to expect. This symbol usually stood on a cultic high place (→ במה *bāmāh*) near an altar and/or an incense altar. The *'asherah* was often associated with a raised stone (→ מצבה *matslsēbhāh*).

Some scholars have supposed that the *'asherah* was an object made out of wood in the form of a pole, perhaps decorated with carved work. Since this stage was probably preceded by a phase in which the raised stone was combined with a living or dead tree, it is possible to assume that the *'asherah* was a stylized tree, as it appears, e.g., on a clay model of a cultic scene from Cyprus. [37] On the other hand, that the same object is called *pesel ha'asherah,* "the graven image of Asherah," in one passage (2 K. 21:7), and simply *ha'asherah,* "the Asherah," in another (23:6), probably favors the view that it was an image of a god. Under no circumstances can the word → פסל *pesel* be interpreted so as to refer to a tree-trunk the branches or protrusions of which were chopped off, because such treatment would have desecrated the tree (cf. the Mishnah *'Abodah Zarah* iii.10). The expression (*pesel*) *hassemel,* "(the image of) the idol," which is used in 2 Ch. 33:7,15, also points to an image of the goddess.

Frequently the Asherim are mentioned in connection with other images of gods (Dt. 7:5; 12:3; 2 K. 17:16; Mic. 5:12f.[13f.]; 2 Ch. 24:18; 33:19; 34:3f.,7). This could give the impression that they are distinguished from "regular" images. It is possible, however, that they are specifically mentioned because they represent the most important female deity. In interpreting the Asherim as an image, the fact that they are always made of wood leaves open the possibility that this image took over the function that formerly belonged to the tree. The frequent combination of *'asherah* and *matstsebhah,* "pillar," is interesting in this regard. Stone and tree were combined at Ugarit, [38] and according to the OT both attributes were found in ancient sanctuaries, as at Shechem (Josh. 24:26), Bethel (Gen. 28:18ff.; 35:8), and Ophrah (Jgs. 6:11,19f.,24ff.). It is noteworthy that the OT often speaks of appearances and revealed messages which were given to the patriarchs and judges at these holy places. Trees and stones were also specifically connected with the oracle at Ugarit. When Hosea says that the people inquire of "a thing of wood" (4:12), this could refer to the *'asherah,* which was later mentioned in connection with the *matstsebhah,* "pillar," instead of the tree. As the *'asherah* is the symbol of the fertility goddess, the *matstsebhah* is the symbol of the fertility god Baal (2 K. 3:2; 10:26f.). We have already seen that the tree-oracle and the stone-oracle were specifically connected with these deities at Ugarit.

---

[37] *BRL,* 35f.; *BHHW,* I, 137.
[38] See above, II.

3. *Religious Significance.* According to the Deuteronomistic historical writers and later chroniclers, there were cult symbols of the goddess Asherah throughout the whole land–both in Judah and in Israel (Dt. 12:2f.; 1 K. 14:23; 2 K. 17:10; 2 Ch. 31:1; 34:6f.). Ophrah (Jgs. 6:25), Bethel (2 K. 23:15), Samaria (1 K. 16:33; 2 K. 13:6), the high places that were east of Jerusalem (2 K. 23:13f.), and for a brief time the temple in Jerusalem (2 K. 21:7; 23:6), are specifically named as cult places where Asherim were kept. Under Ahab the Asherah cult must have become well organized, because 1 K. 18:19 says there were 400 prophets of the Asherah in his day. After the reform of Josiah (2 K. 23), a strict law was made that the *'asherah* had to be destroyed along with all other kinds of heathen practices (Ex. 34:13; Dt. 7:5; 12:3). The Deuteronomistic historical writers condemn the kings who (in this respect the historical tradition is certainly reliable) served the heathen fertility goddess (Jeroboam I, 1 K. 14:15f.; Rehoboam, 14:23; Ahab, 16:33; 18:19; Joash, 2 Ch. 24:18; Jehoahaz, 2 K. 13:6; and Manasseh, 21:3,7). They praise the judge Gideon (Jgs. 6) and the kings (Asa, 1 K. 15:13; Jehoshaphat, 2 Ch. 17:6; 19:3; Hezekiah, 2 K. 18:4; and Josiah, 23:4, 6f.,14f.) who destroyed the symbols of this goddess. They attribute the calamity that comes on the Israelites to the worship of the *'asherah,* among other things (Jgs. 3:7; 2 K. 17:10,16; Jer. 17:2). In the End Time, Israel will turn away from the *'asherah* (Isa. 17:8), and Yahweh will also destroy the last *'asherah* (Mic. 5:13[14]; cf. Isa. 27:9).

Naturally, the severe condemnation of the *'asherah* is to be traced back directly to the first and second commandments of the Decalog. Undoubtedly every other manifestation of the fertility goddess falls under this condemnation in the pre-Deuteronomistic period. Of course, there is involved here a fear that the syncretistic tendency to assimilate Yahweh to → בַּעַל *ba'al* could receive a strong impetus precisely through the possibility of connecting a consort with Yahweh in the form of a fertility goddess. When Manasseh set up an image of Asherah in the Jerusalem temple (2 K. 21:7), choosing, with obvious cleverness, the person of the fertility triad that was the most venerable, but at the same time the least worshipped by the Canaanites of that period, this danger became particularly acute. Therefore, the reform of Josiah was directed especially against this goddess and her symbols (Dt. 16:21; 2 K. 23:4,6). This is also the reason she is so prominent among the gods and goddesses of Canaan who are attacked by the Deuteronomist.

No other source explicitly forbids the worship of the Asherah, although scholars are justified in assuming that the fertility goddess was either worshipped or opposed elsewhere in Israel, even if very likely not under the name Asherah. In Canaan, Asherah was completely absorbed by the figure of the consort of Baal, which must have been better known in this area by the name 'Anat, Astarte, or possibly also *ba'alah,* "mistress," and *malkath hashshamayim,* "queen of the heavens." Thus, it may also be assumed that the worship of 'Anat in connection with that of Yahweh in the Jewish colony of Elephantine was, in reality, hardly different from the service of Asherah described here.

De Moor

┌─────────────┐
│ אַשְׁרֵי *'ashrê* │
└─────────────┘

Contents: I. 1. Lexicographical Matters; 2. Usage. II. 1. Theology of the Blessing in the Psalms; 2. In Proverbs and Late Writings. III. The Blessing in the Development of Biblical Theology.

I. 1. *Lexicographical Matters.* *'ashre* is a masculine plural construct, and was interpreted as a type of interjection at a very early time.[1] Some scholars have taken it to be a segholate noun derived from the root *'šr,* "to go," which is known in Hebrew, Ugaritic, and Arabic. The verb, which is rarely used in the qal (Prov. 9:6), frequently occurs in the piel in Isaiah with the meaning "to lead." But the piel also means that a person "happily" transfers his (implied in the root) property to someone, and thus means "to make (someone) happy." This meaning is found in Gen. 30:13 (probably J) and in seven late passages (Mal. 3:12; Prov. 31:28; Job 29:11; Cant. 6:9; Ps. 72:17; pual, Prov. 3:18; Ps. 41:3 [Eng. v. 2]). Gen. 30:13 presupposes a segholate of another sort, which would be *'osher* according to the MT. Some lexicographers assume a different root related to the root *yšr,* "to be upright," which they identify with the Akk. *wašāru,*[2] but the Akkadian equivalent to *yšr* is *'ešēru,* "to be in order (right, correct)." The Egyptian transcriptions of Semitic names from the period of the Middle Kingdom may also point to a root *'šr* which is distinct from the Ugar. *'tr.*[3] Moreover, Janzen has shown that *'ashre* is not to be interpreted as an antithesis to the cry of woe, *hoy,* "Ah! Alas!"

Just because the blessing formula *barukh,* "Blessed be (is)," in Israel is very old does not mean that the same is true of *'ashre.* This word appears only rarely in J (Gen. 30:13), E (Dt. 33:29 in the final portion of Dt., which is a redactional ending), Isaiah (30:18), and 1 Kings (10:8, which is probably redactional). It occurs most frequently in the Psalms (26 times) and in the Wisdom books (12 times

---

'ashrê. A. Barucq, *L'expression de la louange divine et de la prière dans la Bible et en Egypte* (Cairo, 1962), 262, 482; G. Bertram, "μακάριος," *TDNT,* IV (1967), 364-367; J. Dupont, *Les Béatitudes* (Bruges-Louvain, ²1958); *idem,* "Béatitudes égyptiennes," *Bibl,* 47 (1966), 185-222; A. George, "La 'forme' des béatitudes jusqu'à Jésus," *Mélanges Bibliques en l'honneur de A. Robert* (Paris, 1957), 398-403; W. Janzen, "'Ašrê' in the OT," *HThR,* 58 (1965), 215-226; W. Käser, "Beobachtungen zum alttestamentlichen Makarismus," *ZAW,* 82 (1970), 225-250; C. Keller, "Les Béatitudes de l'AT," *Maqqel Shâqêdh, Hommage à W. Vischer* (Montpellier, 1960), 88-100; R. Kieffer, "Vishet och välsignelse som grundmotiv i saligprisningarna hos Matteus och Lukas," *SEÅ,* 34 (1969), 107-121; E. Lipiński, "Macarismes et psaumes de congratulation," *RB,* 75 (1968), 321-367; S. Mowinckel, *Segen und Fluch in Israels Kult und Psalmendichtung. Psalmenstudien,* V (Oslo, 1923); W. Zimmerli, "Zur Struktur der at.lichen Weisheit," *ZAW,* 51 (1933), 175-204.

[1] *GK,* § 93 l.
[2] *GesB, KBL.*
[3] Albright, *JAOS,* 74 (1954).

outside the Greek portions of Sir.). While *'ashre* is found only once each in Job and Ecclesiastes, it occurs relatively often in Proverbs in antithetical parallelism (which Zimmerli and Lipiński consider to be a distortion of the pure form) in collections which are regarded as the oldest (14:21; 16:20; 20:7; 29:18).

2. *Usage. 'ashre* occurs most often in the Psalms. It opens the Psalter in 1:1, is found at the end of Ps. 2 (Acts 13:33 D considers these two psalms as a unit; cf. *Berakhoth* 9b), is missing from the first two books of the Psalms with the exception of the last psalm in each group (32–41 and 65), occurs in the psalms concluding collections I (41:2[1]), III (89:16[15]), and IV (106:3), and finally appears quite often in the last book (8 times, in particular in 119:1f.).

This evidence will hardly allow one to deny a connection between *'ashre* and the liturgy of the Second Temple. *'ashre* is a liturgical cry, and its late connection with the verb *'šr* points to an act in which believers seek happiness; it was probably the pilgrimage to the temple in the sense of the Deuteronomistic movement and the return from the exile. This act makes the believers "happy," thus explaining the translation by Gk. *makários* and Aram. *ṭûbai.*

II. 1. *Theology of the Blessing in the Psalms.* What is the connection between this cry of happiness and the blessing? According to Mowinckel, there is no difference between the words *'ashre* and *barukh*,[4] but according to Kraus the "more secular" *'ashre* should be distinguished from the sacral-solemn *barukh.*[5] Kraus is probably correct, because this cry of happiness never refers to God (even in Dt. 33:29 Israel is happy because she has been saved by God). The desire for happiness is different from the blessing in that it demands that the believer do certain things: he must come to Zion (Ps. 65:5[4]; 84:5[4]; as well as Isa. 30:18; cf. v. 19), where refuge (*chasah*) is to be found (Ps. 2:12; 34:9[8]; cf. 84:13[12]), and where sins are forgiven (32:1,2). But in harmony with the Deuteronomistic view, happiness depends on the choice (Ps. 33:12) or teaching of God (94:12). The believer must fear God (112:1; 128:1). His behavior must be blameless (119:1f.), and he must obey the Torah and not follow the counsel of the wicked (1:1). Happy is he who considers the poor (41:2[1]), who observes justice and does *tsedhaqah,* "righteousness" (106:3), who receives sons as a gift from God in his youth (127:5), and who executes God's judgment against the enemies of the chosen people (137:8).

2. *In Proverbs and Late Writings.* We find an echo of this view in the parallel constructions in Proverbs. Happiness belongs to those who take refuge in God (Prov. 16:20), who have pity on the oppressed (14:21), who are given children (20:7), and who keep the Torah (29:18). Similarly, the fear of God (which is often made a fundamental demand in this book) as the beginning of wisdom is connected with the blessing that comes on those who fear God (28:14).

---

4 S. Mowinckel, *The Psalms in Israel's Worship* (1962), 47.
5 H.-J. Kraus, *BK,* X/1, 3.

The later literature also takes up this theme. Happy are those who find wisdom, the tree of life (Prov. 3:13), or who listen to the wisdom created by God and watch at her gates (8:33f.). This is connected with the poem concerning the woman whose excellence motivates her children to bless her (31:28). Eliphaz reminds Job that God connects happiness with reproof (Job 5:17). When one heard Job speak formerly, he called him happy (29:11); but now God has thrust him out in misery.

In harmony with election theology, Mal. 3:12 says that the nations will praise Israel. In Ps. 72:17 they bless the sons of David, and in Cant. 6:9 the maidens proclaim the happiness of the female lover.

III. The Blessing in the Development of Biblical Theology. The interpretation of the biblical use of 'ashre would not be complete without an attempt to explain its origin and meaning. Since 'ashre has a peculiar grammatical form and was introduced into the language of the OT at a late period, it is logical to conclude that it is a foreign expression which was taken over into the OT.

In the cuneiform literature there are no satisfactory parallels. To be sure, this material does speak of success and happiness, especially in the omina, [6] and uses the expression ṭūb libbi, "the well-being of the heart," but all this has little to do with the use of 'ashre in the OT. In the Babylonian hymns we encounter cries[7] which prepare the way for the 'ashre of the Psalms. It is even possible that the Akk. ašru, which extols humility and trust[8] and is used especially in the Neo-Babylonian period (ašri kanšu, ašri sanga; wašrum in the Code of Hammurabi), played a certain role in Israel's adoption of the 'ashre-formula, since the happiness of this formula is the humble reply of Israel to the call of God who had chosen her.

According to the study of J. Dupont, the pronouncement of blessings is to be found especially in Egypt. It is particularly noticeable in the late Petosiris, whose contacts with the Bible are well known: "Happy is the man who directs his heart into the way of life ... "; "Happy is the man who comes to his house without sin! ... "; "Happy is the one who loves God! ... "; "Happy is the one who directs his heart into the way of faithfulness!" These kinds of blessings are also found in Rameses II ("Happy is he who understands thee, O Amon!"), in the Tell el-Amarna tablets ("Happy is he who hears thy instruction for life"), in Thutmose III ("Happy is he who carries out the law of God in right actions," Drioton), and even in the Pyramid Texts (476, "Happy are those who look like the Pharaoh rising up to heaven").

The form of this blessing is very instructive: rs.wy is used of a servant who sustains his lord, of one who has God in his heart, and of a land whose lord the Pharaoh has become (Sinuhe); w3d.wy is applied to one who has acted well toward his lord, to him who hearkens to the instruction of life, and to one who reaches Thebes, the blessed city (Leiden Papyrus, Rameses II); snk.wy is used of

---

[6] Cf. F. R. Kraus, "Ein Sittenkanon in Omenform," ZA, 43 (1936), 77-113.
[7] E.g., in ANET, 386, "may my paths be straight"; 387, "may he be happy."
[8] CAD, I, 455; AHw, 82.

him who has stayed at Sinai, of one who has not been intimidated like Rameses II at Kadesh, and of the victorious Merneptah on the Israel stele; *nfr.wy* is applied to one who hearkens to his father (Ptah-hotep), and to him who sees Ra in the sunrise; and *ḥntš.wy* is used of the heart of the lover who meets his sweetheart (Chester Beatty Papyri). In all these expressions the exclamatory particle *wy* is used. This particle can also serve as a dual ending, just as *-ê* in Hebrew can also be a dual construct (although this external agreement is hardly decisive). It would be hard to explain the development of the biblical *'ashre* from Isaiah on, apart from any influence from Egyptian culture, since it is precisely in this period that we are able to trace the influence of the Egyptian scribe and of the wisdom vocabulary on the OT. [9] The divine blessing demands deeds of faithfulness to God and his law in order to give happiness to the faithful; this is precisely the meaning of *'ashre*.

'ashre does not occur in the Qumran literature, but the Rabbinic literature preserves the traditional usage. [10] In Sirach, which uses the verb six times, we encounter the last stage in the development of the pronounced blessing (11 times, often confirmed by the Heb. text: happy is he who has not sinned, who is discreet, who has found perfection). In 37:24, he puts blessing and happiness in parallelism, and this prepares the way for the Sermon on the Mount, where Gk. *makários,* "blessed," is connected with fulfilment of the law.

According to Käser, the OT expression "blessed be (is) ... " is a wisdom form used in expressions commonly connected with the language of the OT. It is "proclamation of the relationship between God and man in the living covenant of grace... which was created by grace; this applies also precisely to the *makarism* that is so often related to the Torah." It has to do with life in the sphere of the Torah. The *makarismic* proclamation is "really eschatological," since it is realized in the covenant of the "Lord who continues to be faithful today and tomorrow." "Blessing is praise of the grace of God which creates salvation for the man who is chosen." [11]

Cazelles

---

9 Fichtner.
10 St.-B., I, 189.
11 Käser, 249f.

```
┌─────────────────────────┐
│  אֵת 'ēth;  עִם 'im      │
└─────────────────────────┘
```

Contents: I. Secular Use: 1. Parallelism, Etymology, and Origin of the Prepositions 'eth and 'im; 2. Scope of the Secular Meaning. II. Theological Use: 1. General Considerations; 2. In the Promises of God; 3. As a Promise, Wish, etc. of Man; 4. In the Affirmative Use; 5. Content, History, and Place of the Formula Using 'eth and 'im in the Faith of Israel. III. 'Immānu 'ēl.

I. Secular Use.

1. *Parallelism, Etymology, and Origin of the Prepositions 'eth and 'im.* In the history of languages, it is extraordinary when two different words belonging to the same chronological period of a language have the same meanings. Yet the OT reflects no essential difference in the meanings or uses of. 'eth and 'im either as to the historical periods when they occur or as to the genres in which they appear. The only thing that is clear is that in both the secular and theological realms, in later texts 'eth is used less and less and 'im is used more and more. Therefore, it seems justifiable to treat both prepositions together. While 'eth (originally 'itt?) [1] has a close affinity with the Akk. itti (Assyr. išti), [2] and (because Semitic prepositions were originally substantives) also is intimately connected with 'idt (fem. form of yd?) or a form of 'nh II, "to meet," [3] 'im has a stronger association with the Northwest Semitic-Aramaic language type (cf. the Aram.; Syr. 'am; Ugar. 'm, intensified to 'mn='imman, cf. Hos. 12:5 [Eng. v. 4]; but also the Arab. 'am, also 'an and ma'a?). [4]

2. *Scope of the Secular Meaning.* The following representative examples should clarify the scope of variation and meaning in the two prepositions 'eth and 'im.

'ēth. W. Beyerlin, *ZAW,* 73 (1961), 191; M. Buber, *VT,* 6 (1956), 137; J. L. Crenshaw, *ZAW,* 80 (1968), 207; R. Kilian, *Die Verheissung Immanuels Jes 7,14. SBS,* 35 (1968); H.-P. Müller, *Ursprünge und Strukturen alttestamentlicher Eschatologie. BZAW,* 109 (1969), 138, 142f., 151, 166f.; H. D. Preuss, " . . . ich will mit dir sein!" *ZAW,* 80 (1968), 139-173; cf. 139, n. 4, for the earlier literature; M. Rehm, *Der königliche Messias im Licht der Immanuel-Weissagungen des Buches Jesaja* (1968); W. Richter, *Die sogenannten vorprophetischen Berufungsberichte. FRLANT,* 101 (1970), 138, 146-151, 171f., 174; Ph. de Robert, *Le berger d'Israël* (Neuchâtel, 1968), 54f., 91; L. Schmidt, *Menschlicher Erfolg und Jahwes Initiative. WMANT,* 38 (1970), 37ff., 74ff., 88ff., 100f., etc.; H. Seebass, *ZAW,* 79 (1967), 162; J. J. Stamm, "Die Immanuel-Perikope im Lichte neuerer Veroffentlichungen," *ZDMG Supplement,* 1 (1969), 281-290; H. W. Wolff, *BK,* XIV/2, 294f.

[1] Cf. *KBL*³, 97.
[2] On 'eth in the field of Northwest Semitic languages, see *DISO,* 28f.; cf. also the Lachish Letters III, 20.
[3] So E. König, *Hebr. und aram. Wörterbuch zum AT* (1910), 31.
[4] Cf. further *DISO,* 215f.

a. *ʾeth* and *ʿim* have the following meanings: (1) "with, together with, in the company or association of": *ʾeth,* Gen. 7:7; Jgs. 9:32f.; 2 S. 16:17; Jer. 3:9; *ʿim,* Gen. 5:24; 13:1; Ex. 22:29(30); Dt. 12:23; Hos. 4:14; Eccl. 2:16;[5] (2) "at, close to, beside, in the midst of": *ʾeth,* Ex. 1:14; Lev. 19:13; Jgs. 4:11; Isa. 53:8; Job 2:13; *ʿim,* Gen. 23:4; 25:11; Dt. 22:2; 2 S. 13:23; 21:4; 1 Ch. 13:14 (*ʾeth* sometimes means "besides" in the sense "except, beyond, contrary to," Ex. 20:23; 33:21); (3) "with the help of, under the protection of": *ʾeth,* Gen. 4:1 (?); 30:29; Jgs. 17:2; *ʿim,* 1 S. 14:45; 1 Ch. 4:23; 12:19(18); (4) "provided with, in the possession of": *ʾeth,* Jer. 23:28; *ʿim,* Gen. 24:25; Ps. 89:14(13); (5) "to strive with someone, to fight with": *ʾeth,* Gen. 14:9; Jgs. 11:27; 1 Ch. 20:5; *ʿim,* Gen. 26:29; Isa. 3:14; Ps. 94:16; Job 14:3.

b. In addition to these primary meanings, *ʾeth* and *ʿim* have the following rarer or figurative meanings: (1) "in, at, upon, with reference (regard) to, for the benefit of": *ʾeth,* 1 S. 7:16; 1 K. 9:25; *ʿim,* Gen. 24:12; Ex. 34:10; (2) "as well as, in the manner of": *ʾeth,* Gen. 6:13; *ʿim,* 18:23; Ps. 73:5.

c. As *ʿim* makes its way into Hebrew more and more, it has a somewhat larger scope of meaning: (1) "to have with him = in mind," Nu. 14:24; Dt. 8:5; Job 23:14; (2) "as long as," Ps. 72:5; (3) "comparable with, in comparison with," Ps. 120:4; Job 9:26; (4) "yet" ("nevertheless"), Isa. 25:11; Neh. 5:18 (late passages); (5) "until" (temporal), Isa. 44:7 (read *ʿim*); (6) "after, toward, to," Jgs. 4:9; Ps. 18:24(23) (2 S. 22:24, *le*); Job 31:5 (cf. Ugar. *ʿm*);[6] (7) "from the way, out of," Gen. 23:4; Ps. 85:5(4); Job 27:13.[7]

The presence of one man with another is often placed in the context of "accompanying him on a journey or a trip" (Gen. 13:1,5; 18:16; 19:30; 24:32,40, 54,58; 31:23).[8] The OT does not know an erotic "association" as a formal expression.[9]

II. Theological Use.

1. *General Considerations.* In the theological realm also, the prepositions *ʾeth* and *ʿim* are used promiscuously. In over 100 passages, the OT makes statements concerning the "presence" of Yahweh[10] with individual men or with groups in the past, present, and future, without further specifying how Yahweh

---

[5] On *krt berith ʿim/ʾeth,* see E. Kutsch, *ZAW,* 79 (1967), 24f., n. 26.

[6] On this cf. M. Dahood, *Ugaritic-Hebrew Philology* (Rome, 1965), 32.

[7] Cf. further the Ugar. *ʿm* in *UT,* 2065, 14f., and M. Dahood, *Psalms,* II. *AB,* XVII (1968), 287; *idem, Bibl,* 50 (1969), 350.

[8] Further examples are mentioned in Preuss, 155, n. 60, to which 1 S. 14:7 should be added; this same note cites similar phrases in the ancient Near East.

[9] But cf. Cant. 4:8 and similar statements from the ancient Near East in Preuss, 165f.

[10] On Elohim, Yahweh Elohim, and El, see Preuss, 139, n. 1, where Job 29:5 with Shaddai should be added.

was with them. These statements appear in the form of a direct divine address as promise and pledge, [11] as promise, prayer, or wish of man, [12] and as a statement by man. [13]

The formula using 'eth and 'im in the theological sense is not used at all in Lamentations and Esther. In the OT Wisdom Literature it appears only in Job 29:5 ('im), and not at all in the Wisdom texts of the ancient Near East. It occurs only three times in the Psalms, and is not connected with specific places or institutions. Thus, it does not appear in predominantly cultic texts (Lev.; Ezk.; Ezk. 34:30 is an explanatory gloss), which means that there are difficulties with categorizing it as a cult formula. Rather, in the OT this formula occurs much more frequently in the narrative genres (three-fourths of the passages), in fact particularly in the patriarchal narratives of Genesis (although not in the Primitive History; this formula does not seem to have been known in the creation myths of the ancient Near East either), and in the books of Joshua, Samuel and Chronicles. However, this does not mean that in general it had the same nuance of meaning or occurred in analogous contexts.

It is worthy of note that thus far texts from the ancient Near East seem to offer only two (Egyptian) parallels which speak of the presence of a deity with a man (here the king). We may add to this two proper names, which possibly are based on the idea of the presence of a deity with a man, but Ithobaal should probably be translated differently. [14] Other Egyptian texts speak only of the presence of a deity with the dead, but they also often speak of the association of a god with other gods (!). [15] Even if additional examples are discovered, it is still remarkable that the formula of the presence of a deity with man is very rare in the ancient Near East, while it appears frequently in the OT, where it expresses a basic element in the Yahweh faith. Is it possible that the content of this formula expresses something typical (if not also equally "genuine"!) for the faith of Israel?

2. *In the Promises of God.* We encounter the formula using 'eth or 'im as a promise or pledge of the deity [16] in the following 30 passages:

Gen. 26:3a (J, 'im; v. 3a is clearly an old element in vv. 3-5); 26:4 (J, 'eth; the connection with the formula "Fear not!" also occurs in Dt. 20:1; 31:8; Isa. 41:10; 43:5; Jer. 1:8; 30:10f.; [46:28]; 42:11; 1 Ch. 28:20; 2 Ch. 20:17; 32:7f.; cf. Gen. 21:17; 46:3; 1 S. 4:20, in which the context does not always point to a cult oracle); Gen. 28:15 (J, 'im); 31:3 (J, 'im; cf. 32:10,13, J, 'im); Ex. 3:12 (E, 'eth; do vv. 14,16f. refer to the 'ehyeh, "I will be," of v. 12?); [17] Dt. 31:23

---

[11] See below, 2.
[12] See below, 3.
[13] See below, 4. Richter, 146-151, lists further differentiations which are of an interrogatory, grammatical, and syntactical nature; these are hardly applicable, however, to the passages in J.
[14] Cf. Preuss, 161-171; but cf. in addition G. Rinaldi, *BeO*, 10 (1968), 68; and H.-J. Zobel, *VT*, 21 (1971), 96.
[15] Also *ANET*, 126.
[16] For a more detailed treatment, cf. Preuss, 141-45.
[17] On Ex. 3f., Jgs. 6, and 1 S. 9f., cf. esp. Richter.

(J? a speech of Yahweh, since v. 23 was originally connected with v. 15; cf. further Josh. 1:5,9,17, *'im*); Josh. 1:9; 3:7 (*'im*); 7:12 (*'im*, here in connection with the Yahweh war); Jgs. 6:12 (*'im*, Gideon's further inquiry in v. 13 excludes the possibility that v. 12 should be understood as a greeting formula; cf. Lk. 1:28; otherwise Ruth 2:4; 2 Ch. 19:6);[18] Jgs. 6:16 (*'im;* promise before a battle); 1 K. 11:38 (*'im;* promise of the God of Israel [v. 31] to those who obey, from the mouth of the prophets, in which the reference back to David is important); Isa. 41:10 (*'im;* promise of salvation to the servant, Israel);[19] 43:2,5 (is v. 5a an addition?— *'eth* occurs twice here in oracles of salvation which state that the exiles who return to Palestine will have an escort on the way); Jer. 1:8 (cf. 1:19; 15:20, *'eth;* also Ex. 3:12; Jgs. 6:12; promise connected with the summons to go and send, connected with war terminology, v. 16; assurance of salvation as a promise that Yahweh will be with Israel); Jer. 30:11 (*'eth;* cf. 46:28; promise of salvation to Israel); 42:11 (*'eth;* promise of Yahweh through Jeremiah to the Jews who were about to leave Babylon); Mic. 6:8 (*'im;* Yahweh wants man to "walk with him" attentively!); Hag. 1:13 (cf. 2:4f., *'eth;* promise of help to the people in a time of distress); Zec. 10:5 (*'im;* promise of help for the battle in which Yahweh's flock is about to engage; cf. Ezk. 34:30, which is an addition; *'im*).

In these passages, no distinction can be made between *'eth* (12 times) and *'im* (18 times), either on the basis of content or of persons speaking or persons addressed. No temporal distinction is possible either (cf. Hag. with Zec.; Deutero-Isaiah has both prepositions; Jer. only *'eth;* J only *'im*, but in Gen. 26:24 *'eth;* E has both prepositions),[20] even if the use of *'im* is somewhat predominant. The formula using *'eth* and *'im* has no exclusive connection with cult places, but the oldest texts use it mainly as a promise that Yahweh will be with the people or an individual before and during journeys (but cf. Mic. 6:8; Isa. 43:2). What is meant here is that Israel is accompanied by God, who also fights for his own on their journey. The Yahweh war is one concretizing aspect of God's presence, and not the only *Sitz im Leben* of this formula.[21] By means of a transposition of motifs, this formula later becomes a general promise of divine help, and as such also enters into the prophetic oracle of salvation; but even after this transposition the concrete primitive situation of the road and of war is often apparent (Isa. 43:2,5; Jer. 1:19; 15:20; Zec. 10:5; Ch.). There is no promise that the deity will be with David (2 S. 7:3 is assertive, and the tense cannot be determined definitely), and thus *'im* is not fundamental to the concept of the Davidic covenant.[22] It should also be observed that the expression *hayah 'eth ('im)*, "to be with," calls to mind the divine name Yahweh or is even used to explain its meaning. In this connection, additional passages from the OT using *'eth* and *'im* can be cited which describe Yahweh as a God who leads, accompanies, goes with, and fights

---

[18] For a discussion of the translation and context of Jgs. 6:12, see Preuss, 142f., n. 11 and 11a.

[19] For a more detailed study of this passage, cf. Preuss, 143, n. 12.

[20] See below.

[21] However, cf. further H. W. Wolff.

[22] Cf. Preuss, 145, with the literature cited there, and Kilian, 57f.

for his own, as shepherd of his flock, etc. (Gen. 26:3; 31:3; Ex. 3:12; Nu. 14:43; Dt. 31:23; Josh. 1:5,17; 3:7; Jgs. 2:18; 6:16; 1 S. 17:37; 18:12; 1 K. 11:38; Zec. 10:5).

3. *As a Promise, Wish, etc. of Man.* The formula using *'eth* or *'im* occurs as a promise, pledge, wish, or question in the mouth of man in the following 33 passages:

Gen. 28:20 (E, *'im;* cf. v. 15: Yahweh!; again, what is really intended is protection on the road); 48:21 (*'im,* J? E?—again the reference is to a trip); Ex. 10:10 (*'im,* from the mouth of the Pharaoh, concerning a trip; cf. 2 Ch. 35:21, from the mouth of Necho); Ex. 18:19 (E, *'im;* a new situation in the wilderness wandering is connected with the wish that God would be with his people); 33:16 (*'im;* the literary source to which this verse belongs is disputed; Yahweh's presence with his people is fundamentally connected with his presence with Moses, cf. v. 13); Nu. 14:43 (J, *'im;* for the situation see v. 42!); Dt. 20:1 (*'im;* promise that Yahweh will be with his people who go forth to fight; cf. vv. 3f.; 31:6; similarly 20:1,4; 31:8 [*'im*], pledges that Yahweh will be with his people and promises that Yahweh will help his people in battle); Josh. 1:17 (*'im;* cf. 1:9; Yahweh will be with his people in the sense of accompanying them and helping them in battle); 14:12; [23] Jgs. 6:13 (*'im;* question pertaining to the divine promise in v. 12; cf. Gen. 28:20); Ruth 2:4 (greeting formula in a late text; cf. 2 Ch. 19:6; *'im*); 1 S. 17:37 (*hayah 'im* with Yahweh; a wish for help); 20:13; 2 S. 14:17 (both using *'im;* wishes that Yahweh would help and accompany David); 1 K. 1:37 (wish that Yahweh would be with Solomon, based on his having been with David!; *'im*); 8:57 (prayer of Solomon that Yahweh would be with his people, *'im, 'immanu,* with a reference to his having been with the fathers, which is typical in Deuteronomistic theology); Ps. 67:2(1) (*'eth,* the statement here does not completely correspond to the usual formula); 1 Ch. 9:20 (*'im;* a wish for a blessing; cf. 2 Ch. 19:11); 1 Ch. 22:11 (*'im;* wish or promise of David to Solomon, concerning building the temple; so also 22:16; 28:20); 2 Ch. 19:11 (*'im;* Yahweh's presence as a promise to the Levites when they do well: *'im hattobh!;* cf. 1 Ch. 9:20); 2 Ch. 20:17 (*'im;* promise through the Levites to the army of Jehoshaphat as well as to Judah and Jerusalem; recalls Ex. 14:13); cf. also 2 Ch. 25:7 (*'im*); 32:7f. (*'im, 'immanu*); 35:21 (deliberately uses Elohim instead of Yahweh, since it is in the mouth of Necho); 36:23 (*'im;* using the formula as a wish for blessing on those who return from captivity, from the mouth of Cyrus, cf. Ezr. 1:3).

These 33 passages regularly use *'im.* Only in Josh. 14:12 do we encounter a questionable *'othi;* Ps. 67:2(1) also has *'eth,* but the formula here is not quite like that found in the other passages in this group. Was *'im* more commonly used in the mouth of man (or at least, did it become standardized later?), while the distribution of *'eth* and *'im* was conservatively retained in the promises of the deity? Also, the presence of God usually means that he accompanies his people on a trip or that he helps them in battle in these passages, and these two concepts

---

[23] The MT has *'othi* here, but cf. *GK,* § 311.

can logically be connected with each other. Passages expressing the hope that God will be with his people in the future, just as he had been with the fathers or had performed his saving deeds (Dt. 20:1!) in the past, are important (Josh. 1:17; 14:12; Jgs. 6:13; 1 S. 20:13; 1 K. 1:37; 8:57; cf. 1 S. 3:19). We also encounter the general use of this formula expressing help in passages that connect it with the idea of protection in war or on a journey (Ex. 18:19f.; 2 S. 14:17; 1 S. 20:13; etc.).

4. *In the Affirmative Use.* In contrast to the 30 passages containing promises from the mouth of God that he would be with his people, and to the 33 passages containing promises or wishes from the mouth of man, there are 41 passages in the OT in which one man or several affirm that Yahweh (or God) was "with him, thee, me, them, you, us." These passages show that from the promises of God an assurance had developed in Israel as self-confidence that Yahweh would be "with" his people as he was with the individual godly person (Am. 5:14!). E.g., P uses the expression "to walk with God" (only in Gen. 5:24 and 6:9) to express the intimate communion between man and God (cf. Ps. 73:23; Mic. 6:8), but we do not find it in P after the story of the flood; now Abraham merely walks "before" God (Gen. 17:1, P). [24]

Actually, the first example of the affirmative use of the formula using *'eth* or *'im* is in Gen. 21:20 (*'eth,* E). God was with Ishmael in the wilderness: without any additional explanation, this formula could already have been mentioned casually as a part of familiar tradition, as a Bedouin motif. [25] 21:22 (*'im,* E) and 26:28 (*'im,* J) reflect similar situations: 21:22 is unique in that it states that God was with Abraham, whereas such a statement is common in the stories of Isaac and Jacob. Also, J does not speak of Yahweh being with Abraham. 31:5 (*'im,* E; cf. v. 3) states that the God of his father was with Jacob as he went on his way; cf. 35:3 (*'im,* E). In 39:2,3,21,23, the narrator expresses his opinion that Yahweh was with (*'eth,* J) Joseph, i.e., he protected and accompanied him, and for this reason he was successful. In Nu. 23:21, even Balaam has to admit that Yahweh was with (*'im,* E) Israel. A fundamental concept in Deuteronomy is that Yahweh alone was with his people during their wandering in the wilderness, and that he alone led them and protected them (Dt. 2:7; 32:12, *'im*). Yahweh was with Joshua at the conquest of Jericho (Josh. 6:27, *'eth*); he was also with Judah and the house of Joseph in their battles to conquer portions of the land of Canaan (Jgs. 1:19, *'eth,* J?; 1:22, *'im*). He was with the different judges of Israel, who fought for Israel against their enemies (Jgs. 2:18, *'im;* Deuteronomistic).

The books of Samuel state that Yahweh was with Samuel and thus fulfilled his promises (1 S. 3:19, *'im*). Saul was told how he would know that God was with him (10:7, *'im*). An Israelite's *"kalokagathía"* [26] (nobility of character) was

---

[24] Richter thinks the affirmative use is the original use of the formula with *'eth* or *'im* expressing help.

[25] So R. Kilian, *Die vorpriesterlichen Abrahamsüberlieferungen literarkritisch und traditionsgeschichtlich untersucht. BBB,* 24 (1966), 237; from the pre-Yahwistic original stratum (*Grundschicht*), so *idem,* 241-43, 247.

[26] Von Rad.

one indication that Yahweh was "with him," as can be seen in the case of David (16:18; 18:14, 'im; cf. 18:12,28, 'im; 2 S. 5:10; 1 Ch. 11:9; 2 S. 7:3,9; 1 Ch. 17:2, always 'im). Here the presence of Yahweh always means "under his help," and in connection with this also (!) "under his blessing," although this is not its primary meaning from a traditio-historical point in view. [27] Yahweh was also with Hezekiah in his conquests (2 K. 18:7, 'im). In the opinion of the Chronicler, he was also with Solomon (and thus Solomon became exceedingly great, 2 Ch. 1:1, 'im), Jehoshaphat (17:3, 'im, because he walked in the ways of his father [David? cf. BHK]), and Asa (15:9, when the Israelites see this, many desert to him, cf. Zec. 8:23). Elsewhere the Chronicler usually states that Yahweh was with a group of people, i.e., with Israel as a people (1 Ch. 22:18, 'im; 2 Ch. 13:12; 15:2 [twice with 'im as a key word]; this verse could also be understood as a prophetic promise). In his trials, Jeremiah is certain that Yahweh is with him as his champion (20:11; note the war figures), and the same is true of the worshipper in Ps. 23 (v. 4, 'im: in direct address to the "shepherd," Yahweh). However, Job (29:5) can look back only plaintively to the time when Yahweh was with him and he was surrounded with divine help and blessing (cf. also 27:13). According to Zec. 8:23, heathen join themselves to the Jews when and where they see that God is with the Jews, as Yahweh Sebaoth himself says. Only in Ps. 91:15 do we encounter an 'immo 'anokhi, "I will be with him," as a quotation from an oracle received by the worshipper. But since this encouragement could hardly be in the 3rd person, there are both textual and contextual questions about it. Finally, a group, viz., the community of the city of God, says that Yahweh Sebaoth is "with us" ('immanu, Ps. 46:8,12[7,11]; also in v. 4[3]?), which is an expression of certainty. Isa. 8:10 as well (also 8:8?) is illuminated from this background. [28]

In these passages where the affirmative use of the formula with 'eth and 'im occurs, it is clear that 'im (34 times) is found much more frequently than 'eth (7 times), and thus the tendency to use 'im exclusively is especially evident (Chronicles uses only 'im). The affirmative use of this formula also betrays a connection with journeys, nomadic life, accompaniment by the deity, and battles fought with his help (Gen. 21:20; 26:28; 31:5; 35:3; Nu. 23:21; Dt. 2:7; 32:12; Josh. 6:27; Jgs. 1:19; 2:18; 2 S. 7:9; 2 K. 18:7; 1 Ch. 22:18; 2 Ch. 13:12; Ps. 23:4; 46:8,12[7,11]; and even Zec. 8:23). This formula is used to express the general help of Yahweh in the Joseph story, the Davidic narratives, and in certain texts in Chronicles.

The promises of God connect the assurance of God's presence to a group only ten times ('eth: Isa. 43:2,5; Jer. 30:11; 42:11; 46:28; Hag. 1:13f.; 2:4; 'im: Josh. 7:12; Isa. 41:10; Zec. 10:5). Human wishes and promises with the assurance of God's presence have a group in mind in 13 passages ('eth: Josh. 14:12; Ps. 67:2 [1]–the text of these two verses is uncertain; 'im: Ex. 10:10; Nu. 14:43; Dt. 20:1, 3f.; 31:6; 1 K. 8:57; 2 Ch. 19:11; 20:17; 25:7; 32:8; 36:23). This survey shows

---

[27] Cf. Preuss, 149, n. 11a; 154, n. 56; on "presence" as "blessing," cf. G. Wehmeier, *Der Segen im AT* (1970), 136, 170, 203f.

[28] See below, III.

that 'im is placed in the mouth of man more often than it is in the mouth of Yahweh. This is emphasized by the 12 examples of the affirmative use which reflect the self-confidence that "Yahweh is with us" (Nu. 23:21; Dt. 2:7; 32:12; Jgs. 1:19,22; 1 Ch. 22:18; Ps. 46:8,12[7,11]; Isa. 8:8,10; Zec. 8:23), where only Jgs. 1:19,22 (J?) has 'eth, while all the other passages have 'im.

5. *Content, History, and Place of the Formula Using 'eth and 'im in the Faith of Israel*. The patriarchal stories of Isaac and Jacob are the first main area in which the formula using 'eth and 'im occurs, with 14 examples out of the total of 104. In these family histories, the presence of God promised to individuals or said to pertain to them is stated as a formula of the accompaniment of the deity on journeys; and here the original concreteness of the formula is clearly an element of nomadic thought and faith. The word of promise that the deity would lead the group was an essential element of this faith. [29] It has been conjectured that this faith in divine guidance was particularly at home in the Isaac tribe. [30] This hypothesis could be supported by the fact that this formula is absent in the stories of Abraham, but is a major aspect of the stories of Isaac, from which came the references to Isaac in Amos (7:9,16) with their possible nomadic background, and his apostrophic allusion to the "presence" of God in 5:14. [31] Gen. 46:1-5a (v. 4a! cf. 26:3) has also been connected with Isaac. [32] Even when later texts address the whole people, frequently we find "Jacob" in them. Since this formula also occurs with analogous concrete content in the stories of Moses and of the Conquest with their sagas of groups and heroes, there seems to be a fundamental nomadic structure of Israelite faith and thought in it: the God who escorts and leads accompanies his own with his protection and help, and also fights for them (Ex. 14:14,25; 15:21; 32:1,4; Dt. 20:1; Josh. 1:17; 6:27; 7:12; 14:12; Jgs. 1:19; 2:18; 6:12,16; etc., even into Ch.). Yahweh's presence is not a static presence, but a dynamic power of God, who rescued his people from Egypt and then went with them, began his way with them, and led them (cf. many texts in Ex.; also Am. 9:7; etc.). Therefore, no one need be afraid. Accordingly, Yahweh's presence is not primarily the gift of the spirit, nor is it only a gift to a man with a special mission, but in the genres found in the oldest texts of the OT it is a concrete promise that Yahweh will be with his own.

In texts from the period of the Davidic monarchy, like the Joseph story and the narratives concerning David himself, a general formula of divine help appears through a transposition of motifs from the concrete promise that Yahweh will be with his own. As such, this formula then penetrates into the prophetic

---

[29] On this subject, cf. the works of V. Maag mentioned by Preuss, 154, n. 55; and also *idem*, "Das Gottesverständnis des AT," *NedThT*, 21 (1967), 161-207, in which pp. 170-79 deal with the nomadic god who accompanied the group; cf. also G. Fohrer, *History of the Israelite Religion* (trans. 1972), 40.

[30] A. Jepsen, "Zur Überlieferungsgeschichte der Vätergestalten," *WZ* Leipzig, 3 (1953/54), 265-281, on this point pp. 274f.; cf. M. Noth, *A History of Pentateuchal Traditions* (trans. 1971), 102ff., 114f.

[31] For another interpretation of this passage, cf. F. Hecht, *Eschatologie und Ritus bei den 'Reformpropheten'* (1971), 158.

[32] A. Weiser, *RGG*3, III, 902, among others.

oracle of salvation, but even here its original concreteness is still preserved or reflected. The Israel that now was to receive rest does not cast off its nomadic thought and faith categories, but remolds them. Various words pertaining to "journey" and "way" are part of the affirmative categories of Israel's history. Texts that speak of general divine guidance represent a change from expressing Yahweh's leadership in specific terms of a journey or the way from A to B (cf. the Joseph Novella and the Succession Narrative). Thus 'im is not a word that is peculiar to the Davidic Covenant, but has already become stereotyped when it is used in this covenant. [33]

Sometimes, when the formula using 'eth or 'im appears in the postexilic period in Chronicles, the presence of Yahweh with his people is connected with the Yahweh war, as it was in the early period. The OT also states that those who return from the exile will travel with the promise that Yahweh will be with them again in their exodus from Babylon. But here also, of course, we encounter the formula using 'eth or 'im in expressions that had already become stereotyped earlier, so that Yahweh is said to be "with" him who walks in his way. Finally, this formula becomes an element in a greeting (2 Ch. 19:6; Ruth 2:4), but it constantly remains connected with history, and does not become a cultic formula in the postexilic period.

Accordingly, the concept of "the presence of Yahweh with his own," which comes from a typically nomadic background, also exhibits the personal character of the Yahweh faith, in which Yahweh was believed to be a God who accompanied, led, protected, and fought for his people. The statement "Yahweh in our midst" is well adapted to this concept of faith (cf. Gen. 46:4; Ex. 3:8,17; 13:17,21; 14:19; 23:20ff.; 33:2f.,5,15f.; 34:5,9f.; Lev. 26:13; Nu. 14:42; Dt. 1:30, 42; 4:37; 20:1,4; 26:8; 31:6,8; 32:12; Jgs. 4:14; 5:13; Isa. 58:11; 63:12f.; Mic. 3:11; Ps. 24:7ff.; 106:9). From the concrete idea of the way and of the journey, in which the traveller was accompanied by Yahweh, came the concept of history as a journey with him, as guidance history; from the promise that Yahweh would accompany his people, a formula of help; and from the nomadic journey, the earthly pilgrimage. This proved to be a good preparation for the references to the presence of God with his people, which frequently were expanded from the viewpoint of salvation history. [34] Various words pertaining to the way, such as "to go," "to guide," "to lead," "to follow," "shepherd and sheep," etc., remain constant in the OT (cf. Am. 9:7; Jer. 2:2,5; etc.), and they are also important in the Qumran literature and the NT. The belief in the presence of God with his people (from Ex. 3 on) is a fundamental component of the concept of salvation history, and in turn eschatology is a function of this belief in God and of historical events. Yahweh's existence, like his name, is frequently manifested by his active presence, i.e., by his works. [35] This sort of OT faith was still active in the

[33] Cf. above under II.3 on 2 S. 7:3, and also Preuss, 156, n. 65.

[34] Cf. under II.3 and 4. On history as a journey with Yahweh, cf. H. D. Preuss, Jahweglaube und Zukunftserwartung (1968), 71ff.; and ZAW, 80, 157f., 171-73 with literature; further F. L. Hossfeld, Studien zur Theologie des Weges im AT (diss., Trier, 1967).

[35] Examples in Preuss, 159.

intertestamental period (cf., e.g., Jth. 5:17; 3 Macc. 6:15). In the Qumran literature, the formula using "with" was used to express the relationship between
angels and men, heaven and earth, and thus was important for the self-understanding of the Qumran community (1QM 12:7f.; 19:1); [36] and the same is true
of the ancient formula "God with us." And in the NT, [37] besides Mt. 1:23; Mk.
3:14; Lk. 1:28; 2:25; 23:43; 24:44; Jn. 3:2; 17:24; Acts 18:10; and Rev. 3:4, [38]
Mt. 28:20 is especially important. [39] Under the influence of the NT, the OT
formula continues to be used even today in the Christian faith as a promise that
God will accompany and help those whom he has exalted, and as a liturgical
greeting, "The Lord be with you!"

III. 'Immānu 'ēl. In section II.4 above, the passages that speak of God's
presence with a group were listed, and it was pointed out that the self-confident
expression "Yahweh is with us" as an affirmative statement or a human wish
occurs more frequently than the promise of God that he would be with his
people. Consequently, the faith in a "God with us" was typical for and in Israel,
as is confirmed also by specific examples of this statement (Isa. 7:14; 8:8,10; Ps.
46:8,12[7,11]; cf. Ps. 23:4), and underscored by prophetic polemic (Am. 5:14).
Perhaps then we are to interpret the prophetic criticism of the patriarchal traditions as referring to the popular belief (cf. Mt. 3:9!) that "God is indeed with us,
as he was with our fathers, whose children we are!" (Hos. 12:3ff.; Jer. 9:14;
Isa. 43:27; also 7:14; 8:8,10?). Yahweh as the shepherd of his flock, who abides
and walks in the midst of his people, also belongs to this sphere of motifs, where
assurance and confidence are expressed in the God who shapes history (Gen.
48:15; 49:24; Hos. 4:16; Ps. 23:4; 68:10f.[9f.]; 74:2[1]; 77:21[20]; 78:52,55,
70-72; 79:13; 80:2[1]; 95:7; 100:3; Isa. 40:11; 63:11-14; Zec. 11:16; Neh.
9:21). [40]

All this background must be taken into consideration when attempting to
determine the meaning of 'immanu 'el. This expression encompasses the entire
content of the Israelite certainty that "God is with us," which is a fundamental aspect of the Yahweh faith that Yahweh is with his people. A number of
faulty interpretations of this term could be avoided if critics would keep this
background in mind. Thus, "Yahweh Sebaoth is with us" (Ps. 46:8,12[7,11];
also at the end of v. 4[3] with *BHK* and several commentators), which is a refrain
in the ancient confident Song of Zion sung by the people in the cult (v. 11[10]!),
and an affirmation of assurance uttered by those who lived in the city of God,
is a guarantee of divine protection in the present and in the future whenever the
floods of chaos or the torrents of the nations have broken in against God's people
(cf. Isa. 8:7f. and the figures used there!). Yahweh was given the more specific
name "Yahweh Sebaoth" (→ צבאות *tsᵉbhā'ôth*), because the context demanded

---

[36] On this, cf. P. von der Osten-Sacken, *Gott und Belial* (1969), 223-26.
[37] Cf. Preuss, 173; W. Grundmann, *TDNT*, VII, 766ff.
[38] On Paul, see above, II.1.
[39] On this, cf. W. Trilling, *Das wahre Israel* (1964), 40f., 43, 50.
[40] Cf. also the examples of "Yahweh in our midst" listed under II.5, above.

with him can and should faithfully trust in Yahweh, as this is congruous with God's promise to David (2 S. 7:16; cf. Isa. 7:2,13: "house of David"!) and as there is great potential in this promise. Vv. 10ff. demand a similar situation, at least as far as content and context is concerned. As a matter of fact, vv. 10-17 are probably the direct continuation of vv. 1-9, only now, after Isaiah has carried out his commission, he and Ahaz have begun a discussion of the prophet's message. Isaiah offers Ahaz a sign, which is intended to support the earlier promise (v. 10 is connected to v. 11 by "Yahweh"; on "your God," cf. 2 S. 7:14: "son"), which Ahaz had declined because he was not willing to abandon his military-political decision. When this happens, Isaiah clearly veers away from the traditionally renewed Davidic promise and from the idea that Yahweh will help his city Jerusalem, by using the expression "my God" (v. 13). He does this because Ahaz is not willing to trust, but disregards God and his promises. This is followed by the word of threat to Ahaz (v. 15), in which Isaiah now announces a sign, although and because Ahaz had refused a sign. V. 14 tells the sign, and vv. 15-17 its results. V. 14b should be translated as follows: "Behold, the young woman is pregnant, (and) will bear a son, and they will call his name 'Immanuel.'"

In order to exegete v. 14, we begin with the following points which are considered to be established from the context of Isa. 7 and especially from the things that have been presented in Section II.

(1) V. 14 is a word of judgment against Ahaz, who has refused the sign. He was spoken of as a representative of the house of David (vv. 2,9,11,13; cf. 2 S. 7:9,14,16; also cf. 2 K. 16:7 with 2 S. 7:14), but he was a failure (cf. also the 'im in the History of David [but not there alone!] for the Immanuel in Isa. 7:14). Now God himself will give Ahaz a sign, which must consist of the birth of a child and his peculiar name.

(2) Consequently, this sign cannot be merely something in the distant future having no present reference to Ahaz. Perhaps it can be futuristic, but it must have already begun. Thus the sign is already underway (the 'almah is already pregnant), but it is yet to be completed (birth and naming of the child; cf. Gen. 16:11; Jgs. 13:3-5). The child's birth will bring judgment upon Ahaz, which probably means that this child will be a threat to Ahaz during his lifetime in that he will be a rival to his successor on the throne;[50] the child will come from the Davidic dynasty, but will not be the son of the queen. Also it is impossible to apply this to "women in general" because only *one* child is involved, and then vv. 14 and 16 could not be harmonized. There will be calamity from the time the child is born until he reaches a certain age (3 years?). But shortly before his accession to the throne,[51] deliverance will come (v. 16).

(3) 'almah is used with the article in Isa. 7:14, which suggests one "who is known to thee" ("whom you know already!"), exclusive of the queen. This must refer to a young woman whom Ahaz knew, who was expecting her first (!) child (by him). A prince will be a threat to Ahaz as his successor. This prince cannot

---

[50] Cf. the Egyptian legends of the Westcar Papyrus, E. Brunner-Traut, *Altägyptische Märchen* (²1965), 11ff.
[51] See below.

be Hezekiah for chronological reasons (2 K. 18:1f.; 2 Ch. 29:1). Chronological difficulties also make it impossible for one to defend the view that this passage has in mind a "mystery" or a remote Messianic future.[52] Furthermore, the phrase "(the) 'almah is pregnant" seems to have been a stereotyped formula for the announcement of the birth of a royal child;[53] it may be compared with the markedly veiled language of Mic. 5:2(3). In light of this, it seems natural to suppose that the 'almah in Isa. 7:14 is a concubine of the royal palace whose pregnancy was well known to Ahaz. Isa. 11:1 also seems to be thinking of an analogous situation. The birth of a son to the queen, or Isaiah's designation of a girl who was standing near by chance, could hardly have been used as the kind of sign required by the context of Isa. 7. It is also impossible to think that the 'almah was Isaiah's wife, because her sons are clearly designated as sons of Isaiah (8:3f.), she could not have been called 'almah, and Isaiah is not the one who gives this child his name.

(4) However, the theological idea of the "presence" of God with his people contained in the name 'immanu'el, "God (is) with us," excludes a unilateral interpretation of v. 14 as a threat, a brief prayer, or a fearful cry ("God help us!"), because faith in the presence of Yahweh involves the assurance that he will accompany and protect his people, and thus the assurance that he will save them. Therefore, neither the terminus technicus nor the context can indicate that "God with us" is exclusively a threat, or that Immanuel is exclusively a cry of distress.[54] On the contrary, v. 14 and the name "Immanuel" are to be understood in a polar sense: on the one hand, this verse is a threat and judgment against Ahaz (as the representative of the Davidic dynasty), who had refused to put his trust in Yahweh and was no longer considered to be standing in the Davidic covenant (cf. also v. 17); on the other hand, it is a promise to a group of people which is not defined more specifically than "us" (cf. Isa. 9:5f.[6f.]; and the figure in 11:1). Judgment and salvation are connected only by God himself, as the one who causes both. The sign again forces each reader and hearer (as Ahaz in Isaiah's day) to decide whether he wishes to belong to the "us," whose saving king in the End Time will be the "Immanuel." In this "us" of 'immanu ("with us"), Ps. 46:8,12(7,11) (cf. Isa. 8:10) again comes into view, where "us" refers to the believing inhabitants of the city of God. This understanding of "us" as a group of people from the city of God as an abiding saved "remnant" is also possible (Isa. 9:5[6]) and demonstrable (8:10; 17:12-14; cf. also 1:8f.; 8:16-18; 14:32; 28:16f.; 30:17[4:3 and 37:32 are late]) for Isaiah, where this remnant is also understood as people set apart by faith (7:3,9; 8:16-18; 28:16; 30:15). In the preaching of Isaiah, the idea of the remnant was intended to apply primarily, of

52 On 'almah, see the survey of M. Rehm, "Das Wort 'almāh in Jes 7,14," BZ, N.F. 8 (1964), 89-101; and idem, Der königliche Messias, 49-63.
53 Cf. H. Ringgren, ZAW, 64 (1952), 131, with reference to CTA, 24 [NK], 7 and an Egyptian text concerning the birth of Hatshepsut.
54 So Th. Lescow, ZAW, 79 (1967), 179; cf. the admission of this discrepancy in Kilian, 104, who otherwise argues that Isaiah uses this expression as a threat of calamity here, pp. 105ff., but then attempts to resolve the difficulties by distinguishing between the word of Yahweh and prophetic reflection, and with the help of secrecy and intuition (considering v. 14 as the word of Yahweh, over against vv. 13,16f.,15? as Isaiah's own reflections).

course, to the period of the Syro-Ephraimitic war (7:3!); but this fits the historical situation of chaps. 7f., and 9:5f.(6f.) is particularly significant for this "us," to whom the future is given.[55] Isaiah also expects a new Davidide and a renewed kingdom for the remnant community as a nucleus of the genuine people of God (cf. 9:1,5f.[2,6f.]; 11:1). In Isaiah, the concept of the remnant and the hope in the renewed house of David are also connected historically during a certain era of his prophecy.[56]

(5) The polar character of the sign to Ahaz, which must be interpreted both as a threat to the king and as a promise of salvation through the "presence" of God with his people, cannot be refuted by the argument that the introductory *lakhen* in v. 14 can stand only before threats (it introduces hope oracles in Ex. 6:6; Nu. 25:12; in prophetic texts such as 2 K. 19:32 par.; 22:20; Isa. 51:21; 53:12; 61:7; Jer. 15:19; 16:14; cf. 23:7; 32:36; Ezk. 11:17; 12:28; 36:7f.,22; 37:12; 39:25; Hos. 2:16[14]; Mic. 5:2[3]!; and in Isa. 10:24 [secondary]; 29:22 [genuine?]; 28:16). Isa. 7:16 also has a promissory character;[57] the possible ambiguity of "milk and honey" (v. 15? or is this rather a gloss?; cf. v. 22, where line a also seems to be an insertion) could support the polar character of this passage.[58]

Thus the child of Isa. 7 brings and means judgment for Ahaz, but the saving presence of God for those who believe.

Preuss

---

[55] H. W. Wolff, *Frieden ohne Ende* (1962), 70, 72.

[56] Cf. S. Herrmann, *Die prophetischen Heilserwartungen im AT* (1965), 139f., who refers to elements of the Davidic royal ritual in 1 K. 3:5ff. in interpreting Isa. 7:15f.; his view has been criticized recently by U. Stegemann, "Der Restgedanke bei Isaias," *BZ*, N.F. 13 (1969), 161-186; on Isa. 7, 184f.

[57] Contra, e.g., Kilian, who considers v. 16c to be an addition.

[58] Cf. further H. W. Wolff, *Frieden ohne Ende*, 44f.; Rehm, 66-73; Kilian, 37-43.

בְּאֵר *be'ēr;* בּוֹר *bôr*

Contents: I. Meaning and Etymology. II. 1. Use and Technology; 2. a. In Place Names; b. In Personal Names. III. Figurative and Religious Meanings.

I. **Meaning and Etymology.** In contrast to a spring (→ עַיִן *'ayin*), in which underground water comes forth in a natural way, the well (*be'er*) is an artificial device in which underground water is obtained by technological means (cf. Gen. 26:19, "a well of living water"). The Ugar. *bỉr*, Aram. *byr'* or *b'r'*, Syr. *bīrā*

---

be'ēr. C. Braunlich, "The Well in Ancient Arabia," *Islamica*, I (1924/25), 41-76, 288-343, 454-528; B. Buffet-R. Evrard, *L'eau potable à travers les âges* (Liége, 1950); G. Dalman, *AuS*, VI, 273-76; T. J. Jones, *Quelle, Brunnen und Zisterne im AT* (1928); R. Patai, "The 'Control of Rain' in Ancient Palestine," *HUCA*, 14 (1939), 251-286; B. Rein, *Der Brunnen im Volksleben* (1912); Ph. Reymond, "L'eau, sa vie et sa signification dans l'AT," *SVT*, 6 (1958), 245-255, with literature.

or *bērā*, and Arab. *bīr* (cf. *ba'ara*, "to dig a well")[1] have the same meaning.

The word *bor*, "cistern,"[2] probably belongs to the same root as *be'er*, and represents a variant in vocalization (cf. Akk. *būru, būrtu,* with the same meaning).

II. 1. *Use and Technology.* The digging and operation of a well presuppose several technological and socio-economic conditions: procuring tools to dig out or to break through (*karah, chatsebh, chaphar,* cf. Jer. 2:13)[3] the soil and rocks, and material to help support the walls of the well. Often a well is the beginning of a human settlement; the digging of the well requires general solidarity, especially in the wilderness. The best illustration of this is the ancient work song in Nu. 21:17f., which has been preserved in connection with a Transjordanian stronghold called Beer (v. 16),[4] and in which the initiative for this important project is said to belong to the leaders of the people. This song by no means excludes echoes of an exorcism directed to the spirit of the spring.[5] This may be compared to the expression common among the Transjordanian Arabs: "The sheik dug this well."[6]

2. a. *In Place Names.* The frequency of geographical names associated with wells or cisterns may easily be explained by the role these played as gathering points and places people must pass by of necessity (cf. Gen. 29). The Hebrew word for "well" (*be'er*) appears in the following place names: Beer, "the well" (Nu. 21:16; Jgs. 9:21); and Beeroth, "the wells" (Josh. 9:17; 18:25; 2 S. 4:2; Ezr. 2:25; Neh. 7:29; gentilic in 2 S. 4:2ff.; 1 Ch. 11:39), which is usually identified with the modern el-Bireh, about 7 kilometers northeast of Gibeon, although the modern name is more closely connected with the Aram. *birah,* "stronghold."[7] A well can be named after the vegetation surrounding it, e.g., Beer-elim, "well of the terebinths" (Isa. 15:8), after ancient battles fought near it, as Beer-esek or Beer-sitnah, "well of the conflict" (Gen. 26:20-22), or ironically Beer-rehoboth, "well of the width." The vital role of wells, especially in a wilderness area, is emphasized by these names. Watering places are reserved exclusively for the clan or tribe (cf. Gen. 21:25; Dt. 10:6, "the well of the sons of Jaakan").

Josh. 15 describes the boundaries between the tribal territories, which sometimes are determined by a watercourse, a spring, or a well (esp. vv. 7,9; cf. the

---

[1] *KBL*[3], 102.

[2] Cf. *br* in the Mesha Inscription, *KAI,* 181.24; 2 S. 23:15,16,20 written בֹּאר *bō'r;* see below, III.

[3] Jones, 8ff.; Reymond, 131-152.

[4] See Eissfeldt, *The OT* (trans. 1965), 88.

[5] Cf. A. Lods, *Histoire de la littérature hébraïque* (1950), 41-43, who gives a complete analysis of the passage.

[6] On technological questions, types of wells and cisterns, etc., see Jones, 4-37; Dalman, *AuS,* VI, 273-76; VII, 47, 89; Reymond, 131ff. Cf. also L. Köhler, "Ein hebr.-arab. Brunnen-Terminus," *ZDPV,* 60 (1937), 135-39, on *'ābhēl,* "covered well," from which a place name has probably been derived, cf. Gen. 29:2.

[7] On this problem, cf. *BRL,* 193-97; M. Weippert, *The Settlement of the Israelite Tribes in Palestine. SBT,* 21 (trans. 1971), 14, n. 30; J. A. Soggin, *Joshua. OTL* (trans. 1972), 115.

picture on a relief of Seti I, where a *mighdol*, "tower," protects a well in the Negeb wilderness). [8]

In Gen. 16:7-14, the angel of Yahweh appears to Hagar at a spring (v. 7, *ʿayin*); v. 14 has an etiological function: Beer-lahai-roi, i.e., "the well (consecrated to) the Living One who sees me." Although the original meaning of this name is still debated (it is also possible to assume a personal name here, i.e., Lehi), [9] undoubtedly we must follow Gunkel in assuming that it preserves the tradition of a divine manifestation (v. 13, *ʾel roʾi*) which was connected with a well and with the time when it was transferred to the God of Israel, not without polemical innuendos directed against the spirits of nature. [10]

In Gen. 21:25-33 (and in the variant readings in 26:33), Beer-sheba, "well of seven" or "well of oath," [11] is a gathering place for nomadic shepherds, the location of a sanctuary associated with the memory of Abraham and Isaac. The dwelling places of their offspring are located around the wells of Beer-sheba and Gerar. Here people come together on certain days to celebrate festivals, which were kept until the time Jerusalem became the only legitimate sanctuary (Am. 5:5; 8:14). Beer-sheba marked the southernmost boundary of the land, and played the same role in the south that Dan did in the north (Josh. 15:28; 19:2; Jgs. 20:1; 1 S. 3:20; 2 S. 24:15; etc.). [12]

b. *In Personal Names.* Personal names containing the root *bʾr* are found at Ugarit, [13] El-Amarna, and Elephantine. In the OT, Beeri, the father-in-law of Esau, is a Hittite; this name is probably not of Semitic origin. [14] Hosea is called ben Beeri, "the son of Beeri"; the term is less toponymic (Ephraimitic) than metaphorical ("my well"), and expresses the delight of the parents in their child. [15]

III. **Figurative and Religious Meanings.** In the earlier period, the fundamental religious significance of *beʾer* is connected with the wells mentioned above, to which religious notions (Gen. 16:7-14) or cultic customs (21:25-33) were attached. Later a number of figurative and/or religious nuances were connected with wells and cisterns. Besides the general symbolism of water, [16] we may note the following.

Negatively, *bor* (probably because of its use as a dungeon, Ex. 12:29; [17] Jer.

---

[8] See Y. Yadin, *The Art of Warfare in Biblical Lands*, I (1963), 97.

[9] So J. Naveh, *BASOR*, 183 (1966), 27f., n. 9.

[10] H. Gunkel, *Genesis*[2], 164-66; P. Jaussen, "Le puits d'Agar," *RB*, N.S. 3 (1906), 595ff.; O. Kaiser, *BZAW*, 78 (1959), 93-95; cf. Fr. Praetorius, *ZDMG*, 61 (1907), 754f.; T. Canaan, "Haunted Springs and Water Demons in Palestine," *JPOS*, 1 (1920), 153-170; T. Fahd, "Le panthéon de l'Arabie centrale à la veille de l'Hégire," *BAH*, 88 (1968), 78-84.

[11] Cf. *KBL*[3], 102.

[12] For the topography, name, and history of Beer-sheba, see H. Haag, "Erwägungen über Beer-Seba," *Sacra Pagina*, I (*Beihefte ETL*, 12-13 [1959]), 335-345.

[13] Gröndahl, *PNU*, 114.

[14] W. Belardi, "Sui nomi ari nell'Asia anteriore antica," *Miscellanea G. Galbiati*, 3 = *Fontes Ambrosiani*, 27 (1951), 63.

[15] Noth, *IPN*, 224.

[16] Reymond, 107-116, 159-162.

[17] Cf. Ch. Clermont-Ganneau, "La citerne de Joseph," *Recueil d'archéologie orientale*, I (1888), 332f.

37:16) denotes the entrance into → שְׁאוֹל *sheʾôl*, "Sheol" (Isa. 14:15; Ezk. 32:23). Therefore, "the dead" are called *yoredhe bhor,* "those who go down to the pit" (Isa. 38:18; Ezk. 26:20; Ps. 28:1; etc.); *beʾer* has a similar meaning in Ps. 69:16 (Eng. v. 15); 55:24(23); cf. Rev. 9:1ff.

In the sexual realm, *beʾer* is used as a figure for a woman giving birth to a child (Lev. 20:18; Isa. 51:1–mother earth?), or a sweetheart and wife (Cant. 4:15; Prov. 5:15; Eccl. 12:6).

Further, the well is a symbol of wisdom as a place of deepening thoughts (cf. Dt. 1:5), and as a source of blessing through the discovery of "water" (Prov. 16:22; Sir. 1:5; Bar. 3:12). On the other hand, a cistern appears occasionally as an expression for disappointment and destruction (Jer. 2:13; [18] cf. Nah. 2:9 [8]), and, even when it performs its function, for the wickedness of Jerusalem (Jer. 6:7).

The religious significance of *beʾer,* which had already been established by the ancient topographical traditions, [19] is also expressed in texts like Isa. 51:1, where Yahweh, as "the well of Judah," [20] is protector and giver of life and of security. In his omnipotence, he cleft open wells in the wilderness (Ps. 74:15) and hewed out cisterns in the promised land (Dt. 6:11). The God of Israel is the one who gives the "living water" (→ מַיִם *mayim,* Jn. 4:14; Rev. 21:6). Using this metaphor, Jeremiah reproves his people because they have forsaken the fountain of living water, and hewed out broken cisterns that can hold no water (Jer. 2:13). Idols are as useless as broken cisterns compared with a good fountain which gives fresh water.

Heintz

---

[18] See below.
[19] See above, II.2.a.
[20] Cf. Reymond, 160f.

> בָּבֶל *bābhel*

Contents: I. The Name. II. The Tower. III. Babylon in the Prophets.

I. The Name. The name *bābhel,* "Babylon," which corresponds to the Akk. *Bābili/u,* is explained in Gen. 11:9 by popular etymology as related to the verb *balal,* "to mix," "to confuse," and is connected with the confusion of tongues. [1] The Babylonians understood it as *Bāb-ili,* "gate of God" (Sum. *ka-dingir-ra*), but this seems to be a learned interpretation. This name, whose original form

---

bābhel. W. Andrae, "Der babylonische Turm," *MDOG,* 71 (1932), 1-11; S. Erlandsson, *The Burden of Babylon* (Lund, 1970); M.-L. Henry, *Glaubenskrise und Glaubensbewährung in den Dichtungen der Jesaja-apokalypse. BWANT,* 5/6 (1967); J. Lindblom, *Die Jesaja-Apokalypse. LUA,* 34/3 (Lund, 1938); A. Parrot, *La tour de Babel* (Paris, 1954); W. von Soden, "Etemenanki und die Erzählung vom Turmbau zu Babel," *UF,* 3 (1971), 253-263; E. Unger, *Babylon, die heilige Stadt* (1931); L. H. Vincent, "De la tour de Babel au temple," *RB,* 53 (1946), 403-440.

[1] See below.

was probably *Babilla,* is neither Sumerian nor Akkadian, and its original meaning is unknown.

II. The Tower. The story of the tower of Babel, Gen. 11:1-9 (J), is a narrative with a twofold etiological thrust. On the one hand it interprets the name *babhel,* "Babylon," [2] and on the other hand it gives an explanation for the many languages in the world. The metropolis of Babylon with its diversified population naturally was particularly suited for this latter motif. Moreover, the idea that prehistoric man had a common language is found in the Sumerian literature (according to the Enmerkar Epic 141-46, the different lands, heaven, and earth praised Enlil "with one [→ אֶחָד *'echādh*] tongue"). The temple tower of E-sag-ila, the temple of Marduk, probably stands behind the idea of the tower in Gen. 11. EnEl VI, 60-62, says concerning the tower of E-sag-ila: "It took a whole year to lay its bricks; when the second year came near, they (the gods) raised up the head of Esagila to the Apsu" (*meḥret apsî ullû rēšašu*), which clearly contains a wordplay on *E-sag-ila,* "the house with elevated head." Apsu here is heaven as the cosmic region of fresh water. The biblical narrative probably also alludes to this when it says: "Let us build ourselves a city, and a tower with its top (head, *ro'sh*) in the heavens." [3]

Theologically, the building of the tower in Gen. 11 is interpreted as an act of human arrogance and rebellion against God; accordingly, Yahweh intervenes against its builders and scatters them over the whole earth. This action of God is both punishment and a preventive measure; it prevents men from going too far in their pride. The common history of all mankind has found its end. The usual positive element of the punishment of prehistoric man is missing here; instead of this, the story of the chosen people of God begins in Gen. 12 with the call of Abraham. [4]

III. Babylon in the Prophets. Babylon is mentioned several times in the rest of the OT, sometimes in purely historical contexts (2 K. 17:24,30, and frequently from chap. 20 on), and sometimes in the prophets in theological contexts.

The earliest passage in the prophets that refers to Babylon seems to be Mic. 4:10, where Zion is threatened: "Now you shall go forth from the city and dwell in the open country; you shall go to Babylon...." This text announces the exile to Babylon. The only question is whether Babylon could have been thought of as an enemy in the time of Micah. Either this verse is a later addition or the name "Babylon" was inserted at a later time to correspond to the later course of history. [5] The conclusion of this verse, "there you shall be rescued," is also questionable. Weiser sees here an inner connection between distress and deliverance, but scholars usually delete these words as a later addition.

Several times, Jeremiah predicts that Judah will be carried away to Babylon, and he does this quite calmly and without any particular overtones, as e.g., in

[2] See above.
[3] Cf. E. A. Speiser, *Or,* 25 (1956), 317-323; however, von Soden identifies the tower with Etemenanki.
[4] Cf. G. von Rad, *Genesis. OTL* (trans. 1961), 148ff.
[5] Weiser, *ATD,* XXIV, 269.

Jer. 20:4, "I will give all Judah into the hand of the king of Babylon; he shall carry them captive to Babylon, and shall slay them with the sword" (cf. vv. 5f.). In chap. 27 he attacks the false prophets who predict the return of the vessels of the temple which had been carried off to Babylon, and in chap. 29 he attacks the prophet Hananiah who had expressed similar hopes. Chap. 29 contains the letter of the prophet to the Jewish captives in Babylon, in which he admonishes them to settle down for a seventy-year stay in this foreign land. Finally, according to 51:59-64, he is said to have compiled his oracles against Babylon in a book, and to have sent it to Babylon, where it was sunk in the Euphrates as a symbolic act.

Occasionally Ezekiel also speaks of Babylon. Oholibah (Jerusalem) had practiced unchastity with the handsome sons of Babylon (23:15,17); now, they will attack her and treat her shamefully (23:23f.). He states quite prosaically that the king of Judah will be carried to Babylon (12:13; 17:12).

The statements in Deutero-Isaiah are much more important. This prophet proclaims that Yahweh will "send to Babylon" and conquer the city (43:14), [6] and that the man whom Yahweh loves (i.e., Cyrus) will perform his purpose on Babylon (48:14). Thus, he sings a satire against Babylon in 47:1ff.: "Come down and sit in the dust, O virgin daughter of Babylon," etc. The proud and beautiful city will be humbled; she will no longer be called "the mistress of kingdoms" (v. 5). To be sure, Yahweh gave his people into the hand of Babylon (v. 6), but Babylon has behaved arrogantly (v. 7), and now she will be smitten with the loss of children and widowhood (v. 9). The gods of Babylon, Bel and Nebo, bow down and go into captivity (46:1f.). Israel will go forth from Babylon and flee from Chaldea in order to return to their land (48:20).

Pride and arrogance are also the characteristics of Babylon in Isa. 13 and 14, which are usually dated in the exilic period. In chap. 13, the fall of Babylon is described as the impending day (→ יוֹם yôm) of Yahweh. Armies will be raised up, warriors will be consecrated, and natural catastrophes will accompany the day of the Lord. The enemies are specifically identified as the Medes (v. 17), and the complete destruction of Jerusalem is announced (vv. 20-22). Moreover, Babylon is mentioned by name only in the superscription and in v. 19. It is significant that in v. 19 Babylon is given the epithet, "the ornament of kingdoms (tsebhi mamlakhoth), the proud splendor of the Chaldeans (tiph'ereth ge'on kasdim)." Chap. 14 describes the fall of the tyrant in a "taunt" (mashal) against the king of Babylon (v. 4): he will be cast into Sheol (v. 15), although at one time he shone arrogantly in heaven as the morning star (helel ben shachar, "day star, son of dawn," v. 12), and wanted to be united with the assembly of the gods. Again, Babylon is mentioned by name only in the superscription and in a definite addition (v. 22). Frequently it is assumed that originally this song was not directed against Babylon, but that this application was first made by the addition of the redactional verses 1-4a and 22f.

However, Erlandsson maintains that these passages are genuinely Isaian and are thinking of Babylon as a part of the Assyrian empire. Israel sought help from the Babylonians against Assyria, but Babylon will fall and this will show that her

---

[6] The text is uncertain; see C. Westermann, Isaiah 40-66. OTL (trans. 1969), 120, 125.

help is worthless. He finds the adaption of this prophecy to the Neo-Babylonian kingdom in Jer. 50f.

Jer. 50 and 51 are dependent on Isa. 13f. It is certain that these chapters are not from Jeremiah, but were written by a redactor, and evidently comprise the book containing the words of disaster mentioned in 51:59ff.[7] As Babylon was once "the foe from the north" for Israel (Jer. 1:14; 6:22ff.), so now Babylon herself will be destroyed by a people from the north (50:3,9,41-46; 51:48). The gods of Babylon will be shattered (50:2; 51:44). Now the Israelites will flee from Babylon (50:8-10; 51:6) in order to return to their land (50:4f.,19). Babylon, which once shattered the nations like a hammer in the hand of Yahweh (50:23; 51:20ff.), will herself be destroyed. The city which intoxicates the nations like a golden cup will be ruined (51:7f.). In her pride and insolence (50:31f.), she has tried to compete with Yahweh (50:24,29), and therefore she will be humbled accordingly. Enemies attack her (50:14-16,21f.; 51:1-6; etc.), the sword comes upon her (50:35-38), she is plundered (50:10) and made a desolation (50:13,16, 39f.; 51:25f.,29). Thus more and more Babylon appears to represent pride which is hostile to God, and which the Almighty will humble.

Ps. 87:4 names Rahab, i.e., Egypt, and Babylon as lands that once knew Yahweh. The choice of the term Rahab indicates that this passage has in mind the archenemy of Yahweh. Ps. 137 twice refers to Babylon as the place of captivity.

According to Lindblom,[8] the allusions to the fallen city in Isa. 24–27 refer to the fall of Babylon to Xerxes in 485 B.C. Thus the text is describing "a great, powerful, towering, well-fortified city" (25:2; 26:5; 27:10). It was a heathen city (qiryath tohu, 24:10), whose inhabitants were an ungodly and unrighteous people (27:11, "without discernment" → בִּין bîn). But now it is broken down by enemies (24:10), and it will become heaps of stones (24:12). It is emphasized in particular that an idol's temple ('armon zarim) will be destroyed (25:2). The fortified city is solitary and forsaken, and calves graze there (27:10f.). This catastrophe is a wonderful deed of Yahweh, by which he is glorified (24:14; 25:1; 26:11). It is also an expression of Yahweh's zeal for his people (26:11).

Other scholars have also suggested that this city be identified with Babylon.[9] But others think it is Samaria, Tyre, Sidon, Carthage, or the capital of Moab.[10] But the concrete statements are not the kind that make it possible for one to determine which city is intended. Perhaps the author did not have any specific city in mind.[11] Henry, who identifies the city with Babylon, finds it difficult "to determine a single historical event" that fits this context,[12] but emphasizes the similarity between Isa. 24–27 and Jer. 50f.,[13] which probably should be dated in the exilic period.

Ringgren

---

[7] See above.
[8] Lindblom, 72-84.
[9] Driver, Ewald, Dillmann, Rudolph, Henry.
[10] See Lindblom, 74f.
[11] Cf. G. Fohrer, *Jesaja,* II (1962), 8: "the urban life style."
[12] Henry, 32.
[13] *Ibid.,* 29.

בֶּגֶד *beghedh,* "clothing" → לבשׁ *lbš*

בָּגַד *bāghadh;* בֶּגֶד *beghedh*

Contents: I. Occurrences, Meaning. II. Range of Usage: 1. Marriage; 2. Covenant; 3. Created Order; 4. Human Agreements.

I. Occurrences, Meaning. The verb *baghadh* occurs 43 times in the OT, and the noun *beghedh* occurs twice. The verb appears only 3 times in the historical books (Ex. 21:8; Jgs. 9:23; 1 S. 14:33). We encounter this word most frequently in the prophetic literature. It occurs 7 times in Jer., 5 times in Mal., and twice each in Hos. and Hab. (Zeph. 3:4 has the form *boghedhoth* with the abstract meaning "faithlessness"). It is found in Isa. 21:2; 24:16; 33:1; and 48:8, in all of which it appears in paronomastic constructions. The verb also occurs in the poetic literature: 9 times in Prov., 5 times in Pss., and once each in Job and Lamentations.

The verb expresses the unstable relationship of man to an existing established regulation, and can be translated "to act faithlessly (treacherously)." It is used when the OT writer wants to say that a man does not honor an agreement, or commits adultery, or breaks a covenant or some other ordinance given by God. The treacherous acts of man stand in contrast to Yahweh's faithfulness to his covenant and trustworthiness (*chesedh ve'emeth*). Thus *baghadh,* "to act treacherously," has primarily a religious function. As a rule, the object of this verb is God. But God-given ordinances also include a man's relationship to his fellow man, and thus occasionally man is also the object of a treacherous act. Sometimes *baghadh* is used to denote the violation of a purely human ordinance. König and others conjecture that this root is connected with *beghedh,* "clothing." In this case, the original meaning of the verb would have been "to clothe, to cover, to veil"; however, this would be weaker than the transferred figurative meaning, "to behave secretively, to do something veiled, to deceive," and thus "to act faithlessly (treacherously)." But this verb occurs in South Arabic with the meaning "to deceive," which can be traced back to two different roots.

II. Range of Usage.

1. *Marriage. baghadh* can be used in connection with faithlessness in marriage, violating a promise, and deserting one's legal partner and establishing a relationship with someone else. The object of faithlessness can be the wife (Ex. 21:8) or the husband (Jer. 3:20). But usually the marriage symbolism in the prophetic texts describes the relationship of the people of Israel or Judah to Yahweh. Here God is the object of the faithless act. In Jer. 9:1 (Eng. v. 2), the people of Judah are called *boghedhim,* "treacherous," which is used in parallelism with *mena'aphim,* "adulterers." In vv. 2ff.(3ff.), additional accusations are added to this indictment which indicate more precisely the nature of their faithlessness

and adultery: the people are characterized by *sheqer*, "lying," and *mirmah*, "falsehood"; they lack stability (trustworthiness, → אמונה *'emûnāh*) and do not speak the truth (→ אמת *'emeth*). Frequently an accusation of faithlessness to God is combined with an accusation of faithlessness and adultery toward men, e.g., in Jer. 3 and Mal. 2:10ff. Jer. 3 contains a detailed description of the two sisters, Israel and Judah, and their adulteries. V. 20 clearly explains the meaning of the symbolism: "Surely as a wife is faithless to (*baghadh min*) her husband, so have you been faithless to (*baghadh be*) me, O house of Israel, says the Lord." It is significant that the expression *baghadh min* is used here in parallelism with the usual construction *baghadh be*. The expression *baghadh min* evidently depends on the expression → זנה *zānāh min*, lit. "to have illicit intercourse away from (someone)," which is common in such contexts. The term *baghodhah*, "false," which is used of Judah in vv. 7 and 10, is synonymous with the expression *'ishshah zonah*, "harlot," in v. 3; the verb *baghadh* runs through this chapter like a thread. Other words used in connection with the verb *baghadh* in this chapter are: *na'aph*, "to commit adultery" (v. 9); *sheqer*, "in pretense" (v. 10); *pasha'*, "to rebel, transgress" (v. 13); and *chata'*, "to sin" (v. 25). But here we come to the realm of covenant ideology, which is often combined with marriage symbolism.

2. *Covenant*. *baghadh* also denotes faithlessness of the people to covenant responsibilities, and is often used as a synonym of verbs like *pasha'*, "to rebel, transgress," and *chata'*, "to sin." In 1 S. 14:33 it is quite clear that a violation of the ordinances of Yahweh is equivalent to a treacherous act (*baghadh*) against God, which is also denoted by the expression *chata' layhvh*, "to sin against Yahweh." In Jer. 3:21, faithlessness and rebellion against God are expressed in a very concrete manner: the people of Judah do not listen to the voice of Yahweh, but "forget" or "neglect" (*shakhach*) their God. In Ps. 78:57, the verb *baghadh* is used in a historical survey, which is entirely covenant ideology. Here, the people commit treacherous acts when they do not observe (*lo' shamar*) God's testimonies (*'edhoth*, v. 56). In Ps. 119:158, the verb *baghadh* is also used in the realm of covenant ideology. Not to act faithlessly means not to swerve (*natah*) from Yahweh's testimonies (v. 157). By way of contrast, the faithless can be recognized in that they do not obey, observe, and keep God's word (*'imrathekha lo' shamaru*, "they do not keep thy commands," v. 158).

In Mal. 2:10ff., covenant ideology and marriage symbolism are combined in order to express the apostasy of the people from Yahweh. The covenant requires that Yahweh's *mishpatim*, "ordinances," be observed, so that the life of the people will be characterized by "fidelity to the covenant" (*chesedh*) and "truth" (*'emeth*) to both God and man. Thus, when it is asked in Mal. 2:10, "Why are we faithless to one another?" this signifies a profaning of the "covenant of our fathers."

The faithlessness of the Israelites to Yahweh is illustrated further by their faithlessness to their lawful wives (*'esheth berithekha*, "your wife by covenant"), and by their having given them a divorce. The result of their marriage to other women is that they worship foreign gods. Consequently, they are no longer "the seed of God" (a godly offspring, *zera' 'elohim*, v. 15). Not unexpectedly, the verb *baghadh* also occurs in Hosea. In Hos. 6:7, the expression *baghedhu bhi,* "they dealt faithlessly with me," is used in connection with the people's transgression (*'abhar*) of the covenant. No one manifests faithfulness; and the love (*chesedh*) of the people is compared with a morning cloud and with the dew that goes early away (v. 4), graphic figures for the unreliability of man. In 5:7, the faithless acts of the people against Yahweh are compared with the birth of illegitimate children (*banim zarim;* cf. Mal. 2:15).

3. *Created Order.* In Proverbs, the verb *baghadh* is used more generally in speaking of man's appeal to the created order. The idea is that one does not wish to continue in and to respect the prevailing conditions and ordinances in the situation in which he has been placed. Therefore, frequently the word *boghedhim,* "treacherous," alternates with → רשעים *reshā'im*, "wicked," e.g., in Prov. 2:22; 11:6f.; 21:18. The *boghedhim* are contrasted with those who live in harmony with the divine order. In Prov. 2:22 *resha'im*, "wicked," and *boghedhim*, "treacherous," stand in contrast to → ישרים *yeshārîm*, "upright," and → תמימים *temimim,* "men of integrity," and the situation is similar in 11:3. Ps. 25:3 and 59:6(5) speak of the judgment upon the treacherous (*boghedhim*). Ps. 73:15 says that the denial of divine justice is faithlessness and treachery against the members of the people of God. Ps. 59:6(5) contains the remarkable expression *boghedhe 'aven*, "those who treacherously plot evil," which evidently is a fusion of the synonymous expressions *po'ale 'aven*, "evildoers, workers of iniquity," and *boghedhim*, "treacherous." In Job 6:15, *baghadh* is used to denote the treacherous acts of men against one another. One thing that is presupposed in trustworthiness and faithfulness is a God-fearing life in communion with the God who provides for the order in the world. Therefore, Job states that the reason for treachery among men is the abandonment (*'azabh*) of the fear of God (v. 14).

With the exception of Isa. 48:8, the verb *baghadh* is used in the book of Isaiah in a way that does not seem to correspond to that which has been suggested above. Among other things, this has led *GesB* to give a special meaning for the verb *baghadh* in Isa. 21:2; 24:16; and 33:1, viz., "to plunder." But this meaning seems rash, and has been rejected by König and others. In Isa. 24:16, the emphatic phrase *beghedh boghedhim baghadhu*, "the treacherous deal treacherously, the treacherous deal very treacherously," stands in a context (24:1-23) in which it is stated that the inhabitants of the earth have broken "the everlasting covenant" (v. 5). Evidently, this refers to the covenant with Noah (Gen. 9:9). To break this covenant, to sin against God's order for man in general, leads to chaos. Thus the term *boghedhim* here has the same meaning as it does in Proverbs, and is synonymous with *resha'im*, "wicked." [1]

4. *Human Agreements.* *baghadh* is also used in speaking of a breach in human agreements and treaties. Thus, this verb is used in Jgs. 9:23 to denote that the men of Shechem were no longer content to submit themselves to the

---

[1] On Isa. 21:2 and 33:1, see II.4.

authority of Abimelech. They "dealt treacherously" with the ordinances of Abimelech. Here *baghadh* is synonymous with "rebel, revolt." In Lam. 1:2 we again encounter the marriage symbolism, but here the verb *baghadh* is used to denote the treachery of one sweetheart to another. Similarly, in Isa. 33:1 this verb describes the relationship of the subject to certain regulations. The tyrant deals treacherously with human regulations; he does not respect ratified covenants (*hepher berith*, "covenants are broken," v. 8). It is quite probable that here *baghadh* includes the idea that the tyrant went beyond the limitations God had allowed him (cf. Isa. 10:7ff.). The term *habboghedh* in Isa. 21:2 can be explained in a similar way. The destructions "of the treacherous one" testify to the rebellion against and lack of respect for ordinances and agreements.

In the MT of Hab. 2:5 we find the words *hayyayin boghedh*. This must refer to the power of wine, which causes a man to act abnormally (chaotically), arrogantly, and rebelliously. 1QpHab 8:3 reads *hon*, "riches," instead of *hayyayin*, "(the) wine." In this case, the appositional *boghedh* refers to the danger that riches might induce a man to act deceitfully and treacherously against his fellow men.

Erlandsson

בָּדַד *bādhādh;* בַּד *badh;*

בָּדַד *bādhadh*

Contents: I. Occurrences, Meaning, Etymology: 1. Outside the OT; 2. In the OT. II. 1. Isolation of Human Communities; 2. Isolation of Individuals; 3. Isolation of God. III. Theological Appraisal of Isolation.

I. Occurrences, Meaning, Etymology.

1. *Outside the OT*. The verb *bdd* appears in Akkadian, Arabic, and Tigriñaic,[1] and possibly also in Ugaritic.[2] The nouns *badd* and *budd*, which are derived from this root, occur in Arabic. In Akkadian in the D stem the verb means "to squander"; in Arabic, "to separate"; in Tigriñaic, "to be omitted"; and in Ugaritic Aistleitner conjectures that it means "to take away" (?). The Arab. nouns *budd* and *badd* are translated "separation," "part of something," and "rafter."

2. *In the OT*. Biblical Hebrew and Middle Hebrew also contain the root *bdd*. However, the verb occurs in the OT only in the qal active participle, and

---

bādhādh. G. Johannes, *Unvergleichlichkeitsformulierungen im AT* (diss., Mainz, 1966), cf. *ZAW*, 81 (1969), 421f.; C. J. Labuschagne, *The Incomparability of Yahweh in the OT* (1966); H. Seidel, *Das Erlebnis der Einsamkeit im AT. Theologische Arbeiten*, 29 (1969).

[1] *KBL³*.
[2] Aistleitner, *WUS*, No. 496.

that only three times. The noun *badh* I is found only two or three times, but it appears in the combination *lebhadh* (which also occurs in Middlé Heb. and Samaritan) approximately 146 times. The other noun **badh* II, which is also attested in Middle Hebrew and Jewish Aramaic, is found 41 times in all in the OT. Also the noun *badhadh* appears 11 times in Biblical Hebrew. These statistics indicate the priority of the nominal aspect of the root *bdd* over the verbal. *badh* I means "part, piece." According to Ex. 30:34, perfumes were to be produced from different kinds of fragrant substances, "an equal part of each" (*badh bebhadh*). Bardtke and Maier[3] translate this expression in a similar way in 1QS 4:16,25.[4] In Job 18:13, *badde* (pl. const. of *badh*), which has a genitival relationship with *'oro*, "his skin," means the "parts" or "pieces" of the skin (and absolutely the "parts" or "members" of the body) consumed by leprosy.

Because of this different meaning of *badh*, most commentators emend the text of Job 18:13a.[5] In Job 41:4 (Eng. v. 12), it is disputed whether *baddav* means "his members (limbs)" or (classifying this word under **badh* IV) "his idle talk (prattle),"[6] or whether to emend the MT.[7] In Am. 3:12, Rabinowitz reads *ubhadh meshoq 'ares*, "and of a piece out of the leg of a bed."[8]

*badh II means both "poles used for carrying" different pieces of cultic furniture (Ex. 25:14f.,27f.; 27:6f.; etc.) and the "shoots (branches)" of the vine (Ezk. 17:6; 19:14). The *lebhadh* listed in the lexicons under *badh I* means as an adverb "alone, by itself," and as a preposition (always in connection with a *min* following it) "besides," "with the exception of," "apart from." The ptcp. *bodhedh* and the noun *badhadh*, which originally was used adverbially, are translated "solitarily," "alone."

This survey indicates that without exception these words must have been derived from a root common to them all, *bdd*, whose original meaning was "to separate, to isolate," a meaning still preserved most clearly in Arabic. Therefore, the root *bdd* (and its derivatives), as a term for isolation, deserves special consideration, since it seems to be a strange peculiarity in OT linguistic usage.

II. 1. *Isolation of Human Communities.* a. The OT repeatedly speaks of an isolation of human communities. In the third song of Balaam we read: "Lo, a people dwelling alone (*lebhadhadh yishkon*)/ and not reckoning itself among the nations!" (Nu. 23:9; E). The very next line in v. 10 extols the innumerable throng of Israel. The concluding portion of the "psalm" in the Blessing of Moses (Dt. 33), which provides the framework for the statements concerning the tribes, sounds very similar. After vv. 26,27a have declared the incomparability of the God of Israel and v. 27b has related the expulsion and destruction of Israel's enemies, v. 28 continues: "So Israel dwelt in safety (*yishkon betach*),/ the foun-

---

[3] H. Bardtke, *Die Handschriftenfunde am Toten Meer*, I (²1953), 92; and J. Maier, *Die Texte vom Toten Meer*, I (1960), 28f.

[4] Contra P. Wernberg-Møller, *The Manual of Discipline* (1957), 84: "separately."

[5] Fohrer, *KAT*, XVI, 298.

[6] Weiser, *ATD*, XIII, 253; Hölscher, *HAT*, 17 (²1952), 96; cf. *KBL*³.

[7] So Fohrer, *KAT*, XVI, 257.

[8] J. Rabinowitz, "The Crux at Amos 3,12," *VT*, 11 (1961), 228-231.

tain of Jacob alone (*badhadh*),/ 'in' a land of grain and wine,/ yea, his heavens drop down dew." These words flow into the enthusiastic exclamation praising the triumphant might and stately power of the people in v. 29: "Happy are you, O Israel! Who is like you?"

In these two songs, which could be regarded as belonging to the genre "Praise of Israel," [9] *badhadh* is connected with *shakhan*, "dwell." As the Blessing of Moses clearly states, and as the narrative context of the Song of Balaam at least intimates when it says that from the bare height the seer saw Israel camped below him in the valley, [10] the idea of Israel dwelling alone refers to her exclusive possession of the land of Canaan. Moreover, the parallelism in Dt. 33:28 indicates that dwelling alone is synonymous with a security based on the power and strength of the people. The same thought is expressed in Nu. 23 by the connection of vv. 9 and 10, i.e., by the combination of Israel's dwelling alone with her innumerable throng.

The same idea appears in Jer. 49:31. In the threat of judgment against Kedar which was supposed to be carried out by the army of Nebuchadrezzar, we read: "Rise up, advance against a nation at ease (*goy shelev*),/ that dwells securely (*yoshebh labhetach*),/ says the Lord;/ that has no gates or bars,/ that dwells alone (*badhadh yishkonu*)." Here also *badhadh* is connected with *shakhan*, "to dwell." Likewise, the adv. *betach*, "securely," belongs to this group of words, and the concept suggested by *badhadh*, "alone," is illustrated further by *shelev*, "at ease," and by the reference to the absence of all fortifications.

Even though the word *badhadh* itself is not used, still the description of the city of Laish in Jgs. 18:7 (cf. 18:10,27) can be included here since the contents of this verse are identical with Jer. 49:31. When Jgs. 18:7 says that the people of the city "dwelt in security" (*yoshebheth labhetach*), "quiet and unsuspecting" (*shoqet ubhoteach*), and that they "were far from the Sidonians and had no dealings with 'Aram,'" it too is speaking of a carefree life of this group of people made secure by their isolation. That the two above-mentioned passages differ from this one in that the people's feeling of security, based on their dwelling alone, is justified in the case of Israel while elsewhere it is an illusion, is not very significant, because this does not affect the positive meaning of *badhadh* that has been ascertained above.

In Hos. 8:9, the scansion of the MT applies "a wild ass wandering alone" to Assyria, which would be a reference to the stubbornness and selfishness of Assyria. [11] But some scholars apply this stich to Ephraim because of the wordplay involving '*ephrayim*, "Ephraim," and *pere*', "wild ass." [12] Even if one accepts this view, however, still it is not clear whether solitude here means the "hopeless condition of the rump state Ephraim" [13] or is to be taken in the sense of a summons to Israel to remain in isolation. [14]

---

[9] G. von Rad, *Deuteronomy*. OTL (trans. 1966), 205: "informative psalm of praise."
[10] Von Rad, *Die Bileamperikope/ 4. Mose 22-24. Deutsches Pfarrerblatt*, 40 (1936), 52f.
[11] Robinson, *HAT*, 14 (³1964), 33.
[12] So Weiser, *ATD*, XXIV, 55; H. W. Wolff, *Hosea* (trans. 1974), 143.
[13] So Weiser.
[14] Cf. Seidel, 110.

b. *badhadh* has another nuance of meaning in Mic. 7:14, as well as in Isa. 27:10 and Lam. 1:1. Mic. 7:14 belongs to an oracle most commentators deny to the prophet Micah and date in the postexilic or even late postexilic period. This oracle is in the form of a popular lament, [15] and its author(s) asks God to restore to the people of Israel the regions of the land east of Jordan which had been lost to them in the catastrophe of 586 B.C. In this context, v. 14 describes the present situation in these words: "'who' dwell alone (*shokhene lebhadhadh*)/ in a forest in the midst of a garden land." To be sure, here also *lebhadhadh* is construed with *shakhan,* "to dwell," but the positive meaning has been transformed into the negative. From the people's security which resulted from dwelling alone has come a deplorable solitude, which is associated with the idea of the forest (*yaʿar*).

Isa. 27:10 and Lam. 1:1, which refer to the city of Jerusalem and personify it, sound similar. Isa. 27:10 is part of a theological reflection (vv. 7-11), which indeed is earlier than the so-called Isaiah Apocalypse, but is still postexilic. [16] The "fortified city," Jerusalem, is "solitary" (*badhadh*), "a deserted habitation" (*naveh meshullach*), "forsaken like the wilderness" (*neʿezabh kammidhbar*). And in the style of the lament of a city that was once densely populated and respected among the nations, Lam. 1:1 says: Now "she sits alone (*yashebhah bhadhadh*), she has become like a widow." Rudolph appropriately observes: "this is not the 'splendid isolation' of Nu. 23:9 and Dt. 33:28[32:12], but the loneliness of a mother deprived of her children." [17]

These observations that *badhadh* means "loneliness," "solitude," for the first time in relatively late passages, that it is used in the genre of lament or at least is closely connected with it, and that it is applied to a city and a people in individualized form, indicate that we are dealing here with a figurative mode of expression. [18]

2. *Isolation of Individuals.* a. *badhadh* is also used of the isolation of individuals. First we may mention certain passages in which this word seems to be neutral. Concerning the approaching Assyrian army among other things, Isa. 14:31 says: "no one is alone (*bodhedh*) in his gathering places" [19] or "in his ranks." [20] At a casual glance the following passages also give the same impression. Ex. 24:2 contains the instruction to Moses that he alone is to come near to Yahweh. According to Jgs. 3:20, Eglon was sitting alone in his cool roof chamber when Ehud went to see him under the pretense of giving him a message from God, murdered him, and closed the doors upon him, which made Eglon's servants think that the king was relieving himself. And according to 1 K. 11:29, that Jeroboam I and Ahijah of Shiloh were alone made it possible

---

[15] Weiser, *ATD,* XXIV, 259.

[16] Eissfeldt, *The OT* (trans. 1965), 324ff.; Fohrer, *Introd OT* (trans. 1968), 369.

[17] W. Rudolph, *KAT,* XVII, 211.

[18] Cf. II.2.b.

[19] Fohrer, *Jesaja²,* I, 201.

[20] Duhm, *Jesaja⁵,* 125; cf. Seidel, 17; otherwise B. Kedar-Kopfstein, "A Note on Isaiah XIV,31," *Textus,* 2 (1962), 143-45.

for Ahijah to give the king a message from God. Consequently, man's solitude is the precondition for the reception or transmission of a divine revelation. But in the account of Jacob crossing the Jabbok, we also are told that while he remained behind alone a man wrestled with him, and finally this man blessed him (Gen. 32:25[24]).[21] The weirdness of this nocturnal attack on Jacob has left its impression on the solitude in this narrative and also throws light on preceding passages.

Abimelech's trembling question to David as he fled from Saul (1 S. 21:2[1]): "Why are you alone?" and Ahithophel's suggestion that he strike down David when he was alone (2 S. 17:2), indicate also that a man's solitude has something terrifying about it, that it is dangerous or "not good," as Gen. 2:18(J) puts it.

b. In the passages cited thus far, solitude conveys the idea that a person is by himself. But in other contexts it means that one is isolated or ejected from human fellowship, i.e., that he is destitute and lonely. According to Lev. 13:46, the leper is to dwell "alone in a habitation outside the camp," i.e., "alone and apart from the company of others."[22] The worshipper in the individual lament, Ps. 102, compares himself in v. 8(7) with a "lonely bird on the housetop."[23] Before this in v. 7(6) he compares himself with "a pelican (?) in the wilderness" (*midhbar*), and "an owl in the ruins" (*charabhoth*). As has been observed above,[24] OT writers evidently liked to describe solitude by using this kind of figure. But it is also clear that the loneliness of the plaintiff in Ps. 102 is due not only to a purely external separation from human fellowship (cf. v. 9[8]), but more strongly to an internal isolation (cf. v. 11[10]), so that Seidel is justified in speaking of an "experience of complete isolation."[25]

Again, Jeremiah complains in one of his confessions: "I did not sit in the company of merrymakers, nor did I rejoice; I sat alone (*badhadh yashabhti*), because thy hand was upon me, for thou hadst filled me with indignation" (15:17). His calling to proclaim Yahweh's word of judgment built this "dividing wall"[26] between him and the people, and this caused him to be alone. And while Jeremiah makes his experience of loneliness the subject of his lament, he gives expression to his deepest inner solitude, which manifests itself in strong protest against God, in fact in doubt and isolation from God (cf. 15:15,18). Lam. 3:28 also reflects the same sort of relationships. In the form of an individual lament, vv. 25-39 are a reflection on the meaning of suffering.[27] The style of this lament is closely connected with that of the Wisdom Literature,[28] and in vv. 28-30 it describes the attitude a man should have toward the yoke God has laid upon him. He is to

---

21 Cf. Seidel, 72.
22 M. Noth, *Leviticus*. OTL (trans. 1965), 106.
23 Cf. N. Airoldi, "Note critiche ai Salmi," *Aug*, 10 (1970), 174-180; H. Ringgren, *The Faith of the Psalmists* (1963), 25f.
24 II.1.b.
25 Seidel, 27.
26 Rudolph, *HAT*, 12 (³1968), 107.
27 Eissfeldt, 502.
28 Weiser, *ATD*, XVI, 328.

"sit alone (*yeshebh badhadh*) in silence" (v. 28), for the Lord has not cast him off (v. 31). Loneliness of the individual within the human community is a result of divine wrath, and again is isolation from God.

However, Lam. 3 is significant in another respect. V. 1 describes the city of Jerusalem with its inhabitants as a man, [29] so that chap. 3 from this point on must be interpreted as referring, not to the fate of a single human being, but to that of the city of Jerusalem. Nevertheless the fact that *badhadh* is construed with *yashabh*, "to sit," and that descriptions of individual and collective isolation coincide even in their specific details, furnish proof of the above-mentioned supposition [30] that here we are dealing with a speech form that was transferred from the individual realm to a collective group.

3. *Isolation of God.* Finally, *badhadh* or *lebhadh* is used in apposition to Yahweh in a number of passages. Isa. 2:11,17, "Yahweh alone will be exalted in that day," which is changed to "his name alone is exalted" in the hymn in Ps. 148:13, emphasizes the majesty and exaltation of the God of Israel (so also Isa. 63:3), and so does the other hymnic expression in Ps. 72:18, "Blessed be Yahweh, the God of Israel, who alone does wondrous things" (cf. Ps. 136:4). From these statements it is only a small step to Dt. 4:35 and 32:12, which, in the form of a commandment (Ex. 22:19[20]; 1 S. 7:3), affirm the uniqueness and incomparability of Yahweh, his exclusive claim to deity. Sometimes his creative acts are mentioned as an indication of this (Isa. 44:24; Job 9:8; Neh. 9:6).

In addition, we also encounter this kind of hymnic or at least hymnlike expressions in a number of prayers of lament and petition: in Solomon's prayer at the dedication of the temple (1 K. 8:39 = 2 Ch. 6:30), in the prayer of Hezekiah (2 K. 19:15,19 = Isa. 37:16,20), in Isa. 26:13, and in the laments in Ps. 4:9(8); 71:16: 83:19(18); and 86:10. They express the confidence of the worshipper in the help of the only powerful God, the God of Israel.

III. **Theological Appraisal of Isolation.** It is significant for the theological appraisal of isolation in the OT that we encounter this concept primarily in hymns and laments, and correspondingly that it may have a positive or a negative connotation.

The passages in the Blessing of Moses and the third Song of Balaam are valuable witnesses to the proud conviction of Israel that she had secure power and strength, indeed that she was unique among the nations. Even though this self-understanding reflects in the Blessing of Moses an emphasis on the national concern over the religious (an emphasis that is well known in the time of David and Solomon), this emphasis is reversed not only in the Elohistic Song of Balaam by the parallel stich which states that Israel did not reckon itself among the nations, but also in the theme of both the Blessing of Moses and the Song of Balaam, "Israel–the people blessed by Yahweh once and for all": here the religious emphasis takes precedence over the national. The peculiarity of Israel

---

[29] Cf. Eissfeldt, 503.
[30] II.1.b.

among the nations is based on her choice by Yahweh. The affirmations of the uniqueness of Yahweh, of his exclusive claim to deity, are connected very intimately with this choice. They also reflect the positive aspect of *badhadh* and bear witness to the acceptance of this idea into the religious language of Israel.

The other idea that the isolation of man, his separation and dissociation from the human community that shelters and protects him, is unnatural, uncertain, artificial, indeed dangerous, certainly also goes back to the earliest times, for in a nomadic or seminomadic environment, a separation from the tribe or from the family meant the renunciation of all social and economic security, and if worse came to worst even the repudiation of one's life. Thus every form of isolation has a negative ring about it. "The Hebrew has no love of isolation." [31]

This consciousness is transformed and deepened by the prophets and their message about the time of the exile. The individualization of man's relationship to God is concurrent with this intensification. Now the believer no longer stands before God as a member of the people or of the community, but as an individual. As can be seen most clearly in Jeremiah, this "state of independence" also means an "insecure dependence upon Yahweh." [32] Thus solitude is no longer merely a deplorable separation from the community, but a much more far-reaching isolation from God, for it originates in a disruption of man's relationship with God. But if life is valid only in communion with God, then solitude is experienced as a hindrance to life, as a threat to existence, as the danger of death, which are appropriately expressed in figures and comparisons like "wilderness," "desert," "ruins," and "depopulated, forsaken places." And since ultimately only Yahweh is able to change this, man turns to him in prayer, which has the form of a lament, the only form suitable to such a situation.

Zobel

---

[31] L. Köhler, *Hebrew Man* (trans. 1956), 157.
[32] Von Rad, *OT Theol*, II (trans. 1965), 58.